Database
Administration

Database Administration

*The Complete Guide to
Practices and Procedures*

Craig S. Mullins

✦✦Addison-Wesley

Boston • San Francisco • New York • Toronto • Montreal
London • Munich • Paris • Madrid
Capetown • Sydney • Tokyo • Singapore • Mexico City

The publisher offers discounts on this book when ordered in quantity for special sales. For more information, please contact:

Pearson Education Corporate Sales Division
201 W. 103rd Street
Indianapolis, IN 46290
(800) 428-5331
corpsales@pearsoned.com

Visit Addison-Wesley on the Web: www.awprofessional.com

Library of Congress Cataloging-in-Publication Data

Mullins, Craig.
   Database administration : the complete guide to practices and procedures / Craig S. Mullins
      p. cm.
   Includes bibliographical references and index.
   ISBN 0-201-74129-6
   1. Database management. I. Title

  QA76.9.D3 M838 2002
  650'.0285'574—dc21

                                           2002024935

ISBN 0-201-74129-6
Text printed in the United States on recycled paper at Courier Stoughton in Stoughton, Massachusetts.

6th Printing   March 2008

To my wife, Beth, for making my journey
through life worthwhile.

Contents

CHAPTER 14   Database Security   385

CHAPTER 15   Database Backup and Recovery   407

CHAPTER 19   Data Warehouse Administration   515

Preface

A database management system (DBMS) is used to create databases. Most of today's applications deploy databases to store information such as names, addresses, and account balances. This information can be accessed and manipulated by application programs to perform business processes like payroll processing, sales processing, and customer billing. Every DBMS requires database administration to ensure efficient and effective use of databases by applications. This means that any user of Oracle, Microsoft SQL Server, DB2, Informix, Sybase, MySQL, Teradata, PostgreSQL, Ingres and any other popular DBMSs will benefit from the information in this book.

This book provides the industry's first non-product-based description of database administration techniques and practices. Many organizations have multiple DBMS products and will benefit from a consolidated view of database administration that does not focus on the internals and nuances of each particular product. Such a view is presented in this text.

The book defines the job of database administrator and outlines what is required of a database administrator, or DBA, in clear, easy-to-understand language. The book can be used

- As a text for learning the discipline of database administration

- As the basis for setting up a DBA group

- To augment a DBMS-specific manual or textbook
- To help explain to upper-level management what a DBA is, and why the position is required

Every organization that deploys databases using a DBMS needs to understand the concepts outlined in this book. Many small- to medium-sized organizations attempt to implement DBMS products without a DBA. This book explains the practice of database administration and underscores the necessity of a DBA for DBMS implementation to succeed. Other organizations implement only subsets of the database administration practices that are covered in this book. With a thorough reading of *Database Administration: The Complete Guide to Practices and Procedures*, it will become quite clear that a comprehensive approach to database administration is required. This book examines and explains each of the components that comprise this discipline.

As technology advances, new IT techniques emerge that impact the discipline of database administration. Two such areas are Internet-enabled database access and the storage of procedural logic in the DBMS in the form of triggers, user-defined functions, and stored procedures. Because the impact of these newer technologies and techniques on the role of the DBA is examined in this book, even seasoned database professionals will find the book useful. Indeed, the book will be helpful for any and all of the following folks:

- DBA managers
- IT professionals who want to become DBAs
- IT professionals new to implementing a DBMS
- Students of database management
- DBAs
- Systems programmers and system administrators who interface with DBAs and need to understand what it is that DBAs do

Because this book covers heterogeneous database administration without focusing on just one DBMS, it can be used by organizations to set up a DBA function when more than one DBMS product is being used. This is particularly important because the single-DBMS shop is a rarity these days. Analysts estimate that most medium- to large-sized organizations have from three to ten different DBMS products in use—all requiring administration.

Additionally, DBA is currently a very hot job. In many cases, DBAs demand and obtain very high salaries. As such, many technicians aspire to become DBAs, and this book will help them to do just that. If you are an IT professional with an interest in becoming a DBA, this book will help you to achieve that objective.

Other books about database administration are available, but they approach the subject from the perspective of a single DBMS. Many of these books are quite good. I wrote one myself about DB2. This book is not intended to replace such books, but to augment them with an independent treatment of database administration tasks.

How to Use This Book

This book can be used as both a tutorial and a reference. The book is organized to proceed chronologically through DBA tasks that are likely to be encountered. Therefore, if you read the book sequentially from Chapter 1 through Chapter 23, you will get a comprehensive sequential overview of the DBA job. Alternatively, you can read any chapter independently because each chapter deals with a single topic. References to other chapters are clearly made if other material in the book would aid the reader's understanding.

Acknowledgments

Writing is a rewarding task, but it also requires a lot of time: researching, writing, reviewing, editing, and rewriting over and over again until you get it just right. But no one can write a technical book in a vacuum. I had many knowledgeable and helpful people to assist me along the way.

First of all, I'd like to thank the many industry experts who reviewed the original book proposal. The following folks provided many useful suggestions and thoughts on my original outline that helped me to create a much better book: Michael Blaha, Keith W. Hare, Michael J. Hernandez, Robert S. Seiner, and David L. Wells. Additionally, I'd like to thank everyone who took the time to listen to my ideas for this book before I began writing. This list of folks is too numerous to include, and I'm sure I'd miss someone—but you know who you are.

I would like to thank the many folks who have reviewed and commented on the text of this book: Dan Hotka, Chris Foot, Chuck Kosin, David L. Wells, and Anne Marie Smith pored over each chapter of various incarnations of the manuscript, and this book is much better thanks to their expert contributions. Special thanks go to data modeling and administration gurus William J. Lewis and Robert S. Seiner, who took extra time to review and make suggestions on Chapter 3.

I'd also like to thank Reggie Moore and Calvin Guidry at BMC Software for providing a work environment conducive to research and growth.

My appreciation goes to Mary Barnard, who did a wonderful job editing this book—making it much more readable in the process. Additionally, thanks to the many understanding and patient folks at Addison-Wesley who worked with me to make this book come to fruition: Patrick Cash-Peterson, Stacie Parillo, and Mary O'Brien were particularly helpful throughout the process of coordinating the production of the book from start to finish.

Thank you, too, to my wonderful wife, Beth, whose understanding and support made it possible for me to write this book. Indeed, thanks go to my entire family for being supportive and helpful all along the way.

And finally, a thank you to all of the people with whom I have worked professionally at BMC Software, Gartner Group, PLATINUM *technology, inc.*, Duquesne Light Company, Mellon Bank, and USX Corporation. This book is a better one due to the many outstanding individuals with whom I have had the honor to work.

About the Author

Craig S. Mullins is Director of Technology Planning for BMC Software, located in Houston, TX. Craig has extensive experience in the field of database management, having worked as an application developer, a DBA, and an instructor with multiple database management systems, including DB2, Oracle, and SQL Server. Additionally, Craig worked as a Research Director with Gartner Group, covering the field of database administration. He is the author of *DB2 Developer's Guide*, the industry-leading book on DB2 for OS/390.

Craig is a frequent contributor to computer industry publications, having authored hundreds of articles in the past several years. His articles have appeared in popular industry magazines including *Database Programming & Design, Data Management Review, DBMS, DB2 Update, DB2 Magazine, Oracle Update, SQL Server Update*, and many others. Craig writes several regular columns, including a monthly column called "The DBA Corner" for *Database Trends and Applications* magazine, a quarterly column called "The Database Report" for *The Data Administration Newsletter* (tdan.com), and a regular column on the impact of the Internet on database administration called "The eDBA" for dbazine.com. Craig is also a consulting editor for dbazine.com and participates as a DB2 expert in the searchdatabase.com portal.

Craig regularly presents technical topics at database industry conferences and events. He has spoken to thousands of technicians about database management and administration issues at such conferences as Database and Client/Server World, SHARE, GUIDE, DAMA Symposium, the DB2 Technical Conference, the International DB2 Users Group (IDUG), and Oracle Open World. He has also spoken at regional database user groups across North America, Europe, Asia, and Australia.

Craig graduated cum laude from the University of Pittsburgh with a double major in computer science and economics, and a minor in mathematics.

Readers can obtain information about this book, including corrections, future editions, and additional writings on database administration by the author at the author's Web site at http://www.craigsmullins.com. The author can be contacted at craig@craigsmullins.com or in care of the publisher.

■ ■ ■ ■ ■ ■ ■ ■ ■ ■ ■

What Is a DBA?

The need for a database administrator is greater today than ever before.

Every organization using a database management system (DBMS) to manage data requires a database administration group to ensure the effective use and deployment of the company's databases. Since most modern organizations of any size use a DBMS, the need for a database administrator (DBA) is greater today than ever before. However, the discipline of database administration is neither well understood nor universally practiced in a coherent and easily replicated manner.

The DBA: Revered or Reviled?

An oft-repeated story about database administration underscores both the necessity for database administration and the lack of understanding of a DBA's function. It goes something like this:

The CIO of Acme Corporation hires a management consulting company to streamline their information technology (IT) operations. The consultant, determined to understand the way Acme works, begins by interviewing the CIO. One of his first questions is: "So, I see that you have a DBA on staff. What does he do?"

> The CIO replies, "Well, I'm told that we need the DBA to make sure our Oracle databases stay online. I know that some of our critical business processes like order entry and inventory use Oracle, but I really don't know what the DBA does. But please don't tell me I need another one, because we can barely afford to pay the one we have!"

This is a sad but too often true commentary on the state of database administration in many organizations. DBMS software is so complex these days that very few people understand more than just the basics (like SQL). However, DBAs understand the complexities of the DBMS, making them a valuable resource. Indeed, sometimes the only source of database management and development knowledge within the organization is the DBA.

The DBA, often respected as a database guru, is just as frequently criticized as a curmudgeon with vast technical knowledge but limited people skills. Just about every database programmer has his or her favorite DBA story. You know, those anecdotes that begin with "I had a problem…" and end with "and then he told me to stop bothering him and read the manual." DBAs simply do not have a "warm and fuzzy" image. However, this perception probably has more to do with the nature and scope of the job than with anything else. The DBMS spans the enterprise, effectively placing the DBA on call for the applications of the entire organization.

The truth is, many database problems require periods of quiet reflection and analysis for the DBA to resolve. Therefore, DBAs generally do not like to be disturbed. However, due to the vast knowledge most DBAs possess (the guru, again), their quiet time is usually less than quiet; constant interruptions to answer questions and solve problems is a daily fact of life.

DBAs need to acquire exceptional communication skills.

DBAs, more than most, need to acquire exceptional communication skills. Data is the lifeblood of computerized applications. Application programs are developed to read and write data, analyze data, move data, perform calculations using data, modify data, and so on. Without data, there would be nothing for the programs to do. The DBA is at the center of the development life cycle—ensuring that application programs have efficient, accurate access to the corporation's data. As such, DBAs frequently interface with many different types of people: technicians, programmers, end users, customers, and executives. However, many DBAs are so caught up in the minutiae of the inner workings of the DBMS that they never develop the skills required to relate appropriately to their coworkers and customers.

A DBA ensures the ongoing operational functionality and efficiency of an organization's databases and applications.

However, we have not yet answered the question: What is a DBA? The short answer is simple: A DBA is the information technician responsible for ensuring the ongoing operational functionality and efficiency of an organization's databases and the applications that access those databases.

The long answer to that question requires a book to answer—this book. This text will define the management discipline of database administration and provide practical guidelines for the proper implementation of the DBA function.

Why Learn Database Administration?

Data is at the center of today's applications; today's organizations simply cannot operate without data. In many ways, business today *is* data. Without data, businesses would not have the ability to manage finances, conduct transactions, or contact their customers. Databases are created to store and organize this data. The better the design and utility of the database, the better the organization will be positioned to compete for business.

Indeed, one of the largest problems faced by IT organizations is ensuring quality database administration. A survey of IT managers conducted by *Information Week* in December 2000 showed that the top two database management execution issues faced by companies are ease of administration and availability of qualified administrators.

Both of these issues were cited by 58% of survey respondents. Additionally, the 1999 Market Compensation Survey conducted by people³, a Gartner Company, shows that DBA positions take longer to fill than any other position. Clearly, there is no lack of demand for DBA skills in today's job market.

A Unique Vantage Point

A good DBA needs to enjoy challenges and be a good problem solver.

The DBA is responsible for designing and maintaining an enterprise's databases, placing the DBA squarely at the center of the business. The DBA has the opportunity to learn about many facets of business and how they interrelate. The DBA can explore groundbreaking technologies as they are adopted by the organization. Exposure to new technology keeps the job stimulating—but frustrating if you are trying to figure out how a new technology works for the first time. The DBA is often working alone in these endeavors; he does not have access to additional expertise to assist when troubles arise. Therefore, a good DBA needs to enjoy challenges and be a good problem solver.

DBA Salaries

You can find no more challenging job in IT than database administration. Fortunately, DBAs are well paid. DICE.com, a career planning and research Web site, provides valuable statistics on DBA compensation. For example, database administration is one of the top ten contract jobs when ranked by salary, as well as one of the top ten jobs for full-time employment. The mean compensation for DBA consultants is $81 per hour; the mean level of experience just 4.98 years. For full-time employees with four or more years of experience, the mean salary ranges from the low $60,000s to over $80,000. Figure 1-1 shows the mean salary for full-time DBAs broken down by years of experience.

Another Web site, searchdatabase.com, a portal of database information for IT professionals, conducted a salary survey of database professionals. As of late January 2001, the average annual salary for all database professionals was more than $62,000. As might be expected, as the years of experience and the number of people managed increases, so does the salary. Of course, DBA salaries, as with all salaries, vary by region of the country. In the United States, DBA salaries are usually higher in the Northeast and on the West Coast than in other regions.

Database administration is a nonstop job.

So, DBAs are well paid, have challenging jobs, and are likely to be engaged in the most visible and important projects. What's not to like? Well, DBAs are expected to know everything, not just about database technologies, but about any-

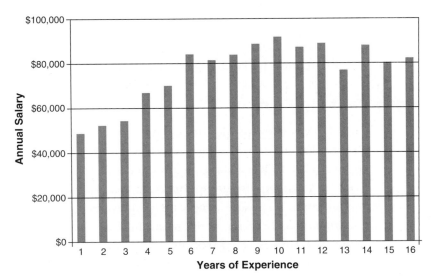

Figure 1-1 *Mean salary for full-time DBAs (Dice.com 2000 IT Rate Survey)*

thing remotely connected to them. Database administration is a nonstop job, and DBAs work long days with lots of overtime, especially when performance is suffering or development projects are behind schedule. DBAs frequently have to work on weekends and holidays to maintain databases during off-peak hours. A DBA must be constantly available to deal with problems, because database applications run around the clock. Most DBAs carry pagers or cell phones so they can be reached at any time. If there is a database problem at 2:00 A.M., the DBA must get out of bed, clear his head, and solve the problem to get the applications back up and running. Failure to do so can result in database downtime, and that can completely shut down business processes. DBAs frequently spend weekends in front of the computer performing database maintenance and reorganizations during off peak hours. You can't bring mission-critical databases down during the nine-to-five day to maintain them. According to industry analysts at the META Group, the average DBA works more than fifty hours per week, including an average of six hours on weekends.

So, database administration is technically challenging and rewarding; it can also be exhausting and frustrating. But don't let that scare you. The positive aspects of the job far outweigh the negative.

Database Technology

This book assumes a basic knowledge of relational database technology and DBMS fundamentals. For readers needing to review these concepts, please refer to Appendix 1. This is not a trivial matter; people sometimes think they know more than they actually do. For example, what is a database? I'll bet most readers believe they know the answer to that question. However, some (perhaps many) of you would be wrong. Oracle is not a database; it is a database management system. You can use Oracle to create a database, but Oracle, in and of itself, is not a database.

A database is an organized store of data wherein the data is accessible by named data elements.

So, what is a database? A *database* is an organized store of data wherein the data is accessible by named data elements (for example, fields, records, and files). And what is a database management system? A *DBMS* is software that enables end users or application programmers to share and manage data. It provides a systematic method of creating, updating, retrieving, and storing information in a database. A DBMS is also generally responsible for data integrity, data security, data access control and optimization, automated rollback, restart, and recovery. Figure 1-2 shows the relationship between a DBMS and a database.

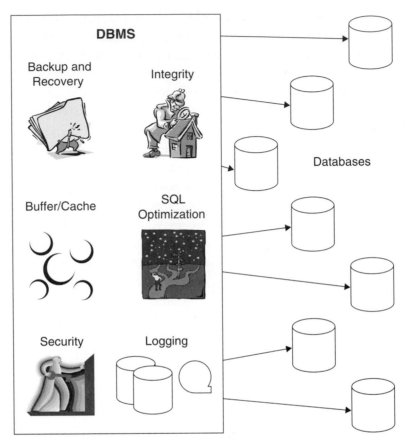

Figure 1-2   *Relationship of DBMS to database*

You might think of a database as a file folder, and a DBMS as the file cabinet holding the labeled folders. You implement and access database instances using the capabilities of the DBMS. Your payroll application uses the payroll database, which may be implemented using a DBMS such as DB2, Oracle9i, or SQL Server.

Why is this important? If we don't use precise terms in the workplace, confusion can result. And confusion leads to over-budget projects, improperly developed systems, and lost productivity.

In addition to database management fundamentals, DBAs must be experts in the specific DBMS in use, and there may be many in the organization. For example, a large organization might use DB2 on the mainframe, Oracle and Informix on several different UNIX platforms, and SQL Server on Windows

2000. Older legacy systems might use IMS databases, and then there is that one crazy application out there that uses a fringe DBMS like Adabas or Ingres.[1]

DBAs must implement decisions based on the best fit of application, DBMS, and platform.

The DBA group, therefore, must have expertise in each of these different management systems and platforms. Furthermore, the DBA must be capable of determining which DBMS and platform is best suited to the needs of each application. This can be a difficult job fraught with politics and conflicting opinions. The DBA group must be able to act impartially and implement decisions based on the best fit of application, DBMS, and platform.

Once again, for a short introduction to DBMS concepts, refer to Appendix 1.

The Management Discipline of Database Administration

Database administration is rarely approached as a management discipline. The term *discipline* implies a plan, and implementation according to that plan. When database administration is treated as a management discipline, the treatment of data within your organization will improve. It is the difference between being reactive and proactive.

All too frequently, the DBA group is overwhelmed by requests and problems. This ensues for many reasons, such as understaffing, overcommitment to supporting new (and even legacy) application development projects, lack of repeatable processes, or lack of budget. The reactive DBA functions more like a firefighter than an administrator; he attempts to resolve problems only after problems occur. The reactive DBA is focused on resolving the biggest problem confronting him.

A proactive DBA develops and implements a strategic blueprint for deploying databases within the organization.

In contrast, the proactive DBA implements practices and procedures to avoid problems before they occur. A proactive database administrator develops and implements a strategic blueprint for deploying databases within the organization. This plan should address all phases of the application development life cycle. A data specialist, usually the DBA, should be involved during each phase of the cycle, as shown in Figure 1-3. During the initiation and requirements gathering phase, the DBA must be available to identify the data components of the project. He can help to determine if the required data already exists elsewhere

---

1. I refer to Adabas and Ingres as "fringe," not because of any functional or technical deficiencies, but only because of their minimal marketshare.

Initiation

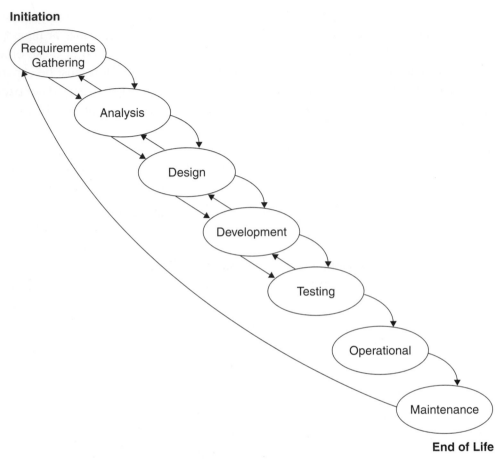

Figure 1-3   *The application development life cycle*

in the organization or if the data is brand new. During the analysis and design phases, the rudimentary data requirements must be transformed into a conceptual and logical data model.

Before development can begin, the logical data model must be translated to a physical database design that can be implemented using a DBMS such as Oracle or DB2. Sample data must be populated into the physical database to allow application testing. Furthermore, the DBA must develop and implement a process to refresh test data to enable repeatable test runs.

When the application moves from development to operational status, the DBA ensures that the DBMS is prepared for the new workload. This preparation includes implementing appropriate security measures, measuring and modifying the storage and memory requirements for the new application, and anticipating the impact of the new workload on existing databases and applications. The DBA is also responsible for migrating the new database from the test environment to the production environment.

While the application is operational, the DBA performs a host of duties including assuring availability, performance monitoring, tuning, backup and recovery, and authorization management. However, no application or database remains static for long. Because business needs change over time, the IT systems that support the business will also change. When maintenance is requested, the DBA becomes engaged in the entire process once again, from requirements gathering to implementation.

Finally, when the application reaches the end of its useful life, the DBA must help to determine the final status of the data used by the application. Is the data no longer required, or do other applications and processes use the data, too? Are there regulations that require the data to be stored longer than the life of the application? Does the business have any privacy policies that impose special rules for handling the data? See the sidebar "Privacy Policies and Data" for further information.

Privacy Policies and Data

The recent bankruptcy of e-business toy seller Toysmart.com provides a good lesson in the impact of privacy policies on corporate data. In May 2000, Toysmart filed for bankruptcy and announced its intention to sell its database of customer information. Toysmart's customer list was estimated to contain information on 250,000 former customers, including their names, phone numbers, street and e-mail addresses, and product preferences. However, Toysmart's own privacy policy, previously posted on its Web site, promised that it would not disclose the personal information of its customers to third parties.

The FTC and a group of state attorneys general blocked the sale on the grounds that the sale would violate Toysmart's privacy policy. They argued that Toysmart's customers conducted business with Toysmart.com under the conditions of the privacy policy. The court ruling further stipulated that the company had to provide an affidavit describing how the list was destroyed.

This is just one example of how privacy policies can impact database administrators and corporate data experts. Of course, you may never work for a company that goes bankrupt, but your company may decide to retire applications and data due to legal regulations, business conditions, or mergers.

The DBA is responsible for managing the overall database environment. Often this includes installing the DBMS and setting up the IT infrastructure to allow applications to access databases. These tasks need to be completed before any application programs can be implemented. Furthermore, ad hoc database access is a requirement for many organizations.

Additionally, the DBA is in charge of setting up an ad hoc query environment that includes evaluating and implementing query and reporting tools, establishing policies and procedures to ensure efficient ad hoc queries, and monitoring and tuning ad hoc SQL.

A good DBA is integral to the entire application development life cycle.

As you can see, a good DBA is integral to the entire application development life cycle. The DBA is "in demand" for his knowledge of data and the way in which data is managed by modern applications.

A Day in the Life of a DBA

A day in the life of a DBA is usually quite hectic. The DBA maintains production and test environments, monitors active application development projects, attends strategy and design meetings, selects and evaluates new products, and connects legacy systems to the Web. And, of course: *Joe in Accounting, he just resubmitted that query from hell that's bringing the system to a halt. Can you do something about that?* All of this can occur within a single workday.

To add to the chaos, DBAs are expected to know everything about everything. From technical and business jargon to the latest management and technology fads, the DBA is expected to be "in the know." And do not expect any private time: A DBA must be prepared for interruptions at any time to answer any type of question—and not just about databases, either.

When application problems occur, the database is "guilty until proven innocent."

When application problems occur, the database environment is frequently the first thing blamed. The database is "guilty until proven innocent." A DBA is rarely approached with a question like "I've got some really bad SQL here. Can you help me fix it?" Instead, the DBA is forced to investigate problems where the underlying assumption is that the DBMS or perhaps the DBA is at fault, when the most common cause of relational performance problems is inefficiently coded applications.

Oftentimes the DBA is forced to prove that the database is not the source of the problem. The DBA must know enough about all aspects of IT to track down errors and exonerate the DBMS and database structures he has designed. So he must be an expert in database technology, but also have semi-expert knowledge of the IT components with which the DBMS interacts: application programming languages, operating systems, network protocols and products, transaction processors, every type of computer hardware imaginable, and more. The need to understand such diverse elements makes the DBA a very valuable resource. It also makes the job interesting and challenging. If database administration still sounds intriguing to you, read on. Actually, the job isn't as bad as it sounds. The work is interesting, there is always something new to learn, and, as previously mentioned, the pay can be good. The only question is: Can anyone do this type of job for twenty or more years without needing a rest? And, oh, by the way, I think I hear your pager going off, so you might want to pause here to see what is wrong.

Evaluating a DBA Job Offer

As a DBA, it is almost inevitable that you will change jobs several times during your career. When making a job change, you will obviously consider requirements such as salary, bonus, benefits, frequency of reviews, and amount of vacation time. However, you also should consider how the company treats their DBAs. Different organizations place different value on the DBA job. It is imperative to your career development that you scout for progressive organizations that understand the complexity and ongoing learning requirements for the position. Here are some useful questions to ask:

- Does the company offer regular training for its DBAs to learn new DBMS features and functionality? What about training for related technologies such as programming, networking, e-business, transaction management, message queueing, and the like?
- Does the company allow DBAs to regularly attend local user groups? What about annual user groups at remote locations?
- Are there backup DBAs, or will you be the only one on call 24/7?
- Are there data administration and system administration organizations, or are the DBAs expected to perform all of these duties, too?
- Does the DBA group view its relationship with application development groups as a partnership? Or is the relationship more antagonistic?
- Are DBAs included in design reviews, budgeting discussions, and other high-level IT committees and functions?

The more "yes" answers you get to these questions, the more progressive the DBA environment is.

Database, Data, and System Administration

Many organizations combine data administration into the database administration role.

Some organizations define separate roles for the business aspects and the technical aspects of data. The business aspects of data are aligned with data administration, whereas the more technical aspects are handled by database administration. Not every organization has a data administration function. Indeed, many organizations combine data administration into the database administration role.

Sometimes organizations also split up the technical aspects of data management, with the DBA responsible for using the DBMS and a system administrator or systems programmer responsible for installing and upgrading the DBMS.

Data Administration

Data administration separates the business aspects of data resource management from the technology used to manage data; it is more closely aligned with the actual business users of data. The data administrator (DA) is responsible for understanding the business lexicon and translating it into a logical data model. Referring back to the ADLC, the DA would be involved more in the requirements gathering, analysis, and design phase, the DBA in the design, development, testing, and operational phases.

Another difference between a DA and a DBA is the focus of effort. The DA is responsible for the following tasks:

- Identifying and cataloging the data required by business users
- Producing conceptual and logical data models to accurately depict the relationship among data elements for business processes
- Creating an enterprise data model that incorporates all of the data used by all of the organization's business processes
- Setting data policies for the organization
- Identifying data owners and stewards
- Setting standards for control and usage of data

The data administrator can be thought of as the Chief Data Officer of the corporation.

In short, the DA can be thought of as the Chief Data Officer of the corporation. However, in my experience, the DA is never given an executive position, which is unfortunate. Many IT organizations state that they treat data as a corporate asset, a statement that is belied by their actions. Responsibility for data policy is often relegated to technicians who fail to concentrate on the nontechnical business aspects of data management. Technicians do a good job of en-suring availability, performance, and recoverability, but are not usually capable of ensuring data quality and setting corporate policies.

In fact, data is rarely treated as a true corporate asset. Think about the as-sets that every company has in common: capital, human resources, facilities, and materials. Each of these assets is modeled: charts of account, organization charts, reporting hierarchies, building blueprints, office layouts, and bills of material. Each is tracked and protected. Professional auditors are employed to ensure that no discrepancies exist in a company's accounting of its assets. Can we say the same thing about data?

A mature DA organization is responsible for planning and guiding the data usage requirements throughout the organization. This role encompasses how data is documented, shared, and implemented companywide. A large responsi-bility of the DA staff is to ensure that data elements are documented properly, usually in a data dictionary or repository. This is another key differentiation between a DA and a DBA. The DA focuses on the repository, whereas the DBA focuses on the physical databases and DBMS.

Furthermore, the DA deals with metadata, as opposed to the DBA, who deals with data. *Metadata* is often described as data about data; more accurately, meta-data is the description of the data and data interfaces required by the business. Data administration is responsible for the business's metadata strategy. Examples of metadata include the definition of a data element, business names for a data element, any abbreviations used for that element, and the data type and length of the element. Data without metadata is difficult to use. For example, the num-ber 12 is data, but what kind of data? In other words, what does that 12 mean? Without metadata, we have no idea. Consider this: Is the number 12

- A date representing December, the twelfth month of the year?
- A date representing the twelfth day of some month?
- An age?
- A shoe size?
- Or, heaven forbid, an IQ?

And so on. However, there are other, more technical aspects of metadata, too. Think about the number 12 again.

- Is 12 a large number or a small one?

- What is its domain (that is, what is the universe of possible values of which 12 is but a single value)?

- What is its data type? Is it an integer or a decimal number with a 0 scale?

Metadata provides
the context by
which data can be
understood and
therefore become
information.

Metadata provides the context by which data can be understood and therefore become information. In many organizations, metadata is not methodically captured and cataloged; instead, it exists mostly in the minds of the business users. Where it has been captured in systems, it is spread throughout multiple programs in file definitions, documentation in various states of accuracy, or in long lost program specifications. Some of it, of course, is in the system catalog of the DBMS.

A comprehensive metadata strategy enables an organization to understand the information assets under its control and to measure the value of those assets. Additional coverage of metadata is provided in Chapter 21.

One of the biggest contributions of data administration to the corporate data asset is the creation of data models. A *conceptual data model* outlines data requirements at a very high level. A *logical data model* provides in-depth details of data types, lengths, relationships, and cardinality. The DA uses normalization techniques to deliver sound data models that accurately depict the data requirements of an organization.

Many DBAs dismiss data administration as mere data modeling, required only because someone needs to talk to the end users to get the database requirements. However, a true DA function is much more than mere data modeling. It is a business-oriented management discipline responsible for the data asset of the organization.

Why spend so much time talking about data administration in a book about database administration? Well, very few organizations have implemented and staffed a DA role. The larger the organization is, the more likely that a DA function exists. However, when the DA role is undefined in an organization, the DBA must assume the mantle of data planner and modeler. Unfortunately, the DBA will usually not be able to assume all of the functions and responsibility of a DA as summarized in this section for a number of reasons:

- The DBA has many other technical duties to perform that will consume most of his time.

- The manager of the DBA group typically does not have an executive position enabling him to dictate policy.

- The DBA generally does not have the skills to communicate effectively with business users and build consensus.

- Frankly, most DBAs are happier dealing with technical issues and technicians than with business issues and nontechnicians.

When DA and DBA functions coexist within the organization, the two groups must work very closely with one another. It is not necessary that both have the same manager, though it would facilitate cooperation. At any rate, it is imperative that some skills cross-pollinate the two groups. The DA will never understand the physical database like a DBA, and the DBA will never understand the business issues of data like a DA, but each job function is more effective with some knowledge about the other.

In short, organizations that are truly concerned about data quality, integrity, and reuse will invariably implement and staff the DA function.

Organizations truly concerned about data quality, integrity, and reuse will invariably implement and staff the DA function.

Database Administration

Database administration is the focus of this entire book, so I will not spend a lot of time defining it in this short section. The rest of the book will accomplish that nicely. This section will quickly outline the functions performed by the DBA group when the DA function exists. The first duty of the DBA is to understand the data models built by the DA and to communicate the model to the application developers and other appropriate technicians. The logical data model is the map the DBA will use to create physical databases. The DBA will transform the logical data model into an efficient physical database design. It is essential that the DBA incorporate his knowledge of the DBMS to create an efficient and appropriate physical database design from the logical model. The DBA should not rely on the DA for the final physical model any more than a DA should rely on a DBA for the conceptual and logical data models. Figure 1-4 depicts this relationship.

The DBA is the conduit for communication between the DA team and the technicians and application programming staff. Of course, the bulk of the DBA's job is ongoing support of the databases created from the physical design and management of the applications that access those databases. An overview of these duties is provided in the DBA Tasks section of this chapter.

The DBA is the conduit for communication between the DA team and the technicians and application programming staff.

System Administration

Some organizations, usually the larger ones, also have a system administrator (SA) or systems programming role that impacts DBMS implementation and operations. The SA is responsible for the installation and setup of the DBMS.

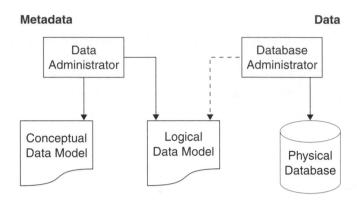

Figure 1-4   *DBA vs. DA*

The SA typically has no responsibility for database design and support. Instead, the DBA is responsible for the databases and the SA is responsible for DBMS installation, modification, and support. (If this distinction is not clear to you, please refer to Appendix 1.)

Furthermore, the SA ensures that the IT infrastructure is implemented such that the DBMS is configured to work with other enabling system software. The SA may need to work with other technicians to configure transaction processors, message queueing software, networking protocols, and operating system parameters to enable the DBMS to operate effectively. The SA ensures that the IT infrastructure is operational for database development by setting up the DBMS appropriately, applying ongoing maintenance from the DBMS vendor, and coordinating migration to new DBMS releases and versions.

As with data administration, there must be cross-training of skills between the SA and DBA. The SA will never understand the physical database like the DBA, but the DBA is unlikely to understand the installation and in-depth technical relationships of system software like the SA. Each job function will be more effective with some knowledge of the other.

If no system administration group exists, or if its focus is not on the DBMS, the DBA assumes responsibility for DBMS-related system administration and programming. Figure 1-5 delineates the responsibilities of the DA, the DBA, and the SA.

DBA Tasks

Ensuring that an organization's data and databases are useful, usable, available, and correct requires the DBA to perform a variety of tasks in a variety of areas. These

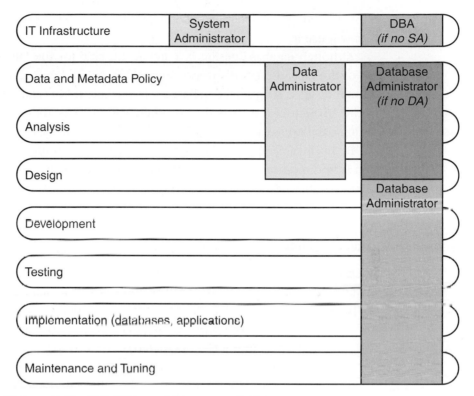

Figure 1-5 *DA, DBA, and SA responsibilities*

areas include database design, performance monitoring and tuning, database availability, security, backup and recovery, data integrity, release migration—really, anything that involves the company's databases. Let's examine each of these topics.

Database Design

To properly design and create relational databases, the DBA must understand and adhere to sound relational design practices. The DBA must understand both relational theory and the specific implementation of the relational database management system (RDBMS) he's using to create the database. Database design requires a sound understanding of conceptual and logical data modeling techniques. The ability to create and interpret entity-relationship diagrams is essential to designing a relational database.

The DBA must be able to transform a logical data model into a physical database implementation. The DBA must ensure that the database design and implementation will enable a useful database for the applications and clients that will use it.

Although database design is a significant skill for the DBA to possess, the job of the DBA is often disproportionately associated with database design. Although designing optimal databases is important, it is a relatively small portion of the DBA's job. A DBA will most likely spend more time administering and tuning databases than in designing and building databases.

A poor relational design can result in poor performance.

By no means, though, should you interpret this to mean that database design is not important. A poor relational design can result in poor performance, a database that does not meet the needs of the organization, and potentially inaccurate data.

Performance Monitoring and Tuning

What is meant by database performance? Let's use the familiar concept of supply and demand. Users demand information from the database, and the DBMS supplies this demand for information. The rate at which the DBMS supplies the information can be termed *database performance*. However, it is not really that simple. Five factors influence database performance: workload, throughput, resources, optimization, and contention.

The *workload* that is requested of the DBMS defines the demand. It is a combination of online transactions, batch jobs, ad hoc queries, data warehousing, analytical queries, and commands directed through the system at any given time. Workload can fluctuate drastically from day to day, hour to hour, minute to minute, and even second to second. Sometimes workload can be predicted (such as heavy month-end processing of payroll, or very light access after 7:30 P.M., when most users have left for the day), but at other times it is unpredictable. The overall workload has a major impact on database performance.

Throughput defines the overall capability of the computer hardware and software to process data. It is a composite of I/O speed, CPU speed, parallel capabilities of the machine, and the efficiency of the operating system and system software. The hardware and software tools at the disposal of the system are known as the *resources* of the system. Examples include the database kernel, disk space, cache controllers, and microcode.

Optimization refers to the analysis of database requests with query cost formulas to generate efficient access paths to data. All types of systems can be optimized, but relational queries are unique in that optimization is primarily accomplished internal to the DBMS. However, many other factors need to be optimized (SQL formulation, database parameters, programming efficiently, and so on) to enable the database optimizer to create the most efficient access paths.

When the demand (workload) for a particular resource is high, *contention* can result. Contention is the condition in which two or more components of the workload are attempting to use a single resource in a conflicting way (for example, dual updates to the same piece of data). As contention increases, throughput decreases.

Therefore, database performance can be defined as the optimization of resource usage to increase throughput and minimize contention, enabling the largest possible workload to be processed.

Whenever performance problems are encountered by an application that uses a database, the DBA is usually the first one called to resolve the problem. Of course, the DBA cannot manage database performance in a vacuum. Applications regularly communicate with other applications, systems, and components of the IT infrastructure. An effective performance monitoring and tuning strategy requires not just DBMS expertise but knowledge outside the scope of database administration. Many performance management tasks must be shared between the DBA and other technicians. In other words, handling performance problems is truly an enterprisewide endeavor.

Many tasks and abilities are required of DBAs to ensure efficient access to databases. Some of these abilities include building appropriate indexes, specifying large enough buffers and caches, aligning the database implementation with the IT infrastructure, monitoring databases and applications, reorganizing databases, and adapting to business changes—more users, more data, additional processing, and changing requirements and regulations.

Database performance can be defined as the optimization of resource usage to increase throughput and minimize contention.

Availability

Ensuring database availability is a multifaceted process.

The *availability* of data and databases is often closely aligned with performance, but it is actually a separate concern. Of course, if the DBMS is offline, performance will be nonexistent because no data can be accessed. However, ensuring database availability is a multifaceted process.

The first component of availability is keeping the DBMS up and running. Vigilant monitoring and automated alerts can be used to warn of DBMS outages and the need for corrective action.

Individual databases also must be maintained so that data is available whenever applications and clients require it. The DBA needs to design the database so that it can be maintained with minimal disruptions, but he also helps developers design applications to minimize conflicts when concurrent access is required.

An additional component of availability is minimizing the amount of downtime required to perform administrative tasks. The faster the DBA can perform administrative tasks that require databases to be offline, the more available the data becomes. Increasingly, the DBMS vendors and ISVs are providing nondisruptive utilities that can be performed on databases while applications read and write from the databases. Additionally, database clustering technologies provide failover techniques that help to reduce downtime. Nevertheless, such technology usually requires more skill and up-front planning to implement.

The DBA must understand all of these aspects of availability and ensure that each application is receiving the correct level of availability for its needs.

Database Security and Authorization

Once the database is designed and implemented, programmers and users will need to access and modify the data. However, to prevent security breaches and improper data modification, only authorized programmers and users should have access. It is the responsibility of the DBA to ensure that data is available only to authorized users.

Typically, the DBA works with the internal security features of the DBMS in the form of SQL GRANT and REVOKE statements, as well as with any group-authorization features of the DBMS. Security must be administered for many actions required by the database environment:

- Creating database objects, including databases, tables, views, and program structures
- Altering the structure of database objects
- Accessing the system catalog
- Reading and modifying data in tables
- Creating and accessing user-defined functions and data types
- Running stored procedures
- Starting and stopping databases and associated database objects
- Setting and modifying DBMS parameters and specifications
- Running database utilities such as LOAD, RECOVER, and REORG

Database security can be enforced in other ways as well. For example, views can be created that block access to sensitive data by end users and programmers. In addition, the DBA interfaces frequently with external security methods when they impact database security. In short, the DBA must understand and be capable of implementing any aspect of security that impacts access to databases.

Backup and Recovery

The majority of recoveries today occur as a result of application software error and human error.

The DBA must be prepared to recover data in the event of a problem. "Problem" can mean anything from a system glitch or program error to a natural disaster that shuts down an organization. The majority of recoveries today occur as a result of application software error and human error. Hardware failures are not as prevalent as they used to be. In fact, analyst estimates indicate that 80% of application errors are due to software failures and human error. The DBA must be prepared to recover data to a usable point, no matter what the cause, and to do so as quickly as possible.

The first type of data recovery that usually comes to mind is a *recover to current*, usually in the face of a major shutdown. The end result of the recovery is that the database is brought back to its current state at the time of the failure. Applications are completely unavailable until the recovery is complete.

Another type of traditional recovery is a *point-in-time recovery*. Point-in-time recovery usually deals with an application-level problem. Conventional techniques to perform a point-in-time recovery remove the effects of *all* transactions since a specified point in time. This can cause problems if valid transactions occurred during that timeframe that still need to be applied.

Transaction recovery is a third type of recovery; it addresses the shortcomings of the traditional types of recovery: downtime and loss of good data. Thus, transaction recovery is an application recovery whereby the effects of specific transactions during a specified timeframe are removed from the database. Therefore, transaction recovery is sometimes referred to as application recovery.

To be prepared for any type of recovery, the DBA needs to develop a backup strategy to ensure that data is not lost in the event of an error in software, hardware, or a manual process. The strategy must be applicable to database processing, so it must include image copies of database files as well as a backup/recovery plan for database logs. It needs to account for any nondatabase file activity that can impact database applications, as well.

Data Integrity

Three aspects of
integrity are rele-
vant to our discus-
sion of databases:
physical, semantic,
and internal.

A database must be designed to store the correct data in the correct way without that data becoming damaged or corrupted. To ensure this process, the DBA implements integrity rules using features of the DBMS. Three aspects of integrity are relevant to our discussion of databases: physical, semantic, and internal.

Physical issues can be handled using DBMS features such as domains and data types. The DBA chooses the appropriate data type for each column of each table. This action ensures that only data of that type is stored in the database. That is, the DBMS enforces the integrity of the data with respect to its type. A column defined as "integer" can only contain integers. Attempts to store non-numeric or non-integer values in a column defined as integer will fail. DBAs can also utilize constraints to further delineate the type of data that can be stored in database columns. Most relational DBMS products provide the following types of constraints:

- *Referential constraints* are used to specify the columns that define any relationships between tables. Referential constraints are used to implement referential integrity, which ensures that all intended references from data in one column (or set of columns) of a table are valid with respect to data in another column of the same or a different table.

- *Unique constraints* ensure that the values for a column or a set of columns occur only once in a table.

- *Check constraints* are used to place more complex integrity rules on a column or set of columns in a table. Check constraints are typically defined using SQL and can be used to define the data values that are permissible for a column or set of columns.

Semantic integrity is more difficult to control and less easily defined. An example of semantic integrity is the quality of the data in the database. Simply storing any data that meets the physical integrity definitions specified to the database is not enough. Procedures and practices need to be in place to ensure data quality. For example, a customer database that contains a wrong address or phone number in 25% of the customer records is an example of a database with poor quality. There is no systematic, physical method of ensuring data accuracy. Data quality is encouraged through proper application code, sound business practices, and specific data policies. Redundancy is another semantic issue. If data elements are stored redundantly throughout the database, the

DBA should document this fact and work to ensure that procedures are in place to keep redundant data synchronized and accurate.

The final aspect of integrity comprises internal DBMS issues. The DBMS relies on internal structures and code to maintain links, pointers, and identifiers. In most cases, the DBMS will do a good job of maintaining these structures, but the DBA needs to be aware of their existence and how to cope when the DBMS fails. Internal DBMS integrity is essential in the following areas:

- *Index consistency.* An index is really nothing but an ordered list of pointers to data in database tables. If for some reason the index gets out of sync with the data, indexed access can fail to return the proper data. The DBA has tools at his disposal to check for and remedy these types of errors.

- *Pointer consistency.* Sometimes large multimedia objects are not stored in the same physical files as other data. Therefore, the DBMS requires pointer structures to keep the multimedia data synchronized to the base table data. Once again, these pointers may get out of sync if proper administration procedures are not followed.

- *Backup consistency.* Some DBMS products occasionally take improper backup copies that effectively cannot be used for recovery. It is essential to identify these scenarios and take corrective actions.

Overall, ensuring integrity is an essential DBA skill.

DBMS Release Migration

The task of keeping the DBMS running and up-to-date is an ongoing effort that will consume many DBA cycles.

The DBA is also responsible for managing the migration from release to release of the DBMS. DBMS products change quite frequently—new versions are usually released every year or so. The task of keeping the DBMS running and up-to-date is an ongoing effort that will consume many DBA cycles. Whatever approach is taken must conform to the needs of the organization, while reducing outages and minimizing the need to change applications.

Jack-of-All-Trades

Databases are at the center of modern applications. If the DBMS fails, applications fail, and if applications fail, business can come to a halt. And if business comes to a halt often enough, the entire business can fail. Database administration is therefore critical to the ongoing success of modern business.

Databases interact with almost every component of the IT infrastructure. The IT infrastructure of today comprises many tools:

- Programming languages and environments such as COBOL, Microsoft Visual Studio, C/C++, and Java
- Database and process design tools such as ERwin and Rational Rose
- Transaction processing systems such as CICS and Tuxedo
- Message queueing software such as MQSeries and MSMQ
- Networking software and protocols such as SNA, VTAM, TCP/IP, and Novell
- Networking hardware such as bridges, routers, hubs, and cabling
- Multiple operating systems such as Windows, OS/390 and MVS, UNIX, Linux, and perhaps others
- Data storage hardware and software such as enterprise storage servers, Microsoft SMS, IBM DFHSM, storage area networks (SANs), and NAS
- Operating system security packages such as RACF, ACF2, and Kerberos
- Other types of storage hardware such as tape machines, silos, and solid state (memory-based) storage
- Non-DBMS data set and file storage techniques such as VSAM and B-tree
- Database administration tools
- Systems management tools and frameworks such as BMC PATROL and CA Unicenter
- Operational control software such as batch scheduling software and job-entry subsystems
- Software distribution solutions for implementing new versions of system software across the network
- Internet and Web-enabled databases and applications
- Client/server development techniques such as multitier, fat server/thin client, thin server/fat client
- Object-oriented and component-based development technologies and techniques such as CORBA, COM, OLE DB, ADO, and EJB
- PDAs such as Palm Pilots and PocketPCs

Although it is impossible to become an expert in all of these technologies, the DBA should have some knowledge of each of these areas and how they interrelate. Even more importantly, the DBA should have the phone numbers of experts to contact in case any of the associated software and hardware causes database access or performance problems.

Types of DBAs

There are DBAs who focus on logical design and DBAs who focus on physical design; DBAs who specialize in building systems and DBAs who specialize in maintaining and tuning systems; specialty DBAs and general purpose DBAs. Truly, the job of DBA encompasses many roles.

Some organizations choose to split DBA responsibilities into separate jobs. Of course, this occurs most frequently in larger organizations, because smaller organizations often cannot afford the luxury of having multiple, specialty DBAs.

Still other companies simply hire DBAs to perform all of the tasks required to design, create, document, tune, and maintain the organization's data, databases, and database management systems. Let's look at some of the more common types of DBA.

System DBA

A system DBA focuses on technical rather than business issues.

A *system DBA* focuses on technical rather than business issues, primarily in the system administration area. Typical tasks center on the physical installation and performance of the DBMS software and can include the following:

- Installing new DBMS versions and applying maintenance fixes supplied by the DBMS vendor
- Setting and tuning system parameters
- Tuning the operating system, network, and transaction processors to work with the DBMS
- Ensuring appropriate storage for the DBMS
- Enabling the DBMS to work with storage devices and storage management software
- Interfacing with any other technologies required by database applications
- Installing third-party DBA tools

System DBAs are rarely involved with actual implementation of databases and applications. They might get involved in application tuning when operating system parameters or complex DBMS parameters need to be altered.

Indeed, the job of system DBA usually exists only if the organization does not have an official system administration or systems programming department.

Database Architect

The database architect is involved in new design and development work only.

Some organizations create a separate position, *database architect*, for design and implementation of new databases. The database architect is involved in new design and development work only; he is not involved in maintenance, administration, or tuning of established databases and applications. The database architect designs new databases for new or existing applications.

The rationale for creating a separate position is that the skills required for designing new databases are different from the skills required to keep an existing database implementation up and running. A database architect is more likely than a general-purpose DBA to have data administration and modeling expertise.

Typical tasks performed by the database architect include:

- Creating a logical data model (if no DA or data modeler position exists)
- Translating logical data models into physical database designs
- Implementing efficient databases, including specifying physical characteristics, designing efficient indexes, and mapping database objects to physical storage devices
- Analyzing data access and modification requirements to ensure efficient SQL and optimal database design
- Creating backup and recovery strategies for new databases

Most organizations do not staff a separate database architect position, instead requiring DBAs to work on both new and established database projects.

Database Analyst

Another common staff position is the *database analyst*. There is really no set definition for this position. Sometimes junior DBAs are referred to as database analysts. Sometimes a database analyst performs a role similar to that of the database architect. Sometimes the data administrator is referred to as the database analyst or perhaps as the data analyst. And sometimes a database analyst is just another term used by some companies instead of database administrator.

Data Modeler

A *data modeler* is usually responsible for a subset of the DA's responsibilities. Data modeling tasks include the following:

- Collecting data requirements for development projects
- Analyzing the data requirements
- Designing project-based conceptual and logical data models
- Creating and updating a corporate data model
- Ensuring that the DBAs have a sound understanding of the data models

Application DBA

The application DBA focuses on database design and the ongoing support and administration of databases for a specific application or applications.

In direct contrast to the system DBA is the *application DBA*. The application DBA focuses on database design and the ongoing support and administration of databases for a specific application or applications. The application DBA is likely to be an expert at writing and debugging complex SQL and understands the best ways to incorporate database requests into application programs. The application DBA must also be capable of performing database change management, performance tuning, and most of the other roles of the DBA. The difference is the focus of the application DBA—it is on a specific subset of applications rather than the overall DBMS implementation and database environment. (See Figure 1-6.)

Not every organization staffs application DBAs. However, when application DBAs exist, general-purpose DBAs are still required to support the overall database environment and infrastructure. When application DBAs do not exist within an organization, general-purpose DBAs are likely to be assigned to support specific applications while also maintaining the organization's database environment.

There are pros and cons to staffing application DBAs. The arguments in favor of application DBAs include the following:

- An application DBA can better focus on an individual application, which can result in better service to the developers of that application.

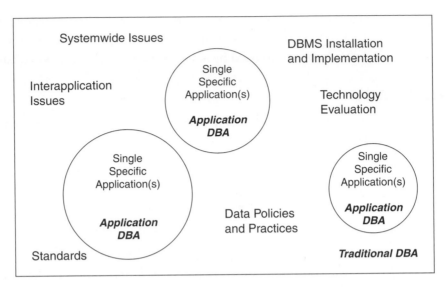

Figure 1-6 *Focus of the application DBA*

- The application DBA is more often viewed as an integral component of the development team and therefore is better informed about new development plans and changes.

- Because the application DBA works consistently on a specific set of applications, he can acquire a better overall understanding of how each application works, enabling him to better support the needs of the application developers.

- With a more comprehensive understanding of the application, an application DBA will have a better understanding of how the application impacts the overall business. This knowledge will likely result in the execution of DBA tasks to better support the organization.

But all is not favorable for application DBAs. There are cons to implementing an application DBA role:

- An application DBA can lose sight of the overall data needs of the organization because of his narrow focus on a single application.

- The application DBA can become isolated. Lack of communication with a centralized DBA group (if one exists) can result in diminished sharing of skills.

- When an application DBA implements useful procedures, it takes more effort to share these procedures with the other DBAs.

- Due to the application-centric nature of the position, an application DBA can lose sight of new features and functionality delivered by the DBMS group.

When staffing application DBAs, be sure to also staff a centralized DBA group.

In general, when staffing application DBAs, be sure to also staff a centralized DBA group. The application DBAs should have primary responsibility for specific applications, but should also be viewed as part of the centralized DBA group.

Task-Oriented DBA

Larger organizations sometimes create very specialized DBAs that focus on a specific DBA task. However, task-oriented DBAs are quite rare outside of very large IT shops. One example of a task-oriented DBA is a backup-and-recovery DBA who devotes his entire day to ensuring the recoverability of the organization's databases.

Most organizations cannot afford this level of specialization, but when possible, task-oriented DBAs can ensure that very knowledgeable specialists tackle very important DBA tasks.

Performance Analyst

Performance analysts are a specific type of task-oriented DBA. The performance analyst, more common than other task-oriented DBAs, focuses solely on the performance of database applications.

A performance analyst must understand the details and nuances of SQL coding for performance and be able to design databases for performance. A performance analyst will have very detailed technical knowledge of the DBMS so that he can make appropriate changes to DBMS and system parameters when required.

However, the performance analyst should not be a system DBA. The performance analyst must be able to speak to application developers in their language in order to help them facilitate appropriate program changes for performance.

The performance analyst is usually the most skilled, senior member of the DBA staff.

The performance analyst is usually the most skilled, senior member of the DBA staff, a role that he has grown into due to his experience and the respect he has gained in past tuning endeavors.

Data Warehouse Administrator

Organizations that implement data warehouses for performing in-depth data analysis often staff DBAs specifically to monitor and support the data warehouse environment. *Data warehouse administrators* must be capable DBAs, but with a thorough understanding of the differences between a database that supports OLTP and a data warehouse. Data warehouse administration requires experience with the following:

- Business intelligence, query, and reporting tools
- Database design for read-only access
- Data warehousing design issues such as star schema
- Data warehousing technologies such as OLAP (including ROLAP, MOLAP, and HOLAP)
- Data transformation and conversion
- Data quality issues
- Data formats for loading and unloading of data
- Middleware

Staffing Considerations

Staffing the DBA organization is not a simple matter. Several nontrivial considerations must be addressed, including the size of the DBA staff and the reporting structure for the DBAs.

How Many DBAs?

One of the most difficult things to determine is the optimal number of DBAs required to keep an organization's databases online and operating efficiently. Many organizations try to operate with the minimal number of DBAs on staff; the idea being that fewer staff members lowers cost. However, that assumption may not be true. An overworked DBA staff can make mistakes that cause downtime and operational problems far in excess of the salary requirements of an additional DBA.

Determining how many DBAs is optimal is not a precise science. It depends on many factors:

- *Number of databases*. The more databases that need to be supported, the more complex the job of database administration becomes. Each database needs to be designed, implemented, monitored for availability and performance, backed up, and administered. There is a limit to the number of databases that an individual DBA can control.

- *Size of the databases.* The larger the databases that need to be supported, the more difficult the job of database administration. A larger database takes longer to create, maintain, and tune. In addition, more potential for confusion arises when SQL takes longer to execute—causing the DBA to spend more time working with developers to tune SQL.

- *Number of users.* As additional users are brought online, optimal database performance becomes more difficult to ensure. Additionally, as the number of users increases, the potential for increase in the volume of problems and calls increases, further complicating the DBA's job.

- *Number of applications.* A single database can be utilized by numerous applications. Indeed, one of the primary benefits of the DBMS is that it enables the sharing of data across an organization. As more applications are brought online, additional pressure is exerted on the database in terms of performance, availability, and resources. As more applications are brought online, more DBAs may be required to support the same number of databases.

- *Service-level agreements (SLAs)*. The more restrictive the SLA, the more difficult it becomes for the DBA to deliver the service. For example, a service-level agreement requiring subsecond response time for transactions is more difficult to support than an agreement requiring three-second response time.

- *Availability requirements*. Database administration becomes easier if databases have an allowable period of scheduled downtime. Some DBA tasks either require an outage, or are easier when an outage can be taken. Considerations such as supporting e-business transactions and the Web drive the need for 24/7 database availability. 24/7 availability is often incompatible with certain DBA tasks.

- *Impact of downtime*. The greater the financial impact of an unavailable database, the greater the pressure on the DBA to assure greater database availability.

- *Performance requirements.* As the requirements for database access become more performance oriented, database administration becomes more complicated.

- *Type of Applications.* The type of applications supported has a direct bearing on the number of DBAs required. The DBMS and database needs of a mission-critical application differ from those of a non-mission-critical application. Mission-critical applications are more likely to require constant monitoring to ensure availability. Likewise, an OLTP application has different characteristics and administration requirements than an OLAP application. OLTP transactions are likely to be of shorter duration than OLAP queries; OLTP applications perform both read and write operations whereas OLAP applications are predominantly read-only. Each has administration challenges that require different DBA procedures.

- *Volatility.* The frequency of database change requests is an important factor in the need for additional DBAs. A static database environment requiring few changes will not require the same level of DBA effort as a volatile, frequently changing database environment. Unfortunately, the level of volatility for most databases and applications tends to change dramatically over time. It's usually very difficult to ascertain how volatile an overall database environment will be over its lifetime.

- *DBA staff experience.* The skill of the existing DBA staff affects the need for additional DBAs. A highly skilled DBA staff will accomplish more than a novice team. Skills, more than experience, dictate DBA staffing requirements. A highly skilled DBA with two years of experience might easily outperform a ten-year veteran who is burned out and unmotivated.

- *Programming staff experience.* If the application developers are not highly skilled in database and SQL programming, the DBAs will need to be more involved in the development process. DBAs will be needed for tasks such as composing complex SQL, analyzing SQL and application code, debugging, tuning, and ensuring connectivity. As the experience of the programming staff increases, the complexity of DBA requirements decreases.

- *End user experience.* When end users access databases directly with ad hoc SQL, their skill level has a direct impact on the complexity of DBA. If the end user has few SQL skills, the DBA will need to be initiate more performance monitoring and tuning.

- *Variety of DBMSs.* The more heterogeneous the environment, the more difficult it becomes to administer. For example, acquiring and maintaining expertise in both Oracle and DB2 is more difficult than gaining expertise in only one of them. Moreover, as multiple DBMSs of different types are installed, database administration becomes even more difficult. For example, a shop with DB2, IMS, and IDMS will have to possess relational (DB2), hierarchical (IMS), and network/CODASYL (IDMS) expertise.

- *DBA tools.* DBMS vendors and a number of ISVs offer tools that automate DBA tasks and make database administration easier. DBA tasks become less complex with the more tools available and the degree to which they are integrated. Lou Agosta, an industry analyst with Giga Group, states that "without [DBA] tools up to twice the number of DBAs might [be] required."

Creating a formula that will dictate the optimal number of DBAs to employ is difficult.

This list of issues notwithstanding, creating a formula that will dictate the optimal number of DBAs to employ is difficult. Industry analysts at the META Group have established a loose formula for calculating DBA level of effort. The formula arrives at a level of effort by applying weights to six factors: system complexity, application immaturity, end-user sophistication, software functionality, system availability, and staff sophistication. After measuring each of these items, you plug in values to the formula to arrive at an estimate for the number of DBAs required. If you are interested in pursuing this metric further, I refer you to the META Group research (META Group, Open Computing & Server Strategies, File: 656, Date: 20-Mar-1998). META Group can be contacted at http://www.metagroup.com or by phone at 1-203-973-6700.

DBA Reporting Structures

To whom should the DBA group report? Different companies have taken different approaches to the DBA reporting structure, but a few reporting hierarchies are quite common. Some reporting structures work better than others, so let's review some of the possibilities.

One of the best structures is a data resource management group that consists of all the data and information specialist of the organization.

One of the best structures is a data resource management (DRM) group that consists of all the data and information specialist of the organization—DA, DBA, data analysts, performance analysts, and so on. This group usually reports directly to the CIO, but might report through a systems programming unit, the data center, or technical support. Figure 1-7 depicts a typical reporting structure.

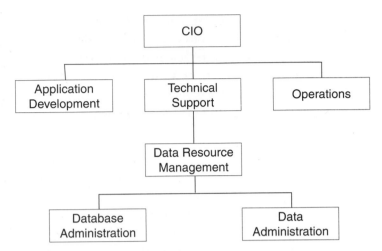

Figure 1-7 *Typical DBA reporting structure*

When an organization staffs application DBAs, they will be spread out in application groups, typically with a direct line of report to the business programming managers. Each application development team has a dedicated application DBA resource as shown in Figure 1-8.

There are problems with both of these reporting structures, though. First, the DRM needs to be placed higher in the IT reporting hierarchy. It's a good idea to have the DRM group report directly to the CIO. When an organization understands the importance of data to the health of the organization, placing the DRM group at this level is encouraged.

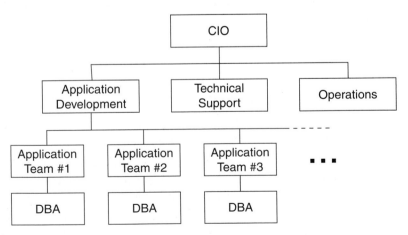

Figure 1-8 *Application DBA reporting structure*

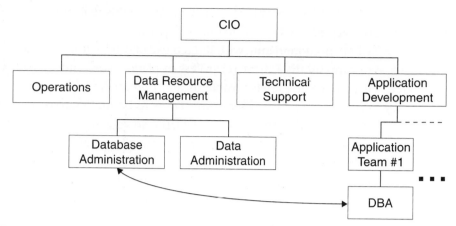

Figure 1-9   *Recommended DRM reporting structure*

Furthermore, when application DBAs exist, they should not report to the application programming manager only. A secondary line of report to the DRM group will ensure that DBA skills are shared and communicated throughout the organization. Figure 1-9 delineates the recommended reporting structure for the DRM group.

Multiplatform DBA Issues

Managing a multi-platform environment complicates the job of database administration.

Managing a multiplatform environment complicates the job of database administration. A whole batch of different problems and issues arise that need to be addressed. The first task is to define the scope of each DBA's job. Does a single DBA administer all of the different DBMSs or does each DBA focus on supporting only one DBMS?

This is a particularly thorny issue. On the one hand, the functionality of a DBMS is strikingly similar regardless of platform and vendor. A DBMS is designed to store, retrieve, and protect data. Programmers, programs, and end users all interact with the DBMS to access and modify data. Administration issues are similar—design, creation, optimization, and so on—though each DBMS implements these items differently. So, the case can be made that a DBA should support multiple DBMSs and databases, regardless of platform or vendor.

On the other hand, each DBMS offers different features, functionality, and technology. Keeping all of the differences and nuances straight is a monumental task. Wouldn't it be better to develop platform-expert DBAs? That way, your Oracle DBAs can focus on learning all there is to know about Oracle, your DB2 DBAs can focus on DB2, and so on.

Every organization will have to make this determination based on their particular mix of DBMSs, features, and DBA talent. If your organization uses one DBMS predominantly, with limited use of others, it may make sense for each DBA to support all of them, regardless of platform or vendor. Sparse usage of a DBMS usually means fewer problems and potentially less usage of its more sophisticated features. By tasking your DBAs to be multi-DBMS and multiplatform, you can ensure that the most skilled DBAs in your shop are available for all database administration issues. If your organization uses many different DBMSs, it is probably wise to create specialist DBAs for the heavily used platforms and perhaps share administration duties for the less frequently used platforms among other DBAs.

When DBA duties are shared, be sure to carefully document the skills and knowledge level of each DBA for each DBMS being supported. Take care to set up an effective and fair on-call rotation that does not unduly burden any particular DBA or group of DBAs. Furthermore, use the organizational structure to promote sharing of database standards and procedures across all supported DBMS environments.

Keep in mind, too, that when multiple DBMSs and platforms are supported, you should consider implementing DBA tools, performance monitors, and scripts that can address multiple platforms. For this reason, DBA tools from third-party vendors are usually better for heterogeneous environments than similar tools offered by the DBMS vendors.

When your organization supports multiple DBMSs, the DBA group should develop guidelines for which DBMS should be used in which situations. These guidelines should not be hard-and-fast rules, but instead should provide guidance for the types of applications and databases best supported by each DBMS. Forcing applications to a given DBMS environment is not a good practice. The guidelines should be used simply to assure best fit of application to DBMS. These guidelines should take into account:

- Features of each DBMS
- Features and characteristics of the operating system
- Networking capabilities of the DBMS and operating system combination
- DBMS skills of the application developers
- Programming language support
- Any other organizational issues and requirements

Test and Production

Separating the test and production environments ensures the integrity and performance of operational work.

At least two separate environments must be created and supported for a quality database implementation: *test* and *production*. Completely separating the test and production environments ensures the integrity and performance of operational work. New development and maintenance work can be performed in the test environment while operational applications are run in the production environment. Failure to separate test and production will cause development activities to impair the day-to-day business of your organization. Errant program code in the early stages of development could access or modify production data and cause production performance problems or invalid data.

The test and production environments need not be identical. While the production environment contains all of the data required to support the operational applications, the test environment needs only a subset of data required for acceptable application testing. Furthermore, the test DBMS implementation will usually not command the same amount of resources as the production environment. For example, less memory will be allocated to buffering and caches, data set allocations will be smaller and on fewer devices, and the DBMS software may be a more recent version in test than in production (to shake out any bugs in the DBMS code itself before it is trusted to run in production).

The test and production environments should be structured similarly though. Both environments should have access to the same system software because the programming staff needs to create applications in the same type of environment in which they will eventually run.

DBAs may need to create multiple copies of databases in the test environment to support concurrent development by multiple programmers. Furthermore, the programming staff must be able to control the contents of the test databases. Because programmers may need to run data modification programs multiple times during the development process, they must be able to ensure that the data at the beginning of each test run is the same. Failure to do so can render the results of the tests invalid. Therefore, the DBA must assist the programming staff in the creation of database load and unload jobs to set up test databases. Prior to a test run, the database must be loaded with the test data. After the test run, the programmer can examine the output from the program and the contents of the database to determine if the program logic is correct. If not, he can repeat the process, loading to reset the data in the database and retesting. Automated procedures can be put in place to unload the databases impacted by the program and compare the results to the load files.

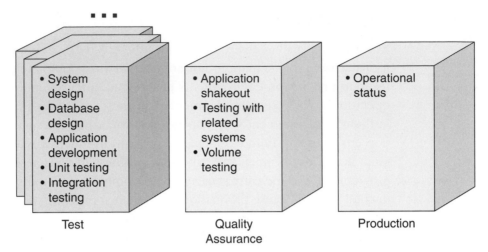

Figure 1-10   *Establishing multiple database environments*

Predicting how test applications will perform once they are moved to production is difficult, but the DBA can assist here as well. A relational DBMS typically provides a method to gather statistical information about the contents of its databases. These statistics are then used by the relational optimizer to determine how SQL will retrieve data. (This topic is covered in more depth in Chapter 12.) But remember, there will be much less data in test databases than in production. In some cases, though, the DBA can set up scripts to read the production statistics and copy them to the test environment, thereby enabling developers to gauge more accurately how test applications will perform in production.

A QA environment may be needed to perform rigorous testing against new and modified programs before they are migrated.

Some organizations implement more than two environments, as shown in Figure 1-10. If special care is needed for complex application development projects, additional levels of isolated testing may need to occur. For example, a unit test environment may exist for individual program development, while an integration testing environment ensures that new programs work together or with existing programs. A quality assurance environment may be needed to perform rigorous testing against new and modified programs before they are migrated to the production environment.

New Technology and the DBA

The DBA is at the center of the action whenever new ways of doing business and new technologies are introduced to the organization. Data is the lifeblood of modern business, data is housed by the database, and the DBA is the expert who understands database technology—and in particular, how databases can be integrated with other new technologies.

Let's examine three specific newer technologies that rely on database administration—at least somewhat—to be effectively implemented: database-coupled application logic, Internet-enabled e-business development, and hand-held computing.

Procedural DBAs: Managing Database Logic

Triggers, user-defined functions, and stored procedures provide the ability to define business rules to the DBMS.

Until recently, the purpose of a database management system was, appropriately enough, to store, manage, and access data. Although these core capabilities are still required of modern DBMS products, additional procedural functionality is slowly becoming not just a nice feature to have, but a necessity. Features such as triggers, user-defined functions, and stored procedures provide the ability to define business rules to the DBMS instead of in separate application programs. These features couple application logic tightly to the database server.

Since all of the most popular RDBMS products provide sometimes-complex features to facilitate database-coupled procedural logic, additional management discipline is required to ensure the optimal use of these features. Typically, as new features are added, their administration, design, and management are assigned to the DBA by default. However, without proper planning and preparation, chaos can ensue. First let's examine how database logic is stored in a DBMS.

Stored Procedures

Stored procedures can be thought of as programs that live in a database. The procedural logic of a stored procedure is maintained, administered, and executed through the database commands. The primary reason for using stored procedures is to move application code from a client workstation to the database server. Stored procedures typically consume less overhead in a client/server environment because one client can invoke a stored procedure that causes multiple SQL statements to be run. The alternative, the client executing multiple SQL statements directly, increases network traffic and can degrade overall application performance.

A stored procedure is a freestanding database object; it is not "physically" associated with any other object in the database. A stored procedure can access and/or modify data in many tables.

Triggers

Triggers are event-driven specialized procedures that are attached to database tables. The trigger code is automatically executed by the RDBMS as data changes in the database. Each trigger is attached to a single, specified table. Triggers can be thought of as an advanced form of rule or constraint that uses procedural logic. A trigger cannot be directly called or executed; it is automatically executed (or "fired") by the RDBMS as the result of a SQL INSERT, UPDATE, or DELETE statement issued on its associated table. Once a trigger is created, it is always executed when its firing event occurs.

User-Defined Functions

A *user-defined function* (UDF) provides a result based on a set of input values. UDFs are programs that can be executed in place of standard, built-in SQL scalar or column functions. A scalar function transforms data for each row of a result set; a column function evaluates each value for a particular column in each row of the results set and returns a single value. Once written, and defined to the RDBMS, a UDF becomes available just like any other built-in database function.

Table 1-1 summarizes the differences between stored procedures, triggers, and UDFs.

Administering Stored Procedures, Triggers, and UDFs

Once developers begin to rely on stored procedures, triggers, and UDFs, DBAs need to take steps to manage them properly. DBAs must grapple with the issues of quality, maintainability, efficiency, and availability. How and when will these procedural objects be tested? The impact of a failure is enterprisewide,

Table 1-1   *Procedural Database Objects*

Object Type	Definition	Executed	How
Stored Procedure	Program logic executed on the database server	By request	Explicit
Triggers	Event-driven procedures attached to database tables	Automatically	Implicit
UDFs	Program logic extending SQL functionality	By request in SQL	Explicit

increasing the visibility and criticality of these objects. Who is responsible if they fail? The answer must be—the DBA.

The role of administering procedural database logic should fall upon someone skilled in that discipline. A new type of DBA is required to accommodate the administration of database procedural logic. This new role can be defined as a *procedural DBA*.

The procedural DBA is responsible for those database management activities that require procedural logic support. He ensures that stored procedures, triggers, and user-defined functions are effectively planned, implemented, shared, and reused. The procedural DBA also takes primary responsibility for coding and testing all triggers. Stored procedures and user-defined functions, although likely to be coded by application programmers, should be reviewed for accuracy and performance by procedural DBAs. (See Figure 1-11.)

The procedural DBA leads the review and administration of all procedural database objects: triggers, stored procedures, and UDFs. Although the procedural DBA is unlikely to be as skilled at programming as an applications programmer

The procedural DBA is responsible for those database management activities that require procedural logic support.

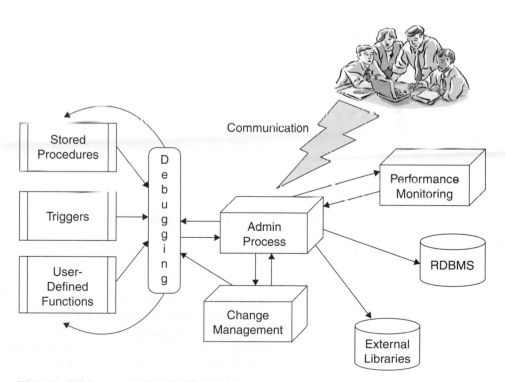

Figure 1-11   *Procedural DBA duties*

or systems analyst, he must be able to write and review program code reasonably well. The skill level required depends on what languages are supported by the DBMS for creating procedural objects, the rate and level of adoption within the organization, and whether an internal organization exists for creating common, reusable programs. Table 1-2 provides a reasonable level of procedural DBA involvement for each type of procedural object. Additionally, the procedural DBA should be on call for any problems that occur with database procedural objects in production.

As shown in Figure 1-11, the procedural DBA requires communication skills as much as he requires technological acumen. In addition to managing and optimizing database procedural objects, the procedural DBA must inform the development community of new triggers, stored procedures, and UDFs. Furthermore, the DBA must promote reuse. If the programmers do not know that these objects exist, they will never be used.

Other procedural administrative functions can be allocated to the procedural DBA. Depending on the number of DBAs and the amount of application development needed, the procedural DBA can be assigned to additional functions such as the following:

- Participating in application code design reviews
- Reviewing and analyzing SQL access paths (from "EXPLAIN" or "SHOW PLAN")
- Debugging SQL
- Writing and analyzing complex SQL statements
- Rewriting queries for optimal execution

Table 1-2 *Procedural DBA Involvement by Object*

Object Type	Level of Procedural DBA Involvement
Stored Procedure	Not likely to write stored procedures; must review all code before migration to production; communicates availability and promotes reuse.
Triggers	Likely to write, test, and debug triggers; communicates deployment of triggers to ensure application awareness.
UDFs	Not likely to write user-defined functions; works closely with the development team to ensure UDF functionality and performance; reviews all code before migration to production; communicates availability and promotes reuse.

Offloading coding-related tasks to the procedural DBA can help the other staff DBAs concentrate on the actual physical design and implementation of databases, resulting in much better designed databases. Procedural DBAs should have the same line of report as traditional DBAs to enable better sharing of skills between the groups. Of course, there will need to be a greater synergy between procedural DBAs and the application programmers. The procedural DBA should typically come from the application programming ranks because this is where the coding skill exists.

The Internet: From DBA to e-DBA

Companies of every size are using Internet technologies to speed up business processes. Indeed, *e-business* has evolved as a new term to describe the transformation of key business processes using Internet technologies. Modern organizations use the Web to communicate with their partners and customers, to connect with their back-end databases, and to conduct transactions (e-commerce). E-business is the integration of traditional information technology with the Internet. This integration creates a more nimble business, prepared for the trials and tribulations of conducting business in the 21st century.

E-businesses must be able to adapt and react to constant change.

E-businesses must be able to adapt and react to constant change. When a business is online, it never closes. People expect full functionality on Web sites they visit regardless of the time. And the Web *is* worldwide. It may be two o'clock in the morning in New York City, but it is always prime time somewhere in the world. An e-business must be available and prepared to engage with customers 24 hours a day, 365 days a year (366 during leap years). Failure to do so risks losing business. When a Web site is down, the customer will go elsewhere to do business because the competition is just a simple mouse-click away. Therefore, those who manage an e-business must be adept, proactive, and ever vigilant.

The frantic pace of an e-business makes extreme demands on those that keep it operational, and DBAs are much affected. The need to integrate the Web with traditional IT services, such as the DBMS, places high expectations on database administrators.

An e-DBA is a DBA who is capable of managing Web-based applications because he understands the special issues that arise because of the Internet.

An e-DBA is a DBA who is capable of managing Web-based applications and their Internet-related issues. With all of the knowledge and training of a traditional DBA, the e-DBA adapts these skills to suit applications and databases that are Internet enabled. When the Web is coupled with traditional applications and databases, a complex infrastructure is the result. (See Figure 1-12.) The e-DBA must be capable of navigating this complex, heterogeneous infrastructure and providing expertise wherever databases interact within this infrastructure.

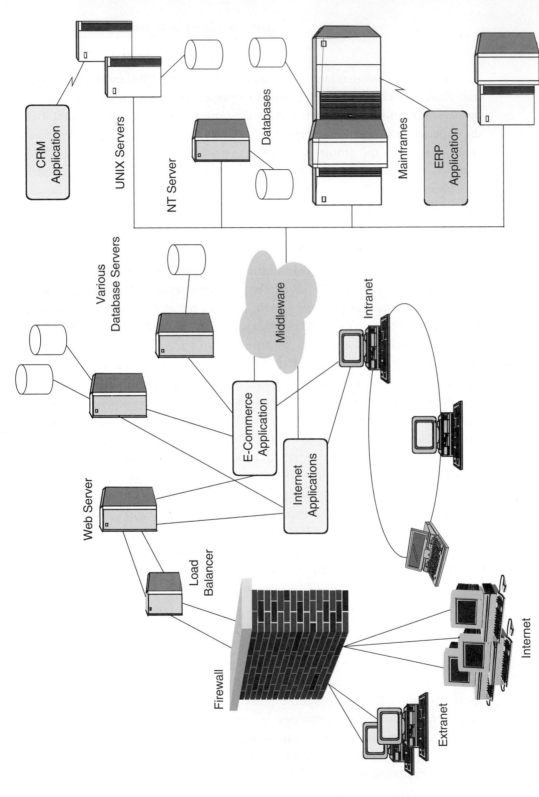

Figure 1-12 *The complex infrastructure enabling Web-to-database capabilities*

Many factors impact database administration when you couple the Internet with database technology. Some of these issues include

- 24/7 data availability
- New technologies such as Java and XML
- Web connectivity
- Integration of legacy data with Web-based applications
- Database and application architecture
- Web-based administration
- Performance engineering for the Internet
- Unpredictable workload

The PDA DBA

Personal digital assistant devices, better known as PDAs, are fast becoming a necessity for modern executives and businessmen. A PDA is a handheld computing device. Whether your PDA of choice is a Palm Pilot or a PocketPC, your PDA may soon have a DBMS running on it. Why is that interesting? Does it change the way you will use your PDA? What will that mean to your IT department?

PDAs offer many benefits. The devices are small and therefore easily transportable. They enhance a mobile worker's ability to be mobile. However, challenges must be faced as organizations incorporate PDAs into their infrastructure. Companies with remote workers such as a distributed sales force or delivery tracking services will most likely be the first impacted. The data on the PDAs must be managed professionally to ensure integrity and reliability. Because the device is remote, sharing of data can be difficult. The data on the PDAs must be reliably synchronized with existing enterprise systems and databases.

All major DBMS vendors provide small-footprint versions of their flagship products to run on PDAs.

All major DBMS vendors provide small-footprint versions of their flagship products to run on PDAs. For example, IBM markets DB2 Everyplace, Oracle sells Oracle8i Lite, and Sybase offers Adaptive Server Anywhere. The general idea is to store a small amount of critical data on the PDA in a database; the local PDA database is later synchronized to long-term data stores on enterprise database servers. Each PDA DBMS provides technology to synchronize data back and forth from the PDA to the enterprise server platforms.

A database the size of those stored on PDAs should not require the in-depth tuning and administration required of enterprise database implementations.

However, DBAs will be called upon to help design appropriately implemented databases for small-form-factor devices like PDAs. However, the biggest impact on the DBA will be the necessity for managing data synchronization from hundreds or thousands of PDAs. When should synchronization be scheduled? How will it impact applications that use large production databases that are involved in the synchronization? How can you ensure that a mobile user will synchronize his data reliably and on schedule?

These are not trivial issues. The DBA staff must be ready to support the organization's inevitable request for this technology by understanding data synchronization technology and the need for remote database users at their organization. Pervasive computing and the mobile workplace are here to stay. The DBA staff must be ready to support these mobile workers with a valid, shared data infrastructure.

As new technology is introduced to the organization, the DBA group is typically the first to examine and use it. The preceding three technologies are merely examples of new trends and technologies that require database administration for efficient and effective implementation.

DBA Certification

Professional certification is a recent trend in IT and is available for many different IT jobs. The availability and levels of certification for database administration have been growing at an alarming rate. Certification programs are available for most of the popular DBMS platforms including IBM DB2, Microsoft SQL Server, and Oracle. The idea behind DBA certification is to ensure that an individual is capable of performing database administration tasks and duties.

This is a noble goal, but the problem is that passing a test is not a viable indicator of success with the complexities of database administration. Some things you just have to learn by doing. I'm not saying that certification is useless: Taking the test and focusing on the questions you miss can help to point out areas of weakness. But does anyone *really* believe that someone passing a formalized test is necessarily as capable as someone with several years of experience as a DBA? Organizations should hire DBAs based on experience that indicates a level of capability. Of course, a DBA with both experience and certification is even better.

Certification will make you more employable.

That said, I do recommend that professional DBAs take the time to study and pass the certification exams. Not because certification will make you a better DBA, but because it will make you more employable. Some companies hire only certified professionals. The trend toward using certification to guide hiring practices will increase because of increasing IT complexity. If you think you might change jobs at some point in your career (and who among us will not?), then certification is a worthwhile pursuit.

Keep in mind that DBA certification tests sometimes ask arcane syntax questions that are not good indicators of a DBA's skills. Getting the syntax 100% accurate is what manuals and design tools are for. Memorizing every detail about SQL syntax and structure is a waste of time because it is complex and changes all the time. It is better to know where to find the syntax, parameters, and answers to your questions when you need them—that is, which manuals and textbooks contain the needed information. DBAs should possess a broad, overarching knowledge of DBMS concepts, IT fundamentals, and the working of their organization's database systems. In other words, it is better to know off the top of your head that something can (or cannot) be done than to know the exact syntax for how to accomplish it.

If you decide to pursue certification, take the time to prepare for the tests. Books and self-learning software titles are available that can be quite useful. These books and programs cover the most common test topics and provide sample questions to help you prepare. In many ways, it is like preparing for a college entrance exam like the SAT.

Finally, once you earn your certification, make sure you display it proudly on your resume and your business card (if your company allows it).

Table 1-3 lists Web sites that contain information about professional certification for the most popular DBMS products.

Table 1-3 *Sources of DBA Certification Information*

DBMS	Web site
Oracle	http://www.oracle.com/education/certification/
Microsoft SQL Server	http://www.microsoft.com/trainingandservices/default.asp?PageID=training
IBM DB2	http://www.ibm.com/certify
Sybase Adaptive Server	http://www.sybase.com/education/profcert/
Informix	http://www.informix.com/informix/training/courses/certific/welcome.htm

The Rest of the Book

This first chapter has introduced you to the world of the DBA. I hope that you have gained respect for the complexity of the position and the qualities required of a good DBA. The remainder of the book will examine the details of the tasks, roles, and responsibilities required of the DBA.

Review

1. What are the primary high-level job responsibilities of a DBA?

2. What is the single biggest problem faced by organizations using relational databases?

3. What is the difference between a data administrator and a database administrator?

4. What factors determine the number of DBAs needed to support an organization's database environment properly?

5. How does new technology impact the job of the DBA?

6. What are the technologies that mandate the need for procedural DBAs?

7. What is the difference between a database architect and a system administrator?

8. Which staff member is most likely to be responsible for installing a new DBMS release?

9. What are the three types of integrity that DBAs must understand?

10. Is a certified DBA necessarily a qualified DBA? Why or why not?

Bonus Question

Why must the DBA be a jack-of-all-trades?

2

Creating the Database Environment

One of the primary tasks associated with the job of DBA is the process of choosing and installing a DBMS. Unfortunately, many business executives and IT professionals without database management backgrounds assume that once the DBMS is installed, the bulk of the work is done. The truth is, choosing and installing the DBMS is hardly the most difficult part of a DBA's job. Establishing a usable database environment requires a great deal of skill, knowledge, and consideration. This chapter will outline the principles involved in establishing a usable database environment.

Defining the Organization's DBMS Strategy

Choosing a suitable DBMS for enterprise database management is not as difficult as it used to be.

The process of choosing a suitable DBMS for enterprise database management is not as difficult as it used to be. The number of major DBMS vendors has dwindled due to industry consolidation and domination of the sector by a few very large players.

Yet, large and medium-sized organizations typically run multiple DBMS products, from as few as two to as many as ten. For example, it is not uncommon for a large company to use IMS or IDMS and DB2 on the mainframe, Oracle and Informix on several different UNIX servers, Microsoft SQL Server on Windows NT servers, as well as pockets of other DBMS products such as Sybase, Ingres, Adabas, and Datacom on various platforms. Not to mention any single-user PC DBMS products such as Microsoft Access, Paradox, or Filemaker. Who chose to install all these DBMSs and why?

Unfortunately, often the answer is that not much thought and planning went into the decision making process. Sometimes the decision to purchase and install a new DBMS is driven by a business need or a new application. This is reasonable if your organization has no DBMS and must purchase one for the first time. This is rarely the case, though. Regardless of whether a DBMS exists on-site, a new DBMS is often viewed as a requirement for a new application. Sometimes a new DBMS product is purchased and installed without first examining if the application could be successfully implemented using an existing DBMS. Or, more likely, the DBAs know the application can be implemented using an existing DBMS but lack the organizational power or support to reject a new DBMS proposal.

There are other reasons for the existence of multiple DBMS platforms in a single organization. Perhaps the company purchased a commercial off-the-shelf application package that does not run on any of the current DBMS platforms. Sometimes the decision to buy a new DBMS is driven by the desire to support the latest and greatest technology. For example, many mainframe shops moving from a hierarchic (IMS) or CODASYL (IDMS) database model to the relational model deployed DB2, result in an additional DBMS to learn and support. Then, when client/server computing became popular, additional DBMSs were implemented on UNIX and Windows NT servers.

Once a DBMS is installed, removal can be difficult because of incompatibilities among the different DBMSs and the necessity of converting application code. Furthermore, when a new DBMS is installed, old applications and databases are usually not migrated to it. The old DBMS remains and must continue to be supported. This complicates the DBA's job.

So what should be done? Well, the DBA group should be empowered to make the DBMS decisions for the organization. No business unit should be allowed to purchase a DBMS without the permission of the DBA group. This is a difficult provision to implement and even more difficult to enforce. Business politics often work against the DBA group because the DBA group frequently possesses less organizational power than other business executives.

The DBA group should be empowered to make the DBMS decisions for the organization.

Choosing a DBMS

The DBA group should set a policy regarding the DBMS products to be supported within the organization. Whenever possible, the policy should minimize the number of different DBMS products. For a shop with multiple operating systems and multiple types of hardware, choose a default DBMS for the platform. Discourage deviation from the default unless a compelling business case exists—a business case that passes the technical inspection of the DBA group.

Most of the major DBMS products have similar features, and if the feature or functionality does not exist today, it probably will within 18 to 24 months. So, exercise caution before deciding to choose a DBMS based solely on its ability to support a specific feature.

When choosing a DBMS, select a product from a tier-1 vendor.

When choosing a DBMS, it is wise to select a product from a tier-1 vendor as listed in Table 2-1. Tier 1 represents the largest vendors having the most heavily implemented and supported products on the market. You cannot go wrong with DB2 or Oracle. Both are popular and support just about any type of database. Another major player is Microsoft SQL Server, but only for Windows platforms. DB2 and Oracle run on multiple platforms ranging from mainframe to UNIX, as well as Windows and even handheld devices. Choosing a DBMS other than these three should be done only under extreme circumstances.

After the big three come Sybase and Informix. Table 2-2 lists these tier-2 DBMS vendors. Both of these vendors provide quality DBMS products, but their

Table 2-1   *Tier-1 DBMS Vendors*

DBMS vendor	DBMS product
IBM Corporation New Orchard Road Armonk, NY 10504 Phone: (914) 499-1900	DB2 Universal Database
Oracle Corporation 500 Oracle Parkway Redwood Shores, CA 94065 Phone: (650) 506-7000	Oracle
Microsoft Corporation One Microsoft Way Redmond, WA 98052 Phone: (425) 882-8080	SQL Server

Table 2-2   *Tier-2 DBMS Vendors*

DBMS vendor	DBMS product
Informix Software, Inc. 50 Washington Street Westborough, MA 01581 Phone: (508) 366-3888	Informix Dynamic Server
Sybase Inc. 6475 Christie Ave. Emeryville, CA 94608 Phone: (510) 922-3500	Adaptive Server Enterprise

installed base is smaller and the companies are smaller, with fewer resources, than IBM, Oracle, and Microsoft, so there is some risk in choosing a DBMS from tier 2 instead of tier 1. The future of Informix is uncertain, though, since IBM acquired it and the future of DBMS technology at IBM will undoubtedly be focused on DB2, not Informix.

Of course, there are other DBMS products on the market, many of which are fine products and worthy of consideration for specialty processing, certain predefined needs, and niche roles. For example, VLDB (very large database) and data warehousing projects may find the architecture and functionality of NCR's Teradata to be the DBMS of choice. If your company is heavily into the "open-source software" movement, PostgreSQL or MySQL might be viable options. If an object DBMS is important for a specific project, you might consider ObjectDesign or Versant.

Choosing any of the lower-tier candidates involves incurring additional risk.

However, for the bulk of your data management needs, a DBMS from a tier-1, or perhaps tier-2, DBMS vendor will deliver sufficient functionality with minimal risk. A myriad of DBMS products are available, each with certain features that make them worthy of consideration on a case-by-case basis. Choosing any of the lower-tier candidates—even such major names as Software AG's Adabas and Computer Associates' Ingres—involves incurring additional risk. Refer to Appendix 2 for a list of DBMS vendors.

I do not want it to sound as if the selection of a DBMS is a no-brainer. You *will* need a strategy and a plan for selecting the appropriate DBMS for your specific situation. When choosing a DBMS, be sure to consider each of these factors:

- *Operating system support.* Does the DBMS support the operating systems in use at your organization, including the versions that you are currently using and plan on using?

- *Type of organization*. Take into consideration the corporate philosophy when you choose a DBMS. Some organizations are very conservative and like to keep a tight reign on their environments; these organizations tend to gravitate toward traditional mainframe environments. Government operations, financial institutions, and insurance and health companies usually tend to be conservative. More-liberal organizations are often willing to consider alternative architectures. It is not uncommon for manufacturing companies, dotcoms, and universities to be less conservative. Finally, some companies just do not trust Windows as a mission-critical environment, and prefer to use UNIX—this rules out some database vendors (Microsoft SQL Server, in particular).

Benchmarks are constantly updated to show new and improved performance measurements.

- *Benchmarks*. What performance benchmarks are available from the DBMS vendor and other users of the DBMS? The Transaction Processing Performance Council (TPC) publishes official database performance benchmarks that can be used as a guideline for the basic overall performance of many different types of database processing. Refer to the sidebar "The Transaction Processing Performance Council" for more details. In general, performance benchmarks can be useful as a broad indicator of database performance, but should not be the only determinant when selecting a DBMS. Many of the TPC benchmarks are run against database implementations that are not representative of most production database systems, and therefore are not indicative of the actual performance of a particular DBMS. In addition, benchmarks are constantly updated to show new and improved performance measurements for each of the major DBMS products, rendering the benchmark "winners" obsolete very quickly.

- *Scalability*. Does the DBMS support the number of users and database sizes you intend to implement? How are large databases built, supported, and maintained—easily or with a lot of pain? Are there independent users who can confirm the DBMS vendor's scalability claims?

- *Availability of supporting software tools*. Are the supporting tools you require available for the DBMS? These items may include query and analysis tools, data warehousing support tools, database administration tools, backup and recovery tools, performance monitoring tools, capacity planning tools, database utilities, and support for various programming languages.

- *Technicians*. Is there a sufficient supply of skilled database professionals for the DBMS? Consider your needs in terms of DBAs, technical support personnel (system programmers and administrators, operations analysts, etc.), and application programmers.

- *Cost of Ownership*. What is the total cost of ownership of the DBMS? The DBMS vendors charge wildly varying prices for their technology. Total cost of ownership should be calculated as a combination of the license cost of the DBMS, the license cost of any required supporting software, the cost of database professionals to program, support, and administer the DBMS, and the cost of the computing resources required to operate the DBMS.

- *Release schedule*. How often does the DBMS vendor release a new version? Some vendors have rapid release cycles, with new releases coming out every 12 to 18 months. This can be good or bad depending on your approach. If you want cutting-edge features, a rapid release cycle is good. However, if your shop is more conservative, a DBMS that changes frequently can be difficult to support. A rapid release cycle will cause conservative organizations either to upgrade more frequently than they would like or to live with outdated DBMS software that is unlikely to have the same level of support as the latest releases.

- *Reference customers*. Will the DBMS vendor supply current user references? Can you find other users on your own who might provide more impartial answers? Speak with current users to elicit issues and concerns you may have overlooked. How is support? Does the vendor respond well to problems? Do things generally work as advertised? Are there a lot of bug fixes that must be applied continuously? What is the quality of new releases? These questions can only be answered by the folks in the trenches.

When choosing a DBMS be sure to take into account the complexity of the products. DBMS software is very complex and is getting more complex with each new release. Functionality that used to be supported only with add-on software or independent programs is increasingly being added as features of the DBMS, as shown in Figure 2-1. You will need to plan for and support all the features of the DBMS. Even if there is no current requirement for certain features, once you implement the DBMS the programmers and developers will find a reason to use just about anything the vendors throw into the DBMS. It is better to plan and be prepared than to allow features to be used without a plan for supporting them.

The Transaction Processing Performance Council

The Transaction Processing Performance Council (TPC) is an independent, not-for-profit organization that manages and administers performance benchmark tests. Its mission is to define transaction processing and database benchmarks to provide the industry with objective, verifiable performance data. TPC benchmarks measure and evaluate computer functions and operations.

The TPC espouses a business definition of "transaction." A typical TPC transaction includes the database updates for items such as inventory control (goods), airline reservations (services), or banking (money). TPC benchmarks measure performance in terms of the number of transactions a given system and database can perform per unit of time—for example, number of transactions per second. The TPC defines four benchmarks:

- TPC-C: Planned production workload in a transaction environment
- TPC-H: Ad hoc processing where transactions are not known and predefined
- TPC-R: Business reporting in a decision report environment
- TPC-W: Transaction processing over the Web

Additional information and in-depth definitions of these benchmarks can be found at the TPC Web site at http://www.tpc.org.

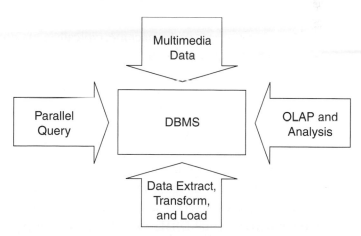

Figure 2-1   *Convergence of features and functionality in DBMS software*

DBMS Architectures

The supporting architecture for the DBMS environment is very critical to the success of the database applications.

The supporting architecture for the DBMS environment is very critical to the success of the database applications. One wrong choice or poorly implemented component of the overall architecture can cause poor performance, downtime, or unstable applications.

When mainframes dominated enterprise computing, DBMS architecture was a simpler concern. Everything ran on the mainframe, and that was that. However, today the IT infrastructure is distributed and heterogeneous. The overall architecture—even for a mainframe DBMS—will probably consist of multiple platforms and interoperating system software. A team consisting of business and IT experts, rather than a single person or group, should make the final architecture decision. Business experts should include representatives from various departments, as well as from accounting and legal for software contract issues. Database administration representatives (DA, DBA, and SA), as well as members of the networking group, operating system experts, operations control personnel, programming experts, and any other interested parties should be included in this team.

Four levels of DBMS architecture are available: enterprise, departmental, personal, and mobile.

Furthermore, be sure that the DBMS you select is appropriate for the nature and type of processing you plan to implement. Four levels of DBMS architecture are available: enterprise, departmental, personal, and mobile.

An *enterprise DBMS* is designed for scalability and high performance. An enterprise DBMS must be capable of supporting very large databases, a large number of concurrent users, and multiple types of applications. The enterprise DBMS runs on a large-scale machine, typically a mainframe or a high-end server running UNIX, Linux, or Windows NT/2000. Furthermore, an enterprise DBMS offers all the "bells and whistles" available from the DBMS vendor. Multiprocessor support, support for parallel queries, and other advanced DBMS features will be core components of an enterprise DBMS.

A *departmental DBMS*, sometimes referred to as a workgroup DBMS, serves the middle ground. The departmental DBMS supports small- to medium-sized workgroups within an organization; typically, it runs on a UNIX, Linux, or Windows NT server. The dividing line between a departmental database server and an enterprise database server is quite gray. Hardware and software upgrades can allow a departmental DBMS to tackle tasks that previously could only be performed by an enterprise DBMS. The steadily falling cost of departmental hardware and software components further contributes to lowering the total cost of operation and enabling a workgroup environment to scale up to serve the enterprise.

A *personal DBMS* is designed for a single user, typically on a low- to medium-powered PC platform. Microsoft Access and Visual dBase are examples of personal database software. Of course, the major DBMS vendors also market personal versions of their more high-powered solutions, such as Personal Oracle and DB2 Everyplace. Sometimes the low cost of a personal DBMS causes a misguided attempt to choose a personal DBMS for a departmental or enterprise solution. However, do not be lured by the low cost. A personal DBMS product is suited only for very-small-scale projects and should never be deployed for multiuser applications.

Finally, the *mobile DBMS* is a specialized version of a departmental or enterprise DBMS. It is designed for remote users who are not usually connected to the network. The mobile DBMS enables local database access and modification on a laptop or handheld device. Furthermore, the mobile DBMS provides a mechanism for synchronizing remote database changes to a centralized enterprise or departmental database server.

A DBMS designed for one type of processing may be ill suited for other uses. For example, a personal DBMS is not designed for multiple users, and an enterprise DBMS will generally be too complex for single users. Be sure to understand the difference between enterprise, departmental, personal, and mobile DBMS software, and choose the appropriate DBMS for your specific data processing needs. You may need to choose multiple DBMS types—that is, a DBMS for each level—with usage determined by the needs of each development project.

If your organization requires DBMS solutions at different levels, favor the selection of a group of DBMS solutions from the same vendor whenever possible. Doing so will minimize differences in access, development, and administration. For example, favor Personal Oracle for your single-user DBMS needs if your organization uses Oracle as the enterprise DBMS of choice.

DBMS Clustering

A modern DBMS offers clustering support to enhance availability and scalability.

Clustering is the use of multiple "independent" computing systems working together as a single, highly available system. A modern DBMS offers clustering support to enhance availability and scalability. The two predominant architectures for clustering are *shared-disk* and *shared-nothing*. These names do a good job of describing the nature of the architecture—at least at a high level.

Shared-nothing clustering is depicted in Figure 2-2. In a shared-nothing architecture, each system has its own private resources (memory, disks, etc.). The clustered processors communicate by passing messages through a network

The main advantage of shared-nothing clustering is scalability.

that interconnects the computers. In addition, requests from clients are automatically routed to the system that owns the resource. Only one of the clustered systems can "own" and access a particular resource at a time. In the event a failure occurs, resource ownership can be dynamically transferred to another system in the cluster. The main advantage of shared-nothing clustering is scalability. In theory, a shared-nothing multiprocessor can scale up to thousands of processors because they do not interfere with one another—nothing is shared.

Shared-disk clustering is better suited to large-enterprise processing in a mainframe environment.

In a *shared-disk* environment, all the connected systems share the same disk devices, as shown in Figure 2-3. Each processor still has its own private memory, but all the processors can directly address all the disks. Typically, shared-disk clustering does not scale as well for smaller machines as shared-nothing clustering. Shared-disk clustering is better suited to large-enterprise processing in a mainframe environment. Mainframes—very large processors—are capable of processing enormous volumes of work. Great benefits can be obtained with only a few clustered mainframes, while many PC and midrange processors would need to be clustered to achieve similar benefits.

Shared-disk clustering is usually preferable for applications and services requiring only modest shared access to data and for applications or workloads that are very difficult to partition. Applications with heavy data-update requirements are probably better implemented as shared-nothing. Table 2-3 compares the capabilities of shared-disk and shared-nothing architectures.

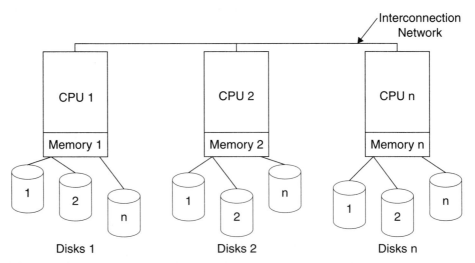

Figure 2-2 *Shared-nothing architecture*

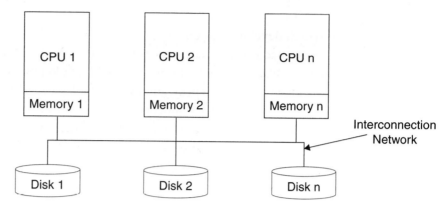

Figure 2-3   *Shared-disk architecture*

Table 2-3   *Comparison of Shared-Disk and Shared-Nothing Architectures*

Shared-disk	Shared-nothing
Quick adaptability to changing workloads	Can exploit simpler, cheaper hardware
High availability	Almost unlimited scalability
Performs best in a heavy read environment	Works well in a high-volume, read-write environment
Data need not be partitioned	Data is partitioned across the cluster

The major DBMS vendors provide support for different types of clustering with different capabilities and requirements. For example, DB2 for OS/390 provides shared-disk clustering with its Data Sharing and Parallel Sysplex capabilities; DB2 Extended Enterprise Edition on nonmainframe platforms uses shared-nothing clustering. Oracle9i's Real Application Clusters provide shared-disk clustering.

For most users, the primary benefit of clustering is the enhanced availability that accrues by combining processors. In some cases, clustering can help an enterprise to achieve five-nines (99.999%) availability. Additionally, clustering can be used for load balancing and failover.

DBMS Proliferation

As a rule of thumb, create a policy (or at least some simple guidelines) that must be followed before a new DBMS can be brought into the organization. Failure to do so can cause a proliferation of different DBMS products that will

A proliferation of different DBMS products can be difficult to support.

be difficult to support. It can also cause confusion regarding which DBMS to use for which development effort.

As mentioned earlier, there are a plethora of DBMS vendors, each touting its benefits. As a DBA, you will be bombarded with marketing and sales efforts trying to convince you that you need another DBMS. Try to resist unless a very compelling reason is given and a short-term return on investment (ROI) can be demonstrated. Even when confronted with valid reasons and good ROI, be sure to double-check the arguments and ROI calculations. Sometimes the reasons specified are outdated and the ROI figures do not take everything into account—such as the additional cost of administration.

Remember, every DBMS requires database administration support. Moreover, each DBMS uses different methods to perform similar tasks. The fewer DBMS products installed, the less complicated database administration becomes, and the better your chances become of providing effective data management resources for your organization.

Hardware Issues

Factor hardware platform and operating system constraints into the DBMS selection criteria.

When establishing a database environment for application development, selecting the DBMS is only part of the equation. The hardware and operating system on which the DBMS will run will greatly impact the reliability, availability, and scalability (RAS) of the database environment. For example, a mainframe platform such as an IBM z900 running z/OS will probably provide higher RAS than a midrange IBM RS/6000 running AIX, which in turn will probably exceed a Compaq server running Windows 2000. That is not to say everything should run on a mainframe: Other issues such as cost, experience, manageability, and the needs of the applications to be developed must be considered. The bottom line is that you must be sure to factor hardware platform and operating system constraints into the DBMS selection criteria.

Installing the DBMS

Once the DBMS has been chosen, you will need to install it. Installing a DBMS is not as simple as popping a CD into a drive and letting the software install itself. (Or for you mainframe folks, just using IEBGENER to copy it off of a tape.) A DBMS is a complex piece of software that requires up-front planning for installation to be successful. You will need to understand the DBMS requirements and prepare the environment for the new DBMS.

DBMS Installation Basics

The very first thing to do when you install a DBMS for the first time is understand the prerequisites. Every DBMS comes with an installation manual or guide containing a list of the operating requirements that must be met for the DBMS to function properly. Examples of prerequisites include ensuring that an appropriate version of the operating system is being used, verifying that there is sufficient memory to support the DBMS, and ensuring that any related software to be used with the DBMS is the proper version and maintenance level.

Read the installation guide from cover to cover.

Once the basics are covered, read the installation guide from cover to cover. Make sure that you understand the process before you even begin to install the DBMS. Quite a few preparations need to be made before installing a DBMS, and reading about them *before* you start will ensure a successful installation. Review how the installation program or routine for the DBMS operates and follow the explicit instructions in the installation guide provided with the DBMS software.

The remainder of this section will discuss some of the common preparations that are required before a DBMS can be installed. If the DBMS is already operational and you are planning to migrate to a new DBMS release, refer to the "Upgrading DBMS Versions and Releases" section of this chapter.

Hardware Requirements

Every DBMS has a basic CPU requirement, meaning a CPU version and minimum processor speed required for the DBMS to operate. Additionally, some DBMSs specify hardware models that are required or unsupported. Usually the CPU criterion will suffice for an Intel environment, but in a mainframe or enterprise server environment the machine model can make a difference with regard to the DBMS features supported. For example, certain machines have built-in firmware that can be exploited by the DBMS if the firmware is available.

Choose the correct DBMS for your needs and match your hardware to the requirements of the DBMS.

Furthermore, each DBMS offers different "flavors" of their software for specific needs. (I use "flavor" as opposed to "version" or "release," which specify different iterations of the same DBMS.) Different flavors of the DBMS (at the same release level) are available for specific environments such as parallel processing, pervasive computing (such as handheld devices), data warehousing, and/or mobile computing. Be sure to choose the correct DBMS for your needs and to match your hardware to the requirements of the DBMS.

Storage Requirements

A DBMS requires disk storage to run. And not just for the obvious reason—to create databases that store data. A DBMS will use disk storage for the indexes to be defined on the databases as well as for the following items:

- The system catalog or data dictionary used by the DBMS to manage and track databases and related information. The more database objects you plan to create, the larger the amount of storage required by the system catalog.

- Any other system databases required by the DBMS, for example, to support distributed connections or management tools.

- Log files that record all changes made to every database. This includes active logs, archive logs, rollback segments, and any other type of change log required by the DBMS.

- Startup or control files that must be accessed by the DBMS when it is started or initialized.

- Work files used by the DBMS to sort data or for other processing needs.

- Default databases used by the DBMS for system structures or as a default catchall for new database objects as they are created.

- Temporary database structures used by the DBMS (or by applications accessing databases) for transient data that is not required to be persistent but needs reserved storage during operations.

- System dump and error processing files.

- DBA databases used for administration, monitoring, and tuning—for example, DBA databases used for testing new releases, migration scripts, and so on.

Factor in every storage requirement of the DBMS and reserve the appropriate storage for its use.

Be sure to factor in every storage requirement of the DBMS and reserve the appropriate storage for its use. Also, be aware that the DBMS will use many of these databases and file structures concurrently. Therefore, it is a good idea to plan on using multiple storage devices even if you will not fill them to capacity. Proper database and file placement will enable the DBMS to operate more effi-

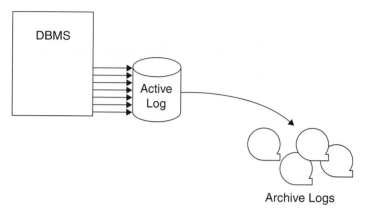

Figure 2-4   *Log offloading*

ciently because concurrent activities will not be constrained by the physical disk as data is accessed.

Disk storage is not the only requirement of a DBMS. Tapes are also required for tasks such as database backups and log offloading. When the active log file fills up, the log records must be offloaded to an archive log either on disk or on tape, as shown in Figure 2-4. Depending on the DBMS being used and the features that have been activated, this process may be automatic or manual. The archive log files must be retained for recovery purposes, and even if originally stored on disk, they must eventually be migrated to tape.

Plan on maintaining multiple tape drives to enable the DBMS to run concurrent multiple processes that require tape, such as concurrent database backups. Database outages can occur if you single-thread your database backup jobs using a single tape drive.

Memory Requirements

Relational DBMSs, as well as their databases and applications, love memory. A DBMS requires memory for basic functionality and will use it for most internal processes such as maintaining the system global area and performing many DBMS tasks.

A DBMS requires a significant amount of memory to cache data in memory structures in order to avoid I/O. Reading data from a disk storage device is always more expensive and slower than moving the data around in memory. Figure 2-5 shows how the DBMS uses a memory structure called a *buffer pool* or *data cache* to reduce physical I/O requests. By caching data that is read into

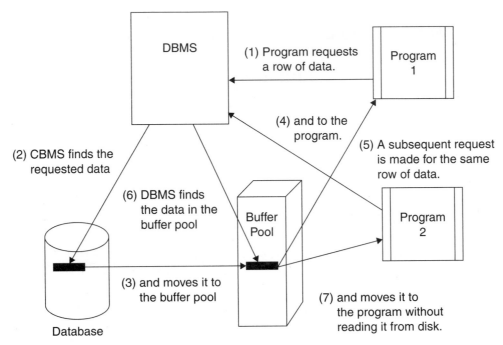

Figure 2-5   *Buffer pool (or data cache)*

a buffer pool, the DBMS can avoid I/O for subsequent requests for the same data, as long as it remains in the buffer pool. In general, the larger the buffer pool, the longer the data can remain in memory and the better overall database processing will perform.

Besides data, the DBMS will cache other structures in memory. Most DBMSs set aside memory to store program structures required by the DBMS to process database requests.[1] The *program cache* will store things like "compiled" SQL statements, database authorizations, and database structure blocks that are used by programs as they are executed. By caching these structures, database processing can be optimized by avoiding additional I/O requests to access them from a physical storage device.

Memory is typically required by the DBMS to support other features such as handling lock requests, facilitating distributed data requests, sorting data, optimizing processes, and processing SQL.

---

1. In DB2, the area used for caching program structures in memory is referred to as the EDM Pool. In SQL Server it is called the SQL Cache, and in Oracle two structures are used, the PGA and the shared pool in the SGA.

Ensure that the
DBMS has a more
than adequate
supply of memory
at its disposal.
Ensure that the DBMS has a more than adequate supply of memory at its disposal. This will help to optimize database processing and minimize potential problems.

Configuring the DBMS

Configuring the system parameters of the DBMS controls the manner in which the DBMS functions and the resources made available to it.[2] Each DBMS allows its system parameters to be modified in different ways, but the installation process usually sets the DBMS system parameters by means of radio buttons, menus, or panel selections. During the installation process, the input provided to the installation script will be used to establish the initial settings of the system parameters.

Each DBMS also
provides a method
to change the sys-
tem parameters
once the DBMS is
operational.
Each DBMS also provides a method to change the system parameters once the DBMS is operational. Sometimes you can use DBMS commands to set the system's parameters; sometimes you must edit a file that contains the current system parameter settings. If you must edit a file, be very careful: An erroneous system parameter setting can be fatal to the operational status of the DBMS.

What do the system parameters control? Well, for example, system parameters control DBA authorization to the DBMS and the number of active database logs; system parameters set the amount of memory used for data and program caching, and turn on or off DBMS features. Although every DBMS has system parameters that control its functionality, each DBMS has a different method of setting and changing the values. And, indeed, each DBMS has different "things" that can be set using system parameters.

Be sure to understand fully the parameters used by your DBMS. Failure to do so can result in an incorrectly configured database environment, which can cause performance problems, data integrity problems, or even DBMS failure.

Connecting the DBMS to Supporting Infrastructure Software

Part of the DBMS installation process is the connection of the DBMS to other system software components that must interact with the DBMS. Typical infrastructure software that may need to be configured to work with the DBMS includes networks, transaction processing monitors, message queues, other

---

2. In DB2, system parameters are set by assembling the DSNZPARM member. SQL Server uses the SP_CONFIGURE system procedure to set system parameters, and Oracle parameters are controlled using INIT.ORA.

types of middleware, programming languages, systems management software, operations and job control software, Web servers, and application servers.

Each piece of supporting infrastructure software will have different requirements for interfacing with the DBMS. Typical configuration procedures can include installing DLL files, creating new parameter files to establish connections, and possibly revisiting the installation procedures for the supporting software to install components required to interact with the DBMS.

Each piece of supporting infrastructure software will have different requirements for interfacing with the DBMS.

Installation Verification

After installing the DBMS, you should run a battery of tests to verify that the DBMS has been properly installed and configured. Most DBMS vendors supply sample programs for this purpose. Additionally, you can ensure proper installation by testing the standard interfaces to the DBMS. One standard interface supported by most DBMSs is an interactive SQL interface where you can submit SQL statements directly to the DBMS.[3]

Create a set of SQL code that comprises SELECT, INSERT, UPDATE, and DELETE statements issued against sample databases. Running such a script after installation helps you to verify that the DBMS is installed correctly and operating as expected.

Furthermore, be sure to verify that all required connections to supporting software are operational and functioning properly. If the DBMS vendor does not supply sample programs, you may need to create and run simple test programs for each environment to ensure that the supporting software connections are functioning correctly with the DBMS.

DBMS Environments

Generally, installing a DBMS involves more than simply installing one instance or subsystem. To support database development, the DBA needs to create multiple DBMS environments to support, for example, testing, quality assurance, integration, and production work. Of course, it is possible to support multiple environments in a single DBMS instance, but it is not prudent. Multiple DBMS installations are preferable to support multiple development environments for a single database. This minimizes migration issues and won't require complex

---

3. In DB2, the SQL interface is referred to as SPUFI. SQL Server calls the interface ISQL, and when using Oracle you can choose to submit SQL using SQL*Plus or the SQL Worksheet in Oracle Enterprise Manager.

database naming conventions to support. Furthermore, segregating database instances makes testing, tuning, and monitoring easier.

Upgrading DBMS Versions and Releases

Change is a fact of life.

Change is a fact of life, and each of the major DBMS products changes quite rapidly. A typical release cycle for DBMS software is 12 to 18 months for major releases, with constant bug fixes and maintenance updates delivered in between major releases. Indeed, keeping DBMS software up-to-date can be a full-time job.

The DBA must develop an approach to upgrading DBMS software that conforms to the organization's needs and minimizes business disruptions due to outages and database unavailability.

You may have noticed that I use the terms *version* and *release* somewhat interchangeably. That is fine for a broad discussion of DBMS upgrades, but a more precise definition is warranted. For a better discussion of the differences between a version and a release, please refer to the sidebar.

A DBMS version upgrade can be thought of as a special case of a new installation. All the procedures required of a new installation apply to an upgrade: You must plan for appropriate resources, reconsider all system parameters, and ensure that all supporting software is appropriately connected. However, another serious issue must be planned for: existing users and applications. An upgrade needs to be planned to cause as little disruption to the existing users as possible. Therefore, upgrading can be a tricky and difficult task.

Version or Release?

Vendors typically make a distinction between a version and a release of a software product. A new version of software is a major concern, with many changes and new features. A release is typically minor, with fewer changes and not as many new features.

For example, moving from Version 7 of Oracle to Oracle8 was a major change—a version change. However, an in-between point such as Oracle8.2 would be considered a release—consisting of a smaller number of changes. Usually the DBMS vendors will increase prices for versions, but not necessarily for releases (but that is not a hard and fast rule).

Usually significant functionality is added for version upgrades, less so for point releases. Nevertheless, upgrading from one point release to another can have just as many potential pitfalls as version upgrades. It depends on the nature of the new features provided in each specific release.

The issues and concerns discussed in this chapter pertain to both types of DBMS upgrades: to a new release and to a new version.

In a complex, heterogeneous, distributed database environment, a coherent upgrade strategy is essential. Truthfully, even organizations with only a single DBMS should approach DBMS upgrades cautiously and plan accordingly. Failure to plan a DBMS upgrade can result in improper and inefficient adoption of new features, performance degradation of new and existing applications, and downtime.

Upgrading to a new DBMS release offers both rewards and risks. The following are some of the benefits of moving to a new release.

- Developers can avail themselves of new features and functionality delivered only in the new release. If development requires a new feature, or can simply benefit from a new feature, program development time can be reduced or made more cost-effective.

- For purchased applications, the application vendor may require a specific DBMS version or release for specific versions of its application to enable specific functionality within the application.

- New DBMS releases usually deliver enhanced performance and availability features that can optimize existing applications. Sometimes a new DBMS release is required to scale applications to support additional users or larger amounts of data.

- DBMS vendors will often provide better support and respond to problems faster for a new release of their software. DBMS vendors are loath to allow bad publicity about bugs in a new and heavily promoted version of their products.

- Production migration to a new DBMS release will align the test and production database environments, thereby providing a consistent environment for development and implementation. If a new release is running in the test environment for too long, database administration and application development tasks become more difficult because the test databases will operate differently than the production databases.

An effective DBMS upgrade strategy must balance the benefits against the risks of upgrading.

However, an effective DBMS upgrade strategy must balance the benefits against the risks of upgrading to arrive at the best timeline for migrating to a new DBMS version or release. The risks of upgrading to a new DBMS release include the following.

- An upgrade to the DBMS usually involves some level of disruption to business operations. At a minimum, databases will not be available while the DBMS is being upgraded. This can result in downtime and lost business opportunities if the DBMS upgrade occurs during normal business hours (or if there is no planned downtime). Clustered database implementations may permit some database availability while individual database clusters are migrated to the new DBMS version.

- Other disruptions can occur, such as having to convert database structures or discovering that previously supported features were removed from the new release (thereby causing application errors). Delays to application implementation timelines are another possibility.

- The cost of an upgrade can be a significant barrier to DBMS release migration. First, the cost of the new version or release must be budgeted for (price increases for a new DBMS version can amount to as much as 10% to 25%). The upgrade cost must also factor in the costs of planning, installing, testing, and deploying not just the DBMS but also any applications using databases. Finally, be sure to include the cost of any new resources (such as memory, storage, additional CPUs) required to use the new features delivered by the new DBMS version.

- DBMS vendors usually tout the performance gains that can be achieved with a new release. However, when SQL optimization techniques change, it is possible that a new DBMS release will generate SQL access paths that perform worse than before. DBAs must implement a rigorous testing process to ensure that new access paths are helping, not harming, application performance. When performance suffers, application code may need to be changed—a very costly and time consuming endeavor. A rigorous test process should be able to catch most of the access path changes in the test environment.

- To take advantage of improvements implemented in a new DBMS release, the DBA may have to apply some invasive changes. For example, if the new version increases the maximum size for a database object, the DBA may have to drop and recreate that object to take advantage of the new maximum. This will be the case when the DBMS adds internal control structures to facilitate such changes.

- Supporting software products may lack immediate support for a new DBMS release. Supporting software includes the operating system, transaction processors, message queues, purchased application, DBA tools, development tools, and query and reporting software.

After weighing the benefits of upgrading against the risks of a new DBMS release, the DBA group must create an upgrade plan that works for the organization. Sometimes the decision will be to upgrade immediately upon availability, but often there is a lag between the general availability of a new release and its widespread adoption.

When the risks of a new release outweigh the benefits, some organizations may decide to skip an interim release if doing so does not impact a future upgrade. For example, a good number of Oracle customers migrated directly from Oracle7 to Oracle8i, skipping Oracle8. If the DBMS vendor does not allow users to bypass a version or release, it is still possible to "skip" a release by waiting to implement that release until the next release is available. For example, consider the following scenario:

ABC Corporation is using DB Version 5 from DBCorp.

DBCorp announces Version 6 of DB.

ABC Corporation analyzes the features and risks and determines not to upgrade immediately.

DBCorp later announces DB Version 7 and that no direct migration path will be provided from Version 5 to Version 7.

ABC Corporation decides that DB Version 7 provides many useful features and wants to upgrade their current Version 5 implementation of DB. However, they have no compelling reason to first implement and use Version 6.

To fulfill their requirements, ABC Corporation first upgrades Version 5 to Version 6 and then immediately upgrades Version 6 to Version 7.

A multiple release upgrade allows customers to effectively control when and how they will migrate to new releases of a DBMS.

Although a multiple release upgrade takes more time, it allows customers to effectively control when and how they will migrate to new releases of a DBMS instead of being held hostage by the DBMS vendor. When attempting a multiple release upgrade of this type be sure to fully understand the features and functionality added by the DBMS vendor for each interim release. In the case of ABC Corporation above, the DBAs will need to research and prepare for the new features of not just Version 7 but also Version 6.

An appropriate DBMS upgrade strategy depends on many things. The following sections outline the issues that must be factored into an effective DBMS release upgrade strategy.

Features and Complexity

Perhaps the biggest factor in determining when and how to upgrade to a new DBMS release is the functionality supported by the new release. Tightly coupled to functionality is the inherent complexity involved in supporting and administering new features.

It is more difficult to delay an upgrade if application developers are clamoring for new DBMS features. If DBMS functionality can minimize the cost and effort of application development, the DBA group will feel pressure to migrate swiftly to the new release. An additional factor that will coerce rapid adoption of a new release is when DBMS problems are fixed in the new release (instead of through regular maintenance fixes).

Regardless of a new release's "bells and whistles," certain administration and implementation details must be addressed before upgrading. The DBA group must ensure that standards are modified to include the new features, educate developers and users as to how new features work and should be used, and prepare the infrastructure to support the new DBMS functionality.

The type of changes required to support the new functionality must be factored into the upgrade strategy. When the DBMS vendor makes changes to internal structures, data page layouts, or address spaces, the risks of upgrading are greater. Additional testing is warranted in these situations to ensure that database utilities, DBA tools, and data extraction and movement tools still work with the revised internal structures.

Complexity of the DBMS Environment

The more complex your database environment is, the more difficult it will be to upgrade to a new DBMS release. The first complexity issue is the size of the environment. The greater the number of database servers, instances, applications, and users, the greater the complexity. Additional concerns include the type of applications being supported. A DBMS upgrade is easier to implement if only simple, batch-oriented applications are involved. As the complexity and availability requirements of the applications increase, the difficulty of upgrading also increases.

Location of the database servers also affects the release upgrade strategy. Effectively planning and deploying a DBMS upgrade across multiple database servers at various locations supporting different lines of business is difficult. It is likely that an upgrade strategy will involve periods of supporting multiple versions of the DBMS at different locations and for different applications. Supporting different versions in production should be avoided if possible, but that is not always possible to achieve.

Finally, the complexity of the applications that access your databases must be considered. The more complex your applications are, the more difficult it will be to ensure their continuing uninterrupted functionality when the DBMS is modified. Complexity issues include the following:

- Usage of stored procedures and user-defined functions.

- Complexity of the SQL—the more tables involved in the SQL and the more complex the SQL features, the more difficult it becomes to ensure that access path changes do not impact performance.

- Client/server processing—network usage and usage of multiple tiers complicates testing the new DBMS release.

- Integration with other infrastructure software such as message queues and transaction processors can complicate migration because new versions of these products may be required to support the new DBMS release.

- The language used by the programs might also impact DBMS release migration due to different support for compiler versions, changes to APIs, or new ways of embedding SQL into application programs.

Reputation of the DBMS Vendor

DBMS vendors have different reputations for technical support, fixing bugs, and responding to problems, which is why customer references are so important when choosing a database.

The better the reputation of the vendor, the greater the likelihood of organizations rapidly adopting a new release.

The better the reputation of the vendor, the greater the likelihood of organizations rapidly adopting a new release. If the DBMS vendor is good at responding to problems and supporting their customers as they migrate to new releases, then their customers will more actively engage in migration activities.

Support Policies of the DBMS

As new releases are introduced, DBMS vendors will retire older releases and no longer support them. The length of time that the DBMS vendor will support an old release must be factored into the DBMS release migration strategy. You should never run a DBMS release in production that is no longer supported by the vendor. If problems occur, the DBMS vendor will not be able to resolve any problems for you.

Sometimes a DBMS vendor will provide support for a retired release on a special basis and at an increased maintenance charge. If you absolutely must continue using a retired DBMS release (for business or application issues) be sure to investigate the DBMS vendor's policies regarding support for retired releases of its software.

Organization Style

Every organization displays characteristics that reveal its style when it comes to adopting new products and technologies. Industry analysts at the Gartner Group have ranked organizations into three distinct groups labeled types A, B, and C. A type-A enterprise is technology driven and, as such, is more likely to risk using new and unproven technologies to try to gain a competitive advantage. A type-B organization is less willing to take risks but will adopt new technologies once others have shaken out the bugs. Finally, a type-C enterprise, very conscious of cost and averse to risk, will lag behind the majority when it comes to migrating to new technology.

Only type-A organizations should plan on moving aggressively to new DBMS releases immediately upon availability and only if the new features of the release will deliver advantages to the company. Type-C enterprises should adopt a very conservative strategy to ensure that the DBMS release is stable and well tested by types A and B companies first. Type-B organizations will fall somewhere between types A and C: Almost never upgrading immediately, the type-B company will adopt the new release after the earliest users have shaken out the biggest problems, but well before type-C enterprises.

DBA Staff Skill Set

The risk of an upgrade increases as the skills of the DBA staff decrease.

Upgrading the DBMS is easier if your DBA staff is highly skilled or experienced. The risk of an upgrade increases as the skills of the DBA staff decrease. If your DBAs are not highly skilled, or have never migrated a DBMS to a new release, consider augmenting your DBA staff with consultants for the upgrade. Deploying an integrated team of internal DBAs and consultants will ensure that your upgrade goes as smoothly as possible. Furthermore, the DBA staff will be better prepared to handle the future upgrades alone.

If consultants will be required, be sure to include their contracting cost in the DBMS release upgrade budget. The budget should allow you to retain the consultants until all production database environments are stable.

Platform Support

When a DBMS vendor unleashes a new release of its product, not all platforms and operating systems are immediately supported. The DBMS vendor will usually first support the platforms and operating systems for which it has the most licensed customers. The order in which platforms are supported for a new release is likely to differ for each DBMS vendor. For example, OS/390 (or MVS) is more strategic to IBM than to Oracle, so a new DB2 release will most likely support OS/390 very quickly, whereas this may not be true of Oracle. The issue is even thornier for UNIX platforms because of the sheer number of UNIX variants in the marketplace. The most popular variants are Sun Microsystem's Solaris, IBM's AIX, Hewlett-Packard's HP-UX, and Linux, the open source version of UNIX. Most DBMS vendors will support these UNIX platforms very quickly upon general availability. Other less popular varieties of UNIX will take longer for the DBMS vendors to support.

When planning your DBMS upgrade, be sure to consider the DBMS platforms you use and try to gauge the priority of your platform to your vendor. Be sure to build some lag time in your release migration strategy to accommodate the vendor's delivery schedule for your specific platforms.

Supporting Software

Carefully consider the impact of a DBMS upgrade on any supporting software.

Carefully consider the impact of a DBMS upgrade on any supporting software. Supporting software includes purchased applications, DBA tools, reporting and analysis tools, and query tools. Each software vendor will have a different time-frame for supporting and exploiting a new DBMS release. Review the "Support vs. Exploit" sidebar to understand the difference between support and exploitation of a new DBMS release.

Some third-party tool vendors follow guidelines for supporting and exploiting new DBMS releases. Whenever possible, ask your vendors to state their policies for DBMS upgrade support. Your vendors will probably not commit to any firm date or date range to support new versions and releases—some DBMS versions are larger and more complicated and therefore take longer to fully exploit.

Fallback Planning

Each new DBMS version or release should come with a manual that outlines the new features of the release and describes the fallback procedures to return to a prior release of the DBMS. Be sure to review the fallback procedures provided by the DBMS vendor in its release guide. You may need to return to a pre-

Support vs. Exploit

Some vendors differentiate specifically between supporting and exploiting a new DBMS version or release. Software that supports a new release will continue to function the same as before the DBMS was upgraded, but with no new capabilities. Therefore, if a DBA tool, for example, *supports* a new version of Oracle, it can provide all the services it did for the last release, as long as none of the new features of the new version of Oracle are used. In contrast, a DBA tool that *exploits* a new version or release provides the requisite functionality to operate on the new features of the new DBMS release.

So, to use a concrete example, IBM added support for large objects (LOBs) in Version 6 of DB2. A DBA tool can *support* DB2 Version 6 without operating on LOBs, but it must operate on LOBs to *exploit* DB2 Version 6.

Prior to migrating to a new DBMS version or release, make sure you understand the difference between supporting and exploiting a new version, and get a schedule for both from your third-party tool vendors for the DBA tools you use.

vious DBMS release if the upgrade contains a bug, performance problems ensue, or other problems arise during or immediately after migration. Keep in mind that fallback is not always an option for every new DBMS release.

If fallback is possible, follow the DBMS vendor's recommended procedures to enable fallback. You may need to delay the implementation of certain new features for fallback to remain an option. Understand fully the limitations imposed by the DBMS vendor on fallback, and exploit new features only when fallback is no longer an option for your organization.

Migration Verification

The DBA should implement procedures to verify that the DBMS release upgrade is satisfactory.

The DBA should implement procedures—similar to those for a new installation—to verify that the DBMS release upgrade is satisfactory. Perform the same steps as with a brand-new DBMS install, but also test a representative sampling of your in-house applications to verify that the DBMS upgrade is working correctly and performing satisfactorily.

The DBMS Upgrade Strategy

In general, design your DBMS release upgrade policy according to the guidelines discussed above. Each specific DBMS upgrade will be unique, but the strategies we've discussed will help you to achieve success more readily. A well-thought-out DBMS upgrade strategy will prepare you to support new DBMS releases with minimum impact to your organization and in a style best suited to your company.

Database Standards and Procedures

Standards and procedures must be developed for database usage.

Before a newly installed DBMS can be used effectively, standards and procedures must be developed for database usage. A recent study conducted by Hackett Benchmarking & Research showed that companies with high levels of standardization reduce the cost of supporting end users by an average of 38% over companies with low levels of standardization.

Standards are common practices that ensure the consistency and effectiveness of the database environment, such as database naming conventions. *Procedures* are scripts that direct the processes required for handling specific events, such as a disaster recovery plan. Failure to implement database standards and procedures will result in a database environment that is confusing and difficult to manage.

The DBA should develop database standards and procedures as a component of corporatewide IT standards and procedures. They should be stored together in a central location as a printed document, in an online format, or as both. Several vendors offer "canned" standards and procedures that can be purchased for specific DBMS products.

Database Naming Conventions

One of the first standards to be implemented should be a set of guidelines for the naming of database objects. Without standard database object naming conventions, it will be difficult to identify database objects correctly and to perform the proper administration tasks.

Database object naming standards should be developed in conjunction with all other IT naming standards in your organization. In all cases, database naming standards should be developed in cooperation with the data administration department (if one exists) and, wherever possible, should peacefully coexist with other IT standards, but not at the expense of impairing the database environment. For example, many organizations have shop conventions for naming files, but coordinating the database object to the operating system file may require a specific format for database filenames that does not conform to the shop standards. (See Figure 2-6). Therefore, it may be necessary to make exceptions to existing shop standards for naming database files.

Be sure to establish naming conventions for all database objects.

Be sure to create and publish naming standards for all database objects that can be created within each DBMS used by your organization. A basic list of database objects supported by most DBMSs includes databases, tables, columns, views, indexes, constraints, programs, user-defined data types, user-defined functions, triggers, and stored procedures. However, this list is incomplete because each DBMS uses other database objects specific to its operation. For example, DB2 uses plans, packages, tablespaces, and storage groups; Oracle uses tablespaces, sequences, and clusters; SQL Server uses filegroups, rules, and defaults.

Minimize name changes across environments.

The database naming standard should be designed to minimize name changes across environments. For example, embedding a T into the name for test and a P for production is a bad idea. It is especially important to avoid this approach for user-visible database objects such as columns, tables, and views. Minimizing name changes simplifies the migration of databases from one environment to another. It is possible to make all the database object names the same by assigning each environment to a different instance or subsystem. The instance or subsystem name, rather than the database object names, will differentiate the environments.

In most cases, for objects not accessed by typical end users, provide a way to differentiate types of database objects. For example, start indexes with *I* or *X*, and databases with *D*. For tables and similar objects though, as discussed earlier, this approach is inappropriate.

In general, do not impose unnecessary restrictions on the names of objects accessed by end users. Relational databases are supposed to be user friendly.

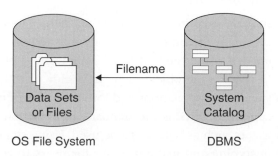

Figure 2-6 *Database objects map to filenames*

A strict database naming convention, if not developed logically, can be antithetical to a useful and effective database environment. Some organizations impose arbitrary length limitations on database tables, such as an 8-byte limit even though the DBMS can support up to 128-byte table names. There is no practical reason to impose a limitation that prohibits the length of database table names.

Table names should be as descriptive as possible, within reason. Furthermore, the same naming conventions should be used for all "tablelike" objects, including views, synonyms, and aliases, if supported by the DBMS. Each of these objects is basically a collection of data accessible as rows and columns. Developing separate naming conventions for each is of no real value. By following this approach, database objects that operate like tables will be defined similarly with a very descriptive name. The type of object can always be determined by querying the DBMS system catalog or data dictionary.

Avoid encoding table names to make them shorter.

Encoding table names to make them shorter is another arbitrary naming standard that should be avoided. Table names should include a 2- or 3-byte application identification prefix, followed by an underscore and then a clear, user friendly name. For example, a good name for the table containing employee information in a human resources system would be HR_EMPLOYEE. You may want to drop the application identification prefix from the table name for tables used by multiple applications.

Keep in mind, too, that some database object names will, in some cases, be externalized. For instance, most DBMSs externalize constraint names when the constraint is violated. There are many types of constraints—triggers, unique constraints, referential constraints, check constraints—each of which can be named. Keeping the names consistent across environments allows the error messages to be consistent. If the DBMS delivers the same error message in the development, test, integration, and production environments, debugging and error correction will be easier.

Standard Abbreviations

Create a list of standard abbreviations.

Although you should keep the database object names as English-like as possible, you will inevitably encounter situations that require abbreviations. Use abbreviations only when the full text is too long to be supported as an object name or when it renders the object name unwieldy or difficult to remember. Create a list of standard abbreviations and forbid the use of nonstandard abbreviations. For example, if "ORG" is the standard abbreviation for "organization," do not allow variants such as "ORGZ" to be used. Using standard abbreviations will minimize mistyping and make it easier for users to remember database object names. Adhering to this practice will make it easier to understand the database objects within your environment.

Other Database Standards and Procedures

Although database naming standards are important, you will need to develop and maintain other types of database standards. Be sure to develop a comprehensive set of standards and procedures for each DBMS used by your organization. Each of the following areas should be covered.

Roles and Responsibilities

The successful operation of a DBMS requires the coordinated management efforts of many skilled technicians and business experts. A matrix of database management and administration functions should be developed that documents each support task and who within the organization provides the support. The matrix can be created at a departmental level, a job description level, or even by individual name. A sample matrix is shown in Table 2-4. An X in the matrix indicates involvement in the process, whereas a P indicates primary responsibility.

Of course, you can create whatever tasks you deem necessary in your roles and responsibilities matrix. You may need additional tasks, or fewer than in this sample. For example, you may wish to differentiate between stored-procedure development, testing, and management, by creating a different task category for each and breaking down the support requirements differently.

Whatever the final format of your roles and responsibilities matrix, be sure to keep it accurate and up-to-date with new DBMS features and tasks. An up-to-date matrix makes it easier to define roles within the organization and to effectively apportion database-related workload.

Data Administration Standards

Include DA standards in the DBA standards as appropriate.

If a DA group exists within your organization, they should develop a basic data administration standards guide to outline the scope of their job role. If a DA group does not exist, be sure to include DA standards in the DBA standards as appropriate.

The data administration standards should include the following items:

- A clear statement of the organization's overall policy with regard to data, including its importance to the company

Table 2-4 *Database Support Roles and Responsibilities*

Task	DBA	DA	SA	Management	Operations	Applications	End Users
DBMS budget	X		X	P		X	X
DBMS installation	P		X		X	X	X
DBMS upgrade	P		X	X	X	X	X
Database usage policy	P	X		X	X	X	
Capacity planning	X		P	X	X	X	
Data modeling and analysis	X	P					X
Metadata policy	X	P					
Database design	P	X				X	
Database creation	P						
System performance	X		P				
Database performance	P		X			X	
Application performance	X		X			P	
Backup and recovery	P		X		X	X	
Disaster recovery	P		X		X		
Database security	P		X		X		
Stored procedures	X					P	
Triggers	P					X	
User-defined functions	X					P	
Application design	X					P	
Application turnover	X				X	P	X
Application design reviews	X	X		X	X	P	X

- Guidelines for establishing data ownership and stewardship

- Rules for data creation, data ownership, and data stewardship

- Metadata management policy

- Conceptual and logical data modeling guidelines

- The organization's goals with regard to creating an enterprise data model

- Responsibility for creating and maintaining logical data models

- Guidelines for tool usage and instructions on how data models are to be created, stored, and maintained

- Organizational data sharing policies

- Instructions on how to document when physical databases deviate from the logical data model

- Guidelines on communication between data administration and database administration to ensure effective database creation and usage

Database Administration Standards

The DBA standards serve as a guide to specific approaches to supporting the database environment.

A basic set of database administration standards should be established to ensure the ongoing success of the DBA function. The standards serve as a guide to the DBA services offered and to specific approaches to supporting the database environment. For example, standards can be developed that outline how requests are made to create a new database or make changes to existing databases, and that specify which types of database objects and DBMS features are favored and under which circumstances they are avoided. Standards can establish backup and recovery procedures (including disaster recovery plans) and communicate the methods used to transform a logical data model into a physical database implementation. An additional set of DBA standards that cover database performance monitoring and tuning may be useful to document procedures for overcoming performance problems.

Although the DBA standards will be most useful for the DBA staff, the application development staff will need them to learn how best to work with the DBA staff. Furthermore, any performance tuning tricks that are documented in the DBA standards should be shared with programmers. The more the application programmers understand the nuances of the DBMS and the role of the DBA, the better the working relationship between DBA and development will be—resulting in a more efficient database environment.

System Administration Standards

Once again, standards for system administration or systems programming are only required if your organization separates the SA function from the DBA function. System administration standards are needed for many of the same reasons that DBA standards are required. Standards for SA may include

- DBMS installation and testing procedures
- Upgrade policies and procedures
- Bug fix and maintenance practices
- A checklist of departments to notify for impending changes
- Interface considerations
- DBMS storage, usage, and monitoring procedures

Database Application Development Standards

The development of database applications differs from typical program development. You should document the special development considerations required when writing programs that access databases. The database application development standards should function as an adjunct to any standard application development procedures within your organization. This set of standards should include

- A description of how database access differs from flat file access
- SQL coding standards
- SQL performance tips and techniques
- Program preparation procedures and guidance on how to embed SQL in an application program
- Interpretations of SQLSTATEs and error codes
- References to other useful programming materials for teleprocessing monitors, programming languages, and general application development standards

Database Security Standards

Outline necessary standards and procedures for administering database security.

The DBA group often applies and administers DBMS security. However, at some shops, the corporate data security unit handles DBMS security. You should provide a resource outlining the necessary standards and procedures for administering database security. It should contain the following information:

- Details on what authority to grant for specific types of situations: For example, if a program is being migrated to production status, what DBMS authorization must be granted before the program will operate successfully in production?

- An definitive list of who can approve what types of database authorization requests.

- Information on any interfaces being used to connect DBMS security with operating system security products.

- Policies on the use of the WITH GRANT OPTION clause of the SQL GRANT statement and how cascading REVOKEs are to be handled.

- Procedures for notifying the requester that database security has been granted.

- Procedures for removing security from retiring, relocating, and terminated employees.

Application Migration and Turnover Procedures

As discussed earlier, the minimum number of environments for supporting database applications is two: test and production. Some organizations, however, create multiple environments to support, for example, different phases of the development life cycle, including

- *Unit testing*—for developing and testing individual programs
- *Integration testing*—for testing how individual programs interoperate
- *User acceptance testing*—for end user testing prior to production status
- *Quality assurance*—for shaking out program bugs
- *Education*—for training end users how to work the application system

Procedures are required for migrating database objects and programs from environment to environment.

When multiple environments exist, procedures are required for migrating database objects and programs from environment to environment. Specific guidelines are needed to accomplish migration in a manner conducive to the usage of each environment. For example, what data volume is required for each environment and how is data integrity to be assured when testing activity occurs? Should data be migrated, or just the database structures? How should existing data in the target environment be treated—should it be kept, or overlaid with new data? Comprehensive migration procedures should be developed to address these types of questions.

The migration and turnover procedures should document the information required before any database object or program can be migrated from one environment to the next. At a minimum, information will be required about the requester, when and why the objects should be migrated, and the appropriate authorization to approve the migration. To ensure the success of the migration, the DBA should document the methods used for the migration and record the verification process.

Design Review Guidelines

All database applications should be subjected to a design review at various stages of their development. Design reviews are important to ensure proper application design, construction, and performance. Design reviews can take many forms. Chapter 6 offers a comprehensive discussion of design reviews.

Operational Support Standards

Operational support assures that applications are run according to schedule.

Operational support is defined as the part of the IT organization that oversees the database environment and assures that applications are run according to schedule. Sufficient operational support must be available to administer a database environment effectively. The operational support staff is usually the first line of defense against system problems. Program failures, hardware failures, and other problems are first identified by operational support before specialists are called to resolve the problems.

Standards should be developed to ensure that the operational support staff understands the special requirements of database applications. Wherever possible, operational support personnel should be trained to resolve simple database-related problems without involving DBAs because the DBA is a more expensive resource.

DBMS Education

Organizations using DBMS technology must commit to ongoing technical education classes for DBAs, programmers, and system administrators. Provide a catalog of available courses covering all aspects of DBMS usage. At a minimum, the following courses should be made available:

- *DBMS Overview:* a one-day management level class that covers the basics of DBMS

- *Data Modeling and Database Design:* a thorough course covering conceptual, logical, and physical database design techniques for DAs and DBAs

- *Database Administration*: in-depth technical classes for DBAs, SAs, and systems programmers

- *Introduction to SQL:* an introductory course on the basics of SQL for every DBMS user

- *Advanced SQL*: an in-depth course on complex SQL development for DBAs and programmers

- *Database Programming*: an in-depth course for application programmers and systems analysts that teaches students how to write programs that use the DBMS

Commit to ongoing technical education classes.

Each of these courses should be available for each DBMS installed in your organization. Furthermore, provide training for any other database-related functionality and software such as proper use of database utilities, query and reporting tools, and DBA tools.

DBMS education can be delivered using a variety of methods including instructor led courses, computer-based training, Web-based training, and distance learning. Sources for DBMS education include the DBMS vendors, ISVs, consultants (large and small, international and local), and training specialists (such as Themis and ProTech).

Finally, be sure to make the DBMS reference material available to every user. Most vendors offer their DBMS reference manuals in an online format using Adobe Acrobat files or Windows Help. Be sure that each user is given a copy of the manuals or that they are available in a central location to minimize the amount of time DBAs will have to spend answering simple questions that can be found in the DBMS documentation.

Summary

Comprehensive advance planning is required to create an effective database environment. Care must be taken to select the correct DBMS technology, implement an appropriate DBMS upgrade strategy, develop useful database standards, and ensure the ongoing availability of education for database users. By following the guidelines in this chapter, you can achieve an effective database environment for your organization.

Nevertheless, setting up the database environment is only the beginning. Once it is set up, you will need to actively manage the database environment to ensure that databases are created properly, used correctly, and managed for performance and availability. Read on to discover how the DBA can accomplish these tasks.

Review

1. Why should database standards be implemented and what are the risks associated with their lack?

2. What are the potential risks of upgrading to a new DBMS release without a plan?

3. What is the difference between a version and a release of a DBMS?

4. Name the four TPC benchmarks and describe how they differ from one another.

5. Describe the four levels of DBMS architecture in terms of the type and nature of processing to which each is best suited.

6. What are the factors to be considered when calculating TCO for a DBMS?

7. Name five requirements that must be planned for when installing a new DBMS.

8. Describe the difference between software that supports a DBMS release and software that exploits a DBMS release.

9. How many standard abbreviations should be supported for a single term? Why?

10. What is wrong with the following SQL code for creating a relational table? (Do not approach this question from a syntax perspective; consider it, instead, in terms database naming standards.)

```
CREATE TABLE tg7r5u99_p
(c1    INTEGER NOT NULL,
 c2    CHAR(5) NOT NULL,
 c9    DATE)
 ;
```

Bonus Question

Your DBMS vendor, MegaDataCorp, just announced the general availability of the latest and greatest version of MDC, the DBMS you use. MDC Version 9 supports several new features that your users and developers have been clamoring for over the past year. You are currently running MDC Version 7.3. Prepare a short paper discussing your plans for upgrading to MDC Version 9 and outline the potential benefits and risks of your upgrade plan.

3

Data Modeling and Normalization

Data modeling
asks the question
"What?"

Data modeling is the process of analyzing the things of interest to your organization and how these things are related to each other. The data modeling process results in the discovery and documentation of the data resources of your business. Data modeling asks the question "What?" instead of the more common data processing question, "How?"

Before implementing databases of any sort, a DBA or DA needs to develop a sound model of the data to be stored. Novice database developers frequently begin with the quick-and-dirty approach to database implementation. They approach database design from a programming perspective. Because novices often lack experience with databases and data requirements gathering, they attempt to design databases like the flat files they are accustomed to using. This is a major mistake. Indeed, most developers using this approach quickly discover problems after the databases and applications become operational in a production environment. At a minimum, performance will suffer and data may not be as readily available as required. At worst, data integrity problems may arise, rendering the entire application unusable.

A proper database design cannot be thrown together quickly by novices. What is required is a practiced and formal approach to gathering data requirements

89

and modeling the data, that is, the discovery and identification of entities and data elements. Data normalization is a big part of data modeling and database design. A normalized data model reduces data redundancy and inconsistencies by ensuring that the data elements are designed appropriately.

It is actually quite simple to learn the basics of data modeling, but it can take a lifetime to master all its nuances. This chapter introduces the concepts of data modeling and normalization, and provides some general guidelines to their proper use.

Experienced data modelers and DAs will probably find the material in this chapter incomplete. This is by design: the intent is to introduce the concept to DBAs and guide them down the right path to producing databases from properly developed data models. A complete treatment of data modeling requires an entire text. Numerous books exist that provide an exhaustive treatment of data modeling and normalization. Consult the suggested references at the end of this chapter for additional details on data modeling.

Data Modeling Concepts

A popular folk story about four blind men and an elephant helps to illustrate the purpose of data modeling:

> Four blind men happened upon an elephant during the course of their journey. The blind men had never encountered an elephant before, but they were a curious group. Therefore, each blind man attempted to learn about the elephant by touching it. The first blind man grabbed the elephant by the trunk and exclaimed, "Oh! An elephant is like a snake—a long, slithery tube." The second blind man reached out, touched the side of the elephant, and remarked, "No, no, the elephant is more like a wall—very flat and solid." The third blind man was confused, so he reached out to touch the elephant but poked his hand on a tusk and said, "No, you're both wrong, the elephant is more like a spear than anything else!" The fourth blind man grabbed the elephant by the leg and shouted, "You're all wrong, an elephant is very much like a tree—round and solid."

Well, each blind man was right, but he was also wrong. The problem was not with the experience of each blind man, but with the scope of that experience. To be a successful data modeler you must learn to discover the entire "truth" of the data needs of your business. You cannot rely on the requirements

The goal of a data model is to record the data requirements of a business process.

of a single user, or even a single expert, because his or her scope of experience will not be comprehensive. The goal of a data model is to record the data requirements of a business process. The scope of the data model for each line of business must be comprehensive. If an enterprise data model exists for the organization, then each individual line-of-business data model must be verified for correctness against the overall enterprise data model.

Data modeling, at the most basic level, begins as a conceptual venture. The first objective of conceptual data modeling is to understand the requirements. A data model, in and of itself, is of limited value. Of course, a data model delivers value by enhancing communication and understanding, and it can be argued that these are quite valuable. However, the primary value of a data model is its ability to be used as a blueprint to build a physical database.

When databases are built from a well-designed data model, the resultant structures provide increased value to the organization. The value derived from the data model exhibits itself in the form of minimized data redundancy, maximized data integrity, increased stability, better data sharing, increased consistency, more timely access to data, and better data usability. These qualities are achieved because the data model clearly outlines the data resource requirements and relationships in a clear, concise manner. Building databases from a data model will result in a better database implementation because you will have a better understanding of the data to be stored in your databases.

A data model can clarify data patterns and potential uses for data.

Another benefit of data modeling is the opportunity to discover new uses for data. A data model can clarify data patterns and potential uses for data that might otherwise remain hidden. Discovery of such patterns can change the

The Enterprise Data Model

An *enterprise data model* is a single data model that describes comprehensively the data needs of the entire organization. This chapter discusses data models as they pertain to individual projects or applications, but not the relatively advanced topic of the enterprise data model. Managing and maintaining an enterprise data model is fraught with many non-database-related distractions such as corporate politics and ROI that is hard to quantify.

If your organization has committed to developing and maintaining an enterprise data model you should definitely take the time to read more about the topic by consulting the books referenced at the end of this chapter and the articles at www.dbazine.com.

way your business operates and can potentially lead to a competitive advantage and increased revenue for your organization.

Data modeling requires a different mindset than requirements gathering for application development and process-oriented tasks. It is important to think "what" is of interest instead of "how" tasks are accomplished. To transition to this alternative way of thinking, follow these three rules.

- *Don't think physical; think conceptual.* Concern yourself with business issues and terms rather than physical storage issues and DBMS constraints.

- *Don't think process; think structure.* How something is done, although important for application development, is not important for data modeling. The things that processes are being applied to are what is important to data modeling.

- *Don't think navigation; think relationship.* The way that things are related to one another is important because relationships map the data model. The way in which relationships are traversed is unimportant to conceptual and logical data modeling.

Keep in mind that as you create your data models, you are developing the lexicon of your organization's business. Much like a dictionary functions as the lexicon of a given language, the data model functions as the lexicon of business terms and their usage.

Entity-Relationship Diagramming

An E/R diagram graphically depicts the entities and relationships of a data model.

Data models are typically rendered in a graphical format using an *entity-relationship diagram*, or E/R diagram for short. An E/R diagram graphically depicts the entities and relationships of a data model. Figure 3-1 shows a sample E/R diagram. This diagram was produced using ERwin, from Computer Associates, a leading data modeling and design tool. Many popular data modeling tools are available from a variety of vendors. Consult Appendix 3 for a list of data modeling tools and vendors.

Multiple diagramming methods and techniques are available for E/R diagramming. Regardless of the method used, an E/R diagram will show the entities in boxes and use lines or arrows to show relationships. The format of the boxes and lines differs with the diagramming method. Several of the most common E/R diagramming methods are shown in Figure 3-2. There is nothing

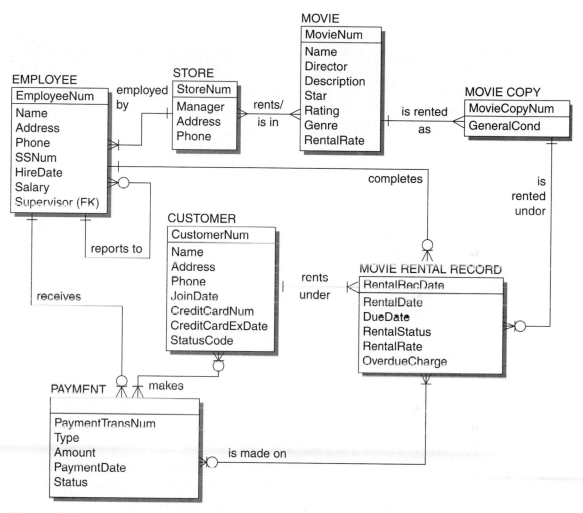

Figure 3-1 *A sample E/R diagram (Diagram created with ERwin.)*

that really makes one method superior to the others, so choose one and try to stick to it to minimize confusion. Allowing different modeling teams to use different diagramming techniques will make sharing the knowledge contained in the data models more difficult. Furthermore, it complicates the consolidation of the data models into an enterprise data model, if one is maintained.

Refer to Figure 3-2 again. The major difference between the diagramming methods is the way in which cardinality is shown. *Cardinality* refers to the maximum number of instances an entity can take on. Each row of Figure 3-2

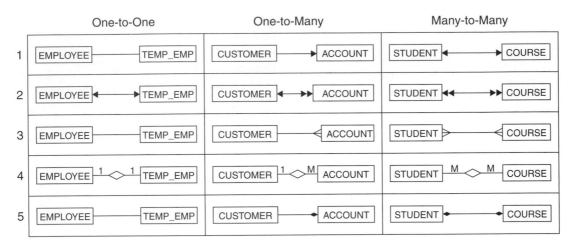

Figure 3-2   *E/R diagramming methods: (1) Ross, (2) Bachmann, (3) Martin, (4) Chen, (5) Rumbaugh*

shows how a different E/R diagramming style handles one-to-one, one-to-many, and many-to-many relationships. The E/R diagramming methods are named after the originator of the technique. By row, the names of the diagramming techniques depicted in Figure 3-2 are Ross, Bachmann, Martin, Chen, and Rumbaugh.

Most modeling tools support one or more of these diagramming techniques. The most popular diagramming techniques are Martin (also known as Information Engineering) and Ross. The E/R diagram in Figure 3-1 was developed using the Martin technique. Popularity aside, each of these techniques is used by many data modelers, and you should select the technique that is easiest for those in your organization to use and understand.

Another popular modeling technique is Unified Modeling Language. UML is a consolidation of several popular object-oriented notations and concepts. It originated from the work of Grady Booch, James Rumbaugh, and Ivar Jacobson. UML provides a standard set of diagrams and notations for modeling object-oriented systems. UML actually defines nine types of diagrams for modeling different types of systems. The UML class diagram can be used to model data, but traditional E/R diagrams capture more information about pure data and are better suited than UML to data modeling and relational database design tasks. Figure 3-3 shows a sample UML class diagram depicting a data model for an airline. Because objects comprise both data and process, UML is more than a data modeling diagramming technique.

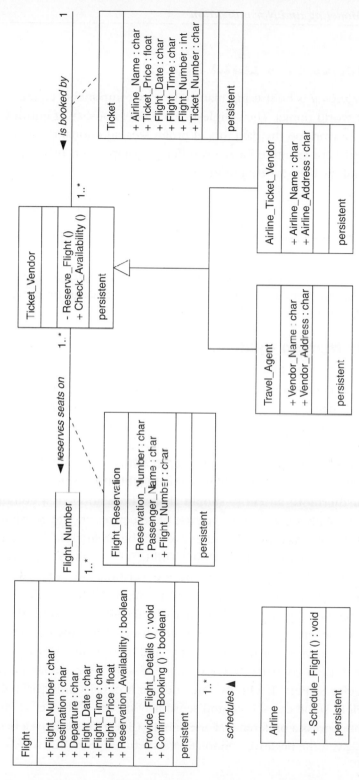

Figure 3-3 *Sample UML class diagram*

From the whitepaper "Modeling Systems with UML" by Lou Varveris, Popkin Software. Diagram created with System Architect.

The Components of a Data Model

A *data model* is built using many different components acting as abstractions of real world things. The simplest data model consists of entities and relationships. As work on the data model progresses, additional detail and complexity is added. Let's examine the many different components of a data model and the terminology used for data modeling.

Entities

An entity is a person, place, thing, concept or event.

An *entity*, at a very basic level, is something that exists and is capable of being described. It is a person, place, thing, concept, or event about which your organization maintains facts. For example, STUDENT, INSTRUCTOR, and COURSE are specific entities about which a college or university must be knowledgeable to perform its business.

Entity Naming Guidelines

It is important to follow a rigorous standard for naming entities within a data model. If developers attempt to communicate using poorly defined and non-standard names, confusion will result. A good standard to follow is to always name entities in singular form using capital letters. An entity should be viewed as a pattern for the occurrences therein, instead of the set of all occurrences for that type of entity. For example, an entity that contains data about your company's employees should be named EMPLOYEE rather than EMPLOYEES.

An entity should always be a noun, or a combination of an adjective with a noun.

Furthermore, an entity should always be a noun, or a combination of an adjective with a noun. However, use of adjectives should be minimized whenever possible. At times, the adjective can be an attribute in disguise. For example, an entity named CONTRACT EMPLOYEE is better expressed as an entity named EMPLOYEE with an attribute describing the status of the employee (where the value of Status can be FULLTIME or CONTRACT).

Promote consistency in the choice of terminology used for entities. In general, use the term favored by the business users. When the business uses multiple terms (synonyms) for the same entity and there is no clear consensus, choose one and use it consistently. For example, if some users prefer VENDOR but others prefer SUPPLIER, choose one and use it consistently throughout the data model. In some cases, common sense may dictate a choice when the business cannot express a preference. For example, CLIENT is perhaps a better term than USER, given the negative connotation sometimes given this word ("drug user").

Finally, remove process-specific artifacts from the entity name. For example, AGENT is better than SELLING AGENT. Remember, the data model should capture the "what" not the "how," and "selling" describes a process.

Entity Occurrences

An occurrence is an instance of an entity.

An *occurrence* is an instance of an entity. For example, AUTHOR is an example of an entity. Craig S. Mullins, along with all my descriptive details, is an occurrence of the AUTHOR entity. It is important to differentiate the abstract entity from the concrete occurrences of the entity. Entity instance is an equivalent term for occurrence.

Attributes

Every attribute does one of three things: it identifies, relates, or describes.

An *attribute* is a characteristic of an entity. Every attribute does one of three things:

- *Identifies*. An attribute that identifies is a *candidate key*. If the value of an identifying attribute changes, it should identify a different entity occurrence. An attribute that identifies should be immutable.
- *Relates*. An attribute that relates entities is a *foreign key*. The attribute refers to the primary key attribute of an occurrence of another (or the same) entity
- *Describes*. An attribute is descriptive if it depicts or express a characteristic of an entity occurrence, but does not identify or relate.

As a rule of thumb, nouns tend to be entities and adjectives tend to be attributes. Nevertheless, this is not a hard and fast rule: Be sure to apply knowledge of the business to determine which nouns and adjectives are entities and which are attributes. Every attribute must identify the entity occurrence, relate the entity occurrence to another entity occurrence (in the same or another entity), or describe the entity occurrence.

An attribute must definitively reflect its specific, intended meaning. The instances of an attribute must be atomic in nature—that is, an attribute represents a singular fact that cannot be further decomposed. For that reason, using Name as an attribute for, say, the entity PERSON, would not be good practice because Name can be decomposed into FirstName, MiddleInitial, and LastName.

Domains

The *domain* defines the universe of valid values for the data element.

Each attribute is assigned a valid domain. The *domain* defines the universe of valid values for the data element. An example of a domain would be "valid positive integer values between 1 and 10." Data type is a component of the domain. The data type specifies, appropriately enough, the type of data that comprises the domain; some examples are Integer, Decimal, Character, Date, Time, and so on.

When an attribute is defined that represents a code, the domain for the code should, if possible, consist of self-documenting values. For example, the domain for an attribute defining a periodic frequency of weekly, monthly, quarterly, and yearly is better defined as ("W", "M", "Q", "Y") than as ("1", "2", "3", "4"). The first domain is self-documenting and easy to remember. The second is not so easy to remember.

Attribute Naming Guidelines

Adhere to a standard format for naming attributes.

Develop and adhere to a standard format for naming attributes. For example, if you name the attributes in singular form with InterCaps ("FirstName"), don't switch back and forth to all lowercase ("first_name"). Choose one form and stick to it. Some potential attribute names for the EMPLOYEE entity might be StreetAddress (or street_address), ZipCode (or zip_code), and EmployeeId (or employee_id). The point is not to spend a lot of time agonizing over the exact standard for naming attributes, but to choose a standard and stick to it to minimize confusion and clarify communication.

An *attribute name* should consist of a prime descriptive word coupled with a class word. A class describes a particular subset of attributes that are common to most information systems. Additional qualifying words can be used if necessary to define the attribute accordingly. The prime descriptive word can be the entity name or another descriptive word. For the class word, establish a valid list of classes for the types of domains in use. A sample list of possible classes is shown in Table 3-1. You may decide to use the entire class name or a standard abbreviation. The following are some sample attribute names:

- VendorID—where Vendor is the entity, and the attribute is an identifier.
- ProductName—where Product is the entity, and the domain of the attribute is an alphabetic, character name.
- ProductYearlySalesAmount—where Product is the entity, and the domain is an amount. However, there may be multiple amounts for each

Table 3-1 *Sample Attribute Class Words*

Class	Class Description	Class Abbreviation
Address	Street address or location	ADDR
Amount	Monetary amount	AMT
Audio	Digital audio or voice recordings	AUD
Code	Codes, types, and classifications	CDE
Date	Calendar dates	DAT
Description	Descriptive text	DSC
Identifier	Unique identifier	ID
Image	Digital images	IMG
Name	Alphabetic, character name	NME
Number	Numeric counter	NUM
Percentage	A numeric ratio or percentage	PCT
Quantity	Numeric units or amounts (nonmonetary)	QTY
Text	Free format text document	TXT
Time	Clock time	TME
Video	Digital video streams; moving pictures	VID

product instance. This particular attribute is further qualified by Yearly, which indicates the period, and Sales, which indicates that the amount is an amount sold, as opposed to, say, an amount purchased.

Class words should not have multiple meanings.

Your list of class words may differ. On the other hand, the list might be the same, with different abbreviations. Either is fine, as long as you develop a list of class words and enforce their usage. Class words should not have multiple meanings. One, and only one class word should be defined for each domain. Also, avoid homonyms and synonyms when defining your class words. (See the sidebar "Homonyms and Synonyms.") Keep in mind that these class words are important for the logical data model only and might not be used in the physical database due to sizing limitations for DBMS object names.

Attribute Values

An *attribute value* is an instance of an attribute. The value "Craig" is an example of an attribute value for the FirstName attribute within the AUTHOR entity. It is important to differentiate the abstract attribute from the concrete values for the attribute.

Homonyms and Synonyms

According to Merriam-Webster's Collegiate® Dictionary, Tenth Edition (1998):

Homonym, *noun*
1: one of two or more words spelled and pronounced alike but different in meaning (as the noun *quail* and the verb *quail*)

Synonym, *noun*
1: one of two or more words or expressions of the same language that have the same meaning or nearly the same meaning in some or all senses

Using homonyms and synonyms in your data modeling can cause confusion. A homonym must be used in context for its meaning to be understood. When two words are spelled and pronounced identically, the only way to differentiate them is to examine how each is being used. For example, if I just say the word "watch," am I referring to a timepiece, or am I requesting that you to look at something? Devoid of context, it is impossible to tell.

Synonyms cause confusion for a different reason. When the same thing is referred to in different ways, it can become unclear that more than one word is being used to refer to the same thing. For example, are clients and customers the same thing?

Although homonyms and synonyms cannot be banned during the course of conducting business, they can be banned within the scope of data modeling and database design. Be sure that as a data modeler you do so. However, don't attempt to force the line of business users to adopt the terminology in place of their current usage habits. Instead, be consistent within the data model and allow the users to continue their current practices without demanding a change of their lexicon. Nevertheless, be sure to capture and document all business usage of homonyms and synonyms.

Nulls and Lack of Value

A null represents missing or unknown information.

A *null* represents missing or unknown information at the attribute level. If an attribute "value" can be null, it means one of two things: the attribute is not applicable for certain occurrences of the entity, or the attribute applies to all entity occurrences, but the information may not always be known. Of course, it could be a combination of these two situations, too.

For example, suppose that an entity, STUDENT, contains an attribute Hair-Color. Further, the HairColor attribute can be null. But what does a null HairColor indicate? Consider three potential entity occurrences: a man with black hair, a woman with unknown hair color, and a bald man. The woman with the unknown hair color and the bald man both could be assigned a null HairColor, but for different reasons. The woman's HairColor would be null, meaning "presently unknown"; the bald man's HairColor would be null, meaning "not applicable."

Be sure to consider the nuances of nulls as you develop your data model. Be sure to determine the nullability for every attribute.

Nulls are sometimes inappropriately referred to as null values. Using the term *value* to describe a null is inaccurate because the term *null* implies the *lack* of a value.

Keys

Keys consist of the attributes that identify entity occurrences and define the relationships between entities.

A *key* consists of one or more attributes, the values of which uniquely identify an entity occurrence and define relationships between entities. Well, more precisely, candidate keys and primary keys identify the entity. A combination of the primary key value of one entity and the foreign key value of another entity identify relationships. For example, if CustNo is the primary key of the CUSTOMER entity, CustNo will be used as the foreign key in a related entity, such as CUSTOMER_CONTACT. A customer can have multiple contacts, so the same CustNo would be registered for each contact for the customer.

A key should contain no embedded meaning. The key's purpose is to identify, not to describe. The other attributes in the entity serve a descriptive purpose. When a key contains an embedded meaning, problems can arise if the meaning changes. Furthermore, the values for any embedded meaning are likely to be outside your immediate control, which can also cause data integrity and modification problems.

Candidate Keys

Each entity can have multiple candidate keys, but it must have at least one. A *candidate key* is an attribute, or set of attributes, that can be used to uniquely identify an occurrence of the entity. If the value of the attribute cannot be used to identify a specific occurrence of the entity, then it does not represent a candidate key.

Primary Key

Each entity will have one, and only one, primary key. The *primary key* is chosen from the set of candidate keys and is used to identify an entity occurrence. Choosing an appropriate primary key is important because the primary key will be used to define the foreign keys in related, dependent entities.

Characteristics of good primary keys include the following.

- The primary key must guarantee the uniqueness of an entity occurrence.
- The value of any component of the primary key cannot be null.
- Primary keys of basic entities should not have embedded meaning.
- Primary keys should be immutable—that is, not capable of or susceptible to change.

Furthermore, you should have control over primary key values. When values are assigned externally, you lose control, causing potential data problems. For one, it is impossible to ensure that the key values will always be unique. As an example, the social security number is a bad primary key choice to identify employees because it is assigned outside of your control. A numeric identifier assigned by your organization is a better choice.

Foreign Keys

Foreign keys reside in dependent entities to establish relationships. The primary key identifies an entity occurrence; foreign keys identify relationships between entity occurrences. For one-to-many relationships, the foreign key will always be on the many side of a relationship. For one-to-one relationships, determination of foreign key placement is more difficult. The basic rule is to analyze the attributes and assign the key to the entity for which it is most characteristic. If one end of the one-to-one relationship is optional, the entity at the optional end should contain the foreign key and the entity at the mandatory end should contain the primary key.

Relationships

Relationships define how the different entities are associated with each other.

Relationships define how the different entities are associated with each other. A relationship name should describe the role played by an entity in its association with another (or perhaps the same) entity. The keys define a relationship: the primary key in the parent entity and the foreign key in the dependent entity.

Relationships are not just the "lines" that connect entities but provide meaning to the data model and should be assigned useful names. The relationship name makes a factual statement about the association between entities. For example, consider the one-to-many relationship between the COURSE and INSTRUCTOR entities: Each COURSE is taught by one, and only one, INSTRUC-

TOR, but an INSTRUCTOR teaches many COURSEs. The name of the relationship, in this case "is-taught-by", coupled with the names of the entities participating in the relationship should form a meaningful sentence.

In an E/R diagram, the relationships should be read clockwise from right to left over the line. Following this convention will assure the legibility of your data models.

Cardinality

Cardinality is the number of occurrences that can exist between a pair of entities.

Cardinality is the number of occurrences that can exist between a pair of entities. Another way of looking at cardinality is as the number of entity occurrences applicable to a specific relationship. Sometimes the term *degree* is used instead of cardinality. Each end of a relationship has a cardinality, or degree, associated with it.

At the simplest level, cardinality is expressed by the way relationships are drawn in the E/R diagram. Recall the diagramming techniques displayed in Figure 3-2. The notion of cardinality is expressed as either "one" or "many." Using the Martin technique (line 3 in the figure), a cardinality of one is expressed as a straight line and a cardinality of many is expressed using crow's feet.

At a more complex level, the data model should capture more information about the specific cardinality of each relationship. A complete data model will record the minimum and maximum cardinality for each end of the relationship as integer values. However, such detailed cardinality information need not be represented on the diagram, especially at the conceptual level.

Optionality

Each end of the relationship will have an optionality characteristic.

The data model must also capture whether relationships are mandatory or optional. This is commonly referred to as the *optionality* of the relationship. Once again, each end of the relationship will have an optionality characteristic.

For the Martin diagramming technique, drawing a bar at the end of the relationship indicates that the relationship is mandatory; a small circle indicates an optional relationship. Refer to the relationship diagrammed in Figure 3-4. This data model fragment clearly states that an EMPLOYEE is employed by a STORE. The STORE can have zero, one, or multiple EMPLOYEEs. If an EMPLOYEE exists, a relationship to a STORE is mandatory. Furthermore, an EMPLOYEE can only work for one store.

Other diagramming techniques use different methods—perhaps different shapes or specific integer values.

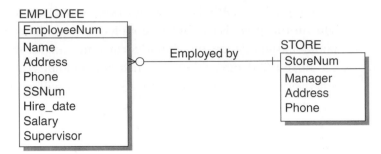

Figure 3-4   *Data model fragment*

So, you can see how a graphical data model that uses well-defined diagramming techniques and notations can clearly communicate the business requirements of data. Knowing nothing more than data modeling techniques, an individual who is unfamiliar with the business can quickly learn and communicate the organization's fundamental business rules.

Discovering Entities, Attributes, and Relationships

At a very high level, the data modeling process can be thought of as *the discovery of entities and their attributes along with the relationships between the entities*. The process of discovering and documenting these items for your business is data modeling. Now, data modeling may sound simple enough, but it takes practice to learn how to listen to business speech and be able to identify and differentiate between entities, attributes, and relationships.

Track the nouns, noun phrases, verbs, and adjectives used by the business experts.

The first trick is to keep track of the nouns, noun phrases, verbs, and adjectives used by the business experts. Nouns are potential entities and attributes, or perhaps entity occurrences and attribute values. Adjectives and prepositional phrases are usually potential attributes. Verbs indicate potential relationships.

Of course, developing a data model is more difficult than merely listening for nouns, adjectives, and the like and transforming them into the entities, attributes, and relationships of a data model. Every noun is not necessarily an entity of interest—likewise for adjectives, verbs, and prepositional phrases. You will need to use your experience to filter the business speech to identify the appropriate entities, attributes, and relationships.

When analyzing business descriptions you will need to place the words in context and ask questions to clearly differentiate between entities and attributes. Remember, attributes identify, relate, or describe entities. Entities are the most important and general "things" the business expert will discuss—the people, places, things, concepts, and events of interest to the business.

Often the terminology used by the business experts will not be appropriate for the data model. You may need to generalize terms, or make them more abstract. For example, business users may speak of doing business with corporations, but business is also conducted with individuals. For the purpose of the data model you may need to create an abstract entity, such as PARTY or some other abstract term that encompasses corporations, other types of organizations, and individuals.

No one individual understands all the data needs of the organization.

When developing a data model, be sure to solicit input from multiple sources. A data model built on the advice of a single expert is sure to be inaccurate. Remember the blind men and the elephant: No one individual understands all the data needs of the organization (or indeed, of any single aspect of the organization). By talking to multiple experts on multiple occasions, the true nature and definition of the data will become clearer.

Keep in mind that patterns in data models tend to repeat. As you work on data modeling projects, you will begin to notice certain patterns that reappear in multiple subject areas. Learning to recognize these patterns can simplify the creation of data models. However, don't make the mistake of jumping to a pattern that you think you recognize, without consulting multiple business experts. Sometimes, what appears to be a recognizable pattern is, in actuality, a completely new pattern.

As with most things, practice will improve your data modeling skills. Don't be discouraged if your initial attempts at creating data models are difficult or error prone. The more you model, the better you will become at data modeling.

Finally, to further clarify the flexibility and usefulness of data modeling, let's look at a data model that incorporates data modeling terms we just learned. Consult the E/R diagram in Figure 3-5. This E/R diagram shows clearly the relationships between the components of a data model.

Conceptual, Logical, and Physical Data Models

Up until now, we have discussed data modeling in general. But there are really three types of data modeling: conceptual, logical, and physical.

Conceptual and *logical* are loose terms that describe different phases of data modeling. A conceptual data model is generally more abstract and less detailed than a complete logical data model. There is no hard and fast boundary

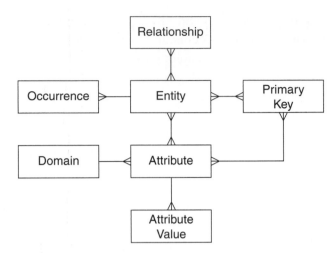

Figure 3-5   *Relationship of data modeling terms*

separating a conceptual data model from a logical data model. But the following generalities are largely accepted in the modeling community.

A conceptual data model depicts a high-level, business-oriented view of information.

A *conceptual data model* depicts a high-level, business-orientated view of information. Noncritical details can be left out of the conceptual data model in order to emphasize the most important entities, attributes, and relationships. The conceptual data model may contain many-to-many relationships. The goal of conceptual modeling is clarity and simplicity. It is not necessary to discover and document every attribute of each entity at the conceptual level. Furthermore, issues such as cardinality, optionality, and data types can be skipped at the conceptual level. Some simple candidate keys may be recorded, but the conceptual data model will not identify most keys because the high level of abstraction makes useful key identification impractical or impossible. Furthermore, every relationship need not be named on the conceptual data model. Remember, the goal of a conceptual data model is clarity at a high level. If the relationship names clutter up the data model diagram then they work against that goal.

The logical data model offers a comprehensive formal structure that serves as a blueprint for business data.

A *logical data model* consists of fully normalized entities with all attributes defined. Furthermore, the domain or data type of each attribute must be defined. A logical data model requires the specification of candidate keys for unique identification of each occurrence in every entity. For those entities having multiple candidate keys, the logical data model must indicate which candidate key to use for identification: that is, the primary key. Foreign key

Associative Entities

An *associative entity* provides additional information about a relationship, if needed. In other words, an associative entity enables attributes to be associated with a relationship. Associative entities also make it possible for many-to-many relationships to be implemented using a relational database.

Every many-to-many relationship can be resolved to a pair of one-to-many relationships between each of the two existing entities, and a new entity—an associate entity, as shown in Figure 3-6.

In the example shown at the top of the figure, a STUDENT can register for many COURSEs, and a COURSE can contain many STUDENTs. This classic many-to-many relationship can be resolved as shown at the bottom of Figure 3-6. A new associative entity is created, in this case, the ENROLLMENT entity. The primary key from each of the previously existing entities is copied to the new entity. And the many-to-many relationship is replaced with two one-to-many relationships, with the many side, in each case, placed on the new associative entity. Now attributes can be assigned to the new entity, which was not possible for a relationship.

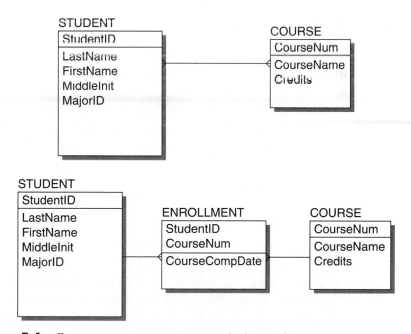

Figure 3-6 *From many-to-many to associative entity*

definitions should be clearly defined or implied by the data relationships. Many-to-many relationships should be translated into associative entities (refer to the sidebar "Associative Entities"), which may acquire additional attributes and identifiers. Additional details, such as cardinality and whether relationships are optional or mandatory, must be documented in the logical data model. All relationships should be clearly and explicitly named. A logical data model should be a complete document from which a physical database can be developed.

The *physical data model* is created to transform the logical data model into a physical implementation using a specific DBMS product such as DB2, Oracle, or SQL Server. The specifics of the physical data model are covered in Chapter 4.

The physical data model transforms the logical data model into a physical implementation using a specific DBMS.

So, a conceptual data model focuses on providing a real-world view of a particular business subject. The conceptual data model makes it easier to understand the business at an abstract level. The logical data model offers a comprehensive formal structure to be used as a blueprint for business data and as input to define databases. And the physical data model specifies exactly how the logical data model will be implemented using a particular DBMS.

What Is Normalization?

Normalization identifyies the one best place where each fact belongs.

In simple terms, *normalization* is the process of identifying the one best place where each fact belongs. Normalization is a design approach that minimizes data redundancy and optimizes data structures by systematically and properly placing data elements into the appropriate groupings. A normalized data model can be translated into a physical database that is organized correctly.

Normalization was created by E. F. Codd, the developer of the relational model, in the early 1970s. Like the relational model of data, normalization is based on the mathematical principles of set theory. Although normalization evolved from relational theory, the process of normalizing data is generally applicable to any type of data.

It is important to remember that normalization is a logical process and does not necessarily dictate physical database design. A normalized data model will ensure that each entity is well formed and that each attribute is assigned to the proper entity. Of course, the best situation is when a normalized logical data model can be physically implemented without major modifications. However, as we will learn in Chapter 4, there are times when the physical database must differ from the logical data model due to physical implementation requirements and deficiencies in DBMS products.

The Normal Forms

As previously mentioned, E. F. Codd was the first to describe data normalization. Codd published several papers in 1971 and 1972 that described the first three normal forms. Subsequent work by Codd and others defined additional normal forms.

First Normal Form

First normal form eliminates repeating groups and nonatomic data from an entity.

The objective of *first normal form* (1NF) is to eliminate repeating groups and nonatomic data from an entity. When data conforms to 1NF, each attribute of the entity is a single discrete fact—in other words, atomic. The term atomic derives from atom, the smallest indivisible particle that can exist on its own.

Definition	A row is in first normal form if and only if all underlying domains contain atomic values only.

To normalize a data model into 1NF, eliminate repeating groups into individual entities. In other words, do not use multiple attributes in a single entity to store similar data. Consider the sample data shown in Table 3-2 for a STUDENT information system for a college or university.

This data contains several violations of 1NF. First, we are tracking courses that really represent a repeating group for STUDENTs. So, the course information should be moved into separate entities. Furthermore, we need to specify identifiers for both entities. The identifier is the primary key for the entity.

Be careful to choose an appropriate primary key for each entity. This can be tricky. Your initial impulse may be to choose CourseNum for the COURSE entity. But in the case of this data, there is more information required to identify the course information. The course completion date applies to a combination of STUDENT and COURSE—a course cannot be completed unless a student has enrolled in the course and is taking it.

A second violation of 1NF is the nonatomic data shown in the Student-Name attribute. A student name can be broken down into pieces: first name, middle initial, and last name. It is not indivisible, and therefore violates first normal form. The end result in 1NF is depicted in Tables 3-3 and 3-4.

Table 3-2 *Unnormalized STUDENT Data*

StudentID	StudentName	MajorID	StudentMajor	CourseNum	CourseName	CourseCompDate
2907	Smith, Jacob R	MAT	Mathematics	MAT0011	Discrete Math	2002-08-01
				MAT0027	Calculus I	2002-04-30
				EGL0010	English Classics I	2001-12-30
4019	Patterson, Jane K	PHI	Philosophy	PHI0010	Intro to Philosophy	2002-04-30
				CS00100	Programming Languages	2002-04-30
5145	Neeld, Norris B	EGL	English Literature	SOC0102	Ascent of Man	2002-08-01
6132	Morrison, Xavier Q	MUS	Music	MUS0002	Origin of Jazz	2002-04-30
				SOC0102	Ascent of Man	2002-08-01
7810	Brown, Richard E	CS	Computer Science			
8966	Juarez, Samantha	EGL	English Literature	EGL0010	English Classics I	2001-12-30
				EGL0101	Shakespeare II	2002-08-01

Table 3-3 *STUDENT Entity in 1NF*

StudentID	LastName	FirstName	MiddleInit	MajorID	StudentMajor
2907	Smith	Jacob	R	MAT	Mathematics
4019	Patterson	Jane	K	PHI	Philosophy
5145	Neeld	Norris	B	EGL	English Literature
6132	Morrison	Xavier	Q	MUS	Music
7810	Brown	Richard	E	CS	Computer Science
8966	Juarez	Samantha		EGL	English Literature

Table 3-4   *COURSE Entity in 1NF*

StudentID	CourseNum	CourseName	CourseCompDate
2907	MAT0011	Discrete Math	2002-08-01
2907	MAT0027	Calculus I	2002-04-30
2907	EGL0010	English Classics I	2001-12-30
4019	PHI0010	Intro to Philosophy	2002-04-30
4019	CS00100	Programming Languages	2002-04-30
5145	SOC0102	Ascent of Man	2002-08-01
6132	MUS0002	Origin of Jazz	2002-04-30
6132	SOC0102	Ascent of Man	2002-08-01
8966	EGL0010	English Classics I	2001-12-30
8966	EGL0101	Shakespeare II	2002-08-01

Second Normal Form

Second normal form ensures that all the attributes of each entity are dependent.

Second normal form (2NF) ensures that all the attributes of each entity are dependent on the primary key. To transform 1NF data into 2NF, create separate entities for sets of attributes that apply to multiple records and assign a foreign key to the new entity to relate it to its previous entity. Simply stated, entity occurrences should not depend on anything other than the entity's primary key.

Definition	A row is in second normal form if and only if it is in first normal form and every non-key attribute is fully dependent on the key.

Let's once again turn our attention to Tables 3-3 and 3-4. Notice that certain courses repeat in the COURSE entity, namely "English Classics I" and "Ascent of Man." This situation indicates a violation of 2NF. To correct the problem, we need to identify the attributes that do not depend on the entire key and remove them. The removed attributes, along with the portion of the primary key on which they depend, are placed in a new entity, ENROLLMENT. The entire primary key of the original entity remains with the original entity.

Another benefit of the normalization process is that you will frequently encounter new attributes that need to be specified for the new entities that are created. For example, perhaps the new COURSE entity causes us to remember that each course is assigned a number of credits that count toward graduation.

Table 3-5   *ENROLLMENT Entity in 2NF*

StudentID	CourseNum	CourseCompDate
2907	MAT0011	2002-08-01
2907	MAT0027	2002-04-30
2907	EGL0010	2001-12-30
4019	PHI0010	2002-04-30
4019	CS00100	2002-04-30
5145	SOC0102	2002-08-01
6132	MUS0002	2002-04-30
6132	SOC0102	2002-08-01
8966	EGL0010	2001-12-30
8966	EGL0101	2002-08-01

Table 3-6   *COURSE Entity in 2NF*

CourseNum	CourseName	Credits
MAT0011	Discrete Math	3
MAT0027	Calculus I	4
EGL0010	English Classics I	3
PHI0010	Intro to Philosophy	3
CS00100	Programming Languages	3
SOC0102	Ascent of Man	3
MUS0002	Origin of Jazz	3

So, we create a new attribute to store the number of credits for each specific course. Of course, we may also decide we need more details on students such as address, phone number, and birth date, but we will omit this from our example to keep it simple.

The end results of normalization to 2NF are depicted in Tables 3-3 (no changes were required for the STUDENT entity), 3-5, and 3-6.

Third Normal Form

Third normal form (3NF) ensures that no relationships between attributes exist within an entity. Every attribute in the entity should depend only on the

Third normal form ensures that no relationships between attributes exist within an entity.

primary key. A tongue-in-cheek expression used to describe a data model in third normal is "Every attribute depends upon the key, the whole key, and nothing but the key, so help me Codd."

Definition	A row is in third normal form if and only if it is in second normal form and every non-key attribute is nontransitively dependent on the primary key.

A rule of thumb for identifying 3NF violations is to look for groups of attributes whose values can apply to more than a single entity occurrence. When you discover such attributes, move them to a separate entity.

It is time to review our STUDENT information again, this time looking for 3NF violations. Examine the STUDENT data in Table 3-3 closely. Notice that students can have the same major and, as such, certain major information can be repeated, specifically two students in our small sample are English Literature majors. To correct the problem, we need to remove major attributes that transitively depend on the key and create a new entity for them. Tables 3-7 and 3-8 show the corrected data, now in 3NF.

Table 3-7 *STUDENT Entity in 3NF*

StudentID	LastName	FirstName	MiddleInit	MajorID
2907	Smith	Jacob	R	MAT
4019	Patterson	Jane	K	PHI
5145	Neeld	Norris	B	EGL
6132	Morrison	Xavier	Q	MUS
7810	Brown	Richard	E	CS
8966	Juarez	Samantha		EGL

Table 3-8 *MAJOR Entity in 3NF*

MajorID	StudentMajor
MAT	Mathematics
PHI	Philosophy
EGL	English Literature
MUS	Music
CS	Computer Science

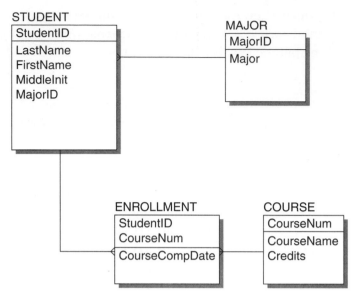

Figure 3-7   *The STUDENT data model*

A Normalized Data Model

To be complete, a diagram should be developed for the 3NF data model we just created for the STUDENT data. Figure 3-7 shows such a data model. Notice that we have not filled in the optionality of the relationships. We could do this based on the sample data we used, but we really need to ask more questions before we can answer questions such as Does a every student have to have a major? The current data shows this to be the case, but in reality, we know that most freshmen, and even upperclassmen, may attend college without having a formally declared major.

Further Normal Forms

Normalization past 3NF does not occur often in normal practice.

Normalization does not stop with 3NF. Additional normal forms have been identified and documented. However, normalization past 3NF does not occur often in normal practice. The following are additional normal forms.

- *Boyce Codd normal form* (BCNF) is a further refinement of 3NF. Indeed, in his later writings Codd refers to BCNF as 3NF. A row is in Boyce Codd normal form if and only if every determinant is a candidate key. Most entities in 3NF are already in BCNF.

- *Fourth normal form* (4NF) states that no entity can have more than a single one-to-many relationship if the one-to-many attributes are independent of each other. An entity is in 4NF if and only if it is in 3NF and has no multiple sets of multivalued dependencies.

- *Fifth normal form* (5NF) specifies that every join dependency for the entity must be a consequence of its candidate keys.

Definition   A *determinant* is any attribute whose value determines other values within an entity occurrence.

Normalization in Practice

Our data models should be normalized as we move from the conceptual level to the logical level. By normalizing our data models, we ensure that we are creating a data blueprint for the best database design possible.

Normalization is a logical process.

But remember, normalization is a logical process. Many times data modelers will try to mandate that the logical model become the physical database design with no changes. But it is not wise to force DBAs and technicians to forgo physical design. In the best of all worlds, a one-to-one logical to physical translation would work, but for many reasons, this strict one-to-one mapping is not practical. We'll discuss the reasons for this in the next chapter.

The only normal form that is absolutely required for implementing a data model as a relational database is 1NF. 1NF ensures tabular data. Of course, further normalization to 3NF will make it easier to manage and maintain the data integrity for a relational database, but 3NF is not a hard-and-fast requirement for relational implementation.

Additional Data Modeling Issues

Please keep in mind that this chapter is intended as a broad overview of data modeling concepts for DBAs. Data modeling can be a full-time occupation for organizations that truly treat their data as a corporate asset. The information in this chapter should be sufficient for DBAs to work toward creating appropriate data models before creating databases. However, organizations that implement data administration will need to tackle more advanced data modeling issues such as the following.

- How should subtypes be handled? Subtypes can be created when a single entity has attributes that apply to only certain entity occurrences. For example, PART-TIME EMPLOYEE and FULL-TIME EMPLOYEE could be subtypes of the EMPLOYEE supertype entity. Subtypes may be needed if different relationships exist for the subtypes or if a sufficient number of attributes apply to only one of the subtypes.

- How is derived data to be treated for the purposes of a logical data model? If it is derived from other data is it necessary to model it or document it?

- When should a domain become an entity? For example, business users in the United States typically know the abbreviations for State by heart. It is usually unnecessary to create an entity to map the State abbreviations to the State names. But not all such decisions are this simple.

- When time is a determining factor for data, how should it be handled in the data model? For example, perhaps a CUSTOMER can purchase only a single BASKET of goods at one time. But over time, the CUSTOMER will purchase multiple BASKETs of goods; a new BASKET is purchased upon each visit.

- When should one-to-one relationships be allowed? Entities participating in a one-to-one relationship may be better collapsed into a single entity. But other issues such as relationships to other entities may impede this practice.

These and other issues will need to be studied and understood by data modelers and DAs in progressive, data-focused organizations.

Summary

Data modeling and normalization provide the foundation for database design. Data modeling is the practice of analyzing the things of interest to your organization and how these things are related to each other. Furthermore, the output is a data model that can be used as a blueprint for the data requirements of the business.

For data to be normalized, each entity must have a primary key for identification. All attributes of every entity must be atomic, indivisible, and not part of a repeating group. Furthermore, each entity contains attributes that apply to that entity only and depend on the full primary key for that entity only.

When data is normalized, facts are grouped into entities that make logical sense. No fact is associated with the *wrong* entity. The primary key wholly and completely identifies each attribute value of each entity occurrence. In other words, a normalized data model is a correct blueprint of the data.

The next phase is to implement a physical manifestation of the logical data model. To do so requires a thorough understanding of the DBMS you plan to use, as well as DBMS and database fundamentals.

Review

1. What is the difference between a conceptual data model and a logical data model?

2. Why is data modeling important for database development?

3. Describe the proper naming guidelines for entities and attributes.

4. Please provide a broad description of the goals of normalization.

5. What is the difference between an entity and an entity occurrence?

6. Review Table 3-9 and explain why the data shown there violates 1NF.

7. Is the LastName attribute a good choice to be the primary key for the CUSTOMER entity? Please elaborate why or why not.

8. How is a relationship specified between two entities?

9. Every attribute will do one of the three things. Name those things and describe them.

10. An attribute, or set of attributes, that identifies an entity occurrence is called what?

Table 3-9   *Sample Data*

AccountNum	CustomerID	AccountTyp	BalanceAmt1	BalanceAmt2	BalanceAmt3
34109	105	A	2,352.47	5,123.31	
34134	113	A	15.95		
34147	422	A	18,549.22	100.00	1,799.85
34147	422	B	15.33		
34155	451	A	3,500.00	1.50	170.44
34162	990	X	500,000.00		
35010	802	X	1,908,190.12	10.88	
37891	999	Z	7.11		

Bonus Question

Read the following paragraph and create a data model for the business under discussion.

"My partner and I own an independent record store. Well, I guess record store is really the wrong word these days since we really don't sell a lot of records anymore. We sell mostly tapes and CDs. We do, however, stock some vinyl records too. Regardless of format (that is CD, tape, or record) we sell long playing albums as well as singles. Every item we sell is priced and we keep track of the number of each individual title in stock on a daily basis. We like to track sales by both title and recording artist. The sales information by title needs to be tallied weekly to send to external ratings services so they can compile their best sellers charts. We often get customers asking us to find certain songs for them. For singles, this is fairly easy because the title of the single is the title of the song. Some singles have multiple songs on them, though. Albums, on the other hand, comprise multiple songs. We need the ability to search for titles by song to let customers know which titles (both singles and albums) contain the songs they are looking for."

Suggested Reading

Brathwaite, Kenneth S. *Systems Design in a Database Environment.* New York, NY: McGraw-Hill (1989). ISBN 0-07-007250-7

Carlis, John, and Joseph Maguire. *Mastering Data Modeling: A User-Driven Approach.* Boston, MA: Addison-Wesley (2001). ISBN 0-201-70045-X

Codd, E. F. "Further Normalization of the Database Relational Model," in *Data Base Systems.* Courant Computer Science Symposia Series, Vol. 6, Englewood Cliffs, NJ: Prentice Hall (1972)

Durell, William R. *The Complete Guide to Data Modeling.* Princeton, NJ: Data Administration, Inc. (1993): No ISBN

D'Souza, Desmond F., and Alan Cameron Wills. *Objects, Components, and Frameworks with UML: The Catalysis Approach.* Reading, MA: Addison-Wesley (1999). ISBN 0-201-31012-0

Hay, David C. *Data Model Patterns.* New York, NY: Dorset House (1996): ISBN 0-932633-29-3

Modell, Martin E. *Data Analysis, Data Modeling, and Classification.* New York, NY: McGraw-Hill (1992). ISBN 0-07-042634-1

Perkinson, Richard C. *Data Analysis: The Key to Database Design.* Wellesley, MA: QED Information Sciences (1984). ISBN 0-89435-105-2

Ross, Ronald G. *Entity Modeling: Techniques and Application.* Boston, MA: Database Research Group (1988). ISBN 0-941049-00-0

Sanders, G. Lawrence. *Data Modeling.* Danvers, MA: Boyd & Fraser Publishing Company (1995). ISBN 0-87709-066-1

Schmidt, Bob. *Data Modeling for Information Professionals.* Upper Saddle River, NJ: Prentice Hall PTR (1999). ISBN 0-13-080450-9

Simsion, Graeme. *Data Modeling Essentials.* New York, NY: Van Nostrand Reinhold (1994). ISBN 0-442-01654-9

4

Database Design

Database design is the process of transforming a logical data model into a physical database design and then implementing the physical model as an actual database. More precisely, database design requires up-front data modeling and normalization as discussed in Chapter 3. A logical data model is required before you can even begin to design a physical database. This chapter assumes that the logical data model is complete. The focus of discussion, therefore, will be on producing a physical database from the logical data model.

From Logical Model to Physical Database

The physical data model is created by transforming the logical data model into a physical implementation.

The physical data model is created by transforming the logical data model into a physical implementation based on the DBMS to be used for deployment. To successfully create a physical database design you will need to have a good working knowledge of the features of the DBMS, including

- In-depth knowledge of the database objects supported by the DBMS and the physical structures and files required to support those objects

- Details regarding the manner in which the DBMS supports indexing, referential integrity, constraints, data types, and other features that augment the functionality of database objects

- Detailed knowledge of new and obsolete features for particular versions or releases of the DBMS

- Knowledge of the DBMS configuration parameters that are in place

- Data definition language (DDL) skills to translate the physical design into actual database objects

Armed with the correct information, you can create an effective and efficient database from a logical data model. The first step in transforming a logical data model into a physical model is to perform a simple translation from logical terms to physical objects. Of course, this simple transformation will not result in a complete and correct physical database design—it is simply the first step. Let's address the transformation step by step.

Transform Entities to Tables

Map each entity in the data model to a table in the database.

The physical counterpart of an entity is a table. Therefore, the first step in transforming a logical data model into a physical database is to map each entity in the data model to a table in the database. The final database that you implement need not adhere to this strict one-to-one entity-to-table mapping. For example, you may need to consolidate or break apart tables—a process called denormalizing—for performance reasons. Denormalization will be covered in detail later in this chapter.

In general, though, do not initially deviate from the simple rule of creating a table for each entity in the logical data model. The logical data model represents the "things" of interest to the business. During the data modeling process, these things were analyzed and designed as entities, each having a specific identity and purpose for existence. The only reason to deviate from this process is if application performance or data availability would be unacceptable without a change.

Transform Attributes to Columns

The attributes of each entity should be mapped to the columns of each respective table.

The physical counterpart of an attribute is a column within a table. When you map entities to tables, map the *attributes* of each entity to the *columns* of each respective table. At least initially, do not change the basic definition of the columns. For example, do not group attributes together into a composite column.

Try to maintain the same naming convention for physical columns as was used for logical attribute names. However, you must understand that the physical constraints of the DBMS being used may limit your ability to do so. Always take into account the capabilities and limitations of the DBMS when creating the physical database from the logical data model.

Transform Domains to Data Types

Map each logical domain to a physical data type, perhaps coupled with additional constraints.

To support the mapping of attributes to table columns you will need to map each logical domain of the attribute to a physical data type and perhaps additional constraints. Each column must be assigned a *data type*. Certain data types require you to specify a maximum length. For example, you could specify a character data type as CHAR(20), indicating that up to 20 characters can be stored for the column. You may need to apply a length to other data types as well, such as graphic, floating point, and decimal (which also require a scale).

Commercial DBMS products do not support domains, so the domain assigned in the logical data model must be mapped to a data type supported by the DBMS. You may need to adjust the data type based on the DBMS you use. For example, what data type and length will be used for monetary values if no built-in currency data type exists? Many of the major DBMS products support user-defined data types, so you might want to consider creating a data type to support the logical domain if no built-in data type is acceptable.

There may be multiple physical data types that can be used successfully for a domain. Consider a logical domain whose valid values are integers between 1 and 10. You could choose an integer data type, of which there may be several (e.g., INTEGER, SMALLINT, TINYINT). Alternatively, you could choose a decimal data type with a zero scale. You might even choose to store the data in a 2-byte character column if no mathematical operations are required. Any of these can work. As the DBA you will need to determine which data type can be most efficiently accessed, stored, maintained, and processed by the applications accessing the data. To make such a decision requires in-depth technical knowledge of the way in which your DBMS physically stores each type of data, as well as knowledge of application processing details.

In addition to a data type and length, you may also need to apply a *constraint* to the column. Consider, once again, the domain of integers 1 through 10. Simply assigning the physical column to an integer data type is insufficient to match the domain. A constraint must be added to restrict the values that can be stored for the column to the specified range of 1 through 10. Without a constraint, negative numbers, zero, and values greater than ten could be stored.

Using check constraints, you can place limits on the data values that can be stored in a column or set of columns. Check constraints are covered in detail in Chapter 13.

Specify the nullability of each column.

The nullability of each column in the table must also be specified. The logical data model should contain information on the nullability of each attribute, and this information can be copied for each requisite column in the physical database. Some DBMS software enables you to assign a default value to be used when a row is to be inserted and no value has been provided for the column. You must assign column default values when you create the table.

For text or character data, you need to make an additional decision: Should the column be fixed length or variable length? A *fixed-length column* occupies a preset and unchanging amount of storage for each row. A *variable-length column* specifies a maximum size, but the actual length used by the column can vary for each row. Variable-length columns can save storage space, but usually require additional manipulation by application code to insert and maintain them. Another negative aspect is that variable-length columns can cause the table to require more frequent attention. Changes made to row size will have the effect of moving rows within the database. If the DBMS offers a compression option, you may be able to save more space by compressing the database than by implementing variable-length columns.

Primary Keys

Specification of a primary key is an integral part of the physical design of entities and attributes. When designing the logical data model, you assigned a primary key for every entity, and as a first course of action you should try to use that primary key. However, multiple candidate keys are often uncovered during the data modeling process. For physical implementation you may decide to choose a primary key other than the one selected during logical design— either one of the candidate keys or another surrogate key.

Most DBMS products provide built-in features to help define primary keys.

If the primary key is unwieldy, you may need to choose another primary key. Perhaps the key is composed of several columns or is a nonstandard data type. In either of these cases it may be better to choose a surrogate primary key. Most DBMS products provide built-in features that can assist in the definition of primary keys. Some examples include support for default values, ROWID data types, and the identity property (see "The Identity Property" sidebar).

Be sure to identify a primary key for each physical table you create.

As a rule of thumb, though, be sure to identify a primary key for each physical table you create. Failure to do so will make processing the data in that table more difficult. If there is no key to uniquely identify rows of the table, it will be

The Identity Property

The *identity property* is a feature supported by several of the most popular relational DBMS products. It can be assigned to a column that has a numeric (usually integer) data type. When the identity property is assigned to a column, the DBMS treats that column in a special way. The database user does not provide values for the column when rows are inserted into the table in which the column exists. Instead, the DBMS increments a counter and automatically uses that value for the column. Usually only one column per table can be assigned the identity property.

The identity property provides an efficient way for ever-increasing sequential values to be populated into a relational table. Before using this feature, make sure that your DBMS supports the identity property and that you completely understand how the feature works and its impact on functionality and performance. For example, does the DBMS provide a way to reset the identity property counter on a table-by-table basis?

difficult for programs to specifically select, modify, and delete individual rows. Furthermore, without a primary key, dependent relationships cannot be defined for that table.

Column Ordering

Before implementing a physical table, be sure to review the order of the columns. The order in which columns are specified is irrelevant from an operational perspective—that is, the DBMS will produce the same results regardless of the sequence of the columns in the table. Nevertheless, the efficiency of how those results are obtained can vary greatly. Column sequencing can impact performance, therefore, for physical implementation you may need to change the sequence recorded in the logical data model.

Let's take a closer look. The way in which the DBMS logs changes can impact performance. DB2, for example, logs database modifications from the first byte changed to the last byte changed. The exception is variable-length rows, in which case DB2 will log a change from the first byte changed to the end of the row.

So, to take advantage of this knowledge about DB2's physical implementation, we should sequence the columns based on how DB2 logs. Infrequently updated nonvariable columns should be grouped together at the beginning of the table, followed by static (infrequently updated) variable columns and then frequently updated columns. This structure will ensure that the least amount of data required is logged, thereby speeding up any data modification processes. Another good idea would be to group together any columns that are frequently modified. This can also reduce the amount of data logged. Because each DBMS logs data differently, you will need to understand how your DBMS logs and how column ordering can impact performance.

Build Referential Constraints for All Relationships

The referential constraint ties the primary key to the foreign key.

The physical counterpart of a relationship is a *referential constraint*. To define a referential constraint you must create a primary key in the parent table and a foreign key in the dependent table. The referential constraint ties the primary key to the foreign key.

Referential Integrity

It is not sufficient merely to identify primary and foreign keys that make up relationships between tables. The functionality of each relationship is greatly affected by the parameters chosen for the referential constraint and the values in the foreign key column(s). A set of rules, which is applied to each relationship, determines the status of foreign key columns when inserted or updated, and of dependent rows when a primary key row is deleted. For example, when a primary key is deleted that refers to existing foreign key values, the rule specifies whether the DBMS should void the primary key deletion, delete the foreign key values too, or set the foreign key values to null.

Referential integrity guarantees that an acceptable value is always in each foreign key column.

In general, a foreign key should either contain a value within the domain of foreign key values or be null. Any other value is unacceptable and the referential constraint will cause the DBMS to reject such values during operation. *Referential integrity*, or RI for short, guarantees that an acceptable value is always in each foreign key column.

It is a good physical design practice to implement referential integrity using database constraints instead of trying to program integrity into application programs. Using database RI will ensure that integrity is maintained whether data is changed in a planned manner through an application program or in an ad hoc manner through SQL statements or query tools.

Of course, there are exceptions to every rule. Cases where you should avoid using database-enforced RI constraints include code tables where the codes do not change frequently and data warehouse implementations where the data is propagated from a referentially intact source. Basically, do not use RI as a substitute for performing data validation and edit checks. Listing valid values in a check constraint can be a better solution than RI for static data with a small number of valid values.

Chapter 13 discusses referential integrity in more detail.

Build Physical Data Structures

Designing and implementing a physical database from a logical data model is not just a simple matter of mapping entities to tables, attributes to columns, and relationships to referential constraints. Quite a few other database design issues must be addressed. One of these issues is preparing for the physical storage of data.

Although relational data is expressed to the user by means of a table, underlying files or data sets must exist to store the actual data—and those files are not necessarily stored as a simple grid of rows and columns. During the physical design process, the DBA must map each table to a physical structure to store the table's data. These physical structures are commonly called *tablespaces* (or *data spaces*). As shown in Figure 4-1, a database comprises one or more tablespaces, and each tablespace contains one or more tables. Depending on the DBMS, a table may be able to span multiple tablespaces, too. The DBA decides how to map tables to tablespaces based on the anticipated usage of the data, the type of tablespace, and the features of the DBMS. Please see the sidebar "SQL Server Filegroups" for information on a similar file structure used by Microsoft SQL Server.

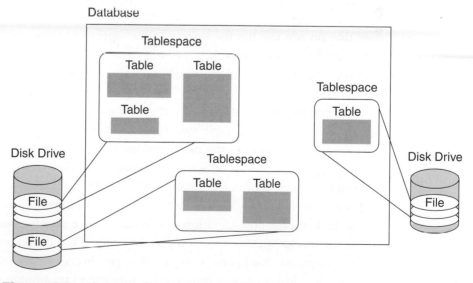

Figure 4-1 *Mapping files to database structures*

SQL Server Filegroups

Microsoft SQL Server provides filegroups to group together the operating system files containing data from a single database. By using a filegroup, the DBA can simplify certain administration tasks. A filegroup is a property of a SQL Server database. A filegroup cannot contain the operating system files of more than one database, though a single database can contain more than one filegroup.

Every database is created on a single filegroup named PRIMARY. After the database is created, additional filegroups can be added.

An additional physical design process is the effective planning for storage and space usage. To calculate the amount of storage required to store a table, the DBA must first establish the *row size*. This is accomplished by adding up the maximum size of all the columns, based on their assigned data type and length. An average size can be substituted for variable-length columns. An estimate for the number of bytes required can be calculated by multiplying the row size by the number of rows planned to be stored in the table. Of course, the DBA must also factor in any storage overhead required by the DBMS for things like row and page headers, pointers, and the like. Because each DBMS uses different techniques, each DBMS will have different overhead requirements.

The DBA must also determine the type of files to be used, based on the operating system being used as the database server. In some cases, database files that do not use the file system of the operating system can be more efficient. Such files are sometimes referred to as *raw files*. Because a raw file can prevent operating system overhead it is often a better choice for database implementation.

> The DBA must determine the size of not only table structures but also index structures.

To prepare storage devices for the database, though, the DBA must determine the size of not only table structures but also index structures. Indexes are covered in more depth in the next section.

The DBA will also build some free space into the database design. By assigning free space within the database, the DBMS can add data more efficiently and with fewer outages for reorganizing and restructuring.

A final storage consideration is whether to use *compression*. Most DBMS products provide methods for compressing data. If the DBMS provides no compression option, third-party compression products can be purchased. With compression, less storage is required to store the same amount of data. A compression routine will algorithmically compress data as it is added to the database and decompress the data as it is retrieved. Compression adds CPU overhead to database processing because access requires the DBMS to compress or decompress the data. However, I/O may be more efficient with compression: Because the data takes up less space on disk, more data can be read with a single I/O operation.

Database Performance Design

When implementing a physical database from a logical data model, you must begin to consider how the database will perform when applications make requests to access and modify data. A basic fact of database processing is that disk access is slower than memory access—slower by orders of magnitude. If the DBMS were required, in every instance, to scan through the database row-by-row, or block-by-block, looking for the requested data, no one could afford to use databases. Fortunately, several good techniques exist to allow data in the database to be accessed more rapidly.

Designing Indexes

One of the best techniques for achieving acceptable query performance is the creation of appropriate indexes on your database tables. Of course, the trick is in determining how many indexes to create and how exactly to define each index. First, let's cover some index basics.

An index is an alternate path to data in the database.

An index is an alternate path to data in the database. The structure of an index makes it easier to find data in the database, with fewer I/O operations. Therefore, queries can perform faster when using an index to look up data based on specific key values.

Many types of indexes are supported by the major DBMS products. Indexes can be unique or nonunique; clustering or nonclustering; single column or multicolumn. An index can be structured as a b-tree or a bitmap. Some DBMS products even support hashing indexes. However, the basic goal of every index is to optimize query processing.

In a relational system, the DBMS—not the programmer—decides whether to use an index. Therefore, the DBA must design indexes based on the type of queries that will be run against the database. The DBA must understand the operation of the relational optimizer and design indexes that are likely to be used during application processing. In the absence of an appropriate index for a query, the DBMS will most likely revert to a *table scan*—every row of the table will be read to determine whether the data matches the query specifications. Table scans are costly if the intent of the query is not to process every row in the table.

In general, try to build indexes on large tables to support the most frequently run queries. Queries that access 25% or fewer of the table's rows are good candidates for indexing. When more than 25% of the table's rows are to be selected, you should determine whether an index would be more efficient than a table scan. This will differ from query to query, and from DBMS to DBMS. Use the tools provided by the DBMS to determine the effectiveness of your indexes. (The SHOW PLAN or EXPLAIN command will show whether an index is used for a particular query.)

Furthermore, you should create indexes on the most-referenced columns in frequently run queries in your application. The order in which columns appear in an index is important. By choosing the right order, you may be able to make a particular index available to many other queries. For example, if quite a few application queries look for items based on ItemType and a few other queries look for items by ItemType and ItemColor, a single composite index on the combination of (ItemType, ItemColor) can satisfy the needs of both these types of queries.

A single table can have multiple indexes defined for it; you are not limited to a single index. Plan on creating indexes for the most common access requirements in each application's SQL WHERE clauses. The following situations should prompt you to consider creating an index.

- *Foreign keys*. Even if the DBMS does not require foreign key columns to be indexed, it is a good idea to do so. Creating an index on foreign key columns can enhance the performance of joins based on the relationships between the tables, but it may also speed up the DBMS's internal processing to enforce referential integrity.

- *Primary keys*. An index is usually required on the primary key columns to enforce uniqueness.

- *Candidate keys*. Even though indexes are not required on candidate keys, it is a good idea to index them if processes will look up data based on the candidate key.

- *Index-only access*. If all of the columns in a data retrieval request exist in an index, it may be possible to satisfy the request using only the

Create indexes on the most-referenced columns in frequently run queries in your application.

index. Avoiding I/O to the table can enhance performance. Therefore, it is sometimes a good idea to overload an index with columns to facilitate index-only access for certain requests.

- *Sorting.* Another reason for building indexes is to minimize sorting. Queries that use JOINs, ORDER BY, GROUP BY, UNION, and DISTINCT can cause the DBMS to sort the intermediate or final results of that query. If indexes are created to support these features, the DBMS may be able to use the index for ordering and avoid invoking a costly sort.

Exercise great care in the creation of an indexing scheme for your databases

Exercise great care in the creation of an indexing scheme for your databases. Be sure to analyze all of the data access requirements of your applications to ensure optimal indexing. You simply cannot design proper indexes without knowledge of how tables are to be accessed. Furthermore, you need a comprehensive view of the access requirements. An index that is the best solution for a particular query can potentially adversely affect the performance of other queries in the system.

Additionally, be aware that indexes do not come for free. The DBMS must keep the indexes updated as the table's data is inserted, updated, and deleted. For that reason, you may want to avoid building indexes on columns that are frequently modified, if you can. Make sure that every index you create provides benefit to the performance of a query or set of queries without significantly degrading the overall performance of the applications accessing the database. Here are some things to consider when determining the cost of an index.

- Additional overhead is incurred to update the index when rows are inserted and deleted, or when indexed columns are updated in the base table.

- Additional disk space is required to store indexes.

- Utilities, such as LOAD and REORG, may take longer to run against a table with many indexes because the indexes must also be maintained during the utility processing.

- Additional files are required to store the indexes, which could potentially cause operating system problems if the number of files that can be open at one time is exceeded.

When building indexes, keep in mind that they will be used in conjunction with the base table data. Consider allocating separate DBMS buffer areas for caching index reads instead of using the same buffers used for data. Index entries will be smaller than a full table row, and as such, more index entries can be kept in memory longer if they are not combined with table data in the database buffers. You might also consider placing the indexes and the table data on different disk drives to minimize disk seek time.

A DBA must learn how each DBMS supports indexing so he can create indexes to support the data access requirements of his database applications. Let's learn a little bit more about the types of indexes that your DBMS may support: b-tree, bitmap, reverse key, partitioned, and ordered.

B-Tree Indexes

A b-tree is a keyed, treelike index structure.

The basic indexing technique supported by most relational database systems is the b-tree index. A *b-tree* is a keyed, treelike index structure. A b-tree index begins at the root page and fans out down to the leaf pages. Figure 4-2 shows the basic structure of a b-tree index.

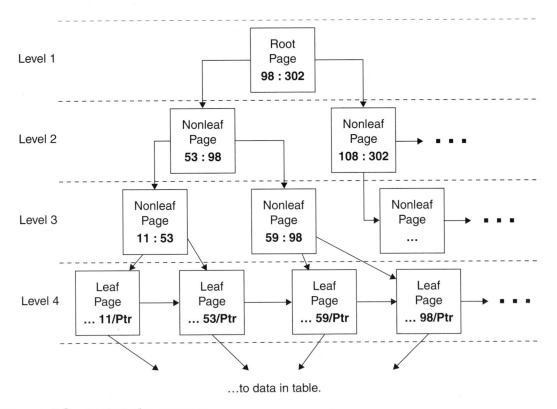

Figure 4-2 *B-tree index structure*

The pages of a b-tree index are referred to as *nodes*. Nodes exist in levels in the b-tree, with nodes above the leaf level containing directory entries and pointers to lower-level b-tree nodes. Nodes at the lowest level are called *leaf pages*. Leaf pages contain entries with the key value and a pointer to individual data rows in the table. As data is added to the table, the b-tree index is updated by storing the new key values in the appropriate location in the index structure. To access data using the index, the DBMS begins at the root page and follows the pointers through the index until the key value is located at the leaf level, where a pointer leads to the actual table data. Each parent node contains the highest key value that is stored in its direct dependent nodes. The leaf pages of a b-tree index can be scanned for ranges of values once the key has been looked up.

Refer to Figure 4-2 again. Suppose a query is run with a search condition requesting data where the key value is equal to 53. The DBMS can traverse the index and in this case will wind up on the second leaf page. This leaf page contains a pointer to the actual row in the table containing the requested key value. A maximum of five I/O requests are required to satisfy this query: one for a page at each level of the index and an additional request for the table page.

An access request using an index can perform better than a table scan because the requested data can be accessed directly using the pointers from the leaf node of the index. This reduces I/O and enhances performance for most data access requests.

Bitmap Indexes

A bitmap index solves only a narrow range of problems, but provides superb performance.

Bitmap indexes are a different type of index supported by some DBMS products. A bitmap index solves only a narrow range of problems, but provides superb performance. A bitmap index is most useful for query-heavy tables that are infrequently modified. Furthermore, bitmap indexes are most useful where the columns to be indexed have a very small number of distinct values, such as sex (Male/Female) or Boolean (True/False) data. Data warehouses and data marts can often benefit from bitmap indexes.

A bitmap index is really quite simple. The implementation of a bitmap index is, appropriately enough, accomplished using a string of zeroes and ones, or bits. For each key value of the bitmap index a separate string of zeroes and ones is stored. The number of distinct key values determines the number of bit strings. For example, a bitmap index defined for the Sex column of the EMPLOYEE table might have three strings, one for male, one for female, and one for unknown. A bitmap index on the State column (for states within the USA) could have 51 strings—one for each state and an extra one for unknown.

To elaborate, let's consider the Sex example again. A bitmap index is created on the Sex column of an EMPLOYEE table that contains ten rows. The bitmap index will contain three strings as indicated previously, each with ten bits. The string is positional. Whatever position has a bit turned on ("1") the Sex column in that row will contain the value for which that particular string was built. Examine the following three bitmaps:

```
'Male' 1000011101
'Female' 0110000010
'Unknown' 0001100000
```

These strings indicate that rows 1, 6, 7, 8, and 10 are males; rows 2, 3, and 9 are females; and rows 4 and 5 are unknown.

Finding the set of records with any of several values that are bitmap indexed simply requires adding the strings for those values. Bitmaps can be much faster than table scans and even b-tree index retrieval under the right circumstances. The strings of the bitmap index can be small enough to maintain in memory, minimizing I/O operations. Even for queries that retrieve large numbers of rows, a complex query using bitmaps can be very efficient.

The problem with bitmaps is that a separate string is needed for each value occurring in a field. When a column can take on a large number of different values, a bitmap index is not practical because too many strings will be required. Additionally, the zeroes and ones of the bitmap cannot be used for calculations or be read directly to determine the actual values they represent. Such limitations make true bitmap indexes impractical for most applications. Some DBMS products have extended the bitmap index to make them more practical for columns with higher cardinality. If your DBMS supports bitmap indexes, make sure you understand the exact nature of the bitmaps being used and the situations under which bitmap indexes are practical.

Reverse Key Indexes

Reverse key indexes can eliminate data hot spots in OLTP applications.

A *reverse key index* is basically a b-tree index where the order of bytes of each indexed column is reversed. The order of the columns within the index is not reversed, just the bytes within each column. Such indexes can be useful to eliminate data hot spots in OLTP applications. By reversing the byte order, adjacent key values are not physically stored together. So reverse key indexes help to distribute the otherwise concentrated index data across leaf nodes, thereby improving performance.

So, if a reverse key index is created on the FirstName column of the EMPLOYEE table, and the value "Craig" is inserted, the value "giarC" is used instead.

If the DBMS you are using does not support reverse key indexes, you might be able to programmatically duplicate the effect. To do so, you will need to use program logic (or perhaps an exit routine, if supported by the DBMS) to reverse the values before inserting them into the columns. Of course, you will need to programmatically unreverse the values when they are retrieved. This process does not work well if the data must be queried in an ad hoc manner, outside the scope of a program.

Partitioned Indexes

Partitioning is usually done to enhance performance.

Partitioned indexes are basically b-tree indexes that specify how to break up the index (and perhaps the underlying table) into separate chunks, or partitions. Partitioning is usually done to enhance performance and increase availability. When data is spread out across multiple partitions, you may be able to operate on one partition without impacting others—for example, to run utilities, to take data offline, or to place the underlying files on separate disks.

Most DBMS products support partitioning, but in different ways. Be sure to understand the nuances of your particular DBMS implementation before partitioning.

Ordered Indexes

Most DBMS products provide an option to specify the order in which b-tree key values are ordered. The order specified, either ascending or descending, will impact the usability of an index to avoid sort operations or to minimize I/O requirements for retrieving MIN or MAX values. Create indexes in the appropriate order to support the types of queries that are to be run against the table.

Index Summary

Indexing is an important component of a physical database design. Indeed, the single most important thing a DBA can do to optimize the performance of database applications is create effective indexes. In order to do so, the DBA needs to know what indexing options are available in the DBMS being used, but more importantly, the DBA must be able to match the DBMS indexing options to the type of processing to be performed against the table. Only by examining the SQL statements that operate on the database tables can an effective indexing strategy be developed. Finally, keep in mind that special processing requirements may require special indexing needs and that add-on products are available from ISVs that can augment the indexing options available to you.

Hashing

Hashing uses key values to enable quick direct access to data.

Hashing is a technique that uses key values to enable quick direct access to data. An algorithm is used to transform the key values into a pointer to the physical location of the rows that have those key values. The algorithm is typically referred to as a randomizer, because the goal of the hashing routine is to spread the key values evenly throughout the physical storage.

In general, the better the randomizing algorithm, the better the results of hashing will be. When the randomizer generates the same pointer for two different key values, a collision occurs. Different techniques can be used to resolve collisions. Typically, the collision resolution algorithm attempts to keep the data on the same page to avoid additional I/O. When pages fill up and collisions force the data to another page, performance rapidly degrades.

Hashing works better with a large amount of free space. A disadvantage of hashing is the amount of space that must be preallocated for data to be hashed into.

Hashing has the big advantage that normally only one database I/O request is needed to retrieve a row of data using the key. Hashing works best for direct data lookup of one row or a small number of rows. If you need to retrieve ranges of data, hashing is not optimal because the data will be spread out instead of clustered and therefore I/O costs will be substantial. Additionally, hashing requires a unique key to minimize collisions.

So, hashing should be considered only when an overwhelming majority of the queries against the table are based on lookups using the key and will return small results sets.

Clustering

Clustering optimizes performance because fewer I/O requests are required to retrieve data.

Clustering describes a way of storing table data physically. The term refers to keeping rows in a specific order on the disk. Through clustering, data that is commonly accessed together can be stored together on the same or contiguous database pages. Clustering optimizes performance because fewer I/O requests are required to retrieve data.

Actually, more accurately, for some products clustering indicates that the DBMS should *attempt* to maintain rows in the sequence of specific column values. If insufficient space is available to maintain clustering when data is inserted or modified, the DBMS typically stores the data without forcing clustering. Therefore, a clustered table may not actually be 100% clustered by the key value at all times.

Usually an index, called a clustering index, is required to support clustering. The columns identified as the index key indicate how the table upon which the index is defined should be clustered.

Consider clustering tables under the following circumstances:

- When a large number of queries retrieve ranges of data based on specific column values.
- If a foreign key exists in the table. A foreign key typically represents the "many" end of a one-to-many relationship. It is common for queries to request data by the foreign key, resulting in large sequential reads.
- When data is frequently sorted together (ORDER BY, GROUP BY, UNION, SELECT DISTINCT, JOINs).

When you cluster a table, be sure to consider the frequency of modification. Inserts and updates can cause data to become unclustered. Favor clustering infrequently modified data over very frequently modified data. However, the primary key is almost always a bad choice for clustering because primary key access tends to be random and clustering optimizes sequential access.

Be sure to understand how your DBMS implements clustering. Some DBMS products merge the table and the clustering index into a single structure, which may require you to modify your administration techniques and procedures. Other clustering differences exist, too. For example, although Oracle supports a structure called a cluster, it does not perform clustering as just described; instead, it interleaves index keys for multiple tables.

Interleaving Data

When data from two tables is frequently joined, it can make sense to use the join criteria to physically interleave the data into the same physical storage structure. *Interleaving* can be viewed as a specialized form of clustering.

To better understand data interleaving, refer to Figure 4-3. The dots indicate rows in different tables. The data is interleaved on the disk, based on the join criteria. Notice that the light dots (table 1) are intermixed in the same file as the dark dots (table 2). When data is interleaved this way, join performance will improve—but only for the specific join that the data was interleaved to optimize.

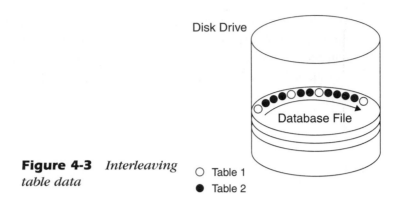

Figure 4-3   *Interleaving table data*

○ Table 1
● Table 2

Different DBMS products support interleaving in different ways. Oracle uses a cluster to support a form of interleaving. For other DBMSs, you may need to develop scripts to organize, sort, and interleave the data before loading it. At any rate, interleaving is useful in a small number of cases and only when the predominant access to the two tables is by means of particular join criteria.

Denormalization

Normalization is the process of putting each fact in the most appropriate place. A normalized database implementation minimizes integrity problems and optimizes updating, perhaps at the expense of retrieval. When a fact is stored in only one place, retrieving many different but related facts usually requires going to many different places. This can slow the retrieval process. Updating is quicker, however, because the fact you're updating exists in only one place.

Denormalization can be thought of as the process of putting one fact in numerous places.

Most applications require very rapid data retrieval. Some applications require specific tinkering to optimize performance at all costs. To accomplish this, sometimes the decision is made to denormalize the physical database implementation. Just as normalization is the process of assembling data in an organized manner to eliminate redundancies, denormalization is the process of deliberately introducing redundancy to your data. In other words, denormalization can be thought of as the process of putting one fact in numerous places. This can have the effect of speeding up the data retrieval process, usually at the expense of data modification.

When to Denormalize

Of course, you should never denormalize data unless a performance need arises or your knowledge of the way your DBMS operates overrides the benefits of a normalized implementation. Many DBMS products have specific deficiencies and inefficiencies that may necessitate denormalizing for performance reasons. Therefore, denormalization is not necessarily a bad decision if implemented wisely. You should always consider the following issues before denormalizing.

- Can the system achieve acceptable performance *without* denormalizing?
- Will the performance of the system *after* denormalizing still be unacceptable?
- Will the system be less reliable due to denormalization?

If the answer to any of these questions is yes, then you should avoid denormalization because the benefits typically will not exceed the cost. If, after considering these issues, you decide to denormalize, be sure to adhere to the general guidelines that follow.

If enough disk space is available, consider creating two sets of tables: one set fully normalized and another denormalized. Populate the denormalized versions by querying the data in the normalized tables and loading or inserting it into the denormalized tables. Your application can access the denormalized tables in a read-only fashion and achieve performance gains, while at the same time modifying the normalized version and avoiding integrity problems in the base data. However, it is important to set up a controlled and scheduled population function to synchronize the normalized table with the denormalized.

If sufficient disk space is not available for two complete sets of tables, then implement only the denormalized tables and maintain them programmatically. Be sure to update each denormalized table representing the same entity at the same time, or use database triggers to keep the redundant data synchronized.

When a column is replicated in many different tables, always update it everywhere simultaneously—or as close to simultaneously as possible—given the physical constraints of your environment. Once again, triggers can be helpful to accomplish this. If the denormalized tables are ever out of sync with the normalized tables, be sure to inform end users that batch reports and online queries may not contain sound data; if at all possible, this should be avoided.

Finally, be sure to design the application so that it can easily be converted from using denormalized tables to using normalized tables.

Every denormalization decision should be documented, including the reason behind the decision and the exact changes made from the normalized logical data model. Such a record will help to ensure that future database changes

Every denormalization decision should be documented.

are made with appropriate knowledge. Documentation will also make it clear that you didn't simply make a design or implementation mistake.

Remember that only one valid reason exists for denormalizing a relational design—to enhance performance. The following criteria can be used to help identify potential denormalization candidates.

- Numerous critical queries or reports require data from more than one table—in other words, joins are required. If these types of requests need to be processed in an online, transaction environment, a denormalization may be able to improve performance.

- Repeating groups need to be processed in a group instead of individually.

- Many calculations need to be applied to one or many columns before queries can be successfully answered. Storing derived or precalculated data can reduce I/O and CPU usage upon retrieval and therefore be more efficient.

- Tables need to be accessed in different ways by different users during the same timeframe.

- Many large primary keys exist that are clumsy to query and consume a large amount of disk space when carried as foreign key columns in related tables.

- Certain columns are queried a large percentage of the time, causing very complex or inefficient SQL to be used.

Of course, these situations do not always require denormalization, but they can be used as broad indications of when denormalization might be considered. Which raises the question: When should the DBA denormalize a database design? Although you might think it would be easier to denormalize at the very beginning of the physical design process, this is usually not the case. DBAs and application designers often decide to denormalize prematurely—before they obtain any concrete evidence for its necessity. Even though it may be difficult to retrofit a partially completed system to work on denormalized structures, it is almost never a good idea to denormalize before you're sure that a normalized design will not perform adequately. Of course, sometimes a DBA will have direct experience for the specific application, DBMS, and version—and in those cases it may be acceptable to denormalize the physical design immediately. However, such a case is actually quite rare.

Be aware that each new RDBMS release usually brings enhanced performance and improved access options that may reduce the need for denormalization. However, most of the popular RDBMS products will require denormalized data structures on occasion. There are many different types of denormalized tables that can resolve the performance problems caused when accessing fully normalized data. The following sections detail the different types and advise on when to consider implementing them.

Never attempt to create a denormalized logical data model.

Never, under any circumstances, should you attempt to create a denormalized logical data model. The logical data model should always be completely normalized. The physical implementation of the database can differ from the data model, but the model should always be fully normalized, and above all, all physical variations from the data model should be documented.

Prejoined Tables

If two or more tables need to be joined on a regular basis by an application, but the cost of the join is prohibitive, consider creating *prejoined tables*. The prejoined tables should

- Contain no redundant columns
- Contain only those columns absolutely necessary to meet the processing needs of the application
- Be created periodically, using SQL to join the normalized tables

The benefit of prejoining is that the cost of the join will be incurred only once—when the prejoined tables are created. A prejoined table can be queried very efficiently because every new query does not incur the overhead of the join process.

However, the negative aspect of prejoining, as with most forms of denormalization, is the difficulty of keeping the data accurate. Prejoined tables may quickly get out of sync with the independent tables from which they were created. For this reason, prejoined tables are more useful for relatively static data than for more dynamic data.

Report Tables

Oftentimes it is impossible to develop an end-user report using only SQL. These types of reports require special formatting or data manipulation. If certain critical or highly visible reports of this nature are required to be viewed in an online environment, consider creating a table that represents the report. This table can then be queried using stand-alone SQL in a query tool or reporting facility. The data for the report should be created by the appropriate mechanism (application program, 4GL, SQL, etc.) in a batch environment and then loaded into the report table in sequence. The report table should

The report table should contain one column for every column of the report.

- Contain one column for every column of the report
- Have its rows physically sequenced in the order in which they should appear on the report so sorting is not required
- Not subvert relational tenets (such as 1NF and atomic data elements)

Report tables are ideal for carrying the results of multiple joins and outer joins, correlated subqueries, or other complex SQL statements. If a complex query is coded, run, and then loaded into a table, a simple SELECT statement can be used to retrieve the results, instead of the complex (and perhaps slower) query that was used to populate the report table.

Mirror Tables

If an application system is very active, it may be necessary to split processing into two (or more) distinct components. Such a split will result in the creation of duplicate, or mirror, tables. For example, consider an application system with very heavy online traffic during the morning and early afternoon hours. This traffic consists of both queries and data modifications. Decision support processing is also performed on the same application tables during the afternoon. The production work in the afternoon always seems to disrupt the decision support processing, causing frequent timeouts and deadlocks.

These disruptions could be corrected by creating mirror tables—a foreground set of tables for the production traffic and a background set of tables for decision support. A mechanism to periodically migrate the foreground data to background tables must be established to keep the application data synchronized. One such mechanism could be a batch job executing UNLOAD and LOAD utilities. Another possibility is to use built-in replication and propagation software, which is sometimes built into the DBMS. At any rate, the data synchronization should be done as often as necessary to sustain the effectiveness of the decision support processing.

It is important to note that the access needs of decision support are often considerably different than the access needs of the production environment. Therefore, different decisions about data definition, such as indexing and clustering, may be made for the mirror tables.

In addition, simple mirror tables may not be sufficient for your decision support needs. Perhaps you will need to create a full-blown data warehouse environment. A data warehouse is just a relational database that is specifically designed or denormalized for decision support and analytical queries.

Split Tables

If separate pieces of one normalized table are accessed by different and distinct groups of users or applications, consider splitting the table into two (or more) denormalized tables—one for each distinct processing group. The original table can also be maintained if other applications access the entire table. In this scenario the split tables should be handled as a special case of mirror tables. If an additional table is not desired, a view joining the tables could be provided instead.

Tables can be split in one of two ways: vertically or horizontally. A *vertically split table* separates the columns of a table into separate tables: One set of columns is placed into a new table and the remaining columns are placed in another new table. The primary key columns are placed in both of the new tables. Designate one of the two new tables as the parent table for the purposes of referential integrity unless the original table still exists, in which case the original table should be the parent table in all referential constraints. If the original table still exists and the split tables are read-only, don't set up referential integrity for the split tables. Because the split tables are derived from a referentially intact source, referential integrity is unnecessary.

If you are splitting a table vertically, always include one row per primary key in each split table. Do not eliminate rows from any of the new tables for any reason. If rows are eliminated, the update process and any retrieval process that must access data from both tables will be unnecessarily complicated.

A *horizontally split table* separates the rows of a table into separate tables. To split a table horizontally, rows are classified into groups via key ranges. The rows from one key range are placed in one table, those from another key range are placed in a different table, and so on. The columns of horizontally split tables are the same. For horizontal splits, avoid duplicating rows in the new

Tables can be split in one of two ways: vertically or horizontally.

tables. To accomplish this, use the primary key to perform the split and ensure that each key value is assigned to only one of the new tables.

Splitting Long Text Columns

A special case of a vertical split can be used to break up very large text columns. For example, consider a table that stores item descriptions of merchandise. The description can be 100 characters long, but most processes require only the first ten characters. For example, consider this CREATE TABLE statement:

```
CREATE TABLE ITEM
   (ItemNum        integer       not null,
    ItemSize       CHAR(1),
    ItemColor      CHAR(10),
    ItemDescr      CHAR(100))
;
```

In such a case, you can split the table into two tables by splitting the description into two columns. One new column, maintained in the old table, would house the first 10 bytes of the description. The second column would be created in a new table with the primary key and the last 90 bytes of the description. For example:

```
CREATE TABLE ITEM
   (ItemNum        INTEGER       NOT NULL,
    ItemSize       CHAR(1),
    ItemColor      CHAR(10),
    ItemDescr      CHAR(10)
;
CREATE TABLE ITEM_DESC
   (ItemNum        INTEGER       NOT NULL,
    ItemDesc       CHAR(90))
;
```

The value of this type of denormalization is better I/O.

The value of this type of denormalization is better I/O: More rows can be stored on each physical page because each row of the main table is smaller. Only those tasks that require all 100 bytes would need to access both tables. Of course, there are variations on this type of denormalization. You might choose to store only the first 10 bytes in the main table, but all 100 bytes in the description table if the other columns do not need to be accessed when the description is accessed. On the other hand, if the description is very large, you might want to break it up into multiple rows in the description table. For example, if the description can be up to 10,000 bytes long but most are under 1,000 bytes, you would not want to create a character column of 10,000 bytes (even if the DBMS allowed you to do so). Instead, you could create a table such as this:

```
CREATE TABLE ITEM_DESC
  (ItemNum         INTEGER       NOT NULL,
   ItemCtr         INTEGER       NOT NULL,
   ItemDesc        CHAR(100))
;
```

In this example, the primary key of the description table is now the combination of ItemNum and ItemCtr, where ItemCtr is a counter of the number of rows of description stored for the ItemNum. This design breaks the description up into 100-byte chunks. For the largest values, 100 rows would be required to store all 10,000 bytes, but for most descriptions, 10 or fewer rows would be required.

Combined Tables

Consider combining tables with a one-to-one relationship into a single combined table.

If tables exist with a one to one relationship, consider combining them into a single combined table. Of course, if each participant in the one-to-one relationship has different relationships to other tables, you will need to take that into account when denormalizing. Sometimes, even one-to-many relationships can be combined into a single table, but the data update process will be significantly complicated because of the increase in redundant data.

For example, consider an application with two tables: DEPT (containing department data) and EMP (containing employee data). You might choose to denormalize by combining the two tables into a large table named, for example, EMP_AND_DEPT. This new table would contain all of the columns of both tables except for the redundant foreign key. So, in addition to all the employee information, all the department information would also be contained on each employee row. This will result in many duplicate instances of the department data. Combined tables of this sort can be considered prejoined tables and treated accordingly.

Tables with one-to-one relationships should always be analyzed to determine whether combination is useful. Sometimes the consolidation of a one-to-one relationship is normalization, not denormalization.

Redundant Data

Sometimes one or more columns from one table are accessed almost every time data is queried in another table. In such cases, consider appending the columns to the queried table as redundant data. By carrying these additional columns, joins can be eliminated and performance perhaps improved. This should be attempted only if the normal data access performs insufficiently.

Consider, once again, the DEPT and EMP tables. If most of the employee queries require the name of the employee's department, the department name column could be carried as redundant data in the EMP table. The column should not be removed from the DEPT table, though. Columns to consider storing redundantly should exhibit the following characteristics.

- Only a few columns are necessary to support the redundancy.
- The columns should be stable, needing infrequent updates.
- The columns should be used by either a large number of users or a few very important users.

Repeating Groups

The normalization process transforms repeating groups into distinct rows instead of separate columns of the same row. Even though the normalization of repeating groups optimizes data integrity and update performance, it usually results in higher disk usage and less efficient retrieval. This happens because there are more rows in the table and more rows need to be read in order to satisfy queries that access the repeating group.

Sometimes, by denormalizing such groups back into distinct columns you can achieve significant performance gains. Nevertheless, these gains come at the expense of flexibility. For example, consider an application that is storing repeating group information in a table such as this:

```
CREATE TABLE CUST_BALANCE
  (CustNum        INTEGER        NOT NULL,
   BalancePeriod  INTEGER        NOT NULL,
   Balance        DECIMAL(15,2),
   constraint PKCB PRIMARY KEY (CustNum, BalancePeriod))
;
```

This table can store an infinite number of balances per customer, limited only by available storage and the storage limits of the DBMS. If the decision were made to string the repeating group, Balance, out into columns instead of rows, a limit would need to be set for the number of balances to be carried in each row. Here is an example of this table after denormalization:

```
CREATE TABLE CUST_BALANCE
 (CustNum          INTEGER        NOT NULL,
  Period1_Balance  DECIMAL(15,2),
  Period2_Balance  DECIMAL(15,2),
  Period3_Balance  DECIMAL(15,2),
  Period4_Balance  DECIMAL(15,2),
  Period5_Balance  DECIMAL(15,2),
  Period6_Balance  DECIMAL(15,2),
  constraint PKCB PRIMARY KEY (CustNum))
;
```

In this example, only six balances may be stored for any one customer. The designer could just as easily have chosen to store eight, twelve, or any arbitrary number of balances. The number six is not important, but the concept that the number of values is limited is important. This reduces the flexibility of data storage and should be avoided unless performance needs dictate otherwise.

Using the first design, six rows would need to be retrieved to obtain six balances. Using the second design, all six balances can be retrieved by reading one row. Therefore, the performance of retrieval may be better using the denormalized design. Before deciding to implement repeating groups as columns instead of rows, be sure the following criteria are met.

- The data is rarely or never aggregated, averaged, or compared within the row.
- The data occurs in a statistically well-behaved pattern.
- The data has a stable number of occurrences.
- The data is usually accessed collectively.
- The data has a predictable pattern of insertion and deletion.

If any of the above criteria are not met, certain types of data retrieval may be difficult to code, making the data less available. This should be avoided because, in general, data is denormalized only to make it *more* readily available.

Derivable Data

If the cost of deriving data using complicated formulas is prohibitive, think about physically storing the derived data in a column instead of calculating it. For example, consider employee data that is scattered across multiple tables. Perhaps the database contains three columns in several tables that store employee compensation data. These columns are Salary, Bonus, and Commission. Furthermore, assume that more often than not, queries require total compensation to be reported, which is the sum of these three columns. It might make sense to include a column in the main EMP table called TotalCompensation that is the sum of Salary, Bonus, and Commission, thereby avoiding a multitable join and a calculation. Even though this example shows a simple addition, certain business calculations can be quite complex, requiring a lot of I/O and CPU processing to accomplish. The more complex the calculation and the more resources it requires, the better the performance gain you can achieve by physically storing it in the database instead of calculating the value every time it is required.

However, when the underlying values that comprise the calculated value change, it is imperative that the stored derived data also be changed, otherwise inconsistent information will be stored. Such incorrect data will adversely impact the usability, effectiveness, and reliability of the database. To avoid such problems, consider storing derived data only when the following criteria are met.

- The source data used for the derivation calculation is relatively static.
- The cost of performing the derivation calculation is quite high.
- The usage pattern of the source tables is such that recalculation can be performed quickly when the source data changes.

Sometimes it is not possible to immediately update derived data elements when the columns change those upon which they rely. Such situations can occur when the tables containing the derived elements are offline or being operated on by a utility. Whenever possible, time the update of the derived data so that it occurs immediately when the source table is made available again. Under no circumstances should outdated derived data be made available for reporting and inquiry purposes.

Hierarchies

Applications requiring hierarchies frequently contain denormalized tables to speed up data retrieval.

A *hierarchy* is a structure that is easy to support using a relational database, but it can cause data retrieval difficulties unless the DBMS supports SQL extensions for traversing the hierarchy. For this reason, applications requiring hierarchies frequently contain denormalized tables to speed up data retrieval.

Most of us have encountered at least one hierarchy in our data processing careers. Two common hierarchical structures are bill-of-materials applications and departmental organization systems. A bill-of-materials application typically records information about parts assemblies in which one part is composed of other parts, which can then be a component of yet another part. A departmental organization system typically records the departmental structure of an organization, indicating which departments report to which other departments. A typical implementation of a hierarchy table for departmental organization would be:

```
CREATE TABLE DEPT
   (ParentDeptNum    INTEGER       NOT NULL,
    DeptName         CHAR(25),
    SupervisorNum    INTEGER,
    ReportsToDeptNum INTEGER,
    constraint PKDN PRIMARY KEY (DeptNum),
    constraint FKCB FOREIGN KEY (ReportsToDeptNum) REFERENCES DEPT
                 ON DELETE RESTRICT))
;
```

To support such a hierarchy, a one-to-many relationship is set up for a single table. In this example the ReportsToDeptNum column is the foreign key that refers to the DeptNum primary key. Each department reports to only one department, but a department can have more than one department reporting to it.

Such a table represents an accurately normalized entity for storing a hierarchy. The complete hierarchy can be rebuilt with the proper data retrieval instructions. However, consider the difficulty of writing SQL to query this table and report on the departmental organization. It is impossible to accomplish such a task using only SQL unless you have some guiding knowledge of the number of levels of reporting that may exist or your DBMS supports SQL extensions for traversing hierarchies.

A very effective
way to denormal-
ize a hierarchy is
to create speed
tables.

A very effective way to denormalize a hierarchy is to create speed tables. The *speed table* contains a pretraversed hierarchy for easy retrieval. Such a speed table is shown here:

```
CREATE TABLE DEPT
    (DeptNum          INTEGER       NOT NULL,
     ChildDeptNum     INTEGER       NOT NULL,
     Level            INTEGER,
     Detail           CHAR(1),
     DeptName         CHAR(25),
     SupervisorNum    INTEGER,
     constraint PKDN PRIMARY KEY (DeptNum, ChildDeptNum))
;
```

The speed table will contain a row for every dependent ChildDeptNum, not just immediate dependents. The primary key for the speed table is the combination of DeptNum and ChildDeptNum. Two additional columns are provided.

- A column named Level contains a numeric value indicating the level within the hierarchy for the ChildDeptNum. For example, if the child resides two levels down in the hierarchy from the parent, Level will contain the value 2.

- A column named Detail contains "Y" if the ChildDeptNum is at the very bottom of the hierarchy, and "N" otherwise.

The speed table must be created programmatically—it cannot be generated using SQL.

Special Physical Implementation Needs

Sometimes the requirements of the database and the physical implementation details of the DBMS will not mix for good performance. For example, some DBMS products have limitations on the physical block sizes that can be specified for database files. At times, the row size of a table in a logical data model may require a very large block size because it will not fit completely in a smaller block size. Some DBMS products treat large block sizes inefficiently. In that case, you may want to denormalize the table by breaking apart the row so it will fit in a smaller block size. This is just one example of a physical DBMS implementation detail that may call for denormalization.

Denormalization Summary

We have discussed ten different types of denormalization. Table 4-1 summarizes the types of denormalization that are available with a short description of when each type is useful.

The decision to denormalize should never be made lightly, because it can cause integrity problems and involve a lot of administration. Additional administration tasks include

- Documenting every denormalization decision
- Ensuring that all data remains valid and accurate
- Scheduling data migration and propagation jobs
- Keeping end users informed about the state of the tables
- Analyzing the database periodically to decide whether denormalization is still required

Any change can alter the need for denormalization

If a database has been denormalized, the data and environment should be regularly reviewed whenever hardware, software, and application requirements

Table 4-1 *Types of Denormalization*

Denormalization	Description
Prejoined tables	Used when the cost of joining is prohibitive
Report tables	Used when specialized critical reports are needed
Mirror tables	Used when tables are accessed concurrently by different types of environments
Split tables	Used when distinct groups use different parts of a table
Combined tables	Used to consolidate one-to-one or one-to-many relationships into a single table
Redundant data	Used to reduce the number of table joins required
Repeating groups	Used to reduce I/O and (possibly) storage usage
Derivable data	Used to eliminate calculations and algorithms
Speed tables	Used to make the processing of hierarchies more efficient
Physical denormalization	Used to optimize for specialized physical DBMS characteristics

change. Any change can alter the need for denormalization. To verify whether denormalization is still a valid decision, ask the following questions.

- Have the processing requirements changed for the application such that the join criteria, timing of reports, and/or transaction throughput requirements no longer dictate a denormalized database?

- Did a new release of the DBMS enhance performance? For example, did the introduction of a new join method or performance technique undo the need for prejoined tables?

- Did a new hardware release change performance considerations? For example, does the upgrade to a new, faster processor provide additional CPU resources so that denormalization is no longer necessary? Or did the addition of memory enable faster data access so that data can be physically normalized?

In general, periodically test whether the extra cost related to processing with normalized tables justifies the benefit of denormalization. You should measure the following criteria:

- I/O saved
- CPU saved
- Complexity of data modification
- Cost of returning to a normalized design

Denormalization is implemented to enhance performance.

Always remember that denormalization is implemented to enhance performance. If the environment changes, it is only reasonable to reevaluate the denormalization decision. Also, it is possible that, given a changing hardware and software environment, denormalized tables may be causing performance degradation instead of performance gains. Simply stated, always monitor and periodically reevaluate all denormalized applications.

Views

Another aspect of physical database design is the creation of *database views* to support specific application data requirements. Views are not required to access a physical database, but they can be helpful to support specific application and user requirements. You can think of a view as a way of turning a SELECT statement into a "table" that is accessible using SQL. Therefore, a view can be considered a logical table. No physical structure is required of a view; it is a representation of data that is stored in other tables (or other views). As shown in Figure 4-4, the data "in the view" is not stored anywhere and only physically exists in the underlying tables. Views can also be based on other views.

Views are flexible and can consist of any combination of the following:

- *Rows from tables.* These can be a subset of rows from a single table, all rows from a single table, a subset of rows from multiple tables, or all rows from multiple tables.

- *Rows from views.* These can be the same combinations as listed for tables.

- *Columns from tables.* These can be a subset of columns from a single table, all columns from a single table, a subset of columns from multiple tables, or all columns from multiple tables.

- *Columns from views.* These can be the same combinations as listed for tables.

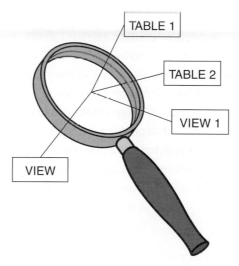

Figure 4-4 *What is a view?*

Views should be created based on their usefulness to application development and ad hoc query users. There are six basic uses for which views excel. Views can allow you to

- Provide row and column level security
- Ensure efficient access paths
- Mask complexity from the user
- Ensure proper data derivation
- Rename tables
- Rename columns

At any rate, be sure to document the intended purpose for every view created so that future structural changes to database tables can be promulgated to any views accessing those changing tables.

Data Definition Language

All physical database objects are created using SQL data definition language.

All physical database objects are created using SQL data definition language, or DDL for short. The basic components of DDL are the CREATE, ALTER, and DROP statements. Appropriately enough, CREATE is used to initially create a database object. Changes to the database object once it has been created can be made using the ALTER statement. But the ALTER statement cannot necessarily be used to change any and every aspect of a database object (which is covered in more detail in Chapter 7). Finally, the DROP statement is used to remove a database object from the system.

Many DBMS products provide a graphical interface for creating and changing database objects. If your DBMS provides such an interface, you may be able to create a physical database without learning the specifics of DDL syntax. I do not recommend this for DBAs, because sometimes the graphical interface does not support all of the syntax and options for every database object. An informed DBA is an effective DBA—and unless you verify that the graphical interface supports every DDL option, you will be better off learning and using DDL statements.

Summary

A logical data model should be used as the blueprint for designing and creating a physical database. But the physical database cannot be created with a simple logical to physical mapping. Many physical design decisions need to be made by the DBA before implementing physical database structures. Many times this will necessitate deviating from the logical data model. But such deviation must be based on in-depth knowledge of the DBMS and the physical environment in which the database will exist.

Review

1. Describe the first, simple steps to convert a logical data model to a physical database.
2. What is the only reason to denormalize a physical data model?
3. Under what circumstances should a bitmap index be considered instead of a b-tree index?
4. Which types of data access will benefit from data clustering?
5. Cite five reasons for creating a database view.
6. A referential constraint is created by specifying a _____ key in the dependent table that refers back to the primary key in the parent table.
7. Describe how a relational database uses indexes.
8. Why might the order in which columns are created in a table be important for physical database design?
9. When should you consider physically storing derived data in a database?
10. If indexes are beneficial to performance, why not create every possible index conceivable just to be on the safe side?

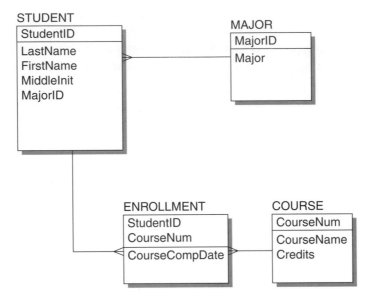

Figure 4-5   *Logical data model*

Bonus Question

Review the very small data model shown in Figure 4-5 and create a physical database implementation for the DBMS of your choice. Assume that there are approximately 25,000 students and that each student enrolls in three to five courses per semester. The most common query requirement is that a student be able to create his or her course schedule. Be sure to specify every physical design decision and create sample DDL statements to implement a basic physical design. Further, indicate where additional information is required to make a physical design decision and why.

Suggested Reading

Fleming, Candace, and Barbara von Halle. *Handbook of Relational Database Design.* Reading, MA: Addison-Wesley (1989). ISBN 0-201-11434-8

Hogan, Rex. *A Practical Guide to Database Design.* Englewood Cliffs, NJ: Prentice Hall (1990). ISBN 0-13-690967-1

Pascal, Fabian. *Practical Issues in Database Management.* Boston, MA: Addison-Wesley (2000). ISBN 0-201-48555-9

Perkinson, Richard C. *Data Analysis: The Key to Database Design.* Wellesley, MA: QED Information Sciences (1984). ISBN 0-89435-105-2

Riordan, Rebecca M. *Designing Relational Database Systems.* Redmond, WA: Microsoft Press (1999). ISBN 0-7356-0634-X

Stephens, Ryan K., and Ronald R. Plew. *Database Design.* Indianapolis, IN: SAMS Publishing (2001). ISBN 0-672-31758-3

5

Application Design

Performance has to be treated as a design issue.

Application design is more than just writing efficient database requests in application programs: Every aspect of the way the program is coded affects the usability and effectiveness of the application. Of course, application design includes database concerns such as interfacing SQL with traditional programming languages and the type of SQL to use. However, each application program must be designed to ensure the integrity of the data it modifies. Additionally, performance has to be treated as a design issue.

At the forefront the DBA must promote the concept of application design based on thorough knowledge of the database. It is unacceptable to allow programmers to design and code applications without considering how the programs will perform as they interact with databases. Some uninformed organizations approach database application development with no proactive performance engineering: The assumption is that any performance problems can be resolved after development by the DBA. However, it may be impossible to tune an improperly designed application program without rewriting it. So why not write it correctly the first time?

The intent of this chapter is not to teach software development methodology or to provide an in-depth treatise on programming—nor is it a primer on SQL. The focus of discussion will be on high-level application design issues that need to be understood when writing applications that use a database for persistent storage of data. Every DBA should understand the concepts in this chapter and be able to effectively communicate them to the developers in their organization.

Chapter 12 provides additional coverage of application performance issues as they pertain to database development.

Database Application Development and SQL

Designing a proper database application system is a complex task.

Designing a proper database application system is a complex and time-consuming task. The choices made during application design will impact the usefulness of the final, delivered application. Indeed, an improperly designed and coded application may need to be redesigned and recoded from scratch if it is inefficient, ineffective, or not easy to use.

To properly design an application that relies on databases for persistent data storage, the system designer at a minimum will need to understand the following issues:

- How data is stored in a relational database
- How to code SQL statements to access and modify data in the database
- How SQL differs from traditional programming languages
- How to embed SQL statements into a host programming language
- How to optimize database access by changing SQL and indexes
- How to use programming methods to avoid potential database processing problems

In general, the developer must match the application development languages and tools to the physical database design and functionality of the DBMS. The first task is to master the intricacies of SQL.

SQL

SQL is the de facto standard for accessing relational databases.

Structured Query Language, better known as SQL (and pronounced "sequel" or "ess-cue-el"), is the de facto standard for accessing relational databases. All RDBMS products, and even some nonrelational DBMS products, use SQL to manipulate data.

Why is SQL pervasive within the realm of relational data access? There are many reasons for SQL's success. Foremost is that SQL is a high-level language that provides a greater degree of abstraction than do traditional procedural languages. Third-generation languages, such as COBOL and C, and even fourth-generation languages, usually require the programmer to navigate data structures. Program logic must be coded to proceed record-by-record through data stores in an order determined by the application programmer or systems analyst. This information is encoded in the high-level language and is difficult to change after it has been programmed.

SQL specifies what data is needed… not how to retrieve it.

SQL, by contrast, is designed such that programmers specify *what* data is needed. It does not—indeed it cannot—specify *how* to retrieve it. SQL is coded without embedded data-navigational instructions. The DBMS analyzes each SQL statement and formulates data-navigational instructions "behind the scenes." These data-navigational instructions are commonly called *access paths*. A heavy burden is removed from the programmer by empowering the DBMS to determine the optimal access paths to the data. Because the DBMS better understands the state of the data it stores, it can produce a more efficient and dynamic access path to the data. The result is that SQL, used properly, provides a quicker application development and prototyping environment than is available with corresponding high-level languages. Furthermore, as the data characteristics and access patterns change, the DBMS can change access paths for SQL queries without requiring the actual SQL to be changed in any way.

Inarguably, though, the single most important feature that has solidified SQL's success is its capability to retrieve data easily using English-like syntax. It is much easier to understand a query such as

```
SELECT    deptnum, deptname
FROM      dept
WHERE     supervisornum = '903';
```

than it is to understand pages and pages of C or Basic source code, let alone the archaic instructions of Assembler. Because SQL programming instructions are easier to understand, they are easier to learn and maintain—affording users and programmers more productivity in a shorter period of time. However, do not underestimate SQL: Mastering all of its intricacies is not easy and will require much study and practice.

SQL also uses a free-form structure that makes it very flexible. The SQL programmer has the ability to develop SQL statements in a way best suited to the given user. Each SQL request is parsed by the DBMS before execution to check for proper syntax and to optimize the request. Therefore, SQL statements do not need to start in any given column and can be strung together on one line or broken apart on several lines. For example, the following SQL statement:

```
SELECT deptnum, deptname FROM dept WHERE supervisornum = '903';
```

is exactly equivalent to the previous SQL statement shown. Another example of SQL's flexibility is that the programmer can formulate a single request in a number of different and functionally equivalent ways—a feature that also can be very confusing for SQL novices. Furthermore, the flexibility of SQL is not always desirable, because different but logically equivalent SQL formulations can result in differing performance results. Refer to the sidebar "Joins vs. Subqueries" for an example.

Finally, one of the greatest benefits derived from using SQL is its ability to operate on sets of data with a single line of code. Multiple rows can be retrieved, modified, or removed in one fell swoop by using a single SQL statement. This feature provides the SQL developer with great power, but also limits the overall functionality of SQL. Without the ability to loop or step through multiple rows one at a time, certain tasks are impossible to accomplish using only SQL. Of course, as more and more functionality is added to SQL, the number of tasks that can be coded using SQL alone is increasing. For example, SQL can be used to create a stored procedure to perform many programming tasks that formerly required a traditional programming language to accomplish. Furthermore, most of the popular relational DBMS products support extended versions of SQL with procedural capabilities. Table 5-1 details the most popular procedural SQL dialects.

Set-at-a-Time Processing and Relational Closure

All SQL data manipulation operations are performed at a set level.

Every operation performed on a relational database acts on a table (or set of tables) and results in another table. This feature of relational databases is called *relational closure*. All SQL data manipulation operations—that is, SELECT, INSERT, UPDATE, and DELETE statements—are performed at a set level. One

Table 5-1   *SQL Usage Considerations*

DBMS	Procedural SQL dialect
Oracle	PL/SQL
Microsoft SQL Server	Transact-SQL
Sybase Adaptive Server Enterprise	Transact-SQL
DB2	SQL Procedure Language

Joins vs. Subqueries

One example of SQL's flexibility is the way in which a single statement can access data from multiple tables. SQL provides two methods: *joins* and *subqueries*. However, a subquery can be converted to an equivalent join. The concept behind both types of queries is to retrieve data from multiple tables based on search criteria matching data in the tables.

Consider the following two SQL statements. The first one is a subquery, where a query is embedded within another query. The second query is a join, where two tables are specified in the FROM clause of a single SELECT statement.

```
SELECT   empno, firstname, lastname
FROM     employee
WHERE    workdept IN
         (SELECT  deptno
          FROM    department
          WHERE   deptname = 'DBA');
SELECT   empno, firstname, lastname
FROM     employee,
         department
WHERE    workdept = deptno
AND      deptname = 'DBA';
```

Both these queries return information about employees who work in the database administration department. The results returned by both queries will be the same, but the performance may vary significantly depending on the DBMS in use, the indexes that are defined for each table, and the complexity of the query itself.

retrieval statement can return multiple rows; one modification statement can modify multiple rows.

To clarify the concept of relational closure, refer to Figure 5-1. A database user initiates SQL requests. Each SQL statement can access one or many tables in the database. The SQL statement is sent to the DBMS, whereupon the query is analyzed, optimized, and executed. The DBMS formulates the access path to the data, and upon completion of the request, the desired information is presented to the user as a set of columns and rows—in other words, a table. The result will consist of one or more columns with zero, one, or many rows. Because SQL performs set-level processing, the DBMS operates on a set of data and a set of data is always returned as the result. Of course, the result set can be empty, or it can contain only one row or column. The relational model and set-level processing

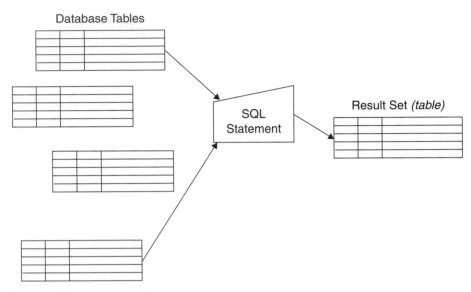

Database Tables

SQL
Statement

Result Set *(table)*

Figure 5-1   *Relational closure*

are based on the mathematical laws of *set theory*, which permits empty and single-valued sets.

Application developers face a potential problem when using relational databases because of the set-at-a-time nature of SQL. Most programming languages operate on data one record at a time. When a program requires relational data, though, it must request the data using SQL. This creates an impedance mismatch. The program expects data to be returned a single row at a time, but SQL returns data a set at a time. There are different ways to get around this mismatch, depending on the DBMS, programming language, and environment. Most DBMS products provide a feature called a *cursor* that accepts the input from a SQL request and provides a mechanism to fetch individual rows of the results set. Some programming environments and fourth-generation languages automatically transform multirow sets to single rows when communicating with the DBMS.

The DBMS determines how best to retrieve the data.

Furthermore, most programmers are accustomed to hard-wiring data navigation instructions into their programs. SQL specifies what to retrieve but not how to retrieve it. The DBMS determines how best to retrieve the data. Programmers unaccustomed to database processing are unlikely to grasp this concept without some training. At any rate, programmers will need to be trained in these high-level differences between nondatabase and database programming techniques. This job usually falls upon the DBA or other highly skilled database technician within the organization. Of course, there are many more details at a lower level that the database programmer needs to know, such as SQL syntax, debugging and testing methods, optimization techniques, and program preparation procedures (compilation, bind, etc.).

Embedding SQL in a Program

Most database applications require a host programming language to use SQL to communicate with the database. A wide range of programming languages can be used with SQL, from traditional languages such as COBOL, FORTRAN, and Assembler to more modern languages such as C/C++, Java, and Visual Basic. Your choice of host programming language can impact the way you will have to code SQL. For example, SQL is embedded directly into a COBOL program, whereas a language like C requires an API like ODBC to issue SQL statements.

Minimize the number of different languages you use.

The choice of development language will likely be limited to just a few at your shop. You should attempt to minimize the number of different languages you use, because it will make supporting and maintaining your applications easier. Furthermore, such limitations will make it easier for DBAs to administer and optimize the database environment. A DBA should be capable of reading and understanding program code for each language used to access databases within the organization.

Some applications development projects use a *CASE tool* or *code generator* to create programs from program specifications. Exercise caution when using this approach: Don't allow the code generator to create SQL for you without first testing it for efficiency. Poor performance can result when using a code generation tool because these tools often have very little knowledge of the DBMS you are using. In most cases the code generator is designed to work for multiple DBMS products and is therefore not optimized for any of them. Test the SQL that is generated and, if necessary, modify the generated SQL or build indexes to optimize the generated SQL before moving the programs to a production environment. The DBA should be responsible for implementing a procedure to ensure that such SQL performance testing occurs.

SQL Middleware and APIs

Application programs require an *interface* for issuing SQL to access or modify data. The interface is used to embed SQL statements in a host programming language, such as COBOL, Java, C, or Visual Basic. Standard interfaces enable application programs to access databases using SQL. There are several popular standard interfaces or APIs (Application Programming Interfaces) for database programming, including ODBC, JDBC, SQLJ, and OLE DB.

ODBC is basically a call-level interface for interacting with databases.

One of the most popular SQL APIs is Open Database Connectivity (ODBC). Instead of directly embedding SQL in the program, ODBC uses *callable routines*. ODBC provides routines to allocate and deallocate resources, control connections to the database, execute SQL statements, obtain diagnostic information, control transaction termination, and obtain information about the implementation. ODBC is basically a call-level interface (CLI) for interacting with databases. Basically, the CLI issues SQL statements against the database by using procedure calls instead of direct embedded SQL statements.

Microsoft invented the ODBC interface to enable relational database access for Microsoft Windows programming. However, ODBC has become an industry-standard CLI for SQL programming. Indeed, every major DBMS today supports ODBC.

ODBC relies on *drivers*, which are optimized ODBC interfaces for a particular DBMS implementation. Programs can make use of the ODBC drivers to communicate with any ODBC-compliant database. The ODBC drivers enable a standard set of SQL statements in any Windows application to be translated into commands recognized by a remote SQL-compliant database.

Another popular SQL API is Java Database Connectivity (JDBC). JDBC enables Java to access relational databases. Similar to ODBC, JDBC consists of a set of classes and interfaces that can be used to access relational data. There are several types of JDBC middleware, including the JDBC-to-ODBC bridge, as well as direct JDBC connectivity to the relational database. Anyone familiar with application programming and ODBC (or any call-level interface) can get up and running with JDBC quickly.

SQLJ enables developers to embed SQL statements in Java programs.

Another way to access databases from a Java program is by using SQLJ. SQLJ enables developers to directly embed SQL statements in Java programs, thus providing static SQL support to Java. A precompiler translates the embedded SQL into Java code. The Java program is then compiled into bytecodes, and a database bind operation creates packaged access routines for the SQL.

Microsoft Database Programming

A lot of database applications run on Microsoft software. Microsoft provides a data access architecture to facilitate database programming in a Microsoft environment. It consists of multiple components that will be discussed briefly here. As a DBA you should understand the basics of these components, but you need not be an expert on any of them. Database developers, though, must be experts in these technologies.

- *COM*, which stands for Component Object Module, is Microsoft's component-based development architecture. By using COM, developers create application components that are pieced together to create application systems. The components can be written by different developers using different programming languages.

- *OLE DB*, which stands for Object Linking and Embedding Database, is an interface that is based on the COM architecture. It is Microsoft's strategic low-level interface to data and the foundation for Microsoft's data access architecture. OLE DB provides greater flexibility than ODBC because it can be used to access both relational and nonrelational data. OLE DB presents an object-oriented interface for generic data access

- *ADO*, which stands for ActiveX Data Objects, is built on top of OLE DB. ADO is an OLE DB consumer, and applications using ADO access the OLE DB interfaces indirectly. ADO provides an object model for database programming and is simpler to use for database programming than OLE DB. To implement an application using OLE DB, the programmer typically uses ADO methods and properties to call the OLE DB interface. ADO provides a high-level interface that can easily be used from within programming and scripting languages such as C++ and Visual Basic, or JScript and VBScript.

Figure 5-2 provides a high level overview of the components of Microsoft's data access architecture. Application programs can access SQL Server by using ADO, which in turn uses OLE/DB, or by using OLE/DB directly.

Object Orientation and SQL

Object orientation can result in a better ROI for program development.

Many organizations have adopted *object-oriented* (OO) programming standards and languages because of the claimed advantages of the OO development paradigm. The primary advantages of object orientation are faster program development time and reduced maintenance costs, resulting in a better ROI. Piecing together reusable objects and defining new objects based on similar object classes can dramatically reduce development time and costs.

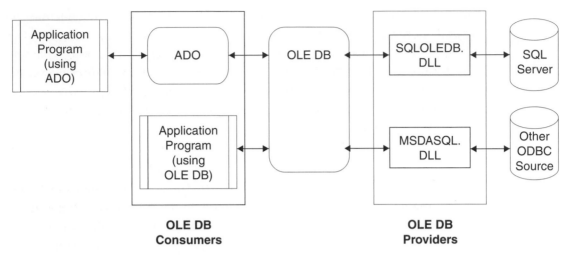

Figure 5-2 *OLE DB and ADO*

With benefits like these, it is no wonder that object-oriented programming and development is being embraced by many IT organizations. Historically, one of the biggest problems faced by IT is a large project backlog. In many cases, end users are forced to wait for long periods of time for new applications because the backlog is so great and the talent needed to tackle so many new projects is not available. This backlog can sometimes result in some unsavory phenomena such as business people attempting to build their own applications or purchasing third-party packaged applications (and all of the potential administrative burdens that packages carry). So, it is very clear why the OO siren song lures organizations.

However, because OO and relational databases are not inherently compatible, OO programmers tend to resist using SQL. The set-based nature of SQL is not simple to master and is anathema to the OO techniques practiced by Java and C++ developers. All too often insufficient consideration has been given to the manner in which data is accessed, resulting in poor design and faulty performance.

Object orientation is indeed a political nightmare for those schooled in relational tenets. All too often organizations are experiencing political struggles between OO programming proponents and the data resource management group. The OO crowd espouses programs and components as the center of the universe; the data crowd adheres to normalized, shared data with the RDBMS as the center of the universe.

Thanks to the hype surrounding object orientation, the OO crowd may win many of these battles, but data-centered thinking will eventually win the war. The use of data normalization and shared databases to reduce redundancy provides far too many benefits in the long run for it ever to be abandoned. Data has an existence independent of process, and the OO way of encapsulating data within methods masks data from other processes and is inefficient for sharing data across an organization. If the focus shifts away from data management and sound relational practices, data quality will deteriorate and productivity will decline.

You will need to marry the relational world to the OO world.

If an OO programming language is to be used against a relational database, you will need to marry the relational world to the OO world. This means your applications will not be object-oriented in the "true" sense of the word because the data will not be encapsulated within the method (that is, the program).

One additional word of caution here: many people believe that object/relational databases resolve all of these issues. But an object/relational database is not truly object oriented. The term *object/relational* means basically that the DBMS supports large multimedia data types and gives the user the ability to define their own data types and functions. All good things, but not object orientation. So don't get confused over the similarity of the terms.

Types of SQL

SQL can be planned or unplanned, embedded in a program or stand-alone, dynamic or static.

SQL, although a single language, comprises multiple types that exhibit different behavioral characteristics and require different development and administration techniques. SQL can be broken down into differing categories based on execution type, program requirement, and dynamism.

- *SQL can be planned or unplanned.* A planned SQL request is typically embedded into an application program, but it might also exist in a query or reporting tool. At any rate, a planned SQL request is designed and tested for accuracy and efficiency before it is run in a production system. Contrast this with the characteristics of an unplanned SQL request. Unplanned SQL, also called *ad hoc SQL*, is created "on the fly" by end users during the course of business. Most ad hoc queries are created to examine data for patterns and trends that impact business. Unplanned, ad hoc SQL requests can be a significant source of inefficiency and are difficult to tune. How do you tune requests that are constantly written, rewritten, and changed?

- *SQL can either be embedded in a program or issued stand-alone.* Embedded SQL is contained within an application program, whereas

Table 5-2   *SQL Usage Considerations*

Situation	Execution type	Program requirement	Dynamism
Columns and predicates of the SQL statement can change during execution.	Planned	Embedded	Dynamic
SQL formulation does not change.	Planned	Embedded	Static
Highly concurrent, high-performance transactions.	Planned	Embedded	Dynamic or static
Ad hoc one-off queries.	Unplanned	Stand-alone	Dynamic
Repeated analytical queries.	Planned	Embedded or stand-alone	Dynamic or static
Quick one-time "fix" programs.	Unplanned	Embedded or stand-alone	Dynamic or static

stand-alone SQL is run by itself or within a query, reporting, or OLAP tool.

- *SQL can be dynamic or static.* A dynamic SQL statement is optimized at run time. Depending on the DBMS, a dynamic SQL statement may also be changed at run time. Static SQL, on the other hand, is optimized prior to execution and cannot change without reprogramming.

Programmers must be able to quantify each SQL statement being developed in terms of these three qualities. Every SQL statement exhibits one of these properties for each criteria. For example, a certain SQL statement can be a planned, embedded, static request, or it could be an unplanned, stand-alone, dynamic request. Be sure to use the right type of SQL for the right situation. Table 5-2 outlines situations and the type of SQL that is most useful for that situation. Of course, the information in this table is meant to serve as a broad suggestion only. You should use your knowledge of your environment and the requirements of the user request to arrive at the correct type of SQL solution.

SQL Coding for Performance

Developing database application programs requires a good amount of effort to ensure that SQL requests are properly coded for performance. A solid understanding of SQL syntax, database structures, and the programming language is imperative. Let's concentrate first on SQL.

Let SQL do the work.

One of the first rules to learn as a database developer is to let SQL, rather than the program logic, do the work. It is much better to filter out unwanted data at the DBMS level than to do so within the program. You'll achieve better efficiency by avoiding the actual movement of data between the DBMS and the program. For example, it is better to add more WHERE clauses to SQL SELECT statements than to simply select all rows and filter the data programmatically.

To use another example, consider the cost of a multitable join statement. It will be easier to tune, say, a four-table join for efficiency than four independent SQL SELECT statements that are filtered and joined using application logic. Of course, this assumes an optimal physical database and the possibility of having to tweak that design (such as by adding indexes).

The more work the DBMS can do to filter data, the greater the efficiency should be, because less data will need to be moved between the DBMS and the application program as it runs. Of course, there is much more to optimizing and tuning SQL than this short discussion of the matter. More details are covered in Chapter 12.

Defining Transactions

A transaction is an atomic unit of work with respect to recovery and consistency.

A *transaction* is an atomic unit of work with respect to recovery and consistency. A logical transaction performs a complete business process typically on behalf of an online user. It may consist of several steps and may comprise more than one physical transaction. The results of running a transaction will record the effects of a business process—a complete business process. The data in the database must be correct and proper after the transaction executes.

When all the steps that make up a specific transaction have been accomplished, a COMMIT is issued. The COMMIT signals that all work since the last COMMIT is correct and should be externalized to the database. At any point within the transaction, the decision can be made to stop and roll back the effects of all changes since the last COMMIT. When a transaction is rolled back, the data in the database will be restored to the original state before the transaction was started. The DBMS maintains a transaction log (or journal) to track database changes.

Transactions exhibit ACID properties. ACID is an acronym for *atomicity, consistency, isolation,* and *durability*. Each of these four qualities is necessary for a transaction to be designed correctly.

- *Atomicity* means that a transaction must exhibit "all or nothing" behavior. Either all of the instructions within the transaction happen, or none of them happen. Atomicity preserves the "completeness" of the business process.

- *Consistency* refers to the state of the data both before and after the transaction is executed. A transaction maintains the consistency of the state of the data. In other words, after running a transaction, all data in the database is "correct."

- *Isolation* means that transactions can run at the same time. Any transactions running in parallel have the illusion that there is no concurrency. In other words, it appears that the system is running only a single transaction at a time. No other concurrent transaction has visibility to the uncommitted database modifications made by any other transactions. To achieve isolation, a locking mechanism is required.

- *Durability* refers to the impact of an outage or failure on a running transaction. A durable transaction will not impact the state of data if the transaction ends abnormally. The data will survive any failures.

Let's use an example to better understand the importance of transactions to database applications. Consider a banking application. Assume that you wish to withdraw $50 from your account with Mega Bank. This "business process" requires a transaction to be executed. You request the money either in person by handing a slip to a bank teller or by using an ATM (Automated Teller Machine). When the bank receives the request, it performs the following tasks, which make up the complete business process. The bank will

1. Check your account to make sure you have the necessary funds to withdraw the requested amount.
2. If you do not, deny the request and stop; otherwise continue processing.
3. Debit the requested amount from your checking account.
4. Produce a receipt for the transaction.
5. Deliver the requested amount and the receipt to you.

Design transactions that ensure ACID properties.

The transaction that is run to perform the withdrawal must complete all of these steps, or none of these steps, or else one of the parties in the transaction will be dissatisfied. If the bank debits your account but does not give you your money, then you will not be satisfied. If the bank gives you the money but does not debit the account, the bank will be unhappy. Only the completion of every one of these steps results in a "complete business process." Database developers must understand the requisite business processes and design transactions that ensure ACID properties.

To summarize, a transaction—when executed alone, on a consistent database—will either complete, producing correct results, or terminate, with no effect. In either case the resulting condition of the database will be a consistent state.

Transaction Guidelines

A transaction should be short in duration.

A transaction should be short in duration because it locks shared resources. Of course, "short" will vary from system to system. A short transaction in a very large system handling multiple thousands of transactions per second will most likely be measured in subseconds.

At any rate, transactions must be designed to remove the human element of "think time" from the equation. When a transaction locks resources, it makes those resources inaccessible to other transactions. Therefore, a good transaction must be designed so that it is not waiting for user input in the middle of the processing.

Unit of Work

A UOW is a series of instructions and messages that guarantees data integrity.

Unit of work (UOW) is another transaction term that describes a physical transaction. A UOW is a series of instructions and messages that, when executed, guarantees data integrity. So a UOW and a transaction are similar in concept. However, a UOW is not necessarily a complete business process—it can be a subset of the business process, and a group of units of work can constitute a single transaction.

Each UOW must possess ACID characteristics. In other words, if the transaction were to fail, the state of the data upon failure must be consistent in terms of the business requirements.

Transaction Processing Systems

A TP system delivers a scheme to monitor and control the execution of transaction programs.

A transaction processing (TP) system, appropriately enough, facilitates the processing of transactions. Such a system is sometimes referred to as a *transaction server* or a *transaction processing monitor*. Regardless of name, a TP system delivers a scheme to monitor and control the execution of transaction programs. The TP system also provides an API—a mechanism for programs to interact and communicate with the TP server. Examples of TP systems include CICS, IMS/TM, Tuxedo, and Microsoft Transaction Server.

The TP system provides an environment for developing and executing presentation logic and business logic components. A TP system is useful for mission-critical applications requiring a high volume of concurrent users with minimal downtime. Used properly, a TP system can efficiently control the concurrent execution of many application programs serving large numbers of on-line users. Another major benefit of some TP systems is their ability to ensure ACID properties across multiple, heterogeneous databases. This is accomplished using a two-phase COMMIT, where the TP system controls the issuance of database commits and ensures their satisfactory completion. If your application requires online access and modification of heterogeneous databases, a TP system is recommended.

A *transaction server* is ideal for building high-performance and reliable distributed applications across heterogeneous environments. A TP system can support the diverse application requirements of front-end e-commerce applications as well as the robust needs of back-office processes. When platform independence is crucial, a TP system can help developers to successfully develop, manage, and deploy online applications that are completely independent of the underlying communications, hardware, and database environment.

Of course, a TP system is not required in order to develop database transactions for every application. The DBMS itself can deliver ACID properties for the data it manages. Yet even in a single-DBMS environment, a TP system can provide development benefits. Take a look at Figure 5-3. It shows the typical application setup: a database server without a TP system. Requests are made by the client through the presentation layer to the database server (DBMS). The client can make data requests directly of the database server, or the client may execute stored procedures to run application logic on the database server.

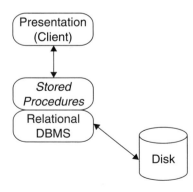

Figure 5-3   *Using a database server*

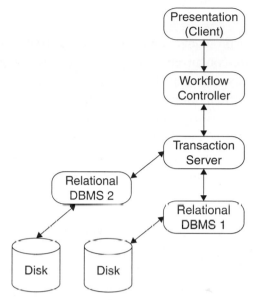

Figure 5-4   *Using a transaction server*

Now let's compare Figure 5-3 with Figure 5-4, which shows an application using a TP system. Database requests are run within the TP system, which helps to control the transaction workflow. Furthermore, the TP system enables the application to make requests of multiple heterogeneous databases and to coordinate database modifications.

Ensure that the DBMS and the TP system are set up to work together in an efficient manner.

If your database applications use a TP system, the DBA should work with the system administrator to ensure that the DBMS and the TP system are set up to work with each other in an efficient manner. Furthermore, both the DBA and the SA will need to monitor the interaction between the DBMS and the TP system on an ongoing basis.

Application Servers

A more recent type of middleware for serving database transactions is the *application server*. An application server usually combines the features of a transaction server with additional functionality to assist in building, managing, and distributing database applications. An application server, such as IBM's WebSphere, provides an environment for developing and integrating components into a secure, performance-oriented application.

Locking

Every programmer who has developed database programs understands the potential for concurrency problems. When one program tries to read data that is in the process of being changed by another program, the DBMS must prohibit access until the modification is complete, in order to ensure data integrity. The DBMS uses a *locking* mechanism to enable multiple, concurrent users to access and modify data in the database. By using locks, the DBMS automatically guarantees the integrity of data. The DBMS locking strategies permit multiple users from multiple environments to access and modify data in the database at the same time.

Locks are used to ensure the integrity of data.

Locks are used to ensure the integrity of data. When a database resource is locked by one process, another process is not permitted to change the locked data. Locking is necessary to enable the DBMS to facilitate the ACID properties of transaction processing.

Data may be locked at different levels within the database. It is the DBA's job to determine the appropriate level of locking for each database object, based on how the data will be accessed and to what extent concurrent users will access the data. Theoretically, database locks can be taken at the following levels:

- Column
- Row
- Page (or block)
- Table
- Tablespace
- Database

The level of locking is known as *lock granularity*. The actual lock granularity levels available will depend on the DBMS in use. Typically the lock granularity is controlled by the DBA when the database object is created, but there may be an overall default lock granularity that is used if none is specified. Nevertheless, it is a good practice for DBAs always to specify the lock granularity when database objects are created.

The lock granularity specification should be based on the needs of the applications and users that will be accessing and changing the data. In general, the smaller the granularity of the lock, the more concurrent access will be allowed, as shown in Figure 5-5. However, the smaller the granularity of the lock, the more resources the DBMS will need to consume to perform locking.

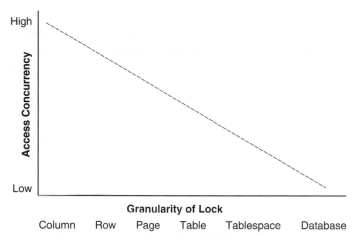

Figure 5-5 *Lock granularity and concurrent access*

The smallest unit that can conceivably be locked is a single column; the largest lock size is the entire database. Neither of these two options is really practical. Locking individual columns would maximize the ability to concurrently update data, but it would require too much overhead. Conversely, locking the database would be cheap to implement, but would restrict concurrency to the point of making the database worthless for anybody but a single user.

Most database implementations choose between row and page locking. For many applications, page locking is sufficient. However, applications needing many concurrent update processes may benefit from the smaller granularity of row locking. Very infrequently, when a specific process will be run when no other concurrent access is needed, table locking can be useful. For this reason many DBMS products provide a LOCK TABLE command that can be issued to override the current locking granularity for a database object during the course of a single process or UOW. The DBA must analyze the application processing requirements for each database object to determine the optimal locking granularity.

Index entries can also be locked, depending on the DBMS and version in use. However, index locking can be a significant impediment to performance. Because index entries are usually quite small, it is not uncommon for locking to block application access—especially when the DBMS locks indexes at the block or page level. Some DBMSs do not require index locks, instead handling integrity by using locks on the data. Remember, there is no data in the index that is not also in a table.

Most database implementations choose between row and page locking.

Index locking can be a significant impediment to performance.

The exact nature of locking and the types of locks taken will differ from DBMS to DBMS. This section will cover the basics of locking that are generally applicable to most DBMS products.

Types of Locks

At a very basic level, a DBMS will take a *write lock* when it writes information or a *read lock* when it reads information. A write occurs for INSERT, UPDATE, and DELETE statements. A read occurs for SELECT statements. But to actually accomplish such locking, the typical DBMS will use three basic types of locks: shared locks, exclusive locks, and update locks.

- A *shared lock* is taken by the DBMS when data is read with no intent to update it. If a shared lock has been taken on a row, page, or table, other processes or users are permitted to read the same data. In other words, multiple processes or users can have a shared lock on the same data.

- An *exclusive lock* is taken by the DBMS when data is modified. If an exclusive lock has been taken on a row, page, or table, other processes or users are generally not permitted to read or modify the same data. In other words, multiple processes or users cannot have an exclusive lock on the same data.

- An *update lock* is taken by the DBMS when data must first be read before it is changed or deleted. The update lock indicates that the data may be modified or deleted in the future. If the data is actually modified or deleted, the DBMS will promote the update lock to an exclusive lock. If an update lock has been taken on a row, page, or table, other processes or users generally are permitted to read the data, but not to modify it. So a single process or user can have an update lock while other processes and users have shared locks on the same data. However, multiple processes or users cannot have both an exclusive lock and an update lock, or multiple update locks, on the same data.

Intent Locks

An intent lock stays in place for the life of the lower-level locks.

In addition to shared, exclusive, and update locks, the DBMS also will take another type of lock, known as an *intent lock*. Intent locks are placed on higher-level database objects when a user or process takes locks on the data pages or rows. An intent lock stays in place for the life of the lower-level locks.

For example, consider a table created with row-level locking. When a process locks the row, an intent lock is taken on the table. Intent locks are used primarily to ensure that one process cannot take locks on a table, or pages in the table, that would conflict with the locking of another process. For example, if a user was holding an exclusive row lock and another user wished to take out an exclusive table lock on the table containing the row, the intent lock held on the table by the first user would ensure that its row lock would not be overlooked by the lock manager.

Lock Timeouts

When data is locked by one process, other processes must wait for the lock to be released before processing the data. A lock that is held for a long time has the potential to severely degrade performance because other processes must wait until the lock is released and the data becomes available. Furthermore, if the application is designed improperly or has a bug, the blocking lock may not be released until the program fails or the DBA intervenes.

The locking mechanism of the DBMS prevents processes from waiting forever for a lock to be released by timing out. Each DBMS provides a parameter to set a *lock timeout value*. Depending on the DBMS, the lock timeout value might be set at the DBMS level, the process level, or the connection level. Regardless of the level, after a process waits for the predetermined amount of time for a lock to be granted, the process will receive an error message informing it that the timeout period has been exceeded. Such an approach assumes that a problem occurs after a certain amount of time is spent waiting for a lock. Timeouts prevent a process from waiting indefinitely for locks—the rationale being that it is better for a process to give up and release its locks than to continue to wait and perhaps block other processes from running.

It is usually a good practice for programs to retry an operation when a lock timeout error is received. If multiple lock timeouts occur for the same operation, the program should log the problem and inform the user that it cannot proceed.

Deadlocks

A deadlock occurs when concurrent processes are competing for locks.

Another locking problem that can occur is deadlocking. A *deadlock* occurs when concurrent processes are competing for locks. Figure 5-6 shows a deadlock situation. Process A holds a lock on row 3 and is requesting a lock on row 7; process B holds a lock on row 7 and is requesting a lock on row 3.

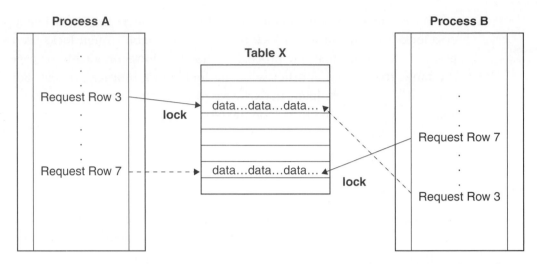

Figure 5-6 *A deadlock situation*

The deadlock is a specific type of lock timeout. It occurs when one process holds a lock that another process is requesting at the same time the second process holds a lock that the first process is requesting. This is also known as a "deadly embrace." The DBMS will choose one of the processes to abort and roll back so the other process can continue.

As with timeouts, it is a good practice for programs to retry an operation when a deadlock error is received. If multiple deadlocks occur for the same operation, the program should log the problem and inform the user that it cannot proceed.

If deadlocks are a persistent problem, application or database design changes may be warranted. One technique is to consider changing the lock granularity (perhaps from page to row) so that less data is locked for each lock request. Another technique is to make application changes. You might rewrite the program to lock all required resources at the beginning of the transaction. However, such a technique is not likely to be possible for most applications. A final method of avoiding deadlocks is to ensure that all database modifications occur in the same order for all programs in your shop. By sequencing the updates in every program, deadlocks can be minimized or eliminated. Perhaps you'll find a logical business order for updates that is reasonable to use for applications. If you don't, consider using an arbitrary policy such as modification in alphabetical order.

Lock Duration

*Lock duration re-
fers to the length
of time that a lock
is held by the
DBMS.*

Lock duration refers to the length of time that a lock is held by the DBMS. The longer a lock is held on a database resource, the longer a concurrent lock request must wait to be taken. As lock durations increase, so does the likelihood of lockout timeouts.

Each DBMS provides parameters that can be set to impact the duration of a lock. Typically these parameters are set at the program, transaction, or SQL statement level. In general, there are two parameters that affect lock duration, isolation level and acquire/release specification.

Isolation Level

The *isolation level* specifies the locking behavior for a transaction or statement. Standard SQL defines four isolation levels that can be set using the SET TRANSACTION ISOLATION LEVEL statement:

- UNCOMMITTED READ

- COMMITTED READ

- REPEATABLE READ

- SERIALIZABLE

*The isolation level
specifies the lock-
ing behavior for
a transaction or
statement.*

The preceding list progresses from lowest to highest isolation. The higher the isolation level, the more strict the locking protocol becomes. The lower the isolation level, the shorter the lock duration will be. Additionally, each higher isolation level is a superset of the lower levels. Let's briefly examine each of the standard isolation levels.

Specifying *UNCOMMITTED READ* isolation implements read-through locks and is sometimes referred to as a *dirty read*. It applies to read operations only. With this isolation level, data may be read that never actually exists in the database, because the transaction can read data that has been changed by another process but is not yet committed. UNCOMMITTED READ isolation provides the highest-level availability and concurrency of the isolation levels, but the worst degree of data integrity. It should be used only when data integrity problems can be tolerated. Certain types of applications, such as those using analytical queries, estimates, and averages are often candidates for UNCOMMITTED READ locking. A dirty read can cause duplicate rows to be returned where none exist, or no rows to be returned when one (or more) actually exists. When choosing UNCOMMITTED READ isolation, the programmer and DBA must ensure that these types of problems are acceptable for the application. Refer to the sidebar "Dirty Read Scenarios" for additional guidance on when to consider using UNCOMMITTED READ isolation.

COMMITTED READ isolation, also called *Cursor Stability*, provides more integrity than UNCOMMITTED READ isolation. When READ COMMITTED isolation is specified, the transaction will never read data that is not yet committed; it will only COMMITTED READ data.

REPEATABLE READ isolation places a further restriction on reads, namely, the assurance that the same data can be accessed multiple times during the course of the transaction without its value changing. The lower isolation levels (UNCOMMITTED READ and COMMITTED READ) permit the underlying data to change if it is accessed more than once. Use REPEATABLE READ isolation only when data can be read multiple times during the course of the transaction and the data values must be consistent.

SERIALIZABLE isolation provides the greatest integrity.

Finally, *SERIALIZABLE* isolation provides the greatest integrity. SERIALIZABLE isolation removes the possibility of phantoms. A phantom occurs when the transaction opens a cursor that retrieves data and another process subsequently inserts a value that would satisfy the request and should be in the result set. For example, consider the following situation:

- Transaction 1 opens a cursor and reads account information, keeping a running sum of the total balance for the selected accounts.
- Transaction 2 inserts a new account that falls within the range of accounts being processed by Transaction 1, but the insert occurs after Transaction 1 has passed the new account.
- Transaction 2 COMMITs the insert.
- Transaction 1 runs a query to sum the values to check the accuracy of the running total. However, the totals will not match.

SERIALIZABLE isolation eliminates this problem. Phantoms can occur for lower isolation levels, but not when the isolation level is SERIALIZABLE.

Most DBMS products support the specification of isolation level at the program or transaction level, as well as at the SQL statement level.

Keep in mind that your DBMS may not implement all of these isolation levels, or it may refer to them by other names. Be sure you understand the isolation

Dirty Read Scenarios

When is using UNCOMMITTED READ isolation appropriate? The general recommendation is to avoid it if your results must be 100% accurate. For example, avoid dirty reads when calculations must balance, data is being retrieved to insert into another table, or for mission-critical data where consistency and integrity are crucial.

Frankly, most database applications are not candidates for dirty reads. However, there are specific situations where permitting uncommitted data to be read is beneficial.

One such situation is when accessing a reference, code, or lookup table that is very static. Because the data is not volatile, an UNCOMMITTED READ would usually be no different than using a stricter isolation level. For those rare occasions where the lookup codes are being modified, the problems should be minimal for concurrent transactions.

When a transaction must perform statistical processing on a large amount of data, a dirty read may be useful. For example, consider a transaction designed to return the average account balance for each type of account. The impact of using UNCOMMITTED READ isolation is minimal because changing a single value should not have a significant impact on the result. Because the result is an average of multiple values, one or perhaps a few "bad" values are unlikely to change the average significantly.

Data warehousing queries are good candidates for dirty reads. A data warehouse is a time-sensitive, subject-oriented store of business data that is used for analytical processing. Other than periodic data propagation and/or replication, access to the data warehouse is read only. An UNCOMMITTED READ can cause little damage because the data is generally not changing.

You might also consider using dirty read for those rare instances where a transaction accesses a table, or set of tables, that is used by a single user only. If only one person can modify the data, the application programs can be coded so that most reads can use UNCOMMITTED READ isolation with no negative impact to data integrity.

Finally, if the data being accessed is already inconsistent, little harm can be done by using a dirty read to access the information.

---

supported by each DBMS you use and its impact on application behavior and lock duration.

Acquire/Release Specification

An additional parameter that impacts lock duration is the treatment of intent locks. Regular transaction locks are taken as data is accessed and modified. However, some DBMS products provide methods to control when intent locks are taken. Intent locks can be acquired either immediately when the transaction is requested or iteratively as needed while the transaction executes. Furthermore, intent locks can be released when the transaction completes or when each intent lock is no longer required for a unit of work.

If the DBMS supports different options for the acquisition and release of intent locks, the parameter will be specified at the transaction or program level.

Lock Escalation

Lock escalation is the process of increasing the lock granularity for a process or program.

If processing causes the DBMS to hold too many locks, lock escalation can occur. *Lock escalation* is the process of increasing the lock granularity for a process or program. When locks are escalated, more data is locked, but fewer actual locks are required. An example of escalating a lock would be moving from page locks to table locks. You can see where this would minimize the number of locks the DBMS needs to track—multiple page locks for a table can be converted into a single lock on the entire table. Of course, this impacts concurrent access because the process locks the entire table, making it inaccessible to other processes.

The DBMS kicks off lock escalation based on preset thresholds. Typically, the DBMS will provide system parameters that can be set to customize the actual manner in which the DBMS escalates locks, or to turn off lock escalation. Also, the DBMS will provide DDL parameters for database objects to indicate on an object-by-object basis whether escalation should occur.

Some DBMSs, such as DB2 and Microsoft SQL Server, provide the capability to escalate locks, whereas others, such as Oracle, do not.

Programming Techniques to Minimize Locking Problems

We have learned that locking is required to ensure data integrity. If application programs are not designed with database locking in mind though, problems can arise. Application developers must understand the impact of locking on the performance and availability of their applications. If locks are held too long, timeouts will make data less available. If applications request locks in a disorganized manner, deadlocks can occur, causing further availability problems.

Standardize the sequence of updates within all programs.

Fortunately, though, there are development techniques that can be applied to minimize locking problems. One such technique is to standardize the sequence of updates within all programs. When the sequence of updates is the same for all programs deadlocks should not occur.

Another programming technique is to save all data modification requests until the end of the transaction. The later modifications occur in a transaction, the shorter lock duration will be. From a logical perspective, it really does not matter where a modification occurs within a transaction, as long as all of the appropriate modifications occur within the same transaction. However, most developers feel more comfortable placing the data modification logic scattered throughout the transaction in a pattern that matches their concept of the processes in the transaction. Grouping modifications such as INSERT, UPDATE, and DELETE statements, and issuing them near the end of the transaction can improve concurrency because resources are locked for shorter durations.

Locking Summary

Database locking is a complex subject with more details than we have covered in this section. Each DBMS performs locking differently, and you will need to study the behavior of each DBMS you use to determine how best to set locking granularity and isolation levels, and to program to minimize timeouts and deadlocks.

Batch Processing

Most of the discussion in this chapter has centered around transaction processing, which is usually assumed to be for online processes. However, many database programs are designed to run as batch jobs with no online interaction required. DBAs must be aware of the special needs of *batch database programs*.

Ensure that data base COMMITs are issued within the program.

The first design concern for batch database programs is to ensure that database COMMITs are issued within the program. Except for very trivial programs that access small amounts of data, database COMMITs should be issued periodically within a batch program to release locks. Failure to do so can cause problems such as a reduction in availability for concurrent programs because a large number of locks are being held, or a large disruption if the batch program aborts because all the database modifications must be rolled back.

Additionally, if a batch program with no COMMITs fails, all of the work that is rolled back must be performed again when the problem is resolved and the batch program is resubmitted for processing. A batch program with COMMITs must be designed for restartability: The batch program must keep track of its progress by recording the last successful COMMIT and including logic to reposition all cursors to that point in the program. When the program is restarted it must check to see if it needs to reposition and, if so, execute the repositioning logic before progressing.

Another problem that occurs frequently with batch database program development is a tendency for developers to think in terms of file processing, rather than database processing. This is especially true for mainframe COBOL programmers who have never worked with database systems. Each developer must be trained in the skills of database programming, including SQL skills, set-at-at-time processing, and database optimization. The responsibility for assuring that developers have these skills quite often falls on the DBA.

Finally, batch programs typically are scheduled to run at predetermined times. The DBA should assist in batch database job scheduling to help minimize the load on the DBMS. Batch jobs that are long running and resource consuming should be scheduled during off-peak online transaction processing hours.

Summary

Application design and development is the job of systems analysts and application programmers. However, the DBA must be involved in the process when programs are being written to access databases. Special skills are required that can be difficult to master. The DBA must first understand these skills and then work to transfer the knowledge to developers. This is a continual job because new programmers are constantly being hired—each with a different level of skill and degree of database experience. Furthermore, DBMS products are constantly changing, resulting in additional development options and features that need to be mastered.

Review

1. Describe what the acronym ACID means and define each component.

2. Under what circumstances should a transaction processing system be considered for database applications?

3. Why is locking required to assure data integrity?

4. Describe the difference between Cursor Stability and REPEATABLE READ isolation levels.

5. Under what circumstance should a UNCOMMITTED READ isolation level be considered?

6. Describe two application design techniques to minimize the impact of locking on application performance.

7. What does "relational closure" mean, and what is its significance on application design?

8. Describe, at a high level, what is required to embed SQL into an application program written in a programming language like C or Visual Basic.

9. What is the difference between a lock timeout and a deadlock?

10. What programming techniques can be used to minimize deadlocks and why?

Bonus Question

Why might the order of database modifications within a transaction impact deadlocks?

Suggested Reading

Bernstein, Philip A., and Eric Newcomer. *Principles of Transaction Processing.* San Francisco, CA: Morgan Kaufmann (1997). ISBN 1-55860-415-4

Carter, John. *Programming in SQL with Oracle, Ingres, and dBase IV.* Englewood Cliffs, NJ: Prentice Hall (1993): ISBN 0-13-014325-1

Date, C. J., with Hugh Darwen. *A Guide to the SQL Standard.* 4th ed. Reading, MA: Addison-Wesley (1997). ISBN 0-201-96426-0

Fronckowiak, John W. *Teach Yourself OLE DB and ADO in 21 Days.* Indianapolis, IN: SAMS Publishing (1997). ISBN 0-672-31083-X

Gray, Jim, and Andreas Reuter. *Transaction Processing: Concepts and Techniques.* San Francisco, CA: Morgan Kaufmann (1993). ISBN 1-55860-190-2

Groff, James R., and Paul N. Weinberg. *LAN Times Guide to SQL.* Berkeley, CA: Osborne/McGraw-Hill (1994). ISBN 0-07-882026-X

Gulutzan, Peter, and Trudy Pelzer. *SQL-99 Complete, Really.* Lawrence, KS: R&D Books (1999). ISBN 0-87930-568-1

Harrington, Jan L. *SQL Clearly Explained.* San Diego, CA: AP Professional (1998). ISBN 0-12-326426-X

Jennings, Roger. *Database Developer's Guide with Visual Basic 6.* Indianapolis, IN: SAMS Publishing (1999). ISBN 0-672-31063-5

Jepson, Brian. *Java Database Programming.* New York, NY: John Wiley & Sons (1997). ISBN 0-471-16518-2

Kline, Kevin, with Daniel Kline. *SQL in a Nutshell.* Sebastopol, CA: O'Reilly (2001). ISBN 1-56592-744-3

Lewis, Philip M., Arthur Bernstein, and Michael Kifer. *Databases and Transaction Processing.* Boston, MA: Addison-Wesley (2002). ISBN 0-201-70872-8

Loosley, Chris, and Frank Douglas. *High-Performance Client/Server.* New York, NY: John Wiley & Sons (1998). ISBN 0-471-16269-8

McClain, Gary. *OLTP Handbook.* New York, NY: McGraw-Hill (1993). ISBN 0-07-044985-6

Melton, Jim. *Understanding SQL's Stored Procedures: A Complete Guide to SQL/PSM.* San Francisco, CA: Morgan Kaufmann (1998). ISBN 1-55860-461-8

Sessions, Roger. *COM+ and the Battle for the Middle Tier.* New York, NY: John Wiley & Sons (2000). ISBN 0-471-31717-9

6

Design Reviews

Decisions made during the database design process and the application development life cycle (ADLC) must be reviewed to ensure correctness. This is the purpose of a design review.

What Is a Design Review?

All aspects of the database and application code are reviewed for efficiency, effectiveness, and accuracy.

Design reviews are an important facet of the ADLC for database applications. It is during the design review that all aspects of the database and application code are reviewed for efficiency, effectiveness, and accuracy. It is imperative that all database applications, regardless of their size, are reviewed to ensure that the application is designed properly, that the coding techniques are cost-effective, and the database can be accessed and modified correctly and efficiently. The design review is an important process for checking the validity of design decisions and correcting errors before applications and databases are promoted to production status.

Multiple design reviews should be conducted over the course of an application's life. For database applications, the DBA must participate in every design review, at every stage. It is imperative that the application be reviewed before, during, and after implementation. Design reviews are critical for ensuring that an application is properly designed to achieve its purpose.

Design reviews address many aspects of the development process and its resulting application. Imposing the design review process on an application exposes it to a thorough review of every underlying component, structure, and nuance of the application. Some of the areas that can be addressed by a design review include

- A validation of the intent and purpose of the application

- An assessment of the logical data model

- An assessment of the physical data model

- A review and analysis of the physical DBMS parameters

- A prediction of SQL performance

- A judgment on the practicality of the programming language techniques deployed

- An analysis of overall performance after production implementation

Subject matter experts, peers, and coworkers should conduct each design review.

A group consisting of subject matter experts and the developer's peers and coworkers should conduct each design review. The DBA usually must act as the focal point for organizing and conducting design reviews. Frankly, if the DBA does not organize design reviews, it is unlikely that any design review will be conducted. In addition, if design reviews are not conducted, the application is more apt to suffer performance and availability problems in a production environment.

Rules of Engagement

All participants should back up their assertions and suggestions with facts, manual references, and experience.

Let's cover the ground rules of a design review before defining each type of review. A design review is conducted by a group of people—each having different backgrounds, skills, expectations, and opinions. When any such group is convened to discuss potential problems and errors, confrontation is unavoidable. Each participant must possess the ability to discuss and reach consensus on issues without turning the review into an unproductive battle or argument. To accomplish this, participants must avoid being combative. Everyone needs to understand that the only goal is to promote the best performing, most usable application possible.

One of the biggest threats to the success of a design review is the possibility that negative criticism will be perceived as a personal attack. If the atmosphere of the review is threatening or the developer perceives it to be so, then the developer is likely to resist contributing to the review or accepting an unbiased critique of the work. To avoid such a scenario, be sure that all participants back up their assertions and suggestions with facts, manual references, and experience. As much as possible, everyone should check his or her emotions at the door.

Design Review Participants

Create formal roles for the design review.

With respect to choosing the design review participants, two guidelines will help to ensure success. The first is to create formal roles for the design review and assign the proper individuals to fulfill those roles. The second is to make sure that participants possess the appropriate skills to actively engage in the design review process.

First, let's discuss the different roles required for a successful design review. Formal roles should include a leader, a scribe, a mediator, and the participants.

The Leader

It is imperative that each design review have only one leader. The leader can change from one design review to the next, but within the scope of a single design review, a single leader must be assigned. The leader's role is multifaceted. The leader

- Acts as a master of ceremonies to keep the review process moving along
- Creates and follows an agenda to ensure that all aspects of the current design review are conducted satisfactorily
- Solicits input from all participants
- Ensures that all participants maintain proper decorum
- Works with the participants before the meeting to ensure that all required documentation will be available
- Addresses other tasks as necessary to ensure a successful design review

The DBA typically acts as the leader of design reviews for applications using a database.

Though it is not mandatory, the DBA typically acts as the leader of design reviews for applications using a database. If the DBA is not the leader, the DBA group must, at a minimum, have the authority to approve the selection of the leader. Sometimes it is a good idea to hire a consultant who has been exposed to more applications at many different sites to lead a design review. Doing so can result in the identification of design flaws that might not be caught otherwise.

The Scribe

The responsibility of the scribe is to capture all points of discussion during the design review. Although the scribe is not an active participant in the design review, a scribe is always required. Failure to record the review can result in loss of vital information from the meeting.

The scribe must be capable of understanding the technical discussion, but need not have a technical position. The scribe could be a member of the development team who has good writing and listening skills. A technically savvy administrative assistant could be another good choice.

The Mediator

The primary role of the mediator is to negotiate settlements when disagreements occur.

The mediator is an optional role, but depending on the project and the dynamics of the design review team, a mediator can be a blessing. The primary role of the mediator is to negotiate settlements when disagreements occur, and given the nature of a design review, disagreements are almost guaranteed. If a disagreement becomes vocal and volatile, the mediator will hear each side of the disagreement and arrive at an equitable decision.

Although a good leader should be able to resolve most disagreements, his or her authority may be compromised by the resentment that can ensue from an intervention. By deferring the most difficult and sensitive decisions to the mediator, the leader can maintain the confidence of the group and keep the design review from breaking down. A technical management representative is the usually the best choice for mediator.

The Participants

Design review participants consist of the other actors with a stake in the project.

Design review participants consist of the other actors with a stake in the project. The participants will differ from project to project, and from one design review to the next. From a high-level perspective, though, the following are the recommended personnel to engage in the design review:

- Application development personnel assigned to this development effort
- Representatives from other applications that are affected by the new application or program
- Data administration representative
- Database administration representative

- Representative end users

- End user management

- IT management for the new application and possibly other impacted applications

- Online support representatives for transaction processing and message queueing systems

- Web support personnel for Internet-enabled applications

- Operational support representatives

- Technical support and systems programming representatives

It is not necessary for each of these participants to be involved in each and every facet of every design review. A single application should be subjected to multiple design reviews—with each review focusing on a particular aspect of the application. The scope of each design review should be determined prior to the scheduling of the review so that only the appropriate participants are invited.

Knowledge and Skills Required

To be considered for a position on a design review team, candidates should be experienced in database development. It is best to form the design review team using participants who possess considerable skills and knowledge. The following criteria should be used to guide the formation of the design review team:

- Strong technical skills: technicians, programmers, and DBAs

- Strong communication skills: all participants

- Good interpersonal skills: all participants

- DBMS fundamentals: all participants to the degree required by their positions

- Background in data modeling and database design: in-depth knowledge for the DA and DBA; good knowledge for programmers and other technicians; some level of knowledge for all other participants

- Strong knowledge of SQL: technicians, programmers, and DBAs

Of course, not every team member will have all of these skills. However, make sure that each member of the design review team is an expert in his or her field of practice. For example, an IT manager may have limited expertise in SQL, but that should not exclude him from the design review team. The manager will contribute from his field of experience and should be chosen based on his exposure to the project and his skills as a manager.

Furthermore, you should strive to maintain the same members of the team throughout the ADLC. Since multiple design reviews are necessary, team member consistency will make design reviews easier because knowledge gained during past design reviews will carry over to subsequent design reviews.

Types of Design Reviews

As previously mentioned, it is best to conduct several design reviews over the course of the ADLC. Multiple design reviews are preferable to a single large design review because it will allow errors and design flaws to be caught earlier in the development process while it is still possible and cost effective to fix the problems. Additionally, it is unreasonable to expect a single design review to be conducted at the end of the development process because too many details will need to be inspected and errors are more likely to fall through the cracks.

The following are the seven basic design review phases for a database application:

- Conceptual design review
- Logical design review
- Physical design review
- Organizational design review
- SQL and application code review
- Pre-implementation design review
- Post-implementation design review

Remember the rendering of the ADLC shown in Figure 1-3? Figure 6-1 points out the relative point within the ADLC where each design review should be conducted.

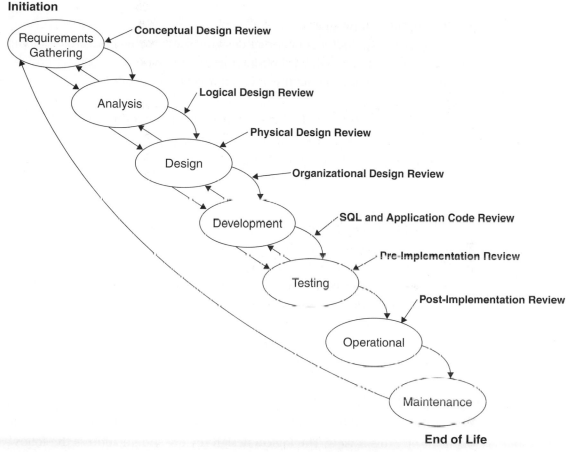

Figure 6-1   *Design reviews in the application development life cycle*

Conceptual Design Review

The conceptual design review validates the concept of the database and application.

The first review to be conducted is the *conceptual design review*. The purpose of this review is to validate the concept of the database and application. The conceptual design review begins with a presentation of an overall statement of purpose and a general overview of the desired functionality to be provided by the application.

The conceptual design review should be conducted as early as possible in the application development lifecycle to determine the overall feasibility of the project. The findings of the conceptual review must verify the purpose of the application and the clarity of the vision for building the databases and supporting application programs.

In order to conduct a conceptual design review a conceptual data model must exist, as well as a high-level design for the application.

Failure to conduct a conceptual design review can result in

- Projects that provide duplicate or inadequate functionality
- Cancellation of projects due to lack of funds, inadequate staffing, poor planning, lack of user participation, or waning management interest
- Projects that run over-budget or take longer to complete than anticipated
- Applications that do not deliver the required features and functionality to support the business

The conceptual design review should have the participation of application development, data administration, and database administration staff; end users; and management representatives from the end user team and IT.

Logical Design Review

The logical design review examines all data elements, descriptions, and relationships.

The *logical design review* follows the conceptual design review. It should be conducted when the first cut of the logical data model has been completed. A thorough review of all data elements, descriptions, and relationships should occur during this review. The logical design review should address the following questions:

- Has the logical data model been thoroughly examined to ensure that all of the required business functionality can be achieved?
- Is the model in (at least) third normal form?
- Have all of the data elements (entities and attributes) required for this application been identified?
- Have the data elements that have been identified been documented accurately?
- Have appropriate data types and accurate lengths been assigned for each attribute?
- Have all of the relationships been defined properly?

The risk of failing to conduct a logical design review is a poorly designed database, which will likely cause data integrity problems. The logical design review helps to ensure that all required data has been identified, designed properly, and fully documented. If changes are made to the logical data model after conducting a logical design review, additional logical design reviews should be scheduled as the project progresses.

Participants in the logical design review should be the same as participated in the conceptual design review. If at all possible, the exact same individuals should attend to maintain a level of consistency from review to review. By having the same participants, less up-front preparation will be required because everyone will already be knowledgeable about the purpose of the application and its high-level conceptual design.

Physical Design Review

The physical design review ensures that all of the proper database parameter settings and other physical design choices have been made.

The *physical design review* comes next—it's the review most often associated with the design review process. In the physical design review, the database is reviewed in detail to ensure that all of the proper database parameter settings and other physical design choices have been made. In addition, the DA and DBA should ensure that a proper translation from logical model to physical database has been made and that all denormalization decisions are formally documented.

The overall operating environment for the application should be described and verified at this stage. The choice of transaction processor and a complete description of the online environment should be provided and verified. An estimation of workload, throughput, and number of concurrent users should be provided and reviewed to ensure that the anticipated requirements can be satisfied. Batch workload should also be reviewed; therefore, a complete description of any batch processes must be provided.

The physical design review may be conducted before all of the SQL that will be used for the application is available. However, general descriptions of all the processes are required to verify the proposed physical database design. Using the process descriptions, the database definitions can be fine-tuned. Furthermore, an initial estimate of whether denormalization could be helpful should be attempted at this point.

Portions of the physical database design may need to be reviewed again as the application development process progresses. Ensuring a valid physical design requires a lot of in-depth attention. As such, the review can be broken into discrete processes that can be repeated as changes are made to the database and the application. For example, as SQL statements are written, indexing requirements will change. As indexes are added, the decision making process should be reviewed to ensure that the indexes are viable for the entire application, not just for a single SQL statement.

Participants in the physical design review should include application development staff, data administration staff, database administration staff, online support representatives, and technical support personnel. If the application or database will affect other applications, or be used by other applications, then it would be wise to include representatives from those areas as well.

Organizational Design Review

The organizational design review gauges the impact of the application on the organization.

Smaller in scope than the physical design review, but no less critical, is the *organizational design review*. This review examines the enterprisewide concerns of the organization with respect to the new application. The following are some common organizational design review questions:

- How does this system interact with other systems in the organization?
- Has the logical data model for this application been integrated with the enterprise data model (if one exists)?
- To what extent can this application share the data of other applications?
- To what extent can other applications share this application's data?
- How will this application integrate with the current production environment in terms of the DBMS resources required?
- Will the implementation of this application cause the batch window to be exceeded?
- Are the requirements of the application such that online response time or data availability are negatively impacted for other users?
- Will the implementation of this application cause the data processing needs of the shop to expand? For example, will more memory, CPU power, or storage be required?

Because the purpose of the organizational design review is to gauge the impact of the application on the organization, all the players listed in the Participants section above should attend this design review. Failure to include everyone could result in missing certain aspects of the application's impact on the organization because of ignorance or oversight.

SQL and Application Code Design Review

The SQL design review is a rigorous review of every SQL statement in the application.

The *SQL design review* is a rigorous review of every SQL statement in the application. Each SQL statement must be reviewed for performance prior to the turnover to production of the application. The review must analyze each statement's access path, the indexes it uses, and possible alternate formulations—resulting in an overall assessment of how it is likely to perform.

Every DBMS provides a command to show the access path that will be used for a SQL statement. Typically the command is called either EXPLAIN or SHOW PLAN, but I will use EXPLAIN as a generic term. Prior to the SQL design review, an EXPLAIN should be run for each SQL statement. It is important that the EXPLAIN command have access to production statistics. The results of the EXPLAIN statement should be analyzed to determine if the most efficient access paths have been chosen.

Furthermore, every program should be reviewed to validate that efficient programming language constructs were used. Although SQL is more likely to be the cause of poor relational performance, it is quite possible to code an inefficient program using COBOL, Visual Basic, C, or whatever language. For example, a very efficiently tuned SQL statement embedded in a loop within a C program might become very inefficient if that loop runs hundreds or thousands of times. Additional application and SQL performance issues are discussed in detail in Chapter 12.

Once again: Every line of code and SQL statement must be reviewed prior to implementation. The SQL and application design review is the appropriate venue for making suggestions for performance improvements prior to moving the application to a production status. Alternate formulations and indexing strategies can be suggested during this review and then tested to determine their impact. If better performance is achieved, the application code, SQL, or database design should be modified.

The application developers and DBA are mandatory participants in the application and SQL design review. Additional participants might include application development managers and perhaps technically savvy end users. In some cases, developers may feel more comfortable while their code is being reviewed if their managers are invited. Such an invitation can make it seem less like the DBA is picking apart months and months of the programmer's hard work. Of course, this decision should be made on a case-by-case basis depending on the developers' comfort level with their management, the personal interaction skills of the DBA, and the skill level of both the DBA and the programmers.

Pre-Implementation Design Review

The preimplementation design review is an overall appraisal of the system components.

A *pre-implementation design review* should be conducted immediately prior to the turning over of the application to production status. This review consists of an overall appraisal of the system components prior to implementation. Each participant must be prepared to discuss the status of any changes required to support the application once it moves to production. Loose ends existing from previous design reviews should be reviewed to verify that necessary modifications were made and tested. A quick, final review of each application component should be performed to make sure that new problems were not introduced as changes were made.

Participants in the pre-implementation design review should include personnel from the application development staff, application development management representatives, database administration staff, online support representatives, and technical support personnel.

Post-Implementation Design Review

A postimplementation design review determines if the application is meeting its objectives.

Finally, we come to the *post-implementation design review*. It is necessary to formally review the application once it has run in the production environment for a while to determine if the application is meeting its objectives, both in performance and in functionality. If any objective is not being met, a plan for addressing the deficiency must be proposed and acted on. Although daily performance monitoring of a new application is a must, it does not preclude the need for a formal post-implementation design review for all new application projects.

Because any portion of the application may be a target for improvement, all the players listed in the Participants section of this chapter may be required to attend the post-implementation design review.

Design Review Output

Output from design reviews should be clear and concise so that any required modifications can be made quickly and correctly.

Output from reviews should be clear and concise so that any required application, SQL, or database modifications can be made quickly and correctly. It is imperative that the scribe captures notes in sufficient detail that a nonattendee can make sense of the discussion. The scribe should edit the notes for grammar and spelling and distribute a copy to all attendees (preferably by e-mail).

An additional result of each design review is a separate list of action items. This list should contain every modification or change discussed during the design review. Each action item should be given a deadline and be assigned to a single person, giving him or her the responsibility to make the change, test its impact, and report the progress back to the entire group.

Summary

By establishing and following a systematic approach to database application design reviews, the likelihood of implementing optimal applications increases. Database development can be very complex. Only by managing and documenting the implementation process can you ensure the creation of successful and useful application systems. The design review process is an efficient way to encourage a rigorous and systematic pre- and post-implementation review of database applications.

Review

1. Name the roles required for each design review.
2. What are the differences between a logical design review and a physical design review?
3. During which type of design review should denormalization be discussed?
4. Why is it important to review application code in addition to reviewing SQL?
5. During which phase of the ADLC should the pre-implementation design review be conducted?
6. During which type of design review should the design be checked for conformance to third normal form?

7. Cite several reasons for including representatives from application development management in design reviews.

8. What output is required of every design review?

9. During which type of design review will the impact of the application on the computing resources of the company be ascertained and analyzed?

10. Why should the DBA lead most of the design reviews?

Suggested Reading

Freedman, Daniel P., and Gerald M. Weinberg. *Handbook of Walkthroughs, Inspections, and Technical Reviews.* New York, NY: Dorset House (1990). ISBN 0-932633-19-6

Ginac, Frank P. *Creating High Performance Software Development Teams.* Upper Saddle River, NJ: Prentice Hall (2000). ISBN 0-13-085083-7

Rothstein, Michael F., and Burt Rosner. *The Professional's Guide to Database Systems Project Management.* New York, NY: John Wiley & Sons (1990). ISBN 0-471-62130-7

7

Database Change Management

Change is the only constant in today's complex business environment.

Although a cliché, it is true that change is the only constant in today's complex business environment. An ever changing market causes businesses to have to continually adapt. Businesses are striving to meet constantly changing customer expectations while trying to sustain revenue growth and profitability at the same time. To keep pace, businesses must constantly update and enhance products and services to meet and exceed the offerings of competitors.

Moreover, the individuals within the business usually find it difficult to deal with change. Change usually implies additional roles and responsibilities that almost inevitably make our job more difficult. Our comfortable little status quo no longer exists. So, we have to change, too—either change aspects of our environment or our approach to doing things. There are many different aspects of managing change, particularly with respect to IT. Each of the following comprises a different facet of the "change management" experience.

- The physical environment or workplace changes to accommodate more employees, fewer employees, or perhaps just different employees with new and different skill sets.

- The organization changes such that "things" like processes or methodology have to adapt to facilitate a quicker pace for product and service delivery.

- The network infrastructure changes to provide support for a growing, and perhaps geographically dispersed, workforce.

- Applications and systems change to perform different processes with existing data or to include more or different types of data.

- The type and structure of data changes, requiring modifications to the underlying database schemata to accommodate the new data.

Many factors conspire to force us into changing our database structures.

Change is inevitable but necessary for business survival and success. Many factors conspire to force us into changing our database structures, including

- Changes to application programs that require additional or modified data elements

- Performance modifications and tweaks to make database applications run faster

- Regulatory changes that mandate storing new types of data, or the same data for longer periods of time

- Changes to business practices, requiring new types of data

- Technological changes that enable databases to store new types of data and more data than ever before

Change will never disappear. Therefore, it is imperative that we have solutions to enable us to better manage these inevitable changes.

Change Management Requirements

To successfully implement effective change management, understanding a set of basic requirements is essential. To ensure success, the following factors need to be incorporated into your change management discipline: proactivity, intelligence, analyses (planning and impact), automation, standardization, reliability, predictability, and quick and efficient delivery.

- *Proactivity.* Proactive change, which can eliminate future problems, is an organization's most valuable type of change. The earlier in the development cycle that required changes are identified and implemented, the lower the overall cost of the change will be.

- *Intelligence*. When implementing a change, every aspect of the change needs to be examined, because it could result in an unanticipated cost to the company. The impact of each change must be examined and incorporated into the change process, because a simple change in one area may cause a complex change in another area. Intelligence in the change management process often requires a thorough analysis that includes an efficient and low-risk implementation plan. True intelligence also requires the development of a contingency plan, should the change or set of changes not perform as projected.

A well-planned change saves time.

- *Planning analysis.* Planning maximizes the effectiveness of change. A well-planned change saves time. It is always easier to do it right the first time than to do it again after the first change proves to be less than effective. An effective organization will have a thorough understanding of the impact of each change before allocating resources to implement the change.

- *Impact analysis.* Comprehensive impact and risk analysis allows the organization to examine the entire problem, and the risk involved, to determine the best course of action. A single change usually can be accomplished in many different ways. However, the impact of each change may be considerably different. Some changes involve more risks: failure, undue difficulty, need for additional changes, downtime, and so on. All considerations are important when determining the best approach to implementing change.

- *Automation.* With limited resources and a growing workload, automating the change process serves to reduce human error and to eliminate more-menial tasks from overburdened staff.

- *Standardization of procedure.* Attrition, job promotions, and job changes require organizations to standardize processes to meet continued productivity levels. An organized and thoroughly documented approach to completing a task reduces the learning curve, as well as the training time.

- *Reliable and predictable process.* When creating any deliverable, a business needs to know that none of the invested effort is wasted. Because time is valuable, a high level of predictability will help to ensure continued success and profitability. Reliability and predictability are key factors in producing a consistently high-quality product.

- *Availability.* Most changes require downtime to implement the change. Applications must come down—the same is true of databases. However, high availability is required of most applications these days, especially for an e-business. This is fast becoming a requirement in the Internet age. Reducing the amount of downtime required to make a change will increase application availability.

- *Quick and efficient delivery.* Consumers demand quick turnaround for most products and services. Profitability is at its best when a product is first to market. Conversely, the cost of slow or inefficient delivery of products can be enormous. So, when implementing change, faster is better. The shorter the duration of an outage to accomplish the change, the quicker the system can be brought to market.

The Change Management Perspective of the DBA

The DBA is the custodian of database changes.

The DBA is the custodian of database changes. However, the DBA is not usually the one to request a change; a programmer, application owner, or business user typically does that. There are times, though, when the DBA will request changes, for example, to address performance reasons or to utilize new features or technologies. At any rate, regardless of who requests the change, the DBA is charged with carrying out the database changes and ensuring that each change is performed successfully and with no impact on the rest of the database.

To effectively make database changes, the DBA needs to consider each of the items discussed in the previous section: proactivity, intelligence, analyses (planning and impact), automation, standardization, reliability, predictability, and quick and efficient delivery. Without a robust, time-tested process that is designed to effect database changes, the DBA will encounter a very difficult job. Why?

Well, today's major DBMS products do not support fast and efficient database structure changes. Each DBMS provides differing levels of support for making changes to its databases, but none easily supports every type of change that might be required. One quick example: Most DBMSs today do not enable a column to be added easily to the middle of an existing row. To accomplish such a task, the DBA must drop the table and recreate it with the new column in the middle. But what about the data? When the table is dropped, the data is gone unless the DBA was wise enough to first unload the data. But what about the indexes on the table? Well, they too are dropped when the table is dropped, so unless the DBA knows this and recreates the indexes too, performance will suffer. The same is true for database security: When the table is dropped, all security for the table is also dropped. And this is but one example of a simple change that becomes difficult to implement and manage.

Adding to this dilemma is the fact that most organizations have at least two, and sometime more, copies of each database. At the very least, a test and production version will exist. But there may be multiple testing environments—for example, to support simultaneous development, quality assurance, unit testing, and integration testing. Each database change will need to be made to each of these copies, as well as, eventually, to the production copy. Furthermore, most organizations have multiple DBMS products, each with varying levels of support for making changes. So, you can see how database change can quickly monopolize a DBA's time.

Types of Changes

Business changes usually necessitate a change to application code or to database structure.

Managing change is a big component of the DBA's job. In fact, if systems and databases could be installed into an environment that never changed, most of the DBA's job would vanish. However, things change. Business changes usually necessitate a change to application code or to database structure. Less obvious business changes also impact the database—for example, when the business grows and more users are added, when additional data is stored, or when transaction volume grows. Additionally, technological changes such as upgrades to the DBMS and changes to hardware components impact the functionality of database software and therefore require DBA involvement.

DBMS Software

As discussed in Chapter 2, the DBA must be prepared to manage the migration to new DBMS versions and releases. The complexity involved in moving from one version of a DBMS to another will depends on the new features and functions supported by the new version. Additional complexity will be introduced if features are removed from the DBMS in a later version, because databases and programs may need to change if the removed features were being used. Furthermore, as functionality is added to, and removed from, the DBMS, the DBA must create the proper policies and procedures for the proper use of each new DBMS feature. This aspect of managing change is a significant component of the DBA's job, as we discussed in depth in Chapter 2.

Hardware Configuration

The DBMS may require hardware upgrades or configuration changes. The DBA will be expected to work in conjunction with the system programmers and administrators responsible for setting up and maintaining the hardware. At times the DBMS may require a different configuration than is commonly used, thereby requiring the DBA to communicate to the SA the reason why a non-standard configuration is required.

Conversely, when hardware changes for other reasons, the DBMS configuration may have to change. Perhaps your organization is changing the disk drives in use with your database server hardware, or maybe adding additional memory to the box. Hardware changes such as these may require changes to database structures and the DBMS configuration. The DBA must be actively engaged with the SA team that configures and maintains the hardware used by the DBMS, and, as discussed earlier, may even have to function as an SA in addition to carrying out his DBA duties.

Logical and Physical Design

When the database changes, the blueprints that define the database must also change.

When the database changes, it is important that the blueprints that define the database also change. This means that you need to keep the conceptual and logical data models synchronized with the physical database. This can be accomplished in several ways.

Organizations adept in data administration may choose to make changes at the conceptual and logical levels first, and then migrate the changes into the physical database. Usually such an approach requires data modeling tools that segregate the logical and physical models. Furthermore, the procedures must facilitate the specification of changes at each level while providing the capability to synchronize the different models—both forward from logical to physical, and backward from physical to logical.

In the absence of robust data modeling tools, the typical approach taken to synchronize models is manual. Whenever the physical database is modified, the DBA must manually update the logical data model (and perhaps the conceptual data model). Such an effort requires a strict approach to change propagation. As with any manual change management scenario, this approach is tedious and error prone. However, it is imperative that the logical model be synchronized with the physical database. Failure to do so invalidates the usefulness of the data model as a blueprint for database development.

Applications

Application changes need to be synchronized with database changes.

Application changes need to be synchronized with database changes; however, this is easier said than done. Whenever changes are made to a physical database structure, application changes usually accompany those changes. For example, simply adding a column to a database table requires application software to populate, modify, and report on the data in the new column.

When the database change is migrated to a production environment, the application change must be migrated as well. Failure to do so will render the database change ineffective. Of course, the DBA could allow the database change to be migrated before the application change to ensure that the database structures are correctly specified. After changing the database in the production environment, the DBA would then inspect the database for accuracy and only then allow the application changes to be migrated.

But the relationship between the database change and the application change is valid. If the application change is backed off, the database change should be backed off, as well. And vice versa. Failure to synchronize changes will likely cause an application error or inefficiency. It is imperative that the DBA understands these relationships and monitors the change management process to ensure that the database and application changes happen in step with one another.

Physical Database Structures

The most complicated type of change for DBAs is making changes to physical database structures.

The most complicated and time consuming type of change for DBAs is planning, analyzing, and implementing changes to physical database structures. But most databases change over time—indeed, the database that remains static once implemented is very rare. So the DBA must be prepared to make changes to the databases under his care. Some changes will be simple to implement, but others are very complex, error prone, and time consuming. The remainder of this chapter discusses how physical database objects can be changed and the problems that DBAs can expect to encounter in the process.

Impact of Change on Database Structures

When the data requirements of your organization change, the databases used to store the data must also change. If the data is not reliable and available, the system does not serve the business—rather, it threatens the health of the business.

So, we need infallible techniques to manage database changes. But even more, we need techniques that are not just fail-safe but also automated, efficient, and easy to use. Unfortunately, today's database systems do not make managing database change particularly easy.

Relational databases are created using *Data Definition Language* (DDL) statements. DDL consists of three SQL verbs: CREATE, DROP, and ALTER. The CREATE statement is used to create a database object initially, and the DROP statement is used to remove a database object from the system. The ALTER statement is used to make changes to database objects.

Not every aspect of a database object can be changed by using the ALTER statement. Some types of changes require the database object to be dropped and recreated with the new parameters. The exact specifications for what can, and cannot, be changed using ALTER differs from DBMS to DBMS.

For example, you can add columns to an existing table using the ALTER statement, but only at the end of the table. In other words, you cannot use ALTER to add a column between two existing columns. Additionally, you cannot remove columns from a table. To add a column anywhere but at the end of the column list, or to remove a column from a table, you must first drop the table and then recreate it with the desired changes. Every DBMS has limitations on what can be changed by using the ALTER statement. Furthermore, not just tables, but most database objects have certain aspects that cannot be changed using ALTER.

The cascading DROP effect complicates the job of changing a database schema.

When making changes to a database requires an object to be dropped and recreated, the DBA must cope with the cascading DROP effect. A *cascading DROP* refers to the effect that occurs when a higher-level database object is dropped: All lower-level database objects are also dropped. (See Figure 7-1 for a depiction of the database object hierarchy.) Thus, if you drop a database, all objects defined in that database are also dropped. The cascading DROP effect complicates the job of changing a database schema.

To understand the complexity involved, let's use an example. Suppose you are working with DB2, and you need to change a segmented tablespace to a partitioned tablespace. To do so, you must drop the segmented tablespace and recreate it as a partitioned tablespace. However, when you drop the segmented tablespace, you are also dropping any tables defined in the tablespace, as well as the table's columns and keys, all indexes defined on those tables, any triggers defined on the tables, any synonyms defined for the table, and all views that access the table. Furthermore, when a database object is dropped, the security information and database statistics are deleted from the system. The DBA must be able to capture all this information prior to dropping the tablespace so that it can be

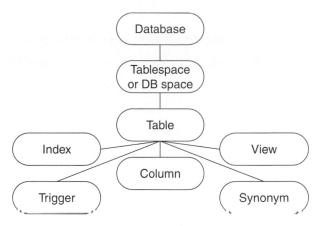

Figure 7-1   *Database object hierarchy*

recreated after the partitioned tablespace is implemented. Capturing the DDL from the system catalog or dictionary and ensuring that the DDL is submitted correctly after the modification can be a tedious, complex, and error-prone process.

The system catalog or data dictionary stores the metadata about each database object. Metadata includes much more than just the physical characteristics of database objects. Additional information about database objects such as security authorizations and database statistics are stored along with the metadata. All of the information required to recreate any database object is readily available if you know where to look for it, and part of the DBA's job is knowing where to look.

A final concern regarding database change: What happens to application program specifications? When database objects that are accessed by a program are dropped, the DBMS may invalidate that program. Depending on the DBMS and the type of program, additional steps may be required to rebind the application to the DBMS after the database objects accessed by the program have been recreated.

The Limitations of ALTER

Many types of database object alteration cannot be performed using the basic SQL ALTER statement; as usual, this varies from DBMS to DBMS and, indeed, from version to version of a single DBMS. However, the actions that are most likely to not be supported by ALTER include

- Changing the name of a database object (however, some objects— usually just tables—can be renamed using the RENAME statement)

- Moving a database object to another database
- Changing the number of tablespace partitions or data files
- Removing a partition from a partitioned tablespace or index
- Moving a table from one tablespace to another
- Rearranging the order of columns in a table
- Changing a column's data type and length
- Removing columns from a table
- Changing the definition of a primary key or a foreign key
- Adding a column to a table that cannot be null
- Adding or removing columns from a view
- Changing the SELECT statement on which the view is based
- Changing the columns of an index
- Changing whether an index is unique
- Changing whether an index is clustering
- Changing whether the index is ascending or descending
- Modifying the contents of a trigger
- Changing a hash key

In some limited cases, it is possible to use ALTER to change the length of certain types of columns. For example, in Oracle you can alter a character column to a larger size, but not to a smaller size. DB2 allows the length of a variable-length column to be changed to a larger size, but not, once again, to a smaller size. Additionally, it may be possible to change a column from one numeric data type to another. However, changes to the data type and length of a column usually require the table to be dropped and recreated with the new data type and length.

Making physical changes to actual database objects is merely one aspect of database change.

Making physical changes to actual database objects is merely one aspect of database change. Myriad tasks require the DBA to modify and migrate database structures. One daunting challenge is to keep test databases synchronized and available for application program testing. The DBA must develop robust procedures for creating new test environments by duplicating a master testing structure. Furthermore, the DBA may need to create scripts to set up the database in a specific way before each test run. Once the scripts are created, they can be turned over to the application developers to run as needed.

Another challenge is recovery from a database change that was improperly specified, or backing off a migration to a prior point in time. These tasks are much more complicated and require knowledge of the database environment both before and after the change or migration.

The preceding discussion justifies the purchase of a database change management tool to streamline and automate database change management. Keep in mind that the list of items above is not exhaustive and that it will differ from DBMS to DBMS. DBA tools exist that manage the change process and enable the DBA to simply point and click to *specify* a change. The tool then handles all of the details of *how* to make the change. Such a tool removes from the shoulders of the DBA the burden of ensuring that a change to a database object does not cause other implicit changes. Database change management tools provide

- A reduction in the amount of time required to specify what needs to change
- A more simple and elegant method of analyzing the impact of database changes
- A reduction in technical knowledge needed to create, alter, and drop database objects
- Ability to track all changes over time
- An increase in application availability by reducing the time it takes to perform changes.

A database change management tool is one of the first tools acquired by most organizations when they implement a database of any size. Such tools reduce the amount of time, effort, and human error involved in managing database changes. The increase in speed and accuracy when using a change management tool provides an immediate return on the investment to the organization. More information on such DBA tools is provided in Chapter 22.

Database Change Scenarios

A DBA will need to make many different types of changes to a database over its lifetime. Some will be simple and easy to implement, other much more difficult and complex.

As discussed earlier, the SQL ALTER statement can be used to make many types of changes to databases. However, other types of changes may require

A simple change is not quite so simple when it has to be propagated to multiple databases on different servers at multiple locations.

additional steps to implement. It is the DBA's job to understand the best way to effect any type of database change. Keep in mind that simple changes often become more difficult in the real world. For example, a simple database change is not quite so simple when it needs to be propagated to multiple databases on different servers at multiple locations.

A single complex change, such as renaming a column, can take hours to implement manually. Changing the name of one column can require hundreds of changes to be scheduled, executed, and verified from development to test to production. Tackling such challenges is the job of the DBA.

Some Database Change Examples

Adding a new column to the end of a table is usually a simple type of change.

Adding a new column to the end of a table is usually a very simple type of change. All that is required to implement the change is an ALTER statement such as:

```
ALTER TABLE Table_1
  ADD COLUMN  new_column   INTEGER   NULL
;
```

The change can be accomplished in a straightforward manner by issuing a single SQL statement. It simply adds a new integer column to Table_1 that can be set to null. However, making the change once is easy, but keeping track of the change is a little more complex. Tracking database changes becomes more difficult as the number of database environments increases and the latency required between changes increases. In other words, a simple change that needs to be populated across twenty distinct database environments over a period of three months becomes more complex because the DBA must be able to track which environment has which changes. Furthermore, there will usually be multiple changes that need to be tracked.

Modifying the amount of free space for a database object is a more difficult change.

A somewhat more difficult change is modifying the amount of free space for a database object. Such a change typically is accomplished by using an ALTER statement, but additional work is required after the ALTER statement has been issued. For example, consider the following ALTER statement:

```
ALTER TABLESPACE TS1
  PCTFREE 25
;
```

This statement changes the free space percentage for the tablespace named TS1 to 25% (from whatever value it was before). However, the additional free space does not magically appear after issuing this ALTER statement. In order to reclaim the free space for the tablespace, the DBA will have to reorganize the tablespace after successfully issuing the ALTER statement. Additional work is also required to ensure that sufficient disk space is available for the increased amount of free space. Therefore, the DBA needs to understand how each parameter that can be altered is actually impacted by the ALTER statement. Furthermore, the DBA needs to understand when additional work is required to fully implement the desired change.

Adding a column to the middle of a table is a very diffi cult change.

Finally, let's examine a very difficult database change: adding a column to the middle of a table. Implementing such a change requires a lot of forethought and planning because it cannot be achieved using a simple ALTER statement. Instead, the table must be dropped and recreated with the new column in the appropriate place. The following steps need to be performed:

1. Retrieve the current definition of the table by querying the system catalog or data dictionary.

2. Retrieve the current definition of any views that specify the table by querying the system catalog or data dictionary.

3. Retrieve the current definition of any indexes defined on the table by querying the system catalog or data dictionary.

4. Retrieve the current definition of any triggers defined on the table by querying the system catalog or data dictionary.

5. Capture all referential constraints for the table and its related tables and determine what their impact will be if the table is dropped (causing all data in the table to be deleted).

6. Retrieve all security authorizations that have been granted for the table by querying the system catalog or data dictionary.

7. Obtain a list of all programs that access the table by using the system catalog, data dictionary, and any other program documentation at your disposal.

8. Unload the data in the table.

9. Drop the table, which in turn drops any views and indexes associated with the table, as well as invalidates any SQL statements against that table in any application programs.

10. Recreate the table with the new column by using the definition obtained from the system catalog.

11. Reload the table, using the unloaded data from step 8.

12. Recreate any referential constraints that may have been dropped.

13. Recreate any triggers, views, and indexes for the table.

14. Recreate the security authorizations captured in step 6.

15. Examine each application program to determine if changes are required for it to continue functioning appropriately.

As you can plainly see, such a complex change requires diligent attention to detail to ensure that it is made correctly. The process is fraught with potential for human error and is very time consuming. In summary, to effectively enact database changes, DBAs must understand all of the intricate relationships between the databases they manage and have a firm understanding of the types of changes supported by the DBMS products they use.

Comparing Database Structures

When managing multiple database environments, the DBA may need to compare one environment to another. Usually changes are made to one database environment, say the test environment, as applications are built and tested. After the changes have been sufficiently tested, they will be promoted to the next environment, perhaps QA, for additional quality assurance testing. In order to appropriately migrate the required changes, the DBA must be able to identify all of the changes that were applied in the test environment.

One approach to change migration is for the DBA to keep records of each change and then duplicate the changes one by one in the new database environment. However, such an approach is likely to be inefficient. The DBA could analyze a series of changes and condense them into a single change or perhaps a smaller group of changes, but once again, this approach is time consuming and error prone.

Use a DBA tool to compare database components.

An alternative approach is to use a DBA tool to compare database components. All of the differences between the environments can be written to a report, or the tool can automatically replicate the structure of the database environment of record to another database environment. To accomplish this, the tool can compare the physical databases using the system catalog, data dictionary, or DDL scripts. A comparison tool is almost a requirement for a very complex database implementation because it is very difficult to track changes from one environment to the next. And the more environments that exist, the more difficult the change management becomes.

If your organization does not have a database change management tool, be sure to save the DDL scripts used to create databases and keep them up-to-date. Every change made to the database must also be made to the DDL scripts. Bear in mind that subsequent ALTER statements can change the database, but will not change the DDL scripts. The DBA will need to either update the DDL scripts either by appending the ALTER statements to the appropriate DDL scripts or by changing the DDL scripts to reflect the effect of the ALTER statement. Both approaches are not ideal: for the first approach, changes may be required that cannot be implemented using ALTER (requiring you to modify the DDL script), and for the second the likelihood of introducing errors is high because a single change is made twice—once to the actual database and once to the saved DDL script.

If you do not store the DDL scripts for your database objects you will need to learn how to query the system catalog or data dictionary tables to recreate the database DDL manually. Both of these approaches, saving DDL and manually recreating DDL, are error prone and time consuming.

Without some type of comparison functionality the DBA must keep track of every single change and accurately record which environments have been changed and which have not. This too is an error-prone process. If the DBA does not keep accurate records then she will have to tediously examine the entire database structure for each database that may have changed using the system catalog or data dictionary in each database environment. Once again, this is also an error-prone and time consuming process.

Requesting Database Changes

The application development team generally requests changes to databases. The DBA is the custodian of the database, but is not the primary user of the database. Business users accessing data by means of application programs and systems tend to be the primary users of databases.

Institute policies governing how changes are to be requested and implemented.

In order to properly coordinate database changes, the DBA group must institute policies and procedures governing how changes are to be requested and implemented. It is not reasonable to expect database changes to be implemented immediately, or even the same day. However, the DBA group should be held accountable to reasonable deadlines for implementing database changes. The DBA must examine each request to determine its impact on the database and on the applications accessing that database. Only after this information is evaluated can the database change be implemented.

An application developer will request database changes only when those changes are viewed as required. In other words, the application has new data usage needs, and the database needs to be changed to support those needs. Of course, not every request will be implemented exactly as it is received. The DBA may need to modify requests based on his knowledge of the DBMS. Any deviations from the request must be discussed with the development team to ensure that they are still workable within the realm of the application.

Standardized Change Requests

Establish standardized forms for implementing database changes.

The DBA group should establish standardized forms for implementing database changes. These forms should be customized for each shop, taking into account things such as environment, development expectations, knowledge, DBA experience, production workload, SLAs, platforms, DBMSs, and naming conventions.

Standardized change request forms prevent miscommunications from occurring during the change management process and, if possible, should be implemented online. The form should include all pertinent information related to each change including, at a minimum, operating system, database subsystem or instance name, object owner, object name, object type, desired change, and date requested. The form should include sign-off boxes for those personnel that are required to sign off on the change before it can be implemented. Required sign-offs should include at least the application development team leader and a senior DBA—but could also include a business unit representative, DA, or SA, depending on the nature of the request.

When the database change is completed, the form should be signed off by the DBA implementing the change and then sent back to the originators. The originators return the form to the DBAs with a requested date for implementing the change in production.

Checking the Checklists

Many DBAs develop checklists that they follow for each type of database change. These checklists may be incorporated into an online change request system so that the DBA can walk through changes as required. Additionally, many application development teams utilize checklists to ensure that every step that is required for an application to run correctly is taken and verified.

Sharing database-change checklists promotes database accuracy.

It is a good practice for the DBA group and the application development teams to share their checklists with each other to verify that each step in the database change and turnover process is completed successfully. Activities performed by DBAs, developers, and technical support personnel often overlap. Allowing the teams to review each other's checklists promotes a better understanding of what steps other units are performing during the change process. Many steps require intricate interaction and communication between the different teams. A formalized review process can correct errors before problems arise.

Communication

DBAs must provide education to development organizations on how to request a database change. They should provide guidance on accessing change request forms, instructions for completing the forms, and guidelines on service expectations.

Unrealistic service expectations can be avoided through education.

Unrealistic service expectations, often the biggest problem, can be avoided through education. For example, if a requester understands that the DBA team could take up to two days to process his request, he will be able to work that delay into his timeline. Clarifying realistic service expectations on an organizational level prevents the DBA team from being deluged by "change this now" requests. These expectations need to be based on solid ground—performance requirements, availability, 24/7 issues, and so on. The DBA must ensure that reasonable timeframes—based on solid requirements—are built into policies and procedures that are readily available to all requesters. Only in this way does change management become a discipline.

Summary

Databases are guaranteed to require changes over the course of their lifetime. The DBA is the custodian of the database and is therefore responsible for implementing change in a responsible manner that ensures the structure, integrity, and reliability of the database. The DBA must create and administer a database change management discipline consisting of tools, procedures, and policies to effect database change appropriately and responsibly.

Review

1. The DBA is usually the initiator of database changes: True or False.

2. Why is it difficult to add a column between two existing columns in an existing table?

3. Name the three types of database comparisons that may be required in a changing database environment.

4. What is the impact of dropping a database?

5. Describe an alternative change method that can be used if your organization does not use a database change management tool.

6. Explain what is meant by the term *cascading DROP*.

7. Why must the DBA understand the relationship between a database change and the application changes that are needed to use the changed data?

8. Your organization does not use a tool to implement changes to database objects. You need to insert a column between the third and fourth column of a table with ten columns. Describe the preparation process you would employ to make such a change.

9. Why would a DBA want to have the capability to compare one database structure to another quickly and simply?

10. If you have to drop an entire table to effect a database change, what other database structures will also be dropped automatically by the DBMS?

8

Data Availability

Availability is the Holy Grail of database administrators. If the data is not available, the applications cannot run. If the applications cannot run, the company is losing business. Therefore, the DBA is responsible for doing everything in his or her power to ensure that databases are kept online and operational. This has been the duty of the DBA since the first days of the database.

It is always prime time somewhere in the world.

However, the need for availability is increasing. The age of the long batch window, where databases can be offline for extended periods to perform nightly processing, is diminishing. Exacerbating this trend is the drive toward e-business. Coupling businesses to the Internet is dramatically altering the way we do business. It has created expectations for businesses to be more connected, more flexible, and importantly, more available. When you integrate the Web with database management, heightened expectations are placed on DBAs to keep databases up and running more smoothly and for longer periods. When your business is online, it never closes. People expect full functionality on Web sites they visit regardless of the time of day. Remember, the Web is worldwide. It may be three o'clock in the morning in New York, but it is always prime time somewhere in the world. Therefore, an e-business must be available and operational 24 hours a day, 7 days a week, 365 days a year (366 for leap years). And if your customer is conducting business at three o'clock in the morning in New York, you better be, too—or you risk losing that customer's business.

On the Web, all of your competitors are just a simple mouse-click away. Studies have shown that if a Web customer does not get the service he wants in three seconds, he will take his business elsewhere. And if he is satisfied by your competitor, chances are he will never come back. So, an e-business site that is down, even for a short period, will result in not just hundreds or thousands of lost hits, but lost business, too. The impact of downtime cannot be measured in the loss of immediate business alone. No, e-business downtime also damages the goodwill and public image of your organization. And once that is lost, it is quite hard to rebuild the trust of your customer and your company's public image.

E-business is not the only driver for increased availability.

Indeed, some pundits use the phrase "Internet time" to describe the rapid rate of change and the rapid development schedules associated with Internet projects. But the DBA can think of Internet time as a simple Boolean equation—there is uptime and there is downtime. During uptime, business is conducted and customers are serviced. During downtime, business is halted and customers are not serviced. So, Internet-age DBAs are sharply focused on maintaining availability.

Of course, e-business is not the only driver for increased availability. Other factors include

- The "fast food" mentality of customers who demand excellent service and demand it "now!"

- "Airline magazine syndrome"—you know, when your manager reads an article from the in-flight magazine during his latest junket that states how a competitor offers round-the-clock service... so your next project has to offer round-the-clock service, too.

- The desire to gain a competitive advantage in the marketplace by offering superior services at a time of the customer's choosing.

- The need to react to competitors who offer better service to customers because of higher data availability.

Defining Availability

Availability is the condition where a given resource can be accessed by its consumers.

Before discussing further the importance of availability, a good definition of availability is needed. After all, we should know what we are talking about. Simply stated, *availability* is the condition where a given resource can be accessed by its consumers. This means that if a database is available, the users of its data—that is, applications, customers, and business users—can access it. Any condition that renders the resource inaccessible causes the opposite of availability: unavailability.

Another definition of *availability* is the percentage of time that a system can be used for productive work. The required availability of an application will vary from organization to organization, within an organization from system to system, and even from user to user.

Database availability and *database performance* are terms that are often confused with each another, and indeed, there are similarities between the two. The major difference lies in the user's ability to access the database. It is possible to access a database suffering from poor performance, but it is not possible to access a database that is unavailable. So, when does poor performance turn into unavailability? If performance suffers to such a great degree that the users of the database cannot perform their job, the database has become, for all intents and purposes, unavailable. Nonetheless, keep in mind that availability and performance *are* different and must be treated by the DBA as separate issues—even though a severe performance problem is a potential availability problem.

Availability comprises four distinct components, which, in combination, assure that systems are running and business can be conducted.

- *Manageability*—the ability to create and maintain an effective environment that delivers service to users

- *Recoverability*—the ability to reestablish service in the event of an error or component failure

- *Reliability*—the ability to deliver service at specified levels for a stated period

- *Serviceability*—the ability to determine the existence of problems, diagnose their cause(s), and repair the problems

All four of these "abilities" impact the overall availability of a system, database, or application.

Increased Availability Requirements

Talk to the DBA group in any major corporation today, and you will hear about an atmosphere of controlled chaos. DBAs are scrambling to address a variety of needs ranging from the design of new applications to keeping business-critical applications operational. All the while, business executives are demanding that

Availability and performance are different and must be treated by the DBA as separate issues.

Availability comprises manageability, recoverability, reliability, and serviceability.

The time available for optimizing performance on business-critical systems and software is shrinking.

DBAs accomplish these tasks with minimal or no downtime. As more businesses demand full-time system availability, and as the cost of downtime increases, the time available for optimizing performance on business-critical systems and software is shrinking.

On the other hand, if routine maintenance procedures are ignored, performance suffers. The DBA is forced to perform a delicate balancing act between the mandate for 24/7 availability and the consequences of deferred system maintenance. The stakes are high, and IT is caught between seemingly contradictory objectives.

The Shrinking Maintenance Window

DBAs need to be increasingly creative to find time to perform routine system maintenance.

All growing businesses accumulate enormous amounts of data. In fact, industry analysts estimate that the average database grew tenfold in size between 1995 and 2000. The largest databases in production at the beginning of the new millennium approached one petabyte in size. At the same time, 24/7 system availability is more a requirement than an exception. DBAs need to be increasingly creative to find time to perform routine system maintenance. High-transaction databases need periodic maintenance and reorganization. With constant use, databases become fragmented, data paths become inefficient, and performance degrades. Data must be put back in an orderly sequence; the gaps created by deletions must be erased. Furthermore, performing defragmentation and reorganization usually results in database downtime.

Decision Support

More and more companies are finding new ways to use core business data for decision support. For example, credit card companies maintain a basic body of information that they use to list purchases and prepare monthly statements. This same information can be used to analyze consumer spending patterns and design promotions that target specific demographic groups and, ultimately, individual consumers. This means that core business data must be replicated across multiple database environments and made available in user-friendly formats. Therefore, the availability of operational data can be negatively impacted by the requirements of decision support users since large amounts of data are not available for update during bulk data unload processing.

Data Warehousing

Just as decision support has expanded the use of operational data, data warehousing has driven overall database growth. Typical data warehouses require

The growth of data warehouses will continue unfettered into the foreseeable future.

the replication of data for use by specific departments or business units. The unloading and loading of external data to operational data stores, and then on to data warehouses and data marts, has increased the number of database utility operations that need to be run and administered. The time taken to propagate data has conversely affected the overall availability window of both the data sources and data targets during unload and load processing. The growth of data warehouses will continue unfettered into the foreseeable future, fed by the informational needs of knowledge workers and the falling cost of storage media.

Full-Time Availability

Just when the latest hardware and software technologies are beginning to bring 24/7 availability within reach, the mandates of the global economy have forced IT departments to reevaluate the situation. Now the buzz phrase is 24/24 availability, because businesses conduct operations in all time zones and data must be available to a new spectrum of users, not all of who work in the same time zone as the operational DBMS.

Airline reservation systems, credit card approval functions, telephone company applications—all must be up and running all day, every day. International finance is one of the best examples of the need for full-time availability. Money never sleeps and the daily flow of Deutschemarks, dollars, pounds, and yen occurs daily and inevitability. So does the global information exchange on which brokers base their buy-and-sell decisions. Large quantities of money are on the line every minute, and downtime simply cannot be tolerated. DBA and IT professionals need techniques that perform maintenance, backup, and recovery in small fractions of the time previously allotted to accomplish these tasks.

Growing IT Complexity

It is hard to find a company of any size that does not operate in a heterogeneous environment.

Any single-vendor system should be clean, precise, and predictable. But today, it is hard to find a company of any size that does not operate in a heterogeneous environment that includes mainframe, midranges, and desktop systems in a client/server infrastructure. As these systems expand in size and functionality, IT staffs must find ways to accommodate operational tuning across a complex, heterogeneous IT environment. This is rarely the seamless process portrayed by the hardware manufacturers. Moreover, the DBMS software itself also can add complexity, with new releases and features being delivered at breakneck speed.

Complexity stems from human factors as well. Downsizing has forced former IT specialists to become generalists. As a result, tasks such as database reorganization—something that used to be simple and straightforward for expert

DBAs—are now complex and lengthy for generalists. Of course, IT is not immune to corporate downsizing; there are now fewer personnel to handle day-to-day computer issues than there were just a few years ago. Finally, mergers and acquisitions force IT staffs to consolidate incompatible systems and data structures.

Cost of Downtime

The cost of downtime varies from company to company. Contingency Planning and Research (a division of Edge Rock Alliance Ltd.) estimates it at approximately $6.5 million per hour at retail brokerage houses. Consult Table 8-1 for additional examples of the estimated hourly cost of downtime by industry. Of course, these numbers are approximations and estimates—each organization needs to determine the actual cost of downtime based on its customers, systems, and business operations.

Outages impact every business.

Some businesses can handle downtime better than others. For brokerages, downtime is a catastrophe. For other businesses that can "get by" using manual systems during an outage, downtime is not as much of a disaster. The truth is, outages impact every business, and any nontrivial amount of downtime will impose a cost on the organization. When estimating the cost of downtime, remember to factor in all of the costs, including

- Lost business during the outage
- Cost of catching up after systems are once again available
- Legal costs of any lawsuits

Table 8-1   *Cost of Downtime*

Type of business	Estimated hourly financial impact of an outage
Retail brokerage	$6.45 million
Credit card sales authorizations	$2.6 million
Home shopping channel	$113,750
Catalog sales centers	$90,000
Airline reservation centers	$89,500
Package shipping service	$28,250
ATM service fees	$14,500

- Impact of reduced stock value (especially for dotcoms that rely on computerized systems for all of their business)

Additionally, downtime can negatively impact a company's image. In this day and age an outage of any length that impacts business, particularly e-business, will be reported by the press—and if the story is big enough, not just the computer press but the business press as well. Let's face it, bad news travels fast. Recovering from negative publicity can be a difficult, if not impossible, task.

Sometimes companies are unwilling to spend money on software and services to improve availability because they do not have an understanding of the true cost of downtime for their business. One line of thought goes something like this: "I know our systems may go down, but the chance of it impacting us is really small, so why should we incur any costs to prevent outages?" Such thinking, however, can be changed when all of the cost and risk factors of downtime are known and understood.

Failure to prepare an estimate of the cost of downtime will make it more difficult to cost-justify the measures a DBA needs to take to ensure data availability.

How Much Availability Is Enough?

Availability is traditionally discussed in terms of the percentage of total time that a service needs to be up. For example, a system with 99% availability will be up and running 99% of the time and down, or unavailable, 1% of the time. Another term used to define availability is MTBF, or mean time between failure. More accurately, MTBF is a better descriptor of reliability than availability. However, reliability has a definite impact on availability. In general, the more reliable the system the more available it will be.

In this Internet age, the push is on to provide never-ending uptime.

So, just how much availability is enough? In this Internet age, the push is on to provide never-ending uptime, 365 days a year, 24 hours a day. At 60 minutes an hour that mean 525,600 minutes of uptime a year. Clearly to achieve 100% availability is a laudable goal, but just as clearly an unreasonable one. The term *five nines* is often used to describe highly available systems. Meaning 99.999% uptime, *five nines* describes what is essentially 100% availability, but with the understanding that some downtime is unavoidable (see Table 8-2).

Even though 100% availability is not reasonable, some systems are achieving availability approaching five nines. DBAs can take measures to design databases and build systems that are created to achieve high availability. However, just because high availability can be built into a system does not mean that every

Table 8-2   *Availability vs. Downtime*

Availability	Approximate downtime per year	
	In minutes	In hours
99.999%	5 minutes	.08 hours
99.99%	53 minutes	.88 hours
99.95%	262 minutes	4.37 hours
99.9%	526 minutes	8.77 hours
99.8%	1,052 minutes	17.5 hours
99.5%	2,628 minutes	43.8 hours
99%	5,256 minutes	87.6 hours
98%	10,512 minutes	175.2 hours (or 7.3 days)

system should be built with a high-availability design. That is so because a highly available system can cost many times more than a traditional system designed with unavailability built into it. The DBA needs to negotiate with the end users and clearly explain the costs associated with a highly available system.

Whenever high availability is a goal for a new system, database, or application, careful analysis is required to determine how much downtime users can really tolerate, and what the impact of an outage would be. High availability is an alluring requirement, and end users will typically request as much as they think they can get. As a DBA, your job is to investigate the reality of the requirement.

The amount of availability that should be built into the database environment will be based on cost. How much availability can the application owner afford? That is the ultimate question. Although it may be possible to achieve high availability, it may not be cost-effective, given the nature of the application and the budget available to support it. The DBA needs to be proactive in working with the application owner to make sure the cost aspect of availability is fully understood by the application owner.

Availability Problems

Because the focus of this book is on database administration, it would be fair to assume that DBAs must manage the availability of the databases under their control. Although this is true, it is an incomplete definition of the DBA's duties with regard to availability. To further understand why this is so, let's first examine all of the potential causes of data unavailability.

Loss of the Data Center

Quite obviously, data will not be available if the data center is lost due to a natural disaster or some other type of catastrophe. Whether the disaster is small from a business perspective and impacts only the computing resources of the business or whether it is large and impacts an entire building or the entire organization, losing the computer means losing the database and any data it contains.

To restore availability in a disaster situation usually requires recreating the database environment (and perhaps much more) at a remote location. Preparing for such a scenario is covered in detail in Chapter 16.

Losing the data center is the worst type of availability problem a DBA could encounter.

From an availability perspective, losing the data center is the worst type of availability problem the DBA could ever encounter. Even after the data and databases have been restored at the remote location, serious availability issues will linger. For example, probably all of the data will not be up-to-date, which may require the DBA and the users to recreate data before allowing general access to the databases. Additionally, ensuring that users have the proper connections to the new location may increase the outage, and problems with an unfamiliar setup can cause subsequent outages. Planning for disasters and developing a good disaster plan will minimize such problems.

Network Problems

If a database server is on a single network switch and that switch incurs an outage, the database will be unavailable. Consider implementing redundant network switches to prevent such outages.

Loss of network access also can cause a database outage. Such problems are usually caused by malfunctioning hardware, such as the network card in the database server. It is wise to have spare networking hardware available for immediate replacement in case such a problem occurs.

However, not all network problems are hardware problems. Installing a new version of the networking software or specifying inaccurate network addresses can cause database outages. The DBA is not a networking expert and cannot be expected to resolve all types of network problems; however, the DBA should be able to recognize when a problem is caused by the network rather than the DBMS, the application, or some other piece of hardware or software used by database applications.

The DBA should build a good working relationship with the networking specialists in his or her organization. When networking problems occur, the DBA can consult with the network specialists right away and ideally learn something from the experience of working with them.

Loss of the Server Hardware

At a basic level, the database server hardware consists of the CPU, the memory, and the disk subsystems holding the databases. Let's examine how the loss of any or all of these components impacts database availability.

Obviously, if the CPU is damaged or becomes unavailable for any reason, the database also will not be available. This is true even if the CPU is the only piece of the database server that is lost. Even if system memory and the disk subsystem remain intact, the database will be inaccessible because the CPU drives all computer processes. However, the database files should remain usable and could possibly be connected to another CPU to bring the database back online.

To avoid outages due to CPU failure, consider using hardware *cluster failover* techniques. When using cluster failover, the loss of a single server causes the system to process on another node of the cluster. The data need not be moved, and failover is automatic.

Another approach is to use a standby system: A copy of the database logs produced on the primary server is shipped to the secondary server, or data from the primary server is replicated to the secondary server. An alternate approach is to keep a second server configured identically to the primary one so that the drives can be pulled out of the primary server and simply inserted into the secondary server.

Any such rapid failover approach will depend on the type of hardware you are using, the ability of the hardware to participate in certain failover techniques, and the cost associated with the technique. Refer to the sidebar "Oracle Standby Database Options" for one approach to database failover.

If system memory fails, the database may or may not be available. If all system memory fails, any database on the system will be unavailable because memory is required for a relational database system to operate. To resolve this situation you will need to replace the failing RAM chips or modules. However, the database may remain available when only some of the system memory fails, although it is likely that performance will suffer. Once again, replacing the faulty memory components should resolve the problem.

If the entire database server is lost or damaged, the failure will be more difficult to address. Loss of an entire server implies that the CPU, memory, and disk subsystem are unavailable. Once again, in such a situation the databases on the server also will be unavailable. If the entire server platform fails, the database will need to be recreated. It is not safe to assume that the data on the disks can be accessed or would be valid even if it could be accessed. The entire database system, including the configuration, connections, and data, would need to be rebuilt. Data would be as accurate and up-to-date as the last database log that is available for the system. Database files would need to be recovered from backup copies, and the changes on the database log reapplied. For more information on database backup and recovery, refer to Chapter 15.

Losing an entire database server is rare if precautions are taken.

Losing an entire database server is rare if precautions are taken, but it is insufficient simply to purchase a reliable server and forget about downtime. Hardware goes bad regardless of built-in ruggedness and availability features. Power spikes, power outages, and human error are the most likely causes of such server failure. The DBA should always ensure that redundant power supplies and UPS systems protect the database server against sudden power loss—and that proper precautions are taken such that any type of outage incurred due to server hardware failure is minimized.

Disk-Related Outages

Database availability is particularly vulnerable to disk failures.

Because databases rely on physical disk structures to actually store the data, database availability is particularly vulnerable to disk failures. Of course, the degree of database unavailability depends on the type of disk system and the type of outage the disk system has suffered. Disk drives fail for numerous reasons: The physical drive mechanism may fail, the controller could fail, or perhaps a connecting wire has loosened.

One of the simplest database implementations is to store the database files on a local disk subsystem attached directly to the database server. Obviously, if the local disk subsystem fails, the database becomes unavailable. Recovery from such a failure typically requires the server to be reconfigured with a new disk subsystem to which the database is restored. Another recovery method is to bring up an entirely new database server and restore the database there. Neither of these options is required if the failing disk subsystem can be fixed.

If you need to restore the database, the DBA can recover the data using backup copies of the database files and logs. RAID disk systems can help to

Oracle Standby Database Options

As of Version V7.3, Oracle supports the ability to create standby databases. A *standby database* is a copy of a functioning database that is kept ready for use in case the original database incurs an outage. Typically, the original database is referred to as the primary, or source, database, and the standby database is referred to as the secondary, or target, database.

It works like this: The transactions applied to the primary database are applied to the standby database using the redo logs of the primary database. When Oracle archives the redo logs, the archived logs are sent to the standby database server and applied. Therefore, the standby database will always be a little less current than the primary database.

If the primary database suffers an outage, the DBA can switch to the standby database. This is done by taking the standby database out of recovery mode, applying all archived redo logs, and then, if possible, applying the transactions from the current redo log. The standby database is then switched to become the primary database. When the original primary database is repaired, it becomes the new standby database.

Oracle also supports standby instances and standby tables when different degrees of availability are required. Of course, there are more implementation details and specifics that an Oracle DBA needs to understand before implementing standby databases. Such implementation-specific details are beyond the scope of this book and the reader is directed to the Oracle product documentation for details.

Keep in mind, though, that the implementation of a standby database does not eliminate the need to make backup copies of either the primary or secondary databases. Nevertheless, standby Oracle databases can help to increase the level of availability in the event of unplanned outages.

minimize outages as well because multiple disk drives must fail before an outage occurs. Chapter 17 provides further details on RAID storage.

Another scenario is a database stored on a storage area network (SAN). A SAN is a grouping of networked disk devices. If the SAN fails, the database will likely become unavailable. SAN failure can occur if multiple disk drives within the network fail, the SAN connections fail, or a power loss occurs.

A failover system, such as a standby database, can help to minimize the outages associated with disk-related failures. With a standby database, the only data likely to be lost because of a disk failure is from uncommitted transactions at the time of the failure.

Operating System Failure

Data will not be available during an OS failure or outage, even if all of the server hardware is operational.

Not all database availability problems are caused by hardware problems. Software also can be the culprit. For example, data will not be available during an operating system (OS) failure or outage, even if all of the server hardware is operational. Typical causes of operating system outages include general OS instability due to inherent bugs, problems encountered when upgrading an OS version, or problems with patches applied to the operating system.

When an OS failure occurs, the only viable options for restoring data availability are to fix the OS problem or to restore the database on another server with a functional operating system. Once again, a failover system can be used to minimize downtime caused by a software failure.

DBMS Software Failure

If the DBMS is not operational, the data in its databases cannot be accessed

Similar to the failure of an operating system, a failure in the DBMS software will cause unavailability. If the DBMS is not operational, the data in its databases cannot be accessed. DBMS failure occurs for similar reasons to those that cause an OS to fail: general DBMS instability due to inherent bugs, problems encountered when upgrading to a new version of the DBMS, or problems when patches are applied to the DBMS software. The DBMS may also fail when resources it needs to operate are not available—such as startup parameters, certain system files, and memory structures. For example, if the database log file is corrupted or missing, the DBMS will not allow data to be modified.

In short, the DBMS will fail when its software has bugs or it cannot gain control of the resources it needs to operate correctly.

Application Problems

Application software also can cause availability problems. If the application is the only way that end users can access data, a data unavailability problem arises when the application fails. An application software failure is unlikely to cause a database outage, but an operational database means little if the users can't use their usual programs to access the data. The DBA and other sophisticated users will be able to access data in the database using alternative methods such as interactive SQL or query tools.

Software bugs and glitches or the loss of program execution modules or libraries can cause application outages. Thorough program testing and quality assurance procedures can minimize the occurrence of application outages.

Security and Authorization Problems

Security-related problems are another cause of database unavailability. This type of problem is caused by improper use or administration of the database. Before data can be accessed, either directly by an end user or by means of a program, authorization must be granted—typically by the DBA or security administrator. If, for any reason, the requesting agent does not have current authorization to access the database, the data will be unavailable to the requester. Security-related problems usually occur immediately after an application goes into production or when a new user attempts to use the system but has yet to receive permission. DBA error can also cause security-related problems: If the DBA accidentally overwrites or removes valid authorizations from the DBMS, valid users will not be able to access data.

Make sure that proper security and authorization procedures are followed at your site.

To avoid security-related problems, make sure that proper security and authorization procedures are followed at your site and use extra caution when changing database security. More information on this topic is provided in Chapter 14.

Corruption of Data

Corrupt data can cause unavailability.

Corrupt data can cause unavailability. Even if the hardware and system software is intact, a database can become unavailable because its contents are inaccurate. Business decisions based on faulty or corrupt data can negatively impact the business. Corrupt data comes from many sources: application program bugs, DBMS software bugs, bad database design, or user error. Old data also can be faulty if newer data was subjected to more rigorous quality and edit checking.

If a sufficient amount of the data becomes corrupt, the DBA will need to take the database offline. Most DBMS systems provide commands to do this. If the database is not taken offline, not only will bad business decisions be made but the data may become more corrupt and processes that use the data may corrupt other, related data. The sooner the DBA takes action to make the data unavailable, the less damage that will ensue. Needless to say, taking a database offline equals lost business.

When data is corrupted, the DBA must work with the application specialists to identify exactly which data is inaccurate and to develop a plan to correct the data. Furthermore, the team must identify the cause of the corruption and take action to correct it. This very time consuming task requires a significant amount of effort.

After identifying the corrupt data elements, the DBA and application specialists may be able to restore access to the unaffected portion of the database while the bad data is cleansed. However, the database should not be brought back online for update processes until the process that was corrupting the data has been identified and corrected.

A different type of availability problem can be caused when data transmissions fail. If users rely on the data in the database to be accurate and up-to-date, a failed data feed can render the database useless, even if there is accurate data in the database, because it will be impossible to determine which data is up-to-date and which is not. Such a failure is similar to data corruption in that the data exists but is not usable. Correcting such problems, though, is usually many times easier than correcting invalid data. At any rate, the DBA must work with the network technicians and SAs to identify and correct data transmission failures. Once the feed is available, the DBA needs to load the new data into the database quickly to resolve the availability problem.

Loss of Database Objects

Inadvertently dropping a database object is another cause of unavailability.

Inadvertently dropping a database object is yet another cause of unavailability. When a tablespace or table is dropped, the data is no longer accessible. The DBA will have to run scripts to recreate the objects (including any related objects that were dropped), reapply any referential constraints, rebuild authorizations, and then reload the data, which may physically still reside on the disk device. Some DBMS products and add-on tools facilitate easy recovery of that data. If such techniques are not available, the data will need to be recovered from backup files and archive logs.

If an index is dropped, the data will be accessible but performance will usually suffer. If performance is bad enough, the user may experience the equivalent of an unavailable database. For example, consider a process that returns a single row from a multimillion-row table. If an index is used, access is rapid because the index is read using a few I/O operations and then a direct pointer to the table data is used to perform a single I/O (usually) to read the data. Without the index, the DBMS will have to scan all the multimillion rows to return the single requested row—and that can take hours, if not days, depending on the DBMS, hardware, and system environment.

Dropping a view will cause availability problems for those users and processes that rely on the view for access to the database. Dropping a view does not delete any data from the database; it simply removes the view definition from the system. However, if a user accesses the database only by means of the view, removing the view results in database unavailability for that user. To rectify the situation, the DBA will need to recreate the view, reapply the view authorizations, and possibly rebind application packages or plans (depending on the DBMS and how that DBMS is being used).

Dropping database objects in error usually is the result of simple human error on the part of a DBA. However, it may also result when inappropriate or unskilled individuals are granted DBA-like authority on the database. You can minimize inadvertent dropping of database objects by creating and ensuring appropriate database security and providing in-depth training for DBAs. Third-party tools are available that automate the restoration of dropped database objects.

Loss of Data

Accidental mass deletes, application program bugs, or even malicious attacks can all cause data loss.

It is possible for data to be unavailable because it no longer exists, which can occur if data is deleted or written over erroneously. Accidental mass deletes, application program bugs, or even malicious attacks can all cause data loss.

When data is deleted in error, the DBA may need to recover the database to a point in time before the data was deleted. This can be accomplished using the RECOVER or RESTORE function of the DBMS in use. The DBA reviews the transaction logs to determine when the error occurred and then restores the data to the point in time just before the error. Analyzing and interpreting the contents of a database transaction log can be a difficult proposition, but there are third-party tools on the market that simplify the task.

If you are using a standby database, there is a slight possibility that you can avoid an outage when data is lost. If there is a sufficient delay in the process that ships the log to the secondary database, the error may not yet have been introduced to the standby database. In which case, you can switch the processing to the secondary database and correct the primary offline.

Data Replication and Propagation Failures

Many databases participate in replication and propagation processes to synchronize data that resides in separate databases. If a replication or propagation task fails, the data will still be accessible, but it may not be as current as the users expect it to be.

There are really two scenarios for replication and propagation failure: one for databases that participate as a subscriber and another for databases that participate as a publisher. Subscribers receive replicated or propagated data from publishers. It is possible that data in the subscriber database will not be up-to-date because the publisher fails to replicate or propagate changes. Such problems can occur for many reasons, including connectivity problems, software failures, or scheduling errors. At any rate, availability problems will result if the data is not up-to-date in the subscriber database.

A second type of problem can occur with the publishing database. If the publishing task fails, the publisher will be up-to-date, but once the replication or propagation is fixed and the service is reinitiated, performance may suffer as the publisher attempts to catch up by sending large amounts of data to the subscriber. This, too, can cause availability problems if the performance degradation is severe enough. Regardless of the scenarios, the DBA needs to develop procedures to detect replication and propagation outages and methods to rapidly restore the replication or propagation process.

Severe Performance Problems

Poor perform ance can make the database unusable.

A severe performance problem can cause unavailability. Even if the database is technically available—with accurate data and running on operational hardware—poor performance can make the database unusable. Any number of problems can cause poor performance, including damaged indexes, improperly defined indexes, data growth, additional users, out-of-data database statistics, and locking problems. The end user does not care what the reason is—she just wants her applications to work. Therefore, even though a performance problem is not technically the same as an availability problem, the DBA must treat it as such if the problem is severe enough to cripple end users' ability to access data.

For more information on monitoring, tuning, and managing database performance refer to Chapters 9 through 12.

Recovery Issues

Your organization's database backup and recovery strategy will have an impact on the availability of your database systems. There are multiple techniques and methods for backing up and recovering databases. Some techniques, while more costly, can enhance availability by recovering data more rapidly.

It is imperative that the DBA team creates an appropriate recovery strategy for each database object. For data with high availability requirements, the backup and recovery strategy should provide the shortest mean time to recover. When it is imperative that the database environment be recovered as quickly as possible after a database crash, using the most effective backup and recovery techniques is critical. Factors that impact recoverability and reinstating availability include operating system configuration, hardware architecture design, database features, backup frequency, and recovery procedures and practices.

Refer to Chapter 15 for in-depth coverage of database backup and recovery practices, as well as procedures for improving database availability.

DBA Mistakes

One of the biggest causes of database downtime is human error.

One of the biggest causes of database downtime is human error. In fact, one major DBMS vendor states that 70% of the calls they receive for database outages are the result of DBA mistakes. While there is nothing you can do to guarantee that mistakes will not be made, proper DBA training and tools can minimize mistakes.

Be sure that all DBAs have received proper training before giving them responsibility for critical-production database systems. Training should consist of both course material (either instructor-led or computer-based training) and on-the-job experience. A DBA's first administration experience should always be with a test system—never with production data.

Additionally, third-party tools can greatly diminish the effort required to keep databases up and running. Database performance monitors can be used to immediately notify DBAs of outages. Simple problems such as "out of space" conditions can be eliminated by proactive performance tools because they can be set up to warn about a potential problem before the problem occurs. The DBA can take corrective action when notified, and a potentially devastating problem that would cause an outage can be averted.

Some database performance tools provide proactive triggers that can be set up to automatically correct problems as they occur. Other DBA tools, such as recovery managers and advanced reorganization tools, can be used to fix problems rapidly when they are encountered. More information on the vast array of available DBA tools can be found in Chapter 22.

Outages: Planned and Unplanned

Most downtime actually is caused by planned outages.

When discussing outages and downtime, many technicians immediately think of unplanned outages. Human error, software bugs and glitches, and hardware failures cause unplanned outages. However, most downtime actually is caused by planned outages. (See Figure 8-1.) Planned outages are caused by regularly

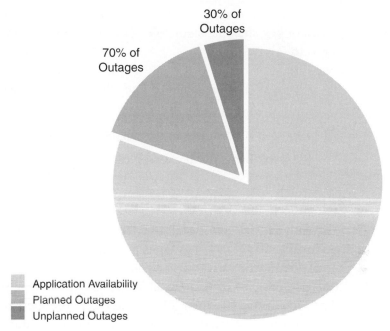

30% of
Outages

70% of
Outages

■ Application Availability
■ Planned Outages
■ Unplanned Outages

Figure 8-1   *Planned and unplanned outages*

scheduled system and database maintenance tasks that require the database to
be offline—for example, database reorganization or changes.

Planned outages represent as much as 70% of downtime; unplanned outages represent the other 30%. Furthermore, studies show that as much as 50%
of unplanned downtime is due to problems encountered during planned
downtime. Therefore, if the majority of outages are caused by planned actions,
it makes sense that DBAs should concentrate more effort on developing techniques to avoid outages during planned database changes and maintenance
activities. It's a given that DBAs need to prepare for the inevitability of downtime due to unplanned outages. However, because planned outages are actually
a greater risk to availability, the DBA can have a more beneficial impact by
developing techniques to reduce them.

Ensuring Availability

Now that we have established that life is challenging for today's DBAs, we will
shift our focus to some techniques that help promote higher availability. Faced
with shrinking budgets and resources, and an ever-increasing volume of data to

manage, IT organizations need to evaluate their critical needs and implement a series of key strategic steps to ensure availability. Good strategy could include steps to

- Perform routine maintenance while systems remain operational.
- Automate DBA functions.
- Exploit the features of the DBMS that promote availability.
- Exploit hardware technologies.

Perform Routine Maintenance While Systems Remain Operational

Utilize the functionality of nondisruptive database utilities.

To address the need for performance optimization while trying to get the most out of smaller IT staffs and budgets, products that simplify and automate maintenance functions are key. DBAs need tools that reduce maintenance time from hours to minutes or none at all, while allowing users continued access to the data they need to do their jobs. Some DBMS products provide built-in features to perform some maintenance tasks while the database is available. If the DBMS does not provide native support, tools are available from ISVs that provide additional database availability. The key is to utilize the functionality of nondisruptive database utilities.

A *nondisruptive utility* is a task that provides both update and read access to a database during execution of database maintenance—and does so without a loss of data integrity. Considerations for deployment of nondisruptive utilities are the number and types of resources needed to perform nondisruptive operations. In general, native database utilities use considerably more CPU and I/O resources than ISV utility solutions, but the ISV utilities can be costly. The types of nondisruptive utilities that are needed most include

- Database reorganization, to maintain performance
- Database backup, to ensure data is available for recovery in the event of application or hardware failure, in addition to disaster recovery preparedness
- Database recovery solutions that can apply recovered data without requiring an outage
- Unloading and loading processes for moving data between source data and operational data stores for decision support systems and data warehouses

- Statistics gathering utilities that can analyze data characteristics and record statistics for use by the database optimizer
- Integrity-checking utilities for both referential integrity and structural data integrity

One example is online database reorganization. Typically, an online REORG is performed by making a duplicate copy of the data and reorganizing the duplicate. Read and write access continues on the original data. When the reorganization of the shadow copy is complete, the REORG process uses the database log to capture the data modifications performed on the original data and applies them to the duplicate. This catching-up process is iterative and may need to be performed multiple times. When the shadow copy has caught up to the original copy, the data sets are switched: The copy becomes the original and the original can be deleted. In this manner, DBAs can reorganize databases with minimal impact to availability. Database reorganization is covered in more depth in Chapter 11.

Most database maintenance tasks impact availability.

But remember, most database maintenance tasks impact availability. Making backups of data, recovering data, checking data for integrity violations, capturing database statistics, and loading new data into a database all can adversely impact availability. Tools that work in conjunction with modern storage devices to minimize or eliminate downtime also are quite useful to maintain databases while they remain online and operational. Some storage devices can make rapid snapshots of files. When database maintenance tasks can take advantage of this technique, outages can be reduced from minutes or hours to seconds.

Making changes to databases can be a major threat to availability. The impact to availability depends on the type of change and how the DBMS implements that change. When simple changes can be made using an ALTER statement, availability, though impacted, is less of a problem because this type of change can be made quickly. Changes to data objects have a greater impact on availability. The DBMS will often need to make the data unavailable as the structural definition of the database object is being changed. As the type of change becomes more complex, the impact to availability becomes greater. Certain changes require objects to be dropped and data to be deleted. Obviously, such as change causes an outage. The longer it takes to make the change, the greater the outage becomes. Using high-speed LOAD and UNLOAD utilities can shrink the duration of the outage. Automating the change, discussed next, can further diminish unavailability. Additional details of implementing database changes can be found in Chapter 7.

Automate DBA Functions

Building more automation into DBA procedures can increase overall database and application availability. When properly created, an automated task will fail less frequently than a manual task. Humans make mistakes. Computers do not make mistakes (unless a human programs them improperly). So, the more complex the task, the more it can benefit from automation.

Automation of changes can improve availability.

Implementing database changes is a complex task. It stands to reason, therefore, that the automation of changes can improve availability. By using an automated DBA tool that understands the DBMS and how to make changes to the database objects, the potential for human error is reduced. Furthermore, the time it takes for a DBA to manually generate change scripts is many times greater than the time it takes a change management tool to generate change scripts. In addition, the tool is unlikely to make errors. So, by automating database changes, less time is required to analyze the requested changes, develop the scripts to make the changes, and to run the scripts to actually change the database. Overall, an automated change process is a boon to availability.

Another task that benefits from automation is database backup and recovery. To ensure that a company can retrieve its data as quickly as possible after an outage or disaster, preplanning is necessary. Taking a proactive approach to backup and recovery management can mean the difference between a minimal outage with no data loss and a situation from which a business can never recover. Most database systems and applications provide little in the way of automated backup and recovery, nor do they provide functions that enable proactive recovery planning. DBAs need products that allow for frequent backups that exert minimal impact on the online system. An additional requirement of backup and recovery software is extremely fast recovery of data in a sequence directly related to the criticality of the business application the data supports. Once it becomes obvious that a recovery is needed to resolve an outage, the DBA needs to ensure the proper recovery of each database object by using the backups and database logs at his disposal. This requires knowledge of the DBMS, the application, and the environment. Add-on products are available that can assist in automating recovery in a crisis situation by analyzing the situation and building the appropriate recovery scripts that will bring the system back in the shortest period of time. For an in-depth discussion of database backup and recovery, consult Chapters 15 and 16.

Exploit High-Availability Features

If the DBMS is engineered to work with clustering and parallel technology, be sure to design databases that work well with that technology. More and more DBMS vendors are aligning their software with the capabilities of modern hardware and operating systems.

Most DBMS vendors have made additional availability features a priority due to the burgeoning need for Internet and Web support in database management systems and applications. Each new DBMS release brings additional availability options and features that can be exploited to enhance uptime and availability. Two obvious examples involve utilities and database system parameters. Running utilities and changing system parameters were tasks that traditionally required an outage. In many cases, running utilities required the database object that was being maintained to be taken offline. Similarly, the entire DBMS had to be taken down to change a system parameter. However, the DBMS vendors are attacking these foes of availability. Many newer DBMS versions provide techniques to change system parameters without bringing down the DBMS (for example, DB2 recently introduced the SET SYSPARM command). DBAs should reexamine old tasks that required database unavailability to see if these tasks can be redesigned to be performed without taking databases or the DBMS offline.

Exploit Clustering Technology

Clustering is an option for increasing the reliability of servers. A *cluster*, quite simply, is a group of interconnected servers. The actual implementation of a server cluster can range from computers that share storage to groups of servers that can redistribute their workload from one to another with the help of special software.

Systems can be kept online and available by adding more servers.

A big advantage of clustering is the ability to increase computing power by adding another server, or node, to the cluster. When throughput increases due to expanding business or publicity, systems can be kept online and available by adding more servers.

Another advantage is reliability. Some clusters are implemented with failover software that can reallocate the workload of one server to another when a server fails. This added reliability minimizes downtime and enhances availability. Each node in the cluster remains in contact with the others. When a node falls out of contact, the cluster recognizes the failure and initiates the failover process.

Clusters can be configured to failover in different ways. For example, when a node fails, failover can direct that processing to another node in a different location. Some configurations have an extra node in the cluster that is usually idle. When failover occurs, the idle node takes over and the cluster capacity isn't compromised. Furthermore, failover can spread the work out over the other existing nodes based on capacity and throughput.

Clustering can enhance availability because failing nodes can be removed from the cluster without an outage. When the node becomes operational, it can rejoin the cluster. This may or may not require an outage, depending on the clustering implementation.

Given all these advantages, why wouldn't every IT organization choose a clustering configuration? Of course, the primary reason is cost. A cluster requires multiple machines—and one machine is always cheaper than multiple machines, at least initially. Another consideration is that applications may need to be modified to enable failover, depending on the cluster implementation.

Most operating systems support some degree of clustering. Windows NT servers can failover if one goes down, but clusters are limited to only four nodes. A cluster of IBM mainframes can completely share system resources and appear for all intents and purposes as one system. Furthermore, from a database perspective, the DBMS software needs to be programmed to understand and take advantage of the clustering support in the operating systems. Some DBMS products do this better than others.

Clustering is useful for masking the impact of routine maintenance.

Additionally, clustering is useful for masking the impact of routine maintenance. When a server node needs to be taken offline for maintenance, its work can be shifted to another server. For example, if memory needs to be added to the motherboard of a server, that server must be shut down. If it participates in a cluster, its workload can be routed to other nodes in the cluster while the maintenance is being performed, resulting in an outage-less maintenance task.

A Few Database Examples

An Oracle standby database is a simple example of one type of cluster. The primary database is mirrored to the standby database, which can step in and take over in the event of a failure. The redundancy can be expensive but is cost effective for businesses that cannot afford long outages.

Another example of a clustered system is IBM's Sysplex multiprocessor line, which splits tasks among parallel processors. Individually, the processors are less powerful than traditional bipolar predecessors, but combined they crunch data faster by assigning work to open processors rather than requiring users to wait for cycles on a single processor. DB2 for z/OS can be set up to take advantage of this type of parallel processing. The sidebar "Data Sharing and DB2 for z/OS" offers more details.

Keep in mind that standard database maintenance software may not run very efficiently on clustered and parallel systems. To reduce costs and improve availability, the tools used by DBAs must be capable of understanding and exploiting the clustering and parallel technologies being used. Otherwise, products that run slowly and inefficiently because they were built for a different hardware environment will negate the benefits of the parallel technology. For example, to reorganize databases and handle backup and recovery functions for parallel processing environments, DBAs need maintenance utilities written specifically to take advantage of parallel processors.

Data Sharing and DB2 for z/OS

DB2 data sharing allows applications running on multiple DB2 subsystems to concurrently read and write to the same data sets. Simply stated, data sharing enables multiple DB2 subsystems to behave as one.

The primary benefit of data sharing is to provide increased availability to data. With data sharing, data is available for direct access across multiple DB2 subsystems. Furthermore, applications can be run on multiple smaller, more competitively priced microprocessor-based machines, thereby enhancing data availability and the price/performance ratio.

An additional benefit is expanded capacity. Capacity is increased because more processors are available to execute the DB2 application programs. Instead of a single DB2 subsystem on a single logical partition, multiple CPCs can be used to execute a program (or even a single query).

DB2 data sharing requires an IBM Parallel Sysplex. An IBM Sysplex is a set of OS/390 (mainframe) images that are connected and coupled by sharing one or more Sysplex timers. A Parallel Sysplex is a basic Sysplex that additionally shares a coupling facility. The coupling facility provides external shared memory and a set of hardware protocols that allow enabled applications and subsystems to share data with integrity by using external shared memory. A Parallel Sysplex enhances scalability by extending the ability to increase the number of processors within a single OS/390 image with the ability to have multiple OS/390 images capable of cooperatively processing a shared workload.

Summary

Organizations have to find a balance between the seemingly incompatible needs for 24/7 uptime and periodic maintenance. A poorly maintained database is a business inhibitor and will be nearly impossible to restore in the event of a crisis. There are alternatives to the native database utilities that can deliver maintenance and backup functionality while providing continuous availability of the database and associated applications. In many instances, critical applications directly affect revenue. Thus, the DBA must implement a maintenance and backup strategy that provides optimum availability.

Additionally, the DBA must remain alert to all of the potential problems that can cause a lack of availability. These causes run the gamut from hardware problems to software bugs to human error. Obviously, each type of database unavailability has different effects on the organization, the users, and the DBA. Although each involves an outage from the end user perspective, some are easier for the DBA to cope with than others. At any rate, the DBA must be prepared to resolve any type of availability problem that impacts a database user's ability to access and modify data. This is a complex and challenging task because its scope is truly enterprisewide—just about every component of the IT infrastructure can impact database availability.

However, if the DBA has the right skills and training, prudent DBA practices and 24/7 availability need not be mutually exclusive. It just takes the right tools, a little planning, and a lot of diligence.

Remain alert to all of the potential problems that can cause a lack of availability.

Review

1. Define what is meant by the term *availability*.

2. Compare and contrast performance problems with availability problems.

3. Describe three types of technology that can help to alleviate availability problems.

4. Hardware and software failures are the only causes of data unavailability: True or False.

5. What impact does corrupt and invalid data have on availability?

6. What factors contribute to the cost of downtime?

7. What is the typical cause of an unplanned outage?

8. What percentage of downtime is caused by planned outages?

9. What are nondisruptive database utilities, and why are they important for maintaining database availability?

10. What are the four (high-level) steps that can be taken to improve database availability?

Suggested Reading

Piedad, Floyd, and Michael Hawkins. *High Availability: Design, Techniques and Processes.* Upper Saddle River, NJ: Prentice Hall PTR (2001). ISBN 0-13-096288-0

Performance Management

When non-DBAs think about what it is that a DBA does, performance monitoring and tuning are quite frequently the first tasks that come to mind. This should not be surprising. Almost anyone who has come in contact with a computer has experienced some type of performance problem. Moreover, relational database systems have a notorious reputation (mostly undeserved) for poor performance.

This chapter, as well as the following three, will discuss performance monitoring, tuning, and management within the context of database administration. This chapter defines performance, discusses the difference between performance monitoring and performance management, looks at managing service levels, and defines three specific subsets of database performance management. Chapters 10 through 12 delve further into the three subsets.

Defining Performance

Performance management is usually reactive.

Most organizations monitor and tune the performance of their IT infrastructure. This infrastructure encompasses servers, networks, applications, desktops, and databases. However, the performance management steps taken are usually reactive. A user calls with a response-time problem. A tablespace runs out of disk storage space in which to expand. The batch window extends into the day. Someone submitted a "query from hell" that just won't stop running. Those of you in the trenches can relate—you've been there, done that.

Handling performance problems is truly an enterprisewide endeavor. However, the task of enterprise performance management frequently becomes the job of the DBA group. Anyone who has worked as a DBA for any length of time knows that the DBMS is usually "guilty until proven innocent." Every performance problem gets blamed on the database regardless of its true cause. DBAs need to be able research and ascertain the source of all performance degradation, if only to prove that it is not caused by a database problem. As such, DBAs must be able to understand at least the basics of the entire IT infrastructure, but they also need to have many friends who are experts in other related fields (such as networking, operating systems, and communication protocols). Possessing a sound understanding of the IT infrastructure enables DBAs to respond effectively when performance problems arise. Event-driven tools exist on the market that can make performance management easier by automatically invoking predefined actions when specific alerts are triggered. For example, an alert can be set to proactively reorganize a database when it reaches its storage capacity or to allocate more memory when the DBMS is reaching its limit. Moreover, other tools exist that can ease the burden of performance management and analysis. However, many of the supposedly proactive steps taken against completed applications in production are truly mostly reactive. Let's face it, DBAs are often too busy taking care of the day-to-day tactical database administration tasks to proactively monitor and tune their systems to the degree they wish they could.

All of this discussion is useful, but it begs the question: Just what do we mean by *database performance*? You need a firm definition of database performance before you can plan for efficiency. Think, for a moment, of database performance using the familiar concepts of supply and demand. Users request information from the database. The DBMS supplies information to those requesting it. The rate at which the DBMS supplies the demand for information can be termed "database performance." However, this definition captures database performance only in a most simplistic form.

We need a more comprehensive definition of database performance. Five factors influence database performance: workload, throughput, resources, optimization, and contention.

The *workload* is a combination of online transactions, batch jobs, ad hoc queries, data warehousing analysis, and system commands directed through the system at any given time. Workload can fluctuate drastically from day to day, hour to hour, and even minute to minute. Sometimes workload is predictable (such as heavy month-end processing of payroll, or very light access after 7:00 P.M., when most users have left for the day), whereas workload is very unpredictable at other times. The overall workload has a major impact on database performance.

Throughput defines the overall capability of the computer to process data. It is a composite of I/O speed, CPU speed, parallel capabilities of the machine, and the efficiency of the operating system and system software. The hardware and software tools at the disposal of the system are known as the *resources* of the system. Examples of resources include the database kernel, disk storage devices, random access memory chips, cache controllers, and microcode.

The fourth defining element of database performance is *optimization*. All types of systems can be optimized, but relational databases are unique in that query optimization is primarily accomplished internal to the DBMS. However, many other factors need to be optimized (such as SQL formulation and database parameters) to enable the database optimizer to create the most efficient access paths.

When the demand (workload) for a particular resource is high, contention can result. *Contention* is the condition where two or more components of the workload are attempting to use a single resource in a conflicting way (e.g., dual updates to the same piece of data). As contention increases, throughput decreases.

Database performance is the optimization of resource use to increase throughput and minimize contention, enabling the largest possible workload to be processed.

Therefore, database performance can be defined as the optimization of resource use to increase throughput and minimize contention, enabling the largest possible workload to be processed. Of course, I do not advocate managing database performance in a vacuum. Applications regularly communicate with other subsystems and components of the IT infrastructure. Each of these must also be factored into the overall performance planning of your organization. However, it is wise to place limits on the DBA's actual responsibility for performance tuning outside the scope of this definition. If the task is not included in the definition above, it probably requires expertise outside the scope of database administration. Therefore, performance management tasks not covered by the above description should be handled by someone other than the DBA—or at least shared among the DBA and other technicians.

A Basic Database Performance Road Map

Planning for database performance management is a crucial component of any application implementation. Therefore, the DBA needs to forge a basic plan to ensure that database performance management and analysis is accomplished for all database applications across the organization. A complete performance management plan will include tools to help monitor application performance and tune the database and SQL.

Following the 80/20 rule (see "The 80/20 Rule" sidebar), the first step should be to identify the most troublesome areas. However, this is not always as easy as it might seem.

The most likely culprit for most database application performance problems is inefficient SQL and application code. In my experience, 75% to 80% of all database performance problems can be traced to poorly coded SQL or application logic. This does not mean that the SQL in applications is necessarily bad to begin with. Although an application may be 100% tuned for rapid relational access when it first moves into the production environment, it can suffer performance degradation over time. This degradation can occur for many reasons, such as database growth, new data access patterns, additional users, changes in the business, and so on.

Of course, the SQL and application code can be just plain bad to begin with, too. Any number of problems can cause poorly performing SQL, including

- Table scans
- Lack of appropriate indexes
- Improper indexing choices
- Not using the available indexes
- Outdated database statistics
- Tables joined in a suboptimal order

The most likely culprit for most performance problems is inefficient SQL and application code.

The 80/20 Rule

The *80/20 rule*, also known as the *Pareto Principle*, is an old maxim stating that 80% of the results come from 20% of the effort. This rule is usually applicable to most efforts. Whether the percentages are precisely 80% and 20%, the underlying logic of the rule holds—namely, that a small amount of effort brings the most rewards.

So, from the perspective of database performance tuning, the wise DBA will concentrate on the most likely causes of performance problems first, because he will receive a high return on his tuning investment.

- Application joins instead of (usually) more efficient SQL joins
- Improper join method (nested loop, merge scan, etc.)
- Efficient SQL inside of inefficient application code (loops)
- Inefficient subquery formulation (exists, not exists, etc.)
- Unnecessary sorting (group by, order by, union)

Finding the SQL statements that are the most expensive in a large shop is an extremely difficult thing to do. Resource hogging SQL statements might be hiding in one of hundreds or even thousands of programs. Interactive users who produce dynamic, ad hoc SQL statements might reside anywhere, and any one person who is generating ad hoc queries can severely affect overall production performance.

A good approach is to use an SQL monitor that identifies all SQL running anywhere in your environment. Typically, these tools will rank SQL statements, based on the amount of resources being consumed, and track the statement back to who issued it and from what program. Once you have identified the top resource consuming statements, you can concentrate your tuning efforts on the most costly statements.

The proper coding and tuning of SQL statements is a detailed endeavor.

However, it is not always obvious how to tune poorly coded SQL statements. The proper coding and tuning of SQL statements is a detailed endeavor. In-depth strategies for SQL tuning and additional application performance management details can be found in Chapter 12.

Of course, other factors can negatively impact database performance. It is wise to periodically check the overall performance of the database instance and the server operating system. Some quick items to check include the following:

- Memory allocation (buffer/cache for data, SQL, authorization)
- Logging options (log cache, log size, Oracle rollback segments)
- I/O efficiency (separation of tables and indexes on disk, database size, fragmented and extended files)
- Overall application and database workload on the server
- Database schema definitions

To assure optimum database performance, plan on combining a good definition of database performance with a detailed performance plan specific to your shop.

Monitoring vs. Management

Unfortunately, the DBA usually attacks performance in a reactive manner. A user calls with a response time problem. A database runs out of space. The batch window extends into the day. The problem has happened and now it needs to be remedied. Such activity is purely reactive.

Even many of the supposedly proactive steps taken against completed production applications might be considered reactive. A change to a completed application that requires code to be rewritten cannot reasonably be considered proactive. A proactive approach would have involved correcting the problem before completing the application.

Some event-driven tools can be used to make performance tuning easier by automatically taking predefined actions when prespecified alerts are triggered. This is the first step toward performance management. Managing performance differs from monitoring performance because it combines monitoring with a detailed plan for resolving problems when they arise.

Performance management consists of three steps: monitoring, analysis, and correction.

Performance management consists of three specific components that need to be performed in conjunction with each other: monitoring, analysis, and correction, as shown in Figure 9-1. *Monitoring* is the first component of performance management. It consists of scanning the environment, reviewing the output of instrumentation facilities, and generally watching the system as it runs. Monitoring is the process of identifying problems.

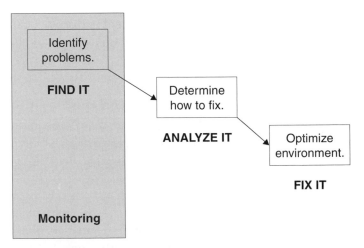

Figure 9-1 *The components of performance management*

Analysis is the second component of performance management. A monitoring task can generate hundreds or thousands of messages, or reams and reams of paper reports. A monitor collects the pertinent information for making performance tuning and optimization decisions, but it is essentially dumb. A monitor cannot independently make decisions based on the information it has collected. This requires analysis—and analysis typically is performed by a skilled technician like a DBA.

Optimization—the corrective action—is the third component of performance management. Some performance tools allow the technician to automate certain aspects of performance management by automatically kicking off corrective actions when the certain prespecified monitoring agent identifies certain conditions. However, most of these tools are limited in scope. Furthermore, a skilled technician must set up the automation to make sure that the appropriate optimization step is taken at the correct time. Eventually performance management tools and solutions will become intelligent—with built-in knowledge of how to optimize a DBMS and with the ability to learn what works best from tuning exercises.

Performance management can be achieved only by using a proactive performance plan. Many problems can be identified and solutions mapped out in advance, before an emergency occurs. With a proper plan, correction of performance problems becomes easier, and indeed, some performance problems can be avoided altogether because a potential problem causing situation can be corrected before a problem occurs.

For true proactive performance management to be achieved, the DBA must plan the performance of an application before it is completed. This requires the DBA to be involved in the application development life cycle and to ensure that performance is designed into the application. Achieving such a high degree of DBA involvement in the application development process can be problematic. DBAs are stressed for time, and it seems like there is always time to do it over later instead of simply doing it right the first time.

> *Performance management can be achieved only by using a proactive performance plan.*

Reactive vs. Proactive

> *Proactive performance management combines forethought, planning, and automation to minimize reactive monitoring and tuning.*

Reactive performance management will always be required because unplanned performance problems will always occur. It is impossible to foresee every type of performance problem; after all, systems and applications change over time. Reactive performance management is not, in itself, a bad thing, but it is a manual, time consuming process. *Proactive performance management* combines forethought, planning, and automation to minimize reactive monitoring and tuning. In other words, proactive performance management reduces the amount time, effort, and human error involved in implementing and maintaining efficient database systems.

Preproduction Performance Estimation

Ideally, DBAs and developers should engineer high performance into their applications during design and construction by implementing a methodology. Such a methodology must address the ADLC by incorporating tactics to achieve high performance into the creation of the database and application code. A rigorous process focusing on verifiable results can build performance into applications and databases, thereby eliminating costly redesign and recoding efforts—at least with respect to most performance problems.

Problems identified earlier in the ADLC are easier to fix and cost less to fix than problems identified later in the application's life, as shown in Figure 9-2. Proactive performance management can reduce the cost of application development because it occurs before the application becomes operational in a production environment. Correcting problems after an application is operational

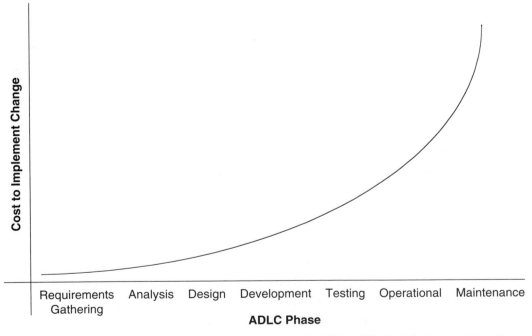

Figure 9-2   *Cost of performance problems across the application development life cycle*

is the costliest method of performance management, because users are relying on the operational application to perform their jobs. Performance problems in a production application can increase the amount of time it takes to perform mission-critical work, such as servicing customers. Moreover, severe performance problems can cause outages, as discussed in the last chapter.

Performance should be modeled for the entire application.

Estimating the performance of applications differs from analyzing and optimizing single database queries. Performance should be modeled for the entire application, because individual queries may optimize at the expense of other queries. A model will show the overall effect of all the queries and how they affect each other's performance. Such a model enables the DBA to optimize overall performance.

Creating an accurate performance model is an iterative process. Each change must be reviewed and updated, and its impact gauged for effectiveness. DBAs, SAs, application developers, and capacity planners must cooperate to share information and address any business requirement issues that may affect the performance criteria.

Historical Trending

Maintaining key historical performance indicators can provide a huge benefit to DBAs.

Capturing and analyzing resource usage trends and performance statistics over time is another valuable performance task. Historical performance and resource trending allows DBAs to predict the need for hardware upgrades weeks, and perhaps months, in advance. Administrators can track key performance statistics (such as buffer hit ratios, file I/O, and log switches) and store that information in *tracker tables* in the database. This provides valuable historical information that can be reported and analyzed. DBAs can track performance and resource consumption and predict when hardware resources will be consumed by increasing usage. Furthermore, historical trends can illuminate periods when database performance is slower than usual due to increased user activity. For example, database applications tend to run slower the first three days of the month due to month-end processing requirements. Maintaining key historical performance indicators can provide a huge benefit to DBAs as they attempt to comprehend the performance characteristics of their applications, databases, and systems.

Service-Level Management

Service-level management (SLM) is the "disciplined, proactive methodology and procedures used to ensure that adequate levels of service are delivered to all IT users in accordance with business priorities and at acceptable cost."[1] In order to effectively manage service levels, a business must prioritize its application and identify the amount of time, effort, and capital that can be expended delivering service for those applications.

A service level is a measure of operational behavior. SLM ensures that applications behave accordingly by applying resources to those applications based on their importance to the organization. Depending on the needs of the organization, SLM can focus on availability, performance, or both. In terms of availability, the service level might be defined as "99.95% uptime from 9:00 A.M. to 10:00 P.M. on weekdays." Of course, a service level can be more specific, stating "average response time for transactions will be two seconds or less for workloads of 500 or fewer users."

For a service-level agreement (SLA) to be successful, all parties involved must agree on stated objectives for availability and performance. The end users must be satisfied with the performance of their applications, and the DBAs and technicians must be content with their ability to manage the system to the objectives. Compromise is essential to reach a useful SLA.

In practice, though, many organizations do not institutionalize SLM. When new applications are delivered, there may be vague requirements and promises of subsecond response time, but the prioritization and budgeting required to assure such service levels are rarely tackled unless the IT function is outsourced. Internal IT organizations are loath to sign SLAs because any SLA worth pursuing will be difficult to achieve. Furthermore, once the difficulties of negotiating an SLA are completed, the business could very well turn around and outsource the SLA to a lower-cost provider than the internal IT group.

But do not misunderstand. The failure of SLM within most businesses lies with both IT organizations and business users. The business users frequently desire better service but are not willing to make the effort to prioritize their needs correctly or to pay additional cash to achieve better service.

Another potential problem with SLM is the context of the service being discussed. Most IT professionals view service levels on an element-by-element basis. In other words, the DBA views performance based on the DBMS, the SA views performance based on the operating system or the transaction processing system, and so on. SLM properly views service for an entire application.

---

1. Sturm, Rick, Wayne Morris, and Mary Jander, *Foundations of Service Level Management,* Indianapolis, IN: SAMS Publishing (2000).

However, it can be difficult to assign responsibility within the typical IT structure. IT usually operates as a group of silos that do not work together very well. Frequently, the application teams operate independently from the DBAs, who operate independently from the SAs, as shown in Figure 9-3. When an application team has staffed an application DBA function, that team may not communicate effectively with the corporate DBA silo. These fractured silos make cooperation toward a common application service level difficult.

To achieve end-to-end SLM, these silos need to be broken down. The various departments within the IT infrastructure need to communicate effectively and cooperate with one another. Failing this, end-to-end SLM will be difficult, if not impossible, to implement.

A robust SLM discipline makes performance management predictable.

SLM is a beneficial practice: A robust SLM discipline makes performance management predictable. SLM manages the expectations of all involved. Without an SLA, how will the DBA and the end users know whether an application is performing adequately? Not every application can, or needs to, deliver sub second response time. Without an SLA, business users and DBAs may have different expectations, resulting in unsatisfied business executives and frustrated DBAs. Not a good situation.

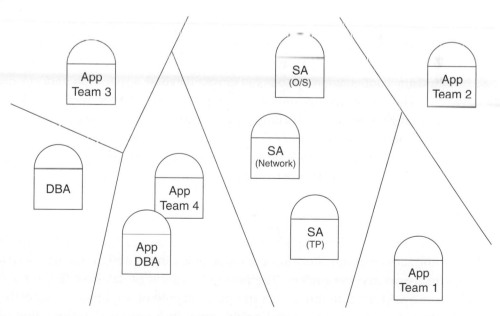

Figure 9-3 *IT silos in a fractured environment*

With SLM in place, DBAs can adjust resources by applying them to the most mission-critical applications as defined in the SLA. Costs will be controlled and capital will be expended on the portions of the business that are most important to the business.

Types of Performance Tuning

A database application requires constant interaction between disparate computing resources in order to operate efficiently and according to specifications. Realistically, though, the tuning of a database application can be broken down into three components: system tuning, database tuning, and application tuning. Indeed, all these areas are related, and certain aspects of tuning require an integrated approach. However, for clarity, we'll discuss these areas separately.

System Tuning

System tuning occurs at the highest level and has the greatest impact on the overall health of database applications because every application depends on the system. For the purposes of this discussion, we will define the system as comprising the DBMS itself and all of the related components on which it relies. No amount of tuning is going to help a database or application when the server it is running on is short on resources or improperly installed.

The DBMS can and must be tuned to assure optimum performance.

The DBMS can and must be tuned to assure optimum performance. The way in which the DBMS software is installed, its memory, disk, CPU, other resources, and any configuration options can impact database application performance.

The other systems software with which the DBMS interacts includes the operating system, networking software, message queueing systems, middleware, and transaction processors. System tuning comprises installation, configuration, and integration issues, as well as ensuring connectivity of the software to the DBMS and database applications.

Database Tuning

The physical location of database files on disk systems impacts the performance of applications accessing the data.

Performance can be impacted by the physical design of the database, including normalization, disk storage, number of tables, index design, and use of DDL and its associated parameters. The physical location of database files on disk systems will have an impact on the performance of applications accessing the data. As more data is stored on the same disk device, the possibility of performance degradation increases.

However, design is not the only component of database performance. The organization of the database will change over time. As data is inserted, updated, and deleted from the database, the efficiency of the database will degrade. Moreover, the files that hold the data may need to expand as more data is added. Perhaps additional files, or file extents, will need to be allocated. Both disorganization and file growth can degrade performance.

Indexes also need to be monitored, analyzed, and tuned to optimize data access and to ensure that they are not having a negative impact on data modification.

Application Tuning

The application itself must be designed appropriately and monitored for efficiency. Most experts agree that as much as 75% of performance problems are caused by improperly coded applications. SQL is the primary culprit; coding efficient SQL statements can be complicated. Developers need to be taught how to properly formulate, monitor, and tune SQL statements.

Not all application problems are due to improperly coded SQL.

However, not all application problems are due to improperly coded SQL. The host language application code in which the SQL has been embedded may be causing the problem. For example, Java, COBOL, C++, or Visual Basic code may be inefficient, causing database application performance to suffer.

Managing the performance for each of these three areas, the system, the database, and the application, will be discussed in depth in Chapters 10, 11, and 12.

Performance Tuning Tools

Many third-party tools can effectively manage the performance of mission-critical database applications.

Database tools are helpful to effectively manage database performance. Some DBMS vendors provide embedded options and bundled tools to address database performance management. However, these tools are frequently insufficient for large-scale or heavily used database applications. Fortunately, many third-party tools will effectively manage the performance of mission-critical database applications. Tools that enable DBAs to tune databases fall into two major categories: performance management and performance optimization.

Many different types of performance management tools are available.

- *Performance monitors* enable DBAs and performance analysts to gauge the performance of applications accessing databases in one (or more) of three ways: real time, near time (intervals), or based on historical trends. The more advanced performance monitors are agent-based.

- *Performance estimation tools* provide predictive performance estimation for entire programs and SQL statements based on access paths, operating environment, and a rules or inference engine.

- *Capacity planning tools* enable DBAs to analyze the current environment and database design and perform "what-if" scenarios on both.

- *SQL analysis and tuning tools* provide graphical and/or textual descriptions of query access paths as determined by the relational optimizer. These tools can execute against single SQL statements or entire programs.

- *Advisory tools* augment SQL analysis and tuning tools by providing a knowledge base that provides tips on how to reformulate SQL for optimal performance. Advanced tools may automatically change the SQL (on request) based on the coding tips in the knowledge base.

- *System analysis and tuning tools* enable the DBA to view and change database and system parameters using a graphical interface (e.g., cache and/or bufferpool tuning, log sizing).

In the performance optimization category, several tools can be used to tune databases.

- *Reorganization tools* automate the process of rebuilding optimally organized databases. Databases can cause performance problems due to their internal organization (e.g., fragmentation, row ordering, storage allocation).

- *Compression tools* enable DBAs to minimize the amount of disk storage used by databases, thereby reducing overall disk utilization and, possibly, elapsed query/program execution time, because fewer I/Os may be required. (Caution: Compression tools can also increase CPU consumption due to the overhead of their compress/decompress algorithms.)

- *Sorting tools* can be used to sort data prior to loading databases to ensure that rows will be in a predetermined sequence. Additionally, sorting tools can be used in place of ORDER BY or GROUP BY SQL. Retrieving rows from a relational database is sometimes more efficient using SQL and ORDER BY rather than SQL alone followed by a stand-alone sort of the SQL results set.

The DBA will often need to use these tools in conjunction with one another.

The DBA will often need to use these tools in conjunction with one another—integrated and accessible from a central management console. This enables the DBA to perform core performance-oriented and database administration tasks from a single platform.

Many DBMS vendors provide solutions to manage their databases only; for example, Oracle provides Oracle Enterprise Manager and Sybase provides SQL Central for this purpose. Third-party vendors provide more robust options that act across heterogeneous environments such as multiple different database servers or operating systems.

In general, it is wise to use the DBMS vendor solution only if your shop has a single DBMS. Organizations with multiple DBMS engines running across multiple operating systems should investigate the third-party tool vendors.

Chapter 22 provides additional information on tools that simplify database administration and performance management tasks.

DBMS Performance Basics

We have defined database performance and discussed it from a high level. Before we delve into the specifics of system, database, and application performance, let's examine some rules of thumb for achieving your DBMS-related performance goals.

- *Do not over-tune*. Most DBAs are more than happy to roll up their sleeves and get their hands dirty with the minute technical details of the DBMS. Sometimes this is required. However, as a DBA, you should always keep in mind the business objectives of the databases and applications you manage. It is wise to manage performance based on the expectations and budget of the business users. Even though it might be an interesting intellectual challenge for you to fine-tune a query to its best performance, doing so may take too much time away from your other duties. It is best to stop tuning when performance reaches a predefined service level for which the business users are willing to pay.

- *Remain focused*. As a DBA, you should understand the goal for each task you perform and remain focused on it. This is important because the DBMS is complex, and when you are tuning one area, you might find problems in another. If so, it is best to document what you found for later and continue with the tuning task at hand. Furthermore, by jumping around trying to tune multiple things at once, you will have no idea of each task's impact on the environment.

- *Do not panic.* The DBA is expected to know everything about the DBMS he manages. However, this is an unreasonable expectation. "I don't know, but I'll find out" is one of the most important phrases in your communications arsenal. A good DBA knows where to look for answers and who to call for help.

- *Communicate clearly.* Communication is key to assuring properly tuned, high-performance database systems. The DBA must be at the center of that communication, coordinating discussions and workload between the business users, programmers, managers, and SAs. Furthermore, the world of IT in general, and database technology in particular, sometimes uses a language all its own. Many similar and confusing terms are thrown about, and folks are expected to understand what they mean. Be sure to clearly define even basic terms so that you're all speaking the same language.

- *Accept reality.* Many organizations talk about being proactive but in reality have very little interest in stopping performance problems before they happen. Yet, every organization is interested in fixing performance problems after the problems occur. This can be a frustrating environment for the DBA, who would rather set up preventative maintenance for the DBMS environment. Alas, this requires budget, time, and effort—all of which are in short supply for strapped IT organizations. As a DBA, you must sometimes be content to accept reality and deal with problems as they occur—even when you know there are better ways of tackling performance management.

Summary

Applications that access relational databases are only as good as the performance they achieve.

Applications that access relational databases are only as good as the performance they achieve. The wise organization will implement a comprehensive performance monitoring, tuning, and management environment that consists of policies, procedures, and integrated performance management tools and utilities.

Review

1. Define database performance.

2. During which phase of the application development life cycle is it most costly to make a change?

3. What are the three "things" that need to be addressed in database application tuning?

4. What does the 80/20 rule mean and how should it be applied to database application performance tuning?

5. Name and describe the three steps of database performance management.

6. Discuss some of the problems involved in implementing service-level management for database applications.

7. What two categories of database tools can be used to help deliver database performance management?

8. What percentage of performance problems do most experts attribute to improperly coded database applications?

9. What is the condition in which two or more components of the workload are attempting to use a single resource in a conflicting way?

10. Compare and contrast reactive and proactive database performance management.

Bonus Questions

Why is it a good idea to capture and store historical performance statistics? What types of questions can historical statistics help a DBA to answer?

Suggested Reading

Dunham, Jeff. *Database Performance Tuning Handbook*. New York, NY: McGraw-Hill (1998). ISBN 0-07-018244-2

Gunther, Neil J. *The Practical Performance Analyst*. Lincoln, NE: Authors Choice Press (2000). ISBN 0-595-12674-X

Koch, Richard. *The 80/20 Principle*. New York, NY: Currency/Doubleday (1998). ISBN 0-385-49170-0

Loosley, Chris, and Frank Douglas. *High-Performance Client/Server.* New York, NY: John Wiley & Sons (1998). ISBN 0-471-16269-8

Shasha, Dennis A. *Database Tuning: A Principled Approach.* Englewood Cliffs, NJ: Prentice Hall (1992). ISBN 0-13-205246-6

Sturm, Rick, Wayne Morris, and Mary Jander. *Foundations of Service Level Management.* Indianapolis, IN: SAMS Publishing (2000). ISBN 0-672-31743-5

10

System Performance

A system problem
can cause all data-
bases and applica-
tions to perform
poorly

A poorly performing system can degrade the performance of all databases and applications deployed on that system. No amount of database, application, or SQL tuning can improve performance when a poorly implemented system is causing performance problems. Applications access databases and both are implemented on an overall system environment, as shown in Figure 10-1. Therefore, a system problem can cause all databases and applications to perform

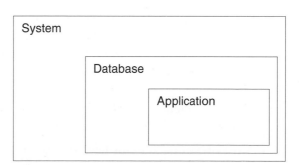

Figure 10-1 *The tuning boxes*

poorly, just like a database problem can cause all applications that access that database to perform poorly.

The system comprises the hardware and software required for the DBMS to operate and for applications to access databases using the DBMS. It is imperative that the DBA understands the system and operating environment where the database applications will be run. The DBA must be able to facilitate changes to any component of the system to tune the database environment. Of course, the DBA cannot be expected to be an expert in every aspect of the system, and therefore the DBA will need to work with other teams within the organization to initiate system changes.

The following sections provide introductory coverage of system-related performance and tuning tactics. They do not provide in-depth treatment of the subjects because that is not the primary focus of the book.

The Larger Environment

A DBMS operates within the context of a larger environment.

A DBMS operates within the context of a much larger environment that consists of other software and hardware components. Each of these components must be installed, configured, and managed effectively for the DBMS to function as required. The DBA needs to understand how the DBMS interacts with the server hardware, the operating system, and any other required software. Tuning and configuring these components and connections properly can have a dramatic impact on system performance.

Interaction with the Operating System

When the operating system experiences a performance problem, all of the software that runs on that operating system may experience performance problems. To help ensure an optimal operating system for your database applications, the DBA should ask the following questions.

- Has a sufficient amount of memory been allocated for operating system tasks?

- Most operating systems have the capability of allocating a specific amount of disk space as a swap area. The swap area is used when the

OS runs out of memory. Has a sufficient amount of disk space been allocated to the swap area?

- How were the database files allocated when the database was implemented? Interaction with the file system can cause some operating systems to create additional overhead. By changing the database files to use raw disk, OS and file system overhead can be eliminated. (Additional information on raw disk usage can be found in Chapter 17.)

- Some operating systems allow the administrator to set the priority of tasks that run under the auspices of the OS. Has each database-related task been assigned a priority? Is the priority appropriate for that specific task?

- Is the operating system at the version and release level recommended by the DBMS vendor? Have any bug fixes been shipped for the OS that are applicable for the particular brand of database server you are running?

- Have the operating system configuration parameters been modified when installing the DBMS? If so, has sufficient testing been done to ensure that the parameters were modified correctly and do not impact any other processes that run on the database server?

Allied Agents

The DBMS has to ally itself with many other software components to deliver service to the end user.

As discussed in previous chapters, the DBMS has to ally itself with many other software components to deliver service to the end user. Examples of allied agent software include

- Transaction processors like CICS and Microsoft Transaction Server
- Networking software such as TCP/IP and SNA
- Message queueing software such as MQSeries and MSMQ
- Web connectivity and development software such as ColdFusion
- Programming languages such as Java, COBOL, and C

Each of these allied agents needs to be configured properly to interact with the DBMS, and it is the DBA's responsibility to understand the setup requirements. In larger shops the DBA might not perform the actual configuration—

leaving it, instead, to more skilled professionals who specialize in administering and managing the software. However, in smaller shops the DBA may have to configure all of the software himself.

Hardware Configuration

The hardware must be installed and set up properly for the DBMS to operate efficiently. The DBMS runs on computer hardware. That hardware may be a large-scale mainframe, an intermediate Unix system, or a PC running Windows. Regardless of its scale, the hardware must be installed and set up properly for the DBMS to operate efficiently.

Again, here are some questions the DBA should ask to assure an optimal hardware environment for the database applications.

- Is the computer hardware and capacity appropriate for the DBMS environment? In other words, does the DBMS vendor recommend this particular hardware implementation?
- Is the computer firmware (e.g., ROM BIOS) up-to-date?
- Has a sufficient amount of memory been installed for all of the system software to be installed (OS, DBMS, and other allied agents)?
- Has an appropriate amount of disk storage space been allocated and configured for use by the DBMS?
- What type of disk storage is being used and is it appropriate for large data volumes and high-speed database queries?
- Are all the network cables connected and functioning properly?
- Are all physical connections (e.g., cables, plugs, and board sockets) fully connected and operational?
- Is the hardware connected to an uninterruptible power supply?
- Is the hardware connected to a surge protection device?

Disk Storage and I/O

One of the biggest bottlenecks for database performance is the physical cost of performing I/O operations. Data resides on a disk, and a disk is a mechanical device. It requires machine parts that move in order to read encoded data from a spinning platter. This physical movement takes time, and anything that can be done to reduce I/O time can enhance performance.

A consideration for optimizing disk access is to utilize solid state devices. A solid state device is actually computer memory that is configured to work like a disk drive. When data is read from a solid state device, there is no physical component to the I/O operation—the data resides in memory and is transferred from memory to the DBMS and then to the requester.

Consider placing database objects with high performance requirements on solid state devices instead of physical disk drives, RAID devices, or storage area networks.

However, implementing solid state devices has some potential problems. The first is cost. Only recently has the initial cost of solid state devices begun to decrease. The second potential problem is persistence. Some solid state devices require a constant supply of power to prevent the data from being erased. In such cases, be sure that solid backup and recovery plans are implemented for database objects.

Components of the DBMS

A DBMS is a very complex system requiring hundreds of thousands of lines of computer code. A DBMS is so complex that multiple programs are required to deliver the requisite data management functionality; each program interoperates with other programs to provide a database management system.

Each DBMS vendor breaks down DBMS functionality into different components. The DBA must study the makeup of the DBMS and gain an understanding of each component piece and how it integrates with the other components of the DBMS. For a high-level overview of the architecture of the Oracle DBMS, refer to the sidebar "The Architecture of Oracle."

The DBA must become an expert on the inner workings of the DBMS in order to ensure an optimized environment for database applications. A failure or problem in any single component of the DBMS can cause severe performance degradation for every application accessing the database.

The Architecture of Oracle

To effectively administer an Oracle environment, the DBA must understand the basic "architectural" blueprint of Oracle. Oracle is composed of five basic components that operate in an integrated manner to provide support for the client tasks: file structures, memory structures, processes, rollback segments, and redo logs.

An Oracle *instance* is the combination of all of the memory structures and background processes that are allocated when an Oracle database is started. Oracle users frequently confuse an Oracle *instance* with an Oracle *database*. An Oracle *database* has both physical structures (data files) and logical structures (table, index). The physical structure of an Oracle database is determined by the files created at the operating system level by the Oracle instance during database creation (e.g., controlfile, logfile) or by the DBA during normal operation (e.g., CREATE tablespace, CREATE controlfile). An Oracle database comprises three physical file structures:

- *Control files*—A small administrative file that is used by the Oracle database.
- *Redo log files*—A record of changes made to data. The redo log files are used in recovery circumstances to ensure that no data is lost should a failure prevent changed data from being written to disk.
- *Database files*—A file that contains the database information, including both system and application data.

An Oracle *parameter file* contains all configuration parameters for an Oracle instance. These parameters can be set to different values to tailor the Oracle instance to the system's operating configuration as well as to the needs of the individual application(s) contained in the Oracle database.

Oracle *database files* contain the data associated with a particular database. All of the files discussed are not absolutely required for normal database operations, but this configuration is highly recommended for a well-designed, efficient environment. Oracle database files can be grouped by the following categories.

- *Control files* record the physical structure of the Oracle database. The control file is read during every database startup.
- *Data files* associated with Oracle tablespaces include system data files, application data files, default data files, temporary files, and rollback files.
- *Redo log files* (the database transaction log) record changes made to data.
- The *config.ora file,* associated with the Oracle client, specifies certain defaults, file, and directory names for the Oracle client.

Additionally, Oracle utilizes specific memory structures to perform DBMS-related tasks. These memory structures are contained in the main memory (RAM) of the computer running the Oracle instance. The basic memory structures for an Oracle instance are the system global area (SGA), the program global area (PGA), and the sort area.

The SGA is a group of shared memory structures allocated by the Oracle instance to contain data and control information. The SGA contains the data cache, redo log buffer, and shared pool for SQL statement parsing and processing.

The PGA is a work area for both user and background processes. Each process has its own PGA. The contents of the PGA will vary, depending on the type of process and Oracle configuration.

The Oracle sort area is a memory structure used to sort, order, and group data whenever a user process requests a sort to be performed.

Finally, we come to the Oracle processes, where most of the data management work is accomplished. Each process is composed of a series of tasks. Oracle has two general types of processes: user processes and Oracle processes. A *user process* is created to execute the program code of an application program. An *Oracle process* is called by another process to perform specific functions on behalf of the invoking process. Oracle processes can be further broken down into server processes and background processes. *Server processes* communicate with user processes acting as a "relay" between the user process and SGA information. *Background processes* perform designated data management and processing functions for the Oracle instance.

Let's examine the functionality of each of the Oracle background processes.

The *process monitor* (PMON) background process performs "cleanup duties" when a user process fails with an error condition. PMON cleans up the cache, releases locks, and performs other miscellaneous tasks.

The *system monitor* (SMON) background process provides instance recovery during startup. SMON also cleans up temporary segments that are no longer in use, compresses free space into contiguous extents, and in a parallel server environment, provides instance recovery for a failed CPU.

The *database writer* (DBWR) process writes data from the data cache contained in memory out to the physical disk files.

The *log writer* (LGWR) manages the redo log buffer. If an Oracle instance takes more checkpoints than the LGWR process can handle, checkpoint duties may be turned over to the checkpoint (CKPT) background process. The archiver (ARCH) process performs log archival by copying online redo log files to auxiliary storage devices as logs fill up.

The *recover* (RECO) background process automatically resolves failures involving distributed transactions.

Finally, Oracle deploys *user* and *server* processes. The user process links the client application to the Oracle instance. The server process parses and executes SQL statements and performs all tasks required to send results back to the requesting application.

This overview of Oracle's architecture is necessarily brief. It is intended to communicate just how specialized the components of a DBMS must be. An Oracle DBA will need to understand all of the above components, how they interact, and how they can be tuned to optimize the performance of the Oracle system and applications.

DBMS Installation and Configuration Issues

Every database management system provides parameters that allow the DBA to configure various aspects of the database environment. Configuration is accomplished in a variety of ways, depending on the DBMS. Some popular configuration methods include executing system procedures to set and reset values, editing files with parameter settings, issuing commands at a DBMS prompt, and assembling parameter specifications using an option within the DBMS. Regardless of the manner of configuring the DBMS, the DBA will be required to specify various parameters to the DBMS that affect the way the DBMS operates.

Default values are usually not sufficient to support the development of robust, production applications.

Most DBMS software ships with default values supplied by the vendor. However, default values are usually not sufficient to support the development of robust, production applications. This section will discuss some of the common configuration parameters and how to tune them.

Types of Configuration

The DBMS can be configured when the DBMS is installed or after the DBMS is operational. During installation, the DBA or SA installing the DBMS will have the option to change the configuration parameters or to allow the parameters to default. However, defaults are almost always wrong. It is almost always better to set the parameters based on knowledge of the data and applications that will be using the DBMS.

Depending on the DBMS, parameters may be changed dynamically, nondynamically, or both.

Once the DBMS is installed and operational, the DBMS will provide a method of changing the configuration parameters. Depending on the DBMS, parameters may be changed dynamically, nondynamically, or both.

Dynamic parameters can take effect without the need to restart SQL Server. Executing the RECONFIGURE command causes dynamic parameters to immediately take effect. After issuing the appropriate commands, the parameter value changes and the DBMS will behave accordingly.

In order for nondynamic parameters to take effect, the DBMS must be shut down and restarted. Of course, the parameter value must be changed—usually in the same or a similar manner as a dynamic parameter. However, a nondynamic parameter will not take effect until the DBMS is restarted.

Memory Usage

Relational databases love memory.

Relational databases love memory. The single biggest system performance tuning task that a DBA will face is configuring RDBMS memory usage. The DBMS uses random access memory to cache data and other resources required by the DBMS. This is done because reading data from memory is much less costly than reading the data from disk. So, as a rule of thumb, the more memory you can provide to the DBMS, the better performance will be. Of course, the DBMS has to be configured properly to use the memory efficiently.

The American Heritage dictionary defines *cache* as "a place for concealing and safekeeping valuables." This is a good starting point for understanding what a cache means to a relational database. The "place" used by the DBMS is memory (as opposed to disk). The "valuables" are data pages, query plans, and other database resources. A typical DBMS will use a cache to keep resources in memory longer. The longer a resource is cached in a memory location, the better the chance for subsequent requests for the resource to avoid incurring costly I/O operations, as shown in Figure 10-2.

There are multiple caches or buffers utilized by DBMS products to reduce the cost of I/O. Each DBMS uses different terminology but generally caches the same resources.

A *data cache* is used to avoid I/O operations when actual data is being read from the database. Accessing data in memory is substantially faster than accessing data on disk. Therefore, all data access from a relational database goes through a caching area. (Refer to Figure 10-3.) Access to memory is typically measured in microseconds, while access to disk I/O is usually measured in milliseconds. When a program needs a row from a table, the DBMS retrieves the page from disk and stores the page in the data cache. Basically, the DBMS uses the cache as a staging area. If the row changes, the change is written to

A data cache is used to avoid I/O operations when actual data is being read from the database

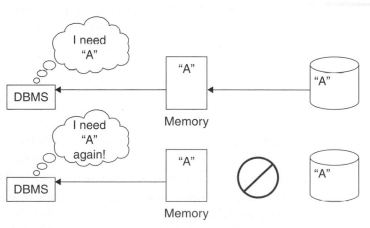

Figure 10-2   *The value of caching resources in memory*

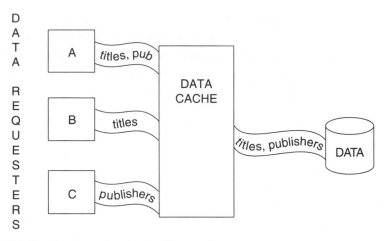

Figure 10-3   *Data cache (or buffer pool)*

the page in the data cache. Eventually, the DBMS will write the page in the data cache back to disk. When data needed by an application is on a page already in the data cache, the application will not have to wait for the page to be retrieved from disk. Depending on the DBMS, this memory structure also may be called a buffer pool.

A *procedure cache* stores SQL and program-related structures. Before SQL statements can be issued to retrieve or modify data, the statement must first be optimized by the DBMS. The optimization process creates an internal structure representing the access path that will be used by the DBMS to read the data. The DBMS can store these access paths in the procedure cache and reuse them each time the program or SQL statement is run. This optimizes application performance because the optimization process need not be performed every time the SQL is run. Instead, optimization occurs the first time the SQL is issued, and subsequent executions retrieve the access path from the procedure cache. Each DBMS provides similar functionality, although with different names and differing features.

The sort cache is used instead of temporary disk storage to store intermediate sort results in memory.

Another memory structure commonly deployed within a DBMS is a *sort cache*. The sort cache is used instead of temporary disk storage to store intermediate sort results in memory. The more sorting functionality that can be performed in memory, the better a sort will perform. Many relational database operations require sorts, for example, grouping, ordering, UNION operations, and certain types of joins.

The DBMS may also use other *internal structure caches*. The implementation of each DBMS is unique. To accomplish relational operations, the DBMS may need to create internal structures that are not necessarily visible to the end user. However, DBAs, and sometimes programmers, will need to know about the internal structures. One example is the internal DBD (database descriptor) structure used by DB2 to manage databases. The DBD is never externalized to users, but every time an application accesses any object within a database, DB2 must load the DBD into a memory area known as the EDM pool. DB2 uses the EDM pool to cache dynamic SQL access paths and other internal structures, as well. DB2 DBAs need to allocate sufficient memory to the EDM pool and monitor the efficiency of the EDM pool as processing requirements and usage patterns change.

The DBMS also may buffer log records to a separate database log cache.

The DBMS also may buffer log records to a separate *database log cache*. Furthermore, the DBMS may implement two log caches, one for log writes and one for log reads. The database log keeps a record of all changes made to the database. The log write cache is used to speed up database modifications. The changed data is written to the log cache, and over time the cache is written asynchronously to disk. By buffering log writes in this way, the database log becomes less of a bottleneck to system and application performance. The log read cache is used for ROLLBACK and RECOVER operations. A rollback or a recovery needs to access the log to undo or reapply database changes. As the log records are requested, they will be buffered in memory in the log read cache.

Additional Areas of Memory Consumption

In addition to the various caches and buffer pools used by relational database systems, memory is required for other purposes. Generally, the DBMS installation or configuration routines allow the DBA to allocate and tune the memory consumption of the DBMS. Some of the more common areas of DBMS memory consumption include

- *User connections.* Each concurrent user connection to the DBMS, regardless of the type of client connection, requires memory for the DBMS to maintain and manage the connection.
- *Devices.* The devices used by databases may require system memory to maintain and use.

- *Open databases.* Most DBMSs provide a parameter to specify the maximum number of databases that can be open at any one time. Each open database requires DBMS memory.

- *Open objects.* Another parameter may exist to identify the maximum number of database objects that can be open at any one time, including tables, indexes, and any other database object in use. Each open database object requires memory.

- *Locks.* Each concurrently held lock will require memory. The DBMS should provide a configuration parameter for the number of concurrent locks that can be held at one time.

- *Caches.* The various caches are discussed in the previous section.

How Much Memory Is Enough?

So, if relational databases love memory, just how much memory should be allocated? This is a difficult (if not impossible) question to answer by using generalities. The tempting answer is "Enough to get the job done," but that does not help the DBA who has to allocate the right amount of memory in the right place.

Every DBMS uses memory, but in different amounts and for different things.

Every DBMS uses memory, but in different amounts and for different things. The best approach is to search your vendor's DBMS manual to determine how much memory is required for each resource. Then you can estimate the usage requirements for each resource and calculate the approximate amount of memory required by the DBMS.

For example, SQL Server requires about 75 bytes of memory per lock. To configure the amount of memory required for locking, the DBA will need to estimate the total number of concurrent transactions and the average number of locks per transaction. After doing so, the calculation for memory required by the DBMS for locking is simple:

Concurrent locks = [# concurrent transactions] $\times$ [# locks per transaction] $\times$ 75

The result of this calculation provides an estimate for the memory (in bytes) used for locking in a SQL Server system. Of course, the number of concurrent transactions and the number of locks per transaction may be difficult to ascertain for your environment. You may be able to substitute the number of concurrent transactions with the DBMS configuration value used for total number of user connections. If locks/transaction is unavailable, you can examine a few typical programs to come up with an estimate. This process is then repeated for each database resource that consumes memory. Of course, the data cache should be treated separately and is covered in the next section.

After repeating this process for each resource, you will arrive at the amount of memory to install for the database server. It is a good practice to leave some breathing room to support the addition of unanticipated application programs, DBMS and operating system upgrades requiring additional memory, and other unforeseen items. This means installing a little bit more memory than you calculate. However, do not leave too much breathing room. The memory was installed to be used, not conserved.

It is a good practice to leave some breathing room.

Data Cache Details

It is important for the DBA to understand the basics of data cache operation. At any given point in time, the data cache will consist of three different types of pages:

- *In-use pages*—pages that are currently being read and updated by the DBMS. These pages are not available to be used for other database processing.

- *Updated pages*—pages where data has been modified in some way, but the data has not yet been written to disk. These pages are not available to be used for other database processing.

- *Available pages*—pages not being used. These pages are available to be used for other database processing. New data can be written to available pages in the data cache.

The performance of the data cache depends on how efficiently memory has been allocated for its use. For example, if unavailable pages dominate the data cache, the DBMS may trigger synchronous writes to increase the space in the data cache. Synchronous writes can slow down database processing because each write request has to wait for the data to be actually physically written to disk. Depending on the type of processing the database applications are using, the DBA may be able to tune data caching parameters and sizes to enable more efficient buffering of data.

Monitoring and Tuning the Data Cache

Ensuring the cache is the proper size is critical.

Ensuring the cache is the proper size is one of the most critical aspects of having an efficient data cache. A data cache that is too large wastes memory and can cause pages in the cache to be moved out to auxiliary storage. A data cache that is too small forces frequent writes to disk and, in the most severe cases, results in swapping the data cache pages back and forth from disk.

The complexity of tuning the data cache varies by DBMS and depends on the configuration and tuning parameters that are available for the data cache. Some DBMSs, such as DB2, provide multiple buffer pools that can be configured and tuned independently with multiple parameters. Others, such as SQL Server, are more basic, with a data cache per database. But regardless of the DBMS, the DBA should monitor the read efficiency of each data cache or buffer pool.

The read efficiency of the data cache is a percentage that tracks how well the cache is performing its primary duty—to avoid physical disk I/O operations. The read efficiency of each data cache is calculated as the number of actual I/Os performed subtracted from the total number of data requests, then divided by the total number of data requests, or:

$$\text{ReadEfficiency} = \frac{(\#\text{database I/O requests}) - (\#\text{physical I/Os})}{(\text{database I/O requests})}$$

In other words, read efficiency shows the percentage of times a data page is found in the data cache (or buffer pool). The higher this percentage is, the more efficient the buffer pool is. When data pages can be found in buffers in memory without requiring a physical I/O, performance will be enhanced.

The actual numbers for I/O requests and actual physical I/O operations can be found by examining DBMS trace records or by using a database performance monitor. Depending on the DBMS, the DBA may need to turn on traces that externalize instrumentation details of the DBMS. Each DBMS has its own set of instrumentation information that can be examined. Also, depending on the type of performance monitor, traces may not need to be started by the DBA because the monitor may start and stop traces as required. The monitor may also use other means to capture the performance information from the DBMS.

An 80% or better read efficiency is good for a data cache.

As a rule of thumb, an 80% or better read efficiency is good for a data cache. Of course, the read efficiency value will depend on the type of processing. Many sequential processes can cause the data cache to be overrun and the efficiency to drop. Furthermore, systems with many processes that access data only weekly or monthly may have lower read efficiencies because less data is frequently reused. The DBA should know the type of database processing that occurs for each data cache and gauge the read efficiency of that data cache in light of the processing that is occuring.

When read efficiency is consistently below 80%, consider tuning by increasing the size of the data cache or reducing the number of tables and indexes assigned to the data cache. Making such changes may impact availability because the DBMS must be stopped and restarted to register the change. Each DBMS has different requirements for making data cache changes.

Large table scans can quickly monopolize a data cache.

Depending on the DBMS, the DBA may be able to configure the data cache better by changing the amount of cache reserved for sequential and parallel operations. Large table scans can quickly monopolize a data cache. By reserving only a subset of the entire cache for sequential scans, the overall performance of the data cache may be improved. Of course, the reverse may be true if the majority of operations that use the data cache are sequential in nature.

Additional possibilities for tuning the data cache—offered by some DBMS vendors or as add-on products—include creating an additional cache to back up the data cache (see the sidebar "DB2 Hiperpools"), pegging specific pages in memory, and automatically growing the size of the data cache as throughput increases.

Monitoring and Tuning the Procedure Cache

The DBA must monitor the effectiveness of the procedure cache to help improve the efficiency of database applications and queries. Although the procedure cache differs dramatically from DBMS to DBMS, the general idea is the same: to keep optimized SQL structures in memory so that they can be reused by subsequent tasks instead of being reformulated or reread from disk.

DB2 Hiperpools

DB2 for OS/390 provides a secondary level of data caching called a *hiperpool*. One hiperpool can be defined for each buffer pool. DB2 can move infrequently accessed pages in the buffer pool to the hiperpool. Only pages that have not been changed, or pages that have changed but have already been written to disk, can be written to a hiperpool.

When a row of data is needed from the hiperpool, the page is written back to the buffer pool. If the row is changed, the page is not written back to the hiperpool until the changed page has been written to disk.

With hiperpools, more data can be maintained in memory for longer periods. Of course, the cost is additional memory that must be installed and configured for use by the DBMS.

DB2's EDM Pool

IBM's DB2 for OS/390 caches SQL in a memory area known as the *environmental descriptor manager pool*, or EDM Pool for short. The EDM Pool contains active and skeleton structures for application plans and packages, as well as optimized dynamic SQL plans, database descriptors, and program authorization lists. The EDM Pool is a sort of catchall memory area for "things" that are used by application programs and SQL statements as they are being run.

An EDM Pool that is too small causes increased I/O activity in the DB2 Directory, a specialized system catalog for internal DB2 structures. An additional symptom that may occur is increased response times as the required structures are read from disk and loaded into memory in the EDM Pool.

The procedure cache must be sized properly to accommodate all the SQL that may be run concurrently.

To ensure optimal performance, the procedure cache must be sized properly to accommodate all the SQL that may be run concurrently. DBAs need information about the application programs that will be run in order to size the procedure cache effectively. The read-efficiency calculation we used for gauging the effectiveness of the data cache can be used for the procedure cache also. In the case of the procedure cache, the read efficiency calculates how often the DBMS needs to reoptimize SQL. Procedure cache read efficiency usually ranges from 60% to 80%. Of course, this percentage range will differ with the type of DBMS and the type of caching performed, as well as with the type of applications and the number of times the same SQL and programs are run. Refer to the sidebar "DB2 EDM Pool" for an example of a procedure cache.

"Open" Database Objects

As database applications process, the DBMS will need to open database objects for access and maintain the open objects. The DBMS will probably have a configuration option for setting this number. However, these numbers are difficult to arrive at originally. As time progresses, the database system can be monitored and better values can be provided.

Each open database object consumes memory.

To begin with, it is not uncommon simply to specify a value such that all production databases and objects can be open. However, each open database object consumes memory. Therefore, it is a good idea to temper this value, taking into account the size of the database implementation, the type of application processing, and the amount of memory available.

Database Logs

All changes to application data in the database are recorded serially in the database log.

The database log is another database system configuration option that can impact performance. The database log, sometimes referred to as the *transaction log*, is a fundamental component of a database management system. All changes to application data in the database are recorded serially in the database log (see Figure 10-4). Using this information, the DBMS can track which transaction made which changes to the database. Furthermore, ROLLBACK and RECOVER operations utilize the database log to reset the database to a particular point in time.

The manner in which the database log is created depends on the DBMS. Some DBMSs specify the log at the database system level, others define a database log for each database that is created within the database system. Some DBMSs provide a parameter to enable and disable logging. In general, avoid disabling database logging for any database or database system where the data is valuable. In other words, consider turning off database logging only for test databases.

Depending on the DBMS, the database log may consist of several files. For example, Oracle uses a transaction log and rollback segments to accomplish all of the functionality described in this section.

During normal database application processing, SQL INSERTS, UPDATES, and DELETES will be issued to modify data in the database. As these database

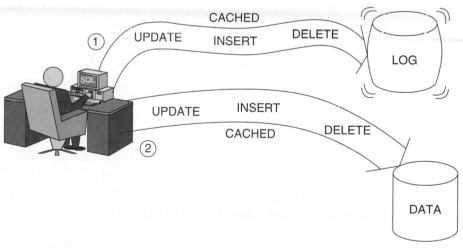

Figure 10-4   *Logging of database transactions.*

modifications are made, the transaction log for the database will grow. Because each database change is logged, the DBA will need to monitor actively the size of the transaction log files. And since data is constantly changing, the log will be continually growing.

The database transaction log is a write-ahead log.

The database transaction log is a *write-ahead log*. This means that changes are made to the transaction log before they are made to the data in the database tables. When the database modification has been fully recorded on the log, recovery of the transaction is guaranteed.

Typically, the DBMS takes a *system checkpoint* to guarantee that all log records and all modified database pages are written safely to disk. The frequency of database system checkpoints can be set up by the DBA using database configuration parameters. Checkpoint frequency is usually set as either a predetermined time interval or a preset number of log records written.

Generally, the following type of information is recorded on the database log:

- Beginning and ending time of each transaction
- Actual changes made to the data and enough information (using "before" and "after" images of the data) to undo the modifications made during each transaction
- Allocation and deallocation of database pages
- Actual COMMIT or ROLLBACK of each transaction

Using this information, the DBMS can accomplish data integrity operations to ensure consistent data. The transaction log is used when the DBMS is restarted, when transactions are rolled back, and to restore a database to a prior state. Let's examine each of these scenarios.

When the DBMS is restarted, each database goes through a recovery process. During restart processing, the DBMS will check to determine which transactions must be rolled forward. This occurs for transactions where it is unknown if all the modifications were actually written from the cache to disk. A checkpoint forces all modified pages to disk. Therefore, it represents the point at which the startup recovery must start to roll transactions forward. Because all pages modified before the checkpoint are guaranteed to be written accurately to disk, there is no need to roll forward anything done before the checkpoint.

When a transaction is rolled back, the DBMS copies "before" images to the database of every modification made since the transaction began.

During a recovery scenario, the DBA can use the transaction log to restore a database.

During a recovery scenario, the DBA can use the transaction log to restore a database. First, a backup copy of the database is restored and then subsequent transaction log backups can be restored. This causes a roll forward of the transaction log. During a roll forward, the DBMS will copy to the database "after" images of each modification. Using the logged data, the DBMS ensures that each modification is applied in the same order that it originally occurred.

You can see where the transaction log is a useful item to have around in case of database or transaction errors, and to ensure data integrity.

Database Log Configuration Considerations

The configuration of the database log can be a complicated task. Depending on the DBMS, the DBA may need to make multiple configuration decisions to set up the database transaction log, such as defining input buffers and output buffers, setting up log offloading, and defining the actual log files.

Defining output buffers for the database log can optimize log write operations. Writing log records to memory instead of directly to disk creates more efficient database processing. The DBMS can write log records asynchronously from the output buffer to the physical log file later. When logging is implemented in this fashion, database processing does not need to wait for synchronous log writes to occur to disk.

Defining input buffers for the database log can optimize operations—such as ROLLBACK and RECOVER—that read the database log.

It is a good idea to set up dual logs.

When configuring the database log, it is a good idea to set up dual logs. With dual logs, the DBMS will log changes to two separate and independent log files. Implementing dual logging provides a redundant log for use in case one of the logs fails. A log can fail for many reasons, including device failure, media problems, or simple carelessness. When setting up dual logging, be sure to define each log on separate devices and on separate controllers to minimize the possibility of both logs failing at the same time.

Another log configuration detail is deciding how database logs are to be handled when they fill up. Once again, the implementation details depend on the DBMS. Some DBMSs provide for automatic log offloading. *Log offloading* is the process of archiving an active log to an archival log and switching log writes to a new active log.

If the DBMS performs automatic log offloading, you can improve performance by offloading to an archive log on disk instead of tape. By archiving to disk, the log offloading process will run faster, and backout and recovery processes can also run faster because the log records will be on disk—meaning not just faster I/O but no wait for tapes to be mounted. The DBA can use a storage management system to automatically migrate archive logs to tape after a predetermined amount of time.

Some DBMSs require the database log to be explicitly backed up. In this case, you will need to implement periodic backups of the transaction log. Typically, the DBMS provides a specific backup command to create a transaction log backup. When the DBMS finishes backing up the transaction log, it truncates the inactive portion of the transaction log to free up space on the transaction log. Truncation of the log enables the DBMS to reuse space.

Of course, as a DBA you will need to learn how each DBMS you use handles backing up the database log. DB2 automatically archives the transaction log; Microsoft SQL Server requires the DBA to back up transaction log files. In fact, Microsoft SQL Server provides some odd features for handling the transaction log; the sidebar "Microsoft SQL Server Log Options" discusses the parameters that can impact the operation of the database log.

Are All Database Operations Logged?

Certain situations and commands may not be logged.

Depending on the DBMS, certain situations and commands may not be logged. To avoid "out of space" conditions caused by rapid growth in transaction log files, the DBMS may turn off logging. For example, some DDL operations and database utility executions might not be logged. Beware of these situations and plan accordingly for your recovery needs.

During some large operations, such as CREATE INDEX, the DBMS will probably not log every new page. Instead, the DBMS will record enough information in the database log to determine that a CREATE INDEX happened, so that it can either be recreated during a roll forward, or removed during a rollback.

Additionally, some DBMSs provide configuration options at the database level to turn off logging for some types of processing. For example, in Microsoft SQL Server, when the SELECT INTO/BULKCOPY database option is set to TRUE, the following operations will not be recorded in the database transaction log: bulk load operations, SELECT INTO statements, and WRITETEXT and UPDATETEXT statements. These four operations usually cause a large volume of data to be changed in the database. As such, logging can slow down these processes, so logging can optionally be disabled for these operations only. However, because these operations are not recorded in the transaction log, SQL Server cannot use the RESTORE operation on the transaction log to recover these operations. If the DBMS has no knowledge of the operations in the log, it cannot recover the data.

Microsoft SQL Server Log Options

Microsoft SQL Server provides a system configuration parameter that affects the behavior of database logging. The TRUNC LOG ON CHKPT option can be changed at the database level. Use the system procedure named SP_DBOPTION to change the configuration settings for a database.

```
EXEC SP_DBOPTION 'pubs', 'trunc. log on chkpt.', 'false'
```

Issuing this command causes the TRUNC LOG ON CHKPT option to be set to FALSE for the pubs database. To see a list of all current database options set for a database, simply issue the system procedure without additional parameters.

```
EXEC SP_DBOPTION pubs
```

The TRUNC LOG ON CHKPT option is potentially quite dangerous. When this option is set to TRUE, every checkpoint operation will cause the database log to be truncated—that is, the database log will be emptied and reset, causing all of the logged changes to be lost. A database cannot be recovered using a log that is truncated on checkpoints.

You might consider setting TRUNC LOG ON CHKPT option to TRUE for test databases during your application development cycle, but not for mission-critical, production databases. The DBA needs to be aware of these options and ensure that the appropriate settings are made, based on the needs of the users of the data and the applications that access that data.

Of course, SQL Server is not the only DBMS that disables logging for certain operations. Another example is the DB2 REORG utility. A parameter is provided to disable or enable logging during the reorganization process. As a DBA, you will need to learn how and when to turn off logging using your DBMS. Moreover, keep in mind that whenever logging is turned off, the data must be backed up both before and after the nonlogged process to ensure point-in-time recoverability.

Locking and Contention

Balance the need for concurrency with the need for performance.

Concurrency operations such as *deadlock detection* and *lock manager settings* can greatly impact database system performance. Database processing relies on locking to ensure consistent data based on user requirements and to avoid losing data during updates. You must balance the need for concurrency with the need for performance. If at all possible, seek to minimize the following situations.

- *Lock suspensions* occur when an application process requests a lock that is already held by another application process and cannot be shared. The suspended process temporarily stops running until the requested lock becomes available.

- *Timeouts* occur when an application process is terminated because it has been suspended for longer than a preset interval. This interval can usually be set by using a configuration parameter.

- *Deadlocks* occur when two or more application processes hold locks on resources that the others need and without which they cannot proceed. The deadlock detection cycle—that is the time interval between checking for deadlocks—can also be set by using a configuration parameter.

When accessing a relational database, the locking process can be quite complex. It depends on the type of processing, the lock size specified when the table was created, the isolation level of the program or SQL statement, the method of data access, and the DBMS configuration parameters. To tune database locking requires a combination of system, database, and application tuning.

The System Catalog

The physical location and setup of the system catalog will have an impact on system performance. The DBA must decide where it will be installed, on what type of disk, and how much space to allocate. These decisions typically are made at installation time.

Place the system catalog on a separate disk device.

As a rule of thumb, place the system catalog on a separate disk device so that it can be managed and tuned independently from other application data. If possible, consider completely dedicating a disk volume or two to the system catalog. Consider placing the indexes and tables on separate disk volumes. In addition, if the DBMS does not already provide a separate data cache for the system catalog, consider isolating the system catalog into its own dedicated data cache. Doing this makes it easer to track the efficiency of system I/O versus application I/O.

When changes need to be made to the system catalog database, utilities such as REORG, COPY, and RECOVER or file system commands need to be used. Changes may need to be made to increase the size of the system catalog, to add a new index, or to migrate to a new release of the DBMS. Usually a migration utility is provided to make system catalog changes.

DBAs should use the system catalog to actively manage their database environment. It is a good practice to actively monitor the database objects in the system catalog and delete obsolete objects. For example, in DB2 for OS/390, IBM delivers sample tables with every new version of DB2. The database object names have the DB2 version number embedded within them. Every new release causes new sample tables to be created. The DBA should delete the old sample tables when new ones are installed. This advice applies to all unused database objects, not just to sample tables. If a tablespace exists that is no longer used, it is consuming valuable resources (disk space, system catalog space, etc.) that can be freed up when the database object is dropped.

Other Configuration Options

Every DBMS will have many configuration and tuning options that are particular to that DBMS. The DBA needs to become an expert in the options that are available and understand the impact of each permissible setting.

Some example configuration options that may be encountered include

- *Nested trigger calls.* Some DBMSs can enable and disable nested trigger calls. A *nested trigger call* is when one trigger causes another trigger to fire. Some DBMSs may provide additional control over trigger nesting by providing a maximum value for it. By setting this value, the DBA can control how many levels of nested trigger calls are allowable. Control over triggers can have an enormous impact on performance. For example, if an application hits the maximum number of nested triggers, all of the changes caused by all previous triggers need to be rolled back— potentially causing considerable performance degradation.

- *Security options.* The functionality of security and authorization can be controlled by DBMS configuration options. Some DBMSs allow database security to be turned over to external security and control software.

- *Identity values.* The identity property can be assigned to a column such that the DBMS automatically assigns numerically sequential values when data is inserted into the table. The DBMS can allow the configuration of the pool size from which identity values are obtained.

- *Distributed database.* To configure a distributed database implementation, the DBMS most likely will provide options for connecting databases at various locations.

General Advice

When configuring your database environment, avoid defaults. Most configuration options will default to a predefined value if no specific value is assigned. The major problem with using default values is that they almost never are the best choice for your particular environment. It is always a good idea to specify the value of every configuration parameter *even if the default value is the one you wish to choose*.

Finally, beware of configuration options that change the behavior of the DBMS. Simply setting a single configuration parameter to the wrong value can cause a lot of damage. Consider the following parameters and their potential impact.

- Oracle provides an optimization-mode parameter to choose between cost-based and rule-based SQL optimization. These two methods can create dramatically different SQL access paths with dramatically different performance.

- Sybase provides a parameter called ALLOW UPDATES that controls whether the system catalog tables can be modified using SQL. When this option is turned on, the system catalog can be changed quite easily. This is to be avoided except under the guidance of Sybase technical support. System catalog changes should be driven by the DBMS itself, not by user-issued SQL.

- DB2 provides several parameters that control the behavior of database operations such as parallel queries, data sharing, and dynamic SQL caching.

System Monitoring

A DBMS environment should be continually monitored for performance degradation and problems. Some DBMSs provide built-in monitors to accomplish rudimentary monitoring. Additional performance monitoring solutions such as BMC Software's PATROL or Omegamon from Candle Corporation can be deployed to provide more robust monitoring functionality, such as dynamic alerting, and proactive management of performance problems. Refer to the sidebar "Sybase SP_MONITOR" for information on the Sybase DBMS performance monitor.

The performance monitor acts as a window into the efficiency of the database system.

Performance monitors are available for every aspect of the system environment, not just the DBMS. So you may be able to monitor the operating system, network, transaction server, and any other system middleware for performance problems. A DBA must be able to operate and understand the output of the monitoring solutions available to him. The performance monitor acts as a window into the efficiency of the database system (or lack thereof).

Sybase SP_MONITOR

The SP_MONITOR system procedure is a rudimentary tool supplied by Sybase with its DBMS. When the procedure is run, it displays DBMS activity in terms of the following performance-oriented numbers:

- **last run:** date and time that SP_MONITOR was last executed
- **current run:** date and time that SP_MONITOR was run to produce this report
- **seconds:** total number of seconds since the last SP_MONITOR was run
- **cpu busy:** CPU time, in milliseconds, that the server CPU spent performing Sybase work
- **io busy:** CPU time, in milliseconds, that the server CPU spent performing Sybase I/O operations
- **idle:** CPU time, in milliseconds, that Sybase has been idle
- **packets received:** number of input packets read by Sybase
- **packets sent:** number of output packets sent by Sybase
- **packet errors:** number of errors detected by Sybase while reading and writing packets
- **total read:** number of disk reads performed by Sybase
- **total write:** number of disk writes performed by Sybase
- **total errors:** total number of errors detected by Sybase while reading or writing
- **connections:** number of logins or attempted logins to Sybase

The numbers are cumulative since the last time SP_MONITOR was executed.

Summary

If the environment where the DBMS must operate is not performing efficiently, it is impossible for the DBMS, and indeed any database access, to perform efficiently. The DBA needs to understand every DBMS configuration value and the impact it can have on the overall performance of the system. Furthermore, the DBA must control the integration of the DBMS with the hardware on which the DBMS runs and any allied agent software.

Review

1. What is the single most important configurable component of a relational database management system?

2. How does the data cache (or buffer pool) improve the performance of database processing?

3. Describe how to determine the read efficiency of the data cache.

4. What components of the DBMS require system memory to control?

5. What three concurrency problems can negatively impact performance?

6. Why are certain database operations not logged?

7. A DBMS is comprised of multiple programs interacting with one another: True or False.

8. What are the three possible statuses of a page in the data cache?

9. What benefits can accrue by caching optimized SQL in memory?

10. What type of information is recorded on the database transaction log?

Bonus Question

When a database operation is not logged, what precautions should the DBA take before and after the nonlogged operation? Why?

Suggested Reading

Baird, Sean, et al. *SQL Server System Administration.* Indianapolis, IN: New Riders (1999). ISBN 1-56205-955-6

Johnson, Robert H. *MVS Concepts and Facilities.* New York, NY: McGraw-Hill (1989). ISBN 0-07-032673-8

Kirkwood, John. *Sybase Architecture and Administration.* New York, NY: Ellis Horwood (1993). ISBN 0-13-100330-5

Mullins, Craig S. *DB2 Developer's Guide.* 4th ed. Indianapolis, IN: SAMS (2000). ISBN 0-672-31828-8

Reiss, Levi, and Joseph Radin, *Unix System Administration Guide.* Berkeley, CA: Osborne/McGraw-Hill (1993). ISBN 0-07-881951-2

Siyan, Karanjit S. *Windows NT Server 4: Professional Reference.* Indianapolis, IN: New Riders (1997). ISBN 1-56205-805-3

Taylor, Ed. *Demystifying SNA.* Plano, TX: Wordware (1993). 1-55622-404-4

———. *Demystifying TCP/IP.* Plano, TX: Wordware (1993). 1-55622-400-1

Terplan, Kornel, and Jill Huntington-Lee. *Distributed Systems and Network Management.* New York, NY: Van Nostrand Reinhold (1995). ISBN 0-442-01873-8

11

Database Performance

Database performance focuses on tuning and optimizing the design, parameters, and physical construction of database objects, specifically tables and indexes, and the files in which their data is stored. The actual composition and structure of database objects must be monitored continually and changed accordingly if the database becomes inefficient. No amount of SQL tweaking or system tuning can optimize the performance of queries run against a poorly designed or disorganized database.

Techniques for Optimizing Databases

The DBA must be cognizant of the features of the DBMS in order to apply the proper techniques for optimizing the performance of database structures. Most of the major DBMSs support the following techniques although perhaps by different names. Each of the following techniques can be used to tune database performance and will be discussed in subsequent sections.

- *Partitioning*—breaking a single database table into sections stored in multiple files.

- *Raw partitions versus file systems*—choosing whether to store database data in an OS-controlled file or not.

- *Indexing*—choosing the proper indexes and options to enable efficient queries.

- *Denormalization*—varying from the logical design to achieve better query performance.

- *Clustering*—enforcing the physical sequence of data on disk.

- *Interleaving data*—combining data from multiple tables into a single, sequenced file.

- *Free space*—leaving room for data growth.

- *Compression*—algorithmically reducing storage requirements.

- *File placement and allocation*—putting the right files in the right place.

- *Page size*—using the proper page size for efficient data storage and I/O.

- *Reorganization*—removing inefficiencies from the database by realigning and restructuring database objects.

Partitioning

One decision that the DBA must make for every table is how to store its data.

A database table is a logical manifestation of a set of data that physically resides on computerized storage. One of the decisions that the DBA must make for every table is how to store that data. Each DBMS provides different mechanisms that accomplish the same thing—mapping physical files to database tables. The DBA must decide from among the following mapping options for each table:

- *Single table to a single file.* This is, by far, the most common choice. The data in the file is formatted such that the DBMS understands the table structure and every row inserted into that table is stored in the same file. However, this setup is not necessarily the most efficient.

- *Single table to multiple files.* This option is used most often for very large tables or tables requiring data to be physically separated at the storage level. Mapping to multiple files is accomplished by using partitioned tablespaces or by implementing segmented disk devices.

- *Multiple tables to a single file.* This type of mapping is used for small tables such as lookup tables and code tables, and can be more efficient from a disk utilization perspective.

Partitioning helps
to accomplish
parallelism.

Partitioning helps to accomplish parallelism. *Parallelism* is the process of using multiple tasks to access the database in parallel. A parallel request can be invoked to use multiple, simultaneous read engines for a single SQL statement. Parallelism is desirable because it can substantially reduce the elapsed time for database queries.

Multiple types of parallelism are based on the resources that can be invoked in parallel. For example, a single query can be broken down into multiple requests each utilizing a different CPU engine in parallel. In addition, parallelism can be improved by spreading the work across multiple database instances. Each DBMS offers different levels of support for parallel database queries. To optimize database performance, the DBA should be cognizant of the support offered in each DBMS being managed and exploit the parallel query capabilities.

Raw Partition vs. File System

For a UNIX-based DBMS environment, the DBA must choose between a raw partition and using the UNIX file system to store the data in the database. A *raw partition* is the preferred type of physical device for database storage because writes are cached by the operating system when a file system is utilized. When writes are buffered by the operating system, the DBMS does not know whether the data has been physically copied to disk or not. When the DBMS cache manager attempts to writes the data to disk, the operating system may delay the write until later because the data may still be in the file system cache. If a failure occurs, data in a database using the file system for storage may not be 100% recoverable. This is to be avoided.

If a raw partition is used instead, the data is written directly from the database cache to disk with no intermediate file system or operating system caching, as shown in Figure 11-1. When the DBMS cache manager writes the data to disk, it will physically be written to disk with no intervention. Additionally, when

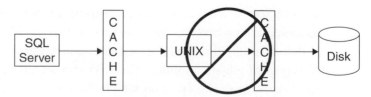

Figure 11-1   *Using raw partitions to avoid file system caching*

using a raw partition, the DBMS will ensure that enough space is available and write the allocation pages. When using a file system, the operating system will not preallocate space for database usage.

From a performance perspective, there is no advantage to having a secondary layer of caching at the file system or operating system level; the DBMS cache is sufficient. Actually, the additional work required to cache the data a second time consumes resources, thereby negatively impacting the overall performance of database operations.

Do not supplement the DBMS cache with any type of additonal cache.

Indexing

Indexes are used to enhance performance.

Creating the correct indexes on tables in the database is perhaps the single greatest performance tuning technique that a DBA can perform. Indexes are used to enhance performance. Indexes are particularly useful for

- Locating rows by value(s) in column(s)
- Making joins more efficient (when the index is defined on the join columns)
- Correlating data across tables
- Aggregating data
- Sorting data to satisfy a query

Without indexes, all access to data in the database would have to be performed by scanning all available rows. Scans are very inefficient for very large tables.

Designing and creating indexes for database tables actually crosses the line between database performance tuning and application performance tuning. Indexes are database objects created by the DBA with database DDL. However, an index is built to make SQL statements in application programs run faster. Indexing as a tuning effort is applied to the database to make applications more efficient when the data access patterns of the application vary from what was anticipated when the database was designed.

Before tuning the database by creating new indexes, be sure to understand the impact of adding an index. The DBA should have an understanding of the access patterns of the table on which the index will be built. Useful information includes the percentage of queries that access rather than update the table, the performance thresholds set within any service level agreements for queries on the table, and the impact of adding a new index to running database utilities such as loads, reorganizations, and recovery.

One of the big unanswered questions of database design is: "How many indexes should be created for a single table?" There is no set answer to this question. The DBA will need to use his expertise to determine the proper number of indexes for each table such that database queries are optimized and the performance of database inserts, updates, and deletes does not degrade. Determining the proper number of indexes for each table requires in-depth analysis of the database and the applications that access the database.

The general goal of index analysis is to use less I/O to the database to satisfy the queries made against the table. Of course, an index can help some queries and hinder others. Therefore, the DBA must assess the impact of adding an index to all applications and not just tune single queries in a vacuum. This can be an arduous but rewarding task.

An index affects performance positively when fewer I/Os are used to return results to a query. Conversely, an index negatively impacts performance when data is updated and the indexes have to be changed as well. An effective indexing strategy seeks to provide the greatest reduction in I/O with an acceptable level of effort to keep the indexes updated.

Some applications have troublesome queries that require significant tuning to achieve satisfactory performance. Creating an index to support a single query is acceptable if that query is important enough in terms of ROI to the business (or if it is run by your boss or the CEO). If the query is run infrequently, consider creating the index before the process begins and dropping the index when the process is complete.

Be sure to thoroughly test the performance of the queries the index supports.

Whenever you create new indexes, be sure to thoroughly test the performance of the queries it supports. Additionally, be sure to test database modification statements to gauge the additional overhead of updating the new indexes. Review the CPU time, elapsed time, and I/O requirements to assure that the indexes help. Keep in mind that tuning is an iterative process, and it may take time and several index tweaks to determine the impact of a change. There are no hard and fast rules for index creation. Experiment with different index combinations and measure the results.

For additional information on the structure of indexes and the types of indexes commonly supported by DBMSs, refer to the section on designing indexes in Chapter 4.

When to Avoid Indexing

There are a few scenarios where indexing may not be a good idea. When tables are very small, say less than ten pages, consider avoiding indexes. Indexed access to a small table can be less efficient than simply scanning all of the rows because reading the index adds I/O requests.

Index I/O notwithstanding, even a small table can sometimes benefit from being indexed—for example, to enforce uniqueness or if most data access retrieves a single row using the primary key.

You may want to avoid indexing variable-length columns if the DBMS in question expands the variable column to the maximum length within the index. Such expansion can cause indexes to consume an inordinate amount of disk space and might be inefficient. However, if variable-length columns are used in SQL WHERE clauses, the cost of disk storage must be compared to the cost of scanning. Buying some extra disk storage is usually cheaper than wasting CPU resources to scan rows. Furthermore, the SQL query might contain alternate predicates that could be indexed instead of the variable-length columns.

Avoid indexing any table that is always accessed using a scan.

Additionally, avoid indexing any table that is always accessed using a scan, that is, the SQL issued against the table never supplies a WHERE clause.

Index Overloading

Query performance can be enhanced in certain situations by overloading an index with additional columns. Indexes are typically based on the WHERE clauses of SQL SELECT statements. For example, consider the following SQL statement.

```
select  emp_no, last_name, salary
from    employee
where   salary > 15000.00
;
```

Creating an index on the salary column can enhance the performance of this query. However, the DBA can further enhance the performance of the query by overloading the index with the emp_no and last_name columns, as well. With an overloaded index, the DBMS can satisfy the query by using *only* the index. The DBMS need not incur the additional I/O of accessing the table data, since every piece of data that is required by the query exists in the overloaded index.

DBAs should consider overloading indexes to encourage index-only access when multiple queries can benefit from the index or when individual queries are very important.

Denormalization

Another way to optimize the performance of database access is to denormalize the tables. Denormalization was covered in detail in Chapter 4, so we will not discuss the topic in depth here. Suffice it to say, *denormalization*, the opposite of *normalization*, is the process of putting one fact in many places. This speeds data retrieval at the expense of data modification. Denormalizing tables can be a good decision when a completely normalized design does not perform optimally.

The only reason to denormalize a relational database is to enhance performance.

The only reason to ever denormalize a relational database design is to enhance performance. As discussed in Chapter 4, you should consider the following options:

- *Prejoined tables*—when the cost of joining is prohibitive.
- *Report table*—when specialized critical reports are too costly to generate.
- *Mirror table*—when tables are required concurrently by two types of environments.
- *Split tables*—when distinct groups use different parts of a table.
- *Combined tables*—to consolidate one-to-one or one-to-many relationships into a single table.
- *Speed table*—to support hierarchies like bill-of-materials or reporting structures.
- *Physical denormalization*—to take advantage of specific DBMS characteristics.

You might also consider

- Storing *redundant data* in tables to reduce the number of table joins required.
- Storing *repeating groups* in a row to reduce I/O and possibly disk space.
- Storing *derivable data* to eliminate calculations and costly algorithms.

Clustering

A clustered table will store its rows physically on disk in order by a specified column or columns.

A clustered table will store its rows physically on disk in order by a specified column or columns. Clustering usually is enforced by the DBMS with a clustering index. The clustering index forces table rows to be stored in ascending order by the indexed columns. The left-to-right order of the columns as defined in the index, defines the collating sequence for the clustered index. There can be only one clustering sequence per table (because physically the data can be stored in only one sequence).

Figure 11-2 demonstrates the difference between clustered and unclustered data and indexes; the clustered index is on top, the unclustered index is on the bottom. As you can see, the entries on the leaf pages of the top index

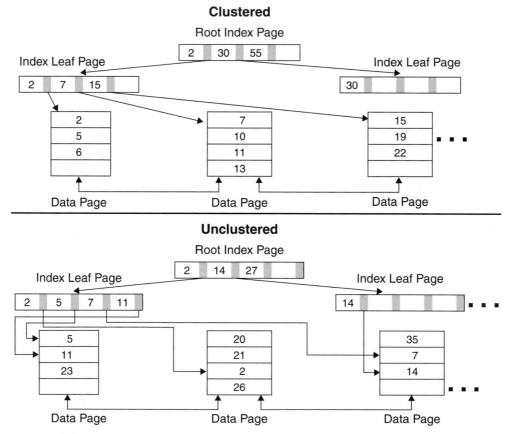

Figure 11-2   *Clustered and unclustered indexes*

are in sequential order—in other words, they are clustered. Clustering enhances the performance of queries that access data sequentially because fewer I/Os need to be issued to retrieve the same data.

Depending on the DBMS, the data may not always be physically maintained in exact clustering sequence. When a clustering sequence has been defined for a table, the DBMS will act in one of two ways to enforce clustering:

1. When new rows are inserted, the DBMS will physically maneuver data rows and pages to fit the new rows into the defined clustering sequence; or

2. When new rows are inserted, the DBMS will try to place the data into the defined clustering sequence, but if space is not available on the required page the data may be placed elsewhere.

The DBA must learn how the DBMS maintains clustering. If the DBMS operates as in the second scenario, data may become unclustered over time and require reorganization. A detailed discussion of database reorganization appears later in this chapter. For now, though, back to our discussion of clustering.

Clustering tables that are accessed sequentially is good practice. In other words, clustered indexes are good for supporting range access, whereas unclustered indexes are better for supporting random access. Be sure to choose the clustering columns wisely. Use clustered indexes for the following situations:

- Join columns, to optimize SQL joins where multiple rows match for one or both tables participating in the join

- Foreign key columns because they are frequently involved in joins and the DBMS accesses foreign key values during declarative referential integrity checking

- Predicates in a WHERE clause

- Range columns

- Columns that do not change often (reduces physically reclustering)

- Columns that are frequently grouped or sorted in SQL statements

In general, the clustering sequence that aids the performance of the most commonly accessed predicates should be used to for clustering. When a table has multiple candidates for clustering, weigh the cost of sorting against the

Clustering tables that are accessed sequentially is good practice.

performance gained by clustering for each candidate key. As a rule of thumb, though, if the DBMS supports clustering, it is usually a good practice to define a clustering index for each table that is created (unless the table is very small).

Clustering is generally not recommended for primary key columns because the primary key is, by definition, unique. However, if ranges of rows frequently are selected and ordered by primary key value, a clustering index may be beneficial.

Page Splitting

The process of creating new pages to store inserted data is called page splitting.

When the DBMS has to accommodate inserts, and no space exists, it must create a new page within the database to store the new data. The process of creating new pages to store inserted data is called *page splitting*. A DBMS can perform two types of page splitting: *normal page splits* and *monotonic page splits*. Some DBMSs support both types of page splitting, while others support only one type. The DBA needs to know how the DBMS implements page splitting in order to optimize the database.

Figure 11-3 depicts a normal page split. To accomplish this, the DBMS performs the following tasks in sequence:

1. Creates a new empty page in between the full page and the next page
2. Takes half of the entries from the full page and moves them to the empty page
3. Adjusts any internal pointers to both pages and inserts the row accordingly

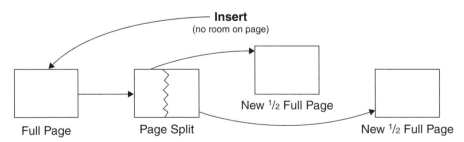

Figure 11-3   *Normal page splitting*

A monotonic page split is a much simpler process, requiring only two steps. The DBMS

- Creates a new page in between the full page and the next page
- Inserts the new values into the fresh page

Monotonic page splits are useful when rows are being inserted in strictly ascending sequence. Typically, a DBMS that supports monotonic page splits will invoke it when a new row is added to the end of a page and the last addition was also to the end of the page.

When ascending rows are inserted and normal page splitting is used, a lot of space can be wasted because the DBMS will be creating half-full pages that never fill up. If the wrong type of page split is performed during database processing, wasted space will ensue, requiring the database object to be reorganized for performance.

Interleaving Data

Interleaving can be viewed as a specialized form of clustering.

When data from two tables is frequently joined, it can make sense to physically interleave the data into the same physical storage structure. This can be viewed as a specialized form of clustering (and, in fact, Oracle uses the term *cluster* to define interleaved data). Interleaving data is covered in Chapter 4 and is mentioned here as a performance tuning technique to consider.

Free Space

Free space, sometimes called *fill factor*, can be used to leave a portion of a tablespace or index empty and available to store newly added data. The specification of free space in a tablespace or index can reduce the frequency of reorganization, reduce contention, and increase the efficiency of insertion. Each DBMS provides a method of specifying free space for a database object in the CREATE and ALTER statements. A typical parameter is PCTFREE, where the DBA specifies the percentage of each data page that should remain available for future inserts. Another possible parameter is FREEPAGE, where the DBA indicates the specified number of pages after which a completely empty page is available.

Ensure a proper
amount of free
space for each
database object.
Ensuring a proper amount of free space for each database object provides the following benefits:

- Inserts are faster when free space is available.
- As new rows are inserted, they can be properly clustered.
- Variable-length rows and altered rows have room to expand, potentially reducing the number of relocated rows.
- Fewer rows on a page results in better concurrency because less data is unavailable to other users when a page is locked.

However, free space also has several disadvantages.

- Disk storage requirements are greater.
- Scans take longer.
- Fewer rows on a page can require more I/O operations to access the requested information.
- Because the number of rows per page decreases, the efficiency of data caching can decrease because fewer rows are retrieved per I/O.

The DBA should monitor free space and ensure that the appropriate amount is defined for each database object. The correct amount of free space must be based on

- Frequency of inserts and modifications
- Amount of sequential versus random access
- Impact of accessing unclustered data
- Type of processing
- Likelihood of row chaining, row migration, and page splits

Don't define a static table with free space—it will not need room in which to expand.

Compression

Compression can be used to shrink the size of a database. By compressing data, the database requires less disk storage. Some DBMSs provide internal DDL options to compress database files; third-party software is available for those that do not provide such features.

When compression is specified, data is algorithmically compressed upon insertion into the database and decompressed when it is read. Reading and writing compressed data consumes more CPU resources than reading and writing uncompressed data: The DBMS must execute code to compress and decompress the data as users insert, update, and read the data.

So why compress data? Consider an uncompressed table with a row size of 800 bytes. Five of this table's rows would fit in a 4K data page (or block). Now what happens if the data is compressed? Assume that the compression routine achieves 30% compression on average (a very conservative estimate). In that case, the 800-byte row will consume only 560 bytes ($800 \times 0.30 = 560$). After compressing the data, seven rows will fit on a 4K page. Because I/O occurs at the page level, a single I/O will retrieve more data, which will optimize the performance of sequential data scans and increase the likelihood of data residing in the cache because more rows fit on a physical page.

Compression always requires a trade-off.

Of course, compression always requires a trade-off that the DBA must analyze. On the positive side, we have disk savings and the potential for reducing I/O cost. On the negative side, we have the additional CPU cost required to compress and decompress the data.

However, compression is not an option for every database index or table. For smaller amounts of data, it is possible that a compressed file will be larger than an uncompressed file. This is so because some DBMSs and compression algorithms require an internal dictionary to manage the compression. The dictionary contains statistics about the composition of the data that is being compressed. For a trivial amount of data, the size of the dictionary may be greater than the amount of storage saved by compression.

File Placement and Allocation

The DBA must make every effort to minimize the cost of physical disk reading and writing.

The location of the files containing the data for the database can have a significant impact on performance. A database is very I/O intensive, and the DBA must make every effort to minimize the cost of physical disk reading and writing.

This discipline entails

- Understanding the access patterns associated with each piece of data in the system

- Placing the data on physical disk devices in such a way as to optimize performance

The first consideration for file placement on disk is to separate the indexes from the data, if possible. Database queries are frequently required to access data from both the table and an index on that table. If both of these files reside on the same disk device, performance degradation is likely. To retrieve data from disk, an arm moves over the surface of the disk to read physical blocks of data on the disk. If a single operation is accessing data from files on the same disk device, latency will occur; reads from one file will have to wait until reads from the other file are processed. Of course, if the DBMS combines the index with the data in the same file, this technique cannot be used.

Another rule for file placement is to analyze the access patterns of your applications and separate the files for tables that are frequently accessed together. The DBA should do this for the same reason he should separate index files from table files.

A final consideration for placing files on separate disk devices occurs when a single table is stored in multiple files (partitioning). It is wise in this case to place each file on a separate disk device to encourage and optimize parallel database operations. If the DBMS can break apart a query to run it in parallel, placing multiple files for partitioned tables on separate disk devices will minimize disk latency.

Database Log Placement

Placing the transaction log on a separate disk device from the actual data allows the DBA to back up the transaction log independently from the database. It also minimizes dual writes to the same disk. Writing data to two files on the same disk drive at the same time will degrade performance even more than reading data from two files on the same disk drive at the same time. Remember, too, every database modification (write) is recorded on the database transaction log.

Distributed Data Placement

Data placement optimizes access by reducing contention on physical devices.

The goal of data placement is to optimize access by reducing contention on physical devices. Within a client/server environment, this goal can be expanded to encompass the optimization of application performance by reducing network transmission costs.

Data should reside at the database server where it is most likely, or most often, to be accessed. For example, Chicago data should reside at the Chicago database server, Los Angeles–specific data should reside at the Los Angeles database server, and so on. If the decision is not so clear-cut (e.g., San Francisco data, if there is no database server in San Francisco), place the data on the database server that is geographically closest to where it will be most frequently accessed (in the case of San Francisco, L.A., not Chicago).

Be sure to take fragmentation, replication, and snapshot tables into account when deciding upon the placement of data in your distributed network.

Disk Allocation

The DBMS may require disk devices to be allocated for database usage. If this is the case, the DBMS will provide commands to initialize physical disk devices. The disk initialization command will associate a logical name for a physical disk partition or OS file. After the disk has been initialized, it is stored in the system catalog and can be used for storing table data.

Before initializing a disk, verify that sufficient space is available on the physical disk device. Likewise, make sure that the device is not already initialized.

Use meaningful
device names to
facilitate more effi-
cient usage.

Use meaningful device names to facilitate more efficient usage and management of disk devices. For example, it is difficult to misinterpret the usage of a device named DUMP_DEV1 or TEST_DEV7. However, names such as XYZ or A193 are not particularly useful. Additionally, maintain documentation on initialized devices by saving script files containing the actual initialization commands and diagrams indicating the space allocated by device.

Page Size (Block Size)

Choosing the
proper page size
is an important
DBA task.

Most DBMSs provide the ability to specify a page, or block, size. The *page size* is used to store table rows (or more accurately, records that contain the row contents plus any overhead) on disk. For example, consider a table requiring rows that are 125 bytes in length with 6 additional bytes of overhead. This makes each record 131 bytes long. To store 25 records on a page, the page size would have to be at least 3275 bytes. However, each DBMS requires some amount of page overhead as well, so the practical size will be larger. If page overhead is 20 bytes, then the page size would be 3295—that is, 3275 + 20 bytes of overhead.

This discussion, however, is simplistic. In general practice, most tablespaces will require some amount of free space to accommodate new data. Therefore, some percentage of free space will need to be factored into the above equation.

To complicate matters, many DBMSs limit the page sizes that can be chosen. For example, DB2 for OS/390 limits page size to 4K, 8K, 16K, or 32K. In this case, the DBA will need to calculate the best page size based on row size, the number of rows per page, and free space requirements.

Consider this question: "In DB2 for OS/390, what page size should be chosen if 0% free space is required and the record size is 2500 bytes?"

The simplistic answer is 4K, but it might not be the best answer. A 4K page would hold one 2500-byte record per page, but an 8K page would hold three 2500-byte records. The 8K page would provide for more efficient I/O, because reading 8K of data would return three rows, whereas reading 8K of data using two 4K pages would return only two rows.

Choosing the proper page size is an important DBA task for optimizing database I/O performance.

Database Reorganization

Relational technology and SQL make data modification easy. Just issue an INSERT, UPDATE, or DELETE statement with the appropriate WHERE clause, and the DBMS takes care of the actual data navigation and modification. In order to provide this level of abstraction, the DBMS handles the physical placement and movement of data on disk. Theoretically, this makes everyone happy. The programmer's interface is simplified, and the RDBMS takes care of the hard part—manipulating the actual placement of data. However, things are not quite that simple. The manner in which the DBMS physically manages data can cause subsequent performance problems.

Query or application slowdowns have many potential causes.

Every DBA has encountered the situation where a query or application that used to perform well slows down after it has been in production for a while. These slowdowns have many potential causes—perhaps the number of transactions issued has increased, or the volume of data has expanded. However, the performance problem might be due to database disorganization. Database disorganization occurs when a database's logical and physical storage allocations contain many scattered areas of storage that are too small, not physically contiguous, or too disorganized to be used productively. Let's review the primary culprits.

- The first possibility is *unclustered data*. If the DBMS does not strictly enforce clustering, a clustered table or index can become unclustered as data is added and changed. If the data becomes significantly unclustered, the DBMS cannot rely on the clustering sequence. Because the data is no longer clustered, queries that were optimized to access data cannot take advantage of the clustering sequence. In this case, the performance of queries run against the unclustered table will suffer.

- *Fragmentation* is a condition in which there are many scattered areas of storage in a database that are too small to be used productively. It results in wasted space, which can hinder performance because additional I/Os are required to retrieve the same data.

- *Row chaining* or *row migration* occurs when updated data does not fit in the space it currently occupies, and the DBMS must find space for the row. With row chaining, the DBMS moves a part of the new, larger row to a location within the tablespace where free space exists. With row migrations, the full row is placed elsewhere in the tablespace. In each case, a pointer is used to locate either the rest of the row or the full row. Both row chaining and row migration will result in the issuance of multiple I/Os to read a single row. Performance will suffer because multiple I/Os are more expensive than a single I/O.

- *Page splits* can cause disorganized databases, too. If the DBMS performs monotonic page splits when it should perform normal page splits, or vice versa, space may be wasted. When space is wasted, fewer rows exist on each page, causing the DBMS to issue more I/O requests to retrieve data. Therefore, once again, performance suffers.

- *File extents* can negatively impact performance. An *extent* is an additional file that is tied to the original file and can be used only in conjunction with the original file. When the file used by a tablespace runs out of space, an extent is added for the file to expand. However, file extents are not stored contiguously with the original file. As additional extents are added, data requests will need to track the data from extent to extent, and the additional code this requires is unneeded overhead. Resetting the database space requirements and reorganizing can clean up file extents.

Let's take a look at a disorganized tablespace by comparing Figures 11-4 and 11-5. Assume that a tablespace consists of three tables across multiple blocks, such as the tablespace and tables depicted in Figure 11-4. Each box represents a data page.

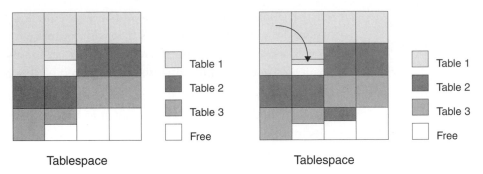

Figure 11-4 *Organized tablespace*   **Figure 11-5** *Disorganized tablespace*

Now, let's make a couple of changes to the data in these tables. First, we'll add six rows to the second table. However, no free space exists into which these new rows can be stored. How can the rows be added? The DBMS requires an additional extent to be taken into which the new rows can be placed. This results in fragmentation: The new rows have been placed in a noncontiguous space. For the second change, let's update a row in the first table to change a variable-length column; for example, let's change the value in a LASTNAME column from WATSON to BEAUCHAMP. Issuing this update results in an expanded row size because the value for LASTNAME is longer in the new row: "BEAUCHAMP" contains 9 characters whereas "WATSON" only consists of 6. This action results in row chaining. The resultant tablespace shown in Figure 11-5 depicts both the fragmentation and the row chaining.

Depending on the DBMS, there may be additional causes of disorganization. For example, if multiple tables are defined within a tablespace, and one of the tables is dropped, the tablespace may need to be reorganized to reclaim the space.

Running a reorganization causes the DBMS to restructure the database object, maximizing the availability, speed, and efficiency of database functions.

To correct disorganized database structures, the DBA can run a database or tablespace reorganization utility, or REORG, to force the DBMS to restructure the database object, thus removing problems such as unclustered data, fragmentation, and row chaining. The primary benefit of reorganization is the resulting speed and efficiency of database functions because the data is organized in a more optimal fashion on disk. In short, reorganization maximizes availability and reliability for databases.

Tablespaces and indexes both can be reorganized. How the DBA runs a REORG utility depends on the DBMS. Some DBMS products ship with a built-in reorganization utility. Others require the customer to purchase the utility. Still others claim that the customer will not need the utility at all when using their

DBMS. I have found the last claim to be untrue. Every DBMS incurs some degree of disorganization as data is added and modified.

Of course, DBAs can manually reorganize a database by completely rebuilding it. However, accomplishing such a reorganization requires a complex series of steps. Figure 11-6 depicts the steps entailed by a manual reorganization.

If a utility is available for reorganizing, either from the DBMS vendor or a third=party vendor, the process is greatly simplified. Sometimes the utility is as simple as issuing a simple command such as

```
REORG TABLESPACE TSNAME
```

A traditional reorganization requires the database to be down. The high cost of downtime creates pressures both to perform and to delay preventive maintenance—a no-win situation familiar to most DBAs. Some REORG utilities are available that perform the reorganization while the database is online. Such a reorganization is accomplished by making a copy of the data. The online REORG utility reorganizes the copy while the original data remains online. When the copied data has been reorganized, an online REORG uses the database log to "catch up" by applying to the copy any data changes that occurred during the process. When the copy has caught up to the original, the online REORG switches the production tablespace from the original to the copy. Performing an online reorganization requires additional disk storage and a slow

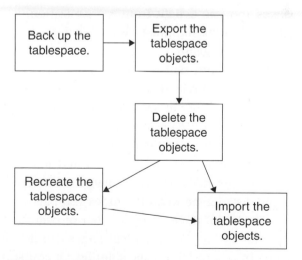

Figure 11-6   *Typical steps for a manual reorganization*

transaction window. If a large number of transactions occur during the online reorganization, REORG may have a hard time catching up.

Determining When to Reorganize

System catalog statistics can help to determine when to reorganize a database object. Each DBMS provides a method of reading through the contents of the database and recording statistical information about each database object. Depending on the DBMS, this statistical information is stored either in the system catalog or in special pages within the database object itself.

Cluster ratio is the percentage of rows in a table that are actually stored in clustering sequence.

One statistic that can help a DBA determine when to reorganize is *cluster ratio*. Cluster ratio is the percentage of rows in a table that are actually stored in a clustering sequence. The closer the cluster ratio is to 100%, the more closely the actual ordering of the rows on the data pages matches the clustering sequence. A low cluster ratio indicates bad clustering, and a reorganization may be required. A low cluster ratio, however, may not be a performance hindrance if the majority of queries access data randomly instead of sequentially.

Tracking down the other causes of disorganization can sometimes be difficult. Some DBMSs gather statistics on fragmentation, row chaining, row migration, space dedicated to dropped objects, and page splits; others do not. Oracle provides a plethora of statistics in dynamic performance tables that can be queried. Refer to the sidebar "Oracle Dynamic Performance Tables" for more details.

Tablespaces are not the only database objects that can be reorganized. Indexes, too, can benefit from reorganization. As table data is added and modified, the index too must be changed. Such changes can cause the index to become disorganized.

A vital index statistic to monitor is the number of levels. Recall from Chapter 4 that most relational indexes are b-tree structures. As data is added to the index, the number of levels of the b-tree will grow. When more levels exist in the b-tree, more I/O requests are required to move from the top of the index structure to the actual data that must be accessed. Reorganizing an index can cause the index to be better structured and require fewer levels.

Another index statistic to analyze to determine if reorganization is required is the distance between the index leaf pages, or *leaf distance*. Leaf distance is an estimate of the average number of pages between successive leaf pages in the index. Gaps between leaf pages can develop as data is deleted from an index or as a result of page splitting. Of course, the best value for leaf distance

Oracle Dynamic Performance Tables

Oracle stores vital performance statistics about the database system in a series of dynamic performance tables. These tables are sometimes referred to as the "V$ tables" because the table names are prefixed with the characters V$.

The V$ tables are used by the built-in Oracle performance monitoring facilities and can be queried by the DBA for insight into the well-being and performance of an Oracle instance. Examples of some of the statistics that can be found in the V$ tables include

- Free space available
- Chained rows
- Rollback segment contention
- Memory usage
- Disk activity

Of course, there is quite a lot of additional performance information to be found in these tables. Oracle DBAs should investigate the V$ tables and query these tables regularly to analyze the performance of the Oracle system, its databases, and applications.

is zero, but achieving a leaf distance of zero in practice is not realistic. In general, the lower this value, the better. Review the value over time to determine a high-water mark for leaf distance that will indicate when indexes should be reorganized.

Automation

Look into using the database utilities or third-party tools to automate reorganizations.

If possible, the DBA should look into using the database utilities or third-party tools to automate reorganizations. The automation tool can be used to query the database statistic and trigger reorganization only for those database objects that have surpassed the high-water mark for a combination of statistics. For example, the DBA may want to automatically reorganize all tablespaces where the cluster ratio is below 85% and all indexes where the leaf distance has a value greater than 100.

Reorganizations can be costly in terms of downtime and computing resources. Furthermore, determining when reorganization will actually create performance gains can be difficult. However, the performance gains that can be accrued are tremendous when data is unclustered, fragmented, or disorganized in any way. The wise DBA will plan for and schedule reorganizations to resolve disorganization problems in their database systems.

Summary

Applications and data are constantly changing. Users require instant response time and 24/7 availability. The database structures that support these applications must be properly maintained to ensure optimal application performance. Proper database design, appropriate choice of clustering, and reorganizing databases based on statistics help to deliver efficient databases. Furthermore, DBAs can ensure database performance by automating these processes to reduce the risk and errors associated with manual database maintenance.

Review

1. What is the best performance tuning technique a DBA can use to improve database performance?

2. What is the only reason to denormalize a physical data model?

3. What is the benefit of clustering data?

4. How many indexes should be defined for a single table?

5. Discuss the pros and cons of providing database objects with free space.

6. What are the causes of database and index disorganization?

7. How can file extents degrade database performance?

8. What performance advantages can be gained by partitioning a table?

9. Explain what the term *leaf distance* means and why it is important for index performance.

10. What is the benefit to allocating tablespaces and indexes on separate disk devices?

Suggested Reading

Besch, David. *MCSE: SQL Server 7 Database Design.* Indianapolis, IN: New Riders (1999). ISBN 0-7357-0004-4

Dunham, Jeff. *Database Performance Tuning Handbook.* New York, NY: McGraw-Hill (1998). ISBN 0-07-018244-2

Informix Software Staff. *Evolution of the High Performance Database.* Upper Saddle River, NJ: Informix Press/PTR (1997). ISBN 0-13-124314-4

Kreines, David C., and Brian Laskey. *Oracle Database Administration: The Essential Reference.* Sebastopol, CA: O'Reilly (1999). ISBN 1-56592-516-5

Mullins, Craig S. *DB2 Developer's Guide.* 4th ed. Indianapolis, IN: SAMS (2000). ISBN 0-672-31828-8

Purba, Sanjiv. *High-Performance Web Databases.* Boca Raton, FL: Auerbach (2001). ISBN 0-8493-0882-8

12

Application Performance

Now that we have discussed performance from the system and database perspective, it is time to turn our attention to performance from the application code perspective. This chapter focuses on tuning and optimizing the application code and SQL statements, as well as ensuring the application interacts with the DBMS appropriately and efficiently. Poorly constructed and formulated application code accounts for the majority of relational database performance problems—as many as 80% of performance problems can be traced back to the application.

Designing Applications for Relational Access

Application design issues were discussed in Chapter 5 and should be revisited when application performance suffers. Perhaps the application was improperly designed and portions of the application, or perhaps the entire application, will need to be rewritten. The application must be designed for performance at the outset—because changing the design of the application later is either impossible, impractical, or too costly to tackle.

Design issues to examine when application performance suffers include

- *Type of SQL.* Is the correct type of SQL (planned or unplanned, dynamic or static, embedded or stand-alone) being used for this particular application?

- *Programming language.* Is the programming language capable of achieving the required performance, and is the language environment optimized for database access?

- *Transaction design and processing.* Are the transactions within the program properly designed to assure ACID properties, and does the program use the transaction processor of choice appropriately and efficiently?

- *Locking strategy.* Does the application hold the wrong type of locks, or does it hold the correct type of locks for too long?

- *COMMIT strategy.* Does each application program issue SQL COMMIT statements to minimize the impact of locking?

- *Batch processing.* Are batch programs designed appropriately to take advantage of the sequential processing features of the DBMS?

- *Online processing.* Are online applications designed to return useful information and to minimize the amount of information returned to the user's screen for a single invocation of the program?

Relational Optimization

The DBA must become intimately familiar with the optimization techniques used by each DBMS in the organization. Of course, application developers must code efficient SQL and understand how to optimize SQL, but in the end it is the DBA who is responsible for the performance of database applications. As such, the DBA must be skilled in SQL coding and tuning SQL for performance.

The optimizer is an inference engine for determining the database navigation strategy.

The *optimizer* is the heart of a relational database management system. It is an inference engine responsible for determining the best possible database navigation strategy for any given SQL request.

The application developer specifies *what* data is needed by coding the SQL statements, the DBMS supplies information about *where* the data is located, and the relational optimizer decides *how* to efficiently navigate the database. The end user needs no knowledge of where and how the actual data is stored. The optimizer knows this information.

To optimize SQL, the relational optimizer must analyze each SQL statement by parsing it to determine the tables and columns that must be accessed. The optimizer will also access statistics stored by the RDBMS in either the system catalog or the database objects themselves. The statistics are used to determine the best method of accomplishing the tasks that need to be performed to satisfy the SQL request. This process is called *relational optimization* and is shown in Figure 12-1.

Relational optimization is very powerful because it allows queries to adapt to a changing database environment. The optimizer can react to changes by formulating new access paths without requiring application coding changes to be implemented. The application can therefore be flexible as tables expand or contract in size, as indexes are added or removed, and as the database becomes disorganized or reorganized.

The separation of access criteria from physical storage characteristics is called *physical data independence.*

Regardless of how the data is physically stored and manipulated, SQL can be used to access data, and the DBMS will take the current state of the database into account to optimize that data access. This separation of access criteria from physical storage characteristics is called *physical data independence.*

Every RDBMS has an embedded relational optimizer that renders SQL statements into executable access paths. Furthermore, each vendor's relational

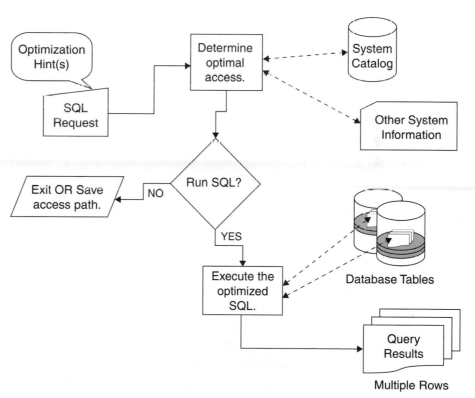

Figure 12-1   *Relational optimization*

optimizer works a little differently, with different steps and using different information. Nevertheless, the core of the process is the same from DBMS to DBMS. The optimizer parses the SQL statement and performs various phases of optimization, typically involving verification of syntactic and semantic correctness, followed by query analysis and formulation of the access paths to satisfy the query.

The relational optimizer can deploy many types of strategies available to the DBMS for optimizing SQL statements. The internal operations and instructions that are used by each DBMS's optimizer are closely guarded secrets. Modern relational optimizers are cost based, meaning that the optimizer will attempt to formulate an access path for each query that reduces overall cost. To function in this manner, the optimizer must evaluate and analyze multiple factors, including estimated CPU and I/O costs, database statistics, and the actual SQL statement.

CPU and I/O Costs

A relational optimizer use formulas and models to estimate the machine cost to run each potential access path for the query being optimized. Based on CPU information, the optimizer can arrive at a rough estimate of the CPU time required to run the query using each optimized access path it analyzes.

Furthermore, a relational optimizer must estimate the cost of the actual writing and retrieval of the data. The optimizer estimates the cost of I/O to the query by using a series of formulas based on the database statistics, the data cache efficiency, and the cost of I/O to intermediate work files. These formulas result in a *filter factor*, which determines the relative I/O cost of the query.

Database Statistics

A relational optimizer is of little use without accurate statistics.

A relational optimizer is of little use without accurate statistics about the data stored in the database. A relational DBMS provides a utility program or command to gather statistics about database objects and to store them for use by the optimizer (or by the DBA for performance monitoring). For example, to collect statistics in DB2, the DBA must execute the RUNSTATS utility; to collect statistics in SQL Server the UPDATE STATISTICS command is issued.

The DBA should collect modified statistics whenever a significant volume of data has been added or modified. Failure to do so will result in the optimizer basing its cost estimates on inaccurate statistics. This may be detrimental to query performance.

Database statistics provide the optimizer with information about the state of the tablespaces, tables, columns, and indexes. The DBMS collects statistical information such as

- Number of rows in the tablespace, table, or index
- Number of unique values stored in the column
- Most frequently occurring values for columns
- Index key density (see "Density" sidebar)
- Details on the ratio of clustering for clustered tables
- Correlation of columns to other columns
- Structural state of the index or tablespace
- Amount of storage used by the database object

When issuing the RUNSTATS command, the DBA specifies which statistics to gather. Of course, the exact statistics collected vary by DBMS to DBMS; additional or fewer statistics may be available within your database system. The key, though, is to keep the statistics as accurate as possible to ensure efficient and useful relational optimization.

Create a script to populate production statistics into the test system.

When developing an application against test databases, the statistics for the test data will not accurately reflect the statistics for the production database. Whenever possible, the DBA should work with the application development team to create a script to populate production statistics into the test system. Depending on the DBMS, this may be accomplished with SQL statements or a data testing tool. Without production statistics, the DBMS will likely choose different access paths in the test environment than in production—potentially causing performance problems when the application goes into production status.

Query Analysis

The more complex the SQL statement, the more work the query analysis must do.

The *query analysis* scans the SQL statement to determine its overall complexity. The formulation of the SQL statement is a significant factor in determining the access paths chosen by the optimizer. The complexity of the query, the number and type of predicates, the presence of functions, and the presence of ordering clauses enter into the estimated cost that is calculated by the optimizer. The more complex the SQL statement, the more work the query analysis

Density

Density is the average percentage of duplicate values stored in the index key column(s) and is recorded as a percentage. For example, a density of 50% means that for a given index key value, we would expect to return 50% of the rows. The following equation determines the average number of rows expected to be returned when accessing a table by the index:

$$\text{Average \# Rows} = \text{Total \# Rows} \times \text{Density}$$

For example, when accessing a table with 1000 rows by an index with a density of 50%:

$$\text{Average \# Rows} = 1{,}000 \times 0.50 = 500$$

When accessing a table with 20,000 rows by an index with a density of 15%:

$$\text{Average \# Rows} = 20000 \times 0.15 = 3{,}000$$

This information is useful to the optimizer because it assists in determining the size of the results set and thus whether an index is helpful for specific access paths.

---

must do to make sense of the SQL statement. During query analysis, the optimizer analyzes aspects of the SQL statement and the database system, such as

- Which tables in which database are required
- Whether any views are required to be broken down into underlying tables
- Whether table joins or subselects are required
- Which indexes, if any, can be used
- How many predicates (WHERE clauses) must be satisfied
- Which functions must be executed
- Whether the SQL uses OR or AND
- How the DBMS processes each component of the SQL statement
- How much memory has been assigned to the data cache(s) used by the tables in the SQL statement
- How much memory is available for sorting if the query requires a sort

In other words, the query analysis breaks down the SQL statement into discrete tasks that must be performed to return the query results.

A large part of query analysis is index selection. After the optimizer determines the indexes available to be used for each predicate, it will decide whether to use a single index, multiple indexes, or no index at all.

Joins

Combining information from multiple tables is known as joining.

When multiple tables are accessed, the optimizer figures out how to combine the tables in the most efficient manner. Combining information from multiple tables is known as *joining*. When determining the access path for a join, the optimizer must determine the order in which the tables will be joined, compute the overall cost estimate of each access path, and choose a join method for the particular query. The DBMS can utilize several different methods for joining tables.

Regardless of the join method, the DBMS must make several decisions and perform certain operations. The first decision is to choose the table to process first—this table is referred to as the *outer table*. Next, a series of operations are performed on the outer table to prepare it for joining. Rows from that table are then combined with rows from the second table, called the *inner table*, as shown in Figure 12-2. A series of operations are also performed on the inner table before the join occurs, as the join occurs, or both.

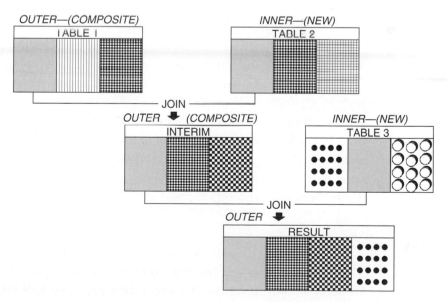

Figure 12-2 *Joining tables.*

Although all joins are similar in functionality, each join method works differently behind the scenes. Let's investigate two common join methods: the *nested-loop join* and the *merge-scan join*.

The *nested-loop join* works by comparing qualifying rows of the outer table to the inner table. A qualifying row is identified in the outer table, and then the inner table is scanned for a match. A *qualifying row* is one in which the predicates for columns in the table match. When the inner table scan is complete, another qualifying row in the outer table is identified. The inner table is scanned for a match again, and so on. The repeated scanning of the inner table is usually accomplished with an index to avoid undue I/O costs. The smaller the size of the inner table, the better a nested-loop join performs, because fewer rows need to be scanned for each qualifying row of the outer table.

A second type of join method is the *merge-scan join*. In a merge-scan join, the tables to be joined are ordered by the keys. This ordering can be accomplished by a sort or by access via an index. After ensuring that both the outer and inner tables are properly sequenced, each table is read sequentially, and the join columns are matched. During a merge-scan join, no row from either table is read more than once. Merge-scan joins are useful when an appropriate index is not available on one (or both) of the tables.

Depending on the DBMS, other join methods may be available.

Join Order

The optimizer reviews each join in a query and analyzes the appropriate statistics to determine the optimal order in which the tables should be accessed to accomplish the join. To find the optimal join access path, the optimizer uses built-in algorithms containing knowledge about joins and data volume. It matches this intelligence against the join predicates, databases statistics, and available indexes to estimate which order is more efficient. In general, the optimizer will deploy an algorithm that minimizes the number of times the inner table must be accessed for qualifying outer table rows. However, none of today's relational optimizers are perfect.

Access Path Choices

The relational optimizer has numerous options for creating SQL access paths. We have already discussed the join access paths; so let's discuss some of the other common types of data access.

Table Scans

Table scans are the simplest form of data access.

Table scans are the simplest form of data access. A table scan is performed simply by reading every row of the table. Depending on the DBMS, an alternate type of scan may exist, called a tablespace scan. The *tablespace scan* reads every page in the tablespace, which may contain more than one table. Obviously, a tablespace scan will run slower than a table scan because additional I/O will be incurred reading data that does not apply.

Another form of scanning is the *partition scan*. If the DBMS can determine that the data to be accessed exists in certain partitions of a multipartition table (or tablespace), it can limit the data that is scanned to the appropriate partitions. A partition scan should outperform a table scan or tablespace scan because the amount of I/O required is reduced.

Typically, the optimizer will choose to scan data for one of the following reasons:

- The query cannot be satisfied using an index possibly because no index is available, no predicate matches the index, or the predicate precludes the use of an index.

- A high percentage of the rows in the table qualify. In this case, using an index is likely to be less efficient because most of the data rows need to be read anyway.

- The indexes that have matching predicates have low cluster ratios and are only efficient for small amounts of data.

- The table is so small that use of an index would actually be detrimental. For small tables, adding index access to the table access can result in additional I/O, instead of less I/O.

Data prefetch is particularly useful for table and tablespace scans.

To assist the performance of a scan, the optimizer can invoke data prefetch. Data prefetch causes the DBMS to read data pages sequentially into the data cache even before they are requested. Essentially, data prefetch is a read-ahead mechanism—when data scans get around to requesting the data, it will already exist in memory. Data prefetch is particularly useful for table and tablespace scans, but can be practical for any type of sequential data access. Whether data prefetch is available, as well as when and how it is used, depends on the DBMS. The optimizer may choose to deploy it when the access path is formulated, or the DBMS may choose to turn on data prefetch when the query is being run. As a DBA, you should learn how and why your particular DBMS prefetches data.

Indexed Access

Of the many decisions that must be made by the optimizer, one of the most important for query performance is whether an index will be used to satisfy the query. To determine this, the optimizer must first discover whether an index exists. An index does not have to be defined before SQL can be written to access a column—you can query any column of any table known to the database.

Of course, before the relational optimizer will use an index to satisfy a query, an appropriate index must already exist. Additionally, at least one indexed column must be referenced within an indexable predicate in the SQL statement. The DBMS is not capable of using an index for every WHERE clause. You must learn what types of predicates can use indexes to ensure that the appropriate indexes are created for the queries in your database applications. Every DBMS has a different list of what is, and what is not, indexable. Furthermore, what is indexable tends to change from version to version of each DBMS.

The simplest type of indexed access is the direct index lookup.

The relational optimizer can choose to use an index in many different ways. The first, and most simple, type of indexed access is the *direct index lookup*. To perform a direct index lookup, the DBMS initiates the following steps:

1. The value in the SQL predicate is compared to the values stored in the root page of the index. Based on this comparison, the DBMS will traverse the index to the next lowest set of pages.

2. If intermediate nonleaf pages exist, the appropriate nonleaf page is read, and the value is compared to determine which leaf page to access.

3. The appropriate leaf page is read; the index leaf page contains pointer(s) to the actual data for the qualifying rows.

4. Based on the pointer(s) in the leaf page index entries, the DBMS reads the appropriate table data pages.

For the DBMS to perform a direct index lookup, values must be provided for each column in the index. For example, consider the following query:

```
SELECT  last_name, first_name, middle_initial, empno
FROM    employee
WHERE   position = 'MANAGER'
AND     work_code = 1
AND     dept = '001000';
```

Furthermore, assume that an index exists on the position, work_code, and dept columns. The DBMS can perform a direct index lookup using the index and the values supplied in the predicate for each of the columns. For a direct index lookup to occur, all three columns must appear in the SQL statement. If only one or two of these columns are specified as predicates, a direct index lookup cannot be chosen because the DBMS cannot match the full index key. Instead, an index scan could be chosen. Recall the previous discussion of table and tablespace scans. Index scans are similar. When an index scan is invoked, the leaf pages of the index are read sequentially, one after the other.

There are two basic types of index scans: matching and nonmatching.

There are two basic types of index scans: matching index scans and non-matching index scans. A *matching index scan* is sometimes called *absolute positioning*. A matching index scan begins at the root page of an index and works down to a leaf page in much the same manner as a direct index lookup does. However, because the complete key of the index is not available, the DBMS must scan the leaf pages of the index looking for the values that are available, until all matching values have been retrieved. To see how a matching index scan works, follow the arrows in Figure 12-3.

To clarify, consider the previous query of the employee table, but this time the query is recoded without the predicate for the dept column. The DBMS

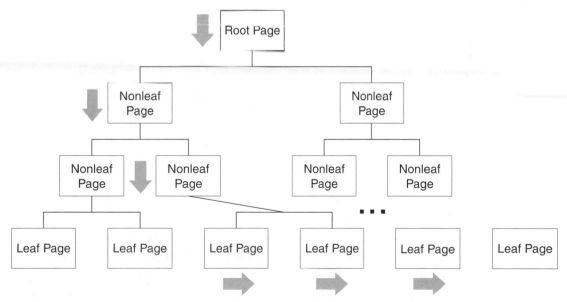

Figure 12-3 *Matching index scan.*

can use a matching index scan. The matching index scan first locates the first leaf page with the appropriate value for `position` and `work_code` by traversing the index starting at the root. However, there can be multiple index entries with this combination of values and different values for `dept`. Therefore, the leaf pages will be scanned sequentially until no more valid entries are found.

For a matching index scan to be requested, you must specify the high-order column in the index key—in other words, for the first column specified in the index DDL. For the preceding example, the high-order column is the `position` column. The high-order column provides the starting point for the DBMS to traverse the index structure from the root page to the appropriate leaf page.

Consider the consequences of not specifying the high-order column in the query. For example, suppose we take the original query and remove the predicate for position, but retain the other two, leaving the following SQL statement:

```
SELECT   last_name, first_name, middle_initial, empno
FROM     employee
WHERE    work_code = 1
AND      dept = '001000';
```

In such situations, the DBMS can deploy a *nonmatching index scan*, sometimes referred to as *relative positioning*. When a starting point cannot be determined because the first column in the index key is not specified, the DBMS cannot use the index tree structure. However, it can use the index leaf pages, as shown in Figure 12-4. A nonmatching index scan begins with the first leaf page in the index and scans subsequent leaf pages sequentially, applying the available predicates.

A nonmatching index scan can be more efficient than a table or tablespace scan, especially if the data pages that must be accessed are in clustered order. Of course, a nonmatching index scan be done on a nonclustered index also.

This brings us to clustered versus unclustered index access. Any of the above methods for indexed access can be used with both clustered and unclustered indexes. However, index scans that must then access table data pages are not likely to be very efficient when the data is not clustered: Clustered index access, as it proceeds from leaf page to leaf page, never requests a read for the same data page twice. Unclustered index access, however, will request the same data page multiple times because the data is spread throughout the table. For clarification of clustering, refer to the discussion and diagrams in Chapters 4 and 11.

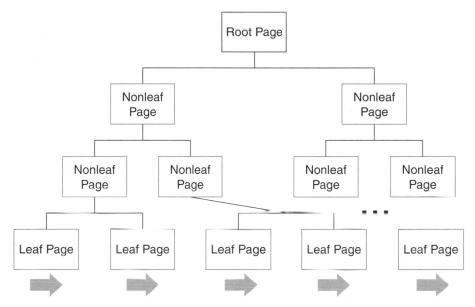

Figure 12-4   *Nonmatching index scan*

Index screening is useful if some columns of a multicolumn index are not specified in the query.

An additional index access technique that can be deployed is *index screening*. With index screening, a matching index scan is done on the leading columns of a multicolumn index, and additional predicates are applied during the scan. This technique is useful if some columns of a multicolumn index are not specified in the query. Consider another sample query:

```
SELECT   last_name, empno
FROM     employee
WHERE    position = 'MANAGER'
AND      work_code = 1
AND      salary > 50000.00;
```

Now assume that an index has been created on the following columns in the following order: position, work_code, dept, and salary. The index can be screened by applying a matching index scan on position and work_code, and then a nonmatching scan for the specified salary values greater than $50,000.00, but only for those rows that matched the position = 'MANAGER' and work_code = 1 predicates.

One of the most efficient types of indexed access is *index-only access*, sometimes referred to as *index covering*. Consider again the query we just examined. Further, assume that an index has been created on the following columns: position, work_code, dept, salary, last_name, and empno. In such a scenario, the DBMS can satisfy the query using only the index because all of the requested data in the SELECT list and the predicates exists in the index. No additional I/O to table data pages is required.

With index-only access, the DBMS can satisfy the query by simply scanning the leaf pages of the index. A nonmatching index-only scan can be much faster than a tablespace or table scan because index entries are generally smaller than table rows, and consequently more data is read with each I/O.

To encourage index-only access, the DBA can overload the index by adding extra columns that appear in the SELECT list of SQL statements. Doing so can provide a large performance payback, but it comes at the cost of additional disk storage requirements because additional columns are being indexed.

With multi-index access, the DBMS uses more than one index to satisfy a single access path.

One final type of indexed access is *multi-index access*. With multi-index access, the DBMS uses more than one index to satisfy a single access path. For example, consider another variation of our employee table query:

```
SELECT   last_name, empno
FROM     employee
WHERE    position = 'MANAGER'
AND      work_code = 1;
```

This time we have two indexes: one on the position column and another on the work_code column. The query specifies two predicates, each of which is supported by a different index. Instead of choosing to use one index or the other, the relational optimizer can combine the two indexes to return the correct data efficiently.

There are two types of multi-index access, depending on whether the predicates are tied together using AND or OR. Some DBMSs support only the AND logical operator, whereas others support both AND and OR. In some cases, the DBA can minimize the number of indexes created by deploying multiple single-column indexes, instead of multiple multicolumn indexes. The DBA should base this decision on the efficiency of the DBMS in using multi-index access and the performance requirements of the applications being deployed.

Using Indexes to Avoid Sorts.   The DBMS may need to sort data to satisfy SQL requests. Sorting is quite cost prohibitive and should be avoided if pos-

Use indexes to avoid sorts by creating them on the columns that need to be sorted.

sible. The DBA can use indexes to avoid sorts by creating them on the columns that need to be sorted. The relational optimizer will try to use indexes to avoid sorts whenever possible. Sorting might occur when the following clauses are specified:

- DISTINCT: When this clause is specified the DBMS requires every column of the resulting data to be in order so that duplicate rows can be removed from the results set.
- UNION: This operation requires the columns in each SELECT list to be ordered because the results set can have no duplicate rows.
- GROUP BY: When this clause is specified, the DBMS requires data to be sorted by the specified columns in order to aggregate data.
- ORDER BY: When this clause is specified, the DBMS will ensure that the results set is sorted by the specified columns.

Consider the following SQL statement:

```
SELECT    last_name, first_name, middle_initial, empno, position
FROM      employee
WHERE     position in ('MANAGER', 'DIRECTOR', 'VICE PRESIDENT')
ORDER BY last_name;
```

If an index exists on the last_name column, the query can use this index and avoid sorting. Using an index to avoid a sort trades off the additional CPU cost required to sort for the additional I/O cost required for indexed access. Of course, if the index is going to be used anyway, the choice is a no-brainer. Whether or not using an index is actually faster than scanning the data and sorting will depend on

- Number of qualifying rows
- Speed of the sort
- Index characteristics (e.g., clustered or nonclustered)

Why Wasn't the Index Chosen? Situations sometimes arise where you think the optimizer should have chosen an index, but it didn't. Any number of reasons can cause the optimizer to avoid using an index. Consult the following checklist for ways to encourage index selection.

- Does the query specify a search argument? If no predicate uses a search argument, the optimizer cannot use an index to satisfy the query.

- Are you joining a large number of tables? The optimizer within some DBMSs may produce unpredictable query plan results when joining a large number of tables.

- Are statistics current? If large amounts of data have been inserted, updated, and/or deleted, database statistics should be recaptured to ensure that the optimizer has up-to-date information upon which to base its query plans.

- Are you using stored procedures? Sometimes the DBMS provides options whereby a stored procedure, once compiled, will not reformulate a query plan for subsequent executions. You may need to recompile or reoptimize the stored procedure to take advantage of up-to-date statistics, new indexes, or any other pertinent database changes.

- Are additional predicates needed? A different WHERE clause might possibly enable the optimizer to consider a different index.

Hashed Access

A hash is similar in operation to a direct index lookup.

The optimizer will also consider using any existing *hashing* structures when formulating access paths. A hash is similar in operation to a direct index lookup. Hashes are most appropriate for random I/O of small amounts of data. To retrieve data based on a hashing algorithm, the DBMS uses a randomizing routine to translate the value supplied for the hash key to a physical location. This algorithm will give the offset of the row in the actual database table.

Parallel Access

Three basic types of parallelism can be supported by the DBMS: I/O, CPU, and system.

The relational optimizer may choose to run queries in parallel. When query parallelism is invoked by the DBMS, multiple simultaneous tasks are invoked to access the data. Three basic types of parallelism can be supported by the DBMS:

- *I/O parallelism* enables concurrent I/O streams to be initiated for a single query. Running parallel I/O tasks can significantly enhance the performance of I/O bound queries. Breaking the data access for the query into concurrent I/O streams executed in parallel can reduce the overall elapsed time for the query.

- *CPU parallelism* enables multitasking of CPU processing within a query. Invoking CPU parallelism also invokes I/O parallelism because each CPU engine requires its own I/O stream. CPU parallelism decomposes a query into multiple smaller queries that can be executed concurrently on multiple processors. CPU parallelism can further reduce the elapsed time for a query.

- Finally, the DBMS can deploy *system parallelism* to further enhance parallel query operations. System parallelism enables a single query to be broken up and run across multiple DBMS instances. By allowing a single query to take advantage of the processing power of multiple DBMS instances, the overall elapsed time for a complex query can be decreased even further.

Ensuring that proper query plans are formulated with the correct index usage is a time consuming process, but one that can pay huge dividends in the form of enhanced performance. The DBA should train the application development staff to understand relational optimization and to create optimal SQL. Of course, the onus falls on the application developer to code efficient SQL and program logic. However, the DBA is the sentry of relational database performance. When performance problems occur, the DBA is the one who has to search for the cause of the problem and suggest remedies to resolve it. Furthermore, the DBA should conduct design reviews to seek out and tune inefficient SQL before suboptimal access paths and programs are migrated to production status.

Additional Optimization Considerations

The optimizer makes additional decisions regarding the manner in which data is accessed for SQL queries that will impact performance. In this section we will discuss some of these additional optimization considerations.

View Access

One of the decisions that must be made during query optimization is how to access data from views. Remember from Chapter 4 that a view is a logical representation of a table that is defined using SQL. Therefore, a query that accesses a view is basically a SQL statement embedded within another SQL statement.

When the optimizer determines the access path for the query containing the view, it must also determine how to resolve the view SQL. Keep in mind that both the view and the SQL accessing the view may reference multiple tables and additional views.

View materialization and view merging can be used to optimize SQL that references views.

Two methods can be used to optimize SQL that references views: view materialization and view merging. The more efficient of the two methods is *view merging*. As the name implies, when view merging is deployed, the SQL in the view DDL is merged with the SQL that references the view. The merged SQL is then used to formulate an access path against the base tables in the views.

The second technique for accessing views is *view materialization*. When the optimizer cannot combine the SQL in the view with the SQL accessing the view, it creates an intermediate work file to hold the results of the view. The SQL accessing the view is then run against the work file that contains the view data. View materialization is not as efficient as view merging because data must be retrieved and stored in a temporary work file.

Each DBMS has its own set of rules that determine when view materialization must be used instead of view merging. Generally, column functions, or operations requiring sorts to be invoked, tend to require view materialization.

Query Rewrite

Some relational optimizers are intelligent enough to rewrite SQL more efficiently during the optimization process. For example, the optimizer might convert a subquery into an equivalent join. Alternatively, it might test out equivalent but different predicate formulations to determine which one creates the better access path. For example, since the following two predicates are equivalent, the optimizer may rewrite the query both ways to see which one produces the best access path:

```
WHERE column1 >= 1 AND column1 <= 100
WHERE column1 BETWEEN 1 AND 100
```

Additionally, the optimizer may rewrite queries by creating inferred predicates. One example of this is a feature known as *predicate transitive closure*, in which the optimizer adds a predicate to the query to improve performance. Consider the following SQL statement:

```
SELECT    d.dept_name, e.last_name, e.empno
FROM      employee   e,
          department d
WHERE     e.deptno = d.deptno
AND       d.deptno = '808';
```

That SQL statement is functionally equivalent to the following SQL statement:

```
SELECT    d.dept_name, e.last_name, e.empno
FROM      employee   e,
          department d
WHERE     e.deptno = d.deptno
AND       e.deptno = '808';
```

The only difference is the second predicate, but because **deptno** is the same in both tables (due to the first join predicate), it does not matter whether we check **deptno** from the employee table or the department table. However, it might make a difference in terms of performance. For example, an index might exist on one of the **deptno** columns, but not the other, or perhaps one of the tables is significantly larger than the other. A query is usually more efficient when the predicate is applied to the larger of the two tables because the number of qualifying rows will be reduced.

If the optimizer can perform predicate transitive closure, the SQL developer need not worry about this. The optimizer will consider the access path for both columns regardless of which is coded in the predicate. In essence, the optimizer will rewrite the query to add the redundant predicate.

The rules for what type of queries can be rewritten varies with DBMS and optimizer.

The DBA should find out whether the relational optimizer in use can perform any form of query rewrite. Additionally, the rules for what type of queries can be rewritten varies from DBMS to DBMS and optimizer to optimizer. For example, the optimizer may not be able to perform predicate transitive closure on some predicates, such as IN or LIKE clauses.

Rule-Based Optimization

The discussion up to this point has focused on cost-based optimization. Most relational optimizers are cost based, meaning they base their access path formulation decisions on an estimation of costs. Lower-cost access paths are favored over costlier access paths.

Oracle provides
both cost-based
and rule-based
optimization.

However, some DBMSs support a different type of optimization that is based on heuristics, or rules. Oracle, for example, provides both cost-based and rule-based optimization.

A *rule-based optimizer* bases its optimization decisions on SQL syntax and structure, placement of predicates, order of tables in the SELECT statement, and availability of indexes. With a rule-based optimizer, the SQL developer has to be aware of the rules as he writes SQL. Query performance can suffer simply by reordering columns in the SELECT list or tables in the FROM clause.

Cost-based optimization is the trend for DBMSs because SQL statements need not be coded following a set of esoteric "rules." Furthermore, an optimizer that estimates the cost of different access paths produces efficient query execution plans more reliably.

Reviewing Access Paths

The programmer or DBA can examine the access paths chosen by the relational optimizer. The commands and process used to accomplish this depend on the DBMS. Usually the command to externalize access paths is EXPLAIN or SHOW-PLAN. Regardless of the name, the general process is depicted in Figure 12-5.

Microsoft SQL Server and Sybase make use of a command called SHOW-PLAN. Figure 12-6 provides a text description of the access path, while Figure 12-7 provides a graphical depiction of the access path.

Oracle and DB2 use a different method, namely the EXPLAIN statement. By prefixing the SQL statement with the EXPLAIN command, the access path

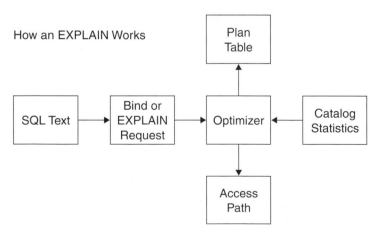

Figure 12-5   *The EXPLAIN process*

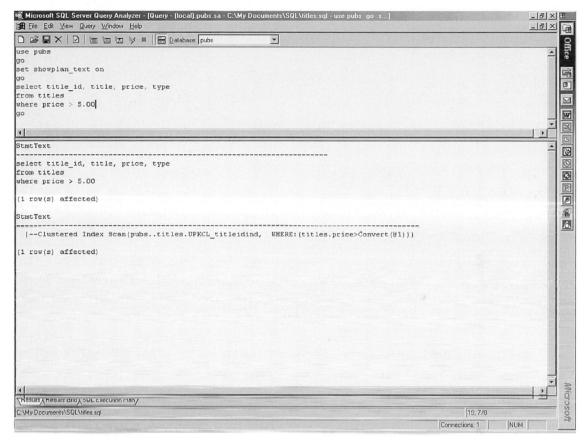

Figure 12-6 *Textual SHOWPLAN example*

information determined by the optimizer is written out to a table called a PLAN_TABLE. The DBA or programmer can then query the PLAN_TABLE to interpret the access paths specified by the optimizer. EXPLAIN can be run on a statement-by-statement basis, or for an entire application program.

For example, consider the following SQL statement:

```
EXPLAIN plan SET STATEMENT_ID = 'emptest' FOR
SELECT   position, last_name, first_name, middle_initial, empno
FROM     employee
WHERE    position IN ('MANAGER', 'DIRECTOR', 'VICE PRESIDENT')
ORDER BY position;
```

By prefixing the SELECT statement with the EXPLAIN command, the relational optimizer will externalize access path information into the PLAN_TABLE.

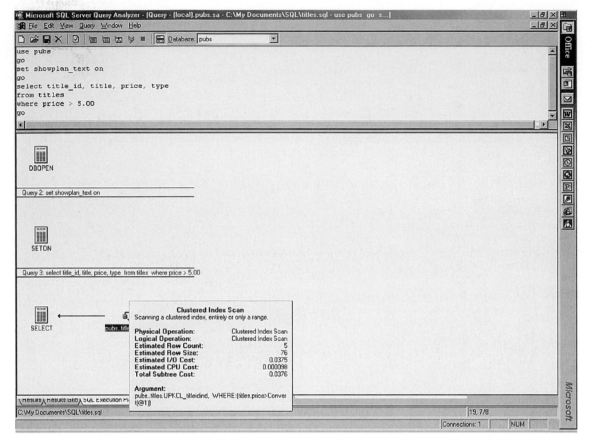

Figure 12-7 *Graphical SHOWPLAN example*

The STATEMENT_ID clause provides an identifier for locating the access path of the SQL statement within the PLAN_TABLE. The PLAN_TABLE contains encoded columns of data that outline the nature of query access paths to be used, such as the following:

- Whether an index is used, and if so, how many
- How many columns of the index match the query
- Whether index-only access is used
- What join method is used
- Whether parallel access is used
- Whether sorting is required

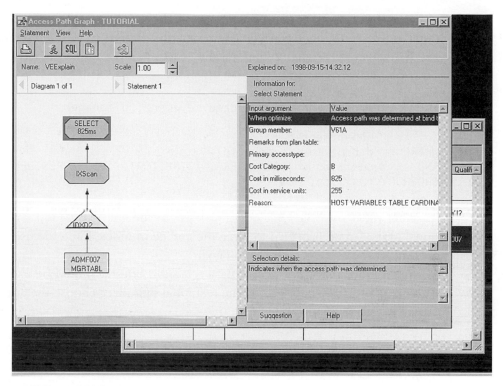

Figure 12-8 *DB2 Visual Explain tool*

Of course, the exact columns and the permissible values of those columns differ from Oracle to DB2.

Analysis tools can make it easier for the DBA to interpret the access paths being used.

Access path analysis tools that interpret the PLAN_TABLE and display English text and graphical access path depictions are available for Oracle and DB2, too. For example, review the graphical output from the DB2 Visual Explain tool shown in Figure 12-8. Such SQL analysis tools frequently provide expert tuning recommendations on how to fix inefficient SQL statements. Analysis tools can make it easier for the DBA to interpret the access paths being used and tune the SQL, if necessary.

Forcing Access Paths

Some DBMSs allow you to force the use of specific access paths or the order in which tables are joined. For example, Microsoft SQL Server provides the FORCE-PLAN option. When FORCEPLAN has been set to ON, the optimizer will join the tables in the order in which they are coded in the SQL statement.

Oracle, on the other hand, provides hints that can be used to guide the relational optimizer to choose specific access paths. Hints are specified directly in the SQL query embedded within /*+ and */, for example:

```
SELECT    /*+ USE_NL */
          e.position, e.last_name, e.empno, d.manager
FROM      employee    e,
          department d
WHERE     d.dept_id = e.dept_id
AND       position IN ('MANAGER', 'DIRECTOR', 'VICE PRESIDENT')
ORDER BY position;
```

This query uses the Oracle hint USE_NL to force a nested-loop join. Additional hints can be provided to force the choice of index, force the use of parallelism, or force other optimization goals.

Techniques that force access path selection criteria should be used with caution. It is usually better to let the relational optimizer choose the appropriate access paths on its own unless

- You have in-depth knowledge of the amount and type of data stored in the tables to be joined
- You are reasonably sure that you can determine the optimal join order better than the optimizer
- Database statistics are not up-to-date, so the optimizer is not working with sufficient information about the database environment

Alternative methods are available to encourage the optimizer to select different access paths.

Alternative methods are available to encourage the optimizer to select different access paths. The general method of encouraging access path selection is to modify the SQL based on in-depth knowledge of the relational optimizer. This is sometimes called tweaking SQL. Since the optimizer within each DBMS is very different, few SQL tweaks are useful across multiple DBMSs.

One common method of tweaking SQL is to change the query such that the results are the same, but the optimizer is incapable of using certain access paths. For example, consider the following SQL statement:

```
SELECT    last_name, first_name, empno, deptno
FROM      employee
WHERE     empno BETWEEN '001000' AND '009999'
AND       (salary > 50000.00 OR 0 = 1)
ORDER by last_name;
```

The results of this query are exactly the same with, or without, the OR 0 = 1 component of the last predicate. However, some DBMS products prohibit the use of an index with such query formulations. In such cases, appending OR 0 = 1 will eliminate the possibility of using an index to support the salary predicate.

The DBA must learn the fundamentals of SQL tuning.

The DBA must learn the fundamentals of SQL tuning and the types of tweaking that make sense for each DBMS that he manages. Furthermore, whenever such tweaks are deployed, be sure to fully document the reason. Without such documentation it is quite likely that a maintenance programmer will remove OR 0 = 1 (or any other tweak) because it is not required.

SQL Coding and Tuning for Efficiency

Coding and tuning SQL is one of the most time consuming DBA tasks. There can be literally thousands of individual SQL statements across hundreds of applications that access databases. The DBA is responsible for ensuring that the following steps occur for each SQL statement in the organization:

1. Identify the business data requirements.
2. Ensure that the required data is available within existing databases.
3. Translate the business requirements into SQL.
4. Test the SQL for accuracy and results.
5. Review the access paths for performance.
6. Tweak the SQL for better access paths.
7. Code optimization hints.
8. Repeat steps 4 through 7 until performance is acceptable.
9. Repeat step 8 whenever performance problems arise or a new DBMS version is installed.
10. Repeat entire process whenever business needs change.

SQL tuning is a complex, time consuming, and error-prone process.

SQL tuning is a complex, time consuming, and error-prone process, indeed. Furthermore, it requires cooperation and communication between the business users and application programmers for the first three steps, and between the application programmers and the DBA for the remaining steps.

Surely, there must be a way to simplify SQL tuning.

SQL Rules of Thumb

In this section, we will examine some rules of thumb that apply generally to SQL development regardless of the underlying DBMS.

Rule 1: "It Depends!"

A successful DBA will know on what it depends.

The answer to every question about database performance is "It depends." A successful DBA will know on what it depends. For example, if someone asks, "What is the best access path for my SQL query?", the best answer is "It depends." Why? Well, if every row must be returned, a table scan is likely to be more efficient than indexed access. However, if only one row is to be returned, direct index lookup will probably perform best. For queries that return between one and all rows, the performance of access paths will depend on how the data is clustered, which version of the DBMS is in use, whether parallelism can be invoked, and so forth.

Be skeptical of tuning tips that use the words "always" or "never." Just about everything depends on other things.

Rule 2: Be Careful What You Ask For

The arrangement of elements within a query can change query performance. To what degree depends on the DBMS in use and whether rule-based optimization is used.

Place the most restrictive predicate where the optimizer can read it first.

A good rule of thumb, regardless of DBMS, is to place the most restrictive predicate where the optimizer can read it first. In Oracle, the optimizer reads WHERE clauses from the bottom up, therefore, the most restrictive predicate should be put at the bottom of the query. It is just the opposite in DB2.

Placing the most restrictive predicate where the optimizer can read it first enables the optimizer to narrow down the first set of results before proceeding to the next predicate. The next predicate will be applied to the subset of data that was selected by the most selective condition, instead of against the entire table.

Rule 3: KISS

Keep it simple, Stupid.

A rule of thumb for all types of IT activities is to follow the KISS principle: Keep it simple, Stupid. However, in the world of SQL there is a trade-off between simplicity and performance.

Keeping SQL simple makes development and maintenance tasks easier. A simple SQL statement is easier to decipher and easier to change. With simple SQL, application developers can perform their job more easily than with complex SQL.

Nevertheless, complex SQL can outperform simple SQL. The more work that can be performed by the DBMS and the optimizer, the better performance is likely to be. Let's look at an example: Some programmers avoid joins by coding multiple SQL SELECT statements and joining the data using program logic. The SQL is simpler because the programmer need not understand how to write SQL to join tables. However, SQL joins usually outperform program joins because less data is returned to the program. Furthermore, the relational optimizer can change the join methodology automatically if the database or data changes. Conversely, program logic must be changed manually by a skilled programmer.

Rule 4: Retrieve Only What Is Needed

Specify the absolute minimum number of columns in the SELECT list.

As simple as this rule of thumb sounds, you might be surprised at how often it is violated. To minimize the amount of data returned by your SQL statements, be sure to specify the absolute minimum number of columns in the SELECT list. If the column is not needed to satisfy the business requirement, do not request it to be returned in the result set.

Programmers frequently copy SQL statements that work well to use as templates for new statements. Sometimes the programmer will forget to trim down the number of columns requested when they only need a subset of the columns in the original query. This can adversely impact performance. The more columns that must be returned by the DBMS, the greater the processing overhead.

Another common problem is requesting unnecessary data. Consider the following SQL statement:

```
SELECT    position, last_name, empno
FROM      employee
WHERE     last_name = 'SMITH';
```

There is no reason to specify the last_name column in the SELECT list of this SQL statement. We know that last_name must be 'SMITH' for the entire result set because of the WHERE clause.

Returning only what is needed does not apply only to columns. You should also minimize the number of rows to be returned by coding the proper WHERE clauses for every SQL statement. The more data that can be filtered out of the result set by the DBMS, the more efficient the query will be because less data must be returned to the requester.

Sometimes application programmers avoid coding appropriate WHERE clauses in a misguided attempt to simplify SQL statements. The more information the optimizer has about the data to be retrieved, the better the access paths it formulates will be. A sure sign of potential abuse is finding a SQL statement embedded in an application program that is immediately followed by a series of IF-THEN-ELSE statements. Try to tune the query by moving the IF-THEN-ELSE statements into SQL WHERE clauses.

Rule 5: Avoid Cartesian Products

Be sure to code predicates matching the columns of every table that will be joined within each SQL statement. Failure to do so will result in severe performance degradation and possibly incorrect results.

The results of a Cartesian product are difficult to interpret.

Whenever predicates do not exist for joining two tables, the RDBMS must perform a Cartesian product. This is the combination of *every* row of one table with *every* row of the other table. Nonmatching rows are not eliminated because there is nothing that can be matched. The results of a Cartesian product are difficult to interpret and contain no information other than a simple list of all rows of each table.

Rule 6: Judicious Use of OR

The OR logical operator can be troublesome for performance.

The OR logical operator can be troublesome for performance. If you can convert a SQL statement that uses OR to one that uses IN, it is likely that performance will improve. For example, consider changing this:

```
SELECT    e.position, e.last_name, e.empno, d.manager
FROM      employee    e,
          department d
WHERE     d.dept_id = e.dept_id
AND       position = 'MANAGER'
OR        position = 'DIRECTOR'
OR        position = 'VICE PRESIDENT'
ORDER BY position;
```

to this:

```
SELECT    e.position, e.last_name, e.empno, d.manager
FROM      employee    e,
          department d
WHERE     d.dept_id = e.dept_id
AND       position IN ('MANAGER', 'DIRECTOR', 'VICE PRESIDENT')
ORDER BY position;
```

Of course, your results may vary depending on the DBMS in use and the nature of the data.

Rule 7: Judicious Use of LIKE

The LIKE logical operator is another troublesome beast.

The LIKE logical operator is another troublesome beast. It is very easy to create performance problems when using LIKE in SQL. For example, consider the following SQL:

```
SELECT    position, last_name, empno
FROM      employee
WHERE     dept_id LIKE '%X'
ORDER BY position;
```

This query will return employee information for all employees working in any department where dept_id ends in 'X'. However, the relational optimizer will have to scan the data in order to resolve this query—there is no way to use an index. Because the high-order portion of the column is not known, traversing a b-tree index structure is impossible.

You might be able to use your knowledge of the data to rewrite this query without a leading wild-card character (%). For example, perhaps all dept_id values start with either 'A' or 'B'. In that case, you could modify the SQL as follows:

```
SELECT    position, last_name, empno
FROM      employee
WHERE     dept_id LIKE 'A%X'
OR        dept_id LIKE 'B%X'
ORDER BY position;
```

In this case, the DBMS may be able to use a nonmatching index scan if an index exists on the dept_id column.

Once again, your results will vary with the DBMS in use and the nature of the data accessed.

Rule 8: Know What Works Best

One way of coding usually provides better performance than the others.

The flexibility of SQL allows the same process to be coded in multiple ways. However, one way of coding usually provides better performance than the others. The DBA should understand the best way to code SQL for each DBMS in use. Furthermore, the DBA should provide information on proper query formulation for performance to the application development staff.

Rule 9: Issue Frequent COMMITs

When coding programs to run as batch transactions, it is important to issue regular SQL COMMIT statements. As discussed in Chapter 5, the COMMIT statement finalizes modifications to the database. When a COMMIT is issued, locks on the modified database objects and data can be released.

An additional consideration for Oracle DBAs is the impact of a COMMIT on the rollback segments. Rollback segments are used by Oracle to store completed transactions before the changes are actually written to the table. When you issue a COMMIT in Oracle, not only is the data finalized to the table but the contents of the rollback segment are removed, too. Oracle rollback segments are used to store before images of the data in case transactions are rolled back before changes are committed.

Issue enough COMMIT statements to minimize the impact of locking on availability.

Therefore, as a DBA you must ensure that application developers issue enough COMMIT statements to minimize the impact of locking on availability and to keep rollback segments to a manageable size.

Rule 10: Beware of Code Generators

Beware of application code generators and similar tools that automatically create SQL. Many of these tools use gateways that require each SQL statement to be recompiled and optimized each time it is requested. However, some gateways provide a caching mechanism to store compiled and optimized SQL on the server. Such a cache can help improve performance for frequently recurring SQL statements.

Rule 11: Consider Stored Procedures

Performance degradation due to repeated network traffic can be minimized by using a stored procedure because only a single request is needed to execute it. Within the stored procedure, multiple SQL statements can be issued, and the results processed and sent to the requesting program or user. Without the stored procedure, each of the multiple SQL statements, as well as all of the results, would have to be sent across the network. Additionally, SQL in stored procedures may perform better than the same SQL outside of the stored procedure if the DBMS parses and compiles the statements before run time.

Additional SQL Tuning Tips

SQL tuning requires a full-length book of its own.

SQL tuning is a complicated task that requires a full-length book of its own. In fact, each DBMS requires its own book-length treatment of SQL tuning to do the topic justice. However, the following SQL tuning suggestions are useful for DBAs to apply, regardless of the DBMS:

- Use indexes to avoid sorting.
- Create indexes to support troublesome queries.
- Whenever possible, do not perform arithmetic in SQL predicates. Use the host programming language (Java, COBOL, C, etc.) to perform arithmetic.
- Use SQL functions to reduce programming effort.
- Build proper constraints into the database to minimize coding edit checks. (See Chapter 13 for more details.)
- Do not forget about the "hidden" impact of triggers. A delete from one table may trigger many more operations. Although you may think the problem is a poorly performing DELETE, the trigger may be the true culprit.

Identifying Poorly Performing SQL

A SQL performance monitor is the best approach to identify poorly performing statements.

A large part of the task of tuning SQL is identifying the offending code. A SQL performance monitor is the best approach to identify poorly performing statements. Such a tool constantly monitors the DBMS environment and reports on the resources consumed by SQL statements. Some DBMSs provide rudimentary bundled support for SQL monitoring, but many third-party tools are available. These tools provide in-depth features such as the ability to identify the worst performing SQL without the overhead of system traces, integration to SQL coding and tuning tools, and graphical performance charts and triggers. Consult Chapter 22 for more information on SQL performance monitors and other DBA tools.

Summary

Application performance management and SQL tuning is a complex area that requires the active participation of programmers and DBAs. Each DBMS operates differently, and DBAs as well as programmers will need to understand all of the minute details of SQL and application performance management for their DBMS.

The relational optimizer combines access path strategies to form an efficient access path for each SQL request. However, the optimizer is a very complex piece of software, and the DBMS vendors do not share with their customers all the intricacies of how the optimizer works. Therefore, quite often, SQL performance tuning becomes an iterative artistic process, instead of a science.

Review

1. Define what is meant by *physical data independence*.

2. Describe the impact of using the LIKE operation with a wild-card character at the beginning of the value.

3. What factors influence the optimizer during SQL access path selection?

4. Name and describe the two predominant relational join methods.

5. Under what circumstances is a nonmatching index scan performed?

6. A query is written to access a single table. Furthermore, that query will return only a single row because an equality operator (=) is coded on the primary key for the table. A unique index exists to support the primary key. What type of access is likely to be the most efficient for that query?

7. How can stored procedures be used to optimize performance in a client/server application?

8. Under what circumstances will a table scan outperform indexed access?

9. Why is it important to use caution before implementing SQL tweaks and hints?

10. Describe the three possible types of parallel query access.

Suggested Reading

Bhamidipati, Kishore. *SQL Programmer's Reference.* Berkeley, CA: Osborne/McGraw-Hill (1998). ISBN 0-07-882460-5

Harrington, Jan L. *SQL Clearly Explained.* San Diego, CA: AP Professional (1998). ISBN 0-12-326426-X

Khoshafian, Setrag, et al. *A Guide to Developing Client/Server SQL Applications.* San Mateo, CA: Morgan Kaufmann (1992). ISBN 1-55860-147-3

Data Integrity

The DBA has
many tools at his
disposal to ensure
data integrity.

Ensuring the integrity of the organization's databases is a key component of the DBA's job. A database is of little use if the data it contains is inaccurate or if it cannot be accessed due to integrity problems. The DBA has many tools at his disposal to ensure data integrity.

Types of Integrity

With respect to databases, we will discuss two aspects of integrity:

- Database structure integrity
- Semantic data integrity

Keeping track of database objects and ensuring that each object is created, formatted, and maintained properly is the goal of database structure integrity. Each DBMS uses its own internal format and structure to support the databases, tablespaces, tables, and indexes under its control. System and application errors can cause faults within these internal structures, and it is the DBA's job to identify and correct such faults before insurmountable problems are encountered.

The second type of integrity is semantic data integrity. This refers to the meaning of data and the relationships that need to be maintained between different types of data. The DBMS provides options, controls, and procedures to define and assure the semantic integrity of the data stored within its databases. DBAs must understand how the DBMS enables automatic semantic data integrity checking. And, as an ongoing component of the job, the DBA has to implement semantic data integrity into the database design, as well as initiate processes to check and correct integrity problems that creep into the database over time.

Database Structure Integrity

The DBMS uses internal structures and pointers to maintain database objects in the proper order.

Structural database integrity and consistency is of paramount importance in the ongoing administration of databases. The DBMS uses internal structures and pointers to maintain database objects in the proper order. If those structures are damaged in any way, database access will be compromised.

Types of Structural Problems

If the pointers do not point to the correct data, the index is useless.

One common problem experienced by relational databases is *index corruption*. You will recall from previous chapters that an index provides an alternate path to data in the database by using an ordered b-tree structure. Basically, the leaf pages of an index are pointers to physical data locations in the base table. If the pointers do not point to the correct data, the index is useless.

An index can become corrupted in several ways, depending on the DBMS in use and the operations performed on the index and the corresponding table. For example, if the table is recovered to a previous point in time, but the index is not rebuilt, the index will not accurately reflect the current contents of the data.

However, indexes are not the only database objects that utilize pointers. When certain data types are used, the DBMS may require pointers. For example, *very large objects* such as DB2 LOB columns or SQL Server text and image columns are not stored contiguously with the rest of the data. Instead, the columns assigned these data types are stored in a separate file, and the primary file for the table contains a pointer to the physical data location of the large object. It is possible for these pointers to get out of sync with the data, rendering the data inaccessible.

Another, though somewhat rare, database structural integrity problem is table data *page header corruption*. Each individual physical page (or block) in the database file stores housekeeping information, known as the *header*, at the beginning of the page. This header enables the DBMS to easily and rapidly read the page contents. If the header becomes corrupted, the DBMS may not be able to interpret the data stored on the page. Such situations usually require the database file to be recovered from backup files. (For more information on backup and recovery operations, refer to Chapter 15).

Backup files are another potential area for a structural integrity problem. Each DBMS formats and maintains a specific structure for its database backup files. If the backup file is not formatted correctly, or if data is in the wrong location in the backup file, it cannot be used by the DBMS for recovery purposes. Media failures, tape degradation, and bugs can cause such problems.

Managing Structural Problems

You can investigate the integrity of a database using DBMS utility programs.

Each DBMS provides different utility programs to check on different aspects of database structural integrity. It is possible to investigate the integrity of a database using these utility programs. For example, Sybase and Microsoft SQL Server provide the DBCC utility program, DB2 supplies the CHECK and REPAIR utilities, and Informix offers the TBCHECK utility.

To elaborate on the functionality of such utilities, let's focus on the DBCC utility. Figure 13-1 shows some of the options for which DBCC can be used.

Database Consistency

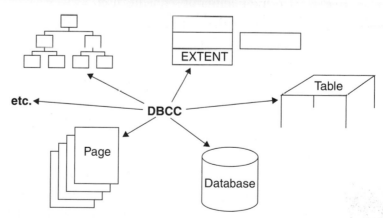

Figure 13-1   *The DBCC utility.*

Use extreme care
when running the
DBCC utility.
The DBA should exhibit extreme care when running the DBCC utility. It is possible to both read and write to database files when using DBCC. To ensure the safety of your database files, never use the write capabilities without guidance from the DBMS vendor's technical support group.

Consistency Options

The DBCC utility provides two options for basic consistency checking:

- DBCC CHECKTABLE(table_name) checks the consistency of the data and index pages of a table. When DBCC is run using this option it will report on the number of data pages, the number of rows, the number of text and image columns, as well as any integrity violations.

- DBCC REINDEX(table_name) checks the consistency of indexes and rebuilds the index if it is found to be corrupted.

Database Checking

Additional DBCC options exist for checking the integrity of a database.

- DBCC CHECKDB(database_name) runs CHECKTABLE (see above) on every table in the database. This option checks the consistency of the data and index pages of all defined tables.

- DBCC CHECKCATALOG(database_name) checks the consistency of the system catalog tables for the specified database. It will report on the size and number of segments used, as well as detect and report on any integrity errors.

- DBCC CHECKALLOC(database_name) checks the consistency of the specified database and reports on the current extent structure. The CHECKALLOC option may find spurious allocation problems if DBCC is run while transactions are modifying the database. This option also reports on the number of allocations and the pages used per allocation.

Memory Usage

The DBCC com-
mand can be used
to monitor current
memory allocation
and usage.
The DBCC command can be used to monitor current memory allocation and usage. By specifying the MEMUSAGE keyword, for example, DBCC MEMUSAGE, the utility will report on the configured memory allocation and memory usage of the top 20 memory users. The following information is displayed:

- *Configured memory*—the amount of memory configured for the DBMS.

- *Code size*—the amount of memory used by code.

- *Kernel and structures*—the amount of memory used for the kernel and the server.

- *Page cache*—the amount of memory used for data cache.

- *Procedure buffers and headers*—the amount of memory used for procedure cache.

- *Buffer cache detail*—a listing of the top 20 users of data cache, indicating the database and object being accessed and how many 2K buffers are being utilized.

- *Procedure cache detail*—a listing of the top 20 users of procedure cache, indicating the type of usage and the memory utilization.

Additional Options

Various other DBCC options are available, including the ability to generate reports containing information on database internals (for example, creation date and internal identifier), to print formatted table pages showing the header contents, as well as to "zap" the database (that is, make quick changes to any of the database contents). Once again, though, it is not a good idea to "zap" the database without guidance from the manufacturer.

Semantic Data Integrity

Semantic data integrity deals with the DBMS features and processes that can be used to ensure the accuracy and viability of the data contents of a database. Whereas structural database integrity refers to the consistency of the "holders" of the data (the database objects), semantic data integrity refers to the consistency of the data itself.

DBAs constantly struggle with the question of how best to enforce data integrity—by using DBMS features or by using application code. This is an important issue and is debated often. In general, using DBMS features to support data integrity usually offers the best solution, for several reasons.

It is easier to discover and maintain a semantic integrity rule using DBMS features than by reading program code. If you prefer to read code, remember that you may need to be able to read several languages (COBOL, Java, Visual

Basic, etc.) in a heterogeneous environment; often, for the same rule. Additionally, you will need to know how to distinguish the active code from the old code from the new enhancement code.

Many forms of semantic data integrity can be enforced by using features of the DBMS.

Many forms of semantic data integrity can be enforced by using features of the DBMS. When DBMS facilities are used to enforce data integrity, less code needs to be written, and therefore less code needs to be tested. This can reduce the time and cost to get the "product" out the door.

Entity Integrity

Entity integrity means that each occurrence of an entity must be uniquely identifiable.

Entity integrity is the most basic level of data integrity provided by relational databases. *Entity integrity* means that each occurrence of an entity must be uniquely identifiable. In other words, entity integrity requires the specification of a primary key for each entity and that no component of the primary key be set to null.

In practice, no major RDBMS product forces entity integrity because entities, or tables, can be created without specifying a primary key. However, it is considered a bad practice to create tables without a primary key because it makes identifying rows of the table difficult.

A primary key is required to set up RI between tables. A primary key constraint can consist of one or more columns from the same table that are unique within the table. A table can have only one primary key constraint, which cannot contain nulls.

The DBMS will require the creation of a unique index on the columns of the primary key constraint to prohibit duplicate column values. Some DBMSs, such as Sybase, will automatically generate the unique index when the primary key constraint is created.

An example of a primary key constraint follows:

```
CREATE TABLE EMP
(empno          INTEGER        PRIMARY KEY,
 emp_address    VARCHAR(70),
 emp_type       CHAR(8),
 emp_dept       CHAR(3)        NOT NULL WITH DEFAULT,
 salary         DECIMAL(7,2)   NOT NULL,
 commission     DECIMAL(7,2),
 bonus          DECIMAL(7,2)
) IN db.ts;
```

This example shows the primary key constraint specified at the column level: it applies to the empno column, which is defined as the primary key for this table. However, in practice it is quite common for primary keys to consist of multiple columns. For this reason, constraints can be defined at the table level, as well. For example, if the primary key of this table were to be defined as the combination of the empno and emp_type columns, you could add the following specification to the end of the table, right after the specification of the last column defined:

```
PRIMARY KEY pkemp
  (empno, emp_type)
```

Of course, the primary key specification would have to be removed from empno at the column level before this would work because you cannot specify more than one primary key per table. Furthermore, notice that we have named the primary key constraint pkemp in this example.

Unique Constraints

A *unique constraint* is similar to a primary key constraint. Each table can have zero, one, or many unique constraints consisting of one or more columns each. The values stored in the column, or combination of columns, must but unique within the table—that is, no other row can contain the same value.

Unique constraints cannot be used to support referential constraints.

Unique constraints differ from primary key constraints in that they cannot be used to support referential constraints. Furthermore, the unique constraint columns may be set to null.

As in the case of primary key constraints, the DBMS will require the creation of a unique index on the columns of the unique constraint to prohibit duplicate column values. The DBA should create unique constraints for columns, or combinations of columns, that must be unique within the table. Unique constraints are more efficient than trying to enforce uniqueness programmatically.

Data Types

Data type and *data length* are the most fundamental integrity constraints applied to data in the database. Simply by specifying the data type for each column when a table is created, the DBMS will automatically ensure that only the correct type of data is stored in that column. Processes that attempt to insert or update the data to the wrong type will be rejected. Furthermore, a maximum length is assigned to the column to prohibit larger values from being stored in the table.

The DBA must
choose the data
type and length
of each column
wisely.

The DBA must choose the data type and length of each column wisely. It is best to choose the data type that most closely matches the domain of correct values for the column. For example, a numeric column should be defined as one of the numeric data types: integer, decimal, or floating point. Specifying a character data type for a column that will contain numeric data imposes additional work on the application programs to edit-check the values. Furthermore, the program is likely to be less efficient at edit-checking data than the DBMS would be. Additionally, data that is inserted or modified outside the scope of an application program will not be edit-checked at all and thereby has the potential of introducing data integrity problems into the database.

User-Defined Data Types

A user-defined
data type extends
the type of data
that can be stored
in databases.

A *user-defined data type,* or UDT for short, provides a mechanism for extending the type of data that can be stored in databases and the way that the data is treated. In other words, the DBA can create user-defined data types to further clarify the legal values for a column. The UDT, once defined and implemented, extends the functionality of the DBMS by enabling the DBA to specify the UDT in CREATE TABLE DDL statements just like built-in data types.

UDTs can be beneficial when you need to store data that is specifically tailored to your organization's requirements. For example, UDTs are useful for organizations that must handle multiple currencies. By creating a separate data type for each currency, errors are less likely to be made in monetary calculations. For example, perhaps your company handles monetary amounts from Canada, the United States, the European Union, and Japan. The DBA can create four UDTs, such as

```
CREATE DISTINCT TYPE canadian_dollar AS DECIMAL(11,2);
CREATE DISTINCT TYPE US_dollar AS DECIMAL(11,2);
CREATE DISTINCT TYPE euro AS DECIMAL(11,2);
CREATE DISTINCT TYPE japanese_yen AS DECIMAL(15,2)
```

After a user-defined data type has been created, it can be used in the same manner as a system-defined data type. Of course, the actual syntax for creating and using UDTs differs with DBMS. Sybase and Microsoft SQL Server use system-stored procedures to create UDTs, whereas Oracle and DB2 use CREATE statements such as those in the previous example.

By creating separate data types, the DBMS enforces strong typing; in other words, the DBMS will prohibit nondefined operations between different types. For example, the following operation will not be allowed due to strong typing:

```
TOTAL_AMT = US_DOLLAR + CANADIAN_DOLLAR
```

If this operation were allowed to proceed, the TOTAL_AMT calculated would be useless because you cannot perform operations on different currencies without converting them to a common currency. So, UDTs and strong typing help us to avoid data integrity problems.

Another benefit of creating user-defined data types is additional consistency throughout the database. For example, if we build a social security number UDT, and use the UDT for every column that contains social security numbers, we ensure that each social security number is stored the same way.

Furthermore, UDTs provide a higher level of abstraction to your database design. It is much easier to discuss the Salary data type (with all its implied definitions, properties, and constraints) than it is to talk about DECIMAL(11,2) or SMALLMONEY data types (with no implied characteristics other than its inherent type).

Default Values

When columns are created within tables, they can be assigned a default value that will be used when SQL INSERT statements are issued that do not provide an explicit value for that column. This allows programmers to ignore columns and the DBMS to automatically provide a default value.

Each column can have only one default value.

Each column can have only one default value. The column's data type, length, and property must be able to support the default value specified. For example, a numeric column cannot be assigned a character default value. Furthermore, the default may be null, but only if the column is created as a nullable column.

Check Constraints

A check constraint is a DBMS-defined restriction placed on the data values that can be stored in a column or columns.

A *check constraint* is a DBMS-defined restriction placed on the data values that can be stored in a column or columns of a table. When a check constraint is defined, it places specific data value restrictions on the contents of a column through the specification of a Boolean expression. The expression is explicitly defined in the table DDL and is formulated in much the same way that SQL

WHERE clauses are formulated. Any attempt to modify the column data (that is, during INSERT and UPDATE processing) will cause the expression to be evaluated. If the modification conforms to the Boolean expression, the modification is permitted to proceed. If not, the statement will fail with a constraint violation.

Check constraints can be defined when the table is created, or added later by altering the table. If you know SQL, it is easy to learn how to code a check constraint because they are written using recognizable SQL syntax. The check constraint syntax consists of two components: a constraint name and a check condition.

The *constraint name* identifies the check constraint to the database. The same constraint name cannot be specified more than once for the same table. If a constraint name is not explicitly coded, the DBMS automatically generates a unique name for the constraint. Each DBMS uses a different algorithm for generating constraint names, but the name is typically derived from the name of the first column in the check condition.

The *check condition* defines the actual constraint logic. The check condition can be defined using any of the basic predicates (>, <, =, <>, <=, >=), as well as BETWEEN, IN, LIKE, and NULL. Furthermore, AND and OR can be used to string conditions together in a check constraint.

Some restrictions, however, apply to creating check constraints:

- The check constraint can refer only to columns in the table in which it is created.

- A limited subset of SQL constructs is permissible within a check constraint definition. Typically, SQL constructs such as subselects, column functions, host variables, negation (i.e., NOT), and special registers are prohibited within check constraints.

- The first operand of the check constraint is the name of a column contained in the table; the second operand is either another column name or a constant.

- If the second operand is a constant, it must be compatible with the data type of the first operand. If the second operand is a column, it must be the same data type as the first column specified.

Check Constraint Benefits

So, what are the benefits of check constraints? The primary benefit is the ability to enforce business rules directly into the database without requiring additional application logic. Once defined, the business rule is physically implemented and cannot be bypassed.

Because there is no additional programming required, DBAs can implement check constraints without involving the application programming staff. This effectively minimizes the amount of code that must be written by the programming staff. With the significant application backlog within most organizations, this can be the most crucial reason to deploy check constraints.

Check constraints provide better data integrity. As check constraints are always executed whenever the data in the column upon which they are defined is to be modified, the business rule is not bypassed during ad hoc processing and dynamic SQL. When business rules are enforced using application programming logic instead, the rules cannot be checked during ad hoc processes.

Check constraints promote consistency. Because they are implemented once in the table DDL—each constraint is always enforced. Constraints written in application logic, on the other hand, must be executed by each program that modifies the data to which the constraint applies. This can cause code duplication and inconsistent maintenance, resulting in inaccurate business rule support.

Typically, check constraints coded in DDL will outperform the corresponding application code to perform the same edit-checking. The overall impact of check constraints is to increase application development productivity while at the same time improving data integrity.

Check Constraint Examples

Check constraints enable the DBA or database designer to specify more robust data integrity rules directly into the database. Consider the following example:

```
CREATE TABLE EMP
(empno          INTEGER        PRIMARY KEY,
    CONSTRAINT check_empno
     CHECK (empno BETWEEN 100 and 25000),
 emp_address  VARCHAR(70),
 emp_type       CHAR(8)
     CHECK (emp_type IN ('temp', 'fulltime', 'contract')),
 emp_dept      CHAR(3)        NOT NULL WITH DEFAULT,
 salary         DECIMAL(7,2)  NOT NULL
    CONSTRAINT check_salary
     CHECK (salary < 50000.00),
 commission    DECIMAL(7,2),
 bonus         DECIMAL(7,2)
) IN db.ts;
```

This CREATE statement for the EMP table contains three different check constraints:

- The name of the first check constraint is check_empno. It is defined on the empno column. The constraint ensures that the empno column can contain values that range from 100 to 25,000 (instead of the domain of all valid integers).

- The second check constraint for this table is on the emp_type column. This is an example of an unnamed constraint and, though possible, is not recommended. It is best to always provide an explicit constraint name in order to ease identification and administration. This specific constraint restricts the values that can be placed into emp_type as: 'temp', 'fulltime', and 'contract'; no other values would be accepted.

- The last check constraint on this table is named check_salary. It effectively ensures that no employee can have a salary of more than $50,000. (Who wants to work there?)

This first check constraint example depicts column-level constraints. However, check constraints also may be coded at the table level. A column-level check constraint is defined in the DDL immediately after the column. Appropriately enough, a table-level check constraint is defined after all of the columns of the table have already been defined.

It is quite common for business data integrity rules to require access to multiple columns within a single table. When this situation occurs, it is wise to code the business rule into a check constraint at the table level, instead of at the column level. Of course, any column-level check constraint can also be defined at the table level, as well. In terms of functionality, there is no difference between an integrity constraint defined at the table level and the same constraint defined at the column level. Let's augment our sample table DDL to add several table-level check constraints:

```
CREATE TABLE EMP
(empno          INTEGER        PRIMARY KEY,
    CONSTRAINT check_empno
      CHECK (empno BETWEEN 100 AND 25000),
 emp_address   VARCHAR(70),
 emp_type      CHAR(8)
      CHECK (emp_type IN ('temp', 'fulltime', 'contract')),
 emp_dept      CHAR(3)        NOT NULL WITH DEFAULT,
```

```
salary         DECIMAL(7,2)  NOT NULL
   CONSTRAINT check_salary
     CHECK (salary < 50000.00),
commission    DECIMAL(7,2),
bonus         DECIMAL(7,2)
   CONSTRAINT comm_vs_salary
     CHECK (salary > commission),
   CONSTRAINT comm_bonus
     CHECK (commission=0 OR bonus=0),
) IN db.ts;
```

Now the CREATE statement for the EMP table has been modified to contain two table-level check constraints having the following ramifications:

- The first table-level check constraint for the EMP table is named `comm_vs_salary`. This constraint ensures that no employee can earn more in commission than in salary.

- The second table-level check constraint is named comm_bonus. This constraint will ensure that an employee cannot earn both a commission and a bonus.

Nulls and Other Potential Problems. An additional consideration for check constraints is the relational null. Any nullable column that is defined with a check constraint can be set to null. When the column is set to null, the check constraint evaluates to unknown. Because null indicates the lack of a value, the presence of a null will not violate the check constraint.

> Any nullable column that is defined with a check constraint can be set to null.

Running database utilities can cause problems with check constraints. For example, depending on the DBMS, the LOAD utility may or may not enforce check constraints as data is being loaded to the table. If constraints are not enforced, data can be loaded that does not conform to the check constraints defined on the table, causing data integrity problems. If constraints are enforced during the LOAD process, someone will have to manually edit the rows that were not loaded so that they adhere to the check-constraint definitions on the table.

Another potential problem with check constraints is inconsistent coding from table to table. It is likely that similar columns of the same data type and length will exist in multiple tables throughout the database. If these columns must all adhere to the same edit-check requirements, the DBA must create the same check constraint on each column across multiple tables. It is possible that errors can be made. Refer to the sidebar "Rules" for a discussion of a different type of constraint available in Sybase and Microsoft SQL Server that helps to alleviate this problem.

Additionally, it is possible to define unworkable check constraints on a table. Relational DBMS products provide the additional capability to specify column defaults. When a row is inserted or loaded into a table and no value is specified for the column, the column will be set to the value that has been identified in the column default specification. For example, the DBA could define a default for the emp_type column of our sample EMP table as follows:

```
emp_type   CHAR(8)   DEFAULT 'fulltime'
           CHECK (emp_type IN ('temp',   'fulltime', 'contract')),
...
```

Rules

Sybase and Microsoft SQL Server both offer a special type of check constraint called a *rule*. Although rules are similar to check constraints, they are "free-standing" database objects.

Like a check constraint, a rule defines the parameters for data validation. Whenever data is inserted or updated, the rule is checked to ensure that the data modification complies with the rule. Both columns and UDTs can have rules defined for them.

After a rule has been created, it must be bound to columns and UDTs before it has any effect on the database. Binding is accomplished using the SP_BINDRULE system procedure. For example, the following statements can be used to create a rule that forces the state code to represent only Illinois, Wisconsin, or Indiana, and then binds the rule to the state column in two different tables.

```
CREATE rule state_rule AS @state IN ("IL", "WI", "IN")
EXEC sp_bindrule "state_rule", "publishers.state"
EXEC sp_bindrule "state_rule", "authors.state"
```

Once a rule is bound to a column or user-defined data type it will function like a check constraint. Whenever data values are inserted or updated, the rule will be invoked to ensure that the values conform to the rule definition. Rules can be removed from columns or user-defined data types by using the SP_UNBIND system procedure when the rule is no longer required.

Rules can be more reliable than check constraints because a rule need be created only once, after which it is bound to the appropriate columns and data types. So, if one constraint applies to multiple columns, less work is required with a rule than with a check constraint. The check constraint must be explicitly coded within the DDL of every table that must be checked.

If a row is inserted without specifying an `emp_type`, the column will default to the value `'fulltime'`. However, most DBMSs are not designed to perform semantic checking on constraints and defaults. For example, the DBMS would allow the DBA to define defaults that contradict check constraints. Furthermore, it is possible for the DBA to define check constraints that contradict one another. Care must be taken to avoid creating this type of problem. Examples of contradictory constraints follow.

In the following case, no value is both greater than 10 and less than 9, so nothing could ever be inserted into the table.

```
CHECK (empno > 10) AND empno < 9)
```

In the next case, the default value is not one of the permitted `emp_type` values according to the defined constraint. No defaults would ever be inserted, so a value must always be provided when rows are inserted.

```
    emp_type  CHAR(8)   DEFAULT 'new'
CHECK (emp_type IN ('temp',   'fulltime', 'contract')), ...
```

In this final case, the constraints are redundant. No logical harm is done, but both constraints will be checked, thereby impacting the performance of applications that modify the table in which the constraints exist.

```
CHECK (empno > 10)
CHECK (empno >= 11)
```

Of course, other potential semantic problems could occur, such as

- When the parent table indicates a neutralizing DELETE RI constraint but a check constraint is defined on the child table stating CHECK (COL1 IS NOT NULL).

- When two constraints are defined on the same column with contradictory conditions.

- When the constraint requires that the column be null, but the column is defined as not null.

Check constraints provide a very powerful vehicle for supporting business rules in the database. They cannot be bypassed and therefore provide better data integrity than corresponding logic programmed into the application. It is a wise course of action for DBAs to define check constraints in the database instead of coding similar edit checking logic into application programs.

Triggers

A trigger is a piece of code that is executed in response to a data modification statement.

Triggers are event-driven specialized procedures that are attached to database tables. A trigger is a piece of code that is executed in response to a data modification statement; that is, an INSERT, UPDATE, or DELETE. To be a bit more precise, triggers are event-driven specialized procedures that are stored in, and managed by, the DBMS. Each trigger is attached to a single, specified table. Triggers can be thought of as an advanced form of rule or constraint that is written using an extended form of SQL. A trigger cannot be directly called or executed; it is automatically executed (or "fired") by the RDBMS as the result of an action—a data modification to the associated table.

Once a trigger is created, it is always executed when its "firing" event occurs (UPDATE, INSERT, or DELETE). Therefore, triggers are automatic, implicit, and nonbypassable. A database with triggers defined on it is sometimes called an *active database* because simple data modification results in additional actions taking place—as defined in the trigger code.

Triggers are similar to stored procedures. Both consist of procedural logic that is stored in or managed by the database. However, stored procedures are not event driven and are not attached to a specific table. A stored procedure is explicitly executed by invoking a CALL to the procedure (instead of being implicitly executed like triggers). Additionally, a stored procedure can access many tables without being specifically associated to any of them.

Triggers are useful for implementing code that must be executed on a regular basis due to a predefined event. By utilizing triggers, scheduling and data integrity problems can be eliminated because the trigger will be fired whenever the triggering event occurs. You need not remember to schedule or code an activity to perform the logic in the trigger—it happens automatically.

Triggers can be implemented for many practical uses. Quite often, it is impossible to code business rules into the database by using only DDL. For example, most DBMSs do not support complex constraints (only value-based CHECK constraints) or certain types of referential constraints (such as pendant DELETE processing or cascading UPDATEs). Using triggers, a very flexible environment is established for implementing business rules and constraints in the DBMS. This is important because having the business rules in the database ensures that everyone uses the same logic to accomplish the same process.

Triggers are quite flexible and can be coded to suit many purposes. For example, triggers can

- Access and modify other tables
- Print informational messages
- Specify complex restrictions

For example, consider a basic student enrollment database as might be used by a college or university. A course can be attended by many students, and a student can attend many courses. Triggers can be used to support scenarios such as the following:

- Perhaps the university places a limit, say five, on the number of courses in which a student can enroll per semester. A trigger can be coded to check that no more than five rows are inserted into the course enrollment table for the same student. Similarly, if a course size limit is required, a trigger can be coded to check that no more students than the limit are inserted into the course enrollment table.
- A trigger can be created to ensure that each professor is assigned to at least one course each semester, or to limit the number of courses each professor can teach each semester
- Triggers can be used to perform calculations such as ensuring that the student has paid the proper tuition for the semester.
- Triggers can be coded to ensure that the student has successfully completed prerequisite courses.

The number of business rules that can be implemented using triggers is limited only by your imagination.

The number of business rules that can be implemented using triggers is truly limited only by your imagination, or more appropriately, your business needs.

When Does a Trigger Fire?

Triggers can be coded to fire at two different times: before the firing activity occurs or after the firing activity occurs. A "before" trigger executes before the firing activity occurs; an "after" trigger executes after the firing activity occurs.

Some DBMSs support both "before" and "after" triggers, whereas others support only one type of trigger. Knowing how the triggers in your database function is imperative. Without this knowledge, properly functioning triggers cannot be coded, supported, or maintained effectively.

Consider, for example, the case where the firing activity occurs before the trigger is fired. In other words, the UPDATE, INSERT, or DELETE occurs first, and as a result of this action, the trigger logic is executed. If necessary, the trigger code may be able to roll back the data modification. What if the trigger is fired before the actual firing event occurs? In this situation, a rollback would not be required for the firing event code because it did not yet occur. However, a rollback may be required for any data modifications that occurred prior to this firing event within the same transaction.

The rule for order of trigger execution depends on the DBMS.

If multiple triggers are coded on the same table, which trigger is fired first? It can make a difference as to how the triggers are coded, tested, and maintained. The rule for order of execution depends on the DBMS. For example, DB2 fires triggers of the same type on the same table in the order in which they were created. For example, if two DELETE triggers exist on the same table, the one that was physically created first would be executed first. Be sure to understand how your DBMS fires triggers and keep the rules in mind as you make changes to your database. If you need to drop a table and recreate it to implement a schema change, make sure you create the triggers in the desired (same) order to keep the functionality the same.

Nested Triggers

As we've already learned, a trigger is fired by an INSERT, UPDATE, or DELETE. However, a trigger also can contain INSERT, UPDATE, and DELETE statements within itself. Therefore, a data modification fires a trigger that can cause another data modification that fires yet another trigger. When a trigger contains INSERT, UPDATE, and/or DELETE logic, the trigger is said to be a nested trigger.

Most DBMSs, however, place a limit on the number of nested triggers that can be executed within a single firing event. If this were not done, it could be quite possible for triggers to fire triggers ad infinitum until all of the data is removed from an entire database.

If RI is combined with triggers, additional cascading UPDATEs and/or DELETEs can occur. If an UPDATE or DELETE results in a series of additional UPDATEs or DELETEs that need to be propagated to other tables, the UPDATE or DELETE triggers for the second table also will be activated. This combination of multiple triggers and referential constraints is capable of setting a cascading effect into motion, which can result in multiple data changes. DB2 limits this cascading effect to 16 levels in order to prevent endless looping; if more than 16 levels of nesting occur, the transaction is aborted. Other DBMSs provide options to enable and disable cascading triggers.

Nesting triggers provides an efficient method for implementing automatic data integrity.

The ability to nest triggers provides an efficient method for implementing automatic data integrity. Because triggers generally cannot be bypassed, they provide an elegant solution to the enforced application of business rules. Use caution, however, to ensure that the maximum trigger nesting level is not reached. Failure to heed this advice can cause an environment where certain types of updates cannot occur at all.

Using Triggers to Implement Referential Integrity

Triggers can be coded to support any type of referential constraint.

One common use for triggers is to support referential integrity (RI). Triggers can be coded, in lieu of declarative RI, to support any type of referential constraint you wish to place on the database. Of course, when you use triggers, it necessitates writing procedural code for each rule for each constraint, whereas declarative RI constraints are coded in the DDL that is used to create relational tables.

Additional guidance on using triggers to support RI can be found later in this chapter.

Transition Variables and Tables

In order to use triggers to support RI rules, it is sometimes necessary to know the values impacted by the action that fired the trigger. For example, consider the case where a trigger is fired because a row was deleted. The row, and all of its values, has already been deleted because the trigger is executed after its firing action occurs. But if this is the case, how can we ascertain if referentially connected rows exist with those values? We may need to access it in its original, unmodified format.

Transition tables are accessible only from triggers.

Each DBMS has a different method of accessing versions of the data both before and after the modification from inside a trigger. In Sybase and Microsoft SQL Server, triggers use tables called INSERTED and DELETED; in DB2 the triggers specify OLD and NEW. Regardless of the specific nomenclature, these tables are generically referred to as *transition tables*. (See Figure 13-2.)

Each trigger has two tables, one with a "before" image of the data and another with an "after" image of the data. Transition tables are accessible only from triggers. For Sybase and Microsoft SQL Server, the transition tables operate as follows:

- When an INSERT occurs, the inserted table contains the rows that were just inserted into the table to which the trigger is attached.

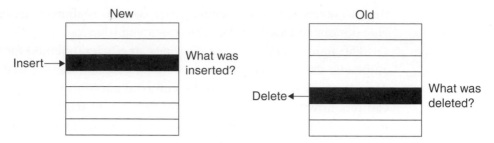

Figure 13-2   *Transition tables*

- When a DELETE occurs, the deleted table contains the rows that were just deleted from the table to which the trigger is attached.

- When an UPDATE occurs, it is treated as a DELETE followed by an INSERT, so the inserted table contains the new values for the rows that were just updated in the table; the deleted table contains the old values (before they were updated) for the updated rows.

The DB2 and Oracle implementation of transition tables (or variables) is simpler, and works as follows:

- When an INSERT occurs, the values inserted can be referenced with the NEW transition variable.

- When a DELETE occurs, the values deleted can be referenced with the OLD transition variable.

- When an UPDATE occurs, the inserted values are referenced using NEW, and the deleted values are referenced using OLD.

A Sample Trigger

Sometimes examining a sample piece of code can help to clarify concepts. So, let's take a quick look at a (DB2) trigger:

```
CREATE TRIGGER salary_update
   BEFORE UPDATE OF salary
   ON emp
   FOR EACH ROW MODE DB2SQL
 WHEN (new.salary > (old.salary * 1.5))
 BEGIN atomic
   SIGNAL SQLSTATE '75001' ('Raise exceeds 50%');
 END;
```

This trigger ensures that the value of the salary column cannot be increased by more than 50% for any individual update. Note the use of transition variables to check the newly updated salary against the previous, old value for salary.

Trigger Granularity

Because SQL is a set-level language, any single SQL statement can impact multiple rows of data. For example, one DELETE statement can actually cause zero, one, or many rows to be removed. Triggers need to take this into account.

Therefore, there are two levels of granularity that a trigger can have: statement level or row level. A *statement-level trigger* is executed once upon firing, regardless of the actual number of rows inserted, deleted, or updated. A *row-level trigger,* once fired, is executed once for each and every row that is inserted, deleted, or updated.

Different business requirements will drive the type of trigger granularity that should be chosen. But keep in mind that a row-level trigger can have a significant impact on performance because it may have to run multiple times for every SQL data modification statement issued.

Trigger Synopsis

Triggers are a powerful feature of modern DBMS products. Triggers enable the DBA to create nonbypassable, event-driven logic that is intrinsically intermingled with data. Before implementing triggers, though, be sure to be aware of the additional DBA duties required to support an active database environment. These issues were discussed in the "Procedural DBA" section of Chapter 1.

Referential Integrity

Referential integrity is a method for ensuring the "correctness" of data within a DBMS. People tend to oversimplify RI, stating that it is merely the identification of relationships between relational tables. It is actually much more than this. However, the identification of the primary and foreign keys that constitute a relationship between tables *is* a component of defining referential integrity.

RI embodies the *integrity* and *usability* of a relationship by establishing rules that govern that relationship. The combination of the primary and foreign key columns and the rules that dictate the data that can be housed in those key columns is the beginning of understanding and utilizing RI to ensure correct and useful relational databases.

RI rules, applied to each relationship, determine the status of foreign key columns when inserted or updated, and of dependent rows when a primary key row is deleted or updated. In general, a foreign key must always either contain a value within the domain of foreign key values (values currently in the primary key column) or be set to null.

The concept of RI is summarized in the following "quick and dirty" definition: RI guarantees that an acceptable value is *always* in the foreign key column. "Acceptable" is defined in terms of an appropriate value as housed in the corresponding primary key, or a null.

The combination of the relationship and the rules attached to that relationship is referred to as a referential constraint. The rules that accompany the RI definition are just as important as the relationship.

Two other important RI terms are *parent table* and *child table*. For any given referential constraint, the *parent table* is the table that contains the primary key, and the *child table* is the table that contains the foreign key. Examine Figure 13-3. The parent table in the employed-by relationship is the DEPT table. The child table is the EMP table. So the primary key (say, DEPT-NO) resides in the DEPT table and a corresponding foreign key of the same data type and length, but not necessarily with the same column name, exists in the EMP table.

Three types of rules can be attached to each referential constraint: an INSERT rule, an UPDATE rule, and a DELETE rule. Let's see how these rules govern a referential constraint.

INSERT Rule

The *INSERT rule* indicates what will happen if you attempt to insert a value into a foreign key column without a corresponding primary key value in the parent table. There are two aspects to the RI INSERT rule:

1. It is *never* permissible to insert a row into a dependent table with a foreign key value that does not correspond to a primary key value. This is known as the restrict-INSERT rule.

2. Whether actual values *must* be specified instead of nulls.

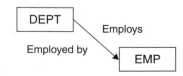

Figure 13-3 *Parent and child tables.*

For each relationship, the DBA must decide whether the foreign key value(s) must be specified when the row is initially inserted into the table. To determine this, ask the following question: "Does it make sense, in business terms, to know the primary key value in the parent table when adding a dependent row?"

If a foreign key value is specified, it must be equal to one of the values currently in the primary key column of the parent table. This implements the restrict-INSERT rule. If a foreign key value is optional, it can be set to null.

UPDATE Rule

The basic purpose of the *UPDATE rule* is to control updates such that a foreign key value cannot be updated to a value that does not correspond to a primary key value in the parent table. There are, however, two ways to view the update rule: from the perspective of the foreign key and from that of the primary key.

Foreign key perspective. Once you have assigned a foreign key to a row, either at insertion or afterward, you must decide whether that value can be changed. Again, this is determined by looking at the business definition of the relationship and the tables it connects. However, if you permit a foreign key value to be updated, the new value must either be equal to a primary key value currently in the parent table or be null.

Primary key perspective. If a primary key value is updated, three options exist for handling foreign key values:

- *Restricted UPDATE.* The modification of the primary key column(s) is not allowed if foreign key values exist.

- *Neutralizing UPDATE.* All foreign key values equal to the primary key value(s) being modified are set to null. Of course, neutralizing UPDATE requires that nulls be permitted on the foreign key column(s).

- *Cascading UPDATE.* All foreign key columns with a value equal to the primary key value(s) being modified are modified as well.

DELETE Rule

Referential integrity rules for deletion define what happens when an attempt is made to delete a row from the parent table. Similar to the primary key perspective of the update rule, three options exist when deleting a row from a parent table:

- *Restricted DELETE.* The deletion of the primary key row is not allowed if a foreign key value exists.

- *Neutralizing DELETE.* All foreign key values equal to the primary key value of the row being deleted are set to null.

- *Cascading DELETE.* All foreign key rows with a value equal to the primary key of the row about to be deleted are deleted as well.

Pendant DELETE

The final type of referential constraint is the *pendant DELETE*. This special type of referential integrity deals with the treatment of parent table rows when no foreign keys from the child table refer back to the primary key. Pendant DELETE RI specifies that the parent table row be deleted after the last foreign key row that refers to it is deleted.

Pendant DELETE processing cannot be implemented using declarative RI. However, triggers can be used to code the program logic to check for this condition and execute the deletion of the primary key row.

Please refer to Table 13-1 for a summary of referential integrity and the rules that apply to its application.

Pendant DELETE processing cannot be implemented using declarative RI.

Table 13-1   *Referential Integrity Rules*

DELETE RESTRICT	If any rows exist in the dependent table, the primary key row in the parent table cannot be deleted.
DELETE CASCADE	If any rows exist in the dependent table, the primary key row in the parent table is deleted, and all dependent rows are also deleted.
DELETE NEUTRALIZE	If any rows exist in the dependent table, the primary key row in the parent table is deleted, and the foreign key column(s) for all dependent rows are set to NULL as well.
UPDATE RESTRICT	If any rows exist in the dependent table, the primary key column(s) in the parent table cannot be updated.
UPDATE CASCADE	If any rows exist in the dependent table, the primary key column(s) in the parent table are updated, and all foreign key values in the dependent rows are updated to the same value.
UPDATE NEUTRALIZE	If any rows exist in the dependent table, the primary key row in the parent table is deleted, and all foreign key values in the dependent rows are updated to NULL as well.
INSERT RESTRICT	A foreign key value cannot be inserted into the dependent table unless a primary key value already exists in the parent table.
FOREIGN KEY UPDATE RESTRICTION	A foreign key cannot be updated to a value that does not already exist as a primary key value in the parent table.
PENDANT DELETE	When the last foreign key value in the dependent table is deleted, the primary key row in the parent table is also deleted.

Setting Up Relationships

A declarative referential constraint is added by coding the primary key in the parent table and one or more foreign keys in dependent tables. Constraints can be added using the CREATE TABLE and ALTER TABLE statements. When implementing declarative referential integrity between a parent and a dependent table, certain rules must be followed.

For the parent table

- A primary key must be identified in the CREATE TABLE or ALTER TABLE statement.
- SQL Server automatically defines a unique clustered index for the primary key when the primary key constraint is specified in the CREATE TABLE or ALTER TABLE statement. Other DBMSs, for example DB2, require the DBA to manually create the unique index to support the primary key.

For the dependent table

- A foreign key that references the parent table must be identified in the CREATE TABLE or ALTER TABLE statement.
- Although not usually required, it is strongly recommended that an index be defined for the foreign key also. An index on the foreign key will not be a unique index unless you are defining a one-to-one relationship. Creating an index on the foreign key will enhance the performance of RI operations.

All constraints will be named, whether explicitly or implicitly. It is better to explicitly name each referential constraint in the DDL. Failure to do so will cause the DBMS to assign a system-generated name, making future referencing of the constraint more difficult.

Declarative RI Implementation Concerns

Sometimes a referential constraint needs to be set up within a single table. For example, a table of departments may need to record which department is subordinate to which other department. A MANAGED_BY_DEPT column may need to be a foreign key of the DEPT_NO primary key—all within the same table. A table is able to reference itself in a declarative RI constraint. This is referred to as a *self-referencing constraint*.

Constraints are checked before triggers are fired. If declarative RI constraints and triggers coexist on the same tables, be sure that they are compatible with one another. For example, you should not code a DELETE trigger to delete foreign keys in conjunction with a declarative constraint, because the declarative constraint will prohibit the trigger from ever firing.

Tables can be altered to add or drop declarative RI. Indeed, sometimes it is not possible to specify all referential constraints within the initial CREATE TABLE statements. A primary key in the parent table must exist before a foreign key can be defined that references the parent table. With self-referencing constraints, the primary key definition can be included when the table is initially created, but the foreign key will have to be added later by using an ALTER TABLE statement.

Tables can be altered to add or drop declarative RI.

DBMS Support for Referential Integrity

Each DBMS supports different levels of declarative RI.

Keep in mind that each DBMS supports different levels of declarative RI and different options for its use. The DBA must learn which RI options are provided by the DBMS in use and provide guidance to the application developers as to what can be handled by the DBMS and what must be coded into the application. Furthermore, the DBA must understand triggers and how they can be used to implement RI when declarative RI support is lacking in the DBMS.

Referential Integrity Using Triggers

If the DBMS you are using does not provide the declarative RI functionality required by your applications, triggers can be coded in lieu of declarative RI. By using triggers, it is possible to support all conceivable RI rules. Of course, when you use triggers, it necessitates writing procedural code for each rule for each constraint. Complete referential integrity can be implemented using four types of triggers for each referential constraint:

1. A DELETE trigger on the parent table can be used to code
   - DELETE restrict
   - DELETE cascade
   - DELETE neutralize
2. An UPDATE trigger on the parent table can be used to code
   - UPDATE restrict
   - UPDATE cascade
   - UPDATE neutralize

3. An INSERT trigger on the dependent table can be used to code
   - INSERT restrict.

4. An UPDATE trigger on the dependent table can be used to code the restriction that a foreign key cannot be updated to a non-primary-key value.

Nested and recursive triggers can be coded to support a very robust implementation of referential integrity

Indeed, nested and recursive triggers can be coded to support a very robust implementation of referential integrity. Furthermore, triggers can be the only automatic method of implementing system-managed RI under certain circumstances:

- When deleted, inserted and updated information needs to be explicitly referenced in order to determine the action to take. Triggers provide a method of doing this, which we will discuss shortly.

- When an RI rule that is not supported by the DBMS is necessary. For example, Sybase declarative RI only supports restricted DELETEs and UPDATEs; the declarative RI provided by DB2 supports restricted DELETEs and UPDATEs, neutralizing DELETEs and UPDATEs, and cascading DELETEs, but not cascading UPDATEs. Each DBMS provides different degrees of declarative RI support.

- When pendant DELETE processing is required. This is sometimes referred to as "reverse" RI. Pendant-DELETE processing is the situation where the parent row must be deleted when the last dependent row that references it is deleted. The only way to implement this type of constraint is with a trigger.

Of course, if your RI needs can be satisfied using declarative RI, you should use declarative RI instead of triggers. Triggers must be hand-coded and tested, meaning that they may contain bugs or function improperly. Declarative RI is built into the DBMS and is unlikely to fail (unless the DBMS itself has bugs). Additionally, declarative RI almost always outperforms trigger-based RI. So, as a rule of thumb, favor declarative RI over trigger-based RI.

Let's examine some sample triggers to clarify how transition tables and variables are properly used. The following (SQL Server) trigger implements the cascading-DELETE RI rule:

```
CREATE TRIGGER title_del
ON titles FOR DELETE
AS
```

```
IF @@rowcount = 0
  RETURN
DELETE titleauthor
  FROM titleauthor, deleted, title
  WHERE titles.title_id = deleted.title_id
RETURN
```

When a row in the parent table (`titles`) is deleted, the `DELETE` is cascaded to the dependent table (`titleauthor`). A second example follows that implements the restricted-INSERT RI rule. When a row in the dependent table (`titleauthor`) is inserted, we must first check to see if a viable primary key exists in the parent table (`titles`):

Let's look at another example. The following trigger is coded to implement the restricted-INSERT RI rule. When a row in the dependent table (`titleauthor`) is inserted, we must first check to see if a viable primary key exists in the parent table (`titles`).

```
CREATE TRIGGER title_ins
ON titleauthor FOR INSERT
AS
DECLARE @rc int
SELECT @rc = @@rowcount
IF @rc = 0
  RETURN
IF (select count(*)
  FROM titles, inserted
  WHERE titles.title_id = inserted.title_id)!=@rc
  BEGIN
      RAISERROR 20001 "Invalid title: title_id
       does not exist on titles table"
      ROLLBACK transaction
      RETURN
  END
RETURN
```

A final (SQL Server) example depicts neutralizing updates:

```
CREATE TRIGGER title_upd
ON titles FOR UPDATE
AS
IF UPDATE (title_id)
  IF (select count(*)
      FROM deleted, titles
      WHERE deleted.title_id = title.titleid) = 0
```

```
BEGIN
  UPDATE titleauthor
          SET titleauthor.titleid = null
  FROM titleauthor, deleted
  WHERE titleauthor.titleid = deleted.title_id
END
RETURN
```

The first check is to see if the `title_id` was actually updated. If so, the trigger checks to make sure that the `title_id` was not updated to the same value it previously held. If it was, the neutralizing update should not occur. If these two checks are passed, the update occurs. When a row in the parent table (`titles`) is updated, we check to see if any corresponding rows exist in the dependent table (`titleauthor`). If so, the foreign key columns must be set to null.

User-Managed vs. System-Managed RI

It may be necessary to support both user- and system-managed RI.

System-managed declarative RI has not always been available, and your installation may have applications with user-managed RI already in place. It may be necessary to support both user- and system-managed RI in this situation.

Furthermore, even though system-managed RI is now available, sometimes user-managed RI may be a more appropriate solution. One such instance is when it is *always* necessary for applications to access the parent and dependent tables (even when system-managed RI is implemented). For example, consider an application program that always inserts the order row into the ORDR_TAB (parent) table before inserting the order item rows into the ORDR_ITEM_TAB (dependent) table; another application always accesses the rows in the ORDR_ITEM_TAB table for historical information before deleting them and then deleting the parent row from the ORDR_TAB table. Since these applications already access both tables, the additional overhead of system-implemented RI may not be worthwhile.

However, the benefit of system-managed RI is that the integrity of the data is enforced during ad hoc access, such as interactive SQL and data warehouse queries. When RI is maintained only in programs, data integrity violations can occur if data modification is permitted outside the scope of the application programs that control RI. It is usually a wise move to implement system-managed rather than user-managed RI. But remember, most DBMSs provide two methods of implementing system-managed RI: declarative constraints and triggers.

RI vs. Check Constraints vs. Program Logic

Referential integrity, check constraints, and writing application program logic are all valid methods of enforcing data integrity. This chapter illustrated the functionality and strengths of each. But let's stop to examine a particular requirement and the impact of implementing it using each of these methods.

Consider comparing the consequences of enforcing a domain. For example, suppose there are three valid employee types when the database is created: T (temporary), F (full-time), and C (contract). Subsequently, after implementation, a fourth employee type is added, say, P (part-time). It will be easier to support the new value using RI by creating an employee-type table to store the values. To support the new type, all that is required is inserting a row to the employee-type table—the referential constraints will now allow the new value.

To support this new value using a check constraint, the DBA most likely will be required to drop and recreate the check constraint. During the period when the check constraint does not exist, an outage will be required, or data integrity violations could occur. Certainly, such a scenario should be avoided when a 24/7 environment is required.

Finally, if program logic is required to support a new value for the domain, a programmer must be deployed to modify the program, test it, and then migrate it to the production environment. This is a lot more work than either of the previous two scenarios.

Use the facilities of the DBMS to enforce data integrity wherever possible.

As a rule of thumb, then, use the facilities of the DBMS to enforce data integrity unless a very compelling reason exists not to do so.

RI Rules of Thumb

Regardless of the type of RI you plan to implement in your databases, you should heed the following rules of thumb.

Be aware that there are certain situations in which referential integrity can be bypassed. This can cause severe data integrity problems as well as significant confusion. One common problem area for most DBMSs is the BULK LOAD utility. Loading data into database tables without checking foreign key references speeds up the load process. However, this also means that data integrity problems may be introduced during the bulk data load process.

Additionally, some DBMSs provide SQL switches that turn RI on and off. Avoid using these. Whenever RI is turned off, it is very likely to cause data integrity problems. Programs and ad hoc data modifications are likely to insert or update foreign key columns to values that do not conform to any existing primary key value in the parent table.

Primary and foreign key columns can have different names, null attribute qualifiers (e.g., NULL vs. NOT NULL), and default values. The column attributes, for example CHAR(5), must be the same. It is not possible to create a declarative constraint between two columns with different attributes. Likewise, though possible, it is not wise to create a trigger-based constraint between columns with differing attributes.

Keep in mind that when multiple relationships exist for the dependent row, they must all be verified before the row can be inserted. It is possible for an insert to pass three of four referential constraints, but to fail on the fourth.

When composite keys are used for a "primary key–foreign key" relationship, a single row must exist in the parent table with key values that match all the columns of the foreign key for the row being inserted into the dependent table.

Referentially related tables must be backed up and recovered together.

In general, avoid using declarative RI to create very large groups of referentially related tables. The larger the group of referentially related tables, the more difficult they become to manage. Keep in mind that referentially related tables must be backed up and recovered together to keep the relationships intact.

Consider using check constraints instead of referential constraints for code tables and reference tables that are small and relatively static in nature. If the number of values in a table is small, a check constraint will probably outperform referential constraints. For example, consider a table that contains status codes for projects, such as the one in Table 13-2. Instead, we could simply code a check constraint consisting of those values on any child tables, for example

```
CREATE TABLE PROJECT
(projno       INTEGER       PRIMARY KEY,
 deptno       INTEGER       NOT NULL,
 mg_empno     INTEGER,
 status       INTEGER       NOT NULL
      CHECK (status BETWEEN 0 AND 3),
 start_date   DATE,
) IN db.ts;
```

The check constraint on the status column performs the same function as creating a foreign key on the status column to the STATUS_CODE column in the PROJECT_STATUS table (Table 13-2). And it will be more efficient. However, if the project status codes change frequently, it will be more difficult to maintain the values using check constraints than it would be to add values to the PROJECT_STATUS table.

Table 13-2 *PROJECT_STATUS Codes*

STATUS_CODE	Description
0	Project not yet started
1	Project begun
2	Project complete
3	Project past deadline

Summary

Today's DBMSs provide a wealth of features to support data integrity. Because one of the major problems plaguing production systems today is data quality, it is imperative that DBAs understand, implement, and administer DBMS features such as constraints, referential integrity, and triggers in their database designs. Failure to do so can be a prescription for disaster.

No DBMS can ensure the integrity of its data 100% reliably all of the time.

However, no DBMS can ensure the integrity of its data 100% reliably all of the time. Other methods—programs, manual inspections, automated data cleansing, and data quality products—may be needed to assure the quality of specific databases.

However, every DBA should take advantage of the mechanisms provided by the DBMS to ensure data integrity. When DBMS-provided methods are used, fewer data integrity problems are likely to be found in the database. More-over, fewer data integrity problems means higher-quality databases and more-proficient end users.

Review

1. Define what is meant by *entity integrity*.

2. Describe the difference between database structural integrity and semantic data integrity.

3. What is the preferred method of implementing referential integrity in a relational database?

4. What is a trigger, and how can triggers be used to enhance data integrity?

5. What is the difference between a check constraint and a rule?

6. What are transition variables and tables, and what benefit do they provide?

7. What is the difference between a primary key constraint and a unique constraint?

8. Name and describe four types of database structural integrity problems that may be encountered by a DBA.

9. What is a user-defined data type, and how can it be used to enhance data integrity?

10. Describe the three RI DELETE rules and the impact of each on foreign key rows in the child table when a DELETE is issued for the primary key row in the parent table.

Suggested Reading

Codd, E. F. *The Relational Model for Database Management, Version 2.* Reading, MA: Addison-Wesley (1990). ISBN 0-201-14192-2

Owens, Kevin T. *Building Intelligent Databases with Oracle PL/SQL, Triggers, and Stored Procedures.* Upper Saddle River, NJ: Prentice Hall PTR (1996). ISBN 0-13-443631-8

Parsaye, Kamran, et al. *Intelligent Databases.* New York, NY: John Wiley & Sons (1989). ISBN 0-471-50345-2

Rob, Peter, and Carlos Coronel. *Database Systems: Design, Implementation, & Management.* Cambridge, MA: Thomson Learning (2000). ISBN 0-7600-1090-0

Widom, Jennifer, and Stefano Ceri. *Active Database Systems: Triggers and Rules for Advanced Database Processing.* San Francisco, CA: Morgan Kaufmann (1996). ISBN 1-55860-304-2

14

Database Security

The basic security and authorization approach taken by DBMS vendors to secure database access is that all database resources are controlled by the DBMS. There are no default authorizations given to any user just because the user logs in to the DBMS. Therefore, for a user to be able to perform any DBMS operation or function, one of the following conditions must exist:

- The user has been granted the ability to perform that function or operation
- That operation or function has been granted generically to all users

Using the security features of the DBMS, the DBA can set up the environment such that only certain users or certain application programs are allowed to perform certain operations to certain data within the database. Each user's function within the organization should determine the authorized level of database access. For example, only general-ledger programmers, batch jobs, and programs can access and modify the general-ledger databases. Different checks can be established for each type of access to each type of information, and different users can be assigned different access rights to different database objects.

The operational challenge of effectively administering database security arises because setting up and managing database authorization requires technical expertise and elevated privilege. Many aspects of database security require different utilities, system procedures, and commands to implement. When users require access to multiple databases, on multiple servers distributed across different physical locations, database security administration becomes quite complicated indeed. The commands must be repeated for each database, and there is no central repository for easily modifying and deleting user security settings on multiple databases simultaneously.

Although the DBA typically is responsible for administering database security, some organizations have transferred this task to a separate security administration function that controls all of the IT security for the company. However, even in many shops where security administration is a separate entity, database security is still handled by the DBA group because database security is handled differently than a typical IT authorization scenario.

The DBA must manage database security as a component of his job.

When the security administration group handles security policies, this group usually relies on third-party security software such as IBM's RACF or Computer Associates ACF2 and Top Secret. These products automate the security function and do not require the administrator to have elevated privileges to manage security policies. However, most of these security administration products run only on mainframes. Additionally, most IT security departments are understaffed and lack the technical DBMS expertise required to administer database security. Granting untrained security personnel the privileges required to administer database security can result in accidental disruption of database service or performance problems. So, the DBA is forced to manage database security as a component of his job.

Database Security Basics

Strong authentication is the cornerstone of any security implementation plan.

Strong authentication is the cornerstone of any security implementation plan. It is impossible to control authorization and track usage without it. Before authorization to use database resources can be granted, a login needs to be established for each user of the DBMS. Logins are sometimes referred to as *accounts*, or user IDs. The login will have a password associated with it such that only those who know the password can use the login ID. Some DBMSs use the operating system login ID and password as the DBMS login ID and password; others require an additional login ID and password to be created specifically for database access and security.

When the DBMS controls the addition of logins, the DBA is required to provide certain information about the login when it is created. Typically, other than the actual login name or ID, the following information either can or must be provided:

- *Password*—the key phrase, word, or character string associated with the new login that must be provided by the user before access to the database is permitted.
- *Default database*—the name of the database to which the user will initially be connected during login.
- *Default language*—the default language assigned to the login when using the DBMS if multiple languages are supported.
- *Name*—the actual full name of the user associated with this login.
- *Additional details*—additional details about the user for which the login has been created: e-mail, phone number, office location, business unit, and so on. This is useful for documentation purposes.

Passwords should be changed regularly over time.

Passwords should be changed regularly over time to make it difficult for hackers and miscreants to gain access to the DBMS surreptitiously. Refer to the sidebar "Password Guidance" for tips on creating useful passwords. As a DBA, you may decide to set up automated procedures—such as an e-mail notification system—to coerce users into changing their login passwords every month or so. Users who do not change their login password can be disabled until the user calls to complain. Of course, this adds to the workload of the DBA, but it does enhance the security of the DBMS.

When a DBMS user no longer requires access to the DBMS, or leaves the company, the DBA should drop his login from the system as soon as possible. However, this could become a complicated task—a login cannot be dropped if the person is currently using a database, or if the user owns any database objects.

Limit the database users who can create database objects to DBAs only.

For this reason it is wise to limit the database users who can create database objects to DBAs only, especially in a production environment.

In lieu of dropping a login, the DBMS may provide an option to lock the login. Locking a login prohibits the user from accessing the DBMS, but it does not actually drop the login from the system. The login can subsequently be unlocked, thereby enabling access to the server. Such a process is very useful if you simply wish to prohibit access, say, for those users who have not recently changed their login password.

Password Guidance

As a DBA, you are responsible for securing the DBMS and granting data access to authorized users. One way of assuring proper DBMS usage is to develop and disseminate tips on creating useful passwords. A password that is useful and proper will be difficult to guess.

If passwords are too simplistic or too related to some aspect of the person using the password, unscrupulous individuals may be able to guess the password and use it to surreptitiously access the database.

The following guidelines should be followed for proper password creation:

- Avoid passwords that are too short. Each password should be at least six characters long, more if possible.

- Each password should consist of at least a combination of alphabetic characters and numeric characters. Using other allowable symbols makes the password harder to guess.

- Avoid creating a password that is a complete word (in either the native language of the user or any foreign language).

- Do not embed personal statistics in the password. Street addresses, social security numbers, phone numbers, and the like are easily guessed and do not belong in passwords.

- Consider concatenating two unrelated words with a symbol or number between them. For example, "toe3star" is a viable password.

Use mnemonic devices to help you remember passwords. For example, use a sentence such as "Moondance by Van Morrison is my favorite album" to remember that your password is "mbvmimfa" (the first letters of each word in the sentence). However, do not make the sentence too obvious—for example, using "My name is Craig S. Mullins" to remember "mnicsm" is not a good idea because it might be quite easily guessed.

As a DBA, you should work with your organization's security administration team to create guidelines such as the above and distribute them to your database users.

Keep in mind that logins that are dropped must be created anew if they are ever required again. For this reason, follow these rules of thumb regarding login administration:

- Lock logins that may need to be reactivated.
- Drop logins that will never need to be reactivated.

Some DBMSs provide additional controls and parameters on logins and passwords. For example, some DBMSs provide profile parameters for passwords that can be used to limit the following:

- Number of failed login attempts before the account is locked
- Number of days a password is valid, the grace period for changing an expired password
- Number of days the account can remain locked when the password expires
- Reusability of passwords (number of days before a password can be reused and the maximum number of times a password can be reused)

When such controls are available, be sure to use them when doling out login accounts to better secure the DBMS environment.

Enforce corporate password standards.

Keep in mind, though, that each DBMS is different, and there may be no capability to force a user to periodically change a password. If a password is never changed, the likelihood of it being compromised increases over time. If the database is able to force a periodic password change, it is often limited in its ability to completely enforce corporate password standards that reduce the risk of the password being guessed. These standards usually include minimum length and alphanumeric requirements. Most DBMSs do not even provide a simple interface by which the end user can change their own password. The problem is compounded if the user has an account on multiple databases across multiple servers.

Database Users

In addition to a login account, which is required to access the DBMS, some database systems require an additional account in order to use specific databases. In this situation, a user name is created for the login account and is attached to each database required by the user. As shown in Figure 14-1, the following accounts may be required:

- A *login*, sometimes called an *account*, is used to access the DBMS, or database server. For this reason, it is sometimes also known as a server user ID, or SUID.

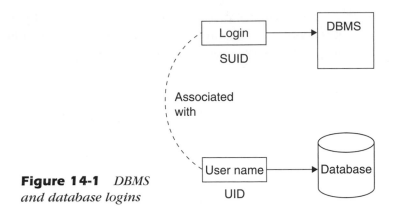

Figure 14-1   *DBMS and database logins*

- A *user name* is sometimes referred to as a *database ID*. The user name is associated with the login account. Users are required by some DBMS implementations to be set up with a database user name in order to access each database.

Guest usage of a database is permitted by configuring a special user name that permits users to access the database as a GUEST. Adding a GUEST user for a database allows any login with the special user name to access the database.

Granting and Revoking Authority

DCL statements comprise two basic types: GRANT and REVOKE.

The DBA controls database security and authorization using Data Control Language, or DCL. DCL is one of three subtypes of SQL. (The other two are DDL and DML.) DCL statements are used to control which users have access to which objects and commands. These statements are the manner in which database security is enacted. DCL statements comprise two basic types:

- *GRANT* assigns a permission to a database user.
- *REVOKE* removes a permission from a database user.

The GRANT statement is issued with two accompanying lists: a list of privileges to be assigned to a list of users. To use the GRANT statement, the user must be the owner of the database object, have been granted high-level group authority, or have been given the WITH GRANT OPTION when he was granted the privilege.

The WITH GRANT OPTION allows a user to pass the authority to grant privileges along to others. Generally, the use of this clause depends on whether an installation practices centralized or decentralized administration of privileges.

- *Decentralized administration* is generally easier to establish, but more difficult to control. As more and more users obtain the authority to grant privileges, the scope of authority is widened and becomes unwieldy.
- *Centralized administration* is generally easier to administer, but places a burden on the centralized administrator as the sole arbiter of privileges within the environment.

Avoid issuing GRANT and REVOKE statements from within an application program. Ideally, an individual who understands the security needs of the organization—usually the DBA—grants database authorization. Furthermore, application programs designed to grant database privileges must be executed by a user who has the appropriate authority to issue the GRANTs and REVOKEs coded into the application program. This could create a loophole in your database security infrastructure.

Types of Privileges

There are different types of privileges that can be granted and revoked from database users. Every DBMS provides certain basic types of privileges, such as the ability to access data, to create database objects, and to perform system functions. Each DBMS will also have additional types of privileges, depending on the features it supports.

The following types of privileges are commonly provided by modern DBMSs:

- *Table:* to control who can access and modify the data within tables
- *Database object:* to control who can create new database objects and drop existing database objects
- *System:* to control who can perform certain types of systemwide activities
- *Program:* to control who can create, modify, and use database programs
- *Stored procedure:* to control who can execute specific functions and stored procedures

Granting Table Privileges

Table privileges are granted to enable users to access tables, views, and columns within tables and views. The following privileges can be granted for tables and views:

- SELECT: to enable the user to select from this table/view
- INSERT: to enable the user to insert rows into this table/view
- UPDATE: to enable the user to update this table/view
- DELETE: to enable the user to delete rows from this table/view
- ALL: to enable the user to select, insert, update, and delete using this table/view

For example, to enable user7 to delete rows from the Titles table, the following statement can be issued:

```
GRANT DELETE on Titles to user7;
```

Some table privileges can be specified at the column level. Doing so can be desirable when certain users must be permitted to modify specific columns of a table but not other columns. The SELECT and UPDATE privileges can be granted for specific columns. For example, to enable user7 to update only the au_id column in the Titles table, the following statement can be issued:

```
GRANT UPDATE on Titles (au_id) to user7;
```

Typically, the DBA will grant table privileges to programmers in a test environment for development purposes. Additionally, programmers and end users may require table privileges on production tables for certain tasks. However, most production access should be controlled using program and stored procedure privileges, instead of direct table privileges.

Granting Database Object Privileges

Database object privileges control which users have the permission to create database structures.

Database object privileges control which users have the permission to create database structures. The actual privileges that can be granted will depend on the DBMS and the types of database objects supported. Generally, the DBMS will provide options to grant CREATE privileges on each type of database object, including databases, tablespaces, tables, indexes, triggers, defaults, and user-defined data types.

For example, to enable `user5` and `user9` to create tables and indexes, the following statement can be issued:

```
GRANT CREATE table,
      CREATE index
TO user5,
   user9;
```

The ability to create database objects is usually reserved for DBAs. If these privileges are granted to others, the number of existing database objects can be quite difficult to control. Furthermore, it becomes very difficult to track which database objects are really being used, and which were created and then abandoned. For these reasons, the DBA should keep this authority to himself, with only rare exceptions perhaps for SAs or very skilled developers.

Granting System Privileges

System privileges control which users can use certain DBMS features and execute certain DBMS commands. The system privileges available will vary from DBMS to DBMS but may include the ability to archive database logs, shut down and restart the database server, start traces for monitoring, manage storage, and manage database caches.

System privileges cannot be granted at the database level. System privileges are granted at a systemwide level across the DBMS. For example, to enable `user6` to start performance traces, the following statement can be issued:

System privileges cannot be granted at the database level.

```
GRANT TRACE
TO    user6;
```

System privileges should be granted with care and should usually be reserved for the DBA and SA.

Granting Program and Procedure Privileges

Granting the EXECUTE privilege gives the user permission to execute a program or a stored procedure. For example, to enable `user1` and `user9` to execute the stored procedure named `proc1`, the following statement can be issued:

```
GRANT EXECUTE on proc1
TO    user1, user9;
```

Granting privileges to users on programs and procedures is easier to control than granting privileges on individual tables and columns. The procedural logic in the program and procedure controls which specific tables and columns can be modified. Furthermore, the DBA can better maintain the integrity of production data if the only way it can be changed is programmatically.

Granting to PUBLIC

As an alternative to granting access to a database user, the DBA can choose to grant a particular authorization to PUBLIC. When authorization is granted to PUBLIC, the DBMS will allow anyone who can log in to the DBMS that particular authority. Grants made to PUBLIC cannot be given with the WITH GRANT OPTION, as everyone is in PUBLIC.

For example, to grant everyone the authority to delete rows from the `titles` table, the following statement can be issued:

```
GRANT DELETE on titles to PUBLIC;
```

Exercise caution when granting any privileges to PUBLIC.

Administering security can be a complex duty. Using the PUBLIC authority to permit blanket access to certain database objects and resources often appears easier than specifically controlling access by user. However, DBAs should exercise caution when granting any privileges to PUBLIC.

Whenever a privilege is granted to PUBLIC, the DBA loses control over that database object or resource—anyone can access or use the object or resource as specified by the GRANT statement. Inevitably, users will abuse PUBLIC resources, and gaining control over the resource again will be quite difficult.

Reserve usage of PUBLIC authority for those few database objects and resources that should be available to everyone. Alternately, PUBLIC authority can be a useful shortcut if another security mechanism is in place. For example, you could grant program authority to PUBLIC for transactions that are run under a transaction processor and use the security facilities of the transaction processor to control access.

Revoking Privileges

The REVOKE statement is used to remove privileges that were previously granted. The syntax for REVOKE is the "flip side" of the GRANT syntax. Additionally, privileges will be automatically revoked by the DBMS when a database object is dropped.

For example, to revoke the ability to update the `au_id` column of the `titles` table from `user7`

```
REVOKE UPDATE on titles (au_id) from user7;
```

Revoking a PUBLIC privilege will not remove that privilege from any user to whom it was granted in a separate GRANT statement.

Cascading REVOKEs

When privileges are revoked, the DBMS must decide whether additional revokes are necessary, based on the privileges being revoked. When one revoke causes the DBMS to revoke additional related privileges, it is called *cascading REVOKEs*. Consider the authority hierarchy depicted in Figure 14-2. Joe has been granted the ability to grant a privilege, say *X*, to others. He grants *X* to Pete and Phil with the GRANT option. Pete in turn grants *X* to Bruce. Joe also grants *X* to Don, but without the grant option.

Now let's investigate the impact of cascading REVOKEs by outlining what happens if we revoke the *X* privilege from Joe. In this case, not only will Joe no longer have the *X* privilege, but the DBMS will also remove the authority from Pete, Phil, and Don. Furthermore, because Phil's *X* privilege was revoked, the effect of the revoke will cascade to Bruce, too.

Cascading REVOKEs

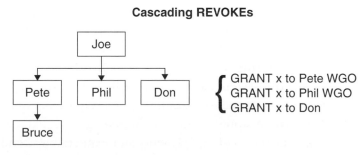

Figure 14-2 *Cascading REVOKEs*

To minimize the impact of cascading REVOKEs, avoid granting privileges using the WITH GRANT OPTION. The fewer users who can grant subsequent privileges, the easier it is to manage and administer a viable DBMS security infrastructure.

Chronology and Revokes

The timing of a GRANT or REVOKE statement may have a bearing on its impact. For example, in some DBMSs it is possible to grant a privilege to all users except a specific user by issuing the following statements:

```
GRANT DELETE on titles to public;
COMMIT;
REVOKE DELETE on titles from userx;
```

The first statement grants everyone the authority to delete data from the `titles` table. Because the REVOKE statement is issued after the GRANT to `public`, the individual `userx` is barred from deleting data from this table. Some DBMSs (e.g., DB2) will not permit such exclusions, because the PUBLIC authority will override any revokes; other DBMSs (e.g., Microsoft SQL Server) will permit such exclusions.

The DBA needs to understand exactly how GRANTs and REVOKEs work for each DBMS being administered in order to properly manage privileges on database objects and resources.

Security Reporting

Once granted, the DBA will need to monitor and report on the privileges held by users. Database security is maintained in the system catalog. The DBA can use SQL to retrieve the needed information from the appropriate system catalog tables. Alternately, some DBMSs provide views and system-stored procedures that simplify the retrieval of database security.

As a further consideration, though, be sure to adequately protect the security of the system catalog, especially within the production system. Only the DBA, SA, and security administrator require access to the database security information stored in the system catalog.

User security requirements and expectations tend to evolve over time. As new applications are added and business requirements change, database security will need to change. Security reviews should be performed on a regular basis to ensure that database security as implemented continues to match the current user requirements. Reports from the system catalog tables can be used to provide the input for such reviews.

Authorization Roles and Groups

In addition to granting privileges to individual users, the DBMS may provide the capability to assign

- Specific privileges to a role, which is then granted to others
- Specific built-in groups of privileges to users

Of course, the terminology is not strict among the major DBMSs. Some DBMSs refer to roles as groups, and vice versa. As a DBA, you will need to understand how each DBMS you manage implements roles and groups and how each of these features can be used to simplify database security administration.

Roles

The DBA can create a role and assign certain privileges to that role.

Once defined, a *role* can be used to grant one or more preassigned privileges to a user. A role is essentially a collection of privileges. The DBA can create a role and assign certain privileges to that role. Then the role can be assigned to one or more users. The administration of database security is simplified in this way. For example, consider the following sequence of statements:

```
CREATE role MANAGER;
COMMIT;
GRANT select, insert, update, delete on employee to MANAGER;
GRANT select, insert, update, delete on job_title to MANAGER;
GRANT execute on payroll to MANAGER;
COMMIT;
GRANT MANAGER to user1;
COMMIT;
```

This script creates a new role named MANAGER, grants privileges on certain tables and procedures to the role, and then assigns user1 the MANAGER role. Additional users can be assigned the MANAGER role, and the DBA will not need to remember to issue each of the individual GRANT statements, because they have already been assigned to the MANAGER role.

Groups

Group-level authority is similar to roles. However, each DBMS provides built-in groups that cannot be changed. Each DBMS implements group-level database security in different ways and with different group names and privileges. However, there are some similarities across DBMSs. The following groups are common among the major DBMSs.

- *System administrator*. Sometimes abbreviated SA or SYSADM, the system administrator group is the most powerful within the DBMS. A user granted SA-level authority typically can execute all database commands and access all databases and objects. The system administrator is usually responsible for installing the DBMS and is viewed as the owner of system resources and system catalog tables.

- *Database administrator*. Sometimes abbreviated as DBADM or DBA, the database administrator group gives all privileges over a specific database, plus the ability to access, but not modify, data in tables within that database. Users assigned DBA-level authority can drop and alter any objects within the database (tablespaces, tables, and indexes).

- *Database maintenance*. Sometimes abbreviated as DBMAINT, the database maintenance group includes the specific database privileges for maintaining database objects (such as the ability to run utilities and issue commands). Like the DBA group, the DBMAINT-level privilege is granted on a database-by-database basis.

- *Security administrator*. The security administrator role has the privilege-set permitting the granting and revoking of database security across the DBMS. Any database security-related activities can be performed by the security administrator, including login and password administration, auditing, security configuration, as well as GRANTs and REVOKEs. Another common name for the security administrator role is SSO.

- *Operations control*. Sometimes referred to as OPER or SYSOPR, the operations control role has the authority to perform operational database tasks such as backup and recovery, or terminating runaway tasks.

Limit the Number of SA Users

A single organization should limit the number of users who are assigned the SA role or group-level authority. A user with SA capabilities is very powerful. Only corporate DBAs and systems programmers should be granted this level of authority. End users, managers, and application development personnel do not need SA authority to do their jobs.

Group-Level Security and Cascading REVOKEs

Depending on the group, some users who have been assigned group-level privileges can grant privileges to other users. If the group-level authority is revoked from that user, any privileges that user granted will also be revoked. This is similar to the cascading REVOKEs that occur as a result of the WITH GRANT option.

Before revoking a group-level authorization from a user, be sure to ascertain the impact of cascading REVOKEs, and be prepared to reapply the required privileges that will be removed due to the cascading effect.

Other Database Security Mechanisms

Modern relational DBMS products support many capabilities and qualities that can aid in securing data. Some of these capabilities are not primarily security features. For example, views and stored procedures can be used for security purposes, even though that is not their main purpose.

Using Views for Security

Most database security is performed using the native security of the DBMS. However, it is possible to simplify some aspects of database security by creating views to protect your data.

Your organization has deployed an employee table that houses pertinent information about all employees. Columns within the table exist to store the employee's first and last name, middle initial, address, telephone, salary, and so on. Granting the SELECT privilege on the employee table to a group of users can cause a security problem. While application security is maintained with this scenario, personal security is not because the user could access the personal details, including salary information, of fellow employees.

A view can be created that omits sensitive information.

A view could be created that omits the sensitive information from the employee table. By creating the view without the sensitive columns, users can be granted the SELECT privilege on the view and will be able to access employee information that is deemed appropriate. For example,

```
CREATE view emp_all
AS
```

```
SELECT  first_name, last_name, middle_initial,
        street_address, state, zip_code
FROM    employee;
```

This simple example shows a view that specifies only certain columns from the base table. Once the view has been created and the user has been granted the SELECT privilege on the view, only the information specified in the view can be retrieved. When a view eliminates columns from a base table it is referred to as *vertical restriction.*

Of course, the definition of sensitive will vary from organization to organization. In our example, the salary and telephone information were removed. It is quite simple to understand why salary is sensitive, but what about telephone number? And if telephone number is sensitive, perhaps the employee's address should be as well. Views allow you to easily specify the column-level security deemed necessary for your organization.

Vertical restriction using views is an alternative to specifying columns when granting table privileges. It also can be easier to implement and administer.

Views can also be used to provide row-level security based on the content of data. This is called *horizontal restriction* and is implemented by coding the appropriate WHERE clauses into the view. For example,

```
CREATE view emp_dept20
AS
SELECT  first_name, last_name, middle_initial,
        street_address, state, zip_code
FROM    employee
WHERE   deptno = 20;
```

When users select from the view, only rows that match the predicate will be returned. This view will return only those employees who work in department 20. When users modify rows of the view, if the WITH CHECK OPTION has been specified, the predicates will ensure that values cannot be updated or inserted out of the range. Additionally, rows that do not match the predicate cannot be deleted using the view when WITH CHECK OPTION is specified.

Using Stored Procedures for Security

The privilege to execute a stored procedure must be explicitly granted or revoked.

Stored procedures can be used to provide an additional level of security. The privilege to execute a stored procedure must be explicitly granted or revoked, regardless of the security implemented on the underlying base tables.

Oracle Virtual Private Database

Oracle9i provides row-level access control through its Virtual Private Database (VPD) technology. VPD is enabled by associating one or more security policies with tables or views. When the table is accessed, either directly or indirectly, the database will consult a function implementing the policy. The policy is basically a SQL predicate (or WHERE clause) that the database appends to the user's SQL statement. This dynamically modifies the user's data access.

With VPD, a user is only able to retrieve and manipulate data that matches the WHERE clause in the policy. In essence, this works something like creating a dynamic view (using WITH CHECK OPTION) that is always applied and enforced.

Stored procedures can be coded that access only row- and/or column-level subsets of data. The ability to execute these stored procedures can then be granted to users. If no privileges on the underlying base tables are granted, the users will be able to access the data only by executing the stored procedure, thereby providing the requisite security.

In addition to providing a level of security, this method can provide better performance if the algorithms in the procedure are coded properly.

Logic-Oriented Security

Sometimes it is necessary to implement security based on an algorithm. For example, what happens if only a subset of users can access a specific table during a specific time of day? This criterion can be coded into the stored procedure. Whenever the stored procedure is executed, it checks the user and the time of day before permitting access.

Some DBMS products offer special functionality for database security. See the sidebar "Oracle Virtual Private Database" for an example of such functionality.

Auditing

Auditing enables DBAs to track the use of database resources and privileges.

Auditing is a DBMS facility that enables DBAs to track the use of database resources and privileges. When auditing is enabled, the DBMS will produce an audit trail of database operations. Each audited database operation produces an audit trail of information including what database object was impacted, who performed the operation, and when. Depending on the level of auditing supported by the DBMS, an actual record of what data actually changed may also be

Threats to Security

External agents trying to compromise your security and access your company data are rightly viewed as a threat to security. However, industry studies have shown that 60% to 80% of security threats are internal—within your organization. The most typical security threat is a disgruntled or malevolent current or ex-employee who has valid access to the DBMS. Auditing is crucial because you may need to find an instance of an unauthorized access by an authorized user.

recorded. Tracking who does what to what data is important because there are many threats to the security of your data. (See "Threats to Security" sidebar.)

Keep in mind that auditing tracks what a particular user has done once access has been allowed. Auditing occurs post activity; it does not do anything to prohibit access. Audit trails help promote data integrity by enabling the detection of *security breaches*, also referred to as *intrusion detection*. An audited system can serve as a deterrent against users tampering with data because it helps to identify infiltrators.

An audit trail can be useful in many situations. Your company's business practices and security policies may dictate a comprehensive ability to trace every data change back to the initiating user. Perhaps government regulations require your organization to analyze data access and produce regular reports. You may be required to produce detailed reports on an ongoing basis, or perhaps you just need the ability to identify the root cause of data integrity problems on a case-by-case basis. Auditing is beneficial for all of these purposes.

Most auditing facilities allow for the selective creation of audit records.

A typical auditing facility permits auditing at different levels within the DBMS—for example, at the database, database object level, and user levels. One of the biggest problems with DBMS audit facilities is performance degradation. The audit trails that are produced must be detailed enough to capture before and after images of database changes. However, capturing so much information, particularly in a busy system, can cause performance to suffer. Furthermore, this audit trail must be stored somewhere, which is problematic when a massive number of changes occur. Therefore, most auditing facilities allow for the selective creation of audit records to minimize performance and storage problems.

Although each DBMS offers different auditing capabilities, some common items that can be audited by DBMS audit facilities include

- Login and logoff attempts (both successful and unsuccessful)
- Database server restarts
- Commands issued by users with system administrator privileges
- Attempted integrity violations (where changed or inserted data does not match a referential, unique, or check constraint)
- SELECT, INSERT, UPDATE, and DELETE operations
- Stored procedure executions
- Unsuccessful attempts to access a database or a table (authorization failures)
- Changes to system catalog tables
- Row-level operations

When the DBMS does not support the level or type of auditing required, log analysis tools from third-party ISVs can be purchased to retrieve all types of information from the database transaction log.

Each DBMS provides different means to view the audited data. Formatted reports and graphical reporting tools that read and present the audit information in a reasonable manner make it easy to identify security problems from among many recorded database operations.

Auditing can also be used for data recovery.

As an additional note, auditing can also be used for data recovery. We will examine this aspect of auditing in Chapter 15.

If you have turned on database auditing at your site, consider the following advice:

- *Auditing can be a large consumer of system resources.* When the audit queue is full, tasks that generate audit records will wait until the auditing task can resume. Consider using a larger audit queue if performance suffers. As a last resort, discontinue auditing when performance is unacceptable.

- *Place the system catalog tables that store security-related information on a separate, inactive disk.* This will enhance auditing performance by decreasing head contention.

- *Ensure that the data set or table used to store audit data does not fill up.* When the audit data set is full, auditing will be disabled, records in the current audit queue will be lost, and any user task attempting to send data to the audit queue will be canceled.

External Security

In addition to database security, the DBA must ensure that certain resources used by the DBMS are protected from being accessed outside the control of the DBMS. If database resources are not accessed using DBMS commands and SQL statements, database security mechanisms cannot be relied on to enforce proper user authentication.

Focus primarily on the data sets and files used by the DBMS.

When using external security mechanisms to protect database-related resources, the DBA should focus primarily on the data sets and files used by the DBMS. Data sets to protect at the operating system or file system level include

- System catalog data files
- Active and archive log files
- User data sets for tablespaces
- User data sets for indexes
- Audit data files
- Performance trace files
- Program and script files (both source and executable code)

Ingenious users intent on mischief may be able to figure out the format of these files and access unauthorized data if you fail to protect these data sets and files. An additional level of protection can be achieved by compressing the data within the DBMS. This places the additional burden on the hacker of trying to decompress the data. Of course, compression is not sufficient protection.

If data encryption software is available for use within database files, consider using it. Data encryption is a security technique that encodes legible data into a scrambled format, making the files unreadable without the encryption key. The general idea is to make the effort of decrypting so difficult as to outweigh the advantage to the hacker of accessing the unauthorized data.

Additional security may need to be applied to DBMS system resources, such as the physical storage and address spaces used to run the DBMS, the DBMS console, and files used to install the DBMS.

Job Scheduling and Security

Most organizations schedules tasks to be run at predetermined times, and when those tasks involve database access, authority must be granted to the scheduler. Scheduling is usually accomplished using a third-party job scheduler such as CA-7, Control-M, or AutoSys. When scheduling software is used to control the submission and scheduling of batch programs and scripts, the DBA will have to determine the best way to grant database security to the scheduler.

It is not a good idea to grant SYSADM authority to the job scheduler.

It is not a very good idea to grant SYSADM authority to the job scheduler. Doing so would permit any job to perform any database task—creating potentially severe security problems. Instead, determine how to grant individual authorization to specific jobs using the facilities of the scheduling package and the DBMS. Many job schedulers can be set up to generate a user ID for each job. The generated ID can be granted the proper authority based on the type of actions that are authorized for that particular job.

Another common security mistake made at some shops is embedding actual passwords into database utility jobs and scripts. If the password is hard-coded into the job, anyone can read it and use it elsewhere in the system. This is not protecting the security of your data.

Non-DBMS DBA Security

The DBA will need to possess a fairly high level of operating system authority in order to perform the job of administering and managing the organization's databases and data. For example, in the UNIX environment some installation tasks require root authority. This situation can be handled in two ways: Either grant the DBA root authority to do the installation, or turn the specific installation tasks requiring root authority over to the UNIX system administrator. Either option is viable. My preference is to grant the authority to the DBAs if the DBA staff possesses the requisite level of UNIX skills to understand the ramifications of having root authority. Either way, though, the DBAs and SAs will need to cooperate in order to create an effective operating system security approach that enables the DBA to perform his job while at the same time protecting the security and integrity of the platform.

Summary

Each DBA should learn the security mechanisms at his disposal.

Database security is an important component of a DBA's job. Without a comprehensive database security plan and implementation, the integrity of your organization's databases will become compromised. Each DBA should learn the security mechanisms at his disposal to assure that only authorized users are accessing and changing data in the company's databases.

Furthermore, the DBA should implement auditing operations to verify that the database security measures being deployed are adequate.

Review

1. What is the purpose of a login?

2. Explain two ways that views can be used to implement data security.

3. Once a password has been established for a login, it cannot be changed: True or False.

4. What two SQL DCL statements are used to establish and remove database privileges?

5. If a password needs to be deactivated for a period of time, but may need to be reactivated later, it can be _____ instead of _____.

6. What is a cascading REVOKE and what effect can it have on database security?

7. Is "2926Glenmore" a good password? Why or why not?

8. What is the effect of granting a privilege to PUBLIC?

9. Why is it important to protect some database resources using security mechanisms external to the DBMS?

10. Explain the purpose for creating an audit trail of database operations.

Suggested Reading

Castano, Silvana, Mariagrazia Fugini, Giancarlo Martella, and Pierangela Samarati. *Database Security.* Wokingham, England: Addison-Wesley/ACM Press (1995). ISBN 0-201-59375-0

15

Database Backup and Recovery

Things break. When a new database is created or a new application goes on-line, everything is fresh and new—and running as designed. But the environment changes over time. New hardware and software is added, along with more users, more data, more requirements—more, more, more. Systems wear down as they are taxed on a daily basis to deliver service.

The DBA must be prepared for situations where a failure impacts the availability, integrity, or usability of a database. Reacting to failures and service disruptions is a key component of the DBA's job. The ability of the DBA to react accordingly depends directly on his having a well-planned approach to database backup and recovery.

Reacting to failures and service disruptions is a key component of the DBA's job.

Preparing for Problems

Numerous daily hazards can cause system failures. As you plan your database backup and recovery strategy, be sure to consider all of these various threats to database integrity and availability. Of course, it is wise to take precautionary measures to prevent failures. Techniques such as UPS systems, mirrored disks, and failover technology can minimize the need to recover, but no amount of planning and regulation can prevent unexpected failures.

407

Database failures that may require recovery can be divided into three categories:

- *Instance failures* are the result of an internal exception within the DBMS, an operating system failure, or other software-related database failure. In some cases, an instance failure can result in corruption of data that requires a recovery, but usually such failures do not damage data, so the DBMS simply needs to be restarted to reestablish normal operations.

- *Application (or transaction) failures* occur when programs or scripts are run at the wrong time, using the wrong input, or in the wrong order. An application failure usually results in corrupt data that requires a database restore or recovery. The sooner an application failure is identified and corrected, the smaller the amount of damage to the database will be.

- *Media failure* is likely to damage data, too. Media failure includes damage to disk storage devices, file system failures, tape degradation or damage, and deleted data files. Although less common in practice, damaged memory chips also can cause data corruption. After a media failure, the database will likely be in a state where valid data is unreadable, invalid data is readable, or referential integrity is violated. Outages due to media failures can often be avoided by implementing modern disk technologies such as RAID, which is covered in more detail in Chapter 17.

It is common for organizations to manage a terabyte or more of data on a single database server.

Businesses today are demanding higher throughput and around-the-clock availability even as they increase the amount of stored and processed data. Not too long ago, we talked about data in terms of gigabytes. Now it is common for organizations to manage a terabyte or more of data on a single database server. Therefore, more data needs to be constantly available and has to be processed faster than ever before. Organizations rely on data to conduct business, so it is imperative that you are prepared with a plan to counteract failures. A sound backup and recovery plan can be thought of as an insurance policy for your data.

Image Copy Backups

A fundamental component of a database backup and recovery plan is creating backup copies of data. When an error occurs that damages the integrity of the database, a backup copy of the data can be used as the basis to recover or restore the database. However, the full story on backing up a database is not quite that simple.

Backing up databases involves making consistent copies of your data.

Backing up databases involves making consistent copies of your data, usually in the form of image copies, which are the output of a COPY utility. The name of the copy utility will vary from DBMS to DBMS. Common names for the backup utility include BACKUP, COPY, DUMP, and EXPORT. Some DBMSs rely on the native operating system's file system commands for backing up data. However, even if the DBMS supplies an internal backup option, the DBA may choose to use facilities that operate outside the realm of the DBMS.

Current and accurate image copies provide the foundation for database recovery. The DBA must assure the currency and accuracy of the image copies and base the backup plan on the recovery needs of the applications. The DBA will use those recovery requirements to determine how often to take image copy backups and how many backup generations must be kept on hand. Furthermore, the DBA must make sure that the appropriate log records are available or backed up for recovery purposes. To decide the frequency with which to back up a database object, consider how much time will be needed to recover that object. Duration of recovery is determined by factors such as

- The number of log records that must be processed to recover
- Whether the log is compacted or compressed
- The time it takes an operator to mount and dismount the required tapes
- The time it takes to read the part of the log needed for recovery
- The time needed to reprocess changed pages

Additionally, recovery duration depends on the architecture of the DBMS. For example, mainframe DB2 keeps track of log range information and reads only the required log files for any recovery operation. However, most other DBMSs require that all the log files be read to scan for information needed for recovery.

Keep in mind that database backups taken while there is read-only activity, or no activity, can be restored back to that point in time using only the backup—no log files are required. This can simplify and minimize the cost of a recovery.

In general, the more often you make an image copy, the less time recovery takes. However, the amount of time required to make an image copy backup must be balanced against the need for concurrent processing during the backup process.

The DBA must decide how many complete generations of backups to keep.

The DBA must decide how many complete generations of backups (for both database object copies and log copies) to keep. By keeping extra generations, you can sometimes recover from an error during recovery by switching to an older backup. At a minimum, the retention period should be at least two full cycles. When you make a scheduled full image copy of a tablespace, the latest full image copy and at least one other previous copy will exist, plus the log created since the earliest image copy. You may want to consider keeping at least two weeks' worth of copies. Of course, the number of copies you decide to keep must be tempered by the number of associated logs that must also be maintained for the backups to remain viable.

The following guidelines on making image copy backups will help assure a recoverable environment.

- Make at least two local copies of each image copy backup to help avoid an unrecoverable state in the case of a media error (for example, a damaged tape).

- Coordinate your local backup strategy with your disaster recovery backup strategy. Many backup utilities permit both local and offsite backups to be created simultaneously.

- Keep at least two generations of image copy backups for each database object. If the most recent image copy fails, you can fall back to the older copy and still be able to recover.

- Consider creating image copy backups to disk, and then migrating them to tape, which can speed up the image copy process. Not only is disk faster than tape but also the recovery will not have to wait for a manual tape mount.

- When image copy backups are migrated to tape, consider compressing the files to reduce the number of tapes needed for large image copy backup files. This usually can be accomplished using the facilities of the tape drive.

- Be sure to include the system catalog database objects in your backup and recovery plans. System catalog data should be backed up at least weekly—perhaps more frequently for very dynamic systems. Whenever you issue DDL, it changes the data in the system catalog. Failing to back up the system catalog after a DDL change may cause the changed database objects to become inaccessible after a recovery.

- Ensure that the backup process is restartable. For example, consider a database backup process that takes three hours to complete. If the process fails after two and a half hours, the restart should require only a half hour to finish. If the backup were not restartable, it would have to start again from the beginning.

- After the backup has completed, use the DBMS's facilities to verify the correctness of the backup, for example, the DB2 db2ckbkp operation or the Sybase BCP utility.

- Data that is not stored in a database, but is used by database applications, should be backed up at the same time as the database objects.

As a rule of thumb, make image copy backups infrequently enough that you do not interrupt daily business, but frequently enough that you can afford the time required to recover the database object. Of course, this is easy to say but hard to accomplish. You will need to keep abreast of the application requirements of each database object in order to strike the right balance for creating image copy backups.

It is often a wise decision to take a full image copy backup of a database object.

Of course, certain database activities make it a wise decision, if not a requirement, to take a full image copy backup of a database object. For example, before reorganizing the system catalog, you should make image copy backups of all system catalog database objects.

In addition, after every reorganization, you should take a full image copy backup of the reorganized database object. If you need to recover the object, you can recover to the reorganized version of the database objects instead of a prior, disorganized version. Alternatively, if the reorganization was logged, you will not need to apply all the log records written during the reorganization.

Another situation requiring an image copy backup is when data is loaded into a table with logging disabled. After you have loaded data into a table using the load utility, immediately make a full image copy backup. Even if you load with logging enabled, it is wise to create a full image copy backup of the data after the load process completes. That way, if you need to recover the object, you will not need to apply the log records written during the load.

Finally, image copy backups should be taken after point-in-time recoveries. This will ensure that the database object can be recovered if another failure occurs.

Full vs. Incremental Backups

There are two
types of image
copy backups that
can be taken: full
and incremental.

Two types of image copy backups can be taken: full and incremental. As a DBA, you will need to learn the difference between the two and implement the proper image copy backup strategy based on application needs and database activity.

A *full image copy backup* is a complete copy of all the data in the database object at the time the image copy was run. An *incremental image copy backup,* sometimes referred to as a *differential backup*, contains only the data that has changed since the last full or incremental image copy was made. The advantage of taking an incremental backup rather than a full backup is that it can sometimes be made more quickly, and it occupies less space on disk or tape. The disadvantage is that recovery based on incremental copies can take longer because, in some cases, the same row is updated several times before the last changes are restored.

For example, suppose you took a full image copy of a database object early Monday morning at 2:00 A.M. and then took an incremental image copy at the same time the following three mornings. (Refer to Figure 15-1.) The full image copy plus all three incremental image copies need to be applied to recover the tablespace. If the same column of the same row was updated on Tuesday to "A", Wednesday to "B", and Thursday to "C", the recovery process would have to apply these three changes before arriving at the final, accurate data. If a full image copy were taken each night, the recovery process would only need to apply the latest image copy backup, which would contain the correct value.

Some DBMSs provide the capability to analyze a database object to determine if a full or incremental backup is recommended or required. This is typically accomplished using an option of the copy utility. If such an option exists, the DBA can run the copy utility to examine the amount of data that has changed since the last image copy backup was taken. Furthermore, the DBA can set a threshold such that a full image copy is taken when more than a specified amount of data has changed; an incremental image copy is taken when the amount of data that has changed is less than the threshold. When this option is not available, the DBA will need to set up the type of image copy backups to be taken based on her knowledge of the applications and their use of the databases.

Most database objects will be set up for full image copy backups instead of incremental image copies. The time saved by incremental copying is useful only when a small amount of data has been changed. However, the additional

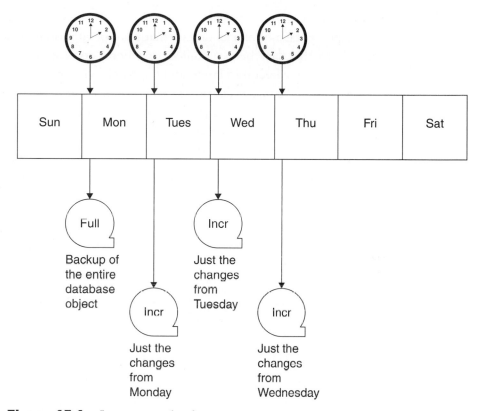

Figure 15-1   *Image copy backups*

work required for a recovery using incremental copies can be troublesome. In general, full image copy backups are recommended for database objects where 30% to 40% or more of the data blocks are modified between backups. The DBMS makes this determination based not just on data volatility but also on factors such as criticality of the data, availability requirements, and the functionality of the DBMS.

Favor full image copies for small database objects. The definition of "small" will vary from site to site and DBMS to DBMS. For large, mainframe-based databases, a "small" database object is probably within the 150GB to 200GB range. For smaller, though still significant UNIX-based databases, a "small" database object is probably about 100GB. For small, workgroup or Windows-based databases, even a 100GB database object is on the large side.

Consider using incremental image copies to reduce the batch processing window for very large database objects that are minimally modified in between

Favor full image copies for small database objects.

image copy backups. The DBA must base the full-versus-incremental decision on the percentage of blocks of data that have been modified, not on the number of rows that have been modified. In general, consider incremental copying as the tablespace becomes larger and the batch window becomes smaller.

Some scenarios are not compatible with incremental image copy backups.

Additionally, some scenarios are not compatible with incremental image copy backups. Some DBMSs permit the user to disable logging during some operations and utilities. Whenever an action is taken that adds or changes data without logging, a full image copy is required.

Merging Incremental Copies

If the DBMS supports incremental image copy backups, it may also support incremental copy merging. A merge utility, sometimes referred to as MERGE-COPY, can be used to combine multiple incremental image copy backups into a single incremental copy backup, or to combine a full image copy backup with one or more incremental image copy backups to create a new full backup.

If your DBMS supports merging incremental copies, consider running the merge utility to create a new full image copy directly after the creation of an incremental copy. The merge utility can be run with no impact to concurrent data access or the batch window. If you wait until recovery is required to run the merge, downtime will be increased because the merge (or similar processing) will occur during the recovery process while the database object is unavailable.

Database Objects and Backups

An image copy backup is made at the database, tablespace, or table level.

Typically, an image copy backup is made at the database, tablespace, or table level. The level(s) supported will depend on the DBMS being used. In general, though, the idea is to back up the database object or objects that contain the data. In general, the more granular control the DBMS provides for backup of database objects, the easier it will be to effectively implement a useful backup and recovery strategy.

Copying Indexes

Some DBMSs support making backup copies of indexes. Indeed, some DBMSs require indexes to be backed up, whereas index backup is optional for others. Index backup can be optional because the DBMS can rebuild an index from the table data. Therefore, a typical recovery scenario would involve recovering tables or tablespaces and then using the table data to rebuild the indexes. If the DBMS supports index backups, you can choose to copy indexes and then recover using the image copy backups of the indexes.

You will need to examine the trade-offs of copying indexes.

As a DBA, though, you will need to examine the trade-offs of copying indexes if your DBMS supports index backup. The question DBAs must answer for each index is "Rebuild or recover?" The more data that must be indexed, the longer an index rebuild will require in a recovery situation. For larger tables, backing up the index can result in a much quicker recovery—although at the expense of the increased time required for backup. When multiple indexes exist on the large table, backing them up, again, leads to faster recovery. However, keep in mind that index backups will require additional time to execute during your regular backup process. As a DBA, you will need to weigh the cost of recovery versus the cost of backup in making your decision.

Be sure to perform data and index backups at the same time if you choose to back up rather than rebuild your indexes. In other words, when you back up a table (or tablespace or database) be sure to also back up all associated indexes. Failure to do so can result in indexes that do not match the recovered data—which will cause applications to be unavailable or, worse, to receive invalid results.

DBMS Control

The degree of control the DBMS asserts over the backup and recovery process differs from DBMS to DBMS. Some DBMSs record backup and recovery information in the system catalog. That information is then used by the recovery process to determine the logs, log backups, and database backups required for a successful recovery. DB2 for OS/390 works this way; refer to the sidebar "DB2 COPY Utility." The more information the DBMS maintains about image copy backups, the more the DBMS can control proper usage during recovery.

Some DBMSs do not record backup and recovery information in the system catalog.

On the other hand, some DBMSs do not record backup and recovery information in the system catalog. If this is the case, the DBA must track image copy backup files and assure their proper usage during a recovery. Microsoft SQL Server is an example of a DBMS that works this way. Whenever a backup is made, the DBA must trap pertinent details of the backup such as the type, the time, and the date. During a recovery situation, the DBA must supply the backups (for both database objects and logs) in the proper sequence to assure a valid recovery.

Backup and recovery for Oracle databases can be handled this way, too; however, most organizations will not choose to do so. Oracle provides a comprehensive method for managing backup and recovery called RMAN. RMAN, which stands for Recovery Manager, is a utility that establishes a connection

The DB2 COPY Utility

The COPY utility is used by DB2 for OS/390 to create image copy backups. This utility maintains a catalog of image copy information in the system catalog. Every successful execution of the COPY utility causes DB2 to record information in the system catalog indicating the status of the image copy, the image copy data set name and file details, the date and time of the backup, and log information. This information is read by the DB2 RECOVER utility to enable automated tablespace and index recovery. Only valid image copies, recorded in the system catalog, can be used by DB2 for recovery.

As time passes, image copy backups become obsolete. New backup copies are made and database objects are recovered to various points in time. The DB2 DBA must maintain the information in the system catalog because outdated and unnecessary backup rows in the system catalog can slow down the recovery process. Backup information in the system catalog is removed by the DBA using the DB2 MODIFY utility.

with a server session and manages the data movement for backup and recovery operations. When using RMAN, Oracle backup and recovery operates similarly to DB2 for OS/390. Refer to the sidebar "Using Oracle RMAN for Backup and Recovery" for more details.

Concurrent Access Issues

Some backup techniques permit concurrent write access to the database object. Using these techniques allows you to keep the data online during the backup process, but it will slow down any subsequent recovery because the DBMS has to examine the database log to ensure accurate recovery.

Some DBMSs and recovery utilities provide the capability to perform change accumulation. The change accumulation process creates an up-to-date image copy backup by merging existing image copies with data from the database logs. This is similar to the merging of incremental image copies.

Some image copy backup techniques allow only read access to the database object. Before the image copy is taken, a QUIESCE (explained in the next section) of the database object establishes a point of consistency. Backups that allow only read access provide faster recovery than those that allow concurrent read-write because the database log is not needed to ensure a proper recovery.

Finally, some image copy backup techniques require the database object to be stopped, or completely offline. Under such conditions, no one can read or

Using Oracle RMAN for Backup and Recovery

RMAN is a powerful program for managing the backup and recovery of Oracle data. The DBA can use RMAN to specify files or archived logs to be backed up using the RMAN BACKUP command. Doing so causes RMAN to create a backup set as output. A backup set is one or more data files, control files, or archived redo logs that are written by RMAN in proprietary format. The only way to recover using the backup set is to use the RMAN RESTORE command. Of course, the DBA can choose to use the COPY command instead. This creates an image copy of a file that is usable outside the scope of RMAN.

RMAN accesses backup and recovery information from either the control file or the optional recovery catalog. The recovery catalog is similar to the DBMS system catalog, but it contains only backup and recovery metadata.

RMAN generally is preferable to other Oracle backup and recovery methods because it is easier to use and more functional. For example, RMAN provide the ability to create incremental backups. Only full image copy backups are available when using traditional Oracle backup and recovery methods.

write to the tablespace. This type of copy provides fast backup because there is no contention for the tablespace.

The DBA must understand the backup capabilities of each DBMS in the organization.

The DBA must understand the backup capabilities of each DBMS in the organization and plan a proper backup strategy that takes into consideration

- The need for concurrent access and modification during the backup process

- The amount of time available for the backup process and the impact of concurrent access on the speed of backing up data

- The speed of the recovery utilities

- The need for access to the database logs

Some DBMSs use the terms *hot backup* and *cold backup* to describe the concurrent access that can occur while the data is being backed up. A cold backup is accomplished by shutting down the database instance and backing up the relevant database files. A hot backup is performed while the database instance remains online, meaning that concurrent access is possible. Depending on the capabilities of the DBMS you are using, hot backups can be problematic because

- They can be more complex to implement.

- They can cause additional overhead in the form of higher CPU, additional I/O, and the additional database log archivals.
- They can require the DBA to create site-specific scripts to perform the hot backup.
- They require extensive testing to ensure that the backups are viable for recovery.

Backup Consistency

Be sure your backup plan creates a consistent recovery point for the database object. In order to ensure backup consistency, you need to be aware of all relationships between the database objects being backed up and other database objects. This includes application-enforced relationships, referential constraints, and triggers. If you use an image copy backup to recover a database object to a previous point in time, you will need to recover any related database objects to the same point in time. Failure to do so will most likely result in inconsistent data.

If your DBMS provides a QUIESCE utility, use it to establish a point of consistency for all related database objects prior to backing them up. The QUIESCE utility will halt modification requests to the database objects to ensure consistency and record the point of consistency on the database log. Use the QUIESCE utility even when some database objects do not need to be copied, so that you can provide a consistent point of recovery for all referentially tied tablespaces.

If the DBMS does not provide a QUIESCE option, you will need to take other steps to ensure a consistent point for recovery. For example, you can place the database objects into a read-only mode, take the database objects offline, or halt application processes—at least those application processes that update the related database objects.

When to Create a Point of Consistency

The DBA should create a point of consistency during daily processing.

If possible, the DBA should create a point of consistency during daily processing. A point of consistency can come in handy if a point-in-time recovery is required. You should consider creating a point of consistency in the following situations:

- *Before archiving the active log.* If you ever lose your active logs, and you need to use your archive logs for recovery, you can safely apply log records only up to the last recovery point. If you apply logs after that point, you can end up with inconsistent data. If the active logs are not automatically archived, you can quiesce your objects just before you offload the active log, which will allow you to use the data all the way to the end of the log without being left in an inconsistent state.

- *Before copying related database objects.* Consider creating a point of consistency before copying sets of related tables. This assures that the image copy backups for all of the related database objects are consistent with each other.

- *Just after creating an image copy backup.* When making image copy backups concurrently with online database changes, you can create a point of consistency after the backup is taken to establish a good recovery point.

- *Just before heavy database modification.* When batch jobs are run out of order, or online programs work incorrectly, partial recoveries are used to restore the data to its state preceding the update activity. By establishing a point of consistency before the update activity, you can consistently recover to that point without having to make image copy backups prior to the heavy update activity.

- *During quiet times.* Establishing a point of consistency can be disruptive during periods of heavy activity. The DBMS must establish a point in time when none of the database objects in question are being updated. By scheduling a QUIESCE during quiet periods, you can avoid such disruptions.

Log Archiving and Backup

All database changes are logged by the DBMS to a log file commonly called the *transaction log* or *database log*. Log records are written for every SQL INSERT, UPDATE, and DELETE statement that is successfully executed and committed. It is possible to review and either recreate or undo the effects of every change made to the database by using the database log.

As time progresses and the number of database changes grows, the database log will increase in size. The database log to which records are currently being written is referred to as the *active log*. When the active database log is filled, the DBMS invokes a process known as log archival or log offloading.

When a database log is archived, the current active log information is moved offline to an archived log file, and the active log is reset. If information cannot be written to the active database log, the DBMS will halt database modifications until the log has been archived and the active log is reset.

The DBA typically controls the frequency of the log archival process by using a DBMS configuration parameter. Most DBMSs also provide a command to allow the DBA to manually request a log archival process. And remember, each DBMS performs log archival and backup differently. Refer to the sidebar "Backing up SQL Server Transaction Logs" for a short discussion of transaction log backup considerations.

The DBA typically controls the frequency of the log archival process.

Determining Your Backup Schedule

Establishing a reasonable backup schedule requires you to balance two competing demands: the need to take image copy backups frequently enough to assure reasonable recovery time, and the need to not interrupt daily business. The DBA must be capable of balancing these two objectives based on usage criteria and the capabilities of the DBMS.

Not all data is created equal.

Not all data is created equal. Some of your databases and tables contain data that is necessary for the core of your business. Other database objects contain data that is less critical or easily derived from other sources. Before you can set up a viable backup strategy and schedule, you will need to analyze your databases and data to determine their nature and value to the business. To do so, answer the following questions for each database object.

- How much daily activity occurs against the data?
- How often does the data change?
- How critical is the data to the business?
- Can the data be recreated easily?
- What kind of access do the users need? Is 24/7 access required?
- What is the cost of *not* having the data available during a recovery?
- What is the dollar value associated with each minute of downtime?

Grade each database object in terms of its criticality and volatility.

It can be helpful to grade each database object in terms of its criticality and volatility. This can be accomplished using the grid shown in Figure 15-2. The vertical axis represents a criticality continuum that ranges from easily replaceable data to data that cannot be easily replaced. The horizontal axis represents

Backing Up SQL Server Transaction Logs

To ensure an efficient and effective backup and recovery strategy for your Microsoft SQL Server databases, you will need to implement periodic transaction log backups. A transaction log backup is created using the BACKUP LOG command. A database can be restored to any point in time contained within the sequence of transaction logs you have backed up, up to the point of failure. If you do not back up your transaction logs before truncating them, you will be able to restore your database to only the last database backup you have created.

When Microsoft SQL Server finishes backing up the transaction log, it truncates the inactive portion of the transaction log. This frees up space on the transaction log. SQL Server can reuse this truncated space instead of causing the transaction log to continuously grow and consume more space. The active portion of the transaction log contains transactions that were still running and had not yet completed at the time of the backup.

Microsoft SQL Server will try to take a checkpoint whenever the transaction log becomes 70% full, or when a "log full" error occurs. Additionally, when SQL Server is shut down (unless the NOWAIT option is specified) it will take a checkpoint for each database.

The transaction log should not be backed up if the TRUNC LOG ON CHKPT database option is set to TRUE. If you specify TRUNC LOG ON CHKPT as true, Microsoft SQL Server will clear out inactive transaction log entries at every checkpoint. This option tells SQL Server that you will not be using the transaction log for restore operations. The transaction log must still be created, though, because it is still required to roll back transactions and for SQL Server to determine how to recover databases when it is restarted. Enable checkpoint log truncation only for systems where it is okay for you to lose transactions during the course of a day because you will be able to restore your database back to only the last database backup that was taken. Applications of this nature are very rare in most production environments.

If a transaction log has been truncated (except by a BACKUP LOG command) you should not back up that log until you take a database backup or differential database backup. A differential database backup will back up only the data that has changed since the last full database backup.

You should also avoid backing up transaction logs in which any nonlogged operations have occurred since the last database backup was created. If this is the situation, create a database backup or a differential database backup instead.

Finally, if any files are added or deleted from the database, a transaction log backup should not be taken. Instead, you should create a full database backup, after which transaction log backups can be created again.

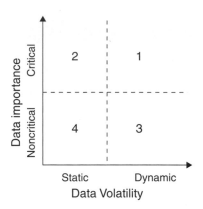

Figure 15-2 *Nature and types of data*

a volatility continuum that ranges from static data that changes infrequently to volatile data that changes frequently. Use this grid to diagram each database object by estimating its relative volatility and importance to the organization. Remember, these terms are somewhat vague; you will need to analyze your data and define it along the axes based on your knowledge of the data and your organization.

Once you have charted your database objects, you can use the diagram as a general indicator of how frequently each database object should be backed up. The DBA in charge of each application must develop the backup thresholds for each different type of data, as suggested by the grid. In general, critical data should be backed up more frequently than noncritical data, and volatile data should be backed up more frequently than static data. The key, however, is how you define the term *frequently*. For example, 1,000 updates per day might be frequent at some shops, whereas 50,000 updates per day might be infrequent at other shops. The DBA uses the grid to determine an appropriate backup schedule for each database object. The method of backup is also affected by user access needs.

Quadrant 1 on the grid identifies the critical/dynamic data in the organization. This data is crucial to your business and it changes rapidly. As such, you must be able to recover it quickly, so you should copy it frequently. As a rule of thumb, the data should be backed up at least on a daily basis. If more than 20% of the data changes daily, be sure to make full rather than incremental backups.

Quadrant 2 represents critical but static data. Even though the data changes little from day to day, you will need to recover the data promptly in the event of an error because it is critical to the business. Be sure to back up this data at least weekly. Consider using incremental backups that are merged immediately upon completion to minimize the work required during a recovery.

Quadrant 3 represents volatile data that is not as vital to your business. You may be able to recreate the data if it becomes corrupted. Depending on the amount of data and the volume of change, you might not even back it up at all. For small amounts of data, a printed report may suffice as a backup. If the data fails, you could simply reenter it from the printed report. Alternatively, if data is recreated nightly in a batch job, you could simply run the batch job to refresh the data. As a DBA, you will need to ensure that the data can be recreated or copied on a regular basis. In general, more than a weekly backup for quadrant-3 data is likely to be overkill.

Quadrant 4 represents static, noncritical data. Such data does not change much and can be replaced easily. It is the least important data and should be addressed only when data in the other three quadrants have been adequately backed up. In fact, quadrant-4 data may never need to be backed up—the DBA could take a similar approach to that described for quadrant 3.

DBMS Instance Backup

Be prepared to recover from failure of the entire DBMS instance or subsystem.

In addition to being prepared for failure of individual database objects, the DBA must be prepared to recover from failure of the entire DBMS instance or subsystem. Be sure to back up all of the crucial components of the database instance, including DBMS files, system catalog and directory objects, database (archive) logs, configuration and setup files, system libraries, tape management libraries, program source libraries, and executable libraries. Of course, each DBMS and platform will have different key components that must be dealt with when planning a recovery strategy for the DBMS instance.

Recovering an entire DBMS instance is relatively rare, but it is not something that can be ignored. The DBMS instance can fail for reasons as diverse as a device failure (when critical DBMS components reside on that device), a botched version upgrade, or human error (deleting a critical file).

In certain dire situations, you may need to resort to the original installation media in order to recover a DBMS component. Of course, when restoring from the original media you may lose any subsequent bug fixes that were applied. Therefore, the recovery process would include reapplying the maintenance as supplied by the DBMS vendor.

Recovering from a DBMS instance failure can be a very complex process. Always refer to the documentation provided with the DBMS when planning your backup and recovery strategy to make sure you are backing up everything that is necessary. Furthermore, always reread the manuals before attempting

DBMS instance recovery, and never attempt to recover the DBMS instance without thoroughly understanding the reason for recovering.

Designing the DBMS Environment for Recovery

Allocate redundant database logs. You should always take advantage of DBMS features to make recovery an easier process. For instance, most DBMSs provide the option of allocating redundant database logs. Take advantage of this option. Always allocate (at least) two copies of the active database log files to separate disk controllers, channels, and volumes. By separating the dual copies in this fashion, you are building in protection against volume failures. If one copy of the active database log is lost or damaged, operations can continue using the other copy.

Alternate Approaches to Database Backup

The backup methods discussed so far have taken the physical data files for a database object and copied them verbatim (or almost verbatim) to a backup device. Such image copy backups provide a fast method of backing up data and are relatively easy to use during a recovery.

The preferred method of backing up data stored in a database is to use the utilities and methods provided by the DBMS. However, other approaches can be used, too. These approaches should be considered as special procedures to be used only under certain circumstances.

Using Database Exports to Create Logical Backups

An alternate approach to database recovery is to create an *export*, or *unload*, of the data stored in the database object. Sometimes the process of backing up just the data, and not the entire physical file, is referred to as a *logical backup*. In instances such as the following, it is quite useful to deploy logical backups:

- *Object or row recovery*. If someone inadvertently drops a table or deletes a few rows from a table, restoring them from a physical backup may be difficult. With a logical backup, the missing data is simply reloaded to the table.

- *DBMS release upgrade*. Sometimes the DBMS vendor changes the underlying database structures for a release migration. When this occurs, it can be useful to have logical backups that can be imported into the new version, instead of trying to convert existing structures—data and all—to the new format.

- *Heterogeneous database migration.* Physical data structures differ between different platforms, even when the same DBMS is being used. For example, an Oracle database on OS/390 will use different physical file structures than the same Oracle database implemented on Windows NT. Logical backups can be used to facilitate the movement of data between different databases on different platforms.

- *Data movement.* Data, once created in the database, will be shifted and moved all over the organization—perhaps to different DBMSs, perhaps to flat files, perhaps to spreadsheets. A logical backup, because it is just the data, can make it easier to move that data wherever it needs to be, whenever it must be there.

Use logical backups to complement your physical backup strategy.

A logical backup is performed with the database up and running, so the only impact on performance will be the possible concurrent access to data by transactions and other production programs. However, as a DBA you must keep the data integrity of the logical backup in mind. Although the DBMS will use its locking mechanism to assure consistent data, referential integrity will not be guaranteed unless efforts are made to quiesce concurrent activity during the data export process.

The regular creation of logical backups can complement your physical backup strategy.

Using Storage Management Software to Make Backup Copies

Storage management software can be utilized to back up files on managed storage devices. Some DBMSs interact with certain storage management software—for example, IBM DFSMS backups can be integrated with DB2 image copy backups.

Special treatment of database files is required when backing up with storage management software.

When using storage management software to back up database objects outside the scope of DBMS control, be sure to disable database write operations for all database objects that are being backed up. To accomplish this, use the DBMS commands to stop the database objects, or start them in read-only mode. Once database modification operations have been suspended, the storage management software can be used to back up the database objects. When the backup is complete, use the DBMS commands to restart the database objects in read/write mode.

Be sure you fully understand both the functionality of the storage management software and the DBMS. For example, some storage management software will not copy open files. However, files containing database data will be open if the DBMS is using them. Failing to understand such details can result in missing backups and unrecoverable data.

Additionally, when recovery is required, the storage management software should be used instead of DBMS utilities or commands. The backups were made by the storage management software and will likely be in a format that is usable only by the same software.

Document Your Backup Strategy

Once your backup strategy has been established and implemented, the backup system can run for a long time without any DBA intervention required. Such automation is a mixed blessing, though. Over time, things can be forgotten and the DBA staff can change, both of which can cause confusion during a hectic database recovery. For this reason it is imperative that the backup and recovery strategy, implementation, and procedures be thoroughly tested and documented by the DBA.

Schedule periodic evaluations of the backup and re-covery plans for every production database.

The most important aspect of any backup plan is to thoroughly test each different type of recovery in a test environment. Be sure that you can recover from a media failure, an instance failure, and several types of application failures. Document the type of backup taken for each database object, along with a schedule of when each is backed up. Be sure that all of your databases can be recovered and that all DBAs on-site have firsthand experience at database recovery. The DBA group should schedule periodic evaluations of the backup and recovery plans for every production database.

Database Object Definition Backups

Database object definitions can change over time.

In addition to regularly backing up data, the DBA should consider regularly backing up the database object definitions. Database object definitions can change over time as parameters are altered and modified. What happens if an object is inadvertently dropped and no record of the DDL used to create and change the object over time is maintained? The answer is, it can be very difficult to recreate the object exactly as it was before it was dropped.

DB2 UDB provides the DB2LOOK utility to do this; Oracle offers the Export utility. If the DBMS you use does not offer such a utility, database object information can be obtained from the DBMS's system catalog. Consider generating regular reports from the system catalog that detail the specific parameters and options in effect for each database object in the production environment.

You may be able to create SQL queries against the system catalog that generate actual DDL statements that can be rerun as needed. For example, consider the following pseudo-SQL query:

```
SELECT "CREATE DATABASE ", dbname, " BUFFERPOOL ", bpname,
       " STOGROUP ", sgname, " ;"
FROM   sysdatabases;
```

This SQL query creates SQL CREATE statements from the metadata in the system catalog. Why is this information important? Consider this tale of woe: A DBA using mainframe DB2 had to drop a partitioned tablespace and recreate it with fewer partitions. There was no way to alter the tablespace to remove partitions. After the change, there was an increased rate of locking problems. Fortunately, the DBA had saved the definition of the tablespace prior to the change. In this case, the original lock size was row, but the current lock size was page. Setting the tablespace back to row locking solved the problem—however, without that original definition, the problem would have been much more difficult to trace and resolve.

Recovery

Database recovery can be a very complex task.

When problems impact the database, the DBA can use the image copy backups and the database log to recover the database. Whatever the cause of the problem, the DBA must be able to recover data quickly so that the business can continue to operate. When data is unavailable, your company may be losing thousands or even millions of dollars. Recognizing the need for a database recovery is quite different from actually performing a recovery in a speedy and proper fashion. Database recovery can be a very complex task that is prone to errors and difficult to manage.

Recovery involves much more than simply restoring an image of the data as it appeared at some earlier point in time. A database recovery will involve bringing the data back to its state at (or before) the time of the problem. Often a recovery involves restoring databases and then reapplying the correct changes that occurred to that database in the correct sequence.

Simply stated, a successful recovery is one where you get the application data to the state you want it—whether that state is how it was last week, yesterday, or just a moment ago. If you planned your backup strategy appropriately, you should be able to recover from just about any type of failure you encounter.

Determining Recovery Options

When a failure occurs, the DBA will need to ascertain whether recovery is required. If recovery is required, you will need to determine what resources (backup copies) are available and how best to perform that recovery. You need to answer several questions to determine the type and extent of failure. Your answers dictate the steps you take to recover the system.

- What type of failure has occurred: media, transaction, or database instance?
- What is the cause of the failure?
- How did the database go down: abort, crash, normal shutdown?
- Did any operating system errors occur?
- Was the server rebooted?
- Are there any errors in the operating system log?
- Are there any errors in the alert log?
- Was a dump produced?
- Were any trace files generated?
- How critical is the lost data?
- Have you attempted any kind of recovery so far? If so, what steps have already been performed?
- What types of backups exist: full, incremental, both?
- What needs to be recovered: the full database, a tablespace, a single table, an index, or combinations thereof?
- Does your backup strategy support the type of recovery required (recover-to-current vs. point-in-time)?
- If you have cold backups, how was the database shut down when the cold backups were taken?
- Are all of the archived database logs available for recovery?
- Do you have recent logical backup (EXPORT or UNLOAD)?
- What concurrent activities were running when the system crashed?
- Can you bring the DBMS instance up?
- Can you access the database objects?
- What are your system availability requirements?

- How much data must be recovered?
- Are you using raw files?

Additionally, DBMS version migration can impact recoverability. For example, consider the following sequence of events:

- A backup copy of TableA is taken while the DBMS is running on Version 5.
- The DBMS is migrated to a new version, say Version 6.
- A problem is encountered, and TableA needs to be recovered.

Investigate the particulars of backup and recovery for each new DBMS version before migration.

Depending on the DBMS and the particulars of the new version, TableA may not be recoverable. Sometimes the DBMS vendors change the format of image copy backup files, rendering any backups using the old format unusable. The same could be true for the log file—the format may have changed for a new version, rendering the old log files unreadable and the data therefore unrecoverable. Perhaps the new version changed the functionality of the RECOVER utility, such that it could not read older backup files. In either case, the DBA is stuck because there is no valid backup that can be used for recovery. For these reasons, be sure to investigate the particulars of backup and recovery for each new DBMS version before migration, and take new image copy backups after migration if the old backups are unusable.

Of course, these are just some of the questions that the DBA must be prepared to answer in order to effectively recover database objects. Additionally, the DBA will need to understand all of the details specific to the DBMS in use—for example, information on the Oracle rollback segments or how to identify a specific log RBA (relative byte address) for DB2 recovery.

When using Microsoft SQL Server 2000, the DBA can select from several recovery models to use for database implementations. Refer to the sidebar "SQL Server Recovery Models" for more details.

General Steps for Database Object Recovery

At a high level, the following steps are common to most database recoveries:

1. *Identify the failure.* The detection of an outage is usually simple: either the database is not responding to the application or the DBMS has

SQL Server Recovery Models

SQL Server DBAs can select recovery models when creating the backup and recovery plan for their databases. A recovery model selects options for recovery based on requirements for performance, transaction log storage, and fault tolerance. There are three recovery models: simple recovery, full recovery, and bulk-logged recovery.

Simple recovery requires less log spaces, but has the greatest potential for data loss. With simple recovery, only full and differential backups are available for recovery.

Full recovery logs everything and trades the extra log space required for a more comprehensive approach to recovery. With full recovery, the DBA can perform point-in-time recovery using the transaction log.

Finally, *bulk-logged recovery* is optimized for bulk operations and offers the best performance of the three options. Bulk operations include BCP executions, SELECT INTO, index creation, and text updating and writing. Bulk-logged recovery does not support point-in-time recovery.

SQL Server DBAs can choose from among these models to fine-tune the backup and recovery operations of their production databases.

---

displayed some type of error message. Some problems are more insidious, though, such as a corrupt control file. This type of problem take more skill to identify.

2. *Analyze the situation.* The DBA must analyze the error to determine the cause, type, and scope of the failure. Based on the results of this analysis, the DBA will choose a recovery method. This is usually the most time consuming recovery task.

3. *Determine what needs to be recovered.* The DBA must determine which database objects (and perhaps other components such as logs) are failing and prepare a recovery script that is appropriate for each component. This task can also consume a significant amount of time, especially for larger systems.

4. *Identify dependencies between the database objects to be recovered.* The failure of one database object can impact other database objects (e.g., indexes and referentially related tables). Loss of data or recovery to a prior point in time will most likely affect related database objects.

5. *Locate the required image copy backup(s).* The closer the image copy backup is to the recovery point in time, the shorter amount of time it

will take to recover. Keep in mind other factors such as the time it takes to find tapes in the library and the possibility of the tape being located at an off-site location.

6. *Restore the image copy backup(s).* Restoration is accomplished using the database recovery utility or file system recovery command of choice.

7. *Roll forward through the database log(s).* To recover to current or to a point in time after the image copy backup was taken, the database logs will need to be processed.

At the very basic level, every database recovery will involve most of these seven steps. However, depending on the situation and the type of recovery requested, certain steps might be eliminated or changed significantly.

Types of Recovery

The first type of recovery is recover to current.

Of the different types of recovery performed, the first one that usually comes to mind is a *recover to current* to handle some sort of disaster. This disaster could be anything from a media failure to a natural disaster destroying a data center. Applications are completely unavailable until the recovery is complete. This process is depicted in Figure 15-3.

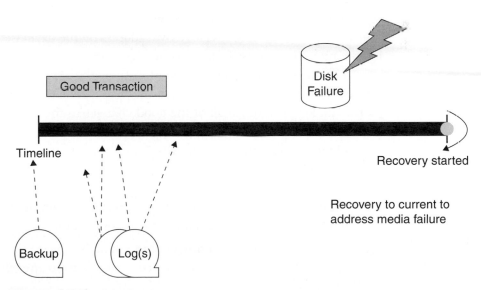

Figure 15-3 *Recover to current*

To successfully recover to current, the recovery process must be able to reset the contents of the database to the way it looked just at (or right before) the point of failure. To recover to current, the recovery process must find a valid, full image copy backup and restore that image copy. Then the recovery will roll forward through the database log, applying all of the database changes.

If the last full image copy is lost or destroyed, it may still be possible to recover if a previous image copy exists. The recovery process could start with the older backup copy, apply any incremental copies, and then roll forward through the archived and active logs. Of course, more database logs will be required in such a case, so the recovery process will take longer.

If no image copy is available as a starting point, it may be possible to recover the database object using just the database log. If the data was loaded and the load process was logged, recovery may be able to proceed simply by applying log records.

Recovery to a point in time removes the effects of all transactions that have occurred since that specified point in time.

Another traditional type of recovery is *point-in-time* (PIT) recovery, which is usually done to deal with an application-level problem. PIT recovery is sometimes referred to as *partial recovery* because only part of the existing data will remain after recovery. Recovery to a point in time removes the effects of all transactions that have occurred since that specified point in time.

To perform a PIT recovery, an image copy backup is restored and then changes are applied by rolling forward through the database log (or log backups). However, only the log records up to the specified time are processed. Sometimes the recovery point is specified as an actual date and time; sometimes it is specified using a relative byte address on the database log. The point-in-time recovery process is depicted in Figure 15-4.

To successfully recover to a point in time, the recovery must be able to reset the contents of the database to the way it looked at a prior consistent point. The key is to retain all of the good changes to the data, while removing all of the "bad." The PIT recovery depicted could be done in one of two ways, depending on the features of the DBMS and the amount of data to be recovered. It could

- Restore the image copy by rolling forward through the logs and applying the database changes up to the recovery point.
- Not restore the image copy, instead rolling backward through the logs and removing the database changes that occurred after the recovery point.

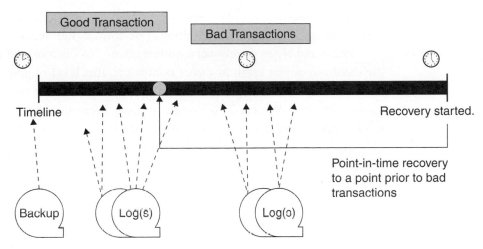

Figure 15-4 *Point-in-time recovery process.*

If the DBMS supports both types of recovery, the DBA should choose to deploy the one that creates the least downtime. If a significant number of changes need to be removed, then restoring and rolling forward usually results in the least downtime. If the number of changes that must be removed are minimal, then rolling backward through the logs should result in less downtime. Few DBMSs support backward log rolling, but third-party products are available that can make it a viable technique.

Regardless of the method used to perform PIT recovery, the DBA must select a *recovery point* that represents a point where the data is consistent. A consistent recovery point will assure data integrity, referential integrity, and transaction integrity. Some DBMSs provide a QUIESCE utility to achieve a point of consistency, whereas others require the database objects to be stopped (or in read-only mode) during the image copy.

An additional issue is determining what exactly has run since the bad transaction or failure from which you are recovering. The DBA can examine the job schedule, format a report from the database logs (if the DBMS provides a utility to produce such a report), and review the computer console for messages to help determine what processes ran after the failure occurred.

Transaction recovery is a third type of recovery; it addresses the shortcomings of the traditional types of recovery: downtime and loss of good data. Thus, transaction recovery is an application recovery whereby the effects of

Third-party software is required to perform a transaction recovery.

specific transactions during a specified timeframe are removed from the database. Third-party software is required to perform a transaction recovery.

Traditional types of recovery, both recovery to current and PIT, recover at the database object level. In direct contrast to this level of granularity, transaction recovery allows a user to recover a specific portion of the database based on user-defined criteria. This can be at a transaction or application program level. In this context, a transaction is defined by the user's view of the process. This might be the set of panels that comprise a new-hire operation, or the set of jobs that post to the general ledger. The important point is that there may or may not be a correlation between the transactions you are trying to fix and transactions (or units of recovery) in the DBMS.

Examples of user-level transaction definitions might be

- All database updates performed by userid DSGRNTLD since last Wednesday at 11:50 A.M.

- All database deletes performed by the application program named PAYROLL since 8:00 P.M. yesterday

Any number of problems such as the following can occur at the application level.

- Edit-checks in the programs or database are not defined properly or contain bugs.

- Somebody changed the job scheduling software or didn't check for valid completion codes, so certain processes were run out of sequence, causing data problems.

- Inadequately tested code hits production.

- Bugs in the system software.

Or maybe there is no problem, but you need to run a program multiple times against the same data. There are times, in particular in test and system test environments, where you may want to run a test and then just roll the results back and try it again (and again and again…).

Once you have identified the transaction to recover, you have three recovery options:

- *PIT recovery.* You can try to identify all of the database objects impacted by the application and perform traditional point-in-time recovery to remove the effects of the transactions. You would then manually rerun or reenter work that was valid.

- *UNDO recovery.* Remove only the effects of the bad transactions.
- *REDO recovery.* Remove all the transactions after a given point in time, and then redo the good transactions only.

PIT recovery was discussed earlier, so we will not cover it again here. The other two forms of transaction recovery are SQL-based application recovery techniques. The basic idea is to read the log and generate the proper SQL statements that can be run to achieve the desired recovery results.

UNDO recovery is the simplest version of SQL-based transaction recovery.

Let's first examine an *UNDO recovery*. UNDO recovery is the simplest version of SQL-based transaction recovery because it involves only SQL. To accomplish an UNDO recovery, the database logs must be scanned for the identified transaction and anti-SQL is produced. Anti-SQL reverses the affect of SQL by

- Converting inserts into deletes
- Converting deletes into inserts
- Reversing the values of updates (e.g., UPDATE "A" to "X" becomes UPDATE "X" to "A")

Once the anti-SQL is generated, it is run using an interactive SQL script to perform an UNDO recovery, which is shown in Figure 15-5. The portion of the database that does not need to be recovered remains undisturbed. When undoing erroneous transactions, recovery can be performed online without suffering an outage of the application or the database. Indeed, the DBMS must be up and running in order to execute the anti-SQL. However, certain applications

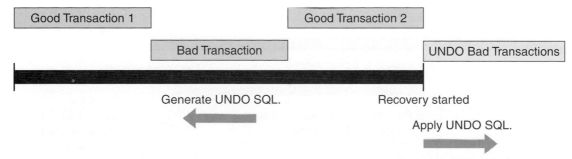

Figure 15-5 *UNDO recovery process*

may need to be brought down for the duration of the UNDO recovery to eliminate the potential for data anomalies causing additional failures.

A REDO recovery is a combination of PIT recovery and UNDO recovery, with a twist. Instead of generating SQL for the bad transaction that we want to eliminate, we generate the SQL for the transactions we want to save. Then we do a standard point-in-time recovery to eliminate all the transactions since the recovery point. Finally, we reapply the good transactions captured in the first step. This process is shown in Figure 15-6.

A REDO recovery is a combination of PIT recovery and UNDO recovery, with a twist.

Unlike the UNDO process, which creates SQL statements designed to back out all of the problem transactions, the REDO process creates SQL statements that are designed to reapply only the valid transactions from a consistent point in time. Since the REDO process does not generate SQL for the problem transactions, performing a recovery and then executing the REDO SQL can restore the database object to a current state that does not include the problem transactions.

When redoing transactions in an environment where availability is crucial,

1. Perform a recovery to a point in time.

2. Bring the application and database online.

3. Redo the subsequent valid transactions to complete the recovery This step must be done while the database is online for concurrent read/write operations.

If your approach to backup and recovery is to use *storage management software*, individual image copy backups for database objects will not exist. In

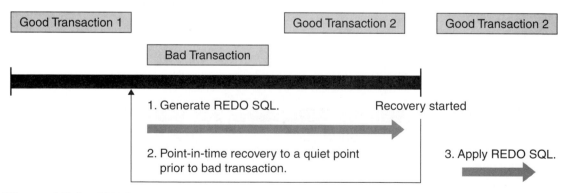

Figure 15-6 *REDO recovery process*

this case, you will need to deploy storage management software to perform the recovery. The actual recovery process will depend on the type of storage management software in use, as well as how (or if) it interacts with the DBMS recovery mechanisms.

Off-site disaster recovery is the most comprehensive type of database recovery.

Off-site disaster recovery is the rarest, but most comprehensive, type of database recovery. An off-site disaster recovery is required when a natural disaster (fire, flood, etc.) or other severe accident makes it impossible to use your primary data processing center. In this case, you need to reestablish your entire system environment, as well as recover your DBMS, database objects, and data. Disaster recovery is discussed in more detail in Chapter 16.

Choosing the Optimum Recovery Strategy

So, what is the best recovery strategy? It depends.

Historically, recovery was performed mostly for disasters and hardware failures, but this is simply not the case any more. In fact, the majority of recoveries these days result from application problems. Recent industry analyst studies have shown that most system downtime is caused by software problems—not hardware problems.

User errors and application failures are the most common reason for database recovery.

In reality, very few DBAs ever need to perform a true disaster recovery except during tests. Though media continues to fail, it fails relatively infrequently these days. User errors and application failures are the *most common* reason for database recovery and thereby the primary cause for system unavailability.

Software problems and bugs might cause only certain transactions to be in error and in need of repair. Unfortunately, as databases grow in size and complexity, so do the chances that bad transactions will corrupt the data on which your business depends. Transaction recovery may seem like the answer to availability problems, but there are a number of cases where transaction recovery is neither possible nor advisable. In determining the type of recovery to perform, the DBA must consider several questions:

- *Transaction Identification.* Can all the problem transactions be identified? You must be able to actually identify the transactions that will be removed from the database for transaction recovery to work. Can all the work that was originally done be located and redone?

- *Data Integrity.* Has anyone else updated the rows since the problem occurred? If they have, can you still proceed? Is all the data that is required still available? Intervening reorganizations, loads, or mass deletes can require the use of an image copy backup, thereby eliminating UNDO recovery. Will the recovery cause any other data to be lost? If so, can the lost data be identified in some fashion and reapplied?

- *Speed.* If multiple techniques are viable, which one is likely to perform the fastest? How many database logs are required to perform the recovery? Can anything be done to reduce the number of logs, such as merging incremental copies?

- *Availability.* How soon can the application become available again? Can you afford to go offline?

- *Invasiveness.* How invasive was the failure to your database? Were decisions made based on bad data? Can *any* subsequent work be trusted?

What is the cost of rework?

All of these questions actually boil down to a question of cost. What is the cost of rework, and is it actually possible to determine what would need to be redone? This cost needs to be balanced against the cost of long scans of log data sets to isolate data to redo or undo and the cost of applying that data via SQL. Of course, an additional question looms large: Which of these recovery techniques are actually available at your site and will they work for the DBMS in question?

Many factors influence the duration of the recovery process. The DBA can implement measures to reduce downtime by developing a smart backup and recovery plan. The following factors can shorten the duration of a recovery.

- The smaller the size of the components that need to be recovered, the shorter the recovery process will be. In general, the less you have to do, the less time it will take.

- Consider partitioning database objects and backing up and recovering at the partition level. Sometimes a failure that would otherwise impact an entire database object can be limited to impacting only a single partition.

- Consider keeping image copy backups and log archive files on disk. Because disk file access is quicker and processes do not need to wait for tape mounts, using disk instead of tape can speed up the recovery process.

- Test your image copy backups to make sure they are valid. Encountering an invalid image copy during the recovery process will lengthen the duration of recovery. When invalid image copy backups are found, steps can be taken to create a new, valid image copy backup before causing a negative impact on recovery.

- Automate your backup and recovery procedures to the greatest extent possible. Automated procedures remove manual error from the equation, thereby minimizing downtime.

- Whenever possible, design databases with as few dependencies as possible. Autonomous database objects can minimize the duration of a recovery because fewer related database objects may need to be recovered at the same time.

- Finally, be sure that every DBA understands the recovery procedures for each database object under his or her control.

Matching Type of Failure to Type of Recovery

Match the type of failure to the appropriate type of recovery.

Matching the type of failure to the appropriate type of recovery is good practice. Of course, there are exceptions to every rule, so the following generalizations should be treated as a starting point only.

Recovering from a *media failure* usually involves a recover to current. When the media fails, the database objects residing on that media most likely will not be able to be accessed or changed. The general desire in such a situation is to recover all database objects on the failing media to the point just before the failure—in other words, the DBA will try to recover all activity and data for these database objects.

Recovering from a *transaction failure* usually involves a point-in-time recovery or a transaction recovery. By definition, a transaction recovery is caused by an erroneous or incorrect execution of a program. The database changes resulting from the improperly run program must be removed from all database objects affected.

Recovering from a *database instance or subsystem failure* will most likely involve a recover to current. The goal of such a recovery is to bring the data in all database objects within that instance or subsystem back to the way it was before the point of failure, and in a consistent state.

Index Recovery

Recall from the previous discussion on image copy backups that there are two options for index recovery:

- Rebuilding the index from the table data
- Recovering the index from a backup copy of the index itself

Most DBMSs provide the capability to rebuild an index from the table data. Some DBMSs support both methods of index recovery. When both methods are available, the DBMS may require you to choose one or the other method for each index that you create. As a DBA, you will need to examine the index recovery methods available to your DBMS and choose the appropriate method for each index.

In general, the larger the amount of data to be indexed, the bigger the actual index will be and the longer it will take to rebuild that index from the data. Therefore, consider using image copy backup and recovery for indexes when the database object is very large. Of course, the definition of "very large" is vague and will differ from organization to organization depending on your database usage and the amount of downtime your company can tolerate.

The index recovery method must be chosen when the tablespace recovery method is selected.

When you choose to use backup and recovery for indexes, be sure to synchronize the backup and recovery with the indexed database objects. In other words, when you make a backup of a tablespace, be sure to also copy any associated indexes. Failure to do so can result in data integrity problems.

Testing Your Recovery Plan

Develop a recovery plan and test it often.

Every DBA should prepare a recovery plan for each database object and test it frequently. A recovery plan describes the procedures you will use to recover in the event of hardware failure or a local site disaster, such as fire. You should develop a recovery plan and test it often.

To develop your recovery plan:

- Write all aspects of the recovery plan out in detail, documenting each step.
- Include all the scripts required to back up and recover each database object.
- Review the plan with everyone who may be called on to implement it.

- Include a contact list with names and phone numbers of everyone who may be involved in the recovery.

- Keep the recovery plan up-to-date by modifying the plan to include every new database object that is created.

Testing your recovery procedures on a regular basis includes running regular recovery tests for individual database objects, databases, and the entire database system. By testing recovery procedures, the DBA assures that the backup and recovery scripts work and that every database object is indeed recoverable. Furthermore, regular recovery testing is on-the-job training for the inevitable, stress-filled production database recovery. A DBA that tests his recovery plan will be more familiar with the tools and scripts needed to perform recovery.

Recovering a Dropped Database Object

Until now, we have focused on backing up and recovering data. However, it is also possible to drop a database object unintentionally. When such an error is recognized, the DBA will need to recover the database object as quickly as possible to avoid availability and integrity problems.

Recovering a dropped object requires extra steps beyond a normal recovery.

Recovering a dropped object requires extra steps beyond a normal recovery. Depending on the DBMS and the tools available, it can sometimes be very complicated.

Typically, each DBMS identifies the database objects under its control by an internal identifier. When an object is dropped and recreated, the internal identifier for that object usually will change. Therefore, recreating the object using the same DDL and running a recovery using a prior image copy backup usually will not work.

To recover a dropped database object, the DBA may need to translate the internal identifier of the old database object to the internal identifier of the new database object. Refer to the sidebar "DB2 and DSN1COPY" for an example. To accomplish this, you must recreate the dropped database object using the exact same definition that was in effect when the image copy backup was taken. If a column definition differs between the dropped object and the newly recovered object, the recovery will probably fail.

Of course, the above scenario does not apply if you have a logical backup file. If that is the case, the DBA should be able to recreate the database object and set up a load script to repopulate the data.

DB2 and DSN1COPY

DB2 for OS/390 supplies a utility called DSN1COPY to enable database files to be copied outside the control of the DBMS. DB2 does not need to be operational for DSN1COPY to be able to run.

Furthermore, the DSN1COPY utility can be used to modify the internal object identifier used by DB2 to identify tablespace and index space data sets. Using the OBIDXLAT option, the DBA can direct DSN1COPY to translate one object identifier to another so that data can be recovered to similar (or restored) database objects, even if the internal identifier does not match the identifier in the image copy backup.

At any rate, regardless of the method used to recover the dropped database object, keep in mind the ramifications of dropping objects. When a database object is dropped, all subordinate database objects are also dropped, as are security authorizations, referential constraints, and check constraints. Once you have recovered a dropped object, you need to address these other issues.

Recovering Broken Blocks and Pages

You can rebuild an index from the data in the tablespace.

A broken block or page is a section of a tablespace or index that contains bad or inconsistent data. Data may be inconsistent due to a broken or orphaned chain, referential constraint violations, a damaged recovery log, a missing or extra index entry, or some other arcane problem. To recover an index with a broken page you can simply rebuild the index from the data in the tablespace.

Tablespaces are a different proposition. Sometimes simply stopping and starting the tablespace or recycling the DBMS instance can fix a broken page. Additionally, some DBMSs come with a repair utility that can be used to pinpoint locations within a file based on offsets and replace data at the bit or byte level. Before using any such repair tool, be sure to completely read the DBMS instruction manuals. Furthermore, be sure that the corrective action will actually fix the broken page. Repair utilities can be invasive and damaging to the contents of the database. Sometimes the DBMS vendor recommends that such activities be performed only under the direction of the DBMS vendor's technical support staff. Heed these recommendations to avoid causing further damage to your data.

Once you have repaired the information, you may need to recover the tablespace to current. The recovery will apply the log records that record the activity that caused the damage.

Populating Test Databases

Populate the test environment with a production database backup.

One of the best ways to populate a test environment is with a production database backup. Such a database backup contains a valid set of data from the production environment at a given point in time. To create the test environment, the DBA can use the RECOVER utility or perhaps an UNLOAD utility that can read backup files.

Creating a test system from a production database can impose specific requirements on the structure and timing of the production backup, as well as the structure of the test environment. If the production database backup is not taken during a period of no activity, then the restore to the test environment will require the production log files as well.

Populating the test environment with production data can be a feasible approach to resolving some types of production problems. For example, consider a 24/7 application with month-end reports and month-end database backups. On the tenth day of the month, a business user finds a problem in the month-end report. To resolve the issue, the programmer needs to know the contents of the database as of the first of the month. However, the database has changed significantly over the past ten days. Restoring the production database with month-end data is not an option—business transactions must continue. In such a scenario, the DBA could use the month-end production database backup to populate the test environment with month-end data. The programmer can now fix the month-end report by using the test database with the month-end production data.

Alternatives to Backup and Recovery

The creation of image copy backups for recovery is the most common and reliable method of insuring against failures and lost data. However, several alternatives exist that either augment or perhaps replace standard backup and recovery methods. The next few sections briefly examine some of these alternatives.

Standby Databases

Oracle introduced the concept of a *standby database* back in version 7. A standby database is an identical copy of an online production database that is close to being up-to-date in terms of its data content. The standby database may not be 100% up-to-date because of system latency between applying updates from the online production database to the standby database. When a failure occurs, control is transferred to the standby database, which is then opened as the online production database to allow normal activity to continue.

Usually, a standby database is created initially by restoring a cold backup. Then, all the archive logs from the production database must be copied to the standby database and applied. For all intents and purposes, the standby database is continuously running in recovery mode because it is applying the archive logs from the production database as operations are performed on the production database.

But, beware. A standby database does not eliminate the need for normal backups to be performed on the production database. Operations performed in error on the production database will be duplicated on the standby database. For example, a row deleted accidentally will also be deleted on the standby machine.

A standby database is fairly easy to implement.

A standby database is fairly easy to implement and provides quick recovery from certain types of failures. However, standby databases are almost never completely up-to-date: If a production archive is lost the standby database becomes unsynchronized, and only an entire database can be duplicated (instead of just certain database objects).

Standby databases can be ideal for disaster recovery.

Replication

Some DBMSs provide automated replication features.

Data replication involves storing and maintaining redundant data in a separate copy of the database. Of course, replicated data can be a subset of the rows and/or columns of the original database. A simple form of replication can be implemented simply by copying entire tables to multiple locations at various times throughout the day. Of course, this is easier said than done. Some DBMSs provide automated replication features, and for those DBMSs without such features, third-party tools are available.

There are two basic technologies for replicating data among databases:

- Snapshot replication
- Symmetric replication

Snapshot replication produces a copy of database tables on a target system based on a query of the source database. At the time a snapshot is initially taken, the specified query (maybe an entire table) is run, and the resulting data is loaded into the target snapshot table. Furthermore, each replica database should contain accurate, up-to-date information. When multiple replicas exist, the DBA must facilitate the update of all replicated copies at the same time. If replicas are updated on different schedules, it becomes burdensome to keep track of the state of each replica.

The advantage of snapshot replication is its ease of implementation. However, snapshot replicas can become out-of-date very rapidly, and refreshing the replica can cause administrative and performance problems.

Symmetric replication is a more robust implementation of replication because it keeps the replicas up-to-date. Symmetric replication can be set up to ensure that no transaction is fully committed until all the modifications have been committed locally for all replicas. Alternatively, it can replicate asynchronously, allowing each database node to run at full speed without holding up local updates because of remote database speed issues. The updates are applied later, after the COMMIT is taken for the master database.

The biggest advantage of symmetric replication over snapshot replication is the automatic synchronization of modifications from the master database to the replicas. However, symmetric replication is more difficult to set up and administer, high transaction volumes can cause performance degradation, and a network failure can cause the database to fail because modifications cannot be synchronized.

Replication is not a substitute for backup and recovery.

Replication is not a substitute for backup and recovery, but it can be helpful in some situations. With snapshot replication, it may be possible to use the snapshot replicas as a point in time before a failure. However, symmetric replication has the same problem as a standby database—the problems would be propagated to the replica. Both types of replication may be useful for a disaster recovery.

Disk Mirroring

Mirroring disk devices can add an extra level of protection for databases. *Disk mirroring* occurs by allocating a secondary device that will contain a duplicate copy of the primary device. All data modifications made to the primary device are also made to the mirrored device. If the primary device fails, the mirrored device can be used without causing a system outage. Of course, disk mirroring consumes double the amount of disk storage for the same amount of data.

Disk mirroring differs from replication in that the data duplication occurs at the device level instead of the database level.

Disk mirroring can remove the need to recover from a media failure.

Once again, disk mirroring does not replace the need for backup and recovery, because the mirrored data will be the same as the data that is experiencing the problem. Disk mirroring, though, can remove the need to recover from a media failure. Instead of recovering database objects on the failing disk, the DBA can switch to the mirrored data.

Summary

An in-depth backup and recovery plan for every database object is an integral part of a database implementation plan. It is the duty of the DBA to ensure that every piece of critical data in the database is protected and can be recovered if a problem arises. Furthermore, the DBA must be able to minimize the amount of downtime associated with recovering from database integrity problems and failures. The longer the database is down, the larger the financial impact will be to the business.

Review

1. What is the difference between a logical backup and an image copy backup?

2. Why is a quiesce point important for a point-in-time recovery?

3. Why can't standby databases, replication, or disk mirroring be used to replace traditional backup and recovery?

4. What factors determine whether a full or incremental image copy backup should be taken for a database object?

5. Name and describe the three types of database failures that may require recovery.

6. Describe two ways to recover an index.

7. What is meant by the term log archival, and why is it important to assure recoverability?

8. Name four factors that impact the duration of a recovery.

9. The DBA should grade each database object in terms of its _____ and _____ to determine how frequently it should be backed up.

10. Name the different types of recovery and discuss the factors that influence when each type of recovery should be performed.

Suggested Reading

Velpuri, Rama. *Oracle Backup & Recovery Handbook.* Berkeley, CA: Osborne/McGraw-Hill (1995). ISBN 0-07-882323-4

16

Disaster Planning

Invest in a disaster recovery plan.

A disaster recovery plan is like insurance—you're glad you have it, but you hope you never need it. With automobile insurance, you pay a regular fee so that you are covered if you have an accident—in other words, it's an investment. A disaster recovery plan is similar in that you invest in it by designating a disaster recovery site, shipping backup copies of the data off-site, preparing recovery jobs, and practicing the recovery procedures.

The Need for Planning

Disaster recovery planning, also called *contingency planning,* is the process of preparing your organization's assets and operations in case of a disaster. But what is a disaster? Sungard Recovery Services (1995) provides a good definition of *disaster*: any unplanned, extended loss of critical business applications due to lack of computer processing capabilities for more than a 48-hour period. Your own definition may be more or less stringent with regard to the timeframe, but the basic definition is a sound one.

The *DB2 Developer's Guide* (Mullins 2000) defines a disaster as "any event that has a small chance of transpiring, a high level of uncertainty, and a potentially devastating outcome." This too, is a workable definition for a disaster.

Most of us have witnessed a disaster, at least on television. Floods, earthquakes, hurricanes, and fires are some examples of natural disasters. Disasters can be man-made, such as electrical failure, bursting pipes, and war. Many of us have had our basements flooded or been in an automobile accident. A disaster does not have to have global consequences in order for it to be a disaster for you.

You must recognize potential disasters and understand their consequences. How these disasters might impact your business is the sole purpose of disaster recovery planning. If your business is on a coast, the likelihood of hurricanes, floods, and tornadoes increases. If your business is located in the north, blizzards and severe cold weather will pose more of a risk. California businesses are more apt to worry about earthquakes.

Even though disasters are unpredictable and unlikely, every organization should have a comprehensive and tested plan to cope with a disaster situation. For example, consider some recent disaster situations. In 1992, Hurricane Andrew impacted 39 data centers and the flood in the Chicago Loop district impacted 33 data centers. The World Trade Center bombing of 1993 impacted 21 data centers. And, closer to home, the 9/11 terrorist attacks on the World Trade Center had severe consequences for any business with a data center in one of the buildings. Furthermore, many disasters are not location specific. Sabotage, computer viruses, vandalism, air conditioning or heating failures, and health or environmental hazards can happen anywhere on the planet.

Just because your organization has not yet experienced a disaster, or is not in a high-risk area, does not absolve you from the need for contingency planning—especially for your databases. In the wake of a disaster, companies with a disaster plan will be able to service their customers again much more quickly than those companies without one. Indeed, a company facing a disaster without a disaster recovery plan may never resume business.

Database disaster recovery must be an integral component of your overall business recovery plan.

Database disaster recovery must be an integral component of your overall business recovery plan. A disaster recovery plan must be global in scope. It must handle business issues such as alternate locations for conducting business, communication methods to inform employees of new locations and procedures, and publicity measures to inform customers how to transact business with the company post disaster. It must restore the IT infrastructure. Finally, and most important to our discussion, a component of that plan must be for the recovery of database and DBMS operations.

However, to what extent should a company take disaster planning? Before your company can ascertain the appropriate level of recoverability, you must analyze the risks and determine the objectives.

Risk and Recovery

The goal of a disaster recovery plan is to minimize the costs resulting from losses of, or damages to, the resources or capabilities of your IT facilities. The success of any database disaster recovery plan depends a great deal on being able to determine the risks associated with data loss. What is the impact to your business if the data is lost?

Evaluate each database object for disaster recovery.

As with local database recovery, the DBA must perform an evaluation of each database object for disaster recovery. Recall from Chapter 15 (Figure 15-2) the grid we used to evaluate database objects for criticality and volatility. Although the emphasis in disaster recovery is more on criticality than volatility, the dynamism of the data still plays a role. Although it is quite likely that each database object will be graded similarly for disaster recovery purposes, it is still a good practice to reevaluate each database object in terms of its complete loss in a disaster.

When analyzing the risk associated with losing data, keep in mind the different types of risk. With regard to data, there are three categories of risk—financial loss, business service interruption, and legal responsibilities—with varying degrees of risk within each category. The unavailability of each application has a different impact on the company's bottom line. Consider a brokerage firm, for example. Having the stock trading system unavailable will cause a greater loss than having the employee payroll application unavailable not only because current business operations cannot be conducted in a timely manner, but because customers will stop trusting the brokerage with future business. And if a major stock exchange like NYSE or NASDAQ incur an outage the impact would be even greater—affecting the global economy.

Business needs must dictate your priorities.

As you create your database disaster recovery plan, remember that business needs must dictate your priorities, and not technical needs and issues. Consider separating your systems into critical and noncritical applications based on business needs. The task of defining *criticality* can become a political nightmare if it is left to each business unit. The decision to rank one system as more critical than another must be made at a high level—with the overall business in mind—and not individually by each business unit.

Rank your applications into groups to determine which applications have the biggest impact if they are down.

It is a good idea to rank your applications into the following groups to determine which applications have the biggest impact if they are not available:

- *Very critical applications.* The most-critical applications in your organization will require current data upon recovery. These applications are the most difficult for which to develop a disaster plan because more steps are required for off-site backup and recovery. Additionally, the most-critical applications in your shop will be the first ones that must be made operational at the recovery site. Try to limit the number of applications designated as very critical; any more than a half dozen or so will be unmanageable in a disaster situation.

- *Business-critical applications.* Business-critical applications are important to your organization and should be the next group to recover after the very critical applications. A business-critical application frequently requires current data, but it may not be available at the remote site within the first couple of days. For example, consider the applications for a telephone service provider. The system that delivers phone service would be a very critical application; customer billing would be a business-critical application.

- *Critical applications.* A critical application differentiates itself from a business critical application by its immediacy or data currency needs. This group of applications, though important, need not be available immediately. However, if the disaster persists for a week or longer, the business requires the application. Critical applications should not be recovered until the very critical and business-critical applications are up. The requirements of these applications vary from up-to-date to possibly day-old or week-old data.

- *Required Applications.* Required applications are not critical but must be backed up such that they can be recovered at the remote site if needed. Data from the last available backup is usually sufficient to support such applications.

- *Noncritical applications.* Noncritical applications need not be supported in the event of a disaster. Very few applications fall into this category—if the application is not critical, why was it developed in the first place?

The criticality of an application must be based on the overall importance of the application to the organization. Factors that impact criticality include the financial cost of the application being unavailable, the legal responsibilities your organization has for each application and its data, and the cost of losing customers and future business due to a delay in bringing the application back online.

As a DBA, you must create the disaster recovery plans with application criticality in mind. In this way, the most critical data can be recovered and made available immediately in the event your company experiences a disaster. Based on these application rankings, an appropriate backup strategy can be deployed for each database object supporting your database applications.

General Disaster Recovery Guidelines

Minimize downtime and loss of data.

During a disaster recovery, your goals are to minimize downtime and loss of data. Whether you achieve these goals is primarily determined by the preparations you have made.

Planning for disaster recovery is an enterprisewide task. Remember that DBMS and database recovery is just one component of an overall disaster recovery plan. When your organization creates a disaster recovery plan, it needs to look at all of its business functions and operational activities—customer interfaces, phone centers, networks, applications, and every company function that can be impacted by a disaster. However, this chapter addresses only DBMS and database-related recovery issues. For a comprehensive discussion of disaster recovery, consult the books listed at the end of the chapter.

The Remote Site

When a disaster strikes, you will need an off-site location where you can set up your company's operations. The site must be located far enough away from your primary site so that a natural disaster will not disrupt both sites. Sometimes the difference between success and failure is simple common sense. For example, your remote location should not be on the same power grid, in the same floodplain, or along the same earthquake faultline as your primary site. Your company may even select several sites for different corporate functions.

If your company is large enough to have more than one data center, you may be able to use each site as a backup for one of the others. For example, if your Houston data center is destroyed, you can move operations to your Pittsburgh data center.

Other companies set up a specific remote location where they send their data on a regular basis. In the event of a disaster, they simply connect to the backup system. This is an expensive alternative, but necessary for some businesses.

Yet another approach is to sign up with a disaster recovery service provider. The service provider maintains the equipment necessary for you to recover your operations on their computers in the event of a disaster. In this case, you are responsible for ensuring that the proper applications and data are available to be installed at the service provider's location if a disaster strikes your site.

Backup materials must be stored for safekeeping.

Storage of backup materials is another issue. Ideally, they would be stored for safekeeping at the recovery site, but if this is not possible, another off-site storage location should be designated. If a disaster occurs, you will need to provide a mechanism to move the recovery materials from the storage location to the recovery location.

The Written Plan

A written plan is the foundation of any good disaster recovery plan. The plan should be distributed to all key personnel in the disaster recovery scenario. Each participant should keep a copy of the plan at home as well as at the office. A copy of the disaster plan should be kept at the recovery site, as well.

Perhaps the biggest challenge to implementing a successful disaster recovery plan is keeping the plan current and relevant. Maintain the plan as a part of your everyday activities. Be sure that your DBA procedures automatically include disaster recovery plan updates. For example, whenever you create a new database object, be sure to incorporate that object into the disaster recover plan. Likewise, whenever a database object is dropped, remove it from the disaster recovery plan. Furthermore, whenever you add a new application to the system, be sure to evaluate the criticality of the application and include it in the disaster recovery plan.

The disaster recovery plan is a living document.

Simply stated, the disaster recovery plan is a living document that will change as your systems, requirements, and usage change. Whenever the plan changes, be sure to destroy all of the outdated copies of the plan and replace them with the new plan.

Writing out the specific procedures and policies to follow for an off-site disaster recovery has several benefits.

- It causes you to formulate the explicit actions to be taken in the event of a disaster.
- It makes you order these actions into specific sequential steps.
- It forces you to be specific about the tools to be used and the exact backup information required.

- It documents the location where all the required information is stored and how it is to be made available at the recovery site.

- It provides a blueprint for others to follow, in case those who are most familiar with the plan are not available.

Another benefit of creating a detailed disaster recovery plan is that it will highlight areas that need to be improved within your backup procedures and organization.

Be sure to include all of the interested parties in the disaster recovery planning process. This includes not just DBAs and systems programmers, but also end users, system operators, business managers, and perhaps even your customers. Your disaster recovery plan should include the following sections:

- *Off-site location.* List the address of the remote location(s), along with the phone number, fax number, and address of the contact at each remote site. Additional useful details could include a list of nearby hotels, options for travel to the recovery site, details of how expenses will be handled, and other pertinent information.

- *Personnel.* List the name and contact information for each member of the recovery team. Be sure to include the work, home, and mobile phone numbers for each team member.

- *Authorizations.* List the security authorizations necessary for the recovery operations and the personnel to whom they've been granted.

- *Recovery procedures and scripts for all system software, applications, and data.* Be sure to provide the complete step-by-step procedures for the recovery of each piece of system software, every application, and every database object, and the order in which they should be restored. Part of this section should be a listing of all the installation tapes for system software as well as the tapes for all maintenance that has been applied. Options for database recovery procedures will be covered later in this chapter.

- *Reports.* List the reports you will need at the recovery site to ensure a complete recovery. The reports should list each backup tape, its contents, when it was produced, when it was sent from the primary location, and when it arrived at the remote site. As an additional component, include a description of the naming conventions for the remote site backup files.

The disaster recovery plan should include instructions for a complete off-site disaster recovery.

The disaster recovery plan should include instructions for a complete off-site disaster recovery. However, before you commit your disaster recovery procedures to paper, you need to make a number of decisions. The first decision to be made is to prioritize your disaster recovery goals. Do you want to get the system up as quickly as possible? Or is it more important to lose as little data as possible? Or perhaps your most important goal is to avoid reprocessing data as much as possible. The disaster recovery plan should be written in accordance with your specific recovery goals.

Testing Your Disaster Plans

Test your disaster recovery plan at the remote recovery site at least once a year.

Once the disaster recovery plan is written, be sure to schedule regular tests. It is a good practice to test your disaster recovery plan at the remote recovery site at least once a year. You should also consider testing the plan after the following events:

- Significant change in daily operations
- Change in system hardware configuration
- Upgrade of the DBMS (or related system software)
- Loss (or hire) of personnel responsible for the recovery
- Move of primary data center to a new location
- Change in daily backup procedures
- Addition of major new applications or significant upgrades of existing critical applications
- Major increase in the amount of data or the number of daily transactions

Use a disaster recovery test to discover weaknesses and errors in the plan. After the test, be sure to update the disaster recovery plan to address the problems. A valid disaster recovery test need not end in a successful recovery—although that is the desired result. A disaster recovery test that reveals weaknesses in the plan serves a useful purpose.

Regular disaster recovery tests assure the readiness of your personnel.

Another consideration for scheduling regular disaster recovery tests is to assure the readiness of your personnel. The best way to prepare for a disaster is to practice disaster recovery. The process of actually implementing the plan forces you to confront the many messy details that need to be addressed during the recovery process. Testing also helps you to become familiar with the tools and procedures you will use during an actual disaster recovery.

Actually, a scheduled test of the disaster recovery plan is probably a poor idea. A disaster recovery test should work more like a pop quiz that doesn't give you the opportunity to prepare. One day your boss should come to work and announce that the building was just destroyed. Who should be called? Is everyone available? How can you get the right people to the remote site for recovery? Can you get your hands on the disaster recovery plan?

The goals of recovery practice are to discover problems with the recovery plan, to provide on-the-job training for key personnel to become familiar with the procedures and tools to be used for disaster recovery, and to raise awareness of the organization's actual level of readiness to confront an actual disaster.

Of course, you might decide that it is impractical to conduct disaster recovery testing without advance warning. This is especially true if out-of-town travel is involved. However, to keep the test as close to the real thing as possible, do not use the advance warning as an opportunity to cheat (perhaps by sending additional materials to the off-site location that would not have been there otherwise).

The disaster recovery test should include all of the components of the written plan. This will include setting up the operating systems, installing the DBMS, recovering applications and data, and testing the recovered environment for success or failure.

As mentioned earlier, you should periodically review the contents of your off-site tapes to ensure that they contain the correct backup data, and not just during a test. At the same time, you should review all additional materials sent off-site to assure that everything that is supposed to be there actually is there.

Personnel

Choosing the right team is essential.

Choosing the right team to design and carry out your disaster recovery plan is essential to the success of that plan. From the perspective of the DBMS, the disaster recovery team must be capable of installing and configuring the DBMS system software, assuring the integration of the DBMS with other system software components, recovering individual databases, testing the integrity of the databases, recovering related data that may not be stored in a database, installing and configuring application software, testing the applications, and taking care of the numerous details along the way. In other words, the team must be multiskilled and very adaptable. Moreover, the team members must possess a combination of IT skills and business skills.

Once the team is assembled, it is imperative that each member be trained to understand the ramifications of disaster recovery. This also means that the

DBAs, programmers, and SAs on the team need to understand the business aspect of disaster recovery and the business users need to understand the IT dimension of disaster recovery—at least at a very high level.

The entire team should meet regularly for cross training and to perform at least annually a disaster recovery test. Remember that each member must be granted the proper authorizations at the remote site to perform his or her part of the disaster recovery. Nothing can stop a disaster recovery faster than lack of authority to perform a crucial task—especially if no one is around with the authority to grant authorizations, which could be the case during a disaster.

Backing Up the Database for Disaster Recovery

Your disaster recovery procedures will be determined in large part by the method you use to back up your data. If you rely on disk volume backups, then your recovery will be one volume at a time. If you create image copies, you will probably use the DBMS's RECOVER utility or a third-party recovery tool. Of course, you might combine several different techniques for off-site backups, depending on the sensitivity and criticality of the data. Let's look at several different backup strategies for disaster recovery.

Tape Backups

You can use the same techniques deployed to create local backup files.

A valid strategy for disaster recovery backups is to use the same techniques deployed to create local backup files. Create multiple output files from the image copy backup process, and send tapes of at least one of the copies to the remote disaster recovery site. Be sure to send the backup files to the disaster site as soon as possible after their creation. The sooner the tapes are shipped off-site, the less likely they can be destroyed in a disaster.

For disaster recovery purposes, you usually don't need to back up indexes. They can always be recreated from the data after it is recovered at the disaster recovery site.

Be sure to produce a daily report of all the backup files that were sent to the remote site. Keep a copy of the report at the local site and ship one to the remote site as well. The report should detail all of the information required to perform a recovery, including file name, type of backup (full or incremental), how the image copy was created (database utility or file system command), date and time of the backup, date and time it was shipped off-site, and the date and time it was received off-site (if possible).

Back up the database logs and ship them to the remote site.

Additionally, you will need to back up the database logs and ship them to the remote site. Failure to ship the log files to the remote site means that you will only be able to recover each database object to the point when the last backup was taken. Refer to Figure 16-1. In this case, we have backed up the database object and sent a copy to the remote site. Subsequent modifications occur to the database object and then a disaster strikes. Without a backup of the database log for the period between the image copy backup and the disaster, all of those changes will be lost. The amount of data lost in an offsite recovery depends on the timeliness of the backup of database log files.

Recovery at the remote site is performed for each database object one by one. Indexes are rebuilt or recreated after the data is recovered. After recovery, the DBA should use whatever tools and utilities are available to identify and resolve any data integrity problems and constraint violations.

Additional preparation may be required, depending on the DBMS and operating system(s) in use. For example, if the DBMS keeps a record of the image copy backups, then the system catalog will need to be recovered to a point where all of the offsite backups are listed in the system catalog—or some of the offsite image copy backups may not be able to be applied.

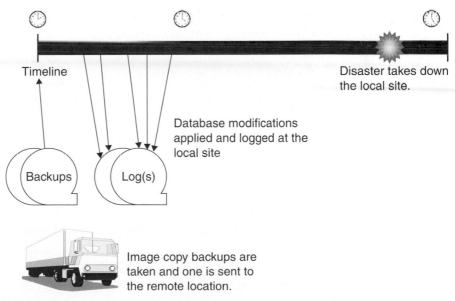

Figure 16-1   *The database log and disasters*

Of course, the system catalog will need to be recovered at the remote site regardless of the DBMS in order to recover any database objects at all. Other DBMS-related files may need to be recovered after the DBMS is installed, as well.

Keep at least three backup tapes at your remote site for each database object. This provides a cushion in case one or more of the image copy tapes is damaged. The extra tapes will allow you to fall back to an older backup in the event of a tape failure. Furthermore, if you have the database logs, you may be able to recover the database object completely, even if the recovery does take longer.

Consult the DBMS documentation for the particulars of remote site recovery.

Finally, when using this approach, be sure to consult the documentation provided by the DBMS vendor for the particulars of remote site recovery for that DBMS.

Storage Management Backups

Use storage management software to make point-in-time copies of entire disk packs.

Another approach to disaster recovery backups is to use storage management software to make point-in-time copies of entire disk packs. Such an approach greatly simplifies disaster recovery preparation and execution, but this strategy can require a significant system outage to accomplish properly. To perform a backup using storage management software, follow these steps:

1. Stop the DBMS to create a systemwide point of stability for recovery.
2. Copy all of the database objects, using storage management software to dump complete disk volumes to tape.
3. When all of the disk volumes containing database objects have been successfully copied, restart the DBMS.
4. Copy the backup tapes and send them to the remote site.

Recovery at the remote site is then performed a complete disk volume at a time using the storage management software. The biggest problem with this approach is the requirement to stop the DBMS. Most organizations cannot tolerate such an outage, due to e-business or global 24/7 requirements.

As an alternative to stopping the entire DBMS, data could be copied application by application. Using such an approach would require a regularly scheduled job to

1. Stop the application.
2. Stop or quiesce the associated database objects.

3. Back up the database objects with the storage management software.

4. Restart the application and database objects after the backup is complete.

Of course, such a compromise complicates the disaster planning and remote site recovery. The files containing the data for the application are not likely to exist on a single disk drive. Thus, identifying the correct disks and files to back up can be more difficult.

In general, stopping the DBMS and using storage management software for disaster recovery backups is effective for organizations that are willing to trade off around-the-clock availability for ease of disaster recovery preparation.

Other Approaches

A WAN can be used to deliver backups to the remote site.

Although the first two approaches are the most commonly implemented disaster recovery strategies, many other approaches and options exist. Deploying a wide-area network (WAN) to assist in the delivery of backups to the remote site is a good tactic to consider. If your primary site can be connected to the remote site using a WAN connection, you can direct your offsite backups to an electronic tape vault at the remote location. Of course, any direct connection between the primary site and the remote site increases the chances of a disaster at one location impacting the other location—although a network connection is probably a very small risk if implemented properly.

Another approach to disaster recovery preparation is the remote mirroring of data to the alternate site over the network. This approach minimizes the amount of preparation required for recovery at the remote site because the data is mirrored there. For this strategy to be effective, *all* changes at the primary site must be mirrored at the remote site including regular database changes (INSERTs, UPDATEs, and DELETEs), database utility operations (LOAD and REORG), and local database recovery operations.

The standby database option for Oracle databases can be used as a disaster recovery approach. As long as the standby database is located at a different physical site than the primary database, the standby database can be a good choice for implementing a disaster recovery plan for an Oracle instance.

Some Guidelines

Adhere to the written plan.

In order for your recovery plan to be effective, you need to adhere to the written plan. Follow all of the routine precautionary measures documented in the plan to assure the recoverability of your critical data in the event of a disaster. Image copy backups or disk backups need to be made as directed and sent to the remote site as quickly as possible. Reports need to be printed and sent off-site. Missing any little detail can render a disaster recovery plan ineffective.

When testing the disaster recovery plan, make sure that each team member follows the written instructions precisely. Of course, it is quite likely that things will come up during the tests that were missed or undocumented in the plan. Be sure to capture all of these events and update the written plan. Keep in mind that during an actual disaster, you may need to rely on less experienced people, or perhaps consultants and others who are not regular employees. The more foolproof the written plan, the better the chance for a successful disaster recovery.

The following are some quick tips and hints to keep in mind as you develop your database disaster recovery plans.

Order of Recovery

Make sure the operating system and DBMS are installed at the correct version and maintenance level before proceeding with any database object recovery at the disaster site. Be sure to follow rigorously the recovery steps as documented in the written plan.

Data Latency

How old is the data? If you take nightly backup tapes to another location, your data could be up to 24 hours old. Sometimes having data that old is unacceptable, and sending backup media to off-site storage more than once a day is too expensive. One solution is to get the data to another location—via log shipping or replication, for example.

Some data may not be fully recoverable.

Database logs at the time of the disaster may not be available to apply at the off-site recovery location. Some data may not be fully recoverable, and there is really no way around this. The more quickly that backup copies of database objects and database logs are sent off-site, the better the disaster recovery will be in terms of data currency.

Remember Other Vital Data

Creating off-site backups for database objects may not be sufficient to ensure a complete disaster recovery plan for each application. Be sure to back up related data and send it off-site as well. Additional data and files to consider backing up for the remote site include

- DDL libraries for database objects, recovery, and test scripts
- Application program source and executable files
- Stored procedure program source and executable files
- User-defined function source and executable files
- Libraries and passwords for critical third-party DBA tools
- Related data files used by the application

Beware of Compression

Be sure that the remote recovery site uses the same tape-compression software.

If your site uses tape-compression software, be sure that the remote recovery site uses the same tape-compression software. If it does not, the image copy backups will not be readable at the remote site. Turn off compression at the primary site for the disaster recovery backups if the remote site cannot read compressed tape files.

Post-Recovery Image Copies

An essential part of the disaster recovery process is to create an image copy backup for each database object after it has been recovered at the remote site. Doing this enables easier recoverability of the data should an error occur after processing begins at the remote site. Without the new image copy backups, the disaster recovery procedure would have to be performed again if an error occurs after remote site processing begins.

Disaster Prevention

Establish procedures and policies to prevent problems in the first place.

DBAs and IT professionals, in general, create procedures and enforce policies. Many of these procedures and policies, such as a disaster recovery plan, are geared toward dealing with situations once they occur. Having such procedures and policies is wise. However, isn't it just as wise to establish procedures and policies to prevent problems in the first place? Although you cannot prevent an earthquake or flood, you can implement policies to help prevent man-made disasters. For example, use surge protectors to prevent power surges from destroying computing equipment and have backup generators on standby in case of electrical outages.

Another good idea is to document and disseminate procedures to end users teaching them how to deal with error messages. You cannot expect every user to understand the impact of responding to every error message. Depending on the application, the wrong user response to an error message can result in data loss. Guidelines can help avoid errors—and manmade disasters.

Disaster and Contingency Planning Web Sites

There are a number of useful sites on the Web that cover disaster and contingency planning in detail. The following sites can afford you a broader view of disaster recovery planning than the database-focused approach we have discussed in this chapter:

- http://www.survive.com
- http://www.thebci.org
- http://www.globalcontinuity.com
- http://www.sungard.com
- http://www.gedisasterrecovery.com

Summary

The DBA must be part of a multi-discipline team for disaster recovery.

A key part of a DBA's job is developing a plan to mitigate damages in the event of a disaster. The primary goal is to bring the applications back online with as little data loss and interruption as possible. There are many components required to create a viable disaster recovery plan, but it is imperative that a comprehensive written plan is created and maintained. Although the DBA's scope of responsibility is primarily assuring database availability and data integrity, the DBA must be part of a multidiscipline team for disaster recovery. Regular planning, testing, and revising are crucial to the creation of a usable disaster recovery plan.

Review

1. What is a disaster?

2. Describe two different approaches to database disaster backup and recovery.

3. What factors should be considered when determining the criticality of a database object for disaster recovery planning?

4. What role does the database log play in disaster recovery?

5. What are the considerations for choosing a viable disaster recovery site?

6. Discuss the capabilities disaster recovery team members must possess to assure a viable recovery.

7. Once the disaster recovery plan is written it should not be changed: True or False.

8. Why is it a good idea to rank your applications and database objects for disaster recovery planning purposes?

9. With regard to data, what are the three categories of risk?

10. It is a good idea to perform a regularly planned disaster recovery test. However, what other events might cause you to test your disaster recovery plan more frequently?

Suggested Reading

Bell, Judy Kay. *Disaster Survival Planning: A Practical Guide for Businesses.* Port Hueneme, CA: Disaster Survival Planning, Inc. (1991). ISBN 0-96305-800-2

Chantico Publishing Company. *Disaster Recovery Handbook.* Blue Ridge Summit, PA: Tab Professional & Reference Books (1991). ISBN 0-8306-7663-5

Mullins, Craig S. *DB2 Developer's Guide.* 4th ed. Indianapolis, IN: SAMS (2000). ISBN 0-672-31828-8

SunGard Recovery Services, Inc. *Action Plan for Disaster.* (1995)

Toigo, Jon William. *Disaster Recovery Planning.* 2nd ed. Upper Saddle River, NJ: Prentice Hall PTR (2000). ISBN 0-13-084506-X

17

Data and Storage Management

All DBMSs rely on data files to store data, and these files, or *data sets,* reside on storage media, or devices. Storage management is thus a key part of the database operations required of a DBA. Typically, storage means fixed disk drives or disk subsystems, but storage can also mean nonvolatile storage, solid state disk, removable storage, optical storage, or tape devices.

Since the DBA deals with database management systems that store data, a good part of the DBA's job will involve planning for the actual storage of database data. In order to perform this part of the job, the DBA must be conversant in the actual physical mechanisms available for data storage. Furthermore, the DBA must understand the ways in which the abstract concept of data as embodied by the database interacts with the physical storage of data on persistent storage media.

Storage Management Basics

Some storage technologies are better suited than others.

As a rule, DBMS vendors do not certify or explicitly support any specific third-party storage products. Instead, the assumption is made that some underlying storage technology is available and will be reliable. To determine what will work best with each DBMS, the DBA must evaluate the many products, technologies, and vendors that provide storage solutions. Although most storage technologies work with most DBMS products, some storage technologies are better suited than others in terms of performance, reliability, usability, and cost.

The predominant storage technology used for data management is the disk drive. Modern disk drives are more reliable than in years past, with an ever-increasing MTBF. It is not unheard of for disk drives to achieve in excess of a hundred thousand hours of availability before failing. However, the mechanical nature of the disk drive renders them more vulnerable to failure than other computer components. As the number of disk drives in a system increases, the vulnerability of the system increases. It is not uncommon for a single organization to rely on hundreds or thousands of disk drives to support its database applications. Furthermore, the ways in which disk drives are used by databases can make storage management unpredictable, as the sidebar "Modern DBMS Disk Usage" points out. Certain modern storage solutions, such as RAID, can be used to address some of the MTBF problems.

However, for mission critical applications data *integrity* can be more important than data *availability*. If the storage media is unreliable and a failure causes data corruption, the lost data can be more of a problem than the downtime. It is imperative, therefore, that database storage solutions protect the data at all costs.

Database performance is I/O dependent.

Database performance is I/O dependent—the faster the DBMS can complete an I/O operation the faster the database application will run. Remember that data retrieval from storage media takes much longer to complete than data retrieval from cache or memory. For this reason, some modern storage systems provide their own caching mechanism to prestage data in memory—thereby reducing the wait time associated with traditional disk I/O operations.

Indeed, storage is becoming more central to business operations. Heterogeneous, multiterabyte database sites are not uncommon these days. The amount of data being stored is greater than ever before, and the data is being

Modern DBMS Disk Usage

DBAs must be prepared for spikes in disk usage. The inherent functionality of modern DBMSs makes them much more likely than their forebears to cause disk usage spikes. Some DBMSs allow the temporary file sizes to expand and contract automatically. Depending on the type and nature of database operations in process, this fluctuation can cause disk usage spikes. Additionally, many online utility operations use shadow objects. Therefore, if a tablespace normally occupies 10 GB of disk space, an online reorg would require 20 GB—10 GB for the normal object and another 10 GB for the shadow object.

stored for longer durations. At an industry conference late in December 2000, Lou Gerstner,[1] former CEO of IBM Corporation, summed up the phenomenal rate of data growth: "Inside IBM we talk about ten times more connected people, a hundred times more network speed, a thousand times more devices, and a million times more data." Mr. Gerstner is not the only one to note this phenomenal growth:

- www.searchdatabase.com, a Web portal for database information, conducted a survey asking its visitors to reveal the size of their largest database or data warehouse. Of the respondents, 29% indicated database sizes of a terabyte or more.

- Winter Corporation publishes a regular survey of the largest databases in the world called the VLDB Report (details at http://www.wintercorp. com/). The most recent Winter VLDB Report projects a 100TB database by 2003. Additionally, the report documents several very large databases, including a 10.5TB UNIX-based data warehouse and a 1.45TB Windows NT-based data warehouse.

- A recent research note[2] from the Giga Research Group tackles the question "How much data is on the planet?" Their research estimates the amount of data to be approximately 201,000 TB, or about 197 PB. Of course, this is just an estimate that Giga believes to be accurate within an order of magnitude, that is, a factor of ten. Indeed, talking about terabyte- and petabyte-sized databases and data warehouses is becoming common these days. Table 17-1 outlines the measurements used when discussing data storage size. Keep in mind, though, that the figures in this chart are "rough" guides. Some people speak about disk storage in terms of "powers of ten" instead of "powers of two"—in other words, they refer to a kilobyte as 1,000 bytes instead of 1,024 bytes. However you choose to measure it, though, disk drive capacity is increasing very rapidly.

Managing storage in today's dynamic environment is a challenging task.

The growth in storage capacity further increases the complexity of managing data and databases. Many organizations are implementing new storage technologies, such as network-attached storage (NAS) and storage area networks (SANs), to

---

1. http://www.informationweek.com/816/gerstner.htm
2. *Giga IdeaByte,* "How Much Data Is on the Planet?" by Lou Agosta, September 20, 2000.

Table 17-1 *Data Storage and Size Terminology*

Abbreviation	Term	Size	Power of 2
B	Byte	8 bits	
KB	Kilobyte	1,024 bytes	2^{10} bytes
MB	Megabyte	1,024 KB	2^{20} bytes
GB	Gigabyte	1,024 MB	2^{30} bytes
TB	Terabyte	1,024 GB	2^{40} bytes
PB	Petabyte	1,024 TB	2^{50} bytes
EB	Exabyte	1,024 PB	2^{60} bytes
ZB	Zettabyte	1,024 EB	2^{70} bytes
YB	Yottabyte	1,024 ZB	2^{80} bytes

help manage the ever-increasing amount of storage required for modern applications. Managing storage in today's dynamic environment is a challenging DBA task. Goals to consider while building a storage system include

- Preventing loss of data—the number-one priority
- Assuring that adequate capacity is available and that the storage solution can easily scale as storage needs grow
- Selecting a solution that provides fast access to data with minimal or no interruptions to service
- Choosing storage solutions that are fault tolerant and that can be repaired quickly when a failure occurs.
- Selecting a storage solution where you can add or replace disks without an outage
- Combining all of the above into a cost-effective storage solution your company can afford

Files and Data Sets

There are many storage issues that must be resolved before a DBA can create a database. One of the most important issues is how much space to allow for the database. A data file corresponds to the tablespace database object as shown in Figure 17-1. Keep in mind that the space calculation must take into account not just tablespaces, but also indexes, and depending on the DBMS, the

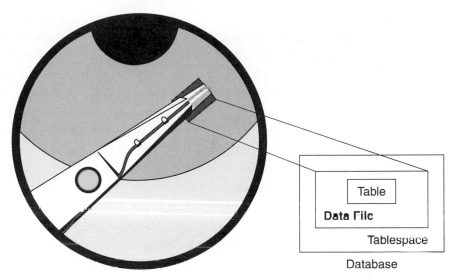

Figure 17-1 *Database storage and data files*

transaction log. Each of these entities will likely require a separate file, or data set, for persistent storage.

The DBA may choose to use multiple storage devices.

After determining the amount of storage required, the DBA must choose an appropriate storage device with sufficient space to store the database and all of its files. The DBA may choose to use multiple storage devices for the different files to

- Align the performance requirements of the file with the appropriate disk device.

- Separate indexes from data for performance reasons.

- Isolate the transaction log on a separate and very fast device.

- Isolate temporary and work files on a single volume; if a disk error occurs, temporary files can be deleted and redefined with no backup and recovery implications.

- Spread the data across multiple devices to facilitate parallel access.

File Placement on Disk

The DBA must determine the optimal placement of files on disk devices. At times, the DBA can achieve performance gains simply by moving files from one physical disk device to another. One common technique is to place index files and data files on separate disk devices. By separating indexes from the data that is indexed, I/O operations can be made more efficient because the physical read-write arm of a single disk device does not need to move multiple times. For the same reason, placing data that is accessed by the same operations on separate physical disk devices is another common file placement technique and provides the same type of performance advantage as separating indexes from data.

Of course, exact file placement is becoming less beneficial with the advent of modern storage devices. If the DBMS is using a modern storage device that creates a virtual disk by spreading the data across multiple physical disks (RAID) explicit file placement is a waste of time. Even if the DBA specifies two different disk devices, the disk array will physically place the files across multiple disks. So, as a DBA, do not waste time on precise file placement when using a modern storage array technology such as RAID.

Place the transaction log on a separate device from the database.

Regardless of the type of storage being used, be sure to place the transaction log on a separate device from the database to backup the transaction log independently from the database. This is a good idea because it increases overall recoverability.

Every DBMS provides different storage options. Microsoft SQL Server offers filegroups, DB2 for OS/390 provides STOGROUPS, and Sybase offers Segments (see "Sybase Segments" sidebar). Be sure to understand the mechanisms your DBMS uses to interact with the storage subsystems and disks to create database files. Improperly created database files can be a significant cause of poor performance.

Sybase Segments

Some databases provide options for controlling the size of tables. For example, Sybase segments can be used to limit table size because a table can never grow larger than its segment allocation. To control growth of a table, the DBA can create it on a specific segment of a specific size. The table will never be able to grow larger (without taking explicit action to extend the segment to another device).

Indexes and tables can be allocated to specific segments to enhance performance. Placing nonclustered indexes on separate segments from the table reduces disk head contention if the segments reside on separate physical disks.

An ideal use of segments is to isolate large, frequently accessed tables. In addition, segments can be used to split a single table across two disks.

Some organizations choose to implement system-managed storage, or SMS. With SMS, the actual location of files and data sets is determined by the system, instead of a DBA or storage administrator. With the new efficient disk technology that is available, SMS is a more viable option than it was in the past.

One possible scenario is to let SMS handle the placement of the majority of your database files. However, for certain performance-sensitive files (such as the transaction log or mission critical database objects), use non-SMS file placement techniques. With this approach, SMS can minimize the effort involved in most database file placement tasks, and the DBA can get involved only for "high-need" database file placement.

Raw Partitions vs. File Systems

A raw partition is the preferred type of physical device to choose when deploying databases on UNIX-based database servers. A *raw partition* is simply a raw disk device with no operating system or file system installed.

Raw partitions are favored because of the way UNIX buffers writes when a file system is utilized. When writes are buffered by the operating system, the DBMS cannot know whether the data has been physically copied to disk or not. When the DBMS writes data from cache to disk, UNIX in all probability, will not. If a failure occurs, data in a database using a disk system file may not be 100% recoverable. This should be avoided.

If a raw partition is used, the data will be physically written to disk with no operating system intervention. Additionally, when using a raw partition, the DBMS is better able to ensure that enough space is available and write the allocation pages as needed. When using a disk file, UNIX will not preallocate the space required; it will instead create a sparse file. Only the allocation pages are written. If other applications are contending for the same physical space, you may not have as much space for storing database data as you believe you do.

The drawback to raw devices is the difficulty of tracking the database files. Since the files were not allocated using the operating system or file system, it is not possible to track them using operating system and file system commands. However, third-party storage management software can be used to get around these problems.

On UNIX, be sure to always use a raw partition for transaction logs, even if you use a file system for database files. It is usually wise to utilize raw partitions for production databases, as well. However, if integrity is not an issue (for example, in a development environment), databases can be created on a disk file system for the sake of simplicity.

Temporary Database Files

Temporary database objects require some form of short-term persistent storage.

Modern DBMSs provide capabilities to create temporary database objects that exist only during the scope of a specific transaction. These objects contain temporary data that is transient and does not require long-term persistent storage. However, these database objects still require some form of short-term persistent storage to use for the duration of their existence.

Depending on the DBMS, the DBA will need to assign disk devices and an amount of storage for use by temporary database objects.

Space Management

Consistently monitor database space usage.

As modifications are applied to database tables, databases will grow in size. Remember, too, that a database is not just the data portion (tables and indexes), but also the log portion. It is wise to periodically and consistently monitor database space usage. This can be done using the tools and utilities provided with the DBMS, storage management software, or third party database tools. As a DBA, you should be able to track the following:

- Number of secondary extents
- Device fragmentation
- Fragment usage information
- Free space available
- Segment or partition size
- Tables and indexes allocated per segment
- Amount of reserved space that is currently unused
- Objects approaching an "out of space" condition

Dealing with a database that has run out of space is a common nuisance for DBAs. But it will occur, so it is best to be prepared with a plan of attack for handling database growth. The first step is to reclaim space by regularly dropping unused database objects. Objects are sometimes created, forgotten about, and never required again. By dropping unused database objects, the space they previously occupied can be made available.

If no unused database objects exist, the DBA must expand the storage available for the database. Typically, this is accomplished using the ALTER statement to specify additional space for the database object. The DBA also may have to allocate an additional storage device to be used by the database object, which may involve moving the files for the database object from one device to another. Be careful when specifying additional space for database objects using the ALTER statement. Some DBMSs require the DBA to specify the amount of increase, whereas others require the specification of a new overall size.

Data Page Layouts

The page layout for a database object usually consists of three basic components.

Each DBMS uses a different format for laying out the pages of database objects. Typically, though, the page layout for a database object will consist of three basic components, as shown in Figure 17-2.

- *Page header*. The very beginning section of a database page will contain several bytes of physical "housekeeping" information. The page header may include a page identifier, forward and backward links to other data pages, an identifier indicating to which table the page belongs, free space pointers, and the minimum row length for the table.

- *Data rows*. A page also will contain the actual rows of the table (or index) containing the user data. Rows will not cross a page boundary except for certain large data types like text, images, and other binary large objects.

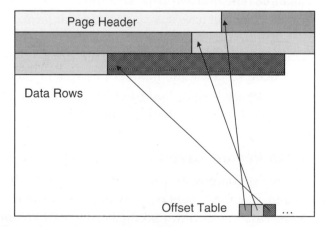

Figure 17-2   *Sample data page layout*

- *Offset table.* An offset table may exist with pointers to each data row on the data page. Some DBMSs always use some form of offset table, whereas others use the offset table only when variable-length rows exist on the data page.

Keep in mind that the actual layout and length of the components of a page will differ from DBMS to DBMS. In addition, the number of rows that can be stored on a database page will depend on the page size. Some DBMSs require a fixed page size for database objects, whereas others permit the DBA to specify the page size.

Allocation Pages

The DBMS uses an allocation page to manage the other pages in the database object.

In addition to data pages, the DBMS will use another type of page to control space usage. Sometimes called a *space map page,* an *allocation page* is used by the DBMS to manage the other pages in the database object. Multiple allocation pages can exist within a database, each one controlling a block of other data pages. These blocks are typically referred to as *allocation units.*

Allocation pages control physical pages. Each physical page is mapped to a single database. Physical pages need not be contiguous on disk and, in fact, frequently will not be. The primary vehicle used by an allocation unit to manage page allocation is the bitmap. A bitmap contains a series of bits that are either turned on ("1") or off ("0"). Each bit refers to pages within the allocation unit and to whether space is available within the page. The DBMS uses this information to facilitate quicker data modification processes. The DBMS may use multiple bitmaps to manage allocation, deallocation, and space usage. The allocation page will have a distinctly different format than a typical data page.

The DBA must factor in the existence of allocation pages to any space calculations he performs to manage the storage used by the database. The DBA will need to know the number of pages in each allocation unit that is controlled by each allocation page. The DBA then adds this additional overhead into the database space usage calculations.

Data Record Layouts

A record contains a row's data contents as well as housekeeping data.

A table is composed of rows and columns. Each single row must be entirely stored on a single data page (with the exception of some large data objects in some DBMSs). Each row is contained within a record that consists of additional housekeeping data along with the actual data contents of the row. Each table record comprises the following elements:

- *Row Header.* Each record typically begins with several bytes of physical "housekeeping" information detailing the structure and composition of the data contents of the row. This might include row length, information on variable-length data, and other control structures.
- *Row Data.* This consists of the actual data contents of the data columns for the row, in the order of their definition. Depending on the DBMS, the variable- and fixed-length columns may be separated.
- *Offset Tables.* Optionally, the record may contain an offset table with pointers to manage and control where variable-length fields are stored within the row.

When calculating the storage required for a table, the DBA must calculate record length, not row length. Record length will include the header and offset table overhead, whereas row length is simply a count of that length of each column in the table. Of course, the DBA must be able to accurately calculate row length, too, because the row length is a component of the overall record length.

To calculate the length of the data portion of the row, the DBA will need to secure documentation that outlines the way to determine the actual, physical length for each data type supported by the DBMS. The actual data types and lengths required to store columns of these data types differs from DBMS to DBMS. The following formulas can be used as general guidelines for calculating the physical size of a row:

Fixed-length rows:

Row Size　=　Length (COL1)
　　　　　+　. . .
　　　　　+　Length (COLn)

Variable-length rows:

Row Size　=　Length (FIXED COL1)
　　　　　+　. . .
　　　　　+　Length (FIXED COLn)
　　　　　+　Average [Length(VAR COL1)]
　　　　　+　. . .
　　　　　+　Average [Length(VAR COLn)]

The length of
a column will
depend on the
data type of
that column.

The length of a column will depend on the data type of that column; each DBMS documents the length of the data types it supports. To calculate the length of the entire record you will need to find the amount of overhead required for the type of rows (variable- or fixed-length) and add that to either calculation.

Calculating Table Size

The size of a page differs from DBMS to DBMS.

Once the page layouts are known and the DBA can accurately calculate record lengths, calculating the size of a table is easy. After calculating the record length, the next step is to determine how many rows will fit on a physical page. The size of a page will differ from DBMS to DBMS, and most DBMSs allow the DBA to specify different page sizes.

For example, assume that a single page consists of 2K of storage, but 32 bytes of that page are required for overhead (header information). This leaves 2016 remaining bytes in which data rows can be stored. Use the following formula to arrive at the number of rows that can fit on a single data page:

$$\text{Rows per page} = \frac{2016}{\text{Row size}}$$

Use the following formula to arrive at the total amount of space required for the table:

$$\text{Table size (in K)} = \frac{\text{Number of rows}}{\text{Rows per page}} \times (2K)$$

Of course, the DBA will need to factor in the free space that is specified for the table, as well. Furthermore, remember to factor in data that is stored externally from the rest of the data, such as text columns in SQL Server or LOB columns in DB2.

Index Page Layouts

When a table has no indexes defined for it, rows are simply added at the end of the table. When there is no additional room to insert new rows to the last page, a new page is obtained (either from the current allocation or by creating a new extent). The data pages of a nonindexed table are linked together with forward and backward pointers. Traversing the linked list causes the data pages to be accessed in order.

A single index row must be entirely stored on a single index page.

Similar restrictions apply to records stored in an index as apply to a data record. A single index row must be entirely stored on a single index page. The typical index record includes the following items:

- *Header information.* As with data pages, each index record typically begins with several bytes of physical "housekeeping" information detailing the structure and composition of the index record.

- *Row length.* For variable-length keys, the index may need to store the actual length of the indexed data.

- *Index key values.* The actual data values for the index key are listed in order of definition.

- *Page pointer.* This points to the physical location of the data page in the table that actually holds the indexed data.

- *Offset and adjust tables.* These may be required to manage and control the position of variable-length fields stored within the index row.

The composition of the pointer component of the index record depends on whether the index is clustered or nonclustered. Clustered indexes require only a pointer to the data page. Nonclustered indexes require both the pointer to the data page and a pointer to the location of the data row within the data page.

Calculating Index Size

The first step in calculating the space required to store an index is to calculate the row size for the index using one of the following formulas:

Fixed length index keys:
Row Size = Length (KEY-COL1)
          + . . .
          + Length (KEY-COLn)

Variable-length index keys:
Row Size = Length (FIXED-KEY-COL1)
          + . . .
          + Length (FIXED-KEY-COLn)
          + Average [Length (VAR-KEY-COL1)]
          + . . .
          + Average [Length (VAR-KEY-COLn)]

Remember, you need to calculate the size of an index record, not just the size of the row. Records are simply the row plus the overhead required to store the row. To calculate the record size you will need to obtain the size of the row overhead required for indexes in the DBMS you are using.

Once you have calculated the record size, you can move on to the next step, which is to calculate the amount of storage space required for the index. Begin by using the following formula to arrive at the number of records that can fit on a single index page:

Entries per page	=	(Block size – Overhead)
	÷	Row size

Then you can use the following formulas to arrive at the total amount of space required for the index:

First-level pages	=	Number of rows
	÷	Entries per page

First-level size	=	First-level pages
	×	(Block size – Page overhead)

Second-level pages	=	First-level pages
	÷	Entries per page

Second-level size	=	Second-level pages
	×	(Block size – Page overhead)

Third-level pages	=	Second-level pages
	÷	Entries per page

Third-level size	=	Third-level pages
	×	(Block size – Page overhead)

And so on. Continue the iteration until the number of pages is one or fewer. At that point, you have reached the root level of the index. Adding together the sizes for each level will result in the total amount of space required to store the index.

Transaction Logs

Arriving at an exact size for the transaction log can be more of an art than a science.

One of the most important files for database processing is the transaction log. Remember, every insert, update, and delete to any database table is recorded (or logged) in the transaction log. Arriving at an exact size for the transaction log can be more of an art than a science, because transaction activity is by nature random.

Database activity is the most important factor in determining an appropriate size for the transaction log. A good rule of thumb is to provide sufficient space for the log file to capture all database modifications that will occur between log archivals during your busiest processing period. The tricky part is determining the most active processing period and the database modification's impact on the log. At any rate, if you do not automatically archive or back up your database logs, you should pay close attention to the size of the database log file(s). Failure to do so can cause data to be unrecoverable or cause processing to slow down or halt completely.

The DBA must specify other database logging parameters that impact disk usage. Most DBMSs supports multiple, redundant logs. The DBA must decide how many transaction logs there should be and on which disk devices they should be allocated. At a minimum, you should run with dual active logging—that way, a problem on one log will not shut down DBMS operations, because the other active log can be used.

Another consideration is how long archive logs should remain on disk. For some implementations, logs can be archived directly to disk. However, from an efficiency standpoint, it makes more sense to archive logs to disk, and then have them roll off to tape later. As a rule of thumb, consider keeping your archive logs on disk for at least 24 hours. Furthermore, plan ahead to make sure you have sufficient disk space to accommodate archive logs for the system throughput on your busiest day.

Storage Options

Once you have calculated the amount of storage required for your database files, you will need to choose the type of storage to be used. There are several storage options available from which the DBA can choose, based on fault tolerance, performance requirements, and budget.

The primary storage medium used by database files will, of course, be direct access disk drives. But other types of media are available. Some newer DBMS

MMDBMS

MMDBMS technology stores data completely in memory. Because disk I/O is avoided, application performance can be greatly enhanced when using a MMDBMS. For read-only applications, the MMDBMS can provide a performance enhancement of ten times or more over disk-based RDBMSs. However, applications with heavy update activity are likely to experience performance gains only three to five times faster than disk-based RDBMSs.

However, organizations that are considering deploying MMDBMS for performance reasons should weigh their decision carefully because the major vendors of RDBMSs and application servers are bolstering their caching abilities. It's probable that such RDBMS augmentation will eventually render the MMDBMS a niche technology.

The leading MMDBMS vendor is TimesTen Performance Systems. Founded in 1996, TimesTen has multiple customers using its production MMDBMS. For more information, refer to http://www.timesten.com.

products, called main-memory database management systems (MMDBMSs), enable the persistent storage of data on solid state devices. Refer to the sidebar "MMDBMS" for additional details.

Tape is also a storage option, as is optical disk, but these are WORM (write once, read many) technologies. Tape is used primarily for backup purposes, while optical disk is a niche technology used primarily for backup and offline data storage.

Disk devices are the predominant storage vehicles used for persistent data storage.

Which brings us back to good old disk. Disk devices are the predominant storage vehicles used by DBAs for persistent data storage. Disk drives are designed for direct read-write access, are cost-efficient, and are capable of storing very large volumes of data. Some disk devices are slower than others; some are smaller. However, an astounding variety of disk drives are available in various speeds, capacities, and price ranges to satisfy just about any type of storage requirement.

RAID

RAID combines multiple disk devices into an array.

Outages due to simple media failures often can be avoided by implementing modern disk technologies such as RAID. *RAID*, an acronym for *redundant arrays of inexpensive disks*, combines multiple disk devices into an array that is perceived by the system as a single disk drive. There are many levels of RAID technology, which deliver different degrees of fault tolerance and performance.

Another desirable aspect of RAID arrays is their ability to use hot-swappable drives; the array does not have to be powered down to replace a failed drive. That a drive can be replaced while the array is up and running is a plus for DBAs needing to manage databases while delivering nonstop data availability.

RAID Levels

Several different levels of RAID are available. Vendors provide varying levels of support for the RAID levels that have been defined. These various levels of RAID support continuous availability through combinations of functions called mirroring, striping, and parity. *Mirroring* occurs when complete copies of the data are made on at least two disk drives, and all changes made to the data are made simultaneously to both copies. If one fails, access is automatically shifted to the remaining copy. *Striping* occurs when subsets of data are spread across multiple disk drives. If any one drive fails, the impact of the failure is limited to the data within the stripe on that disk. Finally, *parity* bits are encoded data that can be used to facilitate the reconstruction of the original data, in the event that all or part of the data cannot be accessed if the drive fails. The lost data can be reconstructed "on the fly" until it can be rewritten to undamaged disks.

Raid-0 (Figure 17-3) is also commonly referred to as *disk striping*. With RAID-0, data is split across multiple drives, which delivers higher data throughput. However, there is no redundancy (which really doesn't fit the definition of the RAID acronym). Because there is no redundant data being stored, performance is usually very good, but a failure of any disk in the array will result in data loss.

RAID-1 (Figure 17-4), sometimes referred to as *data mirroring,* provides redundancy because all data is written to two or more drives. A RAID-1 array will generally perform better than a single drive when reading data and worse when writing data. However, RAID-1 provides data redundancy, so if any drive fails, no data will be lost.

RAID-2 (Figure 17-5) provides error correction coding. RAID-2 is useful only for drives without any built-in error detection.

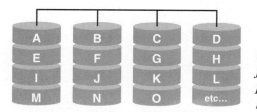

Figure 17-3   *RAID-0 (© 1999 figure courtesy Advanced Computer and Network Corporation [AC&NC])*

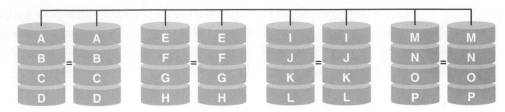

Figure 17-4   *RAID-1 (© 1999 figure courtesy AC&NC)*

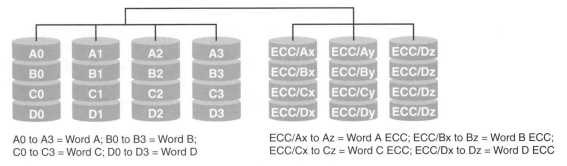

A0 to A3 = Word A; B0 to B3 = Word B;
C0 to C3 = Word C; D0 to D3 = Word D

ECC/Ax to Az = Word A ECC; ECC/Bx to Bz = Word B ECC;
ECC/Cx to Cz = Word C ECC; ECC/Dx to Dz = Word D ECC

Figure 17-5   *RAID-2 (© 1999 figure courtesy AC&NC)*

RAID-3 (Figure 17-6) stripes data at a byte level across several drives, with parity stored on one drive. RAID-3 provides very good data transfer rates for both reads and writes.

RAID-4 (Figure 17-7) stripes data at a block level across several drives, with parity stored on a single drive. For RAID-3 and RAID-4, the parity information allows recovery from the failure of any single drive. The write performance can be slow with RAID-4, and it can be quite difficult to rebuild data in the event of RAID-4 disk failure.

RAID-5 (Figure 17-8) is similar to RAID-4, but it distributes the parity information among the drives. RAID-5 can outperform RAID-4 for small writes in

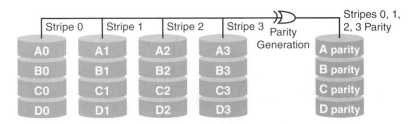

Figure 17-6   *RAID-3 (© 1999 figure courtesy AC&NC)*

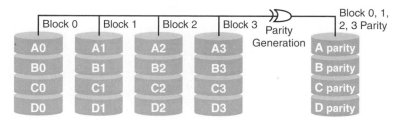

Figure 17-7   *RAID-4 (© 1999 figure courtesy AC&NC)*

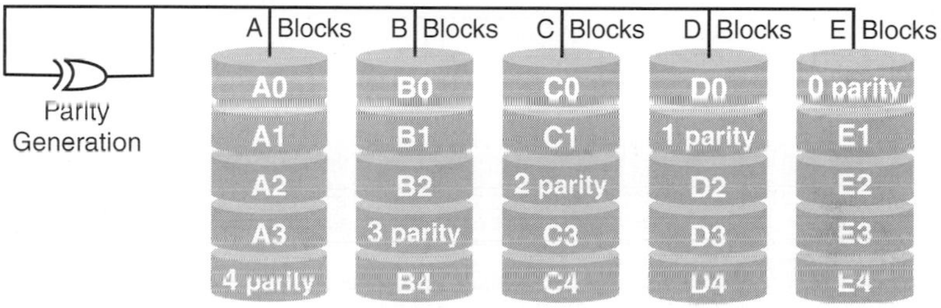

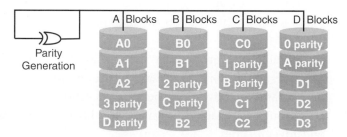

Figure 17-8   *RAID-5 (© 1999 figure courtesy AC&NC)*

multiprocessing systems because the parity disk does not become a bottleneck. However, read performance can suffer because the parity information is on several disks.

RAID-6 (Figure 17-9) is basically an extension of RAID-5, but it provides additional fault tolerance through the use of a second independent distributed parity scheme. Write performance of RAID-6 can be poor.

RAID-10 (Figure 17-10) is a striped array where each segment is a RAID-1 array. Therefore, it provides the same fault tolerance as RAID-1. A high degree of performance and reliability can be delivered by RAID-10, so it is very suitable for high-performance database processing. However, RAID-10 can be very expensive.

Figure 17-9   *RAID-6 (© 1999 figure courtesy AC&NC)*

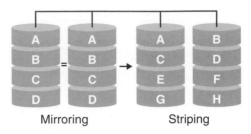

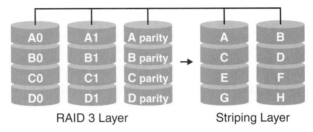

Figure 17-10   *RAID-10 (© 1999 figure courtesy AC&NC)*

Figure 17-11   *RAID-53 (© 1999 figure courtesy AC&NC)*

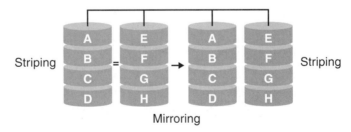

Figure 17-12   *RAID-0+1 (© 1999 figure courtesy AC&NC)*

RAID-53 (Figure 17-11) is a striped array where each segment is a RAID-3 array. Therefore, RAID-53 has the same fault tolerance and overhead as RAID-3.

RAID-0+1 (Figure 17-12) combines the mirroring of RAID-1 with the striping of RAID-0. This couples the high performance of RAID-0 with the reliability of RAID-1.

Proprietary variants and levels of RAID have been defined by the storage vendors.

A number of proprietary variants and levels of RAID have been defined by the storage vendors. If you are in the market for RAID storage, be sure you understand exactly what the storage vendor is delivering. For more details, check out the detailed information at http://www.RAID.edu and http://www. raid-advisory.com.

Choosing the appropriate type of RAID storage for database files is an important aspect of the DBA's job. The level of RAID chosen will directly impact the performance and reliability of your database solution. When evaluating RAID storage solutions for your database files, it is essential that you factor in the cost of the solution to the selection criteria. Table 17-2 compares the fault tolerance, performance, and cost of each level of RAID.

Keep in mind that every DBMS uses files for data, indexes, and transaction logs, each of which serve different purposes and sustain different levels of read and write activity. Different types of storage can be budgeted and procured for the different types of files and the different types of access required for each type. For example, the write activity against a log file tends to be sequential, so it makes sense to isolate log files on a disk system that maximizes write performance. Because log file activity is primarily write activity, you should favor fast-write RAID levels such as RAID-0+1 or RAID-0. RAID-0+1 is optimal, but quite costly, so many organizations decide to live with the reduced write performance and fault tolerance of RAID-1.

When evaluating RAID—or any type of disk system—you must balance your available budget against the reliability and performance requirements of your database systems and applications. The optimal disk configuration for

Table 17-2 *RAID Levels and Performance*

Level	Fault tolerance	Read performance	Write performance	Cost
No RAID	No	Normal	Normal	Inexpensive
Level 0	No	Fast	Fast	Expensive
Level 1	Yes	Normal	Normal	Moderate
Level 2	Yes	Normal	Normal	Moderate
Level 3	Yes	Normal	Normal	Moderate
Level 4	Yes	Normal	Slow	Moderate
Level 5	Yes	Fast	Slow	Expensive
Level 6	Yes	Fast	Slow	Expensive
Level 10	Yes	Fast	Normal	Expensive
Level 53	Yes	Normal	Normal	Expensive
Level 0+1	Yes	Fast	Fast	Very Expensive

your database files might require multiple RAID arrays at different levels. For evaluation purposes, though, consider the following advice:

- Favor fault-tolerant RAID levels for database files. Database files not on fault-tolerant disks are subject to downtime and lost data.

- Choose the appropriate disk system for the type of activity each database object will experience. For example, you might want to implement two separate RAID systems—one at RAID-5 for data that is heavily read-focused, such as analysis and reporting, and another at RAID-1 (or RAID-0+1) for transaction data that is frequently written and updated.

- If you have the budget at your disposal, choose RAID-0+1 because it has fast read, fast write, and fault tolerance.

JBOD

JBOD stands for just a bunch of disks.

JBOD, which stands for *just a bunch of disks,* is a term used to differentiate traditional disk technologies from newer storage technology. Typically, disks are directly connected to a server. Once the DBMS is installed on those disk drives, database files can be created on those disk drives using the facilities of the DBMS.

As the database environment becomes more complex, though, the storage needs become more complex. As the database environment grows, DBAs may need to consider other storage techniques such as SANs and NAS.

Storage Area Networks

No industrywide standard definition of SAN exists.

A *storage area network,* or SAN, generally refers to an interconnected network of storage devices. However, no industrywide standard definition of SAN exists, and it means different things to different folks. To some, a SAN is anything that includes a fiber channel switch. Others define a SAN to be anything with two or more host systems using fiber channel technology. However you define them, SANs offer high speed, coupled with high availability.

Fiber Channel is a serial interface that can deliver a transfer rate of up to 105 MB/second. Fiber Channel is a competitive technology to SCSI, which stands for *small computer system interface* and is pronounced "scuzzy." SCSI is a parallel interface that can deliver transfer rates from 40 MB/second to a maximum of 160 MB/second for Ultra-SCSI. With SCSI, though, repairing or adding storage devices causes significant downtime. Fiber channel offers more fault tolerance by enabling devices to be removed and added without disabling connections.

SAN affords the following benefits:

- Shared storage between multiple hosts
- High I/O performance
- Server and storage consolidation

Network-Attached Storage

Network-attached storage, or NAS, refers to storage that can be accessed directly from the network. With NAS, hosts or client systems can read and write data over a network interface (such as Ethernet, FDDI, or others) using protocols including NFS and CIFS. NAS can be implemented using file servers, host systems running NAS software, or thin servers called appliances.

NAS provides the following benefits:

- Shared storage between multiple hosts
- Simpler management due to reducing duplicate storage
- Application based storage access at file level

Traditional systems use either internal or external storage attached directly to a system, or perhaps use shared storage, such as a large enterprise array. Performance and distance limitations exist with older interfaces (like SCSI and ESCON). The most commonly used NAS software is NFS (Network File System) and CIFS on Windows NT systems.

SAN vs. NAS

A SAN is best utilized as a storage backbone providing basic storage services to host systems and NAS servers. SANs are well suited for sharing storage and building the infrastructure for server and storage consolidation. Applications requiring high performance or large capacities are good candidates for SAN technology. Because it offers high performance and low latency, SAN is ideal for database applications.

NAS is better suited for solving multimedia storage problems, data sharing issues, and sharing of storage for smaller systems. NAS does not efficiently handle the block-based storage used by database systems.

Don't make the mistake of forcing all storage to be of one type.

Do not make the mistake of forcing all storage to be of one type, either SAN or NAS. Match the storage requirements to the access and modification needs of each database and application. You can use a combination of SAN and NAS to solve your data storage and business requirements.

Direct Access File System

DAFS, an acronym for *direct access file system*, is a newer specification that enables disk technologies to take advantage of memory-to-memory interconnect technologies such as VI and InfiniBand. DAFS promises to enhance I/O performance and disk reliability, but DAFS is still early in its development lifecycle.

The DAFS proto-
col promises
to improve per-
formance.

The DAFS protocol promises to improve performance and allow NAS devices to take on more demanding applications while lightening the load of storage servers. DAFS decreases CPU usage by minimizing the data path a server needs to read from and write to a file. Using a direct memory-to-memory transfer, DAFS can bypass application and file servers, allowing data to be transferred directly between appropriately aligned buffers on the communicating machines. Files can be saved directly into memory by an application without having to fill up various operating system and file system buffers across the network. This can optimize I/O operations and reduce network traffic.

DAFS is an emerging technology, and few product implementations are available as of late 2001, although several vendors have created DAFS-based proof-of-concept prototypes. A consortium of vendors has organized as the DAFS Collaborative to support the DAFS protocol and promote the creation of DAFS-based products. Additional information about DAFS can be found on the DAFS Collaborative Web site at http://www.dafscollaborative.org/.

Planning for the Future

Most database implementations are anything but static. Once deployed, databases are queried, updated, loaded, unloaded, and reorganized, and data is deleted and inserted from them on an ongoing basis. As the data composition of a database changes, its storage requirements will change as well.

The DBA must
be ever-vigilant in
planning for future
growth.

The DBA must be ever-vigilant in planning for future growth. The DBA must keep an eye on the amount of data and the number of users accessing the data. When either expands, database storage may have to be modified.

Capacity Planning

Capacity planning is a process whereby the capacity of the entire system is measured and compared against requirements. The goal of this comparison is

Capacity planning measures and compares system capacity against requirements.

to adjust the resources available to the system as appropriate. To successfully embark on a capacity planning exercise requires an understanding of new corporate initiatives and how they are likely to impact the existing infrastructure—that is, your hardware (CPU, storage, network, and memory) and your software (application and system).

By measuring current capacity, gauging the growth of capacity over time, and factoring in the anticipated capacity requirements of new corporate and IT initiatives, you can determine whether your existing infrastructure can sustain the anticipated workload. If the projected growth outpaces the ability of your computing environment to support it, you will need to evaluate the cost of modifying and possibly scaling up your computing infrastructure.

From a storage perspective, this may involve simply adding more disk devices and assigning them to the DBMS. However, it may involve additional tasks to support additional data and users, such as the following:

- Redesigning applications
- Redesigning databases
- Modifying DBMS parameters
- Reconfiguring hardware components
- Adjusting software interfaces

There are multiple perspectives from which to view storage consumption. Each is valid and provides a different view of storage utilization and growth. A systemwide perspective views the rate at which disk space is being consumed on an aggregate level. At a lower level, viewing storage capacity by server determines which computers are consuming disk space at the fastest rate. You can also monitor storage consumption at the file system level to determine which file systems are consuming disk space at the fastest rate. Finally, as a DBA, you will want to view just those files that are associated with the DBMS. The bottom line is that you will need to be able to answer all of the following questions:

- When will more storage be required?
- How much additional storage is needed?
- Where is the additional storage needed?
- What needs to be done to align the additional storage with the DBMS?

Summary

Databases are comprised of data and files that must be stored on reusable media to be useful. The DBA must understand the different storage options available for database objects and files and use the appropriate device for each file that meets capacity, performance, and budgetary objectives.

Storage is a growing field.

Storage is a growing field, with new technologies and products becoming available on a regular basis. DBAs must keep abreast of this technology so that they can meet the storage needs of their databases—and thereby meet the information technology and data processing needs of their organization.

Review

1. Why are most database files stored on disk devices instead of other storage media?

2. What is the difference between SAN and NAS?

3. Name five goals to consider when building a storage system.

4. Your organization has decided to purchase RAID arrays to support your DBMS. Which levels of RAID would you advise them to use and why?

5. What storage management actions should be taken to assure the viability and speed of the transaction log file(s)?

6. Describe the pros and cons of using RAID-4 for database files.

7. When calculating record size for a table, how should you treat the size calculation for variable-length columns?

8. Why is it beneficial to place data files and index files on separate disk devices?

9. What advantages does a SAN have over SCSI devices?

10. Calculating the amount of storage required for a table is as simple as adding up the number of bytes for the columns in a row and multiplying by the total number of rows: True or False.

Suggested Reading

Schur, Stephen G. *The Database Factory.* New York, NY: Wiley & Sons (1994). ISBN 0-471-55844-3

Strauss, Melvin J. *Computer Capacity: A Production Control Approach.* New York, NY: Van Nostrand Reinhold (1981). ISBN 0-442-26243-4

Thornburgh, Ralph H., and Barry J. Shoenborn. *Storage Area Networks.* Upper Saddle River, NJ: Prentice Hall PTR (2000). ISBN 0-13-027959-5

Toigo, Jon William. *The Holy Grail of Data Storage Management.* Upper Saddle River, NJ: Prentice Hall PTR (2000). ISBN 0-13-013055-9

18

Data Movement and Distribution

Data is not sedentary. Once data has been created, organizations tend to move it around to support many different purposes—different applications, different geographies, different users, different computing environments, and different DBMSs.

Rarely is a single copy of any piece of data good enough. Data is copied and transformed and cleansed and duplicated and stored many times throughout the organization. Different copies of the same data are used to support transaction processing and analysis; test, quality assurance, and operational systems; day-to-day operations and reporting; data warehouses, data marts, and data mining; and distributed databases. Controlling this vast sea of data falls on the DBA.

The DBA uses many techniques and technologies to facilitate data movement and distribution. This chapter discusses some of the primary tools that are used to move data from place to place and to support data at multiple locations.

Loading and Unloading Data

One of the simplest ways for the DBA to move data from one place to another is to use the LOAD and UNLOAD utilities that come with the DBMS. The LOAD utility is used to populate tables with new data, and the UNLOAD utility is used to read data from a table and put it into a data file.

The LOAD Utility

A LOAD utility is used to perform bulk inserts of data into database tables.

A LOAD utility is used to perform bulk inserts of data into database tables. It typically can support

- Adding rows to a table, retaining the current data, or
- Replacing all existing rows with the new data.

When loading data, the DBA must take into account many factors to ensure a success. Is the LOAD utility restartable in the event it fails? Although it takes more time to implement a restartable load process, it is easier to support. For the load process to be restartable, the DBA must ensure that any work files used are allocated and that the LOAD utility can restart from where it left off. If the LOAD utility is not restartable and an error occurs that stops the load process, the DBA must choose one of two options:

1. To delete the data that has already been loaded, and to start again from the beginning, or
2. To determine what was already loaded and remove those records from the input data file that is being loaded.

Of course, this task is more difficult when adding rows to existing data using LOAD, because the first option requires a selective delete.

Another consideration for the DBA is whether to presort data before it is loaded into the database. If the table being loaded is clustered, it may make sense to sort the input data by the clustered columns to allow the LOAD utility to process the input data file in clustered order. Failing to sort data into clustering sequence may cause the load process to uncluster the data, depending on the DBMS and the LOAD utility.

Most database LOAD utilities do not cause triggers to fire, which can cause data integrity problems. If the database and application rely on the trigger to calculate data or enforce constraints, loading data without firing triggers can be devastating to the state of the database. The DBA and application developers will need to develop programs or scripts that mimic the triggered action if data is to be loaded regularly and triggers exist.

Other database constraints can pose problems for the LOAD utility, too. If data is being loaded that does not conform to a unique constraint or a check constraint, what will the LOAD utility do? Once again, this depends on the DBMS and the LOAD utility. Some LOAD utilities are flexible enough to provide options to enforce constraints, or not. In such a scenario, the DBA must decide whether invalid data is to be discarded by the LOAD utility, or whether data that does not conform to constraints can be loaded—possibly causing data integrity problems. Some LOAD utilities do not even give the DBA an option—they either load everything or discard nonconforming data automatically. All in all, it is better to have the flexibility, even if it does cause more work for the DBA.

The DBA should favor enforcing constraints when the LOAD utility allows it. Otherwise, you will have to correct the data after it has been loaded or live with data integrity violations. It will be more efficient to process the data once, as it is loaded, than to process the data twice—once to load it and once to correct it.

Before LOAD can be used, the DBA must ensure that all processes and users needing to execute the LOAD utility have the appropriate authority to do so. Some DBMSs provide a specific load authority that can be granted. Most DBMSs permit the owner of the table and those granted administrator-level authority to load data, as well.

Describing the Input File

Using the LOAD utility to populate a table requires an input file containing the data. The DBA must define the layout of the input file to the LOAD utility to enable it to translate raw data into the format required for storage in the database. This is typically accomplished by specifying the data type of each column along with the beginning and ending position within the file where the data exists. Some LOAD utilities also provide specific formats that can be loaded with limited specification such as comma-delimited files or files created using an UNLOAD or EXPORT utility.

The LOAD utility must be capable of handling nulls. Nulls are usually handled with an indicator byte and a specific clause for checking that byte. For example, the LOAD utility could specify a clause such as

The LOAD utility must be capable of handling nulls.

```
LOAD . . . STATUS POSITION (20:25) CHAR(6) NULLIF(26)='F' . . .
```

This statement indicates that the column named STATUS is to be loaded with data from the input file, starting with the 20th character and finishing with the 25th character. However, if the 26th character is equal to the value 'N', the STATUS column is to be set to NULL.

Loading tables with nullable columns can degrade the performance of the LOAD utility because extra processing is required to check whether the data should be null or not. If data is to be loaded to a table on a regular basis, try to avoid nullable columns for those tables.

Some LOAD utilities provide additional controls to allow the DBA to modify the functionality of the load process. For example, clauses to control the loading of default values or to bypass certain records in the input file are common. Be sure to understand all of the parameters of the LOAD utility being used, so that you can control the way in which data is loaded into your tables. Sometimes the LOAD utility can be used instead of an application program to insert data—which reduces the programmers effort because he does not have to write, test, and debug program logic. Instead, the logic exists in the LOAD utility, and the processing can be controlled by the DBA with the parameters and clauses of the utility.

Try to avoid converting data from one data type to another during the load process. Although most LOAD utilities can automatically convert similar data types, additional CPU effort is required to perform such conversions. For example, the LOAD utility may be able to convert an integer value in the input file to a decimal value in the database, but it would be better if the LOAD data were decimal to begin with.

Take special care when loading floating-point data into tables.

Special care must be taken when floating-point data must be loaded into tables. Usually the LOAD utility will require specific information about the format of the data.

Efficient Loading

Create all required indexes before loading data into a table.

It is usually a good idea to create all required indexes before loading data into a table. The LOAD utility is usually more efficient at populating the indexes during the load process than creating new indexes for a fully populated table. Of course, the DBA should verify this to be the case for the DBMS and version in use.

If the LOAD utility is capable of performing tasks in parallel, the DBA should take advantage of this when large amounts of data are being loaded. The LOAD utility might be capable of accepting multiple input files for concurrent loading into different segments or table partitions, or it might be able to build multiple indexes in parallel rather than building each sequentially. Parallel operations like this may increase the amount of CPU required to load data while reducing the overall elapsed time for the LOAD to run.

Another performance-related aspect of loading data is the need to plan for concurrent processing if you are loading multiple tables. Judicious scheduling of concurrent workloads can enable some LOAD utilities to operate concurrently. For example, you might be able to perform concurrent loads on tables from different databases or file groups. The DBA should make every effort to understand the capabilities and limitations of the LOAD utility and to plan concurrent load jobs accordingly.

If the LOAD utility provides an option to turn off logging, consider using it to speed up the load process and minimize overhead. However, the DBA will have to back up the data after the LOAD completes to ensure recoverability. If logging is turned off, the DBMS cannot recover the table without an image copy backup.

It is usually more efficient for the LOAD utility to insert the initial data into a table than it is for a program or multiple SQL INSERT statements to perform the same task. A LOAD utility is optimized for very efficient bulk insertion of data. In addition to the efficiency of LOAD, using a utility is likely to be less error-prone than a corresponding application program.

For some DBMSs, it is more efficient to use LOAD instead of a mass delete. A mass delete is performed when a SQL DELETE statement is issued with no WHERE clause. Using the LOAD utility with an empty input file will have the same result—all rows will be deleted from the referenced table. LOAD is likely to be more efficient, especially if it is possible to turn off logging during the load process.

Running Other Utilities During a LOAD

Some database LOAD utilities take advantage of the fact that they have access to all of the data as it is being loaded. A full-function LOAD utility may enable the DBA to create image copy backups or to create database statistics during the load process. Taking advantage of such capabilities creates efficiencies because the data is read once, but processed multiple times (load, image copy, statistics, etc.).

You may want to schedule a REORG after loading data.

Additionally, you may want to schedule a REORG after loading data. This is an especially good idea if the loaded data was not presorted into clustering sequence and the LOAD utility does not sort for clustering.

The UNLOAD Utility

Information in database tables frequently needs to be moved or copied to other locations. For example, you may want to move data to a different database, from a table to a sequential file for external processing, or possibly to another relational database system or platform. Certain database schema changes require database objects to be dropped and recreated—and when the object is dropped, so is the data. Therefore, you need to unload the data before making database object changes. Perhaps you just want to extract a subset of rows from a table for use as test data. Even to reorganize a database object typically requires the data to be unloaded, optimized, then reloaded.

The purpose of the UNLOAD utility is to read data from a database and write it to an output data file.

The purpose of the UNLOAD utility is to read data from a database and write it to an output data file. Without an UNLOAD utility, database users are forced to use SQL SELECT statements issued by an interactive SQL facility, report writer, or application program in order to unload data. However, these methods are error-prone and slow for large quantities of data. Furthermore, requiring a developer to code an application program to create a file is too inflexible and time consuming for most production database needs. Thus, many DBMSs provide an UNLOAD utility to provide high-speed capabilities and the flexibility to perform most of the bulk data movement tasks performed by DBAs.

Before UNLOAD can be used, the DBA must ensure that all processes and users needing to execute the UNLOAD utility have the appropriate authority to do so. Typically, this involves granting a level of authorization that contains the ability to read (SELECT) data from the table. Depending on the DBMS and utility, additional security may be required.

Concurrency

The level of concurrent activity that can be performed against a table that is being unloaded depends on the parameters and options of the UNLOAD utility. Concurrent read activity is permitted because UNLOAD does not change any data. Most UNLOAD programs enable the user to control whether concurrent data modifications can occur while data is being unloaded. Frequently it is desirable to disable concurrent modifications during an UNLOAD to ensure the creation of a file with consistent data.

Additionally, it may be useful or necessary to prohibit concurrent utilities to be run while data is being unloaded. For example, loading, reorganizing, or recovering data during an UNLOAD will cause unpredictable results because these utilities change data.

Unloading from Image Copy Backups

Modern UNLOAD utilities are capable of unloading data from an image copy backup. Such capabilities are useful because they enhance concurrent data access. Unloading from an image copy backup can be beneficial because the live data is unaffected—meaning no locks are taken on the live data nor is any data read from the actual table on disk. Because the UNLOAD utility reads the data from an image copy backup, the performance and availability of applications running against the live data will be unaffected by the concurrent unload operation.

Of course, the freshness of the data being unloaded may be an issue. If subsequent updates, inserts, and deletes were processed against the table after the image copy backup was taken, those modifications will not be captured in the unloaded data because they were not made to the image copy data set—only to the live data itself.

If you are in the market for an UNLOAD utility, be sure it provides the ability to unload from image copy backups.

A modern UNLOAD utility provides the ability to unload from image copy backups.

Generation of LOAD Parameters

It is common for an UNLOAD utility to provide an option for generating the control statement necessary to use the LOAD utility to reload the data that is being unloaded. Such an option can save time because the DBA will not have to create the LOAD statement by hand. Even if the data is going to be loaded to a different table, it can be useful to generate the LOAD statement during the unload operation. Changing a generated LOAD statement usually will be easier than coding a LOAD statement from scratch.

Data Encoding Scheme

An UNLOAD utility should allow the DBA to specify the encoding scheme to use for the unloaded data. Several common formatting options include EBCDIC, ASCII, and UNICODE. Many DBMSs support multiple code sets for other encoding schemes. Depending on the DBMS and the UNLOAD utility, you may be able to specify another data encoding scheme to be used for the unloaded data.

Floating-Point Data

As with the LOAD utility, special care must be taken when unloading floating-point data. When floating-point data is being unloaded, special parameters may need to be specified to identify the format in which unloaded floating-point numbers should be stored.

Limiting UNLOAD Data

It might make sense to unload only a subset of the total rows.

Sometimes DBAs will need to unload only a portion of the data. That is, the UNLOAD output file will contain only a subset of the rows in the table. Numerous reasons and situations exist where it might make sense to unload only a subset of the total rows, for example to create test data or to inspect only certain rows.

Most UNLOAD utilities provide options to specify a limited number of rows to unload. These options typically take three forms: LIMIT, SAMPLE, and WHEN.

A LIMIT parameter is used to limit the number of rows to be unloaded by the UNLOAD utility. Specifying a parameter like "LIMIT 200" will cause the UNLOAD utility to stop after unloading 200 rows.

A SAMPLE parameter is used to unload a sampling of the data instead of the entire table. The SAMPLE parameter typically requires a decimal condition that specifies the percentage of rows to be sampled. For example, the following parameter indicates that 25.75% of the rows in the table should be unloaded: SAMPLE 25.75.

Finally, a WHEN clause is used to supply SQL predicates to the UNLOAD utility such that only certain data is unloaded. For example, the following condition will cause only rows where the SALARY is greater than 50,000 to be unloaded: WHEN (SALARY > 50000). The UNLOAD utility may also provide the ability to use the ORDER BY clause to sort the data as it is written to the unload file.

Of course, the exact syntax of these three options will differ from DBMS to DBMS and utility to utility, but the general concept remains the same. Each of these options provides the DBA with great flexibility when creating external data files using the UNLOAD utility.

Unloading from Views

Most UNLOAD utilities permit data to be unloaded from views, not just tables. Being able to unload data from a view comes in handy when it is necessary to access data from multiple tables and place it into a single file. By creating the view as a join of those tables and unloading from the view, you can unload data from multiple tables to a single file.

Maintaining Application Test Beds

LOAD and UNLOAD can be used to maintain a consistent test bed of data.

LOAD and UNLOAD can be used to maintain a consistent test bed of data for the purposes of testing application programs, as shown in Figure 18-1. By creating an UNLOAD data file that can be loaded prior to each program test, developers can be sure that each program execution runs against the same data—which is critical for tracking down bugs and assuring that the program code is correct. The DBA can set up the proper LOAD and UNLOAD jobs and then turn them over to the application development teams for their use.

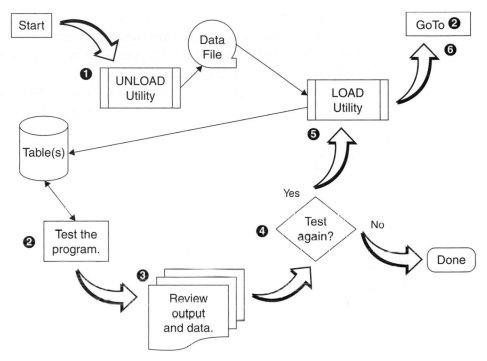

Figure 18-1 *Using LOAD and UNLOAD for program testing*

The UNLOAD utility is quite handy and will be used frequently by most DBAs. There are numerous situations and issues that can be resolved with the UNLOAD utility.

EXPORT and IMPORT

Similar to an UNLOAD utility, an EXPORT utility reads data from a table and places it into an external file. The IMPORT utility will read an external file created by the EXPORT utility and insert the data into a table.

IMPORT and EXPORT facilities typically work with more than just the data, though. Sometimes an EXPORT data file contains the schema for the table along with the data. In such cases, the IMPORT utility can create the table and import the data using just the EXPORT data file. Sometimes the EXPORT file contains more than just a single table. Some EXPORT facilities enable the DBA to specify a single table, and then follow the relationships for that table to extract all of the related files and data.

Some IMPORT/EXPORT facilities provide UNLOAD-like features to sample, subset, and limit the data that is exported (and imported). The difference, though, is the ability to perform such functions across multiple tables and maintain referentially intact data.

Not every DBMS offers IMPORT and EXPORT utilities.

Not every DBMS offers IMPORT and EXPORT utilities. Some third-party vendors (most notably Princeton Softech) provide import and export products.

Bulk Data Movement

The combination of UNLOAD and LOAD is the most common method used by DBAs to move large amounts of data from place to place. However, there are other methods for moving large quantities of data. Let's review a few.

ETL Software

ETL stands for extract, transform, and load.

ETL is a type of software that performs data movement. ETL stands for *extract, transform, and load.* ETL software is primarily used to populate data warehouses and data marts from other databases and data sources.

By using ETL software, the DBA can automate the extraction of data from disparate, heterogeneous sources. For example, data may need to be extracted from legacy IMS databases and VSAM files from the mainframe; relational databases such as Oracle, SQL Server, and DB2 on various platforms; spreadsheets stored on the LAN; as well as from external data feeds. The ETL software can be set up to recognize and retrieve the data from these many different sources.

Once retrieved, the data may need to be transformed in some fashion before it is stored in the target database. ETL software makes it easy to automate these changes. For example, you may wish to transform coded data to recognizable values, perhaps changing 1, 2, and 3 to "Married", "Single", and "Divorced". In addition, ETL software is capable of changing data types, and aggregating and summarizing numerical data.

After the data is transformed to your specifications, it is loaded into the target database. ETL software is much more flexible and useful for complex data movement needs than simple LOAD and UNLOAD utilities.

Replication and Propagation

Another method of moving data is through *replication* and *propagation*. When data is replicated, one data store is copied to one or more data stores, either locally or at other locations. Replication can be implemented simply by

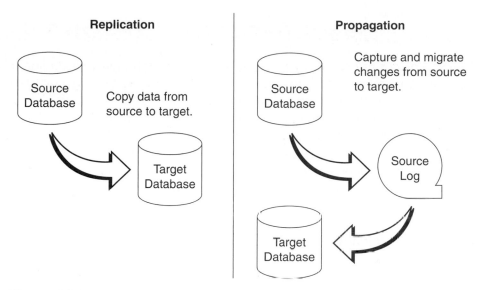

Figure 18-2 *Replication and propagation*

copying entire tables to multiple locations. Alternatively, replicated data can be a subset of the rows and/or columns. Replication can be set up to automatically refresh the copied data on a regular basis.

Propagation, on the other hand, is the migration of only changed data. Propagation can be implemented by scanning the transaction log and applying the results of data modification statements to another data store. Initial population of a data warehouse can be achieved by replication, and subsequent population of changes by either replication (if the data is very dynamic) or propagation.

The difference between replication and propagation is highlighted in Figure 18-2. DBAs can use both of these techniques to move data between different database and data warehouses. More information on managing and administering databases in a data warehouse environment is provided in Chapter 19.

Messaging Software

Messaging software, also known as *message queueing software* or *application integration,* is another popular form of data movement. When using a message queue, data is placed onto the queue by one application or process; the data is read from the queue by another application or process.

Oracle Transportable Tablespaces

Oracle provides the capability to transport an entire tablespace, including its definition and contents, from one database to another. In some cases, transporting a tablespace can be much easier and more efficient than unloading data from one database and loading it into another.

This option requires the same exact database object definitions to exist in each database. Furthermore, the data contents will be the same after you transport the tablespace (after which, of course, you can edit the data).

Transportable tablespaces are quite useful when data must be moved from database to database in an Oracle system. It is usually easier to copy files and run an IMP command on the destination database than it is to use SQL*Loader or a series of export files to accomplish the same thing. Furthermore, neither the source nor target database instance needs to be shut down in order to transport tablespaces.

Messaging software works by providing APIs to read and write formatted messages to and from a queue. An application can read or write messages to and from the queue from any platform supported by the software.

Messaging allows businesses to easily integrate disparate islands of data.

Messaging software provides many benefits for moving data, but primarily the benefit of simple, heterogeneous any-to-any connectivity among disparate platforms from the desktop to mainframes. Messaging allows businesses to easily integrate disparate islands of data in a time-independent manner. As they both use the message queue, two applications can communicate with each other even if they are not running at the same time.

Popular messaging software includes IBM's MQSeries, Microsoft's MSMQ, and Oracle's Advanced Queueing feature.

Other Methods

Of course, many other methods exist for moving data—from the simple, such as using a table editing tool to highlight and copy data, to the complex, such as writing programs to read the database and write to external files or directly to other databases.

Some DBMSs provide additional built-in methods for copying and moving data. For one example, see the sidebar "Oracle Transportable Tablespaces."

Distributed Databases

Sometimes simply moving data from one location to another is not sufficient. Instead, the data needs to be stored at, and accessible from, various locations throughout an organization. In this situation, a distributed database is required.

A *distributed database* permits data to reside at different physical locations in different databases, perhaps using different DBMS software on different operating systems. Consider, for example, an organization with retail outlets that implements a distributed database system. Each retail outlet would have a database, and the headquarters would house a central database. With networking technology and the distributed capabilities of the DBMS, data could be accessed and modified at any location from any location. Furthermore, you could specify which locations have update, or even read, access to certain databases.

In summary, the location of data in a networked environment does require an analysis of many design considerations for fast access time, high integrity, and easy maintainability. The basic premise of distributed database technology is to provide uniform access to data that is logically related but physically distributed in multiple locations. There are multiple types and variations in the way that a distributed database can be implemented.

The characteristics of a distributed environment differ by DBMS

The degree of database distribution that can be achieved is defined by the technology and capabilities of the DBMS in use. The following characteristics of a distributed environment differ by DBMS.

- *Autonomy* represents the degree to which sites within the distributed database implementation can operate independently. An intermediate level of autonomy exists when each site can voluntarily share their data. In contrast, tight coupling represents a high degree of autonomy because each site in the distributed environment has complete knowledge of the state of the system and can control the processing of user requests that span data at multiple sites.

- *Isolation* defines whether each site is aware of the other sites in the distributed environment or if each site is a stand-alone server, unaware of the other sites.

- *Transparency* refers to the shielding of the data location from users and applications.

Each DBMS delivers functionality to implement distributed databases with differing degrees of autonomy, isolation, and transparency. To set up an efficient and effective distributed database environment, the DBA must thoroughly understand the capabilities of the DBMS. Furthermore, the DBA must offer guidance to the application developers. In a system with distribution transparency, the developers need not know the location of data; more typically, distributed programming requires the programmer to explicitly code a connection to a database server location before accessing data from that location.

A distributed database can be set up as a single database or as multiple databases. With the single database setup, a single DBMS process controls all data access. A multidatabase setup, on the other hand, provides multiple independent DBMS processes, each controlling access to its own local database.

A multidatabase setup can be federated or unfederated. A *federated* multidatabase setup spreads control among the distributed databases. The DBA can control each local database component of the federation to determine what data is stored there and who can access it. An *unfederated* multidatabase scheme centralizes the control of these issues. Typically, unfederated multidatabase setups are homogeneous, whereas federated multidatabase setups are heterogeneous.

Setting Up a Distributed Environment

Distributed data can reside on database servers as well as on client nodes.

A distributed DBMS allows data to be physically located on more than one DBMS and at more than one location. Truly distributed data can reside on database servers as well as on client nodes. The more distributed the data, and the closer the data is to the requester, the better the performance is likely to be. However, as data is distributed to more locations, it becomes much more difficult to manage and administer. From a maintenance perspective, the administration required for a large number of desktop DBMSs is quite difficult. A real-life distributed database implementation will often consist of data residing at multiple server locations; and sometimes on client nodes, too.

The DBA must understand the distribution capabilities of the DBMS.

From the perspective of the DBA, some of the most difficult aspects of implementing a distributed database are designing it and setting it up. The DBA's first task is to understand the distribution capabilities of the DBMS. Can it participate in federated or unfederated systems? What additional software is required to support distributed databases? Does the DBMS support two-phase COMMIT? What types of networking protocols are required?

The DBA will need to work with network administrators to assure that the company's networks are properly configured for supporting distributed databases. The DBMS will require configuration parameters to be set that enable distribution and that outline the network location for the remote databases.

Up to this point, we have discussed the physical implementation details. But what about the database design aspects of distributed databases? What data goes where—and why? Suppose you are setting up a distributed database such as depicted in Figure 18-3.

In our sample distributed database, the data resides in Seattle, Washington, and in Sydney, Australia. How does the DBA decide which data should be stored in Seattle and which data should be stored in Sydney? How does the DBA provide the proper authorization and configuration such that users can access the required data regardless of its location?

Data should reside at the server where it is most likely to be accessed.

Frankly, there are no hard and fast rules that answer these questions. There are, though, many guidelines that can be followed. First, data should reside at the server where it is most likely to be accessed. The DBA should analyze the intended usage of data to optimize application performance by reducing transmission costs. For example, data used most frequently in Seattle should reside on the Seattle database server and data used more often in Sydney should reside at the Sydney site.

However, data placement decisions are usually not that simple. In many distributed systems, data may reside in two or three locations, but be accessible from many other locations. What if a certain subset of data is used most frequently in Singapore? Once again, store that data on the closest database server—in our example, Sydney is closer to Singapore than to Seattle.

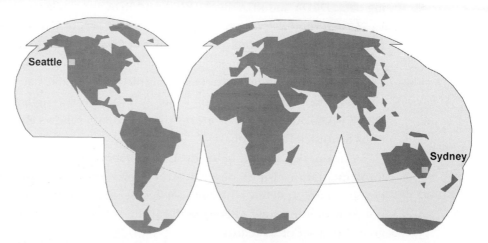

Figure 18-3   *A sample distributed database implementation*

An additional concern arises when data usage is spread almost evenly between the two sites. What if data is required 50% of the time by Sydney processes and 50% of the time by Seattle processes? In such cases, the DBA must choose one location over the other or choose to keep replicas at each site. If replication is not an option, place the data at the location that is most easily managed and monitor the performance of all distributed accesses very closely.

As a DBA, you will need to provide usage guidelines for distributed databases to the application development teams. Such guidelines should cover where data is located, the performance impact of accessing distributed data, and how to optimize distributed relational access. Some of these guidelines will depend on the DBMS implementation, whereas others, such as the following, will be DBMS-independent.

- Minimize network traffic by retrieving only the data that is needed; that is, request no columns or rows in addition to what are absolutely required by the application process.

- Use methods that encourage sending data over network in blocks instead of one row at a time.

- Access local data instead of remote data whenever it is possible to do so.

Data Distribution Standards

There are two common standards supported by the major DBMSs for distributing data: DRDA and RDA. Both DRDA and RDA are similar in their goals.

Distributed Relational Database Architecture, or DRDA, is IBM's protocol for accessing distributed data regardless of its physical location. DRDA provides methods of coordinating communication among distributed locations. This allows applications to access multiple remote tables at various locations and have them appear to the end user as if they were a logical whole. When a DBMS is DRDA-compliant, it means that the DBMS follows the DRDA specifications for distributed databases.

DRDA is IBM's protocol for accessing distributed data regardless of its physical location.

A distinction should be made, however, between the architecture and the implementation. DRDA describes the architecture for distributed data and nothing more. It defines the rules for accessing the distributed data, but it does not provide the actual APIs to perform the access. DRDA is not an actual program, but a set of standards.

RDA is a set of protocols developed by the ISO and ANSI standards committees.

Remote Database Access, or RDA, is a competing set of protocols developed by the ISO and ANSI standards committees. RDA was built to work with a subset of SQL that is available to most DBMSs.

RDA is used to establish a remote connection between a client and a server. The client interfaces to a process that controls data transfers to and from the database. The goal of RDA is to enable applications to interconnect with heterogeneous databases and environments.

As an alternative to DRDA or RDA, a gateway product can be used to access distributed data. Gateways are comprised of at least two components—one for each distributed location—that communicate with each other to permit data to be accessed.

Accessing Distributed Data

Not all methods of access are supported by each DBMS.

The DBA must understand the type of access supported by the DBMS and help the application developers match the DBMS capabilities to application requirements. There are many different types of access possible, but not all are supported by each DBMS, and further limitations will exist with heterogeneous implementations.

The simplest type of distributed database access is a *remote request.* This consists of a single request to a single location within a single unit of work. A remote request allows developers to operate within one DBMS while referring to a different DBMS. This approach is the easiest—but least flexible—method of coding distributed access.

A more complex type of distributed access is called *remote unit of work.* It takes place when a single application program accesses data from multiple locations, but not within the same unit of work. The programmer must know where data is located and build units of work that access data by location. In this scenario,

- Each request must be for a single location.
- Each unit of work can contain multiple SQL statements.
- Each unit of work must access data from a single location only.

Thus, multiple SQL requests per unit of work are permitted, but only to one DBMS per SQL request.

Table 18-1   *Levels of Distributed Database Support*

Distributed access	SQL stmts per UOW	DBMSs per UOW	DBMSs per SQL stmt
Remote request	1	1	1
Remote unit of work	>1	1	1
Distributed unit of work	>1	>1	1
Distributed request	>1	>1	>1

The next step is to remove the unit of work limitation, so that each unit of work can access data from multiple locations. This type of access is referred to as *distributed unit of work*. In this case, more than one DBMS can be accessed per unit of work. Multiple SQL statements can read and/or modify data at multiple database servers within a single unit of work.

The final and most robust form of distributed access is the *distributed request,* where a single SQL statement accesses data from more than one location at a time. Thus, a SQL statement can access multiple database servers, and multiple SQL requests, both distributed and nondistributed, can be contained within a single unit of work. This is the most flexible level of distributed database access.

Frequently an additional product is required to support a distributed request, such as IBM's DataJoiner. Table 18-1 outlines the different types of distributed data access, using the names given to them by the DRDA protocols.

Two-Phase COMMIT

The DBMS must be able to ensure that the modifications are treated as a single operation.

In order to modify distributed data across two different platforms, the DBMS must be able to ensure that the modifications are treated as a single operation. As with any unit of work, all of the SQL statements within the COMMIT scope either succeed or fail. Therefore, for each distributed COMMIT, either the results of all operations are applied to each database, or none of the results are applied—regardless of the database and its location. This requires a two-phase COMMIT, where one phase is the preparation and the other is the COMMIT.

Distributed two-phase COMMIT enables application programs to update data in multiple database servers within a single unit of work. The two-phase COMMIT process coordinates the COMMITs across the multiple platforms. The two-phase COMMIT provides a consistent outcome, guaranteeing the integrity of the data across platforms, regardless of communication or system failures.

One of the database servers acts as the coordinator of the two-phase COMMIT, while the other database servers are participants.

During the preparation phase, each participant prepares for a COMMIT. Each participant informs the coordinator when log records are successfully written and indicates that it is ready to COMMIT changes. When all participants are ready to COMMIT, the second phase, the actual COMMIT, begins. This phase is implemented as a series of communications between the coordinator and its subordinate participants. During the COMMIT phase, success is presumed, even in the case of system failure. Because all participants have elected to continue the COMMIT, success can be presumed with no danger of data integrity violations. However, if any participant fails to COMMIT, the coordinator will need to roll back the changes for all participants.

Whenever applications perform multisite updates within a single unit of work, a two-phase COMMIT must be used to ensure data integrity.

Distributed Performance Problems

The biggest threat to distributed performance is network traffic.

Performance can be particularly troubling in a distributed database environment. As with any system that relies on network activity, the biggest threat to performance is network traffic. The more data that must be sent along the network, the greater the potential for performance problems.

Performance in a distributed environment is defined by throughput and response time.

But let's back up for second. Recall the definition of performance given in Chapter 9: "Database performance is the optimization of resource use to increase throughput and minimize contention, enabling the largest possible workload to be processed." Performance in a distributed environment also is defined by throughput and response time. However, the requester and the server emphasize different aspects of this definition.

The server views performance primarily in terms of throughput. Remember that throughput is the amount of work that can be done in a unit of time. The server must serve multiple requesters. The more requesters that can be serviced, the better the server is performing. The requester, however, views performance more in terms of response time. Response time is the amount of time required to accomplish a predefined set of work. Response time is a more useful indicator to the end user because he is the one who is waiting for a result—the longer the response time, the longer it takes to complete the user's job.

To analyze the throughput of a distributed database request, the DBA must inspect the entire throughput chain required to satisfy that request. Failure to analyze the performance of any one component can result in performance degradation. The throughput chain for a request includes every piece of hardware and software, and every configuration that must be traversed to deliver service to that end user. Typical components of a throughput chain include

- The computer hardware, local operating system, networking software, and local databases for the requester
- The network hardware, wiring, gateways, routers, and hubs
- Any middleware or transaction processing system used by the requester or the server
- The computer hardware, local operating system, networking software, and databases on the server
- Disk storage and storage management software

Each link in the chain is required to complete a given transaction. The best throughput that any given configuration can achieve is always confined by the slowest component on the chain. To tune distributed performance, the DBA should expend more effort on the weaker links in the throughput chain.

Summary

Data is likely to reside in global locations within your organization.

Because data is required at various points throughout an organization, the DBA must understand the various ways of moving data around. This can involve copying data from place to place—either complete copies of the data or a subset of the data. Utilities such as LOAD and UNLOAD, IMPORT and EXPORT, are ideal for accomplishing many of these tasks.

Sometimes the database environment must be designed such that logically related data is distributed to different physical locations. This is a distributed database. The DBA must be capable of designing distributed databases given knowledge of the capabilities of the DBMS, the needs of the organization, and the locations that must be supported.

Data is likely to reside in global locations within your organization. As a DBA, it is your duty to ensure its integrity, efficiency, accessibility, viability, and recoverability.

Review

1. Why is a two-phase COMMIT necessary when data is modified at two locations within a single unit of work?

2. Describe a technique for unloading data from multiple tables into a single UNLOAD file.

3. What techniques can be used to limit the amount of data that is unloaded?

4. What is the biggest threat to efficient performance for a distributed database system?

5. Describe the two-phase COMMIT process.

6. How can LOAD and UNLOAD be used to maintain test beds of data for applications?

7. How are nulls handled when loading data into a table using the LOAD utility?

8. Name and define the three capabilities used to describe distributed technology and databases.

9. What is the difference between replication and propagation?

10. What issues and constructs can cause data integrity problems after a LOAD?

Bonus Question

Read the following paragraph and describe a distributed database implementation that would make sense for the data discussed. Keep in mind the concepts of data placement for distribution efficiency as you outline where each type of data should be kept.

Acme Corporation is headquartered in Phoenix, AZ. It has distribution centers located in Los Angeles, New York City, London, and Tokyo. Acme wishes to build a distributed database for tracking goods from its distribution centers to its retail outlets.

All edible goods are distributed out of the Los Angeles distribution center, except for meat, fish, and poultry, which are distributed from every location. Electronics are distributed out of New York City only. European goods are distributed out of the London center and Asia-Pacific goods are shipped out of the Tokyo center. All other goods can be distributed from any distribution center.

Suggested Reading

Bell, David, and Jane Grimson. *Distributed Database Systems.* Wokingham, England: Addison-Wesley (1992). ISBN 0-201-54400-8

Bobak, Angelo R. *Distributed and Multi-Database Systems.* New York, NY: Bantam Intertext (1993). ISBN 0-553-09156-5

Burleson, Donald K. *Managing Distributed Databases.* New York, NY: John Wiley & Sons (1994). ISBN 0-471-08623-1

Chorafas, Dimitris N., and Heinrich Steinmann. *Solutions for Networked Databases.* San Diego, CA: Academic Press (1993). ISBN 0-12-174060-9

Hackathorn, Richard D. *Enterprise Database Connectivity.* New York, NY: John Wiley & Sons (1993). ISBN 0-471-57802-9

Podcameni, Silvio, et al. *Distributed Relational Database.* Upper Saddle River, NJ: Prentice Hall PTR (1996). ISBN 0-13-570797-8

Schur, Stephen G. *The Database Factory.* New York, NY: John Wiley & Sons (1994). ISBN 0-471-55844-3

19

Data Warehouse Administration

A data warehouse is designed and optimized for a specific type of processing.

The ongoing quest for more and better business intelligence has caused many organizations to develop data warehouses and data marts to serve their analytical needs. Although, at the most basic level, a data warehouse is simply a database that has been designed and optimized for a specific type of processing, DBAs need to administer them differently from typical databases. This chapter outlines why this is so.

What Is a Data Warehouse?

So, just what is a data warehouse, and why should you treat it differently from a DBA perspective? William H. Inmon, recognized as the father of the data warehouse, defines "data warehouse" in his book *Building the Data Warehouse* as follows:

Data Warehouse: A collection of integrated, subject-oriented databases designed to support the DSS function, where each unit of data is specific to some moment of time. The data warehouse contains atomic data and lightly summarized data.

But what exactly does that definition mean? Let's break it down.

- *Subject-oriented.* Data pertains to a particular subject instead of the many subjects pertinent to the company's ongoing operations.

- *Integrated.* Although the data can originate from a variety of disparate sources, the data within a data warehouse is merged into a coherent whole.

- *Time-variant.* Data stored within a data warehouse is identified with a particular time period.

- *Nonvolatile.* Data is stable in a data warehouse. Although data can be added, data cannot be removed. This provides a consistent picture of the business for analysis.

Data warehousing is the process of extracting, integrating, transforming, and cleansing data and storing it in a consolidated database.

For our purposes, data warehousing can be defined as the process of extracting, integrating, transforming, and cleansing data and storing it in a consolidated database. Once consolidated and made available, the data warehouse becomes the only data source that management should access for decision making.

What, then, is a data mart? A data mart is basically a departmental data warehouse defined for a single business unit or area. Actually, there is no universally agreed-on difference between a data warehouse and a data mart. A data mart is not necessarily smaller than an enterprise data warehouse. It may be smaller, but size is determined based on business needs. For example, departmental analysis at the business-unit level may require more historical information than cross-department, enterprisewide analysis.

At any rate, both data marts and data warehouses need to be treated differently than traditional database systems from a DBA perspective.

Analytical vs. Transaction Processing

Data warehouses are designed for analytical processing.

The key difference between a traditional database and a database designed as a data warehouse is the type of processing each supports. The traditional database is designed primarily for transaction processing—that is, supporting the transactions that are required for business operations to be conducted. Transactions read and write data on a regular basis. In contrast, data warehouses are designed for analytical processing—that is, supporting the business intelligence and knowledge discovery needs of the organization. Analytical operations are read-intensive with very few, if any, write operations required.

Terms that are commonly used to describe analytical processing include decision support, DSS, OLAP, data mining, and information center queries. Each of these activities is read-intensive, consisting of queries that sift through the data looking for patterns and trends.

DSS stands for *Decision Support System,* which is a read-only database designed for analytical processing.

OLAP uses a multidimensional view of detail, summary, and aggregate data.

OLAP stands for *online analytical processing*. With OLAP technology, end users can navigate through a data warehouse to derive intelligence from data through interactive and iterative queries against the warehoused data. OLAP uses a multidimensional view of detail, summary, and aggregate data to access information for further analysis. The key term here is *multidimensional*. A dimension is a structural attribute viewed as similar by the end user. For example, years, quarters, months, days, and so on make up the time dimension.

A *dimension* is a modifier of the basic fact that is being analyzed. Examples of *facts* include sales amounts, inventory totals, and expense amounts. Each fact depends on multiple dimensions. For example, sales amounts will differ by geographic region, time, product, and so on. OLAP permits multidimensional analysis of facts by applying complex calculations across dimensions. Additionally, OLAP provides many other capabilities, including analysis and trending over time, subsetting of data, drill-down through varying levels of detail, "reach-through" to operational data, and data comparison methods.

The bottom line is that OLAP, in contrast to OLTP, focuses on analytical, rather than transactional, processing. Table 19-1 compares OLAP and OLTP characteristics.

Table 19-1 *OLAP vs. OLTP*

Characteristics	OLAP	OLTP
Scope of work	Entire database	Single transaction
Amount of data	Individual rows	Groups of rows
Nature of data	Derivative	Primitive
Volatility of data	Low—rarely updated	High—regularly updated
Expected response time	Subsecond	Minutes, perhaps hours
Machine usage	Dynamic and unpredictable	Stable and predictable
Processing priorities	User flexibility	High performance and availability
Type of access	Undefined and dynamic	Predefined and static

Data mining is the process of discovering heretofore-unknown information and patterns lurking within an organization's data. Data mining is fast becoming a requirement for the modern, competitive company. Data mining processes apply heuristic algorithms to historical data to automatically uncover patterns in the data. The quantity and quality of available data and the caliber of the pattern discovery algorithms determine the value of the data mining applications. Consequently, organizations that deploy data mining tend to store more data for longer periods.

OLAP and data mining are methods for searching out patterns in corporate data.

Both OLAP and data mining are methods for searching out patterns in corporate data. However, OLAP is user driven, while data mining is computer driven. This introduction to OLAP and data mining is necessarily brief—an entire book could be devoted to each of these subjects. The key from the DBA perspective is to plan for administering and managing the data warehouse databases in a manner consistent with their usage.

Information Center is an antiquated term that was used for DSS processing in the early 80s. Those readers who recall the proliferation of the Information Center in the 80s will associate it with data warehousing.

Administering the Data Warehouse

The issues of importance when managing a data warehouse differ from those of traditional database administration. Some of the tasks are equivalent, but the implementation and expectations are different.

Data warehouses are accessed mostly by read operations for analytical processing, whereas the traditional database is accessed by a mix of read and write operations for transactional processing. The data warehouse is strategic—it allows users to discover hidden trends and new ways of conducting business. The traditional database is tactical—it allows the business to conduct day-to-day operations.

Be aware of the complexity of data warehouses before undertaking any implementation project. Detailed knowledge of the applications accessing the databases that feed the data warehouse must be available. Be sure to allot development time for learning the complexities of the source systems. Furthermore, the documentation for production systems is often inadequate or nonexistent, so additional time can be lost just trying to understand what already exists. Furthermore, analyzing the source data to determine what level of data scrubbing is required is a time consuming task.

All of these issues must be factored into the task of data warehouse administration. Let's examine some of the different tasks required to administer data warehouses efficiently and effectively.

Too Much Focus on Technology?

A data warehouse project requires more than just sound technology.

When you're developing a data warehouse, be sure to include tools, people, and methods in your warehouse blueprint. Too often, the focus is solely on the technology and tools. A data warehouse project requires more than just sound technology. It needs careful planning and implementation (methods) as well as a means to learn from the efforts of others (people) through mentoring, consulting, education, seminars, and user groups.

Data Warehouse Design

When designing the data warehouse, be sure to create a physical design with the special needs of the data warehouse in mind, instead of just mimicking the design of similar production OLTP databases. For example, the data access requirements for file and table structures, indexes, and clustering sequences in a data warehouse differ from those of OLTP databases.

A common database design for the data warehouse is the star schema.

A common database design for the data warehouse is the *star schema*. This name derives from the pattern formed by the data model when it is diagrammed as in Figure 19-1. In a star schema design, a central fact table stores the primary business activity at the center of the star. This fact table is usually based on a numeric value or a group of numeric values. The fact table is surrounded by the dimensions that affect the activity, and the dimension tables make up the points of the star.

In this simple example, the revenue table is the fact table, and the five dimensions of the star are the movie, theater, customer, market, and time tables. As an end user, you may want to review revenue by any one, or perhaps a combination, of these dimensions.

The star schema is well suited for the design of data warehouses databases for the following reasons.

- The design is flexible enough to facilitate quick changes or additions as the data warehouse grows or the application changes.
- The design is easy to understand for both developers and end users.

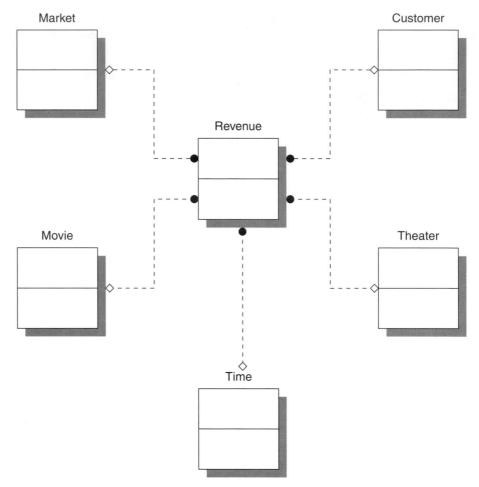

Figure 19-1 *The star schema*

- The design mimics the way end users typically think about and use their business data.
- The design is easily implemented as a physical database and results in efficient queries because many DBMSs are built to recognize and optimize star joins.

Sometimes additional details are required, and the star schema becomes a snowflake schema. A *snowflake schema* is a star schema in which the dimension tables have additional relationships. When additional tables are required that relate to one or more dimension tables, a snowflake schema is borne.

Of course, star schema and snowflake schema designs are not the only aspects of data warehouse design of concern to the DBA. To aid in the performance of certain regularly occurring queries, it is common for some portions of the data warehouse to be denormalized. Because a data warehouse is a read-only database, the DBA should consider the many denormalization options discussed in Chapter 4. Table 19-2 summarizes the various denormalization options to consider.

Proceed with caution when denormalizing the data warehouse design.

As you design the data warehouses, be alert for situations where denormalization may be beneficial. In general, denormalization speeds data retrieval, which may be desirable for a data warehouse. However, proceed with caution when denormalizing the data warehouse design. Denormalization is not mandatory simply because denormalized data is optimized for data access and the data warehouse is primarily "read-only." Because the data must be populated into the data warehouse at some point, a data warehouse is in actuality "read mostly," not read-only. Denormalized data is difficult to maintain and should be avoided if performance is acceptable. So, as with a traditional database implementation, denormalize only when a completely normalized design will not perform optimally.

Another consideration for the physical design of a data warehouse is *data compression*. Because data warehouses tend be substantial in size, compression can be used to reduce storage requirements. The performance impact of

Table 19-2   *Types of Denormalization*

Denormalization	Description
Prejoined tables	Used when the cost of joining is prohibitive
Report tables	Used when specialized critical reports are needed
Mirror tables	Used when tables are accessed concurrently by multiple types of environments
Split tables	Used when distinct groups use different parts of a table
Combined tables	Used to consolidate one-to-one or one-to-many relationships into a single table
Redundant data	Used to reduce the number of table joins required
Repeating groups	Used to reduce I/O and (possibly) storage
Derivable data	Used to eliminate calculations and algorithms
Speed tables	Used to make the processing of hierarchies more efficient
Physical denormalization	Used to optimize for specialized physical DBMS characteristics

compression will depend on the ability of your DBMS to compress data. Sometimes compression aids performance because more rows can be stored in the same amount of space and fewer I/Os are required.

Finally, the DBA should design the physical database for the data warehouse such that it encourages parallel operations. Due to the high volume of data that must be processed by the analytical queries typical of OLAP and DSS, performance is usually enhanced by parallel activities. Consider partitioning tablespaces to take advantage of parallelism features of the DBMS, and consider basing the partitions on the usage patterns of your data warehouse access. In addition, placing indexes and data tablespaces on different disk devices can help parallel tasks to operate more efficiently.

Data Movement

Establishing the data requirements demands a clear understanding of end-user needs.

A big part of any data warehousing effort is establishing the data requirements and then creating methods to capture and move the data into the warehouse. Without a clear understanding of end-user needs, the DBA will have great difficulty determining what data to move, never mind how to move it.

To establish what data is required, the DBA must elicit answers to two important questions:

- What is the purpose of the data warehouse?
- What are the results expected from the data warehouse?

The next step is to ferret out the required data from the OLTP systems and databases. The data warehouse team must understand each piece of data, including its source (where it is created and by whom), its relationship to other data elements, its meaning, and what it needs (if anything) to make it viable for inclusion in the data warehouse. All of this metadata should be captured and maintained so that unanticipated changes to the data in the OLTP systems after the data warehouse goes live can be accommodated.

If a source for the data cannot be found internally, you may need to purchase data from external suppliers and integrate it into your data warehouse.

After all data has been identified, as well as any transformations that are required, processes need to be established for the extraction and movement of the data. Typically, the extraction process gathers the data from the source OLTP databases and places it in an intermediate staging area. However, this still raw data may need to be transformed before it is placed into the data warehouse.

Tools can be used to assist including LOAD and UNLOAD utilities, import and export programs, propagation software, and ETL products. Be sure to include the cost of such software in your data warehousing budget and make sure that all DBAs needing to use this software are sufficiently trained.

Consistent Data Acquisition

As the data in operational systems changes, so must the data in the warehouse.

Businesses react and adapt to industry trends, with resulting changes to data. As the data in operational systems changes, so must the data in the warehouse. Over time, fields will be eliminated, meanings will change, sizes and types will change, and more. You must plan to keep track of physical data changes, as well as changes to the semantics of the data. Regardless of the type of change, you will need utilities, tools, and processes to keep on top of these issues and respond appropriately.

Data Cleansing

The quality of the data in the data warehouse is of utmost importance to the overall usefulness of the data warehouse. If the data is not reliable, or cannot be understood by the users, then the data warehouse will fail. In other words, data in the warehouse is only as good as its source. Failure to clean dirty data can result in the creation of a data outhouse instead of a data warehouse. Therefore, the data warehouse project requires data cleansing and scrubbing tasks to be defined and performed as the data is moved from other sources to the data warehouse.

Transform codes into meaningful values for the user.

Data scrubbing can be used to "clean" data as it is moved into the data warehouse. One component of data scrubbing is the transformation of codes into meaningful values for the user. For example, a CUSTOMER-CODE of 5 means nothing to the typical user, but a CUSTOMER-CODE of "Corporation" or "Individual" is usable and helpful.

A number of insidious data problems can reduce the usefulness of a data warehouse. We've all had the experience of looking at the contents of one of our major files or databases and knowing intuitively that the data is incorrect. There is just no way that an employee was born in 1999. And that next record looks bad, too. How could she have been born in 1979 but hired in 1978?

All too often, these types of data integrity problems are glossed over. "No one would actually take that information seriously, would they?" Well, maybe people won't, but computerized systems will. Incorrect information can be summarized, aggregated, or manipulated in some way, and then populated into another data element. When erroneous data elements are moved into the data warehouse and processed analytically, your company's business can be impacted. What if warehouse data is being analyzed to overhaul hiring practices? Erroneous data could impact employment decisions if enough of those hire and birth dates were inaccurate.

Never cover up data integrity problems.

Never cover up data integrity problems. Document them and bring them to the attention of your manager and the users who rely on the data. Usually, the business units using the data are authorized to modify and validate their business data.

Small data discrepancies can become statistically irrelevant when large volumes of data are averaged. However, averaging is not the only analytical function that is employed by analytical data warehouse queries. What about sums, medians, maximums, minimums, and other aggregate and scalar functions? Even further, can you actually prove that the scope of your data problems is as small as you think it is? The answer is probably no.

This is just one small example of the data integrity violations that many application systems allow into their production data stores. Some of the integrity violations may seem to be inexcusable. For example, most of us have encountered a SEX or GENDER column (or field) that stored everything from "*" to "!" to a blank. Shouldn't it be a simple matter to programmatically force the values to be either "M" or "F"? The short answer is yes, but this simplifies that matter too much, because certain information, by law, has to be optional.

The real problem is that a systematic manner of recording "unknown" values has not been employed. Every program that can modify data should be forced to record a special "unknown" indicator if a data value is not readily available at the time of data entry. Most relational DBMS products enable data columns to store a null to indicate "unknown" or "unavailable" information. Pre-relational DBMS products and data files do not have this option. However, some specific, standard default value can be chosen. The trick is to *standardize* the default value.

Standardization of "unknown" values can be a tedious process.

Standardization of "unknown" values can be a tedious process. Our primitive example used a data element with a simple domain of two valid values. Most data elements have domains that are considerably more complex. Determining which values are valid can be difficult for someone who is not intimately familiar with the application system that allowed the values to be inserted in the first place. Is "1895-01-01" a valid date for that field or is it a default for an "unknown" value?

Only an in-depth analysis of the programs and the metadata in the corporate repository can provide the answer. Nineteenth-century dates may be valid for birth dates, stock issuance dates, account inception dates, publication dates, and any number of other dates with long periods of "freshness." However, just because the program allows it to be entered does not mean it is actually a valid date! It is quite simple for a user to type in 1895 instead of 1985. If the data entry program is not intelligent enough to trap these types of errors, your systems will insert dirty data into production data stores. This type of data integrity problem is the most difficult to spot. It is quite likely that only the end user most familiar with the data could spot these types of problems.

So, what is the solution? Several techniques can be used, but the best approach is to foster an environment in which data is truly treated as a corporate asset. The problem is attracting the appropriate high-level management personnel who can implement a policy that values data. But now we are moving the discussion outside the scope of data warehousing and back to data administration. So, let's get back on track.

Transform the data into useful, queryable information.

A key part of the data movement activities for populating a data warehouse will involve the identification of invalid and coded data, and transforming that data into useful, queryable information. Automated ETL software can help you with this, but it cannot do it all for you.

Data Quality Issues

Maintaining data quality will be an ongoing concern. Both the end users and the data warehouse construction and maintenance team are responsible for promoting and fostering data quality. Data problems will be discovered not only throughout the development phase of the data warehouse but also throughout its useful life.

Establish a policy for the reporting and correction of data anomalies.

Be sure to establish a policy for how data anomalies are to be reported and corrected before the data warehouse is made generally available. Additionally, be sure to involve the end users in the creation and support of this policy; otherwise, it is doomed to fail. Remember, the end users understand the data better than anyone else in the organization, including the data warehouse developers and DBAs.

Do not underestimate the amount of time and effort that will be required to clean up dirty data. Understand the scope of the problems and the processes required to rectify those problems. Take into account the politics of your organization and the automated tools available. The more political the battle, the longer the task will take; the fewer tools available, the longer the task will take. Furthermore, if the tools you do have are not understood properly, the situation will probably be worse than having no tools at all.

Operational Problems

As the previous discussion makes clear, you will encounter problems in the operational systems feeding the data warehouse—problems that may have been running undetected for years. Your options for handling them are few:

- Ignore the problem with the understanding that the problem will exist in the data warehouse too.
- Fix the problem in the operational production system.
- Fix the problem during the data transformation phase of data warehouse population, if possible.

Of course, the second and third options are the favored approaches. Fixing the problem in the operational system is the best solution of all, but you will need to examine the budget and deadlines associated with the data warehouse project to determine if production problems can be remedied during the project. If not, you can fix the data problems as the data flows into the data warehouse. You should also plan on tracking the source of the errors in the production systems, if possible, so that a problem once identified is at least documented.

However, do not mix operational needs into the data warehouse project plan. When a data warehousing project is first initiated, the objectives may be a mix of operational and analytical/informational goals. This is a recipe for disaster. Redefine the project to concentrate on nonoperational, informational needs only. The primary reason for the existence of the data warehouse is to segregate operational processing from reporting.

Data Warehouse Scalability

As a data warehouse becomes accepted within the organization, demand for its services will grow. The need for new reports and summary tables increases, and the data warehouse can explode to several times its original size. Some industry surveys indicate that 60% to 70% of data warehouses are filled with duplicate or redundant data such as summary tables and indexes. This can more than double the disk storage required to store the data warehouse. The more users on the system and the more simultaneous the queries, the more potential for delays in response time. It is important, therefore, to architect the system so that it will be able to scale linearly with demand. The DBA can choose to use parallel processors, parallel databases, bitmapped indexes, data compression, and other techniques to provide better scalability.

Size Issues

One aspect of scalability is size. Many novices incorrectly assume that a data warehouse must be large. While it is true that many data warehouses are quite large and consume massive amounts of storage, a data warehouse can be small and still provide value to the organization. The reality is that size doesn't matter.

Data Warehouse Performance

Data warehouse performance is similar to overall database performance as discussed in Chapter 9. However, different aspects of performance are emphasized. In general, data warehouse performance can be viewed from four perspectives:

- *Extract performance*—how smoothly data is updated and refined in the warehouse

- *Data management*—quality of the data warehouse design and database maintenance

- *Query performance*—how well the database is tuned for analytical processing and how well each query is written

- *Server performance*—the configuration and performance of the hardware

A data warehouse is populated, at least in part, with data extracted from production systems. The efficiency with which data is extracted from the production system impacts the usability and performance of the data warehouse. The longer it takes to gather data and load it to the data warehouse, the longer the period that the data warehouse will not reflect current data. Moreover, that lack of currency can impact the usefulness of any data analysis performed on the data. It is therefore imperative to optimize the speed with which the data warehouse is loaded, unloaded, and accessed. High-speed database utilities can be used to optimize the flow of data throughout the life cycle of the data warehouse.

The design of the data warehouse is intrinsic to its viability. A data warehouse must be designed for easy access and analysis. The DBA must understand how the data is going to be accessed and design the database structures accordingly. With OLTP systems, dynamic activity occurs against live data. Many concurrent updates, inserts, deletes can be going on at any time. The way in which tables are indexed is probably the most crucial element of database design for OLTP systems. In contrast, the OLAP and DSS systems used for data warehousing are read-only systems with no (or limited) online modification capabilities—instead, data is loaded during the off-peak hours. Therefore, the data warehouse may require many finely tuned indexes for daily analytical queries and fewer (perhaps no) indexes during the loads. The DBA must carefully plan to balance the efficiency of the queries versus the efficiency of the load processes.

The data warehouse indexes do not have to be the same indexes that exist in the operational system, even if the data warehouse is nothing more than an exact replica or snapshot of the operational databases. The DBA must optimize the indexes, based on the access patterns and query needs of the decision support environment of the data warehouse. Additionally, consider using bitmap indexes for data warehouses to optimize the performance of your DSS applications.

Furthermore, from a database design perspective, methods for ensuring data integrity during data warehouse operations are not needed. Because data is cleansed and scrubbed during the data transformation process, implementing data integrity mechanisms such as referential integrity, triggers, and check constraints on data warehouse tables is not efficient. Even without a comprehensive cleansing, the data in the warehouse will be as good as the data in the source operational systems (which should utilize RI and check constraints).

The data warehouse is a decision support vehicle. Always remember that the data warehouse is a decision support vehicle. Although the data will be updated and summarized periodically, it should not be updated by the DSS users. If your design calls for a data warehouse in which all the data is modified immediately as it is changed in production, you need to rethink your data warehouse design.

Consider starting data warehouse databases in read-only mode if your DBMS permits. Issuing a START command to enable read-only mode can have the additional effect of eliminating locking on the read-only databases. Of course, when the data warehouse is refreshed, the databases have to be restarted in read-write mode.

From the query performance perspective, everything is different in the data warehouse environment. Subsecond response time is not expected—indeed, a query can run all day long if the results of that query are expected to deliver significant analytical insight. That does not mean that the DBA does not need to monitor data warehouse query performance. It simply means that the goals of monitoring DSS queries are different. The DBA should examine trends instead of absolutes.

For example, in a data warehouse it would be interesting to note that queries running between 3:00 P.M. and 4:00 P.M. from the finance department on expense data average between 10 and 25 seconds response time. The DBA can then examine the daily response time by time ranges to determine whether performance is falling within expected ranges or not. If query response time suddenly and consistently jumps for certain time ranges, the DBA may need to help end users write more efficient queries. Alternatively, he could change the data warehouse implementation to better support the users by building indexes or transforming data by aggregation or summarization, for example.

Because data warehouses are read-only in nature, you should be able to run DSS and OLAP queries using dirty reads. Recall from Chapter 5 that a dirty read is implemented with the UNCOMMITTED READ isolation level. With this isolation level, queries might read data that never actually exists in the database, because the data has been changed by another process but is not yet committed. This is rarely a concern in the data warehouse because of its read-only nature.

The server on which the data warehouse resides requires peak performance around the clock, but this demand is mitigated by the difference between OLTP and OLAP/DSS processing. However, the server hardware and configuration should not become a bottleneck for data warehouse performance, and as such, must be monitored and tuned.

Organizations should use an agent-based performance monitor that collects, analyzes, and stores thousands of performance measures; is configurable for multiple environments; and offers both real-time and historical perspectives on viewing all critical metrics. In this manner, organizations can implement an integrated database performance solution that is capable of monitoring and managing the performance of the following:

- Relational databases in Windows, UNIX, and mainframe environments
- Servers in distributed environments
- Entire enterprise network
- Distributed client/server transactions

Automated Summary Tables

Most experts agree that aggregating records in a data warehouse can palpably enhance the performance of large data warehousing applications. This is so

Aggregating records can palpably enhance the performance of large data warehousing applications.

because the vast amount of detailed information that exists in most data warehouses cannot be easily understood. Summarizing the data into logical groups makes it easier to be assimilated and analyzed in a cogent manner.

> The single most dramatic way to affect performance in a large data warehouse is to provide a proper set of aggregate (summary) records that coexist with the primary base records.[1]

However, summarizing data poses several problems. First, summarizing data can require an enormous amount of processing. Then, once summarized, the data must be stored, which takes up valuable disk space. Even more troubling is the problem of identifying what data should be aggregated.

Many modern DBMSs provide the ability to automate aggregation using automated summary tables, or *materialized views*. The basic concept is to create a new aggregated table from a base table by using basic SQL functions such as COUNT, SUM, AVG, MIN, or MAX. The result is a table that is aggregated at a higher-level dimension.

The DBA controls the creation of summary tables.

Regardless of the actual DBMS implementation, the basic idea is that the DBA controls the creation of summary tables. The summary table is defined by means of a query using SQL functions. Users do not need to even know that summary tables exist. The DBMS optimizer can determine when using a summary table can optimize a query written against the detail data and then automatically rewrite the query to use the summary table. Furthermore, in most cases, the DBMS automatically maintains aggregates. In other words, when underlying data changes, the DBMS automatically updates the summary table data.

In general, automated summary tables can significantly optimize data warehouse performance. However, the DBA will need to monitor which aggregates are used most frequently to ensure that the proper automated summary tables are built. Additionally, the DBA will need to plan for additional disk usage to support the aggregated data.

Data Freshness

Data warehouse processes must be set up to keep data up-to-date.

Because data is constantly changing in the OLTP systems, data warehouse processes must be set up to keep data up-to-date. As business users analyze data in the warehouse, the freshness of the data is an issue. The results of an analytical

---

1. Kimball, Ralph. *The Data Warehouse Toolkit.* New York, NY: John Wiley & Sons (1996).

query issued against data that is up-to-date as of yesterday are likely to be more useful than the same query run against month-old data.

The DBA must establish a means for the business users to determine the freshness of the data. Whenever new or updated data is loaded into the data warehouse, the business users must be capable of ascertaining the validity date of that data. Think of it like the date that is stamped on a carton of milk.

However, do not be confused into thinking that only a completely up-to-date data warehouse is of use. When examining data for patterns and trends, the freshness of the data may be irrelevant—or, perhaps, mostly irrelevant. The importance of data freshness will vary from data element to data element, from business unit to business unit, and from query to query.

The bottom line, though, is that business users should be given an easy way to establish when the data was last loaded and how fresh the data is.

Data Content

The data warehouse administrator may need to provide metadata on the contents of the data warehouse. This metadata could include the types of data being stored, which types of data change most frequently, and how fast certain types of data are growing. Keeping track of growth patterns helps to determine the areas of the data warehouse that may require attention in terms of storage allocation, reorganization, or redesign.

Develop methods to analyze and verify data integrity and relationships in the data warehouse.

Furthermore, it is possible that no matter how closely you manage the population of the data warehouse, invalid or inappropriate data will be loaded. Developing methods to analyze and verify data integrity and relationships in the data warehouse is a worthwhile endeavor.

The primary value of the data warehouse is in its data content. Therefore, it is good practice for the DBA to gain as much understanding of that data content as possible.

Data Usage

A data warehouse management task that is not associated with traditional database administration is the identification of unused data. Maintaining certain data in the warehouse does not make sense when certain thresholds or conditions are met. This situation may occur because of usage reasons (data is no longer used by the business), technology reasons (reaching a capacity limit), regulatory reasons (change in regulations or laws), or business reasons (restructuring data or instituting different processes).

A data warehouse is usually a very large consumer of disk storage. Sometimes users go overboard when designing a data warehouse and store more data than is required. The data warehouse DBA must deploy methods to examine what data has been accessed and how frequently. The DBA should ascertain from the business users whether such inactive data is still required.

If large amounts of unused data are identified, the DBA may decide to remove the data from the warehouse. Such action should not be taken indiscriminately. Only after verifying that the data has been unused for at least a year—to take into account seasonal access variations—should any action be taken on that data.

Purged data should be stored for a period of time.

The unused data may then be purged from the data warehouse or perhaps moved to a cheaper storage media (tape, optical disk, or CDR, for example). Of course, purged data should be stored for a period of time to assure that it was not purged in error.

The capability to track data warehouse activity is a useful administrative goal. For example, the DBA may opt to profile usage on a daily basis, and then summarize it by day of the week, week, or month. Usage by business unit or department is also a useful statistic. The more you can track data at discrete levels—even down to the column level—the better. Furthermore, this information can be coupled with performance monitoring statistics to gauge response time against what was actually accessed. In general, the more you know about who is using what data and when, the better you will be able to manage the data warehouse environment.

Financial Chargeback

In most organizations, data warehouse projects are managed by multiple departments, each of which has its own financial goals. Data warehouse DBAs should ensure that they can charge back appropriate costs to business units and users so that they can meet financial reporting requirements. An integrated solution is required that monitors IT costs by providing critical chargeback services that track information resources used organizationwide.

Measure and track every request made to the data warehouse.

For chargeback purposes, you should consider measuring and tracking every request made to the data warehouse, including who requested the data, the number of rows returned by the request, the CPU cycles spent to return the data, and which tables were accessed. Depending on your particular organizational needs, you may also wish to track the specific time of day the request was made. Some organizations choose to charge different rates based on the activity in the system at specific times.

Even if your organization chooses not to actually bill departments by usage, it can make sense to establish a financial chargeback system to demonstrate the value of the data warehouse to the business units that use it the most.

Backup and Recovery

The DBA must create a backup and recovery plan for the data warehouse even though most access is read-only. Some novices mistakenly view backup and recovery as a non-issue for data warehouses, but this is simply not the case. Data is moved into the data warehouse on a consistent basis—some of it from external sources that might not be easily duplicated.

Furthermore, if warehouse data is lost due to some type of failure, the production data from which it was gathered may no longer exist in the same form. Perhaps the production database was purged to provide space for more transactions. If the data was not archived it will not be able to be reproduced, and even if it was archived, it may be difficult to restore. In addition, data in the data warehouse typically exists in different forms than production data. Data may have been cleansed, transformed, or aggregated before being populated into the data warehouse. Such data may be difficult or impossible to recreate. Furthermore, data warehouses often contain external data that, if lost, may have to be purchased again, creating an unnecessary financial drain on the company.

So, for all of the reasons you need to provide a backup and recovery plan for traditional databases, you need to do the same for the data warehouse databases. Of course, the backups need only be taken whenever data is added to the data warehouse.

Backup and recovery of the data warehouse needs special consideration.

Indeed, backup and recovery needs special consideration within the context of the data warehouse. The data warehouse should have a backup and recovery strategy that will enable the organization to recover all essential data in an emergency. Data warehouses are becoming just as essential to businesses as transaction-oriented databases.

Depending on the size and nature of the data warehouse, you may decide not to back up particular pieces of the data warehouse because you can refresh the data more efficiently. Such cases, however, are more the exception than the rule. Review the cost/benefit of each data warehouse and data mart, keeping in mind how often the data is updated or refreshed and how long a recovery would take to implement.

Finally, disaster recovery requirements must not be overlooked. Organizations are becoming more and more dependent on the information that a data warehouse provides, thereby raising the criticality of data warehouse applications. This means the data warehouse must be treated like any other critical system in terms of disaster recovery planning.

Don't Operate in a Vacuum!

The DBA must be aware of the business requirements of the data warehouse and ensure that these needs are met. This is a challenge, but it is simple when compared to the challenge of keeping the data warehouse accurate and available in light of changing operational systems.

As business needs change, operational systems change. When operational databases and files change, the data warehouse will be affected as well. When a data warehouse is involved, however, both the operational database and the data warehouse must be analyzed for the impact of changing any data formats. This is the case because the data warehouse stores historical data that you might not be able to change to a new format. Before any changes are made to the operational system, the data warehouse team must be prepared to accept the new format as input to the data warehouse and to either maintain multiple data formats for the changed data element or to implement a conversion mechanism as part of the data transformation process.

Conversion can result in lost or confusing data.

Be aware, though, that conversion can result in lost or confusing data. When undertaking a conversion, it is wise to plan thoroughly and automate the process as much as possible with tested, trusted tools and scripts. Relying solely on human conversion will almost surely result in errors to the data.

Summary

Data warehouses can provide organizations with a competitive advantage as users begin to analyze data in conjunction with business trends. Once a data warehouse has been implemented, you cannot turn back because your users will be hooked, your organization will be more profitable, and you'll have the satisfaction of contributing to the success of the business.

DBAs whose duty it is to manage their company's data warehouse need to gain an understanding of the analytical nature of data warehousing. Many of the tasks required to support a data warehouse are similar to the tasks required to support a traditional, OLTP-focused database. However, there are differences that need to be understood and built into your data warehouse administration policies and procedures.

Managing and administering a data warehouse requires a combination of knowledgeable people, full-featured tools, and robust methods. Only through the integration of these disparate resources can the DBA assure that the data warehouse will be built and managed effectively.

Review

1. What is the difference between a data warehouse and a data mart?

2. Is it necessary to develop a backup and recovery plan for the data warehouse since it is a read-only environment?

3. Describe a few data cleansing techniques that may need to be applied to data before it can be loaded to the data warehouse.

4. When designing a data warehouse, how should problems that are identified in the operational OLTP systems be handled?

5. Describe the star schema and why it is an effective design for data warehouse databases.

6. What are the four perspectives of data warehouse performance management?

7. When might data need to be purged from the data warehouse?

8. What is the difference between OLAP and data mining?

9. Discuss the various options that must be considered specifically when creating the physical design of the data warehouse.

10. Denormalization is always a good option for data warehouse databases: True or False.

Suggested Reading

Barquin, Ramon, and Herb Edelstein, eds. *Planning and Designing the Data Warehouse.* Upper Saddle River, NJ: Prentice Hall (1997). ISBN 0-13-255746-0

Bigus, Joseph P. *Data Mining with Neural Networks.* New York, NY: McGraw-Hill (1996). ISBN 0-07-005779-6

Devlin, Barry. *Data Warehouse from Architecture to Implementation.* Reading, MA: Addison-Wesley (1997). ISBN 0-201-96245-2

Hackney, Douglas. *Understanding and Implementing Successful Data Marts.* Reading, MA: Addison-Wesley (1997). ISBN 0-201-18380-3

Inmon, W. H. *Building the Data Warehouse.* 2nd ed. New York, NY: John Wiley & Sons (1996). ISBN 0-471-14161-5

Inmon, W. H., and Richard Hackathorn. *Using the Data Warehouse.* New York, NY: John Wiley & Sons (1994). ISBN 0-471-05966-8

Inmon, W. H., Claudia Imhoff, et al. *Building the Operational Data Store.* New York, NY: John Wiley & Sons (1996). ISBN 0-471-12822-8

Inmon, W. H., John A. Zachman, et al. *Data Stores, Data Warehousing and the Zachman Framework.* New York, NY: McGraw-Hill (1997). ISBN 0-07-031429-2

Kimball, Ralph. *The Data Warehouse Toolkit.* New York, NY: John Wiley & Sons (1996). ISBN 0-471-15337-0

Lewis, William J. *Data Warehousing and E-Commerce.* Upper Saddle River, NJ: Prentice Hall (2001). ISBN 0-13-091154-2

Poe, Vidette. *Building a Data Warehouse for Decision Support.* Upper Saddle River, NJ: Prentice Hall (1996). ISBN 0-13-371121-8

Sprague, Ralph H., and Hugh J. Watson, eds. *Decision Support Systems: Putting Theory Into Practice.* Englewood Cliffs, NJ: Prentice Hall (1993). ISBN 0-13-036229-8

Turban, Efraim. *Decision Support and Expert Systems.* Englewood Cliffs, NJ: Prentice Hall (1995). ISBN 0-02-421701-8

20

Database Connectivity

Installing the DBMS and creating databases is a vitally important part of the DBA's job. However, if the DBMS is not connected to the network, no one will ever be able to access the data.

Client/Server Computing

This section offers a short introduction to client/server computing. The DBA must possess an understanding of the terms commonly used in a client/server processing setting to assure database access in a distributed business environment.

A Historical Look

In the early days of computing, computers required large amounts of power and resources to run. Batch processing was the only operating mode, and users received printed reports as their only source of information. Mainframe programmers communicated with computers through punched cards. As technology progressed in the 1970s, online processing gave the user more power and closer availability to data. In the 1980s and 1990s, personal computers became widely available and affordable. Inexpensive software accelerated the growth of the PC, which today is a machine with considerable power and memory capacity. Some are as powerful as the older mainframes.

PCs were initially used as stand-alone equipment.

Initially, PCs were used as stand-alone equipment with their own resident data and software. The only way users could share data was by copying it to a diskette and giving it to someone else. PCs were also used to emulate mainframe terminals. Although terminal emulation helped somewhat, it did not add significantly to the overall productivity.

As PC usage expanded, end users became more computer literate. This initiated an insatiable desire for more data and more connectivity to corporate systems. Seamless access to corporate databases on many platforms became a requirement. However, for mission-critical applications to achieve productivity enhancements, the computing assets—mainframe, midrange, and personal—of the organization had to be integrated. By deploying the correct computing resources to resolve the issues for which they were best suited, productivity can be optimized. Over time, a company's overall competitiveness could be impacted if end users had to spend an inordinate amount of time and effort simply to access and analyze corporate data—wherever it may reside.

The need to share information gave way to networks of workgroups using the same data, printers, and software. This helped IT departments to include PCs in traditional system management tasks such as backup and technical support. As users grew more accustomed to PCs and their simpler interface, expectations for mainframe and midrange applications grew. The use of icons, dropdown menus, and multiple colors became a requirement of new applications that could be accommodated easily on a high-powered personal computer but were not commonplace for corporate mainframe applications.

Client/server processing is commonplace today.

Organizations have adopted and integrated technology across multiple computing platforms. Today, client/server processing is commonplace and the network keeps these disparate platforms connected. IT personnel need to administer a complex environment to deliver computing services to the business.

Business Issues

Three forces in business have driven the change to client/server environments: downsizing, upsizing, and rightsizing. As the name implies, *downsizing* is a transition downward, from mainframes to networked PC workstations. The proliferation of more-powerful, less-expensive PCs has made downsizing an attractive option for many large mainframe shops. *Upsizing* is the move from stand-alone PCs to a network that connects many PCs together and provides access to corporate databases. Finally, *rightsizing* is the practice of placing applications on the most appropriate platform for the requirements. For example, applications requiring high availability and scalability may require a mainframe, at least for some pieces of the application. In contrast, an application requiring rapid delivery and a highly customized interface will likely require a PC workstation running some version of Windows for some of its components.

What Is Client/Server Computing?

Client/server can be defined as a relationship between two or more computing entities that function together to accomplish a task.

Client/server computing enables a user on a PC to run standard business applications and access corporate shared resources over a network connection. Basically, *client/server* can be defined as a relationship between two or more computing entities that function together to accomplish a task. These entities each perform a portion of the work involved. One entity (the "client") requests services and the other (the "server") fulfills the requests. Of course, a client/server environment may utilize multiple servers, each fulfilling different types of requests—database access, application processing, file access, printing, and so on.

Various interconnected servers enable common computer resources to be shared in a client/server implementation. Most PC-based business software applications access these networked files and printers as if they were directly connected to the desktop PC. For example, in a networked environment, the end user perceives a common pool of disk drives, printers, and other resources without necessarily being able to distinguish between local and remote resources. The most commonly used types of servers include print servers, file servers, database servers, and application servers.

Print servers provide network users access to multiple printers as a sharable resource. Instead of having a printer connected to each desktop PC, print servers provide easy access to a printer by any PC connected on a network.

File servers provide a means of sharing data files among users on the network. *Database servers* advance the data sharing capabilities of the client/ server system by enabling targeted data access. Unlike LAN-based file servers, which require the entire file to be retrieved, a database server is able to accept SQL queries and respond with only the requested data.

Application servers provide services for business applications. One advantage of application servers is their ability to reuse common business logic.

When a client/server system is implemented, the designers must determine which parts of the application should run on which computing assets. A client/server application consists of the following three software layers:

- *Presentation logic* consists of the tasks required to display information on a computer screen. For client/server systems, this usually involves a graphical user interface (GUI) with point-and-click, drag-and-drop capabilities, interactive help facilities, and other ease-of-use functionality.

- *Business logic* delivers the core elements of an application needed by the end user to manipulate information for managing business. This business logic is unique to the particular business at hand and incorporates methods for implementing business strategies, conducting business transactions, and enforcing company policies.

- *Database management systems* are used by most client/server systems to provide quick access to structured data in a secure manner and to facilitate data modification while enforcing data integrity. File storage systems store the data managed by the DBMS (and handle data that is not managed by a DBMS).

The presentation-logic layer is the screen that the user sees.

The presentation-logic layer is the screen (or report) that the user sees—the graphical interface. The application-logic layer provides computer processing that allows business tasks to be accomplished. Underneath both of these software layers is the data-management layer. If a business task requires information from multiple databases, the data access facilities should be consistent and transparent to the front-end software components.

In a client/server environment, each of these components, though independent, interoperate with the other components to provide the end user with a seamless end-to-end application. The end user does not need to know that separate components are being accessed over a network to deliver application functionality. Client/server processing allows the physical placement of two or more components on separate computing platforms and systems, as shown in Figure 20-1.

The *client* computer typically is a PC connected to a network. The client manages the user presentation and provides access to the network resources. When a network service is needed, the client sends a request over the network to the desired server.

Client/Server Processing

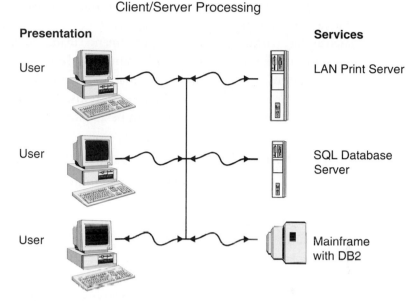

Figure 20-1   *Client/server processing*

*Timely response
from a server is
necessary.*

A *server* typically consists of powerful hardware and the networking components necessary to connect to clients, as well as the software to fulfill service requests made by clients. Servers must be powerful enough to handle multiple
requests from multiple clients. Timely response from a server is necessary to
allow client applications to appear as an integrated and unified application. The
hardware used for the server can be a powerful PC (perhaps with multiple
CPUs), a UNIX-based machine, a midrange computer, or a mainframe computer.
Table 20-1 outlines the types of computing platforms that are most appropriate
for the different client/server component layers.

Table 20-1   *Recommended Hardware for Client/Server Component Layers*

Component	PC	Midrange	Mainframe
User presentation	Excellent	Poor	Poor
Business logic	It depends	Generally good	Generally good
Database management	Poor	Very good	Excellent

From a data management perspective, the database server provides clients with access to shared data. The server must control that access as well as activities such as data backup and recovery, performance management, and error handling.

Of course, solid networking capabilities are required to create a client/server system. The network is the enabling technology for client/server systems and much of modern computing systems. Without networking capabilities, computerized systems would not be able to connect to one another.

Centralized vs. Distributed Processing

Centralized processing utilizes a host computer that is accessed using dumb terminals. PCs can be connected to a centralized system, but their only function in a centralized system is basic terminal emulation. The host-based system cannot access data stored on the PC, and any PC-based applications cannot access host data for local desktop processing. With centralized systems, the PC community is isolated from integrated, seamless processing.

In centralized processing, all data is stored on a large, centralized computer.

In centralized processing, all data is stored on a large, centralized computer, typically a mainframe. All users run predefined applications, sometimes referred to as legacy applications, that have been built to access that data. Maintenance and porting of centralized applications to nonmainframe computer technology is expensive and difficult.

Distributed processing utilizes multiple computers to fulfill a service request.

Distributed processing involves the utilization of multiple computers to fulfill a service request. As the names implies, business tasks are distributed or allocated to multiple processors. The goal is to facilitate processing on the computing platform that is most efficient. A network that links together multiple computers is the first requirement for distributed processing. Additionally, system software must be capable of allocating tasks to different computers.

Another term that is sometimes associated with distributed applications is *cooperative processing*. This refers to the functionality of two nodes *cooperating* and sharing the processing duties for a business problem. For example, one node may run some basic verification routines for new data entered, while the other node performs more rigorous testing of business rules.

Types of Client/Server Applications

In a client/server system, applications are modularized to allow them to execute over two or more nodes. The client application makes requests to a server node, which may be filled by different servers, depending on the type of request. By using software modules, client/server processing allows the sharing of commonly used software and other requested resources.

Client/server networks can be set up in a wide variety of configurations, depending on the needs of the application and the computing resources available to the organization. Keep in mind that a client/server system normally consists of three software layers: the presentation logic, the application or business logic, and the DBMS. How the processing of these layers is distributed will greatly influence the design, implementation, ease of use, and the overall response time. These tasks can be broken apart in various ways across the network as shown in Figure 20-2. The first and last lines in this figure are not client/server models, because all of the processing is centralized—either on a PC workstation or a high-end server. Let's examine a few of the client/server configurations.

Line 2 in the figure shows a common client/server variation: the *distributed user presentation model.* In this model, the user presentation logic is split between the workstation client and the server. The client performs the graphical and menu-driven interface elements and handles some tasks such as physically updating the screens and the rules for how the interface looks and acts. Other presentation level tasks such as data validation may be performed on the client or on the server. Nevertheless, to the end user, the presentation

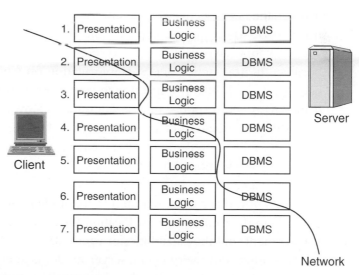

Figure 20-2 *Distributing tasks across the network*

layer appears to be handled entirely by the workstation. Business logic and data management tasks are performed on the server.

Line 3 in the figure shows the *decentralized user presentation model,* where all of the presentation logic is performed on the client workstation. Dividing the processing in this manner works well, especially when client/server technology is to be phased into an organization slowly over time. Ideal applications for this model are ones that require some restructuring, but rewriting is not justified by the business needs.

Line 4 shows an alternative form of decentralization where portions of the business logic are implemented on the client and other portions are implemented on the server. This model is difficult to implement and maintain because application code that controls business functionality resides on multiple platforms.

Line 5, the *centralized data management model,* places all presentation and application logic for business tasks on the client and all data access and management software on the server. A DBMS database server handles all data requests and modifications. This provides a secure environment to administer and control corporate information. It also helps to ensure a high degree of data integrity.

Line 6 shows an alternative approach, the *distributed data management model,* where data resides both on the client node and on the server. The advantage to this approach is that queries to the local DBMS are faster. From a maintenance perspective, the administration required for a large number of distributed DBMSs is more complex. Consider the way in which ATMs work. If you use your own bank's ATM, the response time typically is very fast. This is so because the transaction accesses information on your account locally on the bank's server (probably a mainframe computer). However, if you use another bank's ATM, the response time is often much slower because the transaction goes through a central clearinghouse. In other words, information on bank accounts is distributed among all the banks connected to the clearinghouse.

Line 7, as mentioned before, is not a client/server system; it is a centralized system on a client machine.

As a DBA, you will be required to assist client/server application developers to help determine the best location for data in terms of efficiency, ease of management, and the capabilities of your DBMS.

One of the most popular client/server models in use today is the multitier implementation.

Of course, not every client/server model is adequately described by the simple diagram we have used thus far. Indeed, one of the most popular client/server models in use today is the *multitier implementation*, as shown in Figure 20-3.

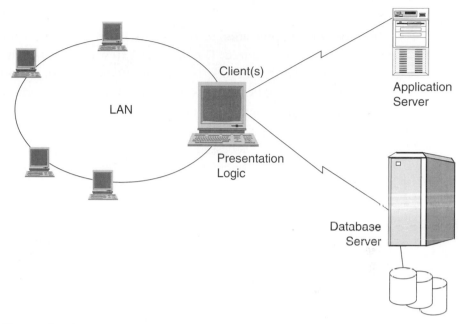

Figure 20-3   *Multitier client/server implementation*

In this client/server implementation, two servers are deployed: one for the application and another for the DBMS. The client handles all (or most) presentation logic duties. This is the model deployed by many popular third-party application vendors such as SAP, PeopleSoft, and Seibel Technologies. Supporting such applications requires networking expertise as well as a high degree of knowledge that spans multiple platforms (because each tier is implemented using a different type of computer).

Thin Client or Fat Client

Distributed and decentralized user presentation client/server implementations are sometimes referred to as *thin client* because only limited functionality resides on the client computer. Client/server models where most of the processing occurs on the client are called *fat client*. Referring back to Figure 20-2, the lines toward the bottom of the diagram (in particular, lines five and six) represent fat client implementations because more logic resides on the client than on the server.

Modern client/ server applications prefer thin client to fat client.

Modern client/server applications prefer thin client to fat client implementations because it is easier to manage and upgrade a thin client. Distributing changes to hundreds, or perhaps thousands of nodes can be difficult when the program logic resides on multiple clients throughout an organization.

Database Gateways

In order for an application to access a database over a network, *database gateway* software is required. The database gateway allows clients to access data stored on database servers. The major DBMS vendors provide gateway software for their DBMS products, and several third-party vendors provide offerings that are more heterogeneous.

The gateway may need to support multiple networking protocols.

When selecting a database gateway, you will need to know what types of databases need to be accessed and what networking protocol will be used. For example, if DB2 and Oracle databases must be accessed, the gateway will need to support both of these DBMS products. Similarly, the gateway will need to support multiple networking protocols if, for instance, a combination of TCP/IP, IPX/SPX, and SNA networking is utilized.

The DBA sets up and configures the database gateway software, usually with the assistance of a network specialist. When setting up the database gateway, you will need to decide whether the gateway should be installed on every client machine or a server should be set up to handle connection requests. If the gateway resides on each client, coordinating software distribution during an upgrade of the database gateway software can be difficult. Implementing the database gateway as a server simplifies software upgrades, but requires connection requests to be routed to the connection server.

Furthermore, the configuration process may require the DBA to set DBMS configuration parameters or update system catalog tables to specify the locations and protocols used by the database gateway. The proper installation and configuration of the database gateway in a client/server system is often one of the most demanding and difficult DBA tasks.

Network Traffic

Network traffic is the primary source of poor performance in client/ server applications.

In general, network traffic is the primary source of poor performance in client/ server applications. The less data that is sent across the network, the better the performance will be. The DBA should look for opportunities to decrease the size of requests sent across the network both from the client to the server and from the server back to the client. Stored procedures can be a useful tactic because issuing a call to a stored procedure over the network usually will require less bandwidth than issuing several SQL statements. Furthermore, the stored procedure, if designed properly, can execute multiple requests on the server and return to the client only the data that is required. This helps to reduce network traffic.

Additional methods can be used to minimize network traffic. For example, design the application programs to minimize the number of individual network requests. Perhaps several requests can be grouped together or combined to reduce network calls.

The DBA should investigate configuration options for the data distribution methods used by the DBMS, as well as database gateway options for reducing network traffic.

Databases, the Internet, and the Web

Connecting databases to the Web is not as difficult as managing the databases once they have been connected. As with any server, the only way to enable access to a database server over the Web is to enable some form of telecommunications connection between the database server and the Internet. This can be accomplished in many ways, from the slow and simple approach of using a dialup connection to permanent and faster connections using frame relay, ISDN, or T1 and T3 lines. Of course, you also may choose to use an Internet service provider (ISP) to host your Web site and the databases used by your Web applications.

By hosting your own databases, you have better control over the data.

Many larger organizations choose to host their own databases instead of turning them over to an ISP. By hosting your own databases, you have a better degree of control over the data—the data resides on site, is accessible by your organization even if the Internet connection goes down, and is more easily secured. When an ISP hosts your database, the data is under the control of an external entity, not your organization. This might be acceptable for smaller databases, noncritical data, or very small organizations lacking the capacity to manage and administer databases in the DBMS environment.

Some service providers simply set up and enable the server hardware, while you install, configure, and maintain the software (DBMS) that is run on that server. This may be a suitable compromise to turning over all control to the ISP. Choosing to host your database server with your ISP can dramatically reduce costs because dedicated connections can be quite expensive.

When you host database servers that are designed to serve Internet users, following these guidelines can help:

- Favor dedicated hardware for the database server. Do not mix and match Web server software and database server software on the same computer. Dedicated hardware makes it easier to separate database and Web resources for tuning and management.

- Favor using the fastest network connections available for connecting the application logic to the database server and the database server to the Internet connection. The faster the network connection is, the better the performance will be.

Internet-Connected Databases

Organizations are rapidly adopting Internet technologies and integrating them into their business processes—in other words, businesses are becoming e-businesses. However, the duties of the DBA become more difficult when it comes to managing databases that are connected to the Internet. The first factor complicating Web database administration is the increased reliance on availability.

Availability

An e-business never closes.

Because an e-business is an online business, it never closes. There is no such thing as a batch window for an e-business application. Customers expect full functionality on the Web regardless of the time of day. And remember, the Web is worldwide—when it is midnight in Chicago it is 3:00 P.M. in Sydney, Australia. An e-business must be available and operational 24 hours a day, 7 days a week, 366 days a year (do not forget leap years). It must be prepared to engage with customers at any time or risk losing business to a company whose Web site is more accessible. Some studies show that if a Web user clicks his mouse and does not receive a transmission back to his browser within seven seconds, the user will abandon that request and go somewhere else.

The net result is that e-businesses are more connected, and therefore must be more available in order to be useful. As e-businesses integrate their Web presence with traditional IT services such as database management systems, they are creating heightened expectations for data availability. In fact, BMC Software uses the term *e-vailability* to describe the increased availability requirements of Web-enabled databases.

Downtime and outages are the enemy of e-vailability.

E-vailability describes the level of availability necessary to keep an e-business continuously operational. Downtime and outages are the enemy of e-vailability. Recall from the discussion in Chapter 8 that 70% of application downtime is caused by planned outages to the system—and only 30% by unplanned outages.

But what does all of this mean for the e-DBA? Because the e-DBA is charged with maintaining the high degree of availability required by e-business, one of his first priorities is to minimize downtime resulting from planned outages. How can an e-DBA accomplish this? The best way to reduce downtime is to avoid it. The following steps can be taken to avoid or reduce downtime.

- Perform routine maintenance while systems remain operational.
- Exploit the features of the DBMS that promote availability.
- Automate DBA functions.
- Consider high-speed utilities and third-party automation solutions.
- Exploit hardware technologies.

Performing tasks faster can shorten the duration of an outage.

These techniques are covered in detail in Chapter 8. Nevertheless, sometimes downtime cannot be avoided. If this is the case, performing tasks faster can shorten the duration of an outage. Be sure that you are using the fastest and least error-prone technology and methods available to you. For example, if a third party RECOVER, LOAD, or REORG utility can be run in half or a quarter of the time of a traditional database utility, consider migrating to the faster technology In many cases, the faster technology will pay for itself much quicker in an e-business than in a traditional business because of the increased availability requirements.

Another way to minimize downtime is to automate routine maintenance tasks. For example, recall from Chapter 7 how changing the database structures can be a difficult task. Tools are available that enable DBAs to make any desired change to a relational database using a simple online interface. By pointing, clicking, and selecting with the tool, scripts are generated that automate the required database changes. When errors are avoided using automation, downtime is diminished, resulting in greater e-vailability. Chapter 7 provides extensive coverage of database change management issues.

New Technologies

New and fundamentally different technologies are used to build and maintain Web-enabled applications and databases. DBAs will need to become experienced in new technologies very rapidly as they are introduced into the organization. Let's examine two of these new technologies—XML and Java.

XML

XML uses tags to describe the data itself.

XML stands for *eXtensible Markup Language*. Like HTML, XML is based on SGML (Standard Generalized Markup Language). HTML uses tags to describe *how* data appears on a Web page. However, XML uses tags to describe the data itself. XML retains the key SGML advantage of self-description, while avoiding the complexity of full-blown SGML. XML allows users to define tags that describe the data in the document. This capability provides users a means to describe the structure and nature of the data in the document. In essence, the document becomes self-describing.

The simple syntax of XML makes it easy to process by machine while remaining understandable to humans. Once again, let's use HTML to help us understand XML. HTML uses tags to describe the appearance of data on a page. For example the tag "<b> text </b>" specifies that the word "text" should appear in boldface letters. XML uses tags to describe the data itself, instead of its appearance. For example, consider the following XML description of a customer address:

```
<CUSTOMER>
<first_name>Craig</first_name>
<middle_initial>S.</middle_initial>
<last_name>Mullins</last_name>
<company_name>BMC Software, Inc.</company_name>
<street_address>2101 CityWest Blvd.</street_address>
<city>Houston</city>
<state>TX</state>
<zip_code>77042</zip_code>
<country>U.S.A.</country>
</CUSTOMER>
```

This data is easily parsed by following the tags. A simple scan of the code will reveal the data elements that make up CUSTOMER, such as first and last name, company name, and address.

XML is actually a metalanguage for defining other markup languages.

XML is actually a metalanguage for defining other markup languages. These languages are collected in dictionaries called *Document Type Definitions* (DTDs), which store definitions of tags for specific industries or fields of knowledge. Therefore, the meaning of a tag must be defined in a *document type declaration*. The DTD in the following code sample defines the tags used in the CUSTOMER XML document shown previously.

```
<!DOCTYPE CUSTOMER [
<!ELEMENT CUSTOMER (first_name, middle_initial, last_name,
         company_name, street_address, city,
         state, zip_code, country*)>
<!ELEMENT first_name (#PCDATA)>
```

```
<!ELEMENT middle_initial (#PCDATA)>
<!ELEMENT last_name (#PCDATA)>
<!ELEMENT company_name (#PCDATA)>
<!ELEMENT street_address (#PCDATA)>
<!ELEMENT city (#PCDATA)>
<!ELEMENT state (#PCDATA)>
<!ELEMENT zip_code (#PCDATA)>
<!ELEMENT country (#PCDATA)>
]
```

The DTD for an XML document can be either part of the document or stored in an external file. The XML code samples shown are meant to be examples only. By examining them, you can quickly see how the document itself describes its contents. This is beneficial for data management professionals because it removes the chore of tracking down the meaning of data elements. One of the biggest problems associated with database management and processing is tracking down and maintaining the meaning of stored data. If the data can be stored in documents using XML, the documents themselves will describe their data content.

Of course, the DTD is a rudimentary vehicle for defining data semantics. Standards committees are working on the definition of an XML Schema to replace the DTD for defining XML tags. The XML Schema will allow for more precise definition of data, such as data types and lengths.

XML is a language that generates other kinds of languages.

The important thing to remember about XML is that it solves a different problem than HTML. HTML is a markup language, but XML is a metalanguage. In other words, XML is a language that generates other kinds of languages. The idea is to use XML to generate a language specifically tailored for each requirement you encounter. It is essential that you understand this paradigm shift in order for you to understand the power of XML. Note that XSL, eXtensible Stylesheet Language, can be used with XML to format XML data for display.

In short, XML allows designers to create their own customized tags, thereby enabling the definition, transmission, validation, and interpretation of data between applications and between organizations. The most important reason to learn XML is that it is quickly becoming the de facto standard for application interfaces.

DBMS products have begun to provide support for XML. One approach is to map the XML document to the database structure. Such a mapping facility is commonly referred to as a *wrapper*. With this approach, the XML documents are decomposed, and their elements and attributes are stored in rows and columns within the DBMS. One example of a wrapperlike implementation is the

XML Extender provided with DB2 Version 7 that enables XML documents to be integrated with DB2 databases. By integrating XML into DB2, you can more directly and quickly access the XML documents. You can search and store entire XML documents using SQL. You also have the option of combining XML documents with traditional data stored in relational tables. When you store or compose a document, you can invoke DBMS functions to trigger an event to automate the exchange of data between applications. An XML document can be completely stored in a single text column, or it can be broken into component pieces and stored as multiple columns across multiple tables.

The DB2 XML Extender provides user-defined data types (UDTs) and user-defined functions (UDFs) to store and manipulate XML in the DB2 database. The XML Extender defines UDTs for XMLVARCHAR, XMLCLOB, and XMLFILE. Once the XML is stored in the database, the UDFs can be used to search and retrieve the XML data as a complete document or in pieces. The UDFs supplied by the XML Extender include

- *Storage* functions to insert XML documents into a DB2 database
- *Retrieval* functions to access XML documents from XML columns
- *Extraction* functions to extract and convert the element content or attribute values from an XML document to the data type specified by the function name
- *Update* functions to modify element contents or attribute values (and to return a copy of an XML document with an updated value)

More and more DBMS products are providing capabilities to store and generate XML. The basic functionality enables XML to be passed back and forth between databases in the DBMS, as shown in Figure 20-4.

Additionally, some vendors have attempted to create XML-based DBMSs. Such DBMS products are based on an architecture that supports the storage of XML documents in their entirety. Typically, this involves using a proprietary database structure in which XML documents form the foundation of the database. These DBMS products will likely garner only niche support and will not supplant relational technology as the leading DBMS technology. An example of such an XML-based DBMS is Tamino from Software AG.

The future of the Web most likely will be defined using XML.

For sharing data within and between organizations, XML is definitely the wave of the immediate future. In fact, the future of the Web most likely will be defined using XML. The benefits of self-describing documents make XML a useful

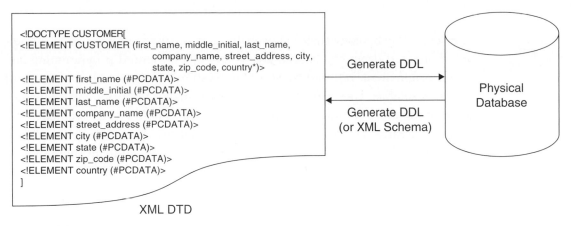

```
<!DOCTYPE CUSTOMER[
<!ELEMENT CUSTOMER (first_name, middle_initial, last_name,
                        company_name, street_address, city,
                        state, zip_code, country*)>
<!ELEMENT first_name (#PCDATA)>
<!ELEMENT middle_initial (#PCDATA)>
<!ELEMENT last_name (#PCDATA)>
<!ELEMENT company_name (#PCDATA)>
<!ELEMENT street_address (#PCDATA)>
<!ELEMENT city (#PCDATA)>
<!ELEMENT state (#PCDATA)>
<!ELEMENT zip_code (#PCDATA)>
<!ELEMENT country (#PCDATA)>
]
```

Generate DDL

Generate DDL
(or XML Schema)

Physical
Database

XML DTD

Figure 20-4 *XML and database integration*

technique for data sharing. Furthermore, being able to use XML to generate an application-specific language is powerful.

XML is being used by more and more organizations to transfer data. In addition, more capabilities are being added to DBMS products to support XML. Clearly, DBAs will need to understand XML as their companies become e-businesses. Learning XML today will prepare DBAs to integrate XML into their data management and application development infrastructure. For more details and specifics regarding XML, refer to the following Web sites: http://www.xml.org and http://www.w3.org/XML/

The capabilities of XML will cause it to gain acceptance, regardless of any drawbacks. And XML does have drawbacks, including

- An increase in the size of data files encoded as XML documents due to the metadata XML tags. Larger documents take longer to transfer across the network than smaller files.

- The need for yet another "model" of storing data. If data is stored in relational databases and incorporated into XML documents for sharing with others, you may be able to mitigate this problem.

- The over-hype of XML. There is a lot of confusion surrounding XML in the industry. Some pundits have claimed that XML will provide metadata where none currently exists, or that XML will replace SQL as a data access method for relational data. Neither of these assertions is true.

Java

One of Java's greatest claims to fame is its cross-platform portability.

The second technology that will probably accompany your sojourn into Internet-connected databases is Java. Java is an object-oriented programming language originally developed by Sun Microsystems. It was modeled after, and closely resembles, C++. However, it requires a smaller footprint and eliminates some of the more complex features of C++, such as pointer management. One of Java's greatest claims to fame is its cross-platform portability. Using Java, developers can create Web application programs once and run them on any platform, regardless of hardware or operating system.

Java Program Types

There are three types of programs that you can implement when accessing data using Java: Java applets, Java servlets, and Java applications.

A *Java applet* is a small application program that must be downloaded before it can be run by a Java-enabled Web browser. Java applets reside on a Web server. When the Web server returns an HTML page that points to a Java applet, the Java-enabled Web browser requests the applet to be downloaded. After the applet is received at the browser, either the browser starts the applet internally, or an external JVM executes it.

Applets typically perform simple operations, such as editing input data or controlling screen interaction, and provide other client functionality. Of course, Java applets can be written to perform more complex functionality, but to load and run non-Java code in the client requires *signed applets*, which have the authority needed to run code in the client machine.

Performance problems can arise because Java applets must be downloaded before they can be run. The time to download the applet must be factored into its service levels. In general, Java applets are small, so the performance impact should be negligible. Nevertheless, even small downloads can be slow if there are network problems. Java applets can be cached by the Web browser, which diminishes the performance impact.

A *Java servlet* is basically server-side Java. A Java servlet runs on the Web server, just like an applet runs in the Web browser. Java servlets can be used to extend the functionality of the Web server. The Web server hands requests to the servlet, and the servlet replies to them. Servlets can be used instead of CGI applications.

Java servlets have security advantages over client-side Java applets. A servlet that runs on a Web server inside a firewall can control access to sensitive data and business logic. Java applets do not inherently provide these security capabilities.

A *Java application* program is basically the same as a program written in any other programming language. It can perform all of the tasks normally associated with programs, including many tasks that Java applets cannot perform. Furthermore, a Java application does not need a browser to be executed. It can be executed in a client or server machine.

Before choosing which Java development style to use, you must know the basics of the environment in which the program will be run. Ask the following questions when deciding what type of Java program is required for your development needs:

- How will the program be executed? Must it run over the Internet, as an intranet or extranet application, Or merely as a stand-alone application?
- What is the business logic that this program must perform?
- How complicated is the program?
- How large (or small) is the program, and can it be quickly downloaded?
- What are the security requirements?
- Who are the target users and at what speed will they be connected to the Web?

Java applications, Java applets, and Java servlets are similar in nature, but a different method is used to invoke each of them. Java applets and servlets are started from an HTML page. Java applications do not require a Web component, but can be used as part of an intranet solution.

An additional capability of Java is its suitability for enabling animation for and interaction with Web pages. Developers can develop and run three types of Java programs, called *applets*, *servlets*, or *applications*. (Refer to the sidebar "Java Program Types" for more details.) Applets and servlets can be run on the Web from an HTML page. However, Java is completely different from HTML, and does not replace it. Java programs are automatically downloaded and executed by users as they surf the Web. Keep in mind that even though Web interaction is one of Java's most touted features, it is a fully functional programming language that can be used for developing general-purpose applications, independent of the Web.

So, to summarize, the major qualities of Java are its

- Similarity to other popular languages
- Ability to enable Web interaction
- Ability to enable executable Web content
- Ability to run on multiple platforms

As your organization moves to the Web, Java will gain popularity. Indeed, the growth of Java usage in recent years mirrors the growth of e-business. Java will be used to write Web applications, and those Web applications will need to access data that is invariably stored in a relational database. However, as DBAs, we know that when programs access data, the opportunity for performance problems is introduced. Therefore, if Java is used to develop Web-based applications that access relational data, DBAs will need to understand Java.

Java can enhance application availability.

There is another reason why Java is a popular choice for Web-based applications. Java can enhance application availability, which is of supreme importance to Web-based applications.

How can Java improve availability? Java is a late-binding language. After a Java program is developed, it is compiled. However, the compiler output is not pure executable code; instead, the compiler produces Java bytecodes. This is what enables Java to be so portable from platform to platform. Each platform has its own Java Virtual Machine (JVM) that interprets the bytecodes. The availability aspect is based on how code changes are introduced. Java code changes can be deployed as components while the application is running. Thus, you do not need to stop the application in order to introduce code changes; the code changes can be downloaded over the Web as needed. In this way, Java can enhance availability. Additionally, Java simplifies complicated turnover procedures and the distribution and management of the DLL files required by most client/server applications.

One of the traditional roles of the DBA is to monitor and manage the performance of database access. With Java, performance can be a problem. Remember that Java is interpreted at run time. A Java program, therefore, is usually slower than an equivalent traditional, compiled program. Just In Time (JIT) compiler technology may be available for your platform of choice. Using a JIT compiler can make Java run faster because it interprets bytecodes into machine language just before they are executed. Such conversion can enhance the performance of a Java program, but even with a JIT compiler, Java is unlikely to deliver the speed of a compiled program because the JIT compiler is still an interpretive process. Another approach is a high-performance Java (HPJ) compiler. The HPJ compiler turns bytecodes into true load modules. It avoids the overhead of interpreting Java bytecodes at runtime. However, remember that not all Java implementations support JIT or HPJ compilers.

DBAs will need to know how to access databases using Java.

Additionally, DBAs will need to know how to access databases using Java. There are two options: *JDBC* and *SQLJ*.

Java Database Connectivity (JDBC) is an API that enables Java to access relational databases. Similar to ODBC, JDBC consists of a set of classes and interfaces that can be used to access relational data. Anyone familiar with application programming and ODBC (or any call-level interface) can get up and running with JDBC fairly quickly. JDBC provides dynamic SQL access to relational databases. The intended benefit of JDBC is to provide vendor-independent connections to relational databases from Java programs. Using JDBC, theoretically at least, you should be able to write an application for one platform, say DB2 for OS/390, and deploy it on another platform, for example, Oracle9i on Sun Solaris. Simply by using the correct JDBC drivers for the database platform, the application should be portable. Of course, this is in theory. In the real world, you need to make sure you do not use any platform-specific extensions or code, or this may not work.

SQLJ provides embedded static SQL for Java. With SQLJ, a translator must process the Java program. (For those of you who are DB2 literate, this is just like precompiling a COBOL program.) Most database vendors plan to use the same generic translator. The translator strips out the SQL from the Java code so that it can be optimized into a database request module. It also replaces SQL calls in the Java program with Java code. Now the entire program can be compiled into bytecodes, and a bind can be run to create a package for the SQL.

SQLJ has a couple of advantages over JDBC.

So, which should you use or recommend to your developers? The answer, of course, is "It depends!" SQLJ has a couple of advantages over JDBC. The first advantage is the potential performance gain that can be achieved using static SQL. This is important because Java has a reputation for being slow. Therefore, if the SQL can be optimized prior to runtime, the overall performance of the program should be improved. Additionally, SQLJ is similar to the embedded SQL programs. If your shop uses embedded SQL to access DB2, for example, then SQLJ will be more familiar to your programmers than JDBC. This familiarity could make it easier to train developers to be proficient in SQLJ than in JDBC. However, you cannot use SQLJ to write dynamic SQL, which can be a drawback if you desire the flexibility of dynamic SQL. However, you can use both SQLJ and JDBC calls inside a single program. Additionally, if your shop uses ODBC for developing programs that access Oracle, for example, then JDBC will be more familiar to your developers than SQLJ.

A final Java issue for DBAs—you will need to have at least a rudimentary understanding of how to read Java code. Most DBAs, at some point in their career, get involved in application tuning, debugging, or designing. Smart organizations ensure that all application code is submitted to a DBA design review process before it is promoted to production status (see Chapter 6 for details). The design review assures that the code is efficient, effective, and properly coded. Moreover, application code and SQL are the single biggest cause of poor relational performance—recall from Chapter 12 that 70% to 80% of poor "relational" performance is caused by poorly written SQL and application logic. So reviewing programs before they are moved to production status is a smart thing to do.

Therefore, it stands to reason that when code is written in Java, the DBA must be able to understand Java to assist in design reviews and performance tuning. If you, as a DBA, do not understand Java, how will you ever be able to provide expert analysis of the code during the review process? How will you be able to tune the application when it encounters problems in the production environment if you do not at least understand the basics of the code? So, plan on obtaining a basic education in the structure and syntax of Java. DBAs do not need expert Java coding knowledge; a beginner level should allow you to read and understand the Java code.

Learn Java before you need to.

Since Java is clearly a part of the future of e-business, e-DBAs will need to understand the benefits of Java. But, clearly, that will not be enough for success. You will also need to understand of how Java works and how to use Java to access relational data efficiently and effectively. Be sure to learn Java before it is used at your shop to access databases, or you will be unprepared to support your Web-enabled database applications.

Database Design

When databases are designed for e-business applications, the tendency is for the DBA to get swept up in the dynamics of Web-based design and development. This can be a dangerous mistake when designing databases. Let's investigate the impact of e-business on the design process and discuss the basics of assuring proper database design.

When a business operates on "Internet time," things move faster.

One of the biggest problems that a DBA will encounter when moving from traditional development to e-business development is coping with the mad rush to "Get it done NOW!" Industry pundits have coined the phrase "Internet time" to describe this phenomenon. Basically, when a business starts operating on "Internet time," things move faster. One "Web month" is said to be equivalent to about three standard months. The nugget of truth here is that Web projects move very fast for a couple of reasons:

- Business executives want to conduct more and more business over the Web to save costs and to connect better with their clients.

- Everyone else is moving fast, so you better move fast, too, or risk losing business.

Rapid application development (RAD) techniques have been around for about two decades now and have been used with varying degrees of success. Sometimes RAD is required for certain projects. But RAD can be bad for database design. Why? Applications are temporary, but data is permanent. Organizations are forever coding and recoding their applications—sometimes developing the next incarnation of an application before releasing the last one.

But when did you ever throw away data? Oh, sure, you may redesign a database or move from one DBMS to another. But what did you do with the data? Chances are, you saved the data and migrated it from the old database to the new one. Some changes had to be made, maybe some external data was purchased to combine with the existing data, but the data lives on. To glean the most value from your data, it is wise to take care when designing the database. It is easier to navigate a well-designed database and therefore easier to retrieve meaningful data from it. Chapters 3 and 4 outline the techniques necessary for designing and implementing a well-constructed database.

But what if you are forced to design a database on "Internet time"?

Be aware of design failures that can result in a hostile database.

Well, the best advice I can give you is to be aware of design failures that can result in a hostile database. A *hostile database* is a database that is difficult to understand, hard to query, and takes an enormous amount of effort to change. Of course, it is impossible to list every type of database design flaw that could be introduced to create a hostile database. However, let's examine some common database design failures.

Assigning inappropriate table and column names is a common design error made by novices. Database names that are used to store data should be as descriptive as possible to allow the tables and columns to self-document themselves, at least to some extent. Application programmers are notorious for creating database naming problems, such as using screen-variable names for columns or coded jumbles of letters and numbers for table names.

Don't design the database with output in mind.

When rushed for time, some DBAs resort to designing the database with output in mind. This can lead to flaws such as storing numbers in character columns because leading zeroes need to be displayed on reports. This is usually a bad idea for a relational database. If the column is created as a character column, the developer will need to program edit-checks to validate that only numeric data is stored in the column. Yet, as discussed earlier, it is better for integrity and efficiency to let the database system perform the edit-checking.

Therefore, data storage should be based on its domain. Users and programmers can format the data for display, instead of forcing the data into display mode for database storage.

Another common database design problem is overstuffing columns. This actually is a normalization issue. Sometimes, for convenience, a single column is used to store what should be two or three columns. Such design flaws are introduced when the DBA does not analyze the data for patterns and relationships. An example of overstuffing would be storing a person's name in a single column instead of capturing first name, middle initial, and last name as individual columns.

Poorly designed keys can wreck the usability of a database.

Poorly designed keys can wreck the usability of a database. A primary key should be nonvolatile, because changing the value of the primary key can be very expensive. When you change a primary key value, you have to ripple through foreign keys to cascade the changes into the child table. A common example is using a social security number for the primary key of a personnel or customer table. This is a flaw for several reasons. First, a social security number is not necessarily unique. Second, social security numbers are unique to the United States, so if your business expands outside the USA, what do you store as the primary key?

Actually, failing to account for International issues can have greater repercussions. For example, when storing addresses how do you define zip codes or postal codes? Many countries use postal codes that are not necessarily numeric. And how do you define state or province? How do you assure that you capture all of the information for every person to be stored in the table, regardless of country? The answer, of course, is proper data modeling and database design.

Denormalization of the physical database is a design option, but it can only be done if the design was normalized to begin with. Actually, a more fundamental problem with database design is improper normalization. By focusing on normalization, data modeling, and database design, you can avoid creating a hostile database.

Without proper up-front analysis and design, the database is unlikely to be flexible enough to easily support the changing requirements of the user. With sufficient preparation, flexibility can be designed into the database to support the user's anticipated changes. Of course, if time is not taken during the design phase to ask the users about their anticipated future needs, you cannot create the database with those needs in mind.

Database design is the armor that protects the heart of e-business.

If data is the heart of today's modern e-business, database design is the armor that protects that heart. Data modeling and database design are the most important part of creating a database application. If proper design is not a component of the database creation process, you will wind up with a confusing mess of a database that may work fine for the first application, but not for subsequent applications. And heaven help the developer or DBA who has to make changes to the database or application because of changing business requirements. That DBA will have to try to tame the hostile database!

Summary

Modern databases are designed and implemented for use across a network where users are connected to the database from many different types of computing platforms. The way in which databases are designed, administered, and supported will impact the usability of connected databases. A different set of issues and problems must be tackled for client/server and Internet-enabled databases. DBAs should be prepared to handle these problems by becoming well versed in not only how to connect databases but also how to manage those databases in an efficient manner once they are connected.

Review

1. Name the three types of Java programs and discuss the pros and cons of each type.

2. Why is database design a potential problem area for Internet-enabled database application development projects?

3. What is the difference between a fat client and a thin client?

4. In a client/server environment, there are always multiple clients communicating with only one server: True or False.

5. A client/server application comprises what three components?

6. What is the biggest DBA challenge when managing an Internet-enabled database?

7. What is a database gateway?

8. Cite examples of flaws introduced during the design phase of an Internet-enabled database that could lead to the creation of a hostile database.

9. What are the two options for accessing relational data from a Java program, and what are the differences between the two methods?

10. What is XML, and how is it different from HTML?

562 *Database Connectivity*

Suggested Reading

Applequist, Daniel K. *XML and SQL: Developing Web Applications.* Boston, MA: Addison-Wesley (2002). ISBN 0-201-65796-1

Eddy, Sandra E. *XML in Plain English.* Foster City, CA: M&T Books (1998). ISBN 0-7645-7006-4

Feiler, Jesse. *Database-Driven Web Sites.* San Francisco, CA: Morgan Kaufmann (1999). ISBN 0-12-251336-3

Gagliardi, Gary. *Client/Server Computing.* Englewood Cliffs, NJ: Prentice Hall PTR (1994). ISBN 0-13-290784-4

Hackathorn, Richard D. *Enterprise Database Connectivity.* New York, NY: John Wiley & Sons (1993). ISBN 0-471-57802-9

Lewis, Philip M., Arthur Bernstein, and Michael Kifer. *Databases and Transaction Processing.* Boston, MA: Addison-Wesley (2002). ISBN 0-201-70872-8

Orfali, Robert, Dan Harkey, and Jeri Edwards. *Essential Client/Server Survival Guide.* New York, NY: Van Nostrand Reinhold (1994). ISBN 0-442-01941-6

Purba, Sanjiv, ed. *High-Performance Web Databases.* Boca Raton, FL: Auerbach (2000). ISBN 0-8493-0882-8

Riccardi, Greg. *Principles of Database Systems with Internet and Java Applications.* Boston, MA: Addison-Wesley (2001). ISBN 0-201-61247-X

Salemi, Joe. *Guide to Client/Server Databases.* Emeryville, CA: ZD Press (1993). ISBN 1-56276-070-X

Sheldon, Tom, ed. *LAN Times Guide to Interoperability.* Berkeley, CA: McGraw-Hill (1994). ISBN 0-07-882043-X

Toledo, Hugo, Jr. *Oracle Networking.* Berkeley, CA: McGraw-Hill/Oracle Press (1996). ISBN 0-07-882165-7

■ ■ ■ ■ ■ ■ ■ ■ ■ ■ ■ ■

21

Metadata Management

In addition to managing data, DBAs need to be able to manage and control the definition of the data elements used in databases. Without an understanding of the structure, limitations, definition, and description of data, it is likely that data will be misinterpreted or misused. Furthermore, data that is not well defined can cause database integrity problems.

What Is Metadata?

Have you ever watched the "Antiques Roadshow" program on television? In this show, people bring items to professional antiques dealers to have them examined and evaluated. The participants hope to learn that their items are long-lost treasures of immense value. The antique dealers always spend a lot of time talking to the owners about their items. They always ask questions like "Where did you get this item?" and "What can you tell me about its history?" Why? Because these details provide knowledge about the authenticity and nature of the item. The dealer also carefully examines the item, looking for markings and dates that provide clues to the item's origin.

Metadata is "data about data."

Users of data must be able to put it into context before the data becomes useful as information. Information about data is referred to as *metadata*. The simplest definition of metadata is "data about data." To be a bit more precise, metadata describes data, providing information like type, length, textual description, and other characteristics. For example, metadata allows the user to know that the customer number is a five-digit numeric field, whereas the data itself might be 56789.

So, using our "Antiques Roadshow" example, the item being evaluated is the "data." The answers to the antique dealer's questions and the markings on the item are the "metadata." Value is assigned to an item only after the metadata about that item is discovered and evaluated.

Metadata characterizes data. It is used to provide documentation such that data can be understood and more readily consumed by your organization. Metadata answers the *who, what, when, where, why, and how* questions for users of the data.

From Data to Knowledge and Beyond

Data is a fact represented as an item or event out of context.

The basic building block of knowledge is data. *Data* is a fact represented as an item or event out of context and with no relation to other facts. Examples of data are 27, JAN, and 010110. Without additional details, we know nothing about any of these three pieces of data. Consider the following:

- Is 27 a number in base ten, or is it in octal (which would translate to 23 in base ten)?

- If 27 is a number in base ten, what does it represent? Is it an age, a dollar amount, an IQ, a shoe size, or something else entirely?

- What does JAN represent? Is it a woman's name (or a man's name)? Or does it represent the first month of the year? Or perhaps it is something else entirely?

- Finally, What about 010110? Is it a binary number? Or is it a representation of a date, perhaps January 1, 1910? January 1, 2010? Or something else entirely?

Because of the lack of context, these are all examples of data. *Information*, on the other hand, adds context by specifying relationships between data, and possibly other information. Data in context with metadata makes information. The relationships may represent information, yet the relations do not actually constitute information until they are understood. In addition, the relationships that represent data have a tendency to be limited in context, mostly about the past or present, with little if any implication for the future.

Webster's New Collegiate Dictionary defines *knowledge* as "the fact or condition of knowing something with familiarity gained through experience or association." Knowledge adds understanding and retention to information. It is the next natural progression after information. To have "knowledge" requires information in conjunction with patterns between data, information, and other knowledge. Therefore, knowledge couples information with understanding and cognition.

Wisdom can be thought of as applied knowledge.

The final step would be to move from knowledge to wisdom. *Wisdom* can be thought of as applied knowledge. You may have the knowledge that fatty foods are bad for you, but if you eat them anyway, you are not wise.

In order for data to be anything more than simply data, metadata is required. Without metadata, data has no identifiable meaning—it is merely a collection of digits, characters, or bits. Metadata gives data its form and makes it usable by information professionals.

Metadata Strategy

A wise organization will develop a metadata strategy to collect, manage, and provide a vehicle for accessing metadata. A sound metadata strategy should address the following:

- A policy for how metadata is used in the organization
- Procedures for identifying and defining data ownership and stewardship
- Identification of the types of metadata that need to be collected
- A description of the purpose for each type of metadata that is identified—a clear and concise reason why each piece of metadata is required by the organization
- Methods for the collection and storage of metadata (typically using a repository)
- Methods for accessing the metadata
- Policies to enforce data stewardship procedures and security for metadata access
- Identification of metadata sources, both internal and external
- Measurements to gauge the quality and usability of metadata

Metadata publicizes and supports the data your organization produces and maintains. By assembling and managing metadata, your organization will have access to relevant facts about your data, making your systems more usable and your databases more useful.

DBAs should participate in the team that develops the metadata strategy, but the data administration organization, if one exists, should be the leader of the metadata effort.

Data Stewardship

A data steward is accountable for actions taken using a defined set of data. A data stewardship policy will identify individuals within the organization whose responsibility it is to create, maintain, and delete data. A data steward is not necessarily the data owner. A comprehensive data stewardship policy will also define the consumers of the data—that is, those who directly use the data during the course of their jobs.

Data Warehousing and Metadata

A data warehousing effort has a critical need for readily available high-quality metadata.

Companies implementing data warehousing systems are more likely than other companies to have embarked on a metadata management strategy. Users require accurate information about the data contained in a warehouse before the data can be used appropriately for business. Therefore, such businesses have a critical need for readily available high-quality metadata. Frequently, though, little if any metadata is captured and managed prior to the onset of a data warehousing effort.

Types of Metadata

Even though all metadata describes data, there are many different types and sources of metadata. At a fundamental level, though, all metadata is one of two types: technology metadata or business metadata. *Technology metadata* describes the technical aspects of the data as it relates to storing and managing the data in computerized systems. *Business metadata*, on the other hand, describes aspects of how the data is used by the business, and is needed for the data to have value to the organization. Knowing, for instance, that the LICNO column is a positive integer between 1 and 9,999,999 is an example of technology metadata. Of course, the business user also requires this information.

Knowing that a number referred to as a LICNO is the practitioner license number for certified course instructors, that it must must be unique, and that every instructor can have one and only one license number is an example of business metadata. (Though, these details also are also useful to the DBA in order to create the database appropriately and effectively.)

For DBAs, the DBMS itself is a good source of metadata. The *system catalog* used to store information about database objects is a vital store of DBA metadata—technology metadata. DBAs and developers make regular use of the metadata in the DBMS system catalog to help them better understand database objects and the data contained therein. Depending on the DBMS, the user can write queries against the system catalog tables or views, or he can execute system-provided stored procedures to return metadata from the system catalog tables. Just about any type of descriptive information about the composition of the data may be found in the system catalog. For example, most DBMSs store all of the following metadata in the system catalog:

The DBMS system catalog is a particularly effective source of metadata.

- Names of every database, table, column, index, view, relationship, stored procedure, trigger, and so on
- Primary key for each table and any foreign keys that refer back to that primary key
- Which tables are in which views
- Data type, length, and constraints for each column of every table
- Names of the physical files used to store database data, as well as information about file storage, extents, and disk volumes
- Authorization and security information detailing which users have what type of authority on which database objects
- Date and time of the last database definition change, as well as the ID of the user who implemented the DDL for the change
- Database organization information

The DBMS system catalog is a particularly effective source of metadata because it is active, integrated, and nonsubvertible. The system catalog is *active* because the metadata is automatically built and maintained as database objects are created and modified. As the DBA creates databases, the DBMS automatically collects and populates metadata in the system catalog. The *integration* of the system catalog and the DBMS, coupled with the active nature of the system catalog, keeps the technology metadata in the system catalog accurate and up-to-date. Additionally, the DBMS system catalog is *nonsubvertible,* meaning that normal DBMS operations are the only mechanism for populating the system catalog. Of course, the subvertibility of the system catalog will differ from DBMS to DBMS. Some DBMSs provide options to enable direct updates to the system catalog, but such an option is to be used only in emergencies and generally under the direction of the DBMS vendor's technical support personnel.

Although a wealth of metadata can be found in the system catalog, this DBMS metadata is usually insufficient to fully describe data. For example, descriptions of database objects are not commonly found in the DBMS system catalog. Some DBMSs provide system catalog description columns that can be populated at the DBA's discretion. However, many DBAs avoid this for fear of disorganizing the system catalog. It's also possible that descriptions for the database objects were not available when the objects were created. Additional metadata that is useful, but not found in the system catalog, includes

- Metadata for nondatabase files (flat or sequential files)
- Modification information regarding when and by whom data in the database was last changed
- Copybook information for the database table (or nondatabase file), as well as which programs use that information
- Information on batch jobs and transactions that access the data
- Operational metadata on IT infrastructure components
- Data model metadata describing the logical database design and how it maps to the physical database implementation
- Data warehousing and ETL metadata defining data source(s), system of record, and other analytical information
- Data ownership and stewardship metadata

Capturing and maintaining metadata makes databases and systems easier to use.

Of course, this is an incomplete list. A myriad of different metadata types and purposes exists that can be cataloged and managed. Capturing and maintaining metadata better documents databases and systems, thereby making them easier to use. The more metadata that you make available to business users, the more value they will be able to extract from their information systems.

Repositories and Data Dictionaries

A repository stores all pertinent metadata for the corporation.

A *repository* stores information about an organization's data assets. In other words, repositories are used to store metadata. A properly implemented repository stores all pertinent metadata for the corporation. It can act as a single, centralized mechanism to assist in the migration of data from the multiple sources to a data warehouse.

In choosing a repository, base your decision on the metadata storage and retrieval needs of your entire organization, not just the databases you wish to support. Typically, a repository can

- Store information about your data, processes, and environment.
- Support multiple ways of looking at the same data. An example of this concept is the three-schema approach, in which data is viewed at the conceptual, logical, and physical levels.
- Store in-depth documentation, and produce detail and management reports from that documentation.
- Support data model creation and administration. Integration with popular ETL, data modeling, and CASE tools is also an important evaluation criterion.
- Support for versioning and change control. Versioning helps to synchronize application development, eliminating rework and increasing flexibility.
- Enforce naming conventions.
- Parse and extract metadata from multiple sources. For example, if your site is a big COBOL shop, the repository vendor should offer tools that automatically examine your COBOL source code to extract metadata.
- Generate copybooks from data element definitions.

These are some of the more common functions of a repository. When choosing a repository for database development, the following features generally are desirable.

- The data stores used by the repository can be stored using database tables in your DBMS. This enables your applications to directly read the data dictionary tables. For example, if you are primarily an Oracle shop, you should favor using a repository that stores its metadata information in Oracle tables. Some repository products utilize multiple DBMSs and allow the user to choose the DBMS to be used.

- The repository should be capable of directly reading the system catalog or views on the system catalog for each DBMS you use. This ensures that the repository will have current information on database objects.

- If the repository does not directly read the system catalog, an interface should be provided to simplify the task of populating the repository using the system catalog information.

- The repository provides an interface to any modeling and design tools used for the generation of database objects.

Most of the popular repository products are mainframe-based and rely on a centralized metadata "database," or repository. This approach is usually better suited for documenting OLTP-based systems. Such a repository may be more difficult to use in a data warehouse environment because a mainframe focus can present challenges when managing metadata in a distributed, state-of-the-art data warehouse implementation. Many ETL tools used in data warehousing projects also contain a repository that is geared toward the needs of the data warehouse. Organizations needing to manage metadata for both OLTP and data warehouses should make sure that the data in their ETL repositories can be migrated successfully to the OLTP repository.

Some repository products are application-centric.

Other repository products are application-centric. Such repository technology focuses on application development metadata—which is useful, but not comprehensive. For example, the Microsoft Repository is focused on Visual Studio and is focused on Microsoft computing assets. Microsoft has partnered with Computer Associates, makers of the market-leading PLATINUM® Repository, to provide additional enterprisewide capabilities for the Microsoft repository technology.

Repository Benefits

Repository technology provides many benefits to organizations properly exploiting their capabilities. The metadata in the repository can be used to integrate views of multiple systems helping developers to understand how the data is used by those systems. Usage patterns can be analyzed to determine how data is related in ways that may not be formally understood within the organization. Discovery of such patterns can lead to business process innovation.

In general, the primary benefit of a repository is the consistency it provides in documenting data elements and business rules. The repository helps to unify the "islands of independent data" inherent in many legacy systems. The repository enables organization's to recognize the value in their legacy systems by documenting program and operational metadata that can be used to integrate the legacy systems with new application development.

Furthermore, a repository can support a rapidly changing environment such as those imposed by Internet development efforts on organizations. The metadata in the repository can be examined to produce impact analysis reports to quickly determine how changes in one area will impact others.

Reusability is a big time saver. If something can be reused instead of being developed again from scratch, not only will time be saved but also valuable resources can be deployed on more crucial projects. Repositories facilitate reuse documenting application components and making this metadata available to the organization.

Finally, repositories are an invaluable aid to data warehousing initiatives.

Repository Challenges

One of the biggest challenges in implementing and using repository technology is keeping the repository up-to-date. The repository must be populated using data from multiple sources—all of which can change at any time. When the composition or structure of source data changes, its metadata most likely will need to change, too.

The process for populating the repository is complicated and should be made as automated as possible. Refer to Figure 21-1. Metadata sources come from multiple areas and locations within an organization and can include

- Application component metadata from program development tools, application programs, and code libraries
- Business metadata from business user input, documents, and memos
- Data modeling metadata from data modeling tools
- Database metadata from the DBMS system catalog
- ETL metadata from data warehousing tools

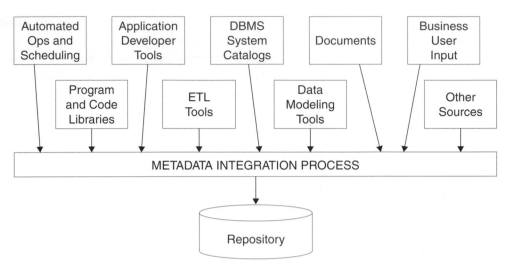

Figure 21-1   *Populating the repository*

- Operational metadata from automated operations and job scheduling tools

- Other types of metadata such as data usage metadata from query tools

To be successful, this information needs to be collected, parsed, and recorded in the corporate metadata repository. The integration process must take into account the frequency of change for each metadata source. Whenever metadata changes at the source, the metadata in the repository will be out of sync until the source metadata is scanned, captured, and integrated into the repository again.

Very few shops own a centralized metadata repository.

Many shops do not own a repository. More accurately, very few shops own a centralized metadata repository. Furthermore, many organizations that do own a repository do not always implement the proper integration and usage procedures, causing the repository to be neglected. As soon as the metadata in the repository becomes outdated, inaccurate, or nonexistent, the repository will cease to be of value. Of course, the fault does not necessarily lie with the repository technology—more likely the fault lies with the organization that does not implement procedures for keeping the metadata in the repository up-to-date. Of course, such an effort requires a significant budget, commitment, and the effort of skilled data management professionals including DAs and DBAs.

Data Dictionaries

The purpose of a *data dictionary* is to manage data definitions.

Data dictionaries were the precursors to repository technology. Data dictionaries were popular in the 1980s. The purpose of a *data dictionary* was to manage data definitions. In general, they offered little automation—the user had to manually key in the definitions. In some cases, the data dictionary was integrated into the DBMS and databases could be defined using the metadata in the data dictionary, but this was prerelational—before DBMS products had system catalogs.

As more and more types of metadata were identified and organizations desired to accumulate and manage such metadata, the data dictionary was transformed into the repository. Use of CASE tools, such as Excelerator and Advantage Gen, for application and database development enabled more metadata to be captured and maintained during the development process. As developers became more sophisticated over time, data dictionaries evolved to provide more than just data attribute descriptions. The products became capable of tracking which applications accessed what databases. Developers who used the data dictionary properly were able to maintain their systems and applications more easily.

Truthfully, IBM's AD/Cycle and Repository Manager initiatives caused much of this transformation. Even though both initiatives ultimately failed in the marketplace, repository technology was forever changed by IBM's ventures into this field. For more information on IBM's initiatives in this area, consult *IBM's Repository Manager/MVS* by Henry C. Lefkovits, the definitive book on the topic.

Summary

This chapter on metadata management has been necessarily brief. As a DBA, you will need to understand the role of metadata as it impacts the DBMS, databases, and database users. Organizations that spend a lot of time managing and maintaining metadata will likely have a data administrator on staff. Alternatively, the data warehouse administrator or architect might focus on metadata management.

DBAs may become involved in certain aspects of metadata management, such as repository selection, installation, and maintenance. However, most DBAs will *use* metadata far more than they will be called upon to store, manage, and maintain metadata.

Review

1. What is metadata?

2. Why is metadata important to an organization?

3. At a high level, what are the two types of metadata?

4. What is the difference between data and information?

5. Describe the purpose of a repository.

6. Why should the DBA participate in developing a metadata management strategy even in organizations with a well-defined data administration function?

7. Discuss the barriers to successful repository implementation.

8. Why is the DBMS system catalog useful for metadata analysis?

9. What is a data steward?

10. A DBA never requires business metadata to do his job, and a business user never needs technology metadata: True or False.

Suggested Reading

Bruce, Thomas A. *Designing Quality Databases with IDEF1X Information Models.* New York, NY: Dorset House (1991). ISBN 0-932633-18-8

Carlis, John, and Joseph Maguire. *Mastering Data Modeling: A User-Driven Approach.* Boston, MA: Addison-Wesley (2001). ISBN 0-201-70045-X

Durell, William R. Data Administration: *A Practical Guide to Successful Data Management.* New York, NY: McGraw-Hill (1985). ISBN 0-07-018391-0

———. *The Complete Guide to Data Modeling.* Princeton, NJ: Data Administration, Inc. (1993). No ISBN

Fleming, Candace, and Barbara von Halle. *Handbook of Relational Database Design.* Reading, MA: Addison-Wesley (1989). ISBN 0-201-11434-8

Hay, David C. *Data Model Patterns.* New York, NY: Dorset House (1996). ISBN 0-932633-29-3

Inmon, W. H. *Data Architecture: The Information Paradigm.* Wellesley, MA: QED Information Sciences (1989). ISBN 0-89435-268-7

Lefkovits, Henry C. *IBM's Repository Manager/MVS.* Wellesley, MA: QED Information Sciences (1991). ISBN 0-89435-349-7

Marco, David. *Building and Managing the Metadata Repository.* New York, NY: John Wiley & Sons (2000). ISBN 0-471-35523-2

Modell, Martin E. *Data Analysis, Data Modeling, and Classification.* New York, NY: McGraw Hill (1992). ISBN 0-07-042634-1

Perkinson, Richard C. *Data Analysis: The Key to Database Design.* Wellesley, MA: QED Information Sciences (1984). ISBN 0-89435-105-2

Ross, Ronald G. *Entity Modeling: Techniques and Application.* Boston, MA: Database Research Group (1988). ISBN 0-941049-00-0

Sanders, G. Lawrence. *Data Modeling.* Danvers, MA: Boyd & Fraser (1995). ISBN 0-87709-066-1

Schmidt, Bob. *Data Modeling for Information Professionals.* Upper Saddle River, NJ: Prentice Hall PTR (1999). ISBN 0-13-080450-9

Seiner, Robert S. "Questions Metadata Can Answer," The Data Administration Newsletter. http://www.tdan.com/i011fe01.htm

Simsion, Graeme. *Data Modeling Essentials: Analysis, Design, and Innovation.* New York, NY: Van Nostrand Reinhold (1994). ISBN 0-442-01654-9

Tannenbaum, Adrienne. *Metadata Solutions.* Boston, MA: Addison-Wesley (2002). ISBN 0-201-71976-2

Wertz, Charles K. *The Data Dictionary: Concepts and Uses.* Wellesley, MA: QED Information Sciences (1986). ISBN 0-89435-180-X

22

DBA Tools

Every major DBMS product provides a complete, functional database management system that can be used out of the box to store and manage data. Although organizations can install and use the DBMS as delivered, many will quickly find that the functionality needed to adequately support large-scale database development is not provided by the DBMS product alone.

The administration and maintenance of database applications is time consuming if you use only the standard features of the DBMS. Fortunately, many DBA tools that enhance the functionality of relational database management systems are available from third-party vendors.

Types and Benefits of DBA Tools

DBA tools reduce the amount of time, effort, and human error involved in maintaining efficient database systems.

A DBA tool reduces the amount of time, effort, and human error involved in maintaining efficient database systems and applications. Such tools ease the administrative burden and reduce the possibility of error.

The need for these tools becomes apparent simply by reviewing the sheer number of products that are available. Most organizations implement at least one add-on tool for their DBMS; many organizations utilize dozens to ease the administrative burdens associated with managing production database development.

Many varieties of tools are available that fulfill market niches not adequately supported by the major DBMS vendors. The remainder of this chapter provides a rundown of the categories and types of products available to the DBA to assist in managing and administering databases.

Data Modeling and Design

Tools specifically supporting your DBMS can significantly reduce development time.

Database modeling and design tools provide a consistent and coherent means of creating conceptual and logical data models and transforming them into physical database designs. Database modeling and design tools do not have to be unique to a specific database, but many are. Tools developed specifically to support your DBMS can significantly reduce development time by automating repetitive tasks and validating the models. However, if you use multiple DBMS products in your organization, you will be better off choosing a tool that can support all of them than choosing multiple tools geared for a specific database.

When choosing a modeling and design tool, look for one that can

- Support the standard tasks associated with logical data modeling such as entity-relationship diagramming and normalization.

- Create a physical data model geared to each of your target DBMS platforms. This model should support all features of each DBMS. For example, for DB2 on the mainframe it should be able to depict all DB2 objects, referential integrity, VCAT (volume catalog)- and STOGROUP-defined tablespaces, and capacity planning.

- Provide an expert system to verify the accuracy of the physical data model and to suggest alternative solutions.

- Cross-reference the logical model to the physical model, capturing text that supports physical design decisions such as denormalization and type of tablespace.

- Generate standard DDL automatically to fully implement the database defined in the physical data model. The DDL created by the tool from the physical model should support all of the options for each DBMS supported.

- Interface with application development tools and repository products used within the organization.

Database Change Management

As we discussed in Chapter 7, making changes to your databases can be an arduous and error-prone job. However, it is a rare database that does not need to undergo some sort of change during its useful life. A variety of tools are available to assist the DBA in managing and effecting database changes. These tools optimize and automate multiple change-management tasks, including database alteration, database comparison, security authorization, audit tracking, catalog querying, space management, and handling referential integrity.

Change Management Tools

The predominant form of change management tool is the database alteration and comparison tool. Although the structure of relational databases can be modified using the ALTER statement, this statement is functionally crippled in most DBMS products. In theory, the DBA should be able to alter all of the parameters that can be specified for an object when it is created, but no current DBMS product supports this. For example, most DBMS products enable you to add columns to an existing table, but only at the end. Furthermore, they do not permit the DBA to remove columns from a table—instead, the table must be dropped and then recreated without the specified columns.

Another problem that DBAs encounter when modifying database structures is the cascading DROP effect. If a change to a database object mandates that it be dropped and recreated, all dependent objects are dropped when the database object is dropped. This includes tables, all indexes on the tables, all primary and foreign keys, any related synonyms and views, any triggers, all authorization, and, of course, the data. Ensuring that DDL is issued after the modification to reverse the effects of cascading DROPs can be a tedious, complex, and error-prone procedure.

Many types of database object alteration cannot be performed using the generic ALTER statement.

Additionally, many other types of database object alteration cannot be performed using the generic ALTER statement. Depending on the DBMS, you may not be able to

- Change the name of a database, table, alias, view, column, tablespace, dbspace, trigger, stored procedure, user-defined function, relationship, or index.

- Change database partitioning.

- Move a table from one database, dbspace, or tablespace to another.

- Rearrange column ordering.

- Change a column's data type and length.

- Remove columns from a table.

- Change the primary key without dropping and adding the primary key.

- Add columns to a view or remove columns from a view.

- Change the SELECT statement on which a view is based.

- Change the indexing columns.

- Change the uniqueness specification of an index.

- Change the clustering of an index or table.

- Change the sequence of the index (ascending or descending).

The burden of ensuring that the database change is performed correctly is moved from the DBA to the tool.

Such a list usually provides all the justification needed to obtain a database alteration tool. Of course, the exact list will differ from DBMS to DBMS. Database alteration tools provide an integrated environment for altering database objects. Such tools usually provide a menu-driven or point-and-click interface allowing the DBA to specify the type of change needed. The burden of ensuring that the database change is performed correctly is moved from the DBA to the tool. At a minimum, an ALTER tool should

- Maintain tables easily without manually requiring the DBA to code DDL.

- Retain or reapply all dependent objects, authorizations, and data affected by the ALTER if a drop is required.

- Navigate hierarchically from object to object.

- Provide GUI-based modification showing before and after definitions of the objects before the changes are applied.

- Batch requested changes into a work list that can be executing in the foreground or the background.

- Analyze changes to ensure that the requested alterations do not violate any DDL rules. For example, if a series of changes is requested and one change causes a subsequent change to be invalid (an object is dropped, for instance), this should be flagged before execution.

- Provide the capability to monitor changes as they are applied.

An automated change management solution enables the DBA to focus on the required change instead of on the arcane details of how the DBMS implements such change. The tool is built to understand not just the discipline of change management but also the DBMS in which the changes are to be made. This built-in intelligence shifts the burden of ensuring that a change to a database object does not cause other implicit changes from the DBA to the tool. Furthermore, once the change has been identified and implemented for one system, it can easily be deployed on other database copies with minimal, or perhaps no, changes.

The impact of changes can be examined prior to implementing any change.

Another benefit of a change management tool is in database analysis and planning. The impact of changes can be examined prior to implementing any change. This is an invaluable resource for ensuring safe and efficient database changes. This type of tool also uses automation to minimize the resources required to implement database change. Instead of writing a new, complex change script from scratch for each database change, the DBA can rely on the change manager to accomplish this. Application and database availability will be enhanced because the product will implement the change in the least intrusive, quickest manner possible.

All in all, a database change management product will improve availability, minimize errors, and speed up your time to market.

Database Comparison Tools

Ensuring that changes are migrated effectively can be a difficult task.

Over time, the DBA will make changes to databases throughout the organization. It is possible that even with an automated database change management solution, some changes will be implemented on some systems but not on others. DBAs at large companies must keep track of dozens, if not hundreds or thousands of database servers. Ensuring that changes are migrated effectively to all of those database servers can be a difficult task.

A database comparison tool enables the DBA to compare one database to another in terms of its database objects and structures. Such tools will identify differences and automatically generate the DDL to make the databases the same—from a structural perspective, not a data content perspective. The database comparison tool should allow the DBA to make the following types of comparisons:

- One live database to another live database (on the same server or another server)

- A live database to a DDL script file
- One DDL script file to another DDL script file

DBAs who manage a large number of database servers should consider using such products. As mentioned earlier, database comparison tools compare only the structure of the database, not the contents. However, some vendors offer tools that can compare the contents of one table to another. Such tools are often useful during application program testing and debugging.

Database Object Migration Tools

Many DBMS products do not provide a feature to migrate database objects from one database server or subsystem to another. Without a tool, you can accomplish this only by manually storing the DDL CREATE statements (and all subsequent ALTER statements) in a script file and then executing the script on the other database server. Manual processes such as this are error prone. In addition, this process does not take into account the migration of table data and database security.

Migration tools facilitate the quick migration of database objects.

Migration tools facilitate the quick migration of database objects from one environment to another (e.g., from test to production). Although similar to a table altering tool, an object migration tool has minimal altering capability (some interface directly with an ALTER tool or are integrated into a single tool). The migration procedure is typically driven by panels or GUI screens that prompt the user for the objects to migrate.

Migration can typically be specified at any level. For example, if you request the migration of a specific database, you could also migrate all dependent objects and security. Capability is provided such that database object names, authorization IDs, and other objects can be renamed according to the standards of the receiving instance, subsystem, or server. When the parameters of the migration have been specified completely, the tool creates a job to implement the requested database objects in the requested environment.

A migration tool can reduce the time required by database administrators to move databases from environment to environment. Quicker turnaround results in a more rapid response to user needs, thereby increasing the efficiency of your business.

Referential Integrity Tools

Referential integrity (RI) is used by relational databases to ensure the validity of primary key to foreign key relationships. However, RI can be difficult to administer and implement. RI tools eliminate this difficulty by

- Analyzing data for both system and user-managed referential integrity constraint violations

- Executing faster than the DBMS-provided integrity checking facility or utility

- Enabling additional types of RI to be supported; for example, by analyzing primary keys for which no foreign keys exist and deleting the primary key row (pendant DELETE processing)

Additionally, tools are available that allow data to be viewed and extracted in referential sets. Such capability makes it easier to create reasonable test data by using a subset of the data in the production databases.

Auditing Tools

Auditing tools provide the ability to audit at a granular level.

An *audit* is the examination of a practice to determine its correctness. Database auditing software helps in monitoring the data control, data definition, and data integrity in the database environment. Most DBMS products provide limited audit mechanisms, but these features are typically difficult to use and maintain. Auditing tools provide the ability to audit at a more granular level and simplify the ability to report on the audit trails. Typical aspects captured by database auditing tools include

- Authorization failures
- SQL GRANT and REVOKE statements
- DDL statements issued
- DML statements issued
- SQL bind requests or new program invocations
- Utility executions

An audit tool should provide five important features.

1. An auditing tool should provide the capability to read the database logs and report on activity as needed. This reduces overhead because it uses the regular processing features of the database instead of an additional tracing feature.

2. The auditing tool should produce a set of prepackaged reports for all data modification from the database logs. The reports should be easy to produce and easy to read.

3. An auditing tool must report who (by user or authorization ID) makes each change and show before and after images of the changed data. The audit trail should also include such pertinent details as the date, time, and program name of the requesting process.

4. The auditing tool should provide the capability to interface with any auditing features of the DBMS, if so desired.

5. Finally, the auditing tool should provide both standard reports and the capability for site-specific reports.

Organizations with strict security and auditing requirements should consider using a database auditing tool because of the weak auditing capabilities of most DBMS products.

Catalog Query and Analysis Tools

The DBA relies on the system catalog to perform his job.

The system catalog or data dictionary contains a wealth of information essential to the operation of the DBMS. Information about all database objects, authority, and recovery is stored and maintained in the system catalog. The DBA relies on this information to perform his job. The system catalog is composed of relational tables and can be queried using SQL and/or vendor-supplied stored procedures. Some DBMS vendors provide system catalog views that are easier to query and monitor. However they are accessed, these tables provide an information base for many monitoring and administrative tasks.

Coding SQL every time the DBA needs to access information in the system catalog can be a very time consuming process. Often, the DBA must combine information from multiple catalog tables to provide the user with facts relevant for a particular task. Moreover, for the most part, the DBMS vendors have made the catalog tables difficult to understand and query by using odd naming conventions, denormalized structures, unused columns, poor data-type choices, and little documentation. As the DBMS vendors add features to new versions of their products, the system catalog becomes more and more difficult to understand as new data is forced into an already ugly system catalog design and implementation. When stored procedures and views are provided, querying the catalog tables is easier; however, crucial information is sometimes missing from these canned "queries."

A GUI is a basic feature common to most catalog tools.

Add-on query tools can ease the burden of developing SQL queries to access the system catalog tables. Sometimes these tools are referred to as *catalog visibility tools* because they make it easier to access information stored in the system catalog. The basic feature common to all catalog tools is the capability to request catalog information using a GUI (or panel-driven) interface without using SQL statements.

System catalog tools that provide only this level of capability are rudimentary tools at best. Most of these tools provide much more functionality. Instead of merely enabling data access, many tools can do one or more of the following tasks:

- Create syntactically correct DDL statements for all database objects by reading the appropriate system catalog tables. These statements are generally executed immediately or saved in a data set for future reference or use.

- Modify any updatable statistical columns using a non-SQL interface.

- Create syntactically correct authorization/security statements from the catalog in the same way that DDL is generated.

- Perform "drop analysis" on a SQL DROP statement. This analysis determines the effect of the cascading DROP by detailing all dependent objects and security that will be deleted as a result of executing the DROP.

- Provide a hierarchic listing of database objects. For example, if a specific table is chosen, the tool can migrate quickly up the hierarchy to show its tablespace and database, or down the hierarchy to show all dependent indexes, views, synonyms, aliases, referentially connected tables, and plans.

- CREATE and DROP database objects, and grant and revoke security from a screen without coding SQL. Additionally, some tools log all DROPs and REVOKEs such that they can be undone in the event of an inadvertent DROP or REVOKE execution.

- Operate directly on the system catalog or on a copy of the system catalog to reduce systemwide contention.

These features aid the DBA in performing his day-to-day duties. Furthermore, a catalog query tool can greatly diminish the amount of time required for a junior DBA (or new staff member) to become a productive member of the DBA team.

Security Tools

Database security is usually provided internal to the database by use of GRANT and REVOKE SQL statements, which grant authorization explicitly and implicitly to database users. Some DBMS products provide authorization exits to enable communication with external security management packages. This eases the administrative burden of database security by enabling the corporate data security function to administer groups of users.

The implementation of security in most relational databases has several problems. Paramount among these deficiencies is the effect of the cascading REVOKE. If authority is revoked from one user who has previously granted authority to other users, all dependent authorizations also are revoked.

A database security add-on tool can address this problem. These tools typically analyze the effects of a REVOKE. These tools enable the user to revoke the authority and optionally reassign all dependent authority either by recreating the appropriate GRANT statements to reapply the authorizations implicitly revoked or by revoking the authority and automatically reapplying all implicit REVOKEs in the background.

A database security add-on tool typically analyzes the effects of a REVOKE.

Database security tools provide other functions. Consider the administrative overhead when database users are hired, quit, or are transferred. Security must be added or removed. A good security tool enables a user to issue a GRANT LIKE command that can copy database authority from one database object to another or from one database user to another.

Suppose that a DBA is transferred to another department. A security tool can assign all of that DBA's authority to another user before revoking his authority. Or suppose that a new table is created for an existing application, and it requires the same authorizations as the other tables in the application. This type of tool enables a user to copy all security from one table to the new table.

A security replacement product supplants database security with an external package.

There is one other type of database security product. Rather than augment database security, however, a *security replacement* product supplants database security with an external package. This product's primary benefit is that it consolidates security administration for the data and the database. A second benefit is that the cascading REVOKE effect can be eliminated because most external data security packages do not cascade security revocations.

Database security replacement tools have their weaknesses too. These tools do not conform to the rigorous definition of the relational model, which states that the DBMS must control security. Some do not provide all types of database security. For example, system-level authorizations are frequently omitted. Another drawback is that if the external security package fails, the data is unprotected.

Table Editors

There are only two methods of updating relational data supplied by most DBMS products out of the box:

- SQL DELETE, INSERT, and UPDATE statements
- Database utilities such as LOAD or IMPORT

SQL statements operate on data a set at a time, so a single SQL statement can affect multiple rows—or even all of the rows. Coding SQL statements for every data modification required during the application development and testing phase can be time consuming. Furthermore, database utilities such as LOAD and IMPORT are not a viable means of making small targeted changes to data. They are designed and optimized for moving data in bulk.

A table editing tool can reduce the time needed to make simple data alterations

A table editing tool can reduce the time needed to make simple data alterations by providing full-screen editing capability for database tables. The user specifies the table to edit, and a table editor launches. The data is presented to the user as a series of rows, with the columns separated by spaces. A header line indicates the column names. The data can be scrolled up and down as well as left and right. To change data, the user simply types over the current data.

This type of tool is ideal for supporting the application development process. A programmer can make quick changes without coding SQL. In addition, if properly implemented, a table editor can reduce the number of erroneous data modifications made by beginning SQL users.

Exercise caution before using a table editor on critical production data. When a table editor is used, all columns are available for update, and a simple miskeying can cause unwanted updates. Native SQL should be used if you must ensure that only certain columns are updated. Tested SQL statements and application programs are characterized by their planned nature—the modification requests were well thought out and tested. This is not true for changes implemented through a table editor.

Performance Management

Assuring optimal performance is one of the biggest problems faced by DBAs on an ongoing basis. The loudest complaints come from users who have to wait longer than they are used to waiting for their applications to respond. This is especially true if the users never had to wait in the past.

However, what causes those formerly fast applications to stall and deliver subpar performance? If there were an easy answer to that question, many DBAs would be out of work. So, let's examine the basics of performance management and optimization that apply to all database applications.

Every database application, at its core, requires three components in order to operate: the system, the database, and the application. To deliver performance, the DBA must be able to monitor and tune each of these components. There are tools available to the DBA for monitoring and optimizing each of these components.

To deliver performance, the DBA must be able to monitor the system, the database, and the application.

System Performance Tools

System performance tools examine the database server, its configuration, and usage. The most commonly used system performance tool is the *performance monitor*. Database performance monitoring and analysis tools support many types of performance-oriented requests in many ways. For example, database performance tools can operate

- In the background mode as a batch job that reports on performance statistics written by the DBMS trace facility

- In the foreground mode as an online monitor that either traps trace information or captures information from the DBMS control blocks as applications execute

- By sampling the database kernel and user address spaces as the program runs and by capturing information about the performance of the job, independent of database traces

- By capturing database trace information and maintaining it in a history file (or table) for producing historical performance reports and for predicting performance trends

- As a capacity planning device that gives statistical information about an application and the environment in which it will operate

- As an after-the-fact analysis tool on a workstation, that analyzes and graphs all aspects of application performance and systemwide performance

Each database performance monitor supports one or more of these features. The evaluation of database performance monitors is a complex task.

Sometimes more than one performance monitor is used at a single site—perhaps one for batch reporting and another for online event monitoring. Maybe an enterprisewide monitoring solution has been implemented and one component of that solution is a database module that monitors your DBMS, but it lacks the details of a more sophisticated DBMS monitor. So, another performance monitor is purchased for daily DBA usage, while the module of the enterprisewide monitoring solution is used for integrated monitoring by system administrators.

Modern database performance tools can set performance thresholds that, once reached, will alert the DBA, perform another task to report on, or actually fix the problem. These tools are typically agent-based. An *agent* is a piece of independent code that runs on the database server looking for problems. It interacts with, but does not rely on, a console running on another machine that is viewed by the DBA. This agent architecture enables efficient database monitoring because the agent is not tied to a workstation and can act independently. The agent sends information to the DBA only when required.

Some system performance tools focus on a specific component of the DBMS such as the data cache

Additionally, some system performance tools are available that focus on a specific component of the DBMS such as the data cache. Such a tool can be used to model the memory requirements for database caching, to capture data cache utilization statistics, and perhaps even to make recommendations for improving the performance of the data cache.

Another type of performance optimization tool enables database configuration parameters to be changed without recycling the DBMS instance, subsystem, or server. These tools are useful when the changes require the DBMS to be stopped and restarted. Such tools can dramatically improve availability, especially if configuration parameters need to be changed frequently and the DBMS does not support dynamic parameter modification.

A few ISVs provide *invasive system performance tools* that enhance the performance of databases by adding functionality directly to the DBMS and interacting with the database kernel. Typically, these products take advantage of known DBMS shortcomings.

Care must be taken when evaluating invasive performance tools.

For example, products are available that enhance the performance of reading a database page or block or that optimize data caching by providing additional storage and control over buffers and their processing. Care must be taken when evaluating invasive performance tools. New releases of the DBMS may negate the need for these tools because functionality has been added or known shortcomings have been corrected. However, this does not mean that you should not consider invasive database performance tools. They *can* pay for themselves after only a short period of time. Discarding the tool when the DBMS supports its functionality is not a problem if the tool has already paid for itself in terms of better performance.

One final caution: Because invasive performance tools can interact very closely with the database kernel, be careful when migrating to a new DBMS release or a new release of the tool. Extra testing should be performed with these tools because of their intrusive nature.

Database Performance Tools

Most DBMSs do not provide an intelligent database analysis capability. Instead, the DBA or performance analyst must use system catalog views and queries, or a system catalog tool, to keep watch over each database and its objects. This is not an optimal solution because it relies on human intervention for efficient database organization, opening up the possibility for human error.

Fortunately, database analysis tools are available that can proactively and automatically monitor your database environment. These database analysis tools typically can

- Collect statistics for tables and indexes: standard statistical information, extended statistics capturing more information (for example, data set extents), or a combination of both.

- Read the underlying data sets for the database objects to capture current statistics, read the database statistics from the system catalog, and read tables unique to the tool that captured the enhanced statistics, or any combination thereof.

- Set thresholds based on database statistics whereby the automatic scheduling of database reorganization and other maintenance tasks can be invoked.

- Provide a series of canned reports detailing the potential problems for specific database objects.

Application Performance Tools

Writing SQL statements to access database tables is the responsibility of an application development team. However, the DBA usually gets involved when it comes to the performance of SQL. With SQL's flexibility, the same request can be made in different ways. Because many of these methods are inefficient, application performance can fluctuate wildly unless the SQL is analyzed and tuned by an expert prior to implementation.

The EXPLAIN or SHOW PLAN commands provide information about the access paths used by SQL queries by parsing SQL in application programs and placing encoded output into a PLAN_TABLE or by producing a standard access path report. To gauge efficiency, a DBA must decode this data and determine if a more efficient access path is available.

SQL code reviews are required to ensure that optimal SQL design techniques are used. As discussed in Chapter 6, an application walkthrough should perform a review of all SQL statements, the selected access paths, and the program code in which the SQL is embedded. The review also includes an evaluation of database statistical information to ascertain whether production-level statistics were used at the time of the EXPLAIN.

SQL analysis tools can automate major portions of the code review process.

A line-by-line review of application source code and EXPLAIN output is tedious and prone to error, and can cause application backlogs. SQL analysis tools greatly simplify this process by automating major portions of the code review process. The SQL analysis tool typically

- Analyzes the SQL in an application program, describing the access paths chosen in a graphic format, an English description, or both.

- Issues warnings when specific SQL constructs are encountered. For example, each time a sort is requested (by ORDER BY, GROUP BY, or DISTINCT), a message informs the user of the requisite sort.

- Suggests alternative SQL solutions based on an "expert system" that reads SQL statements and their corresponding PLAN_TABLE entries and poses alternative SQL options.

- Extends the rules used by the "expert system" to capture site-specific rules.

- Analyzes at the subsystem, instance, server, application, plan, package, or SQL statement level.

- Stores multiple versions of EXPLAIN output, creates performance comparisons, and plans history reports.

Tools that analyze the performance of the application code in which the SQL is embedded are available too. These tools usually capture in-depth information

Application and SQL Analysis

Consider an application program that contains a singleton SELECT inside a loop. The singleton SELECT requests a single row based on a WHERE clause, checking for the primary key of that table. For each iteration of the loop, the program changes the primary key value being searched such that the entire table is read from the lowest key value to the highest key value.

SQL analysis tools will probably not target the SQL statement as inefficient because the predicate value is for the primary key, which should invoke indexed access. The application program analysis tool may flag the section of the code that accesses the data as inefficient, but it will not help you to fix it or tell you why it is inefficient.

A knowledgeable performance analyst or DBA would have to use both tools and interpret the output of each to arrive at a satisfactory conclusion. For example, it could be more efficient to code a cursor, without a predicate, to retrieve every row of the table, and then fetch each row one by one. This method would eliminate index I/O, might use parallel access, and therefore should reduce I/O and elapsed time—thereby enhancing performance.

Only a trained analyst can catch this type of design problem during a code walkthrough. Although a plan analysis tool significantly reduces the effort involved in the code review process, it cannot eliminate it.

about programs as they are run and provide reports that specify which areas of the code consume the most resources. Unfortunately, most of these tools do not necessarily interface to SQL analysis tools. If you are interested in why this might be a problem, see the sidebar "Application and SQL Analysis."

The first feature required of SQL analysis tools is the ability to read and interpret standard EXPLAIN or SHOW PLAN output. The tool should be able to read the plan table or interface directly with the DBMS command to obtain the output. It then must be able to automatically scan the EXPLAIN or SHOW PLAN data and report on the selected access paths and the predicted performance. Advanced tools will provide recommendations for improving the SQL by adding indexes or modifying the SQL.

Backup and Recovery

As we learned in Chapters 15 and 16, assuring the recoverability of database systems is a complex task. In order to do the job properly, DBAs need to understand the backup and recovery features of the DBMS, how it interfaces to the disk storage systems, and the business impact of data to the organization. Sometimes DBAs need a helping hand.

The simplest form of backup and recovery tool is the high-speed utility.

Fortunately, there are a number of tools that streamline and automate the backup and recovery process. The simplest form of backup and recovery tool is the high-speed utility. ISV utilities that speed up the process of making image copy backups and using those backups for recovery can be used to reduce downtime and increase data availability. Some tools also simplify, not just speed up, these processes. For example, many high-speed backup and recovery utilities can back up entire databases or database objects using masking and wildcarding techniques. For example, consider the following command:

```
COPY GL21DBX2.T*
```

A command such as this might be used to make an image copy backup of every tablespace in the database named GL21DBX2 that begins with the letter "T". Not only is this simpler than explicitly listing every tablespace, but the backup script will not need to be edited if a new tablespace is added that conforms to the wildcarded mask.

Additional products are available that automate the entire recovery process. Such tools might be able to accept a recovery request, examine the log and the image copy backups, make a recommendation on how to recover, or, even further, build the scripts to perform the recovery that would result in the most data recovered in the least amount of downtime.

A final type of recovery tool is the *log-based recovery tool*. Such tools can be used to examine the log and produce reverse SQL, as discussed in Chapter 15. For example, assume the DBA issued a DELETE statement in error. Using the log-based recovery tool, the DBA would input the program name and the time it ran. The tool would examine the log, find the DELETE, and create INSERT statements to reproduce the deleted data. Simply by running the INSERT statements, the database is recovered. Of course, this is a simplistic example, but a log-based analysis tool can come in handy when erroneous database modifications need to be identified and rectified quickly.

Database Utilities

Many database utilities that ship free with the DBMS are notorious for poor performance.

Many database utilities that ship free with the DBMS are simple, no-frills programs that are notorious for poor performance, especially on very large tables. However, these utilities are required to populate, administer, and organize your databases. The typical utilities that are provided are LOAD, UNLOAD, REORG, BACKUP, and RECOVER, as well as utilities for integrity checking.

Third-party vendors provide support tools that replace the database utilities and provide the same or more functionality in a more efficient manner. For example, it is not unheard of for third-party vendors to claim that its utilities execute anywhere from four to ten times faster than the native DBMS utilities. These claims must be substantiated for the data and applications at your organization (but such claims are quite believable). Before committing to any third-party utility, the DBA should be sure that the product conforms to at least the following requirements:

- Does not subvert the integrity of the data in the database.

- Provides at a minimum the same features as the corresponding native utility. For example, if the REORG utility reorganizes both indexes and tablespaces, the enhanced REORG tool must be able to do the same.

- Does not subvert standard database features. For example, DB2 image copies are maintained in the DB2 system catalog. An enhanced backup tool for DB2, therefore, should store its image copies there as well.

- Provides an execution time at least twice as fast as the corresponding database utility. For example, if the Sybase DUMP utility requires 20 minutes to back up a table, the enhanced backup tool must dump the same table in at least 10 minutes. Of course, this does not need to be a hard-and-fast rule. Sometimes even a moderate increase in processing time is sufficient to justify the cost of a third-party utility offering.

- Corrects deficiencies in the standard database utilities. For example, if the LOAD utility does not load data in sequence by clustering index, the replacement LOAD utility should do so.

Conduct fair tests when testing utility tools from different vendors.

When testing utility tools from different vendors, be sure to conduct fair tests. For example, always reload or recover prior to testing REORG utilities, or you may skew your results due to different levels of table organization. Additionally, always run the tests for each tool on the same object with the same amount of data, and make sure that the data cache is flushed between each test run. Finally, make sure that the workload on the system is the same (or as close as possible) when testing each product because concurrent workload can skew benchmark test results.

Utility Management Tools

Another variety of database utility offering is the utility manager. This type of tool provides administrative support for the creation and execution of database utility jobstreams. These utility generation and management tools

- Automatically generate utility parameters, JCL, or command scripts.
- Monitor the database utilities as they execute.
- Automatically schedule utilities when exceptions are triggered.
- Restart utilities with a minimum of intervention. For example, if a utility cannot be restarted, the utility manager should automatically terminate the utility before resubmitting it.

Data Warehousing and Business Intelligence

The data warehouse administrator requires a lot of help to automate the management of warehouse databases and to assist the users in effectively querying the data warehouse.

ETL Tools

ETL stands for Extract, Transform, and Load. An ETL tool eases the burden of data movement and transformation because the tool understands the data format and environment of each DBMS it works with. A company's choice of ETL tools depends on the following factors.

- How many DBMS products need to be supported? If the project requires only a single DBMS (unlikely), the ETL features built into that DBMS might be sufficient for the project's needs.
- To what extent must data be replicated across multiple DBMS products?
- Does the data have to be synchronized across DBMS products?
- How much data manipulation and transformation is required as data moves from the OLTP source systems to the data warehouse?
- Is the data static or dynamic?
- If it is dynamic, is it updated online, in batch, or both?

The answers to these questions will help to determine the type of data warehousing tool necessary. Two basic types of data conversion tools are popular in the market today: replication and propagation.

Replication tools extract data from external application systems and heterogeneous databases for population into target database tables. Sometimes the target databases supported by this type of tool are narrow, but the source databases typically are broad. For example, a tool may be able to extract data from IMS, Oracle, SQL Server, nondatabase files, and other structures but will only support loading into a DB2 table. Before choosing a replication tool, be sure you know the full list of source and target data structures that must be supported, and choose your replication tool with care.

Propagation tools capture data as it changes at the source (external applications and heterogeneous databases) and then insert it into target database tables. A propagation tool is similar in function to a replication tool, but propagation tools are active. They constantly capture updates made in the external system, either for immediate application to the target tables or for subsequent batch updating. This differs from the extract tool, which captures entire data structures, not data modifications.

In heterogeneous data processing shops, the same data may need to be stored in multiple DBMS products. In a multiple-DBMS environment, the movement of data from DBMS to DBMS is a tedious task. ETL tools can be useful for converting data from DBMS to DBMS even outside of warehousing needs.

Query and Reporting Tools

Most DBMS products bundle a simple query tool with the product. Usually this tool is very rudimentary and only permits SQL statements to be run with no formatting of the output. Most organizations will find these tools inadequate for developing professional, formatted reports or complete applications. These tools may also be inadequate for inexperienced users or those who want to develop or execute ad hoc queries.

Query and report writing tools address these deficiencies. The capability to format reports without programming is probably their greatest asset. Another important feature is a GUI interface that allows you to develop data manipulation requests without writing complex SQL.

Many vendors provide table query and reporting tools that can be used to enhance ad hoc query capabilities. These products typically

- Provide standard query formats and bundled reports

- Provide access to multiple file formats and heterogeneous databases

- Deliver extensive formatting options

- Offer more analytical functions than SQL

- Use static or dynamic SQL for stored queries

- Execute database commands from the query tool

Fourth-generation languages are popular for accessing relational data.   Database query tools typically use point-and-click, drag-and-drop technology to greatly ease the report generation process. Fourth-generation languages (4GL) are also popular for accessing relational data. These products provide more functionality than a report writing tool, and utilize a GUI front end that makes them easier to use than 3GL programming languages such as Visual Basic, COBOL, or C. Generally, 4GL tools work in one of three ways:

- Queries are developed using 4GL syntax, which then is converted "behind the scenes" into SQL queries.

- SQL is embedded in the 4GL code and executed much like SQL embedded in 3GL code.

- A hybrid methodology is used in which the executed SQL is either difficult or impossible to review.

Newer DBMS versions and releases now include more advanced support of queries, reports, and OLAP activities. For example, Microsoft SQL Server 2000 Analysis Services provides in-depth analytical query capabilities rivaling those of third-party OLAP tools. Of course, these services work for SQL Server only. Organizations having to support analytical and query processing against heterogeneous databases should consider using a third-party tool that supports all of the DBMS products in the organization.

Programming and Development Tools

Some tools straddle the line between DBA tool and programmer tool. For example, third-party vendors offer many tools that enhance the database application development environment. Programmers commonly use these tools, but DBAs quite frequently are involved in the review and analysis of such products.

Some of the tasks that programming and development tools can perform include

- Testing SQL statements in a program editor while the programmer codes the SQL.
- Performing predictive performance estimation for programs and SQL statements.
- Explaining SQL statements in an editing session.
- Generating complete code from in-depth specifications. Some tools even generate SQL. When code generators are used, ensure that the generated code is efficient before promoting it to production status.
- Providing an enhanced environment for coding procedural SQL when creating triggers, stored procedures, and user-defined functions.
- Interfacing with 4GLs to create database access routines.

Because of the many varieties of database programming products, these tools should be evaluated on a case-by-case basis.

Checkpoint/Restart Tools

Some DBMS products provide no inherent capability for storing checkpoint information. When a program fails, a restart is difficult because there is no track of the last data that was committed to the database unless the programmer coded it into the program. Tools are available for some DBMS products to store checkpoint information that can be used by application programs during restarts. Such products are useful for large batch database applications that issue many COMMITs. Many of these products require little, if any, modification of the program.

Testing Tools

Testing tools enable you to issue a battery of tests against a test base and analyze the results. Testing tools typically are used for all types of applications, but some have been specifically extended to support testing against database tables.

Debugging Tools

SQL debugging tools are useful for identifying and fixing syntax and logic errors in difficult SQL statements. These tools are most useful for procedural SQL dialects such as PL/SQL and Transact-SQL.

Miscellaneous Tools

All kinds of niche tools are available.

In addition to the tools we have reviewed already, there are all kinds of niche tools available. Some of them are non-database-specific tools, while others are simply useful single-purpose programs that help when managing database systems. Let's examine some of these miscellaneous tool categories.

Space Management Tools

Most DBMSs provide basic statistics for space utilization, but the in-depth statistics required for both space management and performance tuning are usually inadequate for heavy duty administration. For example, most DBMSs lack the ability to monitor the requirements of the underlying files used by the DBMS. When these files go into extents or become defragmented, performance can suffer. Without a space management tool, the only way to monitor this information is with arcane and difficult-to-use operating system commands. This can be a tedious exercise.

Each DBMS allocates space differently

Additionally, each DBMS allocates space differently. The manner in which the DBMS allocates this space can result in inefficient disk usage. Sometimes space is allocated, but the database will not use it. A space management tool is the only answer for ferreting out the amount of used space versus the amount of allocated space.

Space management tools often interface with other database and systems management tools such as operating system space management tools, database analysis tools, system catalog query and management tools, and database utility generators.

Compression Tools

A standard tool for reducing storage costs is the compression utility. This type of tool operates by applying an algorithm to the data in a table such that the data is encoded in a more compact area. By reducing the amount of area needed to store data, overall storage costs are decreased. Compression tools must compress the data when it is added to the table and subsequently modified, then expand the data when it is later retrieved. Additionally, some tools are available that compress database logs, enabling more log information to be retained on disk before it is offloaded to another medium.

Third-party compression routines are usually specified by using APIs at the database or operating system level. Sometimes tables must be dropped and recreated to apply the compression routine.

In general, a compression algorithm increases CPU costs while it decreases storage and I/O costs. This trade-off is not beneficial for all tables. For example, if a compression routine saves 30% on storage costs but increases CPU consumption without decreasing I/O, the trade-off is probably not beneficial.

A compression tool can reduce the size of the rows to be stored.

A compression tool can decrease storage by reducing the size of the rows to be stored. CPU consumption usually increases because additional processing is required to compress and expand the row. I/O costs, however, could decrease—perhaps dramatically so.

Some DBMSs support compression without requiring a third-party product. The major advantage of third-party compression tools is that most of the vendors provide additional flexibility and multiple compression algorithms for different types of data.

Online Standards Manuals

Products are available that provide "canned" standards for implementing, accessing, and administering databases. These tools are particularly useful for new database shops. By purchasing an online standards manual, new—and even more experienced—shops can quickly come up to speed with each new DBMS.

Online manuals can function as cheap training.

Everyone benefits from these products if the third-party vendor automatically ships updates whenever there is a new version or release of the DBMS product. Online manuals can function as cheap training in the new DBMS release (e.g., migrating from Oracle8i to Oracle9i).

Any product that delivers database standards should

- Provide online networked access so that all developers and DBAs can access the manual
- Be extensible, so additional standards can be added
- Be modifiable, so the provided standards can be altered to suit prior shop standards (e.g., naming conventions, programming standards)

Other Tools

Many types of database tools are available. The categories in this chapter cover the major types of tools, but not all tools can be easily pigeonholed. For example, consider a database space calculator. It reads table DDL and information on the number of rows in the table to estimate space requirements. A space calculator is often provided with another tool such as a space management tool or a database design and modeling tool.

Additionally, some standard system management and programming tools can be used to optimize the database environment. For example, a third-party sorting tool can be used to presort data before loading or to sort output results for comparison during database program testing.

New types of products are announced quite regularly.

Furthermore, new types of products are announced quite regularly. For example, one vendor recently released a product that analyzes the SQL that accesses a particular table and uses a set of expert rules to recommend the most efficient indexes. Be sure to keep your eyes open for new and useful types of tools not mentioned in this chapter.

Evaluating DBA Tool Vendors

Advanced organizations augment their DBA staff with advanced software tools that help to automate the task of database administration. Multiple categories of database tools are available to organizations to improve the efficiency of database administration. Sometimes the DBA will have to choose from a list of similar tools provided by multiple vendors or investigate a new vendor who offers a tool not available from the primary vendor.

The nature and stability of the product vendor is important.

Although the most important aspect of database tool selection is the functionality of the tool and the way it satisfies the needs of your organization, the nature and stability of the product vendor is important also. This section provides suggested questions to ask when you are selecting a database tool vendor.

- How long has the vendor been in business? How long has the vendor been supplying tools for the particular DBMS products you manage? In general, the longer the vendor has been in business, the better, and the longer the vendor has worked with the DBMS products in question, the better.

- Does your company have other DBA or system management tools from this vendor? How satisfied are the users of those tools?

- Are other organizations satisfied with the tool you are selecting? Obtain a list of other companies who use the same tool, and contact several of them.

- Does the vendor provide a 24-hour support number? If not, what are the vendor's hours of operation? Does the vendor have a toll-free number? If not, how far away is the company from your site? You want to avoid accumulating long-distance charges when you are requesting customer support from a vendor.

- Does the vendor provide online technical support? Can you access it to evaluate its usefulness before establishing a relationship with the vendor? If so, scan some of FAQs and reported problems for the tools before committing to the vendor's product.

- Evaluate the response of the technical support number. Call the number with technical questions at least five times throughout the day: before 8:00 A.M., around noon, just before 5:00 P.M., after 9:00 P.M., and just after midnight. These are the times when you could find problems with the level of support provided by the vendor. Was the phone busy? Were you put on hold? For how long? When you got a response, was it accurate and friendly? Did the person who answered the phone have to find someone with more technical knowledge? (This can indicate potential problems.) If you really want to test the vendor, call them after midnight to gauge the response to an after-hours support request.

- Does the vendor provide a newsletter? How technical is it? Does it provide information on the database industry and the vendor's tools, or just on the vendor's tools?

- Does this vendor supply other tools that your organization might need later? If so, are they functionally integrated with this one? Does the vendor supply a full suite of products or just a few? Does the vendor provide solutions in each of the categories discussed above, or in just a few? It is wise to work with a vendor that can satisfy all (or most) of your database administration needs, not just a few of them.

- Are the vendor's tools integrated with other tools? For example, a product that analyzes databases to determine whether a reorg is required should integrate the reorg with your shop's job scheduler.

- Does the vendor provide training? Is it on-site training? Does the vendor supply DBMS training as well as training for its tools? Are installation, technical, and user manuals provided free of charge? If so, how many copies? If not, what is the charge? Is computer-based training available for the vendor's tools?

- Will the vendor answer database questions free of charge in addition to questions about its product? For example, if the vendor provides Oracle tools, are the support personnel skilled enough to answer a question about Oracle database administration? Sometimes vendors will do this, but they do not typically advertise the fact. Try it out by calling the technical support number.

- Does the vendor have a local office? If not, are technicians readily available for on-site error resolution if needed? If so, at what price?

- Will the vendor deliver additional documentation or error-resolution information by overnight mail? Does it publish a fax number? An e-mail address?

- How are software fixes provided? Electronically? By tape? Over the Web? Via FTP? Is a complete reinstallation required? Are fixes typically accomplished using zaps?

- How many man hours, on a short notice, is the vendor willing to spend to solve problems? Is there a guaranteed time limit to resolve severe product problems?

- Is the vendor willing to send a sales representative to your site to do a presentation of the product tailored to your needs? Or is it a "phone sales only" organization? If the vendor will not send someone on-site, it can indicate that you are dealing with a small vendor or a vendor who could be difficult to deal with later.

- Is the vendor a business partner of the DBMS vendors such as Microsoft, IBM, Oracle, and Sybase? How soon will the vendor's tools be modified to support new releases and versions of the DBMS?

- Have the vendor's tools been reviewed or highlighted in any industry publications recently? If so, obtain the publications and read the articles. Sometimes the articles will be available on the Web. Make sure that they were not written by the vendor, but by a neutral third party— preferably a customer, consultant, or industry analyst.

- Will the vendor supply a list of consultants who have used the product and can vouch for its functionality?

- Will the vendor assist in developing a cost justification? Most tool vendors are eager for your business and will be more than willing to provide cost justifications to help you sell upper management on the need for DBA tools.

- Does the vendor provide sample scripts (or JCL for the mainframe) to run its product? Is an easy-to-use "Getting Started" manual available?

- Does the vendor charge an upgrade fee when the processor is upgraded? How flexible are the terms and conditions for the contract?

- Is the vendor willing to set a ceiling for increases in the annual maintenance charge?

- If the vendor is sold or goes out of business, will the vendor supply the source code of the tool? Is the source code escrowed? If not, are the terms and conditions of the contract flexible in the event the vendor is acquired? Given the state of the industry today, with mass vendor consolidation, this is an important item to consider or you may be stuck with unsupported products or a "difficult" vendor post-acquisition.

- Does the vendor supply database administration tools for all of the DBMS products used at your shop? Can the same tool, using the same interface, be used to manage multiple databases across multiple operating systems?

- How does the vendor rank enhancement requests? Is every request ranked equally or are certain customers favored over others? If so, how can you be assured that you will be one of the vendor's "favored" customers?

These questions can provide the basis for your organization's evaluation of DBA tool vendors. Judge for yourself which criteria are most important to your organization. You might consider applying a weighting factor to each question to rate the responses. If you do so, be sure not to inform the vendor of this weighting to ensure that any help the vendor may be supplying you is "honest" help.

Homegrown DBA Tools

Some organizations build homegrown DBA tools to help support their DBMS environments. Such tools are usually developed and maintained by the DBAs or systems programmers. I have seen homegrown tools that address just about every aspect of database administration that vendor-marketed tools address.

Homegrown tools have pros and cons.

There are pros and cons to pursuing a homegrown DBA tool strategy. Most organizations view the biggest benefit as decreased cost. This may be true in some cases, but it often is not. Although homegrown tools will not incur the initial expense of a third-party tool, the ongoing maintenance expense can be prohibitive. Every time a new version or release of the DBMS is installed, a homegrown tool will need to be at least retested and usually recoded. Not only does this incur a cost, it takes valuable management time away from the DBA. Instead of managing the organization's databases, the DBA must maintain the homegrown tools.

New DBAs need to understand the DBA team's tool philosophy when coming onboard. Does the company build its own tools or purchase third-party tools? Sometimes, the answer is a mixture of the two approaches.

Summary

Adopt checklists for product comparisons.

Third-party DBA tools can significantly improve the efficiency of applications that access relational data. When evaluating products, look for features important to your organization. Consider adopting checklists for product comparisons based on the features discussed in this chapter. Remember, most DBMSs leave quite a bit to be desired in the administration, data access, performance monitoring, and application development areas. Third-party DBA tools can help minimize these weaknesses and alleviate your database administration pains.

Review

1. Name the three categories of performance tools and briefly summarize their typical capabilities.

2. If you are asked by management to develop a cost justification for DBA tools, how can you minimize the amount of work it takes to produce such a justification?

3. What type(s) of tool(s) would be most helpful to an organization that is brand new to database management, and why?

4. What is the purpose of a catalog visibility tool?

5. What is the benefit of purchasing database utilities from a third-party vendor when most DBMS products already ship with a set of utilities "in the box"?

6. What type of problem can be caused when using a table editor to modify data in a production database table?

7. What does the acronym ETL mean?

8. Why would it be important to contractually guarantee that the vendor escrow the source code for any tools your organization purchases?

9. What is the difference between a propagation tool and a replication tool?

10. Name the five important features that should be provided by an auditing tool.

23

DBA Rules of Thumb

DBAs should be
armed with a
proper attitude
and sufficient tech-
nical knowledge.

The first 22 chapters of this book cover the practices, policies, and procedures associated with the management discipline of database administration. This chapter provides guidance for DBAs as they embark on the job of implementing those practices, policies, and procedures. Database administration is a very technical discipline; it is also a very political discipline—the DBA is very visible within the organization. DBAs should be armed with a proper attitude and sufficient technical knowledge before attempting to practice database administration.

The Rules

The following sections outline some basic guidelines to help you become a well-rounded, respected, and professional DBA.

Write Down Everything

During the course of performing your job as a DBA, you are likely to encounter many challenging tasks and time consuming problems. Be sure to document the processes you use to resolve problems and overcome challenges. Such documentation can be very valuable should you encounter the same, or a similar, problem in the future. It is better to read your notes than to try to recreate a scenario from memory.

Keep Everything

Be a pack rat.   DBA is just the job for you if you are a pack rat. It is a good practice to keep everything you come across during the course of your job. This includes, but is not limited to,

- Manuals—old and new; online and printed
- Scripts—to make changes, run reorgs, whatever
- Programs—quick fix programs, sample programs, and so on
- Proceedings and presentations—from user groups and conferences
- Notes—from design reviews, specification meetings, team meetings, user groups and conferences, and so on
- Textbooks—from any classes you have attended (as well as additional technical books such as this one)
- White papers
- Reports—from performance monitors, queries, applications, and so on
- Articles—from magazines or links to Web sites (you might consider printing some of your favorite Web links)
- Reference manuals—for all of your DBMS products and tools

Automate!

Why should you do it by hand if you can automate? Anything you do can probably be done better by a computer—if it is programmed properly. Once a task is automated, you save yourself valuable time—that probably will be spent tackling other problems.

Don't reinvent the wheel.   Furthermore, don't reinvent the wheel. Someone, somewhere, at some time may have already solved the problem you are attempting to solve. Look for Web sites that allow you to download and share scripts. If you have the budget, purchase DBA tools as discussed in Chapter 22.

Share Your Knowledge

The more you learn, the more you should share that knowledge with others. Many local database user groups meet quarterly or monthly to discuss aspects of database management systems. Be sure to attend these sessions to learn what your peers are doing. When you have some good experiences to share, put together a presentation yourself. Sometimes you can learn far more by presenting at these events than by simply attending because the attendees will seek you out to discuss your approach.

Use online forums.

Another avenue for sharing your knowledge is using one of many online forums. Web portals and Web-based publications are constantly seeking out content for their Web sites. Working to put together a tip or article for these sites helps you to organize your thoughts and to document your experiences. Furthermore, as the author of an article or column on the Web, you will gain exposure to your peers. Sometimes this type of exposure can help you to land that coveted job.

Finally, if you have the time, considering writing for one of the database-related magazines. Writing an article that gets published will take the most amount of time, but it can bring the most exposure. Furthermore, some of the journals will pay you for your material.

However, the best reason to share your knowledge with others is because you want them to share their knowledge and experiences with you. A spirit of cooperation maintains the community of DBAs who are willing and eager to provide assistance.

Analyze, Simplify, and Focus

As we've learned in the previous chapters, the job of a DBA is complex and spans many diverse technological and functional areas. It is easy for a DBA to get overwhelmed with certain tasks—especially those that are not performed regularly. The best advice I can give you is to remain focused and keep a clear head.

Understand the purpose for each task and focus on performing the steps that will help you to achieve that end. Do not be persuaded to broaden the scope of work for individual tasks unless it cannot be avoided. In other words, don't try to boil the ocean. If nonrelated goals get grouped together into a task, it can become easy to work long hours with no clear end in sight.

Analyze, simplify, and focus. Only then will tasks become measurable and easier to achieve.

Don't Panic!

Panic can cause manual errors.

Problems will occur—nothing you can do can eliminate every possible problem or error. Part of your job as a DBA is to be able to react to problems with a calm demeanor and analytical disposition. When a database is down and applications are unavailable, your environment will become hectic and frazzled. The best things you can do when problems occur are to remain calm and draw on your extensive knowledge and training. As the DBA, you will be the focus of the company (or at least the business units affected) until the database and applications are brought back online. It can be a harrowing experience to recover a database with your boss and your users hovering behind your computer terminal and looking over your back. Be prepared for such events, because eventually they will happen. Panic can cause manual errors—the last thing you want to have happen when you are trying to recover from an error.

The more comprehensive your planning and the better your procedures, the faster you will be able to resolve problems. Furthermore, if you are sure of your procedures you will remain much calmer.

Measure Twice, Cut Once

Being prepared means analyzing, documenting, and testing your DBA policies and procedures. Creating procedures in a vacuum without testing will do little to help you run an efficient database environment. Moreover, it will not prepare you to react rapidly and effectively to problem situations.

The old maxim applies: Measure twice, cut once. In the case of DBA procedures, this means analyze, test, and then apply. Analyze your environment and the business needs of the databases to create procedures and policies that match those needs. Test those procedures. Finally, apply them to the production databases.

Understand the Business, Not Just the Technology

Remember that being technologically adept is just a part of being a good DBA. Although technology is important, understanding your business needs is more important. If you do not understand the impact on the business of the databases you manage, you will simply be throwing technology around with no clear purpose.

Business needs must dictate what technology is applied to what database—and to which applications. Using the latest and greatest (and most expensive) technology and software might be fun and technologically challenging, but it most likely will not be required for every database you implement.

Talk to the users.

Talk to the users—not just the application developers. Get a sound understanding of how the databases will be used before implementing any database design. Gain an understanding of the database's impact to the company's bottom line, so that when the inevitable problems occur in production you will remember the actual business impact of not having that data available. This also allows you to create procedures that minimize the potential for such problems.

Don't Become a Hermit

Work with the application developers. Don't isolate yourself in your own little DBA corner of the world. The more you learn what the applications do and the application requirements, the better you can adjust and tune the databases to support the applications.

Be accessible.   A DBA should be accessible. Don't be one of those DBAs that everyone is afraid to approach. The more you are valued for your expertise and availability, the more valuable you are to your company.

Use All of the Resources at Your Disposal

Remember that you do not have to do everything yourself. Use the resources at your disposal. We have talked about some of those resources, such as articles and books, Web sites and scripts, user groups and conferences. But there are others.

Know where to go to get help to solve the problem.   Do not continue to struggle with problems when you are completely stumped. Some DBAs harbor the notion that they have to resolve every issue themselves in order to be successful. Sometimes you just need to know where to go to get help to solve the problem. Use the DBMS vendor's technical support, as well as the technical support line of your DBA tool vendors. Consult internal resources for areas where you have limited experience, such as network specialists for network and connectivity problems and system administrators for operating system and system software problems.

When you go to user groups, build a network of DBA colleagues whom you can contact for assistance. Many times others have already encountered and solved the problem that vexes you. A network of DBAs to call on can be an invaluable resource (and no one at your company even needs to know that you didn't solve the problem yourself).

Finally, be sure to understand the resources available from your DBMS vendors. DBMS vendors offer their customers access to a tremendous amount of useful information. For example, Oracle provides a MetaLink database (http://metalink.oracle.com/) that users can search to find answers to database problems. IBM customers can use IBM-Link, and Microsoft also supplies a searchable database (click on Knowledge Base) on their Web site (http://www.microsoft.com/).

Some DBAs claim to be able to solve 95% or more of their problems by researching online databases. These resources can shrink the amount of time required to fix problems, especially if your DBMS vendor has a reputation of "taking forever" to respond to issues.

Of course, every DBA should also be equipped with the DBMS vendor's technical support phone number for those tough-to-solve problems. Some support is offered on a pay-per-call basis, whereas other times there is a prepaid support contract. Be sure you know how your company pays for support before calling the DBMS vendor. Failure to know this can result in your incurring significant support charges.

Keep Up-to-Date

Finally, keep up-to-date on technology. Be sure that you are aware of all of the features and functions available in the DBMSs in use at your site—at least at a high level, but preferably in-depth. Read the vendor literature on future releases as it becomes available to prepare for new functionality before you install and migrate to new DBMS releases. The sooner you know about new bells and whistles, the better equipped you will be to prepare new procedures and adopt new policies to support the new features.

Keep up-to-date on technology in general, too. For example, DBAs should understand XML because it deals with data and will impact database design and administration. Don't ignore industry and technology trends simply because you cannot immediately think of a database-related impact. Many non-database-related "things" eventually find their way into DBMS software and database applications.

Keep up-to-date on industry standards—particularly those that impact database technology such as the SQL standard. Understanding these standards before the new features they engender have been incorporated into your DBMS will give you an edge on their management. The DBMS vendors try to support industry standards, and many features find their way into the DBMS because of their adoption by an industry standard.

Attend local and national user groups.

As already discussed, one way of keeping up-to-date is by attending local and national user groups. The presentations delivered at these forums provide useful education. Even more important, though, is the chance to network with other DBAs to share experiences and learn from each other's projects.

Through judicious use of the Internet and the Web, it is easier than ever for DBAs to keep up-to-date. Dozens of useful and informative Web sites provide discussion forums, script libraries, articles, manuals, and how-to documents. Consult Appendix 4 for a list of DBA-focused Web resources. Remember, though, this is just a starting point.

Summary

The job of the DBA is a challenging one—from both a technological and a political perspective. Follow the rules of thumb presented in this chapter to increase your likelihood of achieving success as a DBA.

Final Exam

1. At a high level, discuss the DBA's primary job responsibilities.

2. Is a certified DBA necessarily a qualified DBA? Why or why not?

3. Why must the DBA be prepared to function as a jack-of-all-trades?

4. Why should database standards be implemented, and what are the risks associated with a lack of DBA standards and procedures?

5. Name the four TPC benchmarks and describe how they differ from one another.

6. Name five requirements that must be planned for when installing a new DBMS.

7. What is the difference between a conceptual data model and a logical data model?

8. Why is data modeling important for database development?

9. Describe in broad terms the goals of normalization.

10. What is the difference between an entity and an entity occurrence?

11. Every attribute will do one of the three things. Name those things and describe them.

12. What is the only reason to denormalize a physical data model?

13. Under what circumstances should you consider a bitmap index rather than a b-tree index?

14. Describe how a relational database uses indexes.

15. Why might the order in which columns are created in a table be important for physical database design?

16. If indexes are beneficial to performance, why not create every conceivable index just to be on the safe side?

17. Describe what the acronym ACID means, and define each component.

18. Why does locking assure data integrity?

19. What does *relational closure* mean and what is its significance on application design?

20. What is the difference between a lock timeout and a deadlock?

21. Why is it important to review application code in addition to reviewing SQL?

22. Cite several reasons for including representatives from application development management in design reviews.

23. Why should the DBA lead most of the design reviews?

24. Why is it difficult to add a column between two existing columns in a table?

25. Explain what is meant by cascading DROP.

26. If you have to drop an entire database to effect a database change, what other database structures will also be dropped automatically by the DBMS?

27. Define what is meant by *availability*.

28. What is the typical cause of an unplanned outage?

29. What are nondisruptive database utilities, and why are they important for maintaining database availability?

30. Define *database performance*.

31. What are the three "things" that need to be addressed in database application tuning?

32. What does the 80/20 rule mean, and how should it be applied to database application performance tuning?

33. According to most experts, what is the primary cause of performance problems in database applications?

34. How does the data cache (or buffer pool) improve the performance of database processing?

35. Why are certain database operations not logged?

36. What benefits can accrue by caching optimized SQL in memory?

37. What type of information is recorded on the database transaction log?

38. What is the greatest performance tuning technique a DBA can use to improve database performance?

39. What is the benefit of clustering data?

40. What are the causes of database and index disorganization?

41. What is the benefit of allocating tablespaces and indexes to separate disk devices?

42. Define what is meant by *physical data independence*.

43. What factors influence the optimizer during SQL access path selection?

44. Name and describe the two predominant relational join methods.

45. Under what circumstances will a table scan outperform indexed access?

46. Define what is meant by *entity integrity*.

47. Describe the difference between database structural integrity and semantic data integrity.

48. What is the difference between a primary key constraint and a unique constraint?

49. Name and describe four types of database structural integrity problems that may be encountered by a DBA.

50. Explain two ways that views can be used to implement data security.

51. What two SQL DCL statements are used to establish and remove database privileges?

52. What is a cascading REVOKE and what effect can it have on database security?

53. What is the effect of granting a privilege to PUBLIC?

54. Why is it important to protect some database resources with security mechanisms external to the DBMS?

55. Explain the purpose for creating an audit trail of database operations.

56. Why is a quiesce point important for a point-in-time recovery?

57. What factors determine whether a full or incremental image copy backup should be taken for a database object?

58. Name and describe the three types of database failures that may require recovery.

59. Name the different types of recovery, and discuss the factors that influence when each type of recovery should be performed.

60. Describe what is meant by *disaster* in terms of database administration.

61. What factors should be considered when determining the criticality of a database object for disaster recovery planning?

62. Once the disaster recovery plan is written it should not be changed: True or False.

63. Why are most database files stored on disk devices instead of other storage media?

64. Your organization has decided to purchase RAID arrays to support your DBMS. Which levels of RAID would you advise them to use and why?

65. What advantages does a SAN have over SCSI devices?

66. Calculating the amount of storage required for a table is as simple as adding up the number of bytes for the columns in a row and multiplying the sum by the total number of rows: True or False.

67. Why is a two-phase COMMIT necessary when data is modified at two locations within a single unit of work?

68. What is the biggest threat to efficient performance of a distributed database system?

69. What is the difference between replication and propagation?

70. What is the difference between a data warehouse and a data mart?

71. Is it necessary to develop a backup and recovery plan for the data warehouse, since it is a read-only environment?

72. Describe the star schema and why it is an effective design for data warehouse databases.

73. Discuss the various options to consider specifically when creating the physical design of the data warehouse.

74. Name the three types of Java programs, and discuss the pros and cons of each.

75. What is the difference between a fat client and a thin client?

76. What is the biggest DBA challenge when managing an Internet-enabled database?

77. What is a database gateway?

78. What is metadata, and why is it important?

79. Name the three categories of performance tools, and briefly summarize the typical capabilities they provide.

80. If you are asked by management to develop a cost justification for DBA tools, how can you minimize the amount of work it takes to produce such a justification?

Appendix 1

Database Fundamentals

Most of the readers of this book should understand the basic concepts and fundamentals of database technology. However, many folks who think they understand the basics often do not have the knowledge and understanding they believe they have. Therefore, this appendix serves as a very brief introduction to the fundamentals of database management systems.

What Is a Database?

What is a database? The answer to this question may surprise some readers. Oracle is not a database; neither is DB2 or SQL Server. Each of these is a DBMS, or *database management system*. You can use Oracle, DB2, or SQL Server to create a database, but none of these is itself a database. Many people, even skilled professionals, confuse the overall system—the DBMS—with the creation of the system, the databases.

A database is an organized store of data wherein the data is accessible by named data elements.

So, what is a database? A database is a structured set of persistent data. A phonebook is a database. However, within the world of IT, a database usually is associated with software. A simple database might be a single file containing many records, each of which contains the same set of fields where each field is a certain data type and length. In short, a database is an organized store of data where the data is accessible by named data elements.

A DBMS is a software package designed to create, store, and manage databases. The DBMS software enables end users or application programmers to share data. It provides a systematic method of creating, updating, retrieving, and storing information in a database. DBMS products are usually responsible for data integrity, data access control, automated rollback, restart and recovery.

You might think of a database as a file folder and a DBMS as the file cabinet holding the labeled folders. You implement and access database instances using the capabilities of the DBMS. Your payroll application uses the payroll database, which may be implemented using a DBMS such as IMS, DB2, Oracle9i, or SQL Server.

Why is this distinction important? If we do not use precise terms in the workplace confusion can result, leading to over-budget projects, improperly developed systems, and lost productivity. Therefore, precision is important to us.

Why Use a DBMS?

The main advantage of using a DBMS is to impose a logical, structured organization on the data. A DBMS delivers economy of scale for processing large amounts of data because it is optimized for such operations.

There are four DBMS data models: hierarchical, network, relational, and object-oriented.

A DBMS can be distinguished by the model of data upon which it is based. A *data model* is a collection of concepts used to describe data. A data model has two fundamental components: its structure, which is the way data is stored, and its operations, which is the way that data can be manipulated. The major DBMS products utilize four different data models:

1. Hierarchical

2. Network (or CODASYL)

3. Relational

4. Object-oriented

The *hierarchical data model* arranges data into structural trees that store data at lower levels subordinate to data stored at higher levels. A hierarchy is a network with the additional restriction that access into a record can only be accomplished in one way. IMS is an example of a DBMS based on the hierarchical model.

The *network data model* is structured as a collection of record types and the relationships between these record types. All relationships are explicitly specified and stored as part of the structure of the DBMS. Another common name for the network model is CODASYL. CODASYL is named after the Conference on Data Systems Languages, the committee that formulated the model in the early 1970s. Data is manipulated using the location of a given record and following links to related records. IDMS is an example of a DBMS based on the network model.

The *relational data model* consists of a collection of tables (more properly, *relations*) wherein the columns define the relationship between tables. The relational model is based on the mathematics of set theory. Contrary to popular belief, the relational model is not named after "relationships," but after the relations of set theory. A *relation* is a set with no duplicate values. Data can be manipulated in many ways, but the most common way is through SQL. DB2, Oracle, and SQL Server are examples of DBMS products based on the relational model.

The *object-oriented (OO) data model* consists of a collection of entities, or objects, where each object includes the actions that can take place on that object. In other words, an object encapsulates data and process. With OO systems, data is typically manipulated using an OO programming language. ObjectStore and Jasmine are typical DBMS products based on the OO model.

Each of these four data models is referred to as a data model for the sake of simplicity. In reality, only the relational and network models have any true, formal data model specification. Different models of data lead to different logical and structural data organizations. The relational model is the most popular data model because it is the most abstract and easiest to apply to data, while providing powerful data manipulation and access capabilities.

Advantages of Using a DBMS

Additionally, a DBMS provides a central store of data that can be accessed by multiple users, from multiple locations. Data can be shared among multiple applications, rather than having to be propagated and stored in new files for every new application. Central storage and management of data within the DBMS provides

- Data abstraction and independence
- Data security
- A locking mechanism for concurrent access
- An efficient handler to balance the needs of multiple applications using the same data

- The ability to swiftly recover from crashes and errors
- Robust data integrity capabilities
- Simple access using a standard API
- Uniform administration procedures for data

Levels of Data Abstraction

A DBMS can provide many views of a single database schema. A view defines what data the user sees and how that user sees the data. The DBMS provides a level of abstraction between the conceptual schema that defines the logical structure of the database and the physical schema that describes the files, indexes, and other physical mechanisms used by the database. Users function at the conceptual level—by querying columns within rows of tables, for example—instead of having to navigate through the many different types of physical structures that store the data.

A DBMS makes it much easier to modify applications when business requirements change. New categories of data can be added to the database without disruption to the existing system.

Data Independence

A DBMS provides a layer of independence between the data and the applications that use the data. In other words, applications are insulated from how data is structured and stored. The DBMS provides two types of data independence:

- *Logical data independence*—protection from changes to the logical structure of data
- *Physical data independence*—protection from changes to the physical structure of data

As long as the program uses the API (application programming interface) to the database as provided by the DBMS, developers can avoid changing programs because of database changes.

Note: The primary API to relational databases is SQL. In general, most application SQL statements need not change when database structures change (e.g., a new column is added to a table).

Data Security

Data security prevents unauthorized users from viewing or updating the database. The DBMS uses IDs and passwords to control which users are allowed access to which portions of the database. For example, consider an employee database containing all data about individual employees. Using the DBMS security mechanisms, payroll personnel can be authorized to view payroll data, whereas managers could be permitted to view only data related to project history.

Concurrency Control

A DBMS can serve data to multiple, concurrently executing user programs. This requires a locking mechanism to deliver concurrency control because the actions of different programs running at the same time could conceivably cause data inconsistency. For example, multiple bank ATM users might be able to withdraw $100 each from a checking account containing only $150. A DBMS ensures that such problems are avoided because the locking mechanism isolates transactions competing for the same exact data.

Database Logging

The DBMS uses database logging to record "before" and "after" images of database objects as they are modified. It is important to note that the database log captures information about every data modification (except in circumstances as determined by the DBA). The information on the database logs can be used to undo and redo transactions. Database logging is handled transparently by the DBMS—that is, it is done automatically.

Ensuring Atomicity and Durability

A DBMS can be used to assure the all-or-nothing quality of transactions. This is referred to as *atomicity,* and it means that data integrity is maintained even if the system crashes in the middle of a transaction. Furthermore, a DBMS provides recoverability. After a system failure, data can be recovered to a state that existed either immediately before the crash or at some other requisite point in time.

Data Integrity

The DBMS provides mechanisms for defining rules that govern the type of data that can be stored in specific fields or columns. Only data that conforms to the business rules will ever be stored in the database. Furthermore, the DBMS can be set up to manage relationships between different types of data and to ensure that changes to related data elements are accurately implemented.

Data Access

A DBMS provides a standard query language to enable users to interactively interrogate the database and analyze its data. For relational databases, this standard API is SQL, or *Structured Query Language.* However, SQL is not a requirement for a DBMS to be relational. Furthermore, many DBMS products ship with analytical tools and report writers to further simplify data access.

Summary

This section on DBMS fundamentals is necessarily brief because the focus of this book is on database administration and most readers will find this material to be familiar. If you require additional details on the basic operations and qualities of DBMSs and databases, please refer to the Bibliography for an extensive list of DBMS-related books. My favorites include

- C. J. Date's *An Introduction to Database Systems,* 7th ed., for an academic and theoretical approach to the material

- Fabian Pascal's two books, *Practical Issues in Database Management* and *Understanding Relational Databases*, for an opinionated, but informed approach to the topics

- Joe Celko's *Data & Databases: Concepts in Practice*, for a good practical overview of the topic

- Pratt and Adamski's *The Concepts of Database Management,* 2nd ed., or Rob and Coronel's *Database Systems: Design, Implementation, and Management*, both of which provide a good high-level overview of DBMS concepts

A primary benefit of a DBMS is its ability to maintain and query large amounts of data while assuring data integrity and consistency. It offers transparent recovery from failures, concurrent access, and data independence. In fact, most modern computer applications rely on DBMS and database technology to manage data. Understanding the topic is of benefit to all IT professionals.

The DBMS Vendors

There are many DBMS vendors from which to choose. However, there are definite tiers in terms of popularity, support, and leadership in the DBMS market. In general, the marketplace can be broken down into the following groups:

- *The Big Three*—the three market leaders that comprise the greater part of the DBMS installed base as well as the bulk of any new sales
- *The second tier*—large DBMS vendors with stable products, but lagging behind the Big Three in terms of functionality and number of users
- *Other significant players*— other DBMS vendors with viable, enterprise-capable products
- *Open-source*—DBMS products supported as open-source software
- *Nonrelational*—vendors who supply prerelational DBMS products to support legacy applications
- *Object-oriented*—vendors of ODBMS products that are used in conjunction with OO languages and development projects
- *PC-based*—although many of the other vendors create PC versions of their DBMS products, these companies or products focus exclusively on the PC platform

The Big Three

Oracle Corporation, IBM Corporation, and Microsoft are the leading DBMS vendors, in that order. The installed base for Oracle is greater than any other DBMS, and Oracle is probably used by more people than any other DBMS. IBM's DB2 is in second place and picking up steam. With DB2's near monopoly on the mainframe and its growing UNIX and Windows installed base, IBM can claim to be used by almost as many users as Oracle. In third place overall, but in first place on Windows machines, is Microsoft, with Microsoft SQL Server. Microsoft SQL Server runs only on Windows platforms.

Contact Information

Oracle Corporation
500 Oracle Parkway
Redwood Shores, CA 94065
http://www.oracle.com
Phone: (650) 506-7000

IBM Corporation
New Orchard Road
Armonk, NY 10504
http://www.ibm.com
Phone: (914) 499-1900

Microsoft
1 Microsoft Way
Redmond, WA 98052-6399
http://www.microsoft.com
Phone: (425) 882-8080

The Second Tier

The second-tier DBMS providers comprises companies that were market leaders in the 1980s. Sybase was a leading innovator in database technology, introducing such concepts as the client/server paradigm, stored procedures, and more. Indeed, Microsoft SQL Server is based on Sybase technology. Informix is another former leader who fell on hard times with a misguided development strategy. All of Informix's DBMS assets were acquired by IBM Corporation in the Summer of 2001.

Contact Information

> Sybase Corporation
> 6475 Christie Ave.
> Emeryville, CA 94608
> http://www.sybase.com
> Phone: (510) 922-3555

Other Significant Players

Besides the vendors discussed already, there are several vendors offering relational products with a high degree of functionality and with a reasonable number of installed users. Foremost among these is Ingres, currently marketed by Computer Associates. Ingres began its life as the first relational DBMS implementation at the University of California, Berkeley. The Ingres code was enhanced into a commercial product by Relational Technologies. Relational Technologies became Ingres Corporation, which was purchased by ASK Corporation, which was then purchased by Computer Associates. Ingres still boasts a large number of users, particularly in Europe.

Other significant players include Software AG's Adabas and Tamino DBMS products, and Borland's Interbase. Adabas has its roots as an inverted-list DBMS that was augmented to become relational. Tamino is Software AG's new, XML-based DBMS. Interbase is a highly capable relational DBMS from Borland.

Contact Information

> Borland International
> 100 Enterprise Way
> Scotts Valley, CA 95066
> http://www.borland.com
> Phone: (831) 431-1000
>
> Computer Associates International
> One Computer Associates Place
> Islandia, NY 11788
> http://www.ca.com
> Phone: (516) 342-5224

Software AG
Uhlandstr. 12
64297 Darmstadt
Germany
http://www.softwareag.com
Phone: +49-6151-92-0

Open-Source DBMS Offerings

The rapid acceptance and media glare surrounding Linux has enlivened the open-source community. The term *open source* refers to software that users are free to run, copy, distribute, study, change, and improve. Often "open source" is interpreted to mean free software. This is understandable, but the open-source concept of free is closer to "liberty" than to "no charge." Open-source software adheres to the following beliefs:

- Users are free to run the program, for any purpose.
- Users are free to inspect the actual source code of the program to determine how it works.
- Users are free to modify and adapt the software to their specific needs.
- Users are free to distribute copies to whomever.
- Users are free to release their code improvements to the public, so that the whole community benefits.

There are two leading open-source DBMS products: PostgreSQL and MySQL. In addition to becoming a commercial product, Ingres was enhanced at Berkeley, eventually turning into a second-generation DBMS named Postgres, and eventually a SQL version named PostgreSQL. Red Hat, the Linux distributor, distributes a version of PostgreSQL (http://www.redhat.com/).

MySQL is a true multiuser, multithreaded SQL database server. It is available as a free download from http://www.mysql.com, but it is not technically an open-source DBMS. Because you do not get access to the source code, you cannot modify it. Additionally, you must pay for a license if you sell MySQL, if you charge for administering a server, or if you include MySQL as a component of another product. Furthermore, MySQL is free of charge on UNIX and OS/2 platforms only. For Windows platforms, you must purchase a software license. A free, slower version of MySQL is available for Windows platforms on a 30-day trial period. MySQL is distributed by NuSphere Corporation (http://www.nusphere.com/).

Nonrelational DBMS Vendors

Prior to the commercial acceptance of relational technology in the early 1980s, the DBMS market was primarily mainframe-based and was dominated by two players: IBM and Cullinet. IBM's IMS is a hierarchic DBMS that organizes data into tree structures. Cullinet marketed IDMS, a CODASYL DBMS that organized data into network structures. Cullient was acquired by Computer Associates in the late 1980s.

Object-Oriented DBMS Vendors

At one point in the late 1980s and early 1990s, it looked like object-oriented database management systems (ODBMS) were going to gain rapid acceptance. For many reasons (difficult to query, no solid data model, etc.), this technology did not. Indeed, many of the ODBMS vendors have repositioned their products as e-business solutions or database components for object-oriented application developers. However, there are niche pockets of ODBMS users.

The following vendors still offer ODBMS products and components:

- UniQSL http://www.unisql.com
- Poet http://www.poet.com
- Object Store http://www.odi.com
- Ontos http://www.ontos.com
- Jasmine http://www.ca.com

PC-Based DBMS Vendors

Simpler to use than full-blown enterprise DBMS products, PC-based DBMS products provide structured storage for PC-based data and applications. The following vendors and products are the market leaders in the PC-based DBMS market:

- dBase http://www.dbase.com
- Filemaker http://www.filemaker.com

- Lotus Approach   http://www.lotus.com
- Microsoft Access   http://www.microsoft.com/office/access/
- Visual Foxpro   http://www.microsoft.com/vfoxpro/
- Paradox   http://www.corel.com

Appendix 3

DBA Tool Vendors

In Chapter 22, we covered the wide variety of tools available to ease the burden of database management and administration. Many of the world's largest independent software vendors (ISVs) supply DBA tools. This appendix lists the major players.

The Major Vendors

Although there are many ISVs that manufacture and market DBA tools and utilities, the four vendors that follow are the leading independent DBA tool vendors. These vendors distinguish themselves because they offer tools that work for more than a single DBMS and in more than one tool category. When evaluating DBA tools for a heterogeneous shop with multiple DBMSs, these are the first vendors you should consider.

BMC Software
2101 City West Blvd.
Houston, TX 77042
http://www.bmc.com
Phone: (713) 918-8800

Computer Associates International
One Computer Associates Place
Islandia, NY 11788
http://www.ca.com
Phone: (516) 342-5224

Embarcadero Technologies
425 Market Street, Suite 425
San Francisco, CA 94105
http://www.embarcadero.com/
Phone: (415) 834-3131

Quest Software
8001 Irvine Center Drive
Irvine, CA 92618
http://www.quests.com
Phone: (949) 754-8000

Of course, all of the DBMS vendors themselves also market add-on DBA tools for their respective DBMS products. Refer to Appendix 2 for a listing of the major DBMS vendors and contact information for each.

Other DBA Tool Vendors

In addition to the major DBA tool vendors mentioned above, each of the following vendors market add-on DBA tools. In contrast to the vendors listed above, these vendors are likely to specialize in certain niche areas. For example, some may market only performance management tools, or other may offer tools that work only on Microsoft SQL Server.

The Web sites listed for these vendors will provide additional information on the type of tools offered.

- Allen Systems Group   http://www.asg.com/
- BEZ Systems   http://www.bez.com
- Bradmark Technologies   http://www.bradmark.com/
- Bunker Hill Corporation   http://www.bunkerhill.com/

- Candle Corporation   http://www.candle.com
- CAST Software   http://www.castsoftware.com/
- CDB Software   http://www.cdbsoftware.com
- Compuware Corporation   http://www.compuware.com
- Data Junction   http://www.datajunction.com
- DGI   http://www.database-guys.com/
- DBE Software   http://www.dbesoftware.com/
- Hit Software   http://www.hit.com
- InfoShark   http://www.infoshark.com
- InfoTel Corporation   http://www.infotelcorp.com
- LECCO Technology   http://www.leccotech.com
- NEON Systems   http://www.neonsys.com
- Pentasafe   http://www.pentasafe.com
- Expand Beyond   http://www.pocketdba.com
- Precise Software   http://www.precisesoft.com/
- Princeton Softech   http://www.princetonsoftech.com
- Red Gate Software   http://www.red-gate.com
- Relational Architects   http://www.relarc.com
- Responsive Systems   http://www.responsivesystems.com
- Rocket Software   http://www.rocketsoft.com
- SEGUS Inc.   http://www.scgus.com
- Softbase Systems Inc.   http://www.softbase.com
- SQL Power Tools   http://www.sqlpower.com/
- Tone Software   http://www.tonesoft.com/
- White Sands Technology, Inc.   http://www.whitesands.com
- XPERT Corporation   http://www.planxpert.com

These are not the only vendors marketing add-on DBA tools, but they are some of the bigger and more successful ISVs. Additional tool categories and related ISVs are listed in the following sections.

Data Modeling Tool Vendors

Chen & Associates
chenassoc@aol.com
Product: ER-Modeler

Computer Associates International
http://www.ca.com
Product: ERwin

Datanimic
http://www.datanimic.com
Product: DeZign for Databases

Embarcadero Technologies
http://www.embarcadero.com
Product: ER-Studio

Microsoft Corporation
http://www.microsoft.com
Product: Visio Enterprise

Oracle Corporation
http://www.oracle.com
Product: Oracle Designer

Popkin Software
http://www.popkin.com
Product: System Architect

Powersoft (Open Tools Division of Sybase)
http://www.sybase.com
Product: Power Designer

Rational Software
http://www.rational.com
Product: Rational Rose

Silverrun Technologies
http://www.silverrun.com
Product: Silverrun

Visible Systems
http://www.visible.com/
Product: Visible Analyst, Visible Advantage

Repository Vendors

Adaptive Ltd.
http://www.adaptive.com/
Product: Adaptive Information Manager

Allen Systems Group
http://www.asg.com
Product: ASG-Rochade, ASG-Manager, ASG-Vista

Computer Associates International
http://www.ca.com
Product: PLATINUM Repository

CYRANO
http://www.cyrano.com
Product: Wincap Workbench

Rational Software
http://www.rational.com
Product: ClearCase

Softlab Corporation
http://www.softlab.com
Product: Enabler

Data Movement and Business Intelligence Vendors

The following companies offer data movement and ETL tools:

- Acta Technology   http://www.acta.com/
- Ascential Software   http://www.ascentialsoftware.com/
- CoSort   http://www.cosort.com/
- Data Junction   http://www.datajunction.com
- Data Mirror   http://www.datamirror.com
- DW Soft Corporation   http://www.dwsoft.com/
- Information Builders   http://www.informationbuilders.com
- Lakeview Technology   http://www.lakeviewtech.com/
- MERANT   http://www.merant.com/
- Paladyne   http://www.paladyne.com/
- Sagent   http://www.sagent.com/
- Striva   http://www.striva.com
- Treehouse Software   http://www.treehouse.com

The following companies offer business intelligence and OLAP tools:

- Brio Technology   http://www.brio.com
- Business Objects   http://www.businessobjects.com
- Cardett Associates   http://www.cardett.co.nz/
- Cognos Inc.   http://www.cognos.com
- Computer Associates   http://www.ca.com
- Cross Access   http://www.crossaccess.com/
- Hyperion Solutions   http://www.hyperion.com/
- SAS Institute   http://www.sas.com
- Visual Insights   http://www.visualinsights.com/

Once again, all of the major DBMS vendors offer add-on ETL and business intelligence tools for their respective DBMS products.

Appendix **4**

DBA Web Resources

DBAs are not alone in the Internet-connected world. With the advent of the World Wide Web, DBAs have many online resources at their disposal. By virtue of being Internet-connected, a DBA has access to the vast knowledge and experience of his peers. However, to take advantage of these online resources, the DBA has to know that the resources exist, how to gain access to them, and where to find them. This appendix will discuss several of the Internet resources available to DBAs. Any DBA that does not take advantage of the Internet resources at his disposal is doing himself a disservice.

Usenet Newsgroups

When discussing the Internet, many folks limit themselves to the World Wide Web. However, there are many components to the Internet. One often-overlooked resource is the Usenet newsgroup, which can be a very fertile source of expert information. Usenet, an abbreviation for User Network, is a large collection of discussion groups, called newsgroups. Each newsgroup is a collection of postings pertaining to a single, predetermined topic. Newsgroup names usually reflect their focus. For example, comp.databases.ibm-db2 contains discussions about the DB2 Family of products.

Using newsreader software, any Internet user can access a newsgroup. Refer to Figure A-1 for an example using Forte Free Agent to view messages posted to comp.databases.ibm-db2. The Free Agent newsreader can be downloaded and used free of charge from the Forte Web site at http://www.forteinc. com/. Netscape Navigator also provides newsreader functionality.

There are many newsgroups that focus discussion on database and database-related issues. Table A-1 shows some of the most pertinent newsgroups of interest to the DBA.

Of course, thousands of other newsgroups exist. You can use your newsreader software to investigate the newsgroups available to you and to gauge the quality of their discussions.

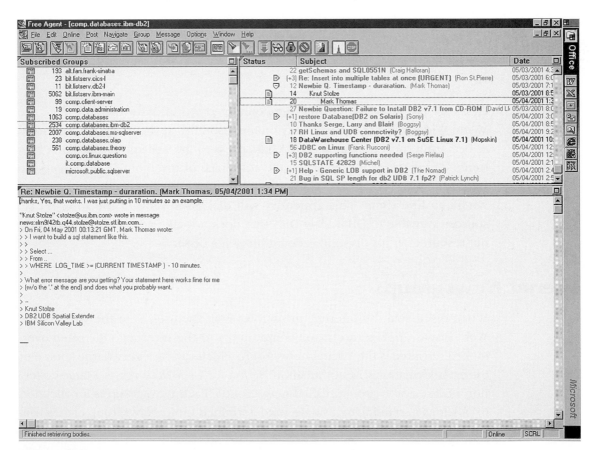

Figure A-1   *Using newsreader software*

Table A-1   *Database-Related Usenet Newsgroups*

Newsgroup	Description
comp.client-server	Information on client/server technology
comp.compression.research	Information on research in data compression techniques
comp.data.administration	Discussion of data modeling and data administration issues
comp.databases	Issues regarding databases and data management
comp.databases.ibm-db2	Information on IBM's DB2 Family of products
comp.databases.informix	Information on the Informix DBMS
comp.databases.ms-sqlserver	Information on Microsoft's SQL Server DBMS
comp.databases.object	Information on object-oriented database systems
comp.databases.olap	Information on data warehouse online analytical processing
comp.databases.oracle.marketplace	Information on the Oracle market
comp.databases.oracle.server	Information on the Oracle RDBMS
comp.databases.oracle.tools	Information about add-on tools for Oracle
comp.databases.oracle.misc	Miscellaneous Oracle discussions
comp.databses.sybase	Information on the Sybase Adaptive Server RDBMS
comp.databases.theory	Discussions on database technology and theory
comp.unix.admin	UNIX administration discussions
bit.listserv.dasig	Database administration special interest group
bit.listserv.db2-1	Information pertaining to DB2 (mostly mainframe)
bit.listserv.ibm-main	IBM mainframe newsgroup (some DBMS discussion)

Mailing Lists

Another useful Internet resource for DBAs is the mailing list. Mailing lists are a kind of community bulletin board. You can think of mailing lists as somewhat equivalent to a mass mailing. However, mailing lists are not spam because users must specifically request to participate before they will receive any mail. This is known as *opting in*.

There are more than 40,000 mailing lists available on the Internet, and they operate by use of a list server. A *list server* is a program that automates the mailing list subscription requests and messages. The two most common list servers are Listserv and Majordomo. Listserv is also a common synonym for mailing list, but it is actually the name of a particular list server program.

Simply by subscribing to a mailing list, information will be sent directly to your e-mail inbox from the list server. The information that you will receive varies from news releases, to announcements, to questions, to answers. This information is very similar to the information contained in a newsgroup forum, except that it comes directly to you via e-mail. Users can also easily respond to mailing list messages, enabling communication with every subscribed user. Responses are sent back to the list server as e-mail, and the list server sends the response out to all other members of the mailing list.

To subscribe to a mailing list, simply send an e-mail to the appropriate subscription address requesting a subscription. Several Web sites, including the following, catalog the available Internet mailing lists.

- http://www.lsoft.com/lists/listref.html
- http://www.listtool.com

Of course, none of these sites track every single mailing list available to you. Vendors, consultants, Web portals, and user groups also support mailing lists of various types. The only way to be sure you know about all the useful mailing lists out there is to become an actively engaged member of the online community. Table A-2 provides details on a few popular database-related mailing lists for DBAs.

Table A-2   *Database-Related Usenet Newsgroups of Interest to DBAs*

Mailing List Name	Subscription Address	Description
ORACLE-L@KBS.NET	E-mail LISTSERV@KBS.NET with the command: SUBSCRIBE ORACLE-L	Discussion about the Oracle DBMS
DB2-L@RYCI.COM	E-mail LISTSERV@RYCI.COM with the command: SUBSCRIBE DB2-L	Discussion about the DB2 family of products
SYBASE-L@LISTSERV.UCSB.EDU	E-mail LISTSERV@LISTSERV.UCSB.EDU with the command: SUBSCRIBE SYBASE-L	Discussion of SYBASE products, platforms, and use
VBDATA-L@PEACH.EASE.LSOFT.COM	E-mail to LISTSERV@PEACH.EASE.LSOFT.COM with the command: SUBSCRIBE VBDATA-L	Discussion for Microsoft Visual Basic DATA ACCESS

Web Sites and Portals

Of course, the Web is also a very fertile source of database- and DBA-related information. However, tracking things down on the Web can sometimes be difficult—especially if you do not know where to look. Several good sources of DBMS information on the Web can be found by reviewing the Web sites of DBMS vendors, DBA tool vendors, magazines, and consultants.

Vendor Web Sites

One of the best DBA resources is the vendor Web site for the DBMS software you use. On such sites you can find up-to-date news, information on release schedules and bug fixes, downloadable manuals, and technical support. Be sure to bookmark the site for your DBMS vendor and visit regularly to keep tabs on what's going on with your favorite database management systems.

The Web sites for the major DBMS vendors are

- IBM DB2   http://www.ibm.com/software/data/db2/
- Informix   http://www.ibm.com/software/data/informix/
- Microsoft SQL Server   http://www.microsoft.com/sql/default.asp
- Oracle   http://www.oracle.com
- Sybase   http://www.sybase.com

Another useful Web resource for DBAs can be found on DBA tool vendor Web sites. The DBA tool vendors employ many DBMS experts and former DBAs who are willing to share tips, techniques, and scripts in order to promote their company and its products. Appendix 3 lists several of the most popular third-party tool vendors along with their Web address and contact information.

Magazine Web Sites

Many useful database and DBA-related articles are published every week in technical magazines of every sort. Several magazines focus almost exclusively on database- and DBA-related issues. Even better, many of these publications are provided free of charge, in return for filling out a subscription request with company and demographic information.

Additionally, most print magazines also host Web sites that offer many, if not all, of their articles online. Some of this content is available to subscribers only, but many periodicals offer some content to all browsers. Some of the better magazine Web sites out there include

- Oracle Magazine   http://www.oracle.com/oramag/index.html
- DB2 Magazine   http://www.db2mag.com
- Database Trends and Applications   http://www.dbta.com
- Data Management Review   http://www.dmreview.com
- Exploring Oracle   http://www.elementkjournals.com/dbm/
- SQL Server Magazine   http://www.sqlmag.com
- Sybase Magazine   http://www.sybase.com/inc/sybmag

Consultant Web Sites

There are a boatload of consultants who specialize in DBMS technology. However, a few consultants have achieved guru status because they are willing to share their knowledge and experience at conferences and events, and by writing articles. Many of these premier consultants have set up content-rich Web sites containing numerous documents, presentations, and tips to anyone visiting the site. The consultants do this to promote their business and gain leads for future business.

Some of the leading consultant Web sites containing interesting and useful information for DBAs include

- Yevich, Lawson & Associates, focusing primarily on DB2 http://www.ylassoc.com.
- TUSC, focusing on Oracle   http://www.tusc.com.
- DBA Direct, focusing on database administration http://www.dbadirect.com.
- Fabian Pascal's site, devoted to debunking erroneous beliefs about relational and other database technologies   http://www.dbdebunk.com.
- And, of course, you can check out the author's Web site at http://www.craigsmullins.com for an exhaustive online catalog of his published writing and more.

Database Portals

There are many Web portals that offer a convenient collection of database- and DBA-related information. A portal typically provides a vast amount of information on a single topic, as well as links to related information, a search engine, customization options, and the ability for users to be notified by e-mail when relevant content is posted. The following Web sites function as portals for database professionals.

DBAzine.com (http://www.dbazine.com) is a regular source of useful information about database administration and data warehouse management issues and solutions. The site is a combination portal and Web-based magazine with regular new content and five channels of links focusing on DB2, Oracle, SQL Server, IMS, and data warehousing.

Searchdatabase.com (http://www.searchdatabase.com) and its sister site searchdatawarehousing.com (http://www.searchdatawarehousing.com) are true portals containing loads of useful information, including tips, articles, discussion boards, "ask the expert" sections, and more.

The Data Administration Newsletter (http://www.tdan.com) is another combination portal/magazine site, which focuses on data administration issues.

There are numerous other portals that provide useful information for DBAs. Some of the best focus on a single DBMS technology. For example, all of the following offer useful services for the specific DBMS they cover:

Oracle links and news	http://www.lazydba.com
	http://www.orafans.com
	http://www.oraworld.com
DB2 links and news	http://www.ruban.de/
	http://db2usa.hypermart.net/eindex.htm
	http://www7b.boulder.ibm.com/dmdd/
SQL Server links and news	http://www.sqlservercentral.com/
	http://www.sql-server-performance.com
	http://www.swynk.com/sql

Other Web Sites

Many other Web sites may prove useful or interesting to DBAs. One of the best things about the Internet is its ability to provide a forum for anyone with information to share. New and intriguing sites are popping up every day. Let's take a look at some of the best Web sites out there for DBAs.

Providing a very useful service for DBAs is DBAjobs.com (http://www. DBAjobs.com). This site lists as its mission "To advance the careers of all database professionals and to recruit the best database talent for its clients." Be sure to visit this site for access to many database-related jobs as well as for assistance in preparing your resume, interviewing tips, salary guidelines, and database news.

Sites hosting information on industry standards can be quite helpful, too. For example, ANSI (American National Standards Institute), ISO (International Standards Organization), and NIST (National Institute of Standards and Technology) all provide Web sites.

- ANSI   http://www.ansi.org
- ISO   http://www.iso.ch
- NIST   http://www.nist.gov

Perhaps closer to the technical information required by a DBA is the SQL standard Web site at http://www.jcc.com/SQLPages/jccs_sql.htm. This site purports to be a central source of information about SQL standards. It contains links to various other sites that document the SQL standard.

NextSLM offers a great site for DBAs focused on performance, specifically service-level management. This site can be found at http://www.nextslm.org and offers an online learning community for SLM practices and issues. If you are working on service-level management, be sure to visit this site for useful articles, discussions, and pointers to other SLM sites and vendors.

DAMA, the Data Management Association, is a coalition of professionals dedicated to the advancement of data resource management. The DAMA Web site (http://www.dama.org) documents the conferences and meetings sponsored by DAMA, but also offers links, resources, newsletters, and publications on data resource management.

User groups have been founded for each of the major DBMS vendors. These groups sponsor annual international conferences and promote the sharing of information by database professionals. The Web sites for these groups offer useful information on conference locations and dates, as well as articles, presentations, and tips.

- International DB2 User Group   http://www.idug.org
- International Oracle User Group   http://www.ioug.org/

- Professional Associates for SQL Server   http://www.sqlpass.org
- International Informix User Group   http://www.iiug.org/
- International Sybase User Group   http://www.sybase.com/ISUG/

There are literally thousands of other Web sites that might be useful to you as you embark on your career as a DBA. Here are a few of the ones I have found to be worthwhile.

- Richard Hackathorn's Web farming site   http://www.webfarming.com
- The XML portal   http://www.xml.com
- The Journal of Conceptual Modeling
  http://www.inconcept.com/JCM/about.html
- The Data Warehousing Institute   http://www.dw-institute.com
- The Metadata Coalition   http://www.mdcinfo.com
- The OLAP Council   http://www.olapcouncil.org/

All of these sites are very useful for obtaining up-to-date information about DBMS releases and versions, management tool offerings, and the like, but bear in mind that the information on this type of site can be very biased. For information that is more likely to be unbiased, you should favor the Web portals over the vendor and consultant sites.

Bibliography

The books listed in this bibliography can be used as guides to further education and research on the topics of database management, database administration, and other data-related technologies.

Database Management and Database Systems

Abiteboul, Serge, et al. *Foundations of Databases.* Reading, MA: Addison-Wesley (1995). ISBN 0-201-53771-0

Atre, Shaku. *Database: Structured Techniques for Design, Performance, and Management.* 2nd ed. New York, NY: John Wiley & Sons (1988). ISBN 0-471-85251-1

Bell, David, and Jane Grimson. *Distributed Database Systems.* Wokingham, England: Addison-Wesley (1992). ISBN 0-201-54400-8

Bobak, Angelo R. *Distributed and Multi-Database Systems.* New York, NY: Bantam Intertext (1993). ISBN 0-553-09156-5

Bontempo, Charles J., and Cynthia Maro Saracco. *Database Management Principles and Products.* Upper Saddle River, NJ: Prentice Hall PTR (1995). ISBN 0-13-380189-6

Bradley, James. *Introduction to Database Management in Business.* New York, NY: Holt, Rinehart, and Winston (1983). ISBN 0-03-061693-X

Brathwaite, Kenneth S. *Systems Design in a Database Environment.* New York, NY: McGraw-Hill (1989). ISBN 0-07-007250-7

Brathwaite, Kenmore S. *The Data Base Environment: Concepts and Applications.* New York, NY: Van Nostrand Reinhold (1990). ISBN 0-442-00300-5

Burleson, Donald K. *Managing Distributed Databases.* New York, NY: John Wiley & Sons (1994). ISBN 0-471-08623-1

Castano, Silvana, et al. *Database Security.* Wokingham, England: Addison-Wesley (1994). ISBN 0-201-59375-0

Celko, Joe. *Data & Databases: Concepts In Practice.* San Francisco, CA: Morgan Kaufmann (1999). ISBN 1-55860-432-4

———. *SQL For Smarties: Advanced SQL Programming.* San Francisco, CA: Morgan Kaufmann (1995). ISBN 1-55860-323-9

Chisholm, Malcolm. *Managing Reference Data in Enterprise Databases.* San Francisco, CA: Morgan Kaufmann (2001). ISBN 1-55860-697-1

Chorafas, Dimitris. *Handbook of Database Management and Distributed Relational Databases.* Blue Ridge Summit, PA: Tab Books (1989). ISBN 0-8306-3253-0

Chorafas, Dimitris N., and Heinrich Steinmann. *Solutions for Networked Databases.* San Diego, CA: Academic Press (1993). ISBN 0-12-174060-9

Codd, E. F. *The Relational Model for Database Management Version 2.* Reading, MA: Addison-Wesley (1990). ISBN 0-201-14192-2

Connolly, Thomas, and Carolyn Begg. *Database Solutions.* Harlow, England: Addison-Wesley (2000). ISBN 0-201-67476-9

———. *Database Systems: A Practical Approach to Design, Implementation, and Management.* 2nd ed. Harlow, England: Addison-Wesley (1998). ISBN 0-201-34287-1

Courtney, James F., and David B. Paradice. *Database Systems for Management.* 2nd ed. Homewood, IL: Irwin (1992). ISBN 0-256-08229-4

Date, C. J. *An Introduction to Database Systems.* 7th ed. Reading, MA: Addison-Wesley (2000). ISBN 0-201-38590-2

———. *An Introduction to Database Systems,* Volume II. Reading, MA: Addison-Wesley (1983, 1985). ISBN 0-201-14474-3

———. *The Database Relational Model.* Reading, MA: Addison-Wesley (2001). ISBN 0-201-61294-1

Date, C. J. and Hugh Darwen. *Foundation for Object/Relational Databases: The Third Manifesto.* Reading, MA: Addison-Wesley (1998). ISBN 0-201-30978-5

Delobel, Claude, et al. *Databases: From Relational to Object-Oriented Systems.* London, England: International Thomson Computer Press (1995). ISBN1-850-32124-8

Dittrich, Klaus R., and Andreas Geppert, eds. *Component Database Systems.* San Francisco, CA: Morgan Kaufmann (2001). ISBN 1-55860-642-4

Dunham, Jeff. *Database Performance Tuning Handbook.* New York, NY: McGraw-Hill (1998). ISBN 0-07-018244-2

Egan, David, et al. *DBA's Guide to Databases on Linux.* Rockland, MD: Syngress Media (2000). ISBN 1-928994-04-0

Feiler, Jesse. *Database-Driven Web Sites.* San Francisco, CA: Morgan Kaufmann (1999). ISBN 0-12-251336-3

Fortier, Paul J. *Database Systems Handbook.* New York, NY: McGraw-Hill (1997). ISBN 0-07-021626-6

Gillenson, Mark L. *Database Step-by-Step* 2nd ed. New York, NY: John Wiley & Sons (1990). ISBN 0-471-61759-8

Gilula, Mikhail M. *The Set Model for Database and Information Systems.* Reading, MA: ACM Press/Addison-Wesley (1994). ISBN 0-201-59379-3

Goldstein, Robert C. *Database Technology and Management.* New York, NY: John Wiley & Sons (1985). ISBN 0-471-88737-4

Grant, John. *Logical Introduction to Databases.* Orlando, FL: Harcourt Brace Jovanovich (1987). ISBN 0-15-551175-0

Gulutzan, Peter, and Trudy Pelzer. *SQL-99 Complete, Really.* Lawrence, KS: R&D Books (1999). ISBN 0-87930-568-1

Hackathorn, Richard. *Enterprise Database Connectivity.* New York, NY: John Wiley & Sons (1993). ISBN 0-471-57802-9

House, William C., ed. *Database Management.* New York, NY: Petrocelli Books (1974). ISBN 0-88405-051-3

Jackson, Glenn A. *Relational Database Design with Microcomputer Applications.* Englewood Cliffs, NJ: Prentice Hall (1988). ISBN 0-13-771841-1

Johnson, James L. Database: *Models, Languages, Design.* New York, NY: Oxford University Press (1997). ISBN 0-19-510783-7

Kim, Won. *Modern Database Systems.* Reading, MA: ACM Press/Addison-Wesley (1995). ISBN 0-201-59098-0

Korth, Henry F., and Abraham Silberschatz. *Database System Concepts.* New York, NY: McGraw-Hill (1986). ISBN 0-07-044752-7

Larson, James A. *Database Directions.* Upper Saddle River, NJ: Prentice Hall PTR (1995). ISBN 0-13-290867-0

Lewis, Philip M., Arthur Bernstein, and Michael Kifer. *Databases and Transaction Processing.* Boston, MA: Addison-Wesley (2002). ISBN 0-201-70872-8

Loucopoulos, Pericles, and Roberto Zicari, eds. *Conceptual Modeling, Databases, and CASE.* New York, NY: John Wiley & Sons (1992). ISBN 0-471-55462-6

Martin, James. *Computer Database Organization.* Englewood Cliffs, NJ: Prentice Hall (1975). ISBN 0-13-165506-X

———. *Managing the Database Environment.* Englewood Cliffs, NJ: Prentice Hall (1983). ISBN 0-13-550582-8

Mattison, Robert M. *Understanding Database Management Systems.* New York, NY: McGraw-Hill (1993). ISBN 0-07-040973

McFadden, Fred R., Jeffrey A. Hoffer, and Mary B. Prescott. *Modern Database Management.* 5th ed. Reading, MA: Addison-Wesley (1999). ISBN 0-8053-6054-9

Melton, Jim. *Understanding SQL's Stored Procedures: A Complete Guide to SQL/PSM.* San Francisco, CA: Morgan Kaufmann (1998). ISBN 1-55860-461-8

O'Neil, Patrick. *Database Principles, Programming, Performance.* San Francisco, CA: Morgan Kaufmann (1994). ISBN 1-55860-219-4

Papadimitriou, Christos. *The Theory of Database Concurrency Control.* Rockville, MD: Computer Science Press (1986). ISBN 0-88175-027-1

Parsaye, Kamran, et al. *Intelligent Databases.* New York, NY: John Wiley & Sons (1989). ISBN 0-471-50345-2

Pascal, Fabian. *Practical Issues in Database Management.* Reading, MA: Addison-Wesley (2000). ISBN 0-201-48555-9

———. *Understanding Relational Databases.* New York, NY: John Wiley & Sons (1993). ISBN 0-471-58538-6

Piattini, Mario, and Oscar Diaz, eds. *Advanced Database Technology and Design.* Boston, MA: Artech House (2000). 0-89006-395-8

Podcameni, Silvio, Manfred Mittelmeir, and Michele Chilanti. *Distributed Relational Database: Cross-Platform Connectivity and Applications.* 3rd ed. Upper Saddle River, NJ: Prentice Hall PTR (1996). ISBN 0-13-570797-8

Pratt, Philip J., and Joseph J. Adamski. *The Concepts of Database Management.* 2nd ed. Cambridge, MA: International Thomsom Publishing (1997). ISBN 0-7600-4925-4

———. *Database Systems Management and Design.* 2nd ed. Boston, MA: Boyd & Fraser (1991). ISBN 0-87835-579-0

Purba, Sanjiv, ed. *Handbook of Data Management 1999.* Boca Raton, FL: Auerbach (1999). ISBN 0-8493-9976-9

———. *High-Performance Web Databases.* Boca Raton, FL: Auerbach (2000). ISBN 0-8493-0882-8

———. *Data Management Handbook.* 3rd ed. Boca Raton, FL: Auerbach (2000). ISBN 0-8493-9832-0

Rishe, Naphtali. *Database Design: The Semantic Modeling Approach.* New York, NY: McGraw-Hill (1992). ISBN 0-07 052955-8

Riccardi, Greg. *Principles of Database Systems with Internet and Java Applications.* Boston, MA: Addison Wesley (2001). ISBN 0-201-61247-X

Rob, Peter, and Carlos Coronel. *Databse Systems: Design, Implementation, & Management.* Cambridge, MA: Thomson Learning (2000). ISBN 0-7600-1090-0

Rothstein, Michael F., and Burt Rosner. *The Professional's Guide to Database Systems Project Management.* New York, NY: John Wiley & Sons (1990). ISBN 0-471-62130-7

Ryan, Nick, and Dan Smith. *Database Systems Engineering.* London, England: International Thomson Computer Press (1995). ISBN1-85032-115-9

Salemi, Joe. *Guide to Client/Server Databases.* Emeryville, CA: ZD Press (1993). ISBN 1-56276-070-X

Saracco, Cynthia Maro. *Universal Database Management: A Guide to Object/Relational Technology.* San Francisco, CA: Morgan Kaufmann (1998). ISBN 1-55860-519-3

Schur, Stephen G. *The Database Factory.* New York, NY: John Wiley & Sons (1994). ISBN 0-471-55844-3

Shasha, Dennis A. *Database Tuning: A Principled Approach.* Englewood Cliffs, NJ: Prentice Hall (1992). ISBN 0-13-205246-6

Shepherd, John C. *Database Management: Theory and Applications.* Homewood, IL: Irwin (1990). ISBN 0-256-07829-7

Simon, Alan R. *Strategic Database Technology.* San Francisco, CA: Morgan Kaufmann (1995). ISBN 1-55860-264-X

Stonebraker, Michael, and Paul Brown. *Object-Relational DBMSs: Tracking the Next Great Wave.* 2nd ed. San Francisco, CA: Morgan Kaufmann (1999). ISBN 1-55860-452-9

Stonebraker, Michael, ed. *Readings in Database Systems.* San Mateo, CA: Morgan Kaufmann (1988). ISBN 0-934613-65-6

Sweet, Frank. *Consultant's Handbook of Database Design.* Jacksonville, FL: Boxes & Arrows (1988). ISBN 0-939479-03-6

Thuraisingham, Bhavani M. *Data Management Systems: Evolution & Interoperation.* Boca Raton, FL: CRC Press (1997). ISBN 0-8493-9493-7

Ullman, Jeffrey D., and Jennifer Widom. *A First Course in Database Systems.* Upper Saddle River, NJ: Prentice Hall (1997). ISBN 0-13-861337-0

Widom, Jennifer, and Stefano Ceri, eds. *Active Database Systems: Triggers and Rules for Advanced Database Processing,* San Francisco, CA: Morgan Kaufmann (1996). ISBN 1-55860-304-2

Yang, Chao-Chih. *Relational Databases.* Englewood Cliffs, NJ: Prentice Hall (1986). ISBN 0-13-771858-6

Zaniolo, Carlo, et al. *Advanced Database Systems.* San Francisco, CA: Morgan Kaufmann (1997). ISBN 1-55860-443-X

Data Administration, Data Modeling, and Database Design

Brathwaite, Kenneth S. *Systems Design in a Database Environment.* New York, NY: McGraw-Hill (1989). ISBN 0-07-007250-7

Bruce, Thomas A. *Designing Quality Databases with IDEF1X Information Models.* New York, NY: Dorset House (1991). ISBN 0-932633-18-8

Carlis, John, and Joseph Maguire. *Mastering Data Modeling: A User-Driven Approach.* Boston, MA: Addison-Wesley (2001). ISBN 0-201-70045-X

Codd, E. F. "Further Normalization of the Database Relational Model," in *Data Base Systems.* Courant Computer Science Symposia Series, Vol. 6. Englewood Cliffs, N.J.: Prentice Hall (1972).

Durell, William R. *Data Administration: A Practical Guide to Successful Data Management.* New York, NY: McGraw-Hill (1985). ISBN 0-07-018391-0

———. *The Complete Guide to Data Modeling.* Princeton, NJ: Data Administration, Inc. (1993). No ISBN

D'Souza, Desmond F., and Alan Cameron Wills. *Objects, Components, and Frameworks with UML: The Catalysis Approach.* Reading, MA: Addison-Wesley (1999). ISBN 0-201-31012-0

English, Larry. *Improving Data Warehouse and Business Information Quality.* New York, NY: John Wiley & Sons (1999). ISBN 0-471-25383-9

Fleming, Candace, and Barbara von Halle. *Handbook of Relational Database Design.* Reading, MA: Addison-Wesley (1989). ISBN 0-201-11434-8

Hay, David C. *Data Model Patterns.* New York, NY: Dorset House (1996). ISBN 0-932633-29-3

Hogan, Rex. *A Practical Guide to Database Design.* Englewood Cliffs, NJ: Prentice Hall (1990). ISBN 0-13-690967-1

Inmon, W. H. *Data Architecture: The Information Paradigm.* Wellesley, MA: QED Information Sciences (1989). ISBN 0-89435-268-7

Kliewer, Bradley D. *Database Modeling in the PC Environment.* New York, NY: Bantam Books (1992). ISBN 0-553-08952-8

Lefkovits, Henry C. *IBM's Repository Manager/MVS.* Wellesley, MA: QED Information Sciences (1991). ISBN 0-89435-349-7

Marco, David. *Building and Managing the Meta Data Repository.* New York, NY: John Wiley & Sons (2000). ISBN 0-471-35523-2

Modell, Martin E. *Data Analysis, Data Modeling, and Classification.* New York, NY: McGraw-Hill (1992). ISBN 0-07-042634-1

Perkinson, Richard C. *Data Analysis: The Key to Database Design.* Wellesley, MA: QED Information Sciences (1984). ISBN 0-89435-105-2

Riordan, Rebecca M. *Designing Relational Database Systems.* Redmond, WA: Microsoft Press (1999). ISBN 0-7356-0634-X

Ross, Ronald G. *Entity Modeling: Techniques and Application.* Boston, MA: Database Research Group (1988). ISBN 0-941049-00-0

Sanders, G. Lawrence. *Data Modeling.* Danvers, MA: Boyd & Fraser Publishing Company (1995). ISBN 0-87709-066-1

Schmidt, Bob. *Data Modeling for Information Professionals.* Upper Saddle River, NJ: Prentice Hall PTR (1999). ISBN 0-13-080450-9

Simsion, Graeme. *Data Modeling Essentials.* New York, NY: Van Nostrand Reinhold (1994). ISBN 0-442-01654-9

Stephens, Ryan K., and Ronald R. Plew. *Database Design.* Indianapolis, IN: SAMS Publishing (2001). ISBN 0-672-31758-3

Wertz, Charles K. *The Data Dictionary: Concepts and Uses.* Wellesley, MA: QED Information Sciences (1986). ISBN 0-89435-180-X

Wurman, Richard Saul. *Information Anxiety.* New York, NY: Doubleday (1989). ISBN 0-385-24394-4

Data Warehousing

Barquin, Ramon, and Herb Edelstein, eds. *Planning and Designing the Data Warehouse.* Upper Saddle River, NJ: Prentice Hall (1997). ISBN 0-13-255746-0

Devlin, Barry. *Data Warehouse from Architecture to Implementation.* Reading, MA: Addison-Wesley (1997). ISBN 0-201-96245-2

Hackney, Douglas. *Understanding and Implementing Successful Data Marts.* Reading, MA: Addison-Wesley (1997). ISBN 0-201-18380-3

Inmon, W. H. *Building the Data Warehouse.* 2nd ed. New York, NY: John Wiley & Sons (1996). ISBN 0-471-14161-5

Inmon, W. H., and Richard Hackathorn. *Using the Data Warehouse.* New York, NY: John Wiley & Sons (1994). ISBN 0-471-05966-8

Inmon, W. H., Claudia Imhoff, et al. *Building the Operational Data Store.* New York, NY: John Wiley & Sons (1996). ISBN 0-471-12822-8

Inmon, W. H., John A. Zachman, et al. *Data Stores, Data Warehousing and the Zachman Framework.* New York, NY: McGraw-Hill (1997). ISBN 0-07-031429-2

Kimball, Ralph. *The Data Warehouse Toolkit.* New York, NY: John Wiley & Sons (1996). ISBN 0-471-15337-0

Lewis, William J. *Data Warehousing and E-Commerce.* Upper Saddle River, NJ: Prentice Hall (2001). ISBN 0-13-091154-2

Poe, Vidette. *Building a Data Warehouse for Decision Support.* Upper Saddle River, NJ: Prentice Hall (1996). ISBN 0-13-371121-8

Object Orientation and Database Management

Barry, Douglas K. *The Object Database Handbook.* New York, NY: John Wiley & Sons (1996). ISBN 0-471-14718-4

Brathwaite, Kenmore S. *Object-Oriented Database Design: Concepts and Application.* San Diego, CA: Academic Press (1993). ISBN 0-12-125882-3

Cattell, R. G. G. *Object Data Management.* Reading, MA: Addison-Wesley (1992). ISBN 0-201-53092-9

Hughes, John G. *Object-Oriented Databases.* New York, NY: Prentice Hall (1991). ISBN 0-13-629882-6

Kroha, Petr. *Objects and Databases.* London, England: McGraw-Hill (1993). ISBN 0-07-707790-3

Loomis, Mary. *Object Databases. The Essentials.* Reading, MA: Addison-Wesley (1995). ISBN 0-201-56341-X

Taylor, David A. *Object-Oriented Technology: A Manager's Guide.* Reading, MA: Addison-Wesley (1990). ISBN 0-201-56358-4

Related Topics

Applequist, Daniel K. *XML and SQL: Developing Web Applications.* Boston, MA: Addison-Wesley (2002). ISBN 0-201-65796-1

Bell, Judy Kay. *Disaster Survival Planning: A Practical Guide for Businesses.* Port Hueneme, CA: Disaster Survival Planning, Inc. (1991)

Bernstein, Philip A., and Eric Newcomer. *Principles of Transaction Processing.* San Francisco, CA: Morgan Kaufmann (1997). ISBN 1-55860-415-4

Bhamidipati, Kishore. *SQL Programmer's Reference.* Berkeley, CA: Osborne/McGraw-Hill (1998). ISBN 0-07-882460-5

Carter, John. *Programming in SQL with Oracle, Ingres, and dBase IV.* Englewood Cliffs, NJ: Prentice Hall (1993). ISBN 0-13-014325-1

Chantico Publishing Company, Inc. *Disaster Recovery Handbook.* Blue Ridge Summit, PA: Tab Professional & Reference Books (1991). ISBN 0-8306-7663-5

Date, C. J., with Darwen, Hugh. *A Guide to the SQL Standard.* 4th ed. Reading, MA: Addison-Wesley (1997). ISBN 0-201-96426-0

Eddy, Sandra E. *XML in Plain English.* Foster City, CA: M&T Books (1998). ISBN 0-7645-7006-4

Freedman, Daniel P., and Gerald M. Weinberg. *Handbook of Walkthroughs, Inspections, and Technical Reviews.* New York, NY: Dorset House (1990). ISBN 0-932633-19-6

Fronckowiak, John W. *Teach Yourself OLE DB and ADO in 21 Days.* Indianapolis, IN: SAMS Publishing (1997). ISBN 0-672-31083-X

Gagliardi, Gary. *Client/Server Computing.* Englewood Cliffs, NJ: Prentice Hall PTR (1994). ISBN 0-13-290784-4

Ginac, Frank P. *Creating High Performance Software Development Teams.* Upper Saddle River, NJ: Prentice Hall (2000). ISBN 0-13-085083-7

Gunther, Neil J. *The Practical Performance Analyst.* Lincoln, NE: Authors Choice Press (2000). ISBN 0-595-12674-X

Gray, Jim, and Andreas Reuter. *Transaction Processing: Concepts and Techniques.* San Francisco, CA: Morgan Kaufmann (1993). ISBN 1-55860-190-2

Groff, James R., and Paul N. Weinberg. *LAN Times Guide to SQL.* Berkeley, CA: Osbourne McGraw-Hill (1994). ISBN 0-07-882026-X

Gulutzan, Peter, and Trudy Pelzer. *SQL-99 Complete, Really.* Lawrence, KS: R&D Books (1999). ISBN 0-87930-568-1

Harrington, Jan L. *SQL Clearly Explained.* San Diego, CA: AP Professional (1998). ISBN 0-12-326426-X

Jennings, Roger. *Database Developer's Guide with Visual Basic 6.* Indianapolis, IN: SAMS Publishing (1999). ISBN 0-672-31063-5

Jepson, Brian. *Java Database Programming.* New York, NY: John Wiley & Sons (1997). ISBN 0-471-16518-2

Johnson, Robert H. *MVS Concepts and Facilities.* New York, NY: McGraw-Hill (1989). ISBN 0-07-032673-8

Khoshafian, Setrag, et al. *A Guide to Developing Client/Server SQL Applications.* San Mateo, CA: Morgan Kaufmann (1992). ISBN 1-55860-147-3

Kline, Kevin, with Daniel Kline. *SQL in a Nutshell.* Sebastopol, CA: O'Reilly (2001). ISBN 1-56592-744-3

Koch, Richard. *The 80/20 Principle.* New York, NY: Currency/Doubleday (1998). ISBN 0-385-49170-0

Loosely, Chris, and Frank Douglas. *High Performance Client/Server.* New York, NY: John Wiley & Sons (1998). ISBN 0-471-16269-8

McClain, Gary. *OLTP Handbook.* New York, NY: McGraw-Hill (1993). ISBN 0-07-044985-6

Melton, Jim. *Understanding SQL's Stored Procedures: A Complete Guide to SQL/PSM.* San Francisco, CA: Morgan Kaufmann (1998). ISBN 1-55860-461-8

Orfali, Robert, Dan Harkey, and Jeri Edwards. *Essential Client/Server Survival Guide.* New York, NY: Van Nostrand Reinhold (1994). ISBN 0-442-01941-6

Piedad, Floyd, and Michael Hawkins. *High Availability: Design, Techniques and Processes.* Upper Saddle River, NJ: Prentice Hall PTR (2001). ISBN 0-13-096288-0

Reiss, Levi, and Joseph Radin. *Unix System Administration Guide.* Berkeley, CA: Osborne McGraw-Hill (1993). ISBN 0-07-881951-2

Sheldon, Tom, ed. *LAN Times Guide to Interoperability.* Berkeley, CA: McGraw-Hill (1994). ISBN 0-07-882043-X

Siyan, Karanjit S. *Windows NT Server 4: Professional Reference.* Indianapolis, IN: New Riders (1997). ISBN 1-56205-805-3

Sessions, Roger. *COM+ and the Battle for the Middle Tier.* New York, NY: John Wiley & Sons (2000). ISBN 0-471-31717-9

Strauss, Melvin J. *Computer Capacity: A Production Control Approach.* New York, NY: Van Nostrand Reinhold (1981). ISBN 0-442-26243-4

Sturm, Rick, Wayne Morris, and Mary Jander. *Foundations of Service Level Management.* Indianapolis, IN: SAMS Publishing (2000). ISBN 0-672-31743-5

Sungard Recovery Services, Inc. *Action Plan for Disaster* (1995)

Taylor, Ed. *Demystifying SNA.* Plano, TX: Wordware (1993). 1-55622-404-4

———. *Demystifying TCP/IP.* Plano, TX: Wordware (1993). 1-55622-400-1

Thornburgh, Ralph H. and Barry J. Shoenborn. *Storage Area Networks.* Upper Saddle River, NJ: Prentice Hall PTR (2000). ISBN 0-13-027959-5

Toigo, Jon William. *The Holy Grail of Data Storage Management.* Upper Saddle River, NJ: Prentice Hall PTR (2000). ISBN 0-13-013055-9

Toigo, Jon William. *Disaster Recovery Planning.* 2nd ed. Upper Saddle River, NJ: Prentice Hall PTR (2000). ISBN 0-13-084506-X

DB2

Chamberlin, Don. *A Complete Guide to DB2 Universal Database.* San Francisco, CA: Morgan Kaufmann (1998). ISBN 1-55860-482-0

Mullins, Craig S. *DB2 Developer's Guide.* 4th ed. Indianapolis, IN: SAMS (2000). ISBN 0-672-31828-8

Werman, Aaron. *DB2 Handbook for DBAs.* New York, NY: McGraw-Hill (1992). ISBN 0-07-069460-5

IMS

Geller, Joseph R. *IMS Administration, Programming, and Database Design.* New York, NY: John Wiley & Sons (1989). ISBN 0-471-62185-4

Hogan, Rex. *Diagnostic Techniques for IMS Databases.* Wellesley, MA: QED Information Sciences (1986). ISBN 0-89435-174-5

Hubbard, George U. *IMS (DL/1) Database Organization and Performance.* New York, NY: Van Nostrand Reinhold (1986). ISBN 0-442-23583-6

Informix

Lumbley, Joe. *Informix Database Administrator's Survival Guide.* Upper Saddle River, NJ: Informix Press/PTR (1995). ISBN 0-13-124314-4

Multiple Authors. *Evolution of the High Performance Database.* Upper Saddle River, NJ: Informix Press/PTR (1997). ISBN 0-13-124314-4

Oracle

Ault, Michael R. *Oracle8 Administration and Management.* New York, NY: John Wiley & Sons (1998). ISBN 0-471-19234-1

———. *Oracle DBA Test 1 and Test 2 Exam Cram.* Scottsdale, AZ: Coriolis Group (1998). ISBN 1-57610-262-9

Caffrey, Melanie, and Douglas Scherer. *Oracle DBA Interactive Workbook.* Upper Saddle River, NJ: Prentice Hall PTR (2001). ISBN 0-13-015742-2

Greene, Joe, et al. *Oracle8 Server Unleashed.* Indianapolis, IN: SAMS (1998). ISBN 0-672-31207-7

Kreines, David C., and Brian Laskey. *Oracle Database Administration: The Essential Reference.* Sebastapol, CA: O'Reilly (1999). ISBN 1-56592-516-5

Loney, Kevin. *Oracle8 DBA Handbook.* Berkeley, CA: McGraw-Hill/Oracle Press (1998). ISBN 0-07-882406-0

Theriault, Marlene, et al. *Oracle DBA 101.* Berkeley, CA: McGraw-Hill/Oracle Press (2000). ISBN 0-07-212120-3

Toledo, Hugo, Jr. *Oracle Networking.* Berkeley, CA: McGraw-Hill/Oracle Press (1996). ISBN 0-07-882165-7

Velpuri, Rama. *Oracle Backup & Recovery Handbook.* Berkeley, CA: Osborne/McGraw-Hill (1987). ISBN 0-07-882323-4

SQL Server

Baird, Sean, et al. *SQL Server System Administration.* Indianapolis, IN: New Riders (1999). ISBN 1-56205-955-6

Besch, David. *MCSE: SQL Server 7 Database Design.* Indianapolis, IN: New Riders (1999). ISBN 0-7357-0004-4

Panttaja, Jim, et al. *The Microsoft SQL Server Survival Guide.* New York, NY: John Wiley & Sons (1996). ISBN 0-471-12743-4

Patton, Robert, and Jennifer Ogle. *Designing SQL Server 2000 Databases for .NET Enterprise Servers.* Rockland, MA: Syngress (2001). ISBN 1-928994-19-9

Spenik, Mark, and Orryn Sledge. *Microsoft SQL Server 2000 DBA Survival Guide.* Indianapolis, IN: SAMS (2001). ISBN 0-672-32007-X

Stanek, William R. *Microsoft SQL Server 7.0 Administrator's Pocket Consultant.* Redmond, WA: Microsoft Press (1999). ISBN 0-7356-0596-3

Sybase

Hitchcock, Brian. *Sybase Database Administrator's Handbook.* Upper Saddle River, NJ: Prentice Hall PTR (1996). ISBN 0-13-357477-6

Kirkwood, John. *Sybase Architecture and Administration.* New York, NY: Ellis Horwood (1993). ISBN 0-13-100330-5

———. *Sybase SQL Server 11—An Administrator's Guide.* London, England: International Thomson Computer Press (1996). ISBN 1-85032-287-2

Index

Note: Italicized page locators refer to tables/figures.

and lock escalation, 184
parameters provided by, 290
and relational data model, 621
Web site for, 641
DB2 Developer's Guide (Mullins), 447
DB2 Everyplace, 45, 57
DB2 Extended Enterprise Edition, and shared-nothing clustering, 59
DB2 for OS/390, 289
    COPY utility used by, 415, 416
    Data Sharing and Parallel Sysplex, 59
    and page sizes, 310
    STOGROUPS with, 470
DB2 for z/OS, 245
DB2 magazine, Web site for, 642
DB2 REORG utility, logging disabled with, 287
DB2 UDB, DB2LOOK utility, 426
DBWR. *See* Database writer
DCL. *See* Data Control Language
DDL. *See* Data Definition Language
Deadlines, for database change implementation, 218
Deadlocks, 179, *180*, 184, 185
    detecting, 287, 288
    minimizing, 288
"Deadly embrace," 180
Deallocation, 474
Debugging tools, 582, 598
Decentralized administration, of privileges, 391
Decentralized user presentation model, 544
Decimal data type, 123, 358
Decision Support System, 517, 522
Declarative referential constraints, 375, 376, 377
Dedicated hardware, for database server, 547–548
Default configuration options, avoiding, 290
Default databases, 387
Default data files, and Oracle tablespaces, 272
Default language, 387
Defaults, 77
Default values
    and DBMS software, 274
    standardizing, 524
Defragmentation, 224
Degree, of relationship, 103
DELETED table, 369
DELETE privilege, granting, 392
DELETE RI constraint, 365
DELETE rule, 373–374
DELETE statement, 66, 162, 185, 283, 371, 587, 593
    and data modification, 310
    log records for, 419
    and transition tables, 370
    and triggers, 40, 366, 368

DELETE trigger, for referential constraints, 376
Delivery, and change management, 206
Demographics, 224
Denormalization, 122, 138–152, 296
    and database design, 560
    and database performance, 301
    documenting decisions for, 139–140, 151
    guidelines for, 139
    of hierarchies, 150
    need for, 138
    and performance, 152
    and repeating groups, 146
    and splitting long text columns, 144–145
    types of, *151, 521*
Denormalized logical data models, avoiding, 141
Denormalized tables, synchronizing with normalized tables, 139
Density, 323, 324
Departmental DBMS, 56, 57
Dependent tables, 379
DEPT_NO primary key, 375
Derived data, 116, 148, 301
Design
    database, 558–561
    data warehouse, 519–522
Design reviews, 189–201
    areas addressed by, 190
    conceptual, 194, 195–196
    description of, 189
    guidelines for, 84
    logical, 194, 196–197
    organizational, 194, 198–199
    output, 201
    participants in, 191–194
    physical, 194, 197–198
    post-implementation, 194, 200
    pre-implementation, 194, 200
    rules of engagement, 190–191
    SQL and application code, 194, 199–200
    types of, 194–200
Design review team, knowledge and skills required by, 193–194
Desktops, 249
Determinants, defined, 115
Development life cycle, 83
Development tools, 597–598
Devices, and database memory consumption, 277
DFSMS backups, IBM, 425
Dialup connections, 547
DICE.com, 4
Differential backup, 412
Dimension, 517

Also Available from Addison-Wesley

0-201-74129-6

0-201-43336-2

0-201-69471-9

0-201-70309-2

0-201-61638-6

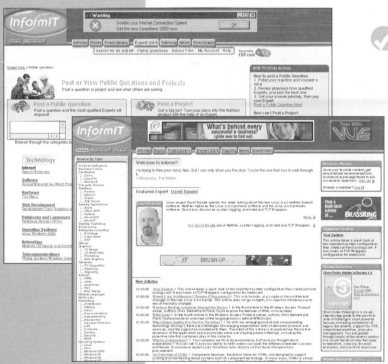

The Java™ Series